THE VIETNAM WAR
AND INTERNATIONAL LAW

The Vietnam War
and International Law

AMERICAN SOCIETY OF
INTERNATIONAL LAW

EDITED BY

RICHARD A. FALK

Princeton University Press

Princeton, New Jersey

1968

Printed in the United States of America

by Princeton University Press

Note of Acknowledgments

THERE are many who deserve thanks in connection with the production of this volume. With the exception of the article by Eliot D. Hawkins, the contents of this book have appeared previously. We thank collectively the authors and publishers who have given us their permission to reprint material here and thereby enabled us to present in one volume the scattered writing pertinent to the legal issues raised by the United States involvement in Vietnam. Detailed permissions appear in the back of this volume.

I would also like to thank the Civil War Panel for working to produce this volume as part of its overall undertaking and the Carnegie Corporation for the grant to the American Society of International Law for the civil war project. The Executive Vice President and Director of the Society, Stephen M. Schwebel, has given indispensable help and encouragement.

The Princeton Press has cooperated closely with the American Society of International Law in the effort to achieve prompt publication. I am grateful to William McClung for his early interest in this volume and to Marjorie Putney for editing the whole with such care under pressure of time. Finally, I wish to thank Priscilla Bryan of the secretarial staff of the Center of International Studies at Princeton University for helping with so many of the countless details and for keeping control over the complex confusion that attends putting together a volume of this sort on behalf of a participating panel.

RICHARD A. FALK

Contents

Introduction

THE VIETNAM WAR
AND INTERNATIONAL LAW

Introduction*

THIS volume of readings and documents has been brought together under the auspices of the Civil War Project of the American Society of International Law. The principal objective of the collection is to enable a reader to consider the various major positions that have been taken by United States international lawyers who have written about the legal character and the consequences for world order of the United States' involvement in the Vietnam War. The Panel believes it to be important to present a selection of scholarly writing that exhibits the wide, and often contradictory, divergence on matters of both fact and law pertaining to the Vietnam War. There is too much that remains, and may always remain, controversial with regard to a legal appraisal of the United States' involvement in the Vietnam War to allow one legal interpretation to be singled out as authoritative by a Panel that seeks to be representative of American international lawyers as a whole.

The Intellectual Setting

The legal situation relating to the American presence in Vietnam is sufficiently unclear to allow reasonable men of professional competence to arrive at diametrically opposed conclusions on the principal legal issues. The selections in the volume illuminate the nature of these disagreements. Three kinds of disagreements dominate these legal analyses of the United States' role in the Vietnam War:

1. Disagreements as to questions of fact (e.g. to what extent was the formation of the National Liberation Front instigated and controlled by North Vietnam? To what extent is the NLF controlled by North Vietnam? At what periods of time and in what quantities did North Vietnam infiltrate men and supplies to the Vietcong?).

2. Disagreements as to whether factual circumstances produce specific legal consequences (e.g. is South Vietnam "a state"? If so, as of what date? At what stage of the conflict, if any, has it been legally persuasive to regard the war in Vietnam as "a civil war"? At what point, if ever, would it have been legally persuasive to regard the involvement of North Vietnam in the war as "an armed attack"? To what extent was the Government in Saigon bound to comply with the terms of the 1954 Geneva Accords? What were the effects on the respective rights and duties of North Vietnam, South Vietnam, the United States,

* This Introduction was prepared on behalf of the Panel by Richard A. Falk.

and the National Liberation Front of various departures from the terms of the Geneva Accords?) .

3. Disagreements as to the world order consequences of validating American action against North Vietnam as a legitimate exercise of the rights of collective self-defense (i.e. the argumentation as to whether it is preferable to treat the pattern of military force used by the United States in Vietnam—both North and South of the Seventeenth Parallel—as a legal precedent or as a violation of international law).

These three classes of disagreements are not rigidly separable, but they do point to the kind of legal questions posed for international lawyers. Most of these disagreements converge on the underlying question as to whether in terms of facts, legal expectations, and policies at stake it is legally appropriate to treat Vietnam-style wars as "civil wars" or as a peculiar modern species of international war. Put differently, the central issue is whether from the perspective of international law it is desirable to differentiate, and if so in what respects, the Korea-style war initiated by an overt attack across an international frontier from the Vietnam-style war in which it is difficult to identify clearly the timing and significance of external involvement and, consequently, in which it is impossible to gain broad agreement as to the relative weighting of internal and external factors in considering the causal sequence leading to the armed struggle for control of the society. President Lyndon Johnson in a speech delivered at Baylor University in May of 1965 expressed the view that appears to have been guiding the United States Government ever since when he said, "With the enemies of freedom talking about wars of national liberation, the old distinction between civil war and international war has already lost much of its meaning." Assent to or dissent from President Johnson's conclusion may turn out to be one of the major world order issues of our time. More careful analysis of its specific implications may help to identify relatively neutral criteria by which to measure whether a given instance of strife is properly treated as "a civil war" or as "an international war." The very bloody struggle in 1965-66 for control of Indonesia appeared to be sufficiently insulated from outside involvement that there would be no genuine basis for treating it as an international war; the locus of violence seems to have been predominantly domestic too in the relatively bloodless changes of government in Greece (1967) and Algeria (1966).

Therefore, the real class of cases over which legal controversy centers involves those in which there is present either the allegation or the actuality of a substantial covert involvement on the side of the anti-incumbent faction.[1] In this class of cases, most dramatically in the instance of Vietnam, but also with respect to the struggle for control of the Dominican Republic in 1965 or the ongoing internal armed struggles in Thailand, Laos, or Aden, the assessment of the legal status of the conflict depends upon information and belief as to the following sorts of mixed questions of fact and law:

1. The timing, extent, and nature of external involvement on behalf of the contesting factions;

2. The absolute and relative degree of autonomy possessed by the contending factions;

3. The permissible levels of incumbent response (either individually or collectively with external assistance) given various levels and forms of external participation on behalf of a substantial and violent effort by an anti-incumbent faction to seize control of the state.

Persuasive answers for these kinds of questions are made more difficult because international society lacks impartial fact-finding procedures and because there is so little prospect of reaching an authoritative interpretation of the international legal status or of the relative legal rights and duties of third party states sympathetic with one side or the other in a particular struggle.[2] The unavoidable result of this deficiency in centralized procedures of inquiry and decision is to produce a divergence of position based on adversary perspective. As one might suspect this divergence of perspective is also reflected somewhat in scholarly analysis. It could not be otherwise given the limited degree of legal integration at the international level and given the sharpness of the rivalry for power and prestige carried on by the principal sovereign states.

Until very recently there has been relatively little serious analysis of the legal status of armed conflict on the blurred boundary between

[1] The anti-incumbent faction may lack any substantial separate identity if it is itself "the agent" or "puppet" of a foreign state; but so might the incumbent. Problems of international law may also be created by disputes as to the identity of the incumbent and anti-incumbent regimes. For example, in 1956 the Soviet Union insisted upon treating the Kadar regime as "the incumbent" whereas the non-Communist world regarded the Nagy regime as entitled to the status of "incumbent." There have been also attempts by international law to prohibit premature recognition of rebel factions, although these attempts have been frustrated by the absence of objective procedures to determine when a condition of prematurity exists.

[2] In the Vietnam context there was operative after 1954 an International Control Commission charged with the task of implementing the Geneva Accords. For survey of its activities between 1954 and 1965 see David W. Wainhouse and others, *International Peace Observation—A History and A Forecast*, Baltimore, Johns Hopkins, 1966, pp. 489-524.

civil war and international war. The literature of international law is extensive with regard to case-studies of some specific civil wars, most especially of the Spanish Civil War (1935-37), and with regard to the legal consequences that attach to a conflict once it is regarded as "a civil war." However, there is almost no serious writing to date—other than the literature provoked by the Vietnam War and contained in this volume—as to the appropriate criteria by which to identify whether from the standpoint of international law a particular conflict is or is not a civil war. And it is this initial act of identification that seems to predetermine so many of the other legal issues in dispute.

As with other problems contained in the international law of war, it may be worth pondering whether the classical dichotomy between civil war and international war is adequate to the requirements of either legal analysis or world legal order.[3] It might be desirable to orient analysis in terms of a factual continuum that incorporates the ratio between external involvement and the internal struggle and derives legal right and duties from a sequence of thresholds, i.e. if the ratio as to external guidance, equipment, or personnel rose from an estimated 1:4 to 1:1, then the international legal status of the conflict would be altered correspondingly. Given the present state of international fact-finding procedures, it would be normally difficult, of course, to get an objective presentation of the critical data and assessments of external involvement would usually consist of contradictory, adversary accounts. Additionally, and more simply, it might be useful to orient legal analysis in terms of a specific intermediate category of struggle, perhaps denominated "international civil war" for which respective legal rights and duties could be described in a manner that was different from either of the two traditional categories—"civil war" and "international war."

In working in this problematic setting of international violence there is also a need to differentiate between legally permissible and legally impermissible forms of involvement in foreign societies.[4] The

[3] For discussion in the broader context of the dichotomy between "peace" and "war" see Philip C. Jessup, "Should International Law Recognize an Intermediate Status Between Peace and War?" 48 *American Journal of International Law* 98 (1954) ; and generally Myres S. McDougal and Florentino P. Feliciano, *Law and Minimum World Public Order*, New Haven, Yale, 1962, pp. 1-12.

[4] A question separate from the matter of rights and duties—but not unrelated, particularly as regards the development of new rights and duties—is the self-interest of states in situations of "international civil war." Hopefully the two major world powers, though suspicious of each other, share the view that external participation in a civil war disrupts world order and thereby militates against their own interests. In this analysis the problem facing both the United States and Russia would be how to take

overall interdependence of international society, accentuated by inter-relations between sovereign units of vastly unequal capabilities, necessarily assures the existence of flows of influence from the more powerful and energetic to the less powerful and passive. Such interdependence is desirable in many respects; it is, in any event inevitable and irreversible. The consequent flows of influence also reflect ideological, cultural, and national patterns of competition for the allegiance of uncommitted, weakly committed, or divided foreign societies. Such activities as foreign aid and cultural exchange programs are clearly designed to include some exertion of influence by the donor upon the donee state, but appear to create no legal problem. The transmission of hostile and misleading information about a foreign government across international boundaries creates a borderline case that has prompted some inquiry into the regulation of propaganda. The effect of domestic struggles for power upon these normal influence flows is one of the more elusive questions caught up in this area. Are foreign states entitled to supply a constituted government with unlimited assistance to enable it to suppress a threat to its own survival? Is there a ratio between external support and the government's own capabilities that should be set forth as an approximate upper threshold? Should this threshold be fixed by a comparison between the external-internal ratios on the two sides in the struggle for control? Is there enough reliable data to establish ratios that might command any degree of general support in the world community? Could the necessary measurements be made in the actual circumstances of conflict? As has been pointed out by Bernard Fall and others, the idea of a ratio in a situation of struggle of the guerrilla variety must take into account the need of the incumbent for much higher force levels to neutralize, let alone defeat, the guerrilla factions.[5] Therefore, the notion of *equivalent* external involvement on the two sides of struggle needs to be adapted to battlefield realities and cannot be a mechanical equivalent imported as an abstraction.

In normative terms these issues have been dealt with by international lawyers long before the Vietnam War. The American Revolution and the French Revolution initiated an intense controversy about the comparative merits of stabilizing the control of the constituted government

---

steps to strengthen world order despite the absence of prior agreement with their chief adversary. Cf. also G.A. Res. 2131 (XX) (Dec. 21, 1965) and G.A. Res. 2160 (Nov. 30, 1966).

[5] For a discussion of ratios of equivalence in the guerrilla contexts of Vietnam see Bernard B. Fall, *The Two Viet-Nams*, New York, Praeger, 2nd rev. edn., 1967, pp. 338-54.

over its own society and encouraging the free interplay of domestic struggle for power. Those international lawyers concerned with the stability of international life tended to emphasize the prerogatives of the constituted government, including its discretion to request and receive external assistance to suppress a domestic challenge to its control. Those international lawyers, in contrast, concerned with the self-determination of peoples tended to emphasize the duties of third parties to remain aloof from civil strife in a foreign society by proclaiming the obligation to treat the government and its opponents impartially and to respect the doctrine of non-intervention.

A third variant in the approach of international lawyers emphasized the obligation of states to act on behalf of the just side in a civil war. The criteria of justice were never set forth with clarity, but emphasized promoting various notions of what constituted a good society. The continuing struggle against colonial regimes in Southern Africa relies on this kind of legal logic.

None of these three broad perspectives taken by international law is entirely relevant to the sort of conflict taking place in Vietnam. In Vietnam the two sides in the struggle for the control of South Vietnam are deeply intermeshed with outside states, so much so that the prospects for settlement of the war presently appear to depend not only upon the will of the main internal participants—the Saigon Government and the National Liberation Front—but upon the will of the main external participants—the United States and North Vietnam—as well.[6] In trying to comprehend the legal status of such a conflict it is important to take some account of this very large relative role being played by states outside the society wherein the struggle rages.

The Civil War Panel of the American Society of International Law

The Civil War Panel has functioned under the general auspices of the Board of Review and Development of the American Society of International Law since 1966. Both the Panel and the Board are made up of persons with special competence and experience in international affairs; they are drawn from academic life, from the practice of law, and to some extent, from the ranks of government and international institutions. The Society is a scholarly and professional association without affiliation to the United States Government and without any

---

[6] Additional significant external participants in the Vietnam War include the Soviet Union, Peoples Republic of China, Thailand, Australia, and South Korea; additionally, and to a lesser degree, the Philippines and New Zealand.

ideology of its own other than a concern with the progressive development of international law and the settlement of international disputes on the basis of law and justice. The work of the Civil War Panel has been most generously supported by a grant to the Society from the Carnegie Corporation.

The basic objective of the Panel is to attempt a reinterpretation of the international law of civil war adequate to the needs of current international life. The literature of international law on this subject appeared to be very inadequate as a basis for the work of the Panel. Accordingly, the Panel gave first priority to the task of gathering together the relevant descriptive and analytic material that could then serve as the basis for further generalization. In this spirit, it was thought desirable to obtain studies in depth of important civil war phenomena. The Panel thus commissioned case studies of civil wars each of which has been selected to illustrate certain distinctive features of the overall problem. For example, the Spanish Civil War was selected because it broke out during the period of the League of Nations and because it both illustrated the unsuccessful attempt of certain foreign states to limit their participation by formal agreement and the effect of other foreign states engaging simultaneously in extensive intervention. The Congo (1960-64) was selected to illustrate a post-colonial instance of civil strife in which international institutions played a significant role, whereas the Algerian war (1954-62) was selected to illustrate a war of independence that did not result in significant involvement by principal outside states nor did it lead to a major role for international institutions. Thus these case studies were organized around certain focal problems of world legal order, problems that will be at the center of the Panel's subsequent attempt at a general reinterpretation of international law in this sphere. Competent scholars were approached to do the work in each case according to a common set of guidelines provided them by the Panel. The purpose of these guidelines has been to standardize the inquiry of various scholars sufficiently to facilitate the comparison of the studies with one another.

In addition to these case studies, the Panel felt that it was important to gain insight into the diplomatic practice and policy processes of those sovereign states that were most heavily involved in foreign civil strife. To gain this insight, time-studies covering relevant historical periods have been planned to provide the Panel with information about important patterns of involvement, such as the United States involvement in the upheavals of Latin America and the Soviet involvement, since the end of World War II, in the suppression and prevention of civil strife in Eastern Europe.

The Vietnam War was of obvious concern to the Panel, both because it seemed to be such a central instance of a conflict on the borderline between civil war and international war and because its world order implications were perceived in such different ways by the membership of the Panel. Serious study of the Vietnam War is made especially difficult because it is unfinished and because there is so little agreement on the central characteristics of the conflict. Despite these obstacles, the Panel felt that it could not conduct a general inquiry into the legal aspects of contemporary civil warfare without dealing seriously with the Vietnam War, if only to shed some light on whether, in view of its international dimensions, it properly belonged within the Panel's mandate to study the phenomena of civil war. After considerable Panel discussion, it was decided that two kinds of effort were worthwhile: first, to bring together the present collection of scholarly writing concerned with the legal status of the United States involvement in the Vietnam War and, thereby, to encourage further reflection and consideration of this most basic issue; secondly, to commission Professor Percy Corbett to do a case study on the Vietnam War that would focus on legal questions other than those relating to the United States involvement. A preliminary version of Professor Corbett's study is expected to be available for the Panel by the end of 1967.

A brief description of what remains to be done will complete this summary account of the Panel's work. The case studies will be revised and edited for eventual publication. The Panel will endeavor to draft its interpretation of the international law of civil war taking into account the case studies completed during Phases I and II of the project. The present timetable calls for the completion of the project during 1969.

The Arrangement of the Volume

The readings included in this volume reflect the overall approach described in the preceding section. To be specific, we wish to enable a reader to have an adequate intellectual basis for appraising the issues caught up in the legal controversy about the United States involvement in Vietnam. But more than that, we want to present the legal controversy that has arisen in the Vietnam War as an intellectual setting, of exceptional political importance, in which to appraise the various policy arguments that pertain to the general status in international law of armed struggle that arises on the borderline between civil war and international war.

In Part I, we offer the reader a framework by presenting a series of selections that raise most of the legal issues, but in a setting largely independent of the Vietnam War. Among other objectives, this section attempts to connect the legal perspectives on violence of this sort with the interconnected perspectives of international politics and international morality. In addition, the excerpt from Vattel and the essay by Mill are intended to convey some minimal historical context so that the reader will resist the temptation to exaggerate the uniquely modern extent of "international civil warfare" or of the problems posed by the Vietnam War.

In Part II, the selections develop the opposing interpretations of the main questions of fact and law that touch upon whether, and in what respects, the United States involvement in Vietnam is lawful or not. These selections, although controversial in matters of both analysis and conclusion, adhere to scholarly standards of argument and presentation, and are not to be regarded as an exhibition of legal polemics. Although a particular author is likely to resolve all the main issues in one direction or the other—as will normally a judge delivering an opinion on behalf of a tribunal—the argument and analysis proceeds by relying upon supporting documentation and reasoning; moreover, the arguments available to the other side in the debate are usually considered and reasons given for their unacceptability. The selections in Part II set before the reader the main legal arguments that have been so far made in connection with the war in Vietnam.

Part III continues the focus upon the legal status of involvement in the war in Vietnam, but enlarges the horizon of concern to present assessments of the world order consequences thought to ensue from the various stages of United States involvement. A particular object of attention is the extent to which there is reason to differentiate legally between the military response of the United States within South Vietnam and the extension of this military response to the territory of North Vietnam after February 1965. The broad and crucial world order question involves the conditions under which it is and should be legally permissible for a government (and its allies) to expand the geographical arena of violence to include the territory of the state giving substantial support to an insurgent group or "agent." The question at issue is: Was the United States legally entitled, as of February 1965, to treat the support given by North Vietnam to the National Liberation Front as "an armed attack" upon South Vietnam that justified recourse to "collective self-defense" including proportional uses of defensive force against the territory of North Vietnam? The authors in Part III explain the reasons for their very different responses to the question by reference to the management of violence in international society and by explanations of their differing assessments of the specific world order consequences that can be attributed to the form and extent of the United States involvement in the Vietnam War.

The selections of Dean Rusk and Secretary General U Thant are intended to convey the world order perspectives on the Vietnam War taken by these two important officials—the one located at the pinnacle of the national bureaucracy, the other at the pinnacle of the international bureaucracy. Each of these two distinguished civil servants has, of course, an individual perspective on these problems as well as a perspective shaped to some uncertain extent by his bureaucratic role.

The final selection by the social psychologist, Ralph White, might have been located in a different part of the volume. The decision to place it at the end of Part III reflects the view that its discussion of the prospect of simultaneous contradictory inferences of "aggression," each reached by parties to the conflict in good faith, might represent the most troublesome world order aspect of the extra-legal setting within which international civil warfare of the Vietnam-type arises. White's argument, in effect, challenges the psychological premises that are relied upon by those who would define the legal position of the United States in either direction.

Part IV presents certain source materials frequently relied upon by the authors of the selections in Parts II and III. These primary materials establish the formal network of relationships whose interpretation is at the center of the legal controversy. Their inclusion is primarily to encourage a student of the legal issues to compare conflicting interpretations of official position in light of the unabridged text of the document in question. It is obvious that these documentary materials are only the starting point of comprehensive analysis and need to be supplemented in many ways, most obviously by reference to more general instruments of international law concerned with the regulation of force. The Charter of the United Nations is the most important of the general documents. Much of the legal argument generated by the Vietnam War has concerned the interaction of Articles 2 (4) and 51 of the Charter in light of the specific circumstances of Vietnam. The legal argument stresses different conclusions as to the interaction of these provisions in terms of textual interpretation, patterns of practice, and opinions of leading scholarly commentators.

In describing the contents of *The Vietnam War and International Law* it is important to explain one central omission. There has been a considerable amount of polemical writing by critics and defenders of the legality of United States participation in the Vietnam War. In Congress, in professional associations, and in citizen groups reports on the legal issues have been issued. Some of these adversary efforts have possessed considerable scholarly merit. Others of these reports or "briefs" have been fraught with fervor and have presented their issues on a basis unconvincing to anyone not previously a partisan of the position advocated. Such polemical literature is an inevitable and healthy by-product of public debate on controversial policy questions in a democratic society—a debate that has proceeded in the United States without interference from the Government throughout the course of the Vietnam War. The use of legal argument in public debate is itself worthy of careful study to enable a better appreciation of who is using international law arguments for what purposes and with what effects, but such an inquiry is sufficiently removed from the main work of the Civil War Panel to make it necessary to exclude these materials and avoid adding to an already bulky volume.

Richard J. Barnet
Thomas Ehrlich
Tom J. Farer
Lawrence S. Finkelstein
Wolfgang Friedmann
G. W. Haight
Eliot D. Hawkins

Brunson MacChesney
Myres S. McDougal
John Norton Moore
Stephen Schwebel
John R. Stevenson
Howard J. Taubenfeld
Richard A. Falk, *Chairman*

I. A FRAMEWORK FOR LEGAL INQUIRY

Civil War*

EMMERICH DE VATTEL

IT IS a much-discussed question whether the sovereign must observe the ordinary laws of war in dealing with rebellious subjects who have openly taken up arms against him. A flatterer at court or a cruel tyrant will immediately answer that the laws of war are not made for rebels, who deserve nothing better than death. Let us proceed more temperately and argue the matter upon the incontestable principles laid down in an earlier chapter. In order to understand clearly what conduct a sovereign should observe towards his rebellious subjects we must first of all remember that the rights of the sovereign are derived wholly from the rights of the State itself or of the civil society, from the duties intrusted to him, and from the obligation he is under to watch over the welfare of the Nation, to procure its greatest happiness, and to maintain order, peace, and justice within the country (see Book I, Chap. IV). Next, we must distinguish the nature and the degree of the various disorders which may disturb the State and force the sovereign to take to arms, or to substitute forcible measures where his authority has failed.

The name of *rebels* is given to all subjects who unjustly take up arms against the ruler of the society, whether with the design of deposing him from the supreme authority, or of merely resisting his orders in some particular instance and making him accept their terms.

A popular tumult is a disorderly gathering of people who refuse to listen to the voice of their superiors, whether they be disaffected towards their superiors themselves or merely towards certain private individuals. These violent movements occur when the people believe themselves harassed, and they are more often caused by tax-collectors than by any other class of public officers. If the anger of the people is directed particularly against the magistrates or other officers invested with the public authority, and if it is carried so far as to result in positive disobedience or acts of violence, the movement is called a *sedition*. And when the evil extends and wins over the majority of the citizens in a town or province, and gains such strength that the sovereign is no longer obeyed, it is usual to distinguish such an uprising more particularly by the name of an *insurrection*.

* *The Law of Nations or The Principles of Natural Law*, by Emmerich de Vattel, originally published in 1758, Book III, Chapter XVIII (reprinted from pages 336-340 of the Carnegie Endowment for International Peace's edition in the Classics of International Law series; trans. by Charles G. Fenwick).

All these acts of violence disturb the public order and are crimes against the State, even when they are based upon just grounds of complaint, for violent measures are forbidden in civil society; persons who are injured should go to the magistrates for relief, and if they can not obtain justice from them they can carry their complaints to the foot of the throne. Every citizen should suffer patiently evils that are not unendurable rather than disturb the public peace. It is only a denial of justice on the part of the sovereign, or deliberate delays, that can excuse the violence of a people whose patience is exhausted, and can even justify it, if the evils are intolerable and the oppression great and manifest. But how is the sovereign to treat the insurgents? I answer, in general in the manner that is at once most in accord with justice and conducive to the welfare of the State. If he must suppress those who unnecessarily disturb the public peace, he should show clemency towards the unfortunate persons who have just grievances and whose only crime is that of having undertaken to obtain justice for themselves; they are wanting in patience rather than in loyalty. Subjects who rise up against their prince without cause deserve the severest punishment. But here, also, the number of the guilty forces the sovereign to show mercy. Shall he depopulate a town or a province in order to quell its rebellious citizens? Certain forms of punishment, however just in themselves, become cruelty when extended to too great a number of persons. Even had the Netherlands rebelled without cause against Spain, we should still remember with horror the Duke of Alva, who boasted of having caused twenty thousand heads to fall under the axe of the executioner. Let not his bloody imitators hope to justify their excesses on the plea of necessity. Who was ever treated more shamefully by his subjects than the great Henry IV? Yet he always pardoned the conquered, and in the end he obtained a victory worthy of so noble a prince—he won over his enemies to be loyal subjects; whereas the Duke of Alva lost for his master the United Provinces. When the crime is shared in by many, the punishment should be meted out to them as a body; the sovereign may deprive a town of its franchises, at least until it has fully acknowledged its guilt, while he will reserve severer punishment for the authors of the disturbance, for those firebrands who incite the people to revolt. But only a tyrant will treat as rebels those brave and resolute citizens who exhort the people to protect themselves from oppression and to maintain their rights and privileges. A good prince will commend those noble patriots, provided their zeal is tempered with moderation and prudence; if he puts justice and duty first, if he aspires to the lofty and immortal honor of being the father of his people, let him distrust the selfish suggestions of the minister who represents to him as rebels all citizens who do not hold out their hands to the chains of slavery and who refuse to bow without a murmur under the rod of a despotic rule.

The surest method of appeasing seditions, and at the same time the most just one, is to satisfy the grievances of the people. If they have revolted without cause, which perhaps is never the case, the sovereign must even then, as we have just observed, grant an amnesty to the greater number of them. Once the amnesty has been published and accepted, all the past must be forgotten, and no one is to be called to account for what happened at the time of the disturbance; and, in general, the sovereign, scrupulous in the observance of his word, must be faithful in keeping whatever promises he has made even to the rebels— I mean to those of his subjects who have revolted without reason or without necessity. If his promises are not inviolable there will be no security for the rebels in treating with him; once they have drawn the sword they will have to throw away the scabbard, as one of the ancients expressed it: the prince will be deprived of the gentler and more effective means of quelling the revolt, and the only means left to him will be the complete extermination of the rebels. Despair will strengthen their resistance; sympathy will bring them help and increase their numbers, and the State will find itself endangered. What would have become of France if the League had been unable to trust the promises of Henry the Great? Accordingly, the same reasons which should make fidelity to promise a sacred and inviolable duty between individual and individual, sovereign and sovereign, enemy and enemy (Book II, §§ 163, 218, and foll.; Book III, § 174), hold good to their fullest extent between the sovereign and his rebellious subjects. However, if they have extorted from him unreasonable terms which are contrary to the welfare of the Nation and the safety of the State, in such case, since he has no right to do anything or grant anything in opposition to that high standard which is the rule of his conduct and the measure of his authority, he may justly revoke injurious concessions, after obtaining the consent of the Nation, whose opinion he must ask in the manner and after the forms prescribed in the Constitution of the State. But this remedy is to be used with reserve, and only where great interests are at stake, lest the principle of fidelity to promises should be impaired.

When a party is formed within the State which ceases to obey the sovereign and is strong enough to make a stand against him, or when a Republic is divided into two opposite factions, and both sides take up arms, there exists a *civil* war. Some authors limit the term to a just uprising on the part of subjects against their sovereign, in order to distinguish such lawful resistance from the open and unlawful resistance which is termed a *rebellion*. But what name will they apply to a war which breaks out in a Republic between two contending factions, or in a monarchy between two claimants to the throne? Custom applies the name of civil war to every war between the members of the same political society; if the war is between a body of the citizens on the one hand and the sovereign with those loyal to him on the other, nothing further is required to entitle the insurrection to be called *civil war,* and not *rebellion,* than that the insurgents have some cause for taking up arms. The term *rebellion* is only applied to an uprising against lawful authority, which is lacking in any semblance of justice. The sovereign never fails to stigmatize as *rebels* all subjects who openly resist his authority; but when the latter become sufficiently strong to make a stand against him, and to force him to make formal war upon them, he must necessarily submit to have the contest called civil war.

It is not here in place to consider the reasons which may authorize and justify civil war; we have elsewhere treated of the cases in which subjects may resist the sovereign (Book I, Chap. IV). Putting aside, therefore, the justice of the cause, it remains for us to consider the principles which should regulate civil war, and to determine whether the sovereign in particular is obliged to observe the ordinary laws of war.

Civil war breaks the bonds of society and of government, or at least suspends the force and effect of them; it gives rise, within the Nation, to two independent parties, who regard each other as enemies and acknowledge no common judge. Of necessity, therefore, these two parties must be regarded as forming thenceforth, for a time at least, two separate bodies politic, two distinct Nations. Although one of the two parties may have been wrong in breaking up the unity of the State and in resisting the lawful authority, still they are none the less divided in fact. Moreover, who is to judge them, and to decide which side is in the wrong and which in the right? They have no common superior upon earth. They are therefore in the situation of two Nations which enter into a dispute and, being unable to agree, have recourse to arms.

That being so, it is perfectly clear that the established laws of war, those principles of humanity, forbearance, truthfulness, and honor, which we have earlier laid down, should be observed on both sides in a civil war. The same reasons which make those laws of obligation between State and State render them equally necessary, and even more so, in the unfortunate event when two determined parties struggle for the possession of their common fatherland. If the sovereign believes himself justified in hanging the prisoners as rebels, the opposite party will retaliate; if he does not strictly observe the capitulations and all the conventions made with his enemies, they will cease to trust his word; if he burns and lays waste the country they will do the same; and the war will become cruel, terrible, and daily more disastrous to the Nation. The shameful and barbarous excesses of the Duke de Montpensier against the reformed party in France are well known. He delivered up the men to the executioner and the women to the brutality of one of his officers. What was the result? The reformed party became exasperated; they avenged the barbarous treatment shown them, and the war, already a cruel one, as being both a civil and religious conflict, became even more dreadful and destructive. Who can read without horror of the savage cruelties of Baron des-Adrets? By turns Catholic and Protestant, he was conspicuous for his barbarity on both sides. Finally he was driven to abandon his authority as judge over men who were able to maintain their cause sword in hand, and who thus forced him to treat them not as criminals, but as enemies. Soldiers themselves have frequently refused to serve in a war in which the cruelties of the prince exposed them to retaliation on the part of the enemy. While ready to shed their blood in his service on the field of battle, officers of the highest sense of honor have considered themselves under no obligation to expose themselves to an ignominious death. Accordingly, whenever a large body of citizens believe themselves justified in resisting the sovereign, and are sufficiently strong to take to arms, war should be carried on between them and the sovereign in the same manner as between two different Nations, and the belligerents should have recourse to the same means for preventing the excesses of war and for re-establishing peace as are used in other wars.

When the sovereign has conquered the party in arms against him, when he has brought them to submit and to sue for peace, he may except from the amnesty the authors of the disturbance, the leaders of the party, and may judge them according to the laws, and punish them if they are found guilty. He may follow this course especially when dealing with those disturbances which are occasioned less by popular grievances than by the designs of certain nobles, and which deserve rather the name of *rebellion* than of *civil war*. Such was the fate of the unfortunate Duke de Montmorency. He took up arms against the King in support of the Duke of Orleans, but being defeated and taken prisoner at the battle of Castelnaudarri, he died upon a scaffold by decree of the Parliament of Toulouse. If he was generally pitied by men of principle it is because he was regarded less as a rebel against the

King than as an opponent of the exorbitant power of a despotic minister, and because his heroic virtues seemed to correspond to the purity
of his motives (a).

(a) See the historians of the reign of Louis XIII.

When, without ceasing to acknowledge the authority of the sovereign,
subjects take up arms merely to obtain redress for grievances, there are
two reasons for observing in their regard the customary laws of war:
(1) the fear of rendering the civil war more cruel and destructive, from
the fact, as we have already observed, that the insurgents will retaliate
upon the severities of the prince; (2) the danger of committing great
injustice, as a result of too great haste in punishing those we are regarding as rebels. The heat of passion attending civil strife is not favorable to the administration of pure and sacred justice; a time of
greater tranquillity must be awaited. The prince will act wisely in keeping the rebels prisoners until, having restored tranquillity to the country, he is in a position to have them judged according to the laws.

As regards the other effects which the Law of Nations attributes to
public war (see Chap. XII of this Book), and particularly as regards the
acquisition of property captured in war, it must be observed that subjects who take up arms against their sovereign, without ceasing to acknowledge his authority, in general can not claim the benefit of those
effects. Only the booty—the personal property carried off by the enemy
—is regarded as lost to the owners, owing to the difficulty of identifying
it, and because of the many inconveniences attending an attempt to
reclaim it. These matters are ordinarily regulated in the edict issued
upon the re-establishment of peace, or in the act of amnesty.

But when the Nation is divided into two absolutely independent parties, who acknowledge no common superior, the State is broken up and
the war between the two parties falls, in all respects, into the class of
a public war between two different Nations. If a Republic is split up
into two factions, each of which claims to form the body of the State, or
if a Kingdom is divided between two claimants to the throne, the contending parties which thus sever the Nation will mutually regard each
other as rebels. Here, then, we have two bodies which claim to be absolutely independent and which have no judge to decide between them
(§ 293). They settle their dispute by having recourse to arms, just as
two distinct Nations would do. The obligation upon the two parties to
observe towards each other the customary laws of war is therefore absolute and indispensable, and the same which the natural law imposes
upon all Nations in contests between State and State.

Foreign Nations must not interfere in the domestic affairs of an independent State (Book II, § 54 and foll.). It is not their part to decide between citizens whom civil discord has driven to take up arms, nor between the sovereign and his subjects. The two parties are equally alien to them, and equally independent of their authority. It only remains for them to interpose their good offices for the re-establishment of peace, and this they are called upon to do by the natural law (see Book II, Chap. I). But if their efforts are without avail, those Nations which are not bound by treaty obligations may, in order to determine upon their own conduct, decide for themselves the merits of the case, and assist the party which seems to have justice on its side, should that party ask for their help or accept the offer of it; they may do so, I say, just as they are at liberty to take up the quarrel of one Nation with another, if they find it a just one. As for the allies of a State which is torn apart by civil war, they will find the rule for their conduct in the nature of their alliances considered in the light of existing circumstances. We have treated of this subject elsewhere (see Book II, Chap. XII, and particularly §§ 196, 197).

A Few Words on Non-Intervention[1]

JOHN STUART MILL

THERE is a country in Europe, equal to the greatest in extent of dominion, far exceeding any other in wealth, and in the power that wealth bestows, the declared principle of whose foreign policy is, to let other nations alone. No country apprehends or affects to apprehend from it any aggressive designs. Power, from of old, is wont to encroach upon the weak, and to quarrel for ascendancy with those who are as strong as itself. Not so this nation. It will hold its own, it will not submit to encroachment, but if other nations do not meddle with it, it will not meddle with them. Any attempt it makes to exert influence over them, even by persuasion, is rather in the service of others, than of itself: to mediate in the quarrels which break out between foreign States, to arrest obstinate civil wars, to reconcile belligerents, to intercede for mild treatment of the vanquished, or finally, to procure the abandonment of some national crime and scandal to humanity, such as the slave-trade. Not only does this nation desire no benefit to itself at the expense of others, it desires none in which all others do not as freely participate. It makes no treaties stipulating for separate commercial advantages. If the aggressions of barbarians force it to a successful war, and its victorious arms put it in a position to command liberty of trade, whatever it demands for itself it demands for all mankind. The cost of the war is its own; the fruits it shares in fraternal equality with the whole human race. Its own ports and commerce are free as the air and the sky: all its neighbours have full liberty to resort to it, paying either no duties, or, if any, generally a mere equivalent for what is paid by its own citizens; nor does it concern itself though they, on their part, keep all to themselves, and persist in the most jealous and narrow-minded exclusion of its merchants and goods.

A nation adopting this policy is a novelty in the world; so much so, it would appear, that many are unable to believe it when they see it. By one of the practical paradoxes which often meet us in human affairs, it is this nation which finds itself, in respect of its foreign policy, held up to obloquy as the type of egoism and selfishness; as a nation which thinks of nothing but of out-witting and out-generalling its neighbours. An enemy, or a self-fancied rival who had been distanced in the race, might be conceived to give vent to such an accusation in a moment of ill-temper. But that it should be accepted by lookers-on, and should

1 *Fraser's Magazine*, December 1859.

pass into a popular doctrine, is enough to surprise even those who have best sounded the depths of human prejudice. Such, however, is the estimate of the foreign policy of England most widely current on the Continent. Let us not flatter ourselves that it is merely the dishonest pretence of enemies, or of those who have their own purposes to serve by exciting odium against us, a class including all the Protectionist writers, and the mouthpieces of all the despots and of the Papacy. The more blameless and laudable our policy might be, the more certainly we might count on its being misrepresented and railed at by these worthies. Unfortunately the belief is not confined to those whom they can influence, but is held with all the tenacity of a prejudice, by innumerable persons free from interested bias. So strong a hold has it on their minds, that when an Englishman attempts to remove it, all their habitual politeness does not enable them to disguise their utter unbelief in his disclaimer. They are firmly persuaded that no word is said, nor act done, by English statesmen in reference to foreign affairs, which has not for its motive principle some peculiarly English interest. Any profession of the contrary appears to them too ludicrously transparent an attempt to impose upon them. Those most friendly to us think they make a great concession in admitting that the fault may possibly be less with the English people, than with the English Government and aristocracy. We do not even receive credit from them for following our own interest with a straightforward recognition of honesty as the best policy. They believe that we have always other objects than those we avow; and the most far-fetched and unplausible suggestion of a selfish purpose appears to them better entitled to credence than anything so utterly incredible as our disinterestedness. Thus, to give one instance among many, when we taxed ourselves twenty millions (a prodigious sum in their estimation) to get rid of negro slavery, and, for the same object, perilled, as everybody thought, destroyed as many thought, the very existence of our West Indian colonies, it was, and still is, believed, that our fine professions were but to delude the world, and that by this self-sacrificing behaviour we were endeavouring to gain some hidden object, which could neither be conceived nor described, in the way of pulling down other nations. The fox who had lost his tail had an intelligible interest in persuading his neighbours to rid themselves of theirs: but we, it is thought by *our* neighbours, cut off our own magnificent brush, the largest and finest of all, in hopes of reaping some inexplicable advantage from inducing others to do the same.

It is foolish attempting to despise all this—persuading ourselves that it is not our fault, and that those who disbelieve *us* would not believe though one should rise from the dead. Nations, like individuals, ought to suspect some fault in themselves when they find they are generally worse thought of than they think they deserve; and they may well know that they are somehow in fault when almost everybody but themselves thinks them crafty and hypocritical. It is not solely because England has been more successful than other nations in gaining what they are all aiming at, that they think she must be following after it with a more ceaseless and a more undivided chase. This indeed is a powerful predisposing cause, inclining and preparing them for the belief. It is a natural supposition that those who win the prize have striven for it; that superior success must be the fruit of more unremitting endeavour; and where there is an obvious abstinence from the ordinary arts employed for distancing competitors, and they are distanced nevertheless, people are fond of believing that the means employed must have been arts still more subtle and profound. This preconception makes them look out in all quarters for indications to prop up the selfish explanation of our conduct. If our ordinary course of action does not favour this interpretation, they watch for exceptions to our ordinary course, and regard these as the real index to the purposes within. They moreover accept literally all the habitual expressions by which we represent ourselves as worse than we are; expressions often heard from English statesmen, next to never from those of any other country—partly because Englishmen, beyond all the rest of the human race, are so shy of professing virtues that they will even profess vices instead; and partly because almost all English statesmen, while careless to a degree which no foreigner can credit, respecting the impression they produce on foreigners, commit the obtuse blunder of supposing that low objects are the only ones to which the minds of their non-aristocratic fellow-countrymen are amenable, and that it is always expedient, if not necessary, to place those objects in the foremost rank.

All, therefore, who either speak or act in the name of England, are bound by the strongest obligations, both of prudence and of duty, to avoid giving either of these handles for misconstruction: to put a severe restraint upon the mania of professing to act from meaner motives than those by which we are really actuated, and to beware of perversely or capriciously singling out some particular instance in which to act on a worse principle than that by which we are ordinarily guided. Both these salutary cautions our practical statesmen are, at the present time, flagrantly disregarding.

We are now in one of those critical moments, which do not occur once in a generation, when the whole turn of European events, and the course of European history for a long time to come, may depend on the conduct and on the estimation of England. At such a moment, it is difficult to say whether by their sins of speech or of action our statesmen are most effectually playing into the hands of our enemies, and giving most colour of justice to injurious misconception of our character and policy as a people.

To take the sins of speech first: What is the sort of language held in every oration which, during the present European crisis, any English minister, or almost any considerable public man, addresses to Parliament or to his constituents? The eternal repetition of this shabby *refrain*—'We did not interfere, because no English interest was involved;' 'We ought not to interfere where no English interest is concerned.' England is thus exhibited as a country whose most distinguished men are not ashamed to profess, as politicians, a rule of action which no one, not utterly base, could endure to be accused of as the maxim by which he guides his private life; not to move a finger for others unless he sees his private advantage in it. There is much to be said for the doctrine that a nation should be willing to assist its neighbours in throwing off oppression and gaining free institutions. Much also may be said by those who maintain that one nation is incompetent to judge and act for another, and that each should be left to help itself, and seek advantage or submit to disadvantage as it can and will. But of all attitudes which a nation can take up on the subject of intervention, the meanest and worst is to profess that it interferes only when it can serve its own objects by it. Every other nation is entitled to say, 'It seems, then, that non-interference is not a matter of principle with you. When you abstain from interference, it is not because you think it wrong. You have no objection to interfere, only it must not be for the sake of those you interfere with; they must not suppose that you have any regard for their good. The good of others is not one of the things you care for; but you are willing to meddle, if by meddling you can gain anything for yourselves.' Such is the obvious interpretation of the language used.

There is scarcely any necessity to say, writing to Englishmen, that this is not what our rulers and politicians really mean. Their language is not a correct exponent of their thoughts. They mean a part only of what they seem to say. They do mean to disclaim interference for the sake of doing good to foreign nations. They are quite sincere and in earnest in repudiating this. But the other half of what their words express, a willingness to meddle if by doing so they can promote any interest of England, they do not mean. The thought they have in their minds, is not the interest of England, but her security. What they would say, is, that they are ready to act when England's safety is threatened, or any of her interests hostilely or unfairly endangered. This is no more than what all nations, sufficiently powerful for their own protection, do, and no one questions their right to do. It is the common right of self-defence. But if we mean this, why, in Heaven's name, do we take every possible opportunity of saying, instead of this, something exceedingly different? Not self-defence, but aggrandizement, is the sense which foreign listeners put upon our words. Not simply to protect what we have, and that merely against unfair arts, not against fair rivalry; but to add to it more and more without limit, is the purpose for which foreigners think we claim the liberty of intermeddling with them and their affairs. If our actions make it impossible for the most prejudiced observer to believe that we aim at or would accept any sort of mercantile monopolies, this has no effect on their minds but to make them think that we have chosen a more cunning way to the same end. It is a generally accredited opinion among Continental politicians, especially those who think themselves particularly knowing, that the very existence of England depends upon the incessant acquisition of new markets for our manufactures; that the chase after these is an affair of life and death to us; and that we are at all times ready to trample on every obligation of public or international morality, when the alternative would be, pausing for a moment in that race. It would be superfluous to point out what profound ignorance and misconception of all the laws of national wealth, and all the facts of England's commercial condition, this opinion presupposes: but such ignorance and misconception are unhappily very general on the Continent; they are but slowly, if perceptibly, giving way before the advance of reason; and for generations, perhaps, to come, we shall be judged under their influence. Is it requiring too much from our practical politicians to wish that they would sometimes bear these things in mind? Does it answer any good purpose to express ourselves as if we did not scruple to profess that which we not merely scruple to do, but the bare idea of doing which never crosses our minds? Why should we abnegate the character we might with truth lay claim to, of being incomparably the most conscientious of all nations in our national acts? Of all countries which are sufficiently powerful to be capable of being dangerous to their neighbours, we are perhaps the only one whom mere scruples of conscience would suffice to deter from it. We are the only people among whom, by no class whatever of society, is the interest or glory of the nation considered to be any sufficient excuse for an unjust act; the only one which regards with jealousy and suspicion, and a proneness to hostile criticism, precisely those acts of its Government which in other countries are sure to be hailed with applause, those by which territory has been acquired, or political influence extended. Being in reality better than other nations, in at least the negative part of international morality, let us cease, by the language we use, to give ourselves out as worse.

But if we ought to be careful of our language, a thousand times more obligatory it is upon us to be careful of our deeds, and not suffer ourselves to be betrayed by any of our leading men into a line of conduct on some isolated point, utterly opposed to our habitual principles of action—conduct such that if it were a fair specimen of us, it would verify the calumnies of our worst enemies, and justify them in representing not only that we have no regard for the good of other nations, but that we actually think their good and our own incompatible, and will go all lengths to prevent others from realizing even an advantage in which we ourselves are to share. This pernicious, and, one can scarcely help calling it, almost insane blunder, we seem to be committing on the subject of the Suez Canal.

It is the universal belief in France that English influence at Constantinople, strenuously exerted to defeat this project, is the real and only invincible obstacle to its being carried into effect. And unhappily the public declarations of our present Prime Minister not only bear out this persuasion, but warrant the assertion that we oppose the work because, in the opinion of our Government, it would be injurious to the interest of England. If such be the course we are pursuing, and such the motive of it, and if nations have duties, even negative ones, towards the weal of the human race, it is hard to say whether the folly or the immorality of our conduct is the most painfully conspicuous.

Here is a project, the practicability of which is indeed a matter in dispute, but of which no one has attempted to deny that, supposing it realized, it would give a facility to commerce, and consequently a stimulus to production, an encouragement to intercourse, and therefore to civilization, which would entitle it to a high rank among the great industrial improvements of modern times. The contriving of new means of abridging labour and economizing outlay in the operations of industry, is the object to which the larger half of all the inventive ingenuity of mankind is at present given up; and this scheme, if realized, will save, on one of the great highways of the world's traffic, the circumnavigation of a continent. An easy access of commerce is the main source of that material civilization, which, in the more backward regions of the earth, is the necessary condition and indispensable machinery of the moral; and this scheme reduces practically by one half, the distance, commercially speaking, between the self-improving nations of the world and the most important and valuable of the unimproving. The Atlantic Telegraph is esteemed an enterprise of world-wide importance because it abridges the transit of mercantile intelligence merely. What the Suez Canal would shorten is the transport of the goods themselves, and this to such an extent as probably to augment it manifold.

Let us suppose, then—for in the present day the hypothesis is too un-English to be spoken of as anything more than a supposition—let us suppose that the English nation saw in this great benefit to the civilized and uncivilized world a danger or damage to some peculiar interest of England. Suppose, for example, that it feared, by shortening the road, to facilitate the access of foreign navies to its Oriental possessions. The supposition imputes no ordinary degree of cowardice and imbecility to the national mind; otherwise it could not but reflect that the same thing which would facilitate the arrival of an enemy, would facilitate also that of succour; that we have had French fleets in the Eastern seas before now, and have fought naval battles with them there, nearly a century ago; that if we ever became unable to defend India against them, we should assuredly have them there without the aid of any canal; and that our power of resisting an enemy does not depend upon putting a little more or less of obstacle in the way of his coming, but upon the amount of force which we are able to oppose to him when come. Let us assume, however, that the success of the project would do more harm to England in some separate capacity, than the good which, as the chief commercial nation, she would reap from the great increase of commercial intercourse. Let us grant this: and I now ask, what then? Is there any morality, Christian or secular, which bears out a nation in keeping all the rest of mankind out of some great advantage, because the consequences of their obtaining it may be to itself, in some imaginable contingency, a cause of inconvenience? Is a nation at liberty to adopt as a practical maxim, that what is good for the human race is bad for itself, and to withstand it accordingly? What is this but to declare that its interest and that of mankind are incompatible—that, thus far at least, it is the enemy of the human race? And what ground has it of complaint if, in return, the human race determine to be *its* enemies? So wicked a principle, avowed and acted on by a nation, would entitle the rest of the world to unite in a league against it, and never to make peace until they had, if not reduced it to insignificance, at least sufficiently broken its power to disable it from ever again placing its own self-interest before the general prosperity of mankind.

There is no such base feeling in the British people. They are accustomed to see their advantage in forwarding, not in keeping back, the growth in wealth and civilization of the world. The opposition to the Suez Canal has never been a national opposition. With their usual indifference to foreign affairs, the public in general have not thought about it, but have left it, as (unless when particularly excited) they leave all the management of their foreign policy, to those who, from causes and reasons connected only with internal politics, happen for the time to be in office. Whatever has been done in the name of England in the Suez affair has been the act of individuals; mainly, it is probable, of one individual; scarcely any of his countrymen either prompting or sharing his purpose, and most of those who have paid any attention to the subject (unfortunately a very small number) being, to all appearance, opposed to him.

But (it is said) the scheme cannot be executed. If so, why concern ourselves about it? If the project can come to nothing, why profess gratuitous immorality and incur gratuitous odium to prevent it from being tried? Whether it will succeed or fail is a consideration totally irrelevant; except thus far, that if it is sure to fail, there is in our resistance to it the same immorality, and an additional amount of folly; since, on that supposition, we are parading to the world a belief that our interest is inconsistent with its good, while if the failure of the project would really be any benefit to us, we are certain of obtaining that benefit by merely holding our peace.

As a matter of private opinion, the present writer, so far as he has looked into the evidence, inclines to agree with those who think that the scheme cannot be executed, at least by the means and with the funds proposed. But this is a consideration for the shareholders. The British Government does not deem it any part of its business to prevent individuals, even British citizens, from wasting their own money in unsuccessful speculations, though holding out no prospect of great public usefulness in the event of success. And if, though at the cost of their own property, they acted as pioneers to others, and the scheme, though a losing one to those who first undertook it, should, in the same or in other hands, realize the full expected amount of ultimate benefit to the world at large, it would not be the first nor the hundredth time that an unprofitable enterprise has had this for its final result.

There seems to be no little need that the whole doctrine of non-interference with foreign nations should be reconsidered, if it can be said to have as yet been considered as a really moral question at all. We have heard something lately about being willing to go to war for an idea. To go to war for an idea, if the war is aggressive, not defensive, is as criminal as to go to war for territory or revenue; for it is as little justifiable to force our ideas on other people, as to compel them to submit to our will in any other respect. But there assuredly are cases in which it is allowable to go to war, without having been ourselves attacked, or threatened with attack; and it is very important that nations should make up their minds in time, as to what these cases are. There are few questions which more require to be taken in hand by ethical and political philosophers, with a view to establish some rule or criterion whereby the justifiableness of intervening in the affairs of other countries, and (what is sometimes fully as questionable) the justifiableness of refraining from intervention, may be brought to a definite and rational test. Whoever attempts this, will be led to recognise more than one fundamental distinction, not yet by any means familiar to the public mind, and in general quite lost sight of by those who write in strains of indignant morality on the subject. There is a great difference (for example) between the case in which the nations concerned are of the same, or something like the same, degree of civilization, and that in which one of the parties to the situation is of a high, and the other of a very low, grade of social improvement. To suppose that the same international customs, and the same rules of international morality, can obtain between one civilized nation and another, and between civilized nations and barbarians, is a grave error, and one which no statesman can fall into, however it may be with those who, from a safe and unresponsible position, criticise statesmen. Among many reasons why the same rules cannot be applicable to situations so different, the two following are among the most important. In the first place, the rules of ordinary international morality imply reciprocity. But barbarians will not reciprocate. They cannot be depended on for observing any rules. Their minds are not capable of so great an effort, nor their will sufficiently under the influence of distant motives. In the next place, nations which are still barbarous have not got beyond the period during which it is likely to be for their benefit that they should be conquered and held in subjection by foreigners. Independence and nationality, so essential to the due growth and development of a people further advanced in improvement, are generally impediments to theirs. The sacred duties which civilized nations owe to the independence and nationality of each other, are not binding towards those to whom nationality and independence are either a certain evil, or at best a questionable good. The Romans were not the most clean-handed of conquerors, yet would it have been better for Gaul and Spain, Numidia and Dacia, never to have formed part of the Roman Empire? To characterize any conduct whatever towards a barbarous people as a violation of the law of nations, only shows that he who so speaks has never considered the subject. A violation of great principles of morality it may easily be; but barbarians have no rights as a *nation*, except a right to such treatment as may, at the earliest possible period, fit them for becoming one. The only moral laws for the relation between a civilized and a barbarous government, are the universal rules of morality between man and man.

The criticisms, therefore, which are so often made upon the conduct of the French in Algeria, or of the English in India, proceed, it would seem, mostly on a wrong principle. The true standard by which to judge their proceedings never having been laid down, they escape such comment and censure as might really have an improving effect, while they are tried by a standard which can have no influence on those practically engaged in such transactions, knowing as they do that it cannot, and if it could, ought not to be observed, because no human being would be the better, and many much the worse, for its observance. A civilized government cannot help having barbarous neighbours: when it has, it cannot always content itself with a defensive position, one of mere resistance to aggression. After a longer or shorter interval of forbearance, it either finds itself obliged to conquer them, or to assert so much authority over them, and so break their spirit, that they gradually sink into a state of dependence upon itself: and when that time arrives, they are indeed no longer formidable to it, but it has had so much to do with setting up and pulling down their governments, and they have grown so accustomed to lean on it, that it has become morally responsible for all evil it allows them to do. This is the history of the relations of the British Government with the native States of India. It never was secure in its own Indian possessions until it had reduced the military power of those States to a nullity. But a despotic government only exists by its military power. When we had taken away theirs, we were forced, by the necessity of the case, to offer them ours instead of it. To enable them to dispense with large armies of their own, we bound ourselves to place at their disposal, and they bound themselves to receive, such an amount of military force as made us in fact masters of the country. We engaged that this force should fulfil the purposes of a force, by defending the prince against all foreign and internal enemies. But being thus assured of the protection of a civilized power, and freed from the fear of internal rebellion or foreign conquest, the only checks which either restrain the passions or keep any vigour in the character of an Asiatic despot, the native Governments either became so oppressive and extortionate as to desolate the country, or fell into such a state of nerveless imbecility, that every one, subject to their will, who had not the means of defending himself by his own armed followers, was the prey of any-body who had a band of ruffians in his pay. The British Government felt this deplorable state of things to be its own work; being the direct con-sequence of the position in which, for its own security, it had placed itself towards the native governments. Had it permitted this to go on indefinitely, it would have deserved to be accounted among the worst political malefactors. In some cases (unhappily not in all) it had en-deavoured to take precaution against these mischiefs by a special article in the treaty, binding the prince to reform his administration, and in future to govern in conformity to the advice of the British Government. Among the treaties in which a provision of this sort had been inserted, was that with Oude. For fifty years and more did the British Govern-ment allow this engagement to be treated with entire disregard; not without frequent remonstrances, and occasionally threats, but without ever carrying into effect what it threatened. During this period of half a century, England was morally accountable for a mixture of tyranny and anarchy, the picture of which, by men who knew it well, is appalling to all who read it. The act by which the Government of British India at last set aside treaties which had been so pertinaciously violated, and assumed the power of fulfilling the obligation it had so long before incurred, of giving to the people of Oude a tolerable government, far from being the political crime it is so often ignorantly called, was a criminally tardy discharge of an imperative duty. And the fact, that nothing which had been done in all this century by the East India Company's Government made it so unpopular in England, is one of the most striking instances of what was noticed in a former part of this article—the predisposition of English public opinion to look unfavour-ably upon every act by which territory or revenue are acquired from foreign States, and to take part with any government, however un-worthy, which can make out the merest semblance of a case of injustice against our own country.

But among civilized peoples, members of an equal community of nations, like Christian Europe, the question assumes another aspect, and must be decided on totally different principles. It would be an affront to the reader to discuss the immorality of wars of conquest, or of conquest even as the consequence of lawful war; the annexation of any civilized people to the dominion of another, unless by their own spontaneous election. Up to this point, there is no difference of opinion among honest people; nor on the wickedness of commencing an aggressive war for any interest of our own, except when necessary to avert from ourselves an obviously impending wrong. The disputed question is that of interfering in the regulation of another country's internal concerns; the question whether a nation is justified in taking part, on either side, in the civil wars or party contests of another; and chiefly, whether it may justifiably aid the people of another country in struggling for liberty; or may impose on a country any particular government or institutions, either as being best for the country itself, or as necessary for the security of its neighbours.

Of these cases, that of a people in arms for liberty is the only one of any nicety, or which, theoretically at least, is likely to present conflicting moral considerations. The other cases which have been mentioned hardly admit of discussion. Assistance to the government of a country in keeping down the people, unhappily by far the most frequent case of foreign intervention, no one writing in a free country needs take the trouble of stigmatizing. A government which needs foreign support to enforce obedience from its own citizens, is one which ought not to exist; and the assistance given to it by foreigners is hardly ever anything but the sympathy of one despotism with another. A case requiring consideration is that of a protracted civil war, in which the contending parties are so equally balanced that there is no probability of a speedy issue; or if there is, the victorious side cannot hope to keep down the vanquished but by severities repugnant to humanity, and injurious to the permanent welfare of the country. In this exceptional case it seems now to be an admitted doctrine, that the neighbouring nations, or one powerful neighbour with the acquiescence of the rest, are warranted in demanding that the contest shall cease, and a reconciliation take place on equitable terms of compromise. Intervention of this description has been repeatedly practised during the present generation, with such general approval, that its legitimacy may be considered to have passed into a maxim of what is called international law. The interference of the European Powers between Greece and Turkey, and between Turkey and Egypt, were cases in point. That between Holland and Belgium was still more so. The intervention of England in Portugal, a few years ago, which is probably less remembered than the others, because it took effect without the employment of actual force, belongs to the same category. At the time, this interposition had the appearance of a bad and dishonest backing of the government against the people, being so timed as to hit the exact moment when the popular party had obtained a marked advantage, and seemed on the eve of overthrowing the government, or reducing it to terms. But if ever a political act which looked ill in the commencement could be justified by the event, this was; for, as the fact turned out, instead of giving ascendancy to a party, it proved a really healing measure; and the chiefs of the so-called rebellion were, within a few years, the honoured and successful ministers of the throne against which they had so lately fought.

With respect to the question, whether one country is justified in helping the people of another in a struggle against their government for free institutions, the answer will be different, according as the yoke which the people are attempting to throw off is that of a purely native government, or of foreigners; considering as one of foreigners, every government which maintains itself by foreign support. When the contest is only with native rulers, and with such native strength as those rulers can enlist in their defence, the answer I should give to the question of the legitimacy of intervention is, as a general rule, No. The reason is, that there can seldom be anything approaching to assurance that intervention, even if successful, would be for the good of the people themselves. The only test possessing any real value, of a people's having become fit for popular institutions, is that they, or a sufficient portion of them to prevail in the contest, are willing to brave labour and danger for their liberation. I know all that may be said. I know it may be urged that the virtues of freemen cannot be learnt in the school of slavery, and that if a people are not fit for freedom, to have any chance of becoming so they must first be free. And this would be conclusive, if the intervention recommended would really give them freedom. But the evil is, that if they have not sufficient love of liberty to be able to wrest it from merely domestic oppressors, the liberty which is bestowed on them by other hands than their own, will have nothing real, nothing permanent. No people ever was and remained free, but because it was determined to be so; because neither its rulers nor any other party in the nation could compel it to be otherwise. If a people—especially one whose freedom has not yet become prescriptive—does not value it sufficiently to fight for it, and maintain it against any force which can be mustered *within* the country, even by those who have the command of the public revenue, it is only a question in how few years or months that people will be enslaved. Either the government which it has given to itself, or some military leader or knot of conspirators who contrive to subvert the government, will speedily put an end to all popular institutions: unless indeed it suits their convenience better to leave them standing, and be content with reducing them to mere forms; for, unless the spirit of liberty is strong in a people, those who have the executive in their hands easily work any institutions to the purposes of despotism. There is no sure guarantee against this deplorable issue, even in a country which has achieved its own freedom; as may be seen in the present day by striking examples both in the Old and New Worlds: but when freedom has been achieved *for* them, they have little prospect indeed of escaping this fate. When a people has had the misfortune to be ruled by a government under which the feelings and the virtues needful for maintaining freedom could not develope themselves, it is during an arduous struggle to become free by their own efforts that these feelings and virtues have the best chance of springing up. Men become attached to that which they have long fought for and made sacrifices for; they learned to appreciate that on which their thoughts have been much engaged; and a contest in which many have been called on to devote themselves for their country, is a school in which they learn to value their country's interest above their own.

It can seldom, therefore—I will not go so far as to say never—be either judicious or right, in a country which has a free government, to assist, otherwise than by the moral support of its opinion, the endeavours of another to extort the same blessing from its native rulers. We must except, of course, any case in which such assistance is a measure of legitimate self-defence. If (a contingency by no means unlikely to occur) this country, on account of its freedom, which is a standing reproach to despotism everywhere, and an encouragement to throw it off, should find itself menaced with attack by a coalition of Continental despots, it ought to consider the popular party in every nation of the Continent as its natural ally: the Liberals should be to it, what the Protestants of Europe were to the Government of Queen Elizabeth. So, again, when a nation, in her own defence, has gone to war with a despot, and has had the rare good fortune not only to succeed in her resistance, but to hold the conditions of peace in her own hands, she is entitled to say that she will make no treaty, unless with some other ruler than the one whose existence as such may be a perpetual menace to her safety and freedom. These exceptions do but set in a clearer light the reasons of the rule; because they do not depend on any failure of those reasons, but on considerations paramount to them, and coming under a different principle.

But the case of a people struggling against a foreign yoke, or against a native tyranny upheld by foreign arms, illustrates the reasons for non-intervention in an opposite way; for in this case the reasons themselves do not exist. A people the most attached to freedom, the most capable of defending and of making a good use of free institutions, may be unable to contend successfully for them against the military strength of another nation much more powerful. To assist a people thus kept down, is not to disturb the balance of forces on which the permanent maintenance of freedom in a country depends, but to redress that balance when it is already unfairly and violently disturbed. The doctrine of non-intervention, to be a legitimate principle of morality, must be accepted by all governments. The despots must consent to be bound by it as well as the free States. Unless they do, the profession of it by free countries comes but to this miserable issue, that the wrong side may help the wrong, but the right must not help the right. Intervention to enforce non-intervention is always rightful, always moral, if not always prudent. Though it be a mistake to *give* freedom to a people who do not value the boon, it cannot but be right to insist that if they do value it, they shall not be hindered from the pursuit of it by foreign coercion. It might not have been right for England (even apart from the question of prudence) to have taken part with Hungary in its noble struggle against Austria; although the Austrian Government in Hungary was in some sense a foreign yoke. But when, the Hungarians having shown themselves likely to prevail in this struggle, the Russian despot interposed, and joining his force to that of Austria, delivered back the Hungarians, bound hand and foot, to their exasperated oppressors, it would have been an honourable and virtuous act on the part of England to have declared that this should not be, and that if Russia gave assistance to the wrong side, England would aid the right. It might not have been consistent with the regard which every nation is bound to pay to its own safety, for England to have taken up this position single-handed. But England and France together could have done it; and if they had, the Russian armed intervention would never have taken place, or would have been disastrous to Russia alone: while all that those Powers gained by not doing it, was that they had to fight Russia five years afterwards, under more difficult circumstances, and without Hungary for an ally. The first nation which, being powerful enough to make its voice effectual, has the spirit and courage to say that not a gun shall be fired in Europe by the soldiers of one Power against the revolted subjects of another, will be the idol of the friends of freedom throughout Europe. That declaration alone will ensure the almost immediate emancipation of every people which desires liberty sufficiently to be capable of maintaining it: and the nation which gives the word will soon find itself at the head of an alliance of free peoples, so strong as to defy the efforts of any number of confederated despots to bring it down. The prize is too glorious not to be snatched sooner or later by some free country; and the time may not be distant when England, if she does not take this heroic part because of its heroism, will be compelled to take it from consideration for her own safety.

The Morality and Politics
of Intervention

MANFRED HALPERN*

I. *Intervention Redefined*

IT IS not inevitable that men should ask whether it is moral to intervene in the internal affairs of other nations. To some, it has obviously become a mere question of posture—how to keep a straight face while intervening, how to smile piously when discovered, and how to win converts during the moral upsurge that should accompany the exposure of others in the great game of intervention. Some are convinced that the Communist world represents a menace so evil that any action against this threat, as long as it is successful, is by definition moral, or else merely a problem of techniques.

If the question of morality is evaded by the technicians of power and the secular crusaders, the meaning of intervention

* This essay has been reprinted, in somewhat revised form, from a pamphlet of the same title originally published by the Council on Religion and International Affairs (New York, 1963). Its permission is gratefully acknowledged. The essay also appeared in *International Aspects of Civil Strife*, ed. James N. Rosenau (Princeton University Press, 1964).

I am deeply indebted to Ernest W. Lefever, Washington consultant to the Council on Religion and International Affairs, for first inviting me to explore these ideas under the intellectually hospitable and rewarding auspices of the Council; to Robert E. Osgood, Robert C. Good, John Courtney Murray, S.J., Robert C. Tucker, Arthur Hertzberg, Robert Gordis, William A. Lybrand, Samuel P. Huntington, Kenneth W. Thompson, and William Lee Miller, who served as chairman or first discussants during Council consultations; and to the board of trustees and the staff of the Council, and to more than fifty government officials, men of religion, and scholars who joined for several intensive hours in Washington and New York to discuss an earlier draft; and to Gregory Massell, Thomas P. Thornton, and Betsy Steele Halpern, who read this paper at various stages. The ideas offered here owe much to their criticism and suggestions even if, at times, these revisions may only have served to clarify and sharpen differences of opinion. Needless to say, I speak for no one in this essay but myself.

is often obscured by traditional preconceptions. Only at first glance does "intervention" seem an obviously identifiable act carrying obvious consequences. In a world built upon national sovereignties and jurisdictions and the equality of independent states, any state that intervenes in the internal affairs of another undermines the institutional and legal foundations on which its own existence rests. This is a truth of great consequence to which we shall have to return. But it is not the only truth. Intervention, which by its nature subverts the foundations of the existing international system, takes place in a system which is by its nature fundamentally unstable. States in fact are not equal: nations can exploit the rules and opportunities of the present international system to enlarge their power over others and so risk death on a vast scale. We live at a time when intervention, by subverting the sovereignty of national independence, may further undermine the only rules of the game that now maintain order, yet when intervention alone may be able to restore the free operation of these rules, save freedom in a nation or, indeed, help to create a more secure and more freely interdependent world order. In our world, intervention can be moral or immoral, or simultaneously illegal and justifiable. The morality of intervention is determined both by the principles it creates or destroys and by the contingencies of circumstances. Intervention therefore involves a realm of morality in which a discussion of principles is essential but in which no discussion of principles has relevance for the next act of intervention or nonintervention until the circumstances surrounding that act have also been discussed.

It is an illustration of the unstable character of the present international system that there is no agreement on the definition of the two acts most likely to destroy the sovereignty, independence, and equality of any participant in the system, or perhaps even the system itself—namely, aggression and intervention. That is not to say that there is no agreement whatever. There is enough agreement to make the system endure; not sufficient agreement to make it stable. Nonetheless, to say that intervention is interference (falling short of aggressively crossing the frontiers with military force) in the internal affairs of another sovereign state is almost to obscure the question. We live, more now than ever, in an interdependent world. Almost everything that a powerful nation does (or almost everything that a weak nation, like the Congo, is powerless to do) vitally affects the internal affairs of many other nations.

A Great Power intervenes in the domestic realm of other states when it says "yes" and when it says "no"; indeed, by its sheer existence. By our very model of life we set an example for the Russians which stings Khrushchev to competition and not a few of his citizens to an emulation subversive of the official ideal of Bolshevik Man, even if not directly of the Soviet government. We intervene when we say "no" to the Aswan Dam, without which Egypt's standard of poverty would further deteriorate; we intervene correspondingly when we say "yes" to the Volta Dam in Ghana.[1]

It has been said that if the American economy sneezes, the world's economy, and especially countries depending on the export of a single raw material, catch pneumonia. A socialist is entitled to say that deliberate nonintervention by governments in their own richer and more powerful domestic economies may cause as much suffering, not only at home but abroad, as the deliberate exploitation of poorer and weaker foreign economies. The capitalist recognizes the potency of such economic intervention in the affairs of other sovereign

[1] Robert Batchelder has raised the question of what responsibilities the American government ought to accept when a private U.S. corporation establishes a plant abroad which, by virtue of the scope of its activities in an otherwise underdeveloped country, not only dominates that economy but sets in motion a social and political transformation which the local government is too weak to guide into channels conducive to domestic welfare and national independence. On the more limited question of the rights of private companies abroad, the U.S. government has for several decades now adhered to the policy that each nation has the right to nationalize foreign property, provided it pays fair compensation.

states both when he opposes and when he supports selective domestic subsidies and foreign aid. Intentions alone do not keep actions from being interventionist. The Western democracies' intention not to intervene in the Spanish Civil War was one of the crucial factors intervening in favor of General Franco's victory.

Intervention may include propaganda, espionage, discriminatory economic policies, assistance to legitimate governments in their domestic tasks [2] no less than aid to subversive movements, and support or denial of support to governments or opposition parties in domestic crises where such foreign support might prove to be decisive. There is no validity in confining the term only to those actions which the *legitimate* government of the country considers to be intervention. In an age of social and colonial revolutions, any prudent government will be as sensitive to the reactions of the future rulers of Angola or Iran to intervention and its consequences as to the reactions of the present ruling regimes. In trying to distinguish intervention from other actions that have consequences across frontiers, one can only set outer limits: intervention is any action, beginning with deliberate or remediable interaction among nations, that significantly affects the public internal realm of another sovereign state and which stops short of aggressive crossing of international frontiers.[3] Intervention is action along

---

[2] For example, agreeing to the holding of a summit conference because, among other reasons, it may benefit the British Conservatives in a forthcoming election, or training the Iranian police in more effective techniques of coping with anti-government activities.

[3] It may be argued that the threat of aggression, and even aggression itself, may constitute intervention. The United States has repeatedly moved military forces into Caribbean states for the sake of altering their internal policies without, however, staying long or taking sovereign title to the countries involved. The question is difficult to decide. The British army "intervened" in Egypt in 1882 and stayed for seventy-four years without taking title to the country. Is that therefore merely to be called "intervention"? This ambiguity illustrates the difficulties of defining the most desperate encounters nations may have, and how readily intervention can shade into the ultimate kind of force.

a continuum of possible choices. The range of alternative courses once men have decided to intervene (or indeed, not to intervene) is far greater than is usually thought of when men debate intervention. Our political and moral responsibility in the realm of intervention is therefore far greater than we usually assume.

Several objections may be raised against so broad a definition of intervention. Certainly it would not be helpful for USIA to speak of such constructive American policies as the application of the Truman Doctrine in Greece and Turkey, or our successful efforts to deter the French from deposing in 1951 the nationalist-minded King of the then French Protectorate of Morocco, as a policy of intervention. To refer to American policy publicly as a "diplomacy of involvement" may be no less accurate, but more agreeable—reserving the harder word "intervention" to describe the actions of unfriendly nations. In the present clinical discussion, however, a single term is more fitting for describing this singular form of national behavior.

A more profound and substantive objection may be raised —namely, that giving such wide compass to the meaning of intervention will tend to undermine precious distinctions between coercion and persuasion in international diplomacy. These distinctions are vital, but they do not take the simple form often ascribed to them. No serious Great Power tries to persuade another nation unless it means to convince. Whether it wins its case or strikes a bargain depends not only on the soundness of its arguments but also on the coercive weight of power that each interested nation has experienced or wishes to avoid experiencing. In international affairs, coercion begins at the moment of persuasion. There is only one important exception—namely, where two nations have agreed on overlapping national interests in a situation in which one nation is not invidiously dependent on the other. In all other cases, the crucial distinction in international relations does not lie in the separation of power and persuasion, but in the difference among the means and ends of power and persuasion—or among types of intervention (discussed below). It still makes a considerable difference whether the coercive component in intervention is assassination and terror or whether it is a deliberate reduction in economic aid. Men who in the present world order are inclined to draw a fundamental contrast between persuasion and coercion in international affairs tend to become either impotent idealists or else seeming realists who hand over to the technicians of power any problem not yet solved by discussion. Those who know that persuasion and coercion are inseparable in the uses of authority may require experts in covert activities and armed combat, but they have no need for men who specialize solely in power, or else in morality.

II. *The Relevance of Morality to Intervention*

At this point, some may be ready to respond to the complex interrelationship of power and morality by relaxing into moral ambiguities or, what is the same thing, platitudes. Others may be content to trust instead to individual moral leadership, forgetting that the same man who rightly would not read another man's mail must find standards by which he would enthusiastically break another nation's code. A man who would not hesitate physically and immediately to avenge an insult to his wife's honor may not act with similar assurance when a hundred million dead become the price of avenging a nation's honor.

Complexity must not deter us. The need for wisdom has grown: intervention is likely to become more common than ever before precisely as we succeed, through military technology, in making gains through outright aggression less probable, even while the conflict between ourselves and expansionist communism remains unresolved. Under these terms also, the danger of uncontrolled intervention escalating into unintended but destructive aggression rises—but so also rises the price of nonintervention whenever Communist nations are already intervening. The greater our power and our responsibility, the greater the need also to find a valid and moral code for our actions in history.

There is no obvious synthesis between morality and intervention. It is a cruel simplicity that makes a virtue of necessity or a necessity of virtue. To balance the demands of morality against the demands of victory in order to strike a mere compromise is almost bound to frustrate action and damage morality. Nor is morality merely an added decoration or only an ultimate grace: morality, especially when it serves to strengthen lawful stability or stabilizing change, has obvious practical consequences. These we ignore at our peril whenever we are tempted to gain only the practical results of power, and imitate the tactics of conflict management developed by Communists or sometimes attributed to them by our own secular crusaders, who compliment Communists beyond reason by believing them to be omnipotent and omnipresent in conspiracy and subversion. Surely the problem deserves to be resolved in terms of choices based on our own values of world order.

Nothing is easier than to state the solution in abstract terms: we must choose the right means for the right ends, and then apply our full force to achieve our goals. But what can this mean in practice? I would attach myself to a view voiced for about two and a half millennia: morality is not the highest value, and neither is power or knowledge. What matters is the best and most relevant relationship among these three—a union which in its contemplative aspect may be called wisdom, and, in its active phase, justice. Nothing is more difficult, or more necessary, to achieve in practice.[4]

Let us see just how difficult it can be. On July 14, 1958, the State Department in Washington received a telegram from the President of Lebanon requesting the landing of American

---

[4] Rabbi Robert Gordis has suggested that morality is the highest good, since, unless it includes honesty and intelligence, it is simply moralism. I do not put it this way because I want to make sure that we explore anew the power and knowledge that have become part of our morality.

forces within twenty-four hours in order to save that country's political integrity and independence. The issues seemed clear enough. The President of Lebanon had been the only Middle Eastern leader to endorse the Eisenhower Doctrine, which committed the United States to come to the aid of any Middle Eastern country which requested assistance "against armed aggression from any country controlled by international communism." Here, explained President Eisenhower, was a government that had been democratically elected, and that was now threatened by subversion armed and encouraged from outside. Here, as the State Department briefed the press, appeared to be a clear-cut case: we must demonstrate that we are ready to support our allies when they need us. American inaction, especially at a moment when pro-Western leaders had just been overthrown in Iraq, could result in the dominance of the Middle East by Soviet or Nasser imperialism, "assuming," as American officials expressed it at that time, "that these are or could remain separate." In a recent prize-winning series of articles on communism, *Life* recalled our Lebanese intervention as a major demonstration that we could stop communism in its tracks.

The real story, however, did not begin in July 1958. Early in 1957, Lebanese President Chamoun faced the bitter truth that during the preceding decade, the birth rate had shifted the balance of power in his country. In 1943, when Christian Arabs were still the majority in the country, the Moslem Arabs and the other minorities had agreed that Christians would always assume the position of President, Foreign Minister, and Commander-in-Chief of the Army, while Moslems would always assume the office of the Prime Minister and the Speaker of Parliament. All other positions in the state were similarly frozen on the basis of sectarian strength. By 1957 it had become clear to everyone that Moslems were turning into a majority, and that most Moslems and an appreciable number of Christians were being attracted to Nasser's neutralist, socialist, and authoritarian Arab nationalism.

Chamoun was unwilling, in a state founded upon ten Christian sects, three Moslem sects, and several "others," and hence viable, if at all, only by compromise, to strive for a new bargain consonant with the changing situation. He might have eased the transition to a system in which Moslems would have gained more responsibility or to a secular state in which all jobs were indiscriminately open to all men of talent and in which Lebanese Christians, thanks to their superior education and prosperity, would have remained at least equal in influence for a long time to come. Instead, in order to make up in foreign backing for what he had lost in domestic support, he agreed to the Eisenhower Doctrine. Then, in order to perpetuate the *status quo*, Chamoun rigged the 1957 election enough to give himself that two-thirds parliamentary majority required to amend the constitution so that Parliament could reelect him for a second six-year term.[5]

When the majority had thus been deprived of the effective use of the ballot while the country, hitherto neutral in intra-Arab conflicts, was being transformed into a pro-Western bulwark against the spread of neutralist Arab nationalism, the opposition resorted to bullets and the civil war began. Into this civil war, Nasser soon sent arms, money, and men, and we, after several months, our own armed forces.

One other fact has to be mentioned. Most politically active Lebanese believe that there is conclusive evidence that the Lebanese President and Foreign Minister, though they failed to consult other members of their government, had from the start acted in concert with CIA. The American intervention in Lebanon seemed to them, as to most other observers, to be part of American efforts after the Suez crisis of late 1956 to stem the growing influence of Nasser's neutralist nationalism. This nat-

[5] Oddly enough, Chamoun had become President in 1952 after helping to overthrow President Khuri—a man who had greatly increased the number of his enemies by his attempt to amend the Constitution so that he might serve an additional six-year term.

urally raises a major question to which we shall have to return: does our knowledge of Middle Eastern forces and trends suggest that it is a moral or necessary use of American power to intervene against neutralist nationalism?

By July 14, 1958, however, there were some additional issues at stake. By the day the telegram arrived, U.N. observers had already contributed materially to the reduction of the level of UAR intervention in Lebanon. The Commander-in-Chief of the Lebanese army, who had used his Christian-officered, but Moslem-and-Christian-manned army to umpire the civil war rather than to fight the opposition, was already laying the groundwork for the compromise that would end the war and make him President. It had also become evident that we were progressively less eager to have Chamoun cash the blank check we had given him —calling for the intervention of American troops. On the other hand, the telegram was sent a few hours after a coup in Iraq overthrew the only Arab government bound to the West by a defense pact. Since no one in Beirut or Washington had anticipated this coup at this moment, nor knew much about its main actors, ignorance conjured up fears and fears led some to think about being close enough, if necessary, to intervene in Iraq.

In addition to seeming new dangers, those who had to answer the telegram now also had to face fundamental and conflicting moral issues only distantly related to their original intentions. Could they, seeing the Lebanese situation itself now closer to solution, afford to say "no," and so let it be said by our allies in NATO and elsewhere that when it comes to a showdown, the United States is likely to have second thoughts? How reliable would that make us as an ally? Who would trust our pledge in the future? Yet should the United States now add a larger, more dramatic commitment to support a *status quo* that had already been undermined by the kind of forces against which Marines lack adequate weapons—birth rates and nationalism? What would have been a wise and just decision?

We chose to land troops. The troops fired on no one; the

American mediator who entered in their wake strengthened and secured the compromise that had already been in the making. But our landing of 10,000 troops in a country half the size of New Jersey also had various other consequences. The compromise brought about the departure from his country of the all too pro-Western Foreign Minister, Charles Malik, and gave the rebels the Premiership, but under the firm neutral leadership of the new President, General Chehab. The compromise has also led to a new, yet deeply frustrating, deadlock among Lebanese factions. As a result, little has been done since 1958 to resolve the imbalance between political structure and political reality which helped to produce the civil war.

The case must be summed up in paradoxes. We concluded that our international status demanded our intervention at a time when we were beginning to feel that the situation in Lebanon itself no longer required it. We demonstrated to the world the solidity of our commitment to our friends by intervening with immediate, well-coordinated, and major force, but we also exposed to the world our incapacity to airlift more than 10,000 troops to more than one trouble-spot at one time.[6] The compromise solution we helped to fashion left our closest friends without further power, so that other Middle Eastern governments could draw various valid lessons: the United States, whether in a right or wrong cause, will not deny itself the use of force and therefore must always be reckoned with; it will employ its horses and its men in its own national interests, and not necessarily in trying to put even an apparently pro-Western Humpty Dumpty together again. Even so, the Humpty Dumptys on our side may still take comfort: we do not use our strength to make structural changes; we merely put others on top of the wall. A U.N. resolution propounded with remarkable unanimity by all Arab states (presumably the kind of unity which we had earlier viewed with reserve) provided the basis on which our forces agreed to leave Lebanon. And

[6] Our military mobility has much improved since that time.

contemporary Lebanese governments find it more difficult to act on our advice for dealing with their still searing problems of social change than the pre-1958 government with whom we so eagerly agreed to repress the problems of change.

I have dealt with the Lebanese intervention in such detail because no wise and just action is ever hypothetical. Unlike our interventions in Cuba or Laos, the Lebanese case also is neither familiar nor (oddly enough) controversial, and hence may most easily lead to fresh insights. For from this one example (with suitable footnotes to other similar actions), we shall be able to raise most of the relevant questions and, possibly, conclusions for the general problem we are considering.

Needless to say, I consider most aspects of our intervention in Lebanon as an unhappy demonstration of American power, morality, and knowledge. Our difficulties stem from failures in each of these three realms and from the faulty connections we fashioned among them.

III. *The Relevance of Knowledge to Moral Intervention*

To begin with knowledge, we have scarcely begun to develop theories of social change that would allow us to understand the fundamental revolutions now in progress in the world, and hence to develop doctrines of intervention relevant to the politics of modernization.[7] Khrushchev has a theory. It is a dogmatic one, and it has led him into error as often as not. But he has a theory which sensitizes him to the great fact of rapid historical transformation that constitutes the modern age. It makes him more aware than we are to the probability that govern-

---

[7] I have dealt with this issue specifically in relation to "Perspectives on U.S. Policy in Iran," published in the SAIS *Review* (Washington), April 1962. This and the next two paragraphs are largely drawn from that article. A more extended analysis of the politics involved in the revolution of modernization may be found in my studies, *The Politics of Social Change in the Middle East and North Africa* (Princeton: Princeton University Press, 1963), and "The Social Revolution," in *The Developmental Revolution in the Middle East*, ed. by William Polk (Washington: The Middle East Institute, 1963).

ments owing their power to deadlocked sectarian parochialism or to absentee landlords are not long for this world. Communists are not responsible for having started the revolution of modernization and Khrushchev is dogmatically wrong about the inevitability of the next stage of social development. But if we compete against his partially correct theory about social change with no theory at all, he may well turn out to be right about the next stage as well, not because of his theory but because of our errors and omissions.

Lacking a theory that would help us understand the transformation of societies, we have tended to play for possible lucky breaks in history, though the breaks have not always come or do not always linger. Or else we have tended to be hardheadedly manipulative, but without a sense of theory or ideology. We are the inventors of a new kind of revolution—the hit-and-run revolution. We help make it and go home and leave the politics of social change, which alone can justify and fulfill a revolution, almost entirely to others who have even less appreciation of the problems of social transformation than we do.

We are not entirely without knowledge. If we do not yet possess a major theory about social change as broad in its concerns and as related to action as Marx's but a hundred years younger and less dogmatic (for it would lead to mischief merely to look for a countercreed), we still have available a number of insights that would form part of any such theory. One such proposition, for example, is that improved administrative efficiency, economic amelioration, and political concessions offered by a regime that is morally and politically isolated from the most important newly emergent classes cannot preserve political stability. When a social structure is radically changing and the political consensus has broken down, the price of political stability in modern times is to overcome the moral and political isolation between ruler and ruled. This certainly requires, among other things, economic and administrative progress, but these cannot substitute for political enterprise that goes to the root of the matter. Another proposition is that the longer repression succeeds in postponing the political adjustments to the transformation of a society's structure and values, the more likely it is that the more extreme and violent elements will gain leadership of the opposition. From these propositions alone it would follow that you can, if you must, use Marines to intervene in a rebellion affecting a change in top personnel. You cannot, even if you try, use Marines effectively to intervene in a revolution that is transforming what men believe, how they live, and how they relate to each other.

The revolution of the peoples of the underdeveloped areas to build institutions that would put them in command rather than at the mercy of the forces of modernization is more searing than any that ever confronted the West. It takes place, for the most part, in the face of fewer resources and skills, greater poverty and population pressure, and in societies that were, until a few decades ago, sure of their ancient truths and traditions. They are now driven by the pressure of sheer needs and new aspirations and the pain of backwardness and powerlessness in the presence of the industrialized nations to pass through their revolution in telescoped time.

If we have failed to understand the dimensions of the forces now transforming Asia, Africa, and Latin America, and viewed them frequently from the shallower perspective of cliques and personalities struggling for power, the fault has not only been in the inadequate state of our intellectual knowledge. The experience that would make us receptive to such knowledge has until recently been lacking. Our own society has been in the midst of constant change, but we have always, barring one civil war, been able to maintain a consensus on our basic social, economic, moral, and political values and institutions. We have been able to pay so much attention to the individual because we could afford to take our institutions for granted. We are only now beginning to experience the pain of bafflement and frustration that comes from living in a world changing both hopefully and dangerously, and certainly quickly and seemingly beyond control. We are coming to recognize that our institutions are not yet adequate to maintain peace, eliminate ignorance, bigotry, and poverty, deal with the sheer growth of the number of people, facts, and institutions, master technology, and preserve and spread beauty. We are only gradually becoming interested in the theory and practice of social change.

We cannot yet effectively capitalize on our knowledge in this field because we have so far invested much more in power than in the knowledge on which the prudent and effective exercise of power must be based. We intervene about as often in the internal affairs of other nations as the USSR, but the world is (and we ourselves ought to be) harder on us when we do. Since intervention when it involves duress is normally neither a legal nor a democratic exercise, we must when we intervene have better reasons, founded on better values and sounder knowledge, than are offered by Communist dogma.

One reason for our intervention is, of course, partly beyond our control: we cannot be secure in a world where domestic political life is in turmoil or guided by dogmatic or cynical adventurers. Within limits, the USSR can prosper from such instability. But not all burdens which this invidious problem imposes on us are inescapable. Had we really explored the roots and implications of neutralism when we intervened against it in Lebanon and Laos? Have we explored all mechanisms by which internal conflicts can be insulated from the cold war?

Our lack of knowledge and foresight about problems of Asian, African, and Latin American stability in which we have an intrinsically greater stake than the USSR also often forces us into intervention against our expectations. We often fail to anticipate crises. Yet there is a world of difference between the range of choices and the decisions one can make when one is aware of the forces and trends of history and the decision at a moment of crisis—when you are no longer free to pick the issue but when you must say yea or nay. On July 14, 1958, we were no longer free to say nay in Lebanon and break our word, yet many were the options we had before that day.

The position of the United States in world affairs, for the sake of power and morality alike, puts a premium on adequate knowledge. Yet the institutional barriers remain high against overcoming our historical ignorance and preconceptions about our rapidly changing world. Until very recently, we were governed by a generation whose education did not include knowledge about that majority of the world which lives in Asia, Africa, and Latin America. A large number of our policy-makers are lawyers, and many lawyers tend to see history as moving from case to case, instead of as a ceaseless trial that can sometimes be made to move in one direction rather than another but that has no final solutions. We are also, as a people, so action-minded that many of our best and most devoted policy-makers are seldom tempted enough, and therefore seldom find time enough, after their intense preoccupation with the evils that are sufficient unto the day, to think about the relevance of their actions to the long-term forces and trends of history. The machinery they have built over the years reflects their predilections. It swarms with facts; it seethes (if not always productively) with action; but few sections of the State Department or CIA are smaller than those whose task it is to devote themselves, full time, to long-range analysis and estimates.

Knowledge, however, bears an effective relationship not only to power but also to morality. One major reason why there is not yet a controlling international sense of morality is that the world does not yet share a single structure of knowledge, values, and sanctions. This moral deficiency in turn demands and perpetuates a hierarchical inequality of knowledge in each nation. This is an issue of intrinsic and not altogether avoidable danger. Precisely on the most vital questions of power, where emotions most require the discipline of knowledge and life itself may be at stake, knowledge can least of all be prudently shared with others who will certainly experience the consequences of action. Just prior to intervention and war, security is likely to dictate the greatest restrictions, even within the government itself, on men's "need to know."

Granting all this, I believe nonetheless that we have let secrecy hinder the application of knowledge and advice so far that both morality and power have suffered. This is worth saying, especially since all the pressures are still moving in the direction of narrowing the spread of knowledge and the range of debate: witness President Kennedy's pleas for voluntary press censorship after the Cuban intervention. As long as rivalries among independent sovereignties force citizens to accept an inequality of knowledge about questions of security, it remains all the more essential to insist that the leaders of our nation persist in constant exchange with the moral and political consensus of their community. Yet their isolation from that consensus is proceeding apace. We are, as a nation, approaching the moral disability of the international system as a whole. Differences in power positions are leading to growing differences in knowledge, values, and sanctions available to different segments of our community.

The fact that the community can no longer arrive at a sense of wisdom and justice because it lacks adequate knowledge and power in the crucial fields of subversion, weapons technology, and social change in strange civilizations makes its notions about the morality of intervention often impractical or else seemingly relevant only because its maxims survived from an earlier age when our institutions were being created, and knowledge, power, and morality were still more closely entwined with each other. Compensations for this weakness are possible, but they are seldom brought into play. Our leaders do not, on the basis of their own special knowledge, take much more time to lead the discussion that could clarify our national purpose than they now take for clarifying the historical and moral context of their acts of intervention. On the contrary, they sometimes feel impelled right up to the moment of intervention to speak enthusiastically against it.[8] Congress seems to have yielded its legislative and educational power on fundamental national issues to the Supreme Court, but the Supreme Court will not be able to guide us with equal strength on foreign affairs. Congress has a watchdog committee over the Atomic Energy Commission, which can transform matter, but it still neglects to appoint a similar committee over CIA, which can transform men and history.

Most of the press west of the Potomac is of little help in discussing and clarifying issues that could lead to intervention. Bipartisanship among our political leaders helped to turn the failure of our 1961 intervention in Cuba into a numbing celebration of national unity before the discussion had scarcely begun, and it inhibits debate on Laos or Vietnam. In contrast to democratic Britain, we also suffer from a peculiar form of patriotism. While the British Parliament sharply debated the merits of the Suez invasion of 1956 while it was in progress, and similarly argued about British troop landings in Jordan contemporary with American landings in Lebanon in 1958, the Speaker of the House of Representatives, Mr. Rayburn, effectively stopped debate in Congress during the Lebanese intervention by saying that "in times like these we had better allow matters to develop rather than make remarks about them." Though our national interest had become deeply involved, our survival as a nation was not at stake in Lebanon. Why then should the noble sentiment of patriotism turn into a crippling disease of eye, ear, nose, and throat? Is a congressional, instead· of a parliamentary, system doomed to either irrelevance or irresponsibility in the conduct of today's foreign affairs?

The top decision-makers are thus usually left to pursue the

[8] Mr. Nixon, one of the earliest and strongest advocates of intervention in Cuba, in retrospect perceives only the electoral ironies that arose from his having declared on TV in August 1960, while preparations for the invasion were under way: "We would lose all of our friends in Latin America, we would probably be condemned in the United Nations, and we would not accomplish our objectives."

national interest, especially in the field of intervention, without any lively, free, or constant touch with the moral and intellectual consensus of the nation or its most representative institutions. What is more, this relative isolation of the decision-makers from the community's consensus, rendered painless by the community's widespread stereotyped acquiescence, persists in institutionalized form almost to the pinnacles of power. Few are the experts in government who are consulted prior to an intervention. What is publicly known about our intervention in Cuba in 1961 illustrates this. Considerations of security, curbing the security-cleared government official's access to information, may well at times have harmed our security.

It is my impression that there are very few among our experts at intervention who are not hard-working, intelligent, imaginative, and courageous far above the average of men. It is also my impression, however (and this one is more likely to be erroneous than the first), that just as the Office of War Information during World War II tended to attract an unusually large number of men who responded to the grandly heroic, hopefully liberal, and victory-promising aspects of the war, so CIA has attracted a core of men similarly attuned to one aspect of their task and their age. They know they are engaged in a cold war without foreseeable end, in an institution which reflects America's recent reaction against its long infatuation with idealistic legalism and its tough-minded discovery of the morality of power. They are involved in a task that must avoid publicity as much as possible, engaged in acts they would not countenance as citizens in their own country, blocked from discussing their problems with anyone but their immediate colleagues, under attack more often from the liberal moralist than the rightist actionist. They have rejected the ideological historicism of their enemy, but they have not yet developed a systematic understanding of their own concerning the forces of history. It is not surprising, therefore, that CIA should have attracted to its ranks of expert interventionists especially the technician of power and the energetic but doctrineless conservative. They are not the only kind of person working at CIA, but their presence inhibits that concern with the linking of knowledge, morality, and power that ensures, as far as it can be ensured by man, wise and just intervention.[9]

We have been fortunate so far that at the very top of power, in the Presidency, and often close to it, the country has been blessed ever since our final initiation as a world power—during the months preceding our entrance into World War II—with leadership of intelligence and morality. If the actions and interventions of this leadership have not always lived up to expectations, it is in part because our leaders are human and not omnipotent. It is in part also because they have been most intimately in touch with two, not entirely helpful, collections of men. On issues of intervention, the broad American constituency acquiesces in any seeming success against communism and is most erratic in the interpretation and punishment of what it, or some segment of the public, considers failures. (Compare the public's reaction to China, Cuba, Lebanon, and the Congo.) The other group, the President's most immediate advisers on intervention, have labored under the limitations which we have been describing, affecting the state of the art and constituting a profession more skilled in surgery than in the

[9] Readers of the *New York Times* and *Time* before, during, and after the Cuban intervention should have no difficulty recalling evidence for this view. We seemed to have lacked adequate knowledge about a country 90 miles from home, or at least failed to utilize knowledge that was available; we ruthlessly manipulated men and groups among Cuban exiles; we gave unconcerned support (or showed pragmatic and instinctive favoritism) to ex-Batista or pre-Batista men, rather than men willing to deal with the discontent that Castro had exploited. Had we insisted on the military success of this particularly ill-conceived venture, it would have been a moral and political tragedy.

There are also outstanding men at CIA who have produced major and imaginative projects in what will be defined below as constructive precautionary intervention. Their successes, by nature, evolve slowly and lack the drama of failure. It is my impression, however, based on inadequate knowledge, that the failures at intervention deserve the greater weight of attention.

problems of disease. The final responsibilities of the President cannot be lessened, but under present circumstances the handicaps under which any President must decide on intervention are dangerously high. A wiser American consensus on the merit and uses of intervention has become a necessity for clarifying and sustaining that final decision which only one man can make in each concrete case. Informed public discussion of at least the fundamental issues and types of intervention is essential to this end. But discussion is no longer a simple task. It could easily make intervention of any kind more difficult to carry out. It could arouse public pressure for crusades in behalf of moralism. Practice and passion have outrun discussion. Whatever the perils, there is no way of creating a relevant consensus except by discussion.

IV. *Types and Uses of Intervention*

As one contribution to such a discussion, I should like to examine several types of intervention and ask to what degree each might be wise or just.

Counter-intervention: No other kind of intervention is as easy to justify. It is an action designed to help free a country from the interventionist manipulations of another power and so enable it to regain its sovereign integrity and independence —that is, to stand free again of all interventions. It is coercion intended to create options rather than, as in the Soviet interventions in Hungary, to foreclose them.

Easy to justify, it is not at all easy to do well. For while it is not unreasonably difficult to define the point at which intervention becomes imperative, it is most difficult to help create that degree of internal stability which makes it prudent again to end intervention. Intervention involves, clearly, not merely a manipulation of power, but a sharing in the historical trials of others.

Intervention through indirect imperialist rule: Though its advocates may wish to call it "preventive intervention," it closely resembles that form of colonialism known as "indirect rule." We intervene to impose rulers who promise to be resolutely anti-Communist, but we leave them otherwise free to pursue any domestic policy they please. This indirect imperialist form of intervention has caused the United States more harm than any other kind of initiative we have undertaken, in particular because—for a number of good reasons—it can usually be counted upon to produce the very dangers we most feared when we first embarked on such adventures.

The initial argument raised in favor of indirect imperialist intervention is normally not confined to the reasonable proposition that if the USSR or its agents are about to intervene, why let the USSR gain the initiative—why wait until the legal government can no longer seek our aid and we are forced to embark on the more difficult path of helping to organize a counterrevolution? Such clear and present danger would justify *pre-emptive intervention.* (And the final justification of such a pre-emptive purchase of time is, of course, what constructive use we make of it.) The argument for indirect imperialist intervention goes further. It does not trust the existing government —one composed, say, of Laotian neutralists—to invite our aid *if* pressed by the USSR or its agents. It does not trust Mosadeq of Iran or Kassim of Iraq to know when or how to stop short of opportunistic collaboration with local Communists. Or, in the form of an Anglo-French argument, it does not trust Nasser to keep the Suez Canal open or run it efficiently. One could readily list more examples: it has been our favorite form of forceful intervention, and it has almost invariably backfired. Why?

It was founded, in part, on insufficient knowledge. In an Asia, Africa, and Latin America that have a highly sensitive pride in their new nationalism, the danger that neutralist nationalists might willingly yield to Soviet control has usually been less than we have feared. On the other hand, the danger that "pro-

Western" regimes, by stifling popular nationalist and reformist impulses, would sap their internal support has been far greater than we have usually anticipated. We have also tended to underestimate the readiness and effectiveness, as in the Congo, or in Syria between 1954 and 1958, with which nationalists will turn to whichever Great Power did not intervene first for countervailing force against the original transgressor. The results might have been much worse had it not been possible to mobilize U.N. intervention to counter national interventions which the United States did not support, as at Suez, or about which it had second thoughts, as in the Congo.

Indirect imperialist intervention has been pernicious morally because it has invariably been invoked against nationalist neutralists instead of Communists, apparently on the devil-ridden notion, happily on the decline since about 1960, that those who are not with us are against us. It has thus obscured the moral distinction between our sense of world order and that of the Communists—all the more so since the USSR has, from about 1951, based its foreign policy on the premise that those who were not against it were potentially for it.

In the realm of power, indirect imperialist intervention has therefore alienated rather than won people. It has never been truly preventive. In no instance—neither in Iran nor Lebanon nor Laos nor in other places not to be mentioned—was power first devoted to the creation of that dynamic stability that might produce a resilience and immunization to subversion by extremist forces. In the future, indirect imperialist intervention may prove even less pertinent as an exercise in power than before. Given the state of the international Communist movement, not every local Communist coup may be automatically interpreted as a Moscow initiative. It may be a new thorn in Moscow's (or Peking's) side. Yugoslavia may not be the only Communist nation we can afford to live with.

Precautionary intervention: This involves a kind of action which our government and our people have least discussed. Let me, therefore, for the moment merely outline some of the pros and cons of such intervention.

Among the most significant examples of how we failed to intervene in time are Hitler's Germany three decades ago and Algeria, where French colonial policy had reached a dead end more than a decade ago. Today the most foreboding case is probably the Republic of South Africa. Our own moderate Southerner need not fear: there is an obvious distinction between a policy intent upon achieving rapid equality, with deliberate speed, and a policy bent on perpetuating and deepening racial inequality. There is a technical strategic question (there usually is): can we defend ourselves successfully against missiles looped around the South Pole without the cooperation of the Republic of South Africa? But there is also one obvious estimate to be made: within the next few years, the Republic of South Africa is going to be a bloodier battleground within the free world than Algeria, because the Republic has no imperial overlord that can act as final arbiter, because the white settlers do not have an obvious place to which to return (though there are available areas for emigration), and the grievances of the non-Europeans are obviously worse than in Algeria. Do we intervene now or after the bloodbath starts? Do we insist on a solution now, or after the Communists gain greater influence among the Africans, and other African nations also covertly intervene?

The objections to such intervention can be phrased in terms applicable to both the Republic of South Africa and other similar areas. Is the United States to intervene in the domestic affairs of countries with which we have satisfactory foreign relations? Are we to intervene wherever men are oppressed and exploited? Do we not establish a mischievous breach in international law if we proclaim our right to overthrow tyrants who, however brutal at home, trespass on none of their neighbors? After all, we do not intervene against Communism because it is tyrannous, but because it is expansionist and threatening us. If precautionary intervention from outside seems prudent, should it not be reserved for the collective action of the states of the region or, when that appears infeasible, the United Nations?

The contrary position is not destroyed by these arguments, however. The various regions of the world suffer from various limitations in handling precautionary intervention by agreement among their constituent states. Neither Asia as such, nor any important subregion within it, possesses the requisite unity for this kind of joint positive action. Africa might be able to act in unison, but only against European, not African, leadership on that continent. The Americas cannot act without us, and might not act with us. U.N. action, affected by these differences among and within regions, therefore depends powerfully on the response of the United States. What do we stand for in the world? We no longer, to be sure, intervene to collect our debts. Some of our best friends are now our debtors. But shall we only intervene against tyranny which expands abroad, and take obviously milder measures against other evils, so that we seem to become champions of the *status quo* while the USSR makes itself the champion of racial equality and the abolition of poverty and exploitation?

I am not yet sure how to resolve all these questions, in principle. When it comes to practice, however, I am certain that the gassing of millions of human beings, or the official suppression of elemental human rights for millions of others because of the color of their skin, must not be placed beyond remedy as a "domestic issue." I must confess that I liked very much the last paragraph of President Kennedy's letter answering Chairman Khrushchev's protest against our 1961 Cuban intervention: "I believe, Mr. Chairman, that you should recognize that free people in all parts of the world do not accept the claim of historical inevitability for Communist revolution. What your government believes is its business; what it does in the world is the world's business. The great revolution in the history of man, past, present and future, is the revolution of those determined to be free." [10] But the letter ends at that point, and the operating clause that would show how this statement could be made effective is missing, just as it was from the Cuban intervention in the Bay of Pigs.

I think it may be possible, however, to distinguish among (1) countries which, despite tyranny (or its obverse, instability), are yet some distance from internal warfare involving extremists, or foreign adventurism inviting aggression; (2) countries which, like Ataturk's Turkey, have chosen an authoritarian road that is intended to lead to democracy; and (3) countries which, like the Republic of South Africa, are clearly heading for the kind of catastrophic internal or external explosion that will make intervention by outside powers unavoidable. In the first two categories, the United States might well undertake the kind of joint precautionary and constructive diplomatic and economic measures that constitute *intervention in partnership*,[11] even though the disparity of power and needs between the collaborating parties seldom permits this kind of partnership to proceed without friction. In this sense, the "Alliance for Progress" with Latin America is an agreement giving the United States and other participating states the right to create effective pressures for altering the social, economic, and political structure of Latin American states for the sake of ultimately putting an end to tyranny, instability, and poverty. In the third category of countries, is not the real choice between precautionary intervention and subsequent intervention under much more unfavorable terms? Our little-publicized but morally and politically sound intervention against the Trujillo dictatorship in the Dominican Republic soon after our Cuban

[10] *New York Herald Tribune*, April 9, 1961.
[11] In the pamphlet published as an earlier version of this essay, I had designated this kind of action more cumbersomely as "positively accepted intervention."

fiasco demonstrates our ability to act prudently despite encumbrances in the realm of precautionary intervention.

There are other forms of intervention. One is equivalent to bearbaiting without invitation in other people's gardens—as when, for a time, we subsidized Chinese Nationalist troops on Burmese soil—but it would not be rewarding to explore further in that direction. Another is constructive, though it seldom earns credit in the short run, as when we inject ourselves powerfully as arbiters in disputes that touch us only because they divide two countries friendly with us. Espionage is also a form of intervention when it involves entering without permission into areas, on the ground or in the air, that fall under the national jurisdiction of other states. This kind of intervention, having the commendable purpose of expanding the world's knowledge, is based upon rules of the game implicitly agreed upon among nations. As an activity, it damages the international system less than adultery damages the institution of marriage. Like adultery, it damages the formal system of intercourse whenever the culprit is caught or insists on publicly championing his right to adultery. That was our compounded sin in the U-2 incident. Unlike adultery, which can damage most by the act itself—that is, by betraying love and trust—no love or trust is present to be undermined in the international system, a vital point to which we shall return in our conclusion.

V. *Toward the Limitation of Intervention*

Surely it is a symptom of the aberrant state of the world that the preceding section might well have been entitled, "Toward a Wise and Just American Intervention in the Internal Affairs of Other Nations." I submit that such a discussion is necessary, but I cannot bring myself to suppose that it would be wise or just to stop here. No state has the sovereign right to intervene in the internal affairs of another sovereign state. Such a "right" is not merely a contradiction in terms but an attack on the very system on which the freedom of every nation rests. It cannot be dismissed as a "mere" breach of international law. It undermines the very structure of a world order which is most imperfect, but in whose survival we have a far greater stake than does the USSR; for, unlike the intended Communist international system, the present international order contains the actuality of national freedom and the potentiality of voluntary collaboration.

We have two choices especially worth discussing. We can accept the world as a jungle in which right and wrong do not apply but only survival matters, and we concentrate on improving the skill and thrust of our power. Since we are still in a jungle, it would be foolish not to do so. But since we do not want to remain where we are, since our very lingering is likely to spell our doom, we must also act to limit the terms of the competition and enlarge the effective power of law.

At the moment we are doing badly. We accept as inescapable the proposition that the challenge posed by the USSR gives us the right and duty to intervene, and that we can deny the same right of intervention to the USSR by threatening to escalate the kind of forces we shall enlist in the fray.[12] To ease the burden

---

[12] The following quotations illustrate our position. On our right to counter Soviet interventions: "Let the record show that our restraint is not inexhaustible. . . . This Government will not hesitate in meeting its primary obligations, which are to the security of our Nation." (President Kennedy, "The Lesson of Cuba," *Department of State Bulletin*, XLIV [May 8, 1961], p. 659.) On the USSR's claiming the same rights: "If you consider yourself to be in the right to implement such measures against Cuba which have been lately taken by the United States of America, you must admit that other countries, also, do not have lesser reason to act in a similar manner in relation to states on whose territories preparations are actually being made which represent a threat against the security of the Soviet Union. If you do not wish to sin against elementary logic, you evidently must admit such a right to other states." (Mr. Khrushchev's Message to President Kennedy, *ibid.*, p. 665.) On escalation: "We are resolved," said Secretary of Defense Robert S. McNamara, "to continue the struggle in all its forms," coping with Soviet long-range ballistic missiles armed with nuclear warheads as well as subversion and indirect warfare, "until such a time as the Communist leaders, both Soviet and Chinese, are convinced that their aggressive policies, motivated by their drive to communize the world, endanger their security as well as ours." (*New York Times*, January 20, 1962.)

and danger of our vigilante activities in a lawless world, we have tried several methods. We have tried to explain to the world the superior justice of our cause. Most people might well grant that ours is a better country to live in than the USSR, but the appreciation of the justice of our cause has often been marred by the kind of interventions by which we have tried to translate justice into practice and by our declarations—perhaps justifiable on other grounds but certainly far more frightening than any uttered by the USSR—about the risks we would take in behalf of justice. And though some are tempted, there is one attitude toward the justice of our cause which we cannot afford to adopt. "Intimidation," Trotsky wrote, "is a powerful weapon of policy, both internationally and internally. . . . The revolution works the same way: it kills individuals, and intimidates thousands. . . . 'But, in that case, in what do your tactics differ from the tactics of Tsarism?' we are asked by the high priests of Liberalism. . . . You do not understand this, holy men? We shall explain it to you. The terror of Tsarism was directed against the proletariat. . . . Our Extraordinary Commissions shoot landlords, capitalists, and generals who are striving to restore the capitalist order. Do you grasp this—distinction? Yes? For us Communists it is quite sufficient. . . ." [13] Should means no longer matter to us, justice will become a remote question.

We have also tried to ease our burden by emphasizing order above social change, taking care to improve the repressive machinery of other governments, and employing economic aid to diminish the political violence which often topples rulers in rapid succession in Asia, Africa, and Latin America. We have often neglected, however, to develop the political enterprise by which they and we might limit the international consequences of such internal warfare. By giving priority to order, we found it more difficult to seize such political initiative, for

[13] Trotsky, *Terrorism and Communism,* 1920; English translation, *Dictatorship vs. Democracy: A Reply to Karl Kautsky* (New York: Workers' Party of America, 1922), pp. 54, 57–59.

while it is true that control of rapid social change itself requires strong, stable authority, such resilient stability is unlikely to arise in most underdeveloped areas until many more fundamental changes have taken place.

In a similar vein, we have championed world law without adequate study of how law might play a constructive role in a rapidly and fundamentally changing world. Our concept of law is fit largely for a world in which political conflicts no longer touch the very purpose and character of life. We have, moreover, failed to live up to international law which we have helped to shape.[14] For example, we agreed in Article 15 of the Charter of Bogotá (1948) that "no state or group of states has the right to intervene directly or indirectly, for any reason whatever, in the internal or external affairs of any other state. The foregoing principle prohibits not only armed attack but also any other form of interference or attempted threat against the personality of the state or against the political, economic and cultural elements." In Article 16, we agreed that "no state may use or encourage the use of coercive measures of an economic or political character in order to force the sovereign will of another state or obtain from it advantages of any kind."

It is true that in subsequent treaties we and the Latin Americans agreed on collective intervention against the encroachments of communism in this hemisphere, that we and they could not agree on effective action against Guatemala and Cuba, and that we therefore had no alternative, as our government saw it, but to proceed unilaterally against a danger condemned in principle by collective agreement. I would not

[14] I am greatly indebted for insights into the relationship of international law to the politics and morality of intervention, and for information, to three contributions by Professor Richard A. Falk: "The United States and the Doctrine of Non-Intervention in the Internal Affairs of Independent States," *Howard Law Journal*, v (June 1959), pp. 163–89; "American Intervention in Cuba and the Rule of Law," *Ohio State Law Journal*, xxii (Summer 1961), pp. 546–85; and *Law, Morality, and War in the Contemporary World* (New York: Frederick A. Praeger, 1963).

worry so much about such a few, somewhat ambiguous breaches of law—hope, patience, and fortitude have sustained the international system as much as law, and these are not as gravely damaged yet by such actions as is the law—except that I foresee no end to such breaches, and it is this which makes me fearful. We have already reached a dangerous point. After our Lebanese intervention, our Secretary of State, forgetful of the origins of our travail, thought of asking for a U.N. resolution against "indirect aggression," but relented when he remembered how vulnerable we would be both in the debate and through the intended law.

One may sympathize with those who would judge our record in this field with some forbearance, pointing out that our nation has only recently arrived fully as a world power. (Our interventions prior to World War II had an impact only on our immediate region and only an indirect effect on the world order.) But one must not sympathize too long, for we shall not be given much time to learn our lessons. It is imperative to move on, if not yet to world government, at least to a system based on self-restraint, constructive forms of intervention, and a broader overlap of national interests.

I do not think such a movement is impossible. Self-restraint would mean, for example, rejecting Edmond Taylor's recent proposal in *The Reporter* for "encouraging and explicitly accepting responsibility for the revolutionary forces behind the Iron Curtain. . . . We should oppose only premature and uncoordinated insurrections." [15] It would mean curing ourselves of the anxious and dogmatic aggressiveness that has caused us to intervene against neutralists and authoritarian socialists in usually unjustified fear of the next stage in their development. It would require us not to treat every Communist challenge—as in 1961 in Cuba—as an issue of survival, and not to turn any confrontation that could affect survival into alternatives that must lead either to complete victory or complete defeat.

[15] *The Reporter,* September 14, 1961.

Such a strategy would also involve forbearance when non-Communists challenge the *status quo*. Imposing the high standards of American political comfort on the rest of the world, we have scarcely paused to be surprised by how the passing of traditional society has been accompanied by far less violence in most of Asia, Africa, and Latin America than during a similar period in Western Europe. But we must not expect this historical transformation to be an entirely peaceful event, nor prepare to intervene whenever it is not.

We shall have to be more tolerant of violence connected with the end of the system of colonial domination than with violence threatening the system which governs the relationship among independent states. (India's usually justifiably high ideals have often fallen short of India's sometimes justifiable and sometimes unjustifiable practices. Our reaction to Goa, however, was an idealistic exaggeration, unmindful of the distinction I have suggested.) I believe we should insist that the arbitrary and artificial frontiers drawn by Europeans for African and Middle Eastern states must not be altered by direct aggression, but forbearance of a kind unjustified in Europe may also be in order when such kindred peoples intervene, short of aggression, in each other's affairs. We need neither become involved in their rivalries nor protect them from such excesses in their attempts to achieve unity. Counter-intervention would be justified, however, to keep other Great Powers from exploiting such rearrangements.

Above all, we need to rid ourselves of the erroneous notion that whenever a privileged Western position in Asia, Africa, or Latin America is lost, the USSR correspondingly gains. The conversion of a pro-Western nation like Iraq to neutralism is not a loss to the West. On the contrary, it usually rids the West of a discreditable relationship and, in bringing about a neutralist state, creates a situation with which we, by virtue of our sense of world order, can live but which the USSR is pledged to alter. Whether our subsequent relationship with a former client state is satisfactory or not depends on our mutual ability to transform our relationship by cementing overlapping national interests and enhancing such a country's internal stability.

That brings us to the second major task in moving toward a more lawful world—namely, finding more constructive forms of intervention. Self-restraint may be helpful in reducing instability and tension within the international system as a whole, but it cannot prevent or cure the internal conflicts within countries of the non-Communist world that incite the interventions of the Great Powers. We also need to develop wiser and more just forms of precautionary intervention and counter-intervention.

A number of possibilities may be suggested. Diplomacy and, at worst, the threat of unilateral intervention may be employed for the specific purpose of persuading the reluctant smaller nations of a region to act or even intervene collectively themselves in order to avoid the intervention of a Great Power. This, after much waste motion, was the final outcome in Lebanon when all the usually disunited Arab states agreed not to intervene, and was achieved even more effectively and with greater dispatch in Kuwait when the Arab states agreed collectively to protect that country against Iraqi intervention. Increasingly it may be possible to parlay the threat of Great Power intervention, as in the Congo, or earlier in Lebanon, into U.N. intervention.[16] Since Great Power intervention is initially masked in most instances, and there is no international law-enforcement agency that can investigate and act in time, the counter-intervention may have to be initiated by the United States. But such action should from the first moment be accompanied by a pledge to withdraw as soon as a U.N. or regional peace force can take its place, while those employing force under the duress

[16] What cannot be used as an effective threat, however, is collective intervention by NATO in the non-European and non-Communist areas of the world. Those who would neglect the U.N. in favor of NATO do not appreciate the limited usefulness of common action by the white partners of a military alliance in the rest of the world.

or discipline of a great foreign power withdraw their threat.[17] An international police force should therefore be organized so as to be in constant readiness.

Precautionary intervention could also be internationalized to a considerable degree. Societies that are already deeply split politically and therefore are unwilling to become dependent on a single Great Power should be helped in larger (and not merely technical) measure through the U.N.[18] Aid from the USSR should also be welcomed, even for joint projects, for what counts is not the source of the money and not even the prestige it earns for a foreign power, but the constructive use to which it is put inside the country.

Neither our self-restraint nor more constructive forms of intervention will help, however, unless the USSR reciprocates in like fashion. Is there any hope that the two powers might develop and enlarge an overlap of national interests in the realm of intervention? It is just such reciprocity that finally creates international law. Fortunately, such an overlap already exists to a significant degree, though amid the sound and fury we have paid little attention to it.

We are now operating on implicit rules that keep the USSR from intervening in sufficient measure within the Western community and the Western Hemisphere to make it the decisive force in placing its local men in power and protecting them there. We have accepted the same restrictions within the Soviet satellite area. This does not mean that the Soviets or the

---

[17] It will be noted that I speak only of intervention against elements employing *force* under the duress or discipline of a *great* foreign power. Threats from smaller nations can surely be handled in less spectacular ways. In restricting counter-intervention to a reply against force, I should like to reject the other alternative with entire clarity. If, as a result of an inadequate performance by democratic forces in India and the West, for example, Indians turn to communism in a free election, I would not for a moment regard the forceful reconversion of India into a Western colony as a morally justifiable or politically prudent alternative.

[18] For a discussion of problems of political therapy involved in U.N. intervention, see Manfred Halpern, "The U.N. in the Congo," *worldview*, Vol. 6 (October 1963), pp. 4–8.

West refrain from intervening in each other's realm in a great many other ways. But Hungary and Cuba indicate the limits of the game with precision. In October 1962, it had clearly become necessary to take bold measures to remind the USSR of these tacit rules as they affect Cuba. Moscow agreed with no resistance and little delay. We, however, offered only to pledge ourselves not to undertake an outright invasion.

In the uncommitted but hitherto non-Communist areas of the world, the USSR is willing to take risks, but not as many as we do in intervening. We have never been deterred from intervention in these areas by fear of the Soviet reaction. By contrast, in several instances where the USSR had excellent opportunities for assisting Communists in seizing control (as in Iran in 1953, Syria in 1955–1958, and Iraq in 1958–1960),[19] the USSR restrained itself for fear of the international consequences. It is also noteworthy that the USSR no less than the smaller states in the U.N. agreed that it would be better, even after the murder of the undoubtedly popular Lumumba, to let Congolese fight each other as Congolese rather than as Great Power puppets. Nor are these instances accidental. One of the chief conflicts between the USSR and China concerns the risks the USSR does not think it prudent to take in assisting "national wars of liberation."

What can we do to harden and to multiply the number of these restricting rules of the game? The first (there is no avoiding it) must be to keep ourselves strong enough to convince the USSR, and increasingly also China, that the risks of intervention on their part remain too high to allow them to take chances. Secondly, we must take diplomatic initiatives to reduce the incitements to intervention. It might be useful to explore, for example, whether it would help to agree to neu-

[19] For detailed documentation of this point, see my essay on "The Middle East and North Africa," in Cyril E. Black and Thomas P. Thornton (eds.), *Communism and Revolution* (Princeton: Princeton University Press, 1964).

tralize the Middle East—outlawing all foreign military alliances and foreign bases, agreeing on limitations of arms shipments to the area, and on collective steps from outside to prevent any border from being changed by military aggression.[20] Such steps might lessen tensions within the region, allow a major shift of local resources from military preparedness to projects that could enhance economic, social, and political stability, lessen the dangers flowing from actual Communist involvement in locally endemic *coups d'état* from reaching the dimensions of a serious crisis, and restrict the possible need for counter-interventions to those more generally acceptable to the international community—namely, to keep neutrals from being subverted from their neutrality.

It would indeed serve to improve international order for us to help all non-Communist states, whether neutralist or not, to cope with the unbalancing forces of uncontrolled social change and so help them lay foundations on which to build independent and responsible foreign and domestic policies. However much we may prefer a policy of close alignment, it might well be acknowledged that the great majority of neutralists in Asia and Africa have demonstrated both the will and the skill to make sure that both the West and the Communist bloc remain on hand competing for advantage among them, each ensuring that the other shall not gain predominance in the area. The interplay of these countervailing forces, and the extraordinary nationalist sensitivity of these new states to any new form of colonialism, constitute powerful new forces at work since the 1950's in restricting the intervention of the Great Powers. The weaker nations of the world are thus for the first time beginning to help define the rules of international relationships.[21]

20 Between 1956 and 1958, the USSR several times publicly indicated its interest in such a proposal.

21 In the realm of intervention, as one perceptive member of the Department of State has pointed out, these new rules of the game demand far more skill and prudence than the old. For example, for a Great Power overtly to extend support to any local faction, whether in the government

Among diplomatic initiatives, it might also be worth exploring whether our explicit acknowledgment of the *status quo* in Eastern Europe might have two worthwhile consequences. It could help to institutionalize the rules of the game of intervention. It might also have a more fundamental outcome. By diminishing our pressure on Eastern Europe, we would make it harder for the foes of relaxed controls within the Communist world to justify their position, and thus we might help ultimately both to ease the pressures within the Soviet elite for adventurous interventions abroad and ease pressures for conformity among the satellites. Accepting the *status quo* might thus make changes in the *status quo* more likely—and thus become a most constructive form of intervention.

The USSR is unlikely in the foreseeable future to accept our conception of international order. Though the threat which Soviet behavior thus raises for us may tempt us to copy Soviet techniques, it behooves us instead to work harder by far to attain standards of world law and justice to which the uncommitted might be won, and which the USSR could ignore only at the cost of incurring international sanctions.

This task is no longer as easy as it might have sounded in the 1920's. Today it is painfully apparent that the demands of international law and international justice do not yet coincide—in part, because the old historical order which molded our present standards has become dangerously fragile; in part, because our present standards are not shared by our principal adversary, or even by all the rest of the world. To argue that in such a world our self-interest and what we hold to be our superior values

---

or the opposition, may in this highly nationalist environment turn out to be the kiss of death. In a world in which the Soviet bloc has become an alternate source of support and supplies, we may also not always be able to afford to let a country that refuses to abide by the conditions of our aid suffer the consequences. But the more moral and more useful course of action has also become clearer: it is no longer enough to pick a strong man and intervene in his behalf. The politics of social change demand intervention in behalf of *programs* relevant to societies in rapid and fundamental transformation.

justify our intervention, however coercive, as long as it succeeds, is to risk the attainment of the surer morality based on
law for the sake of moralism based on power. It would certainly
lead to a conflict with the USSR in which no holds were barred
except on grounds of inefficiency, and hence the present difference in values between us would cease. To argue, on the other
hand, that until intervention achieves in the international order
that lawful status which it now possesses in all domestic societies, there should be a moral and political presumption against
intervention abroad, is to champion law at the expense of justice and ultimately to threaten law itself. Let us observe and
insist on respect for national sovereignty, and try to resolve conflicts through bargaining among these sovereignties. But if
national sovereignty is threatened, or itself clearly threatens
peace, freedom, or justice, wisdom demands intervention, but
in such forms as will best enhance these values and improve the
opportunities for the growth of an international order in which
these values could endure.

VI. *God, Man, and the Purpose of Intervention*

This essay must not end, however, without speaking of two elements which have so far been ignored in this analysis of the
morality of intervention. We have talked only about national
states. We have said nothing about the human being as individual and nothing about God.

The Austrian writer Kraus gave the last line in one of his
plays to God, who, contemplating the destruction of the world
proceeding under his eyes, declared, "I did not will it." A recent
writer in *worldview* has wondered whether nuclear death might
not save more Christian souls for eternal life than life under
atheistic communism. I hesitate to conclude that any man
could know God's earthly preferences with such precision. We
have been given the capacity to distinguish life that is based on
loving one's neighbor from life based on killing him or being
indifferent to him. This is the core of our knowledge and of our

guide to action; the rest is deduction, induction, or dogmatic assertion. We also know how fragile, uncertain, and even absurd this knowledge is, for God has obviously left himself free not only to love but to destroy.

I have therefore spoken in this essay only about our responsibility to act wisely, justly, and with love. I think it is most fortunate for the potentials of justice in international relations that this responsibility arises whether one believes in God or not. It would be fearful if it were not so, for the world which is unlikely to be converted soon to the same view of intervention is even less likely to be converted soon to the same theology. Some men also know how this fits in with God's plans, but I believe that our inescapable ignorance on this subject imposes (as does faith in God) the added responsibility of humility in international relations.

If we commonly err by confusing God's will with our concrete aims in foreign policy, we usually also err by ignoring the existence of concrete individual human beings in discussing the justice of foreign interventions by the abstract collectivity known as the nation-state. If law is not yet an alternative to force in international relations, and indeed requires force, law cannot rest on force alone. The moral individual, however, will not be content with justice; he will prefer a world in which public authority establishes an area of security and justice in which love becomes possible. Instead, he is often confronted by the obvious idiocy of politics in which, to take a recent example, his family is shelled only on odd days on an offshore island that has no military value in preparation for interventions which neither side is in a position to pursue. He knows that interventions are concerned with issues of national power far more often than with poverty, tyranny, or exploitation. As if in compensation for this neglect of the daily concerns of most men, his national leaders make policies based in part on estimates of the personal sincerity or trust or good will of a Nasser or Eden, as if international relations already allowed for more than the identification and enhancement of common national interests. What we share with any rational leaders, whatever their personal morality, is a common interest in the right of their nations to establish foundations which will allow them (and all other nations) to pursue responsibly independent foreign and domestic policies. In such a common interest lie the potentials both for public justice among nations and for personal dignity and love among individuals within nations.

The technicians of power, having shrewdly rejected the illusion that national and individual morality are automatically the same, stop short and do not see that the unfinished task is to relate national purpose to the kind of international justice that gives security and freedom for justice and love to develop among individuals. Indeed, they tend through the prestigious position of their manipulative power to diminish the citizen's concern with love, until he feels embarrassed by the very mention of it in a context of power. In the insecure world in which we live, national loyalty and solidarity have become more precious to most peoples than justice and love. Still, the existence of a nation, any nation, is not justified except as it and its interventions preserve and enhance the individual's capacity to be wise, just, and to love. Mere security can most cheaply be purchased by surrender.

The Legal Regulation of Minor
International Coercion:
A Framework of Inquiry[1]

WILLIAM T. BURKE

AT A TIME when the world trembles lest an inadvertent outburst of violence by one of the nuclear powers provide the spark igniting catastrophic destruction, the problem of the deliberate use of minor coercion assumes increasing importance. The principal purpose of this brief paper is to suggest the outlines of an inquiry into the legal regulation of the less intense forms of international coercion and to raise questions concerning the community policies at stake in such regulation. The need for a framework of inquiry permitting the performance of the intellectual tasks customarily indispensable for solving legal problems is indicated by the multiple confusions that sometimes mar attempts at policy clarification by officials and scholarly observers.

Confusion stems in part from the profusion and ambiguous reference of doctrines that are offered as relevant to the problem of regulation. The main legal doctrines in customary law seem to be expressed in terms of "intervention" and "nonintervention," but there are numerous equivalents, including retorsion, reprisal, measures short of war, international tort, self-help, pacific blockade, breach of the peace, threat to the peace and so on.[2] The confusion of this prolixity of labels is of course heightened by the various shifting references ascribed to each of them.

The same observer sometimes uses a single label to designate very different phenomena, and of course an occasional similarity in labels adopted by different observers by no means implies similarity in factual or legal reference. Among the major identifiable confusions of this type are the employment of the same terms to refer to the facts of coercive conduct and to supposed legal consequences and the use of identical concepts to refer, without qualification, to both lawful and unlawful

---

[1] I wish to acknowledge a substantial debt to Professor Myres S. McDougal of the Yale Law School, for his assistance on this specific problem. It is apparent, in addition, that I have drawn heavily from the general intellectual orientation and framework of inquiry elaborated by Professor McDougal and Dr. Florentino P. Feliciano in their study of major coercion. See McDougal and Feliciano, *Law and Minimum World Public Order* (1961). See also Lasswell and Kaplan, *Power and Society* (1950).

[2] See generally Grob, *The Relativity of War and Peace*, ch. 2 (1949); Briggs, *The Law of Nations* (2d ed. 1952); 2 Hyde, *International Law* 1654-78 (2d ed. 1945).

coercion. An accompanying confusion is to be seen in the common failure to attempt to distinguish between varying intensities of coercion.

The use of terminology that makes a shifting reference from facts to legal conclusions and back again is particularly evident in discussions of the key term "intervention." Observers seek factual orientation by offering definition of intervention in terms of "acts" or "behavior," but at the same time they employ the term to refer to legal conclusion. Thus the latest comprehensive study of the regulation of minor international coercion defines "intervention" as certain conduct by a state or group of states and then proceeds to refer to an alleged "right" of intervention under international law.[3] Dr. Schwarzenberger apparently envisages intervention both as conduct and as a technical legal term denoting illegality under customary international law.[4] The confusion and difficulties stemming from inquiry handicapped with such tools as these were sharply identified by Professor Grob:

> It is not too much to say that there are almost as many textbook definitions of intervention as there are of war. Almost all of these definitions, like almost all of the textbook definitions of war, are unsubstantiated. As regards the few writers who have gone to the trouble of arguing their definitions, it is easy to show that they have made one or another of the mistakes that have been made in arguing the question as to what legally constitutes war. To give an example, the fact that a certain way of conduct has been *called* intervention, no matter where and by whom, is no reason for considering it as legally constituting "intervention."[5]

Even the content of the legal conclusions supposedly connoted by such terms as "intervention" is highly uncertain. Though the latter concept is usually understood to denote unlawful conduct, that is not always the case, and the word is sometimes used by both officials and observers to signify that certain acts are permissible. On occasion the corollary term "nonintervention" is employed to define conduct as "legal," "illegal," and "extra-legal," perhaps creating some uncertainty of reference. In similar fashion some have urged that such less than precise terms of the United Nations Charter as "threat to the peace" and "breach of the peace" are useful because they allegedly carry no implications of legality or illegality.[6]

---

[3] Thomas and Thomas, *Non-Intervention* 71, 74-78 (1956).

[4] G. Schwarzenberger, *A Manual of International Law* 272 (4th ed. 1960).

[5] Grob, *op.cit. supra* note 2, at 227.

[6] E.g., Stone, *Aggression and World Public Order* 21-26 (1958).

A further source of confusion in efforts at policy clarification is trace-able to the failure to develop methods and indicia for distinguishing between varying intensities of coercion. None of the key concepts as-sociated with efforts at regulation of minor coercion is in any way re-lated to differences in the scope and comprehensiveness of coercion. Traditionally, states have sought to preserve a considerable ambiguity in the legal concepts that supposedly limit the use of international co-ercion, and, as a corollary, the processes of coercion to which such con-cepts pertain remain largely undifferentiated. Intervention, measures short of war, reprisals, blockade, and equivalent expressions have been invoked in the greatest variety of contexts, ranging from the minimum coercion in an offer of diplomatic advice to the maximum of violent military invasion and occupation. It seems doubtful, for example, whether clarification of basic community policies about regulation of coercion is assisted by employing the notion of "intervention" to refer both to a comprehensive military attack and the failure to extend diplomatic recognition.[7]

The source of much of this confusion, apart from the traditional overemphasis of lawyers upon doctrines and principles and rules di-vorced from the context of conditions and policies,[8] perhaps derives

[7] Virtually all of the foregoing confusions are illustrated nicely by Professor Fisher's paper "Intervention: Three Problems of Policy and Law," *supra* pp. 3-30. In classic demon-stration he uses the term "intervention" to refer without discrimination to both major and minor coercions, as if no differences in law or policy, to use his distinction, turn on vary-ing intensities in the actual exercise of coercion. On other occasions the term is appar-ently intended to express legal conclusion, principally to imply illegal action (pp. 8-9), though legality is not necessarily excluded by referring to a situation as "intervention" (pp. 19-20). One confusion mentioned in the text above that Professor Fisher tries espe-cially, but unsuccessfully, to avoid is that concerning the legal "rules" relating to the use of force. Though he thinks that "there is much room for discussion," he finds that "the basic rules of international law are reasonably clear" (p. 7). Unfortunately, this sup-posed clarity of legal rule fails to survive even his own analysis for he subsequently an-nounces that "we shall have to clarify the rules beyond the basic propositions stated above" (p. 14) as well as "develop criteria for distinguishing" internal revolution from external interference (p. 14), and, finally, he submits, "we should not forget . . . the lack of any standards for defining intervention . . ." (p. 15).

[8] Professor Fisher again provides convenient and wholly adequate illustration of these tendencies. He cautions us not to identify law with policy in this context and urges us especially not to equate lawfulness with reasonableness (*id.* at 3-4). Perhaps I might caution against the uncritical acceptance of such views by indicating some of the mis-conceptions that underlie them. Chief among them is the suggestion that a policy-oriented approach to jurisprudence precludes any useful resort to legal rules; the notion that law consists solely of a body of "rules" and that the lawyer's task is merely to discover the "rule" and lay it before the decision-maker; the belief that inherited rules provide always but one answer to a controversy, removing any necessity for choice between com-peting principles, policies, and sets of values; the question-begging assumptions about the inclination of courts to apply the "law as it is," accompanied by simplistic statements

from the fact that, traditionally, major coercions were regarded as lawful. Prior to the conditional prohibition of major coercion established by the League of Nations Covenant, international prescriptions did not prohibit resort to war, in the sense of the most intense form of violence. There were, however, a few prescriptions that purported to govern "measures short of war," such as "reprisals," "intervention," and "pacific blockade," restricting the lawful application of minor coercion "to cases in which a prior unlawful act, or a culpable failure to perform international obligations, was attributable to the states against which coercion was applied."[9] The principal function of these prescriptions, as anomalous as they appear, presumably was to localize the use of coercion by conferring positive community approval upon a quick settlement of disputes through superior strength. The participant seeking to remedy an alleged injury could invoke such labels as "intervention" and "reprisals" as a means of signaling other participants that the object of the coercion was not to achieve a significant increment in its power position. The communication served the purpose of allaying the fears of other states and avoided the possibility of their participation in order to maintain their relative power position. The methods utilized in these "measures short of war" were frequently indistinguishable from those employed in undertakings to which the label "war" was attached.

The continued availability of these labels to justify the use of coercion became the focus of considerable attention after the promulgation of the League of Nations Covenant obliged members not to "resort to war" under certain limited conditions. The ambiguity of the term "war" seemed to place a considerable premium on the use of other terms to describe the employment of coercion. If it was only "resort to

---

purporting to describe how decision-makers behave; the contention that it would "produce disorder" if international decision-makers were to apply a standard of reasonableness by measuring the permissibility of their conduct in terms of criteria established in accord with the common interests of states; and, finally, the intellectually sterile suggestion that it is important to distinguish the systems of the "domestic scene" from the "international arena" because in the former "we have a government of laws and not of men."

[The editor has kindly shown me the two new footnotes above and allowed me a brief note in response. There seems little reason to explain the quotations taken out of context from which Mr. Burke constructs a straw man—a nineteenth-century straw man at that. Professor McDougal has properly been concerned with questions of process, and with the role to be played in that process by objective norms. As I see it, the task of the present papers is to seek useful ways of thinking about the problems involved when one country takes action which another may regard as "intervention." I find it more useful to try to suggest a few new general criteria for decision than it is to inventory and catalogue some of the almost limitless factual variables to which McDougal has previously called attention. —*Roger Fisher*]

9 McDougal and Feliciano, *op.cit. supra* note 1, at 137.

war" which the Covenant conditionally proscribed, then it might be contended, and was, that force was still permissible "if the participants used some verbal symbol other than 'war,' such as 'reprisal' or 'intervention' or other 'measure short of war,' in designating their exercises of coercion, and if they disclaimed any intention to institute a 'legal state of war.' "[10]

The Treaty for the Renunciation of War did not materially reduce the ambiguity of the Covenant in this respect, for it recorded in Article 1 the contracting parties' declaration "to condemn recourse to war for the solution of international controversies and renounce it as an instrument of national policy in their relations with one another."[11] The potential lacunae in the term "war" were, however, in the view of some commentators, remedied by the agreement expressed in Article 2 that settlement of disputes "shall never be sought except by pacific means."[12] Other observers were less confident that all measures of force were prohibited by this injunction to use "pacific means," arguing that "measures short of war" were "pacific means," even if compulsive,[13] or that force was still permissible if aimed at an objective other than settling a dispute.[14]

The United Nations Charter avoids the difficulties created by the legalistic invocation of the word "war," but the basic distinction established by the Charter between permissible and impermissible coercion has by no means quieted the controversy about the permissible employment of certain coercion. Some distinguished scholars contend that the fundamental policies projected by the Charter, the promotion of peaceful change and the prohibition of resort to coercion, require that the prohibition of coercion embrace not only the more intense forms that all admit justify the use of similar coercion in self defense, but also the less intense coercions that might be used to remedy certain minor deprivations or violations of international law.[15] Proponents of this Charter interpretation would forbid not only the use of force which attained a certain intensity but also any other form of coercion that reached such intensity.[16] Other commentators assert that the Charter has a somewhat more restrictive compass in that it prohibits armed force of a certain intensity but does not similarly proscribe other forms of

[10] *Id.*, at 140.
[11] 4 Hudson, *International Legislation* 2524-25 (1932).
[12] 2 Oppenheim, *International Law* 184 (7th ed. Lauterpacht 1948).
[13] *Id.*, at 184.
[14] Stone, *Legal Controls of International Conflict* 286 (2d rev. ed. 1959).
[15] McDougal and Feliciano, *op.cit. supra* note 1, at 207 n. 193.
[16] *Id.*, at 142-43.

coercion having the same intensity, such as the manipulation of the economic and ideological instruments.[17]

Professor Julius Stone offers a far more limited view of the Charter prohibition of force. He appears not only to argue that lesser forms of coercion survive the Charter,[18] but that even the more intense coercion of "war" is lawful under the Charter as a response to those prior deprivations of rights enjoyed under international law that do not justify action in self-defense.[19] According to Professor Stone, for example, it continues to be lawful to employ military force for a variety of purposes other than self-defense, but especially as a means of protecting against deprivations, not necessarily amounting to coercion, that are left unsanctioned by the collective community through the procedures of the United Nations. Apparently Dr. Bowett also would authorize the use of force in the event of certain lesser deprivations which he regards as threatening security, though, in contrast to Professor Stone, he justifies this by reference to self-defense.[20]

The policy justifications offered in support of these divergent positions are not dissimilar, at least in terms of long-term community objectives. Professor McDougal and Dr. Feliciano, in urging that the "prescriptions and policies embodied in the U.N. Charter forbid the unilateral use of force and violence by way of reprisal for lesser wrongs or 'tortious' conduct," contend:

> The overwhelming common interest in basic order, and the exorbitant potential costs of exercises of force by contemporary weapons, would appear to counter-balance losses states may occasionally incur from lesser wrongs left inadequately redressed because of deficiencies in available remedial procedures or the limited ability of a poorly organized community to create effective remedies for all wrongs.[21]

Professor Stone begins by assuming that the "liberty" to resort to war is still a wide one even under the United Nations Charter and urges that prohibition of resort to lesser degrees of force "may tend to drive States to seek to vindicate their claims by war, in circumstances when they might otherwise well have been content with measures less disturbing to international order."[22] The major difference between these proponents of opposing Charter interpretations may thus be seen to

---

17 See, e.g., Goodrich and Hambro, *Charter of the United Nations* 104 (2d ed. 1949).
18 Stone, *op.cit. supra* note 14, at 288.
19 Stone, *op.cit. supra* note 6, at 92-103.
20 Bowett, *Self-Defense in International Law* 23-25 (1958).
21 McDougal and Feliciano, *op.cit. supra* note 1, at 207-208 n. 193.
22 Stone, *op.cit. supra* note 14, at 288.

relate not to divergent demands about the use of major forms of coercion but to differing expectations about the consequences of resort to lesser forms of force. Nonetheless, it is obvious that the conditions under which the common interest of the community may be secured are very differently conceived. One version identifies the common interest in avoiding comprehensive violence as requiring the community to permit the use of lesser forms of coercion. In the other version this common interest is served only by prohibiting such use. If one assumes the realism of the expectations underlying one of these positions, it is obvious that a choice made according to the alternative interpretation, if made effective, could have catastrophic consequences.

Our purpose here is not to make arbitrary choice between these divergent expectations about the compatibility of lesser forms of coercion with the provisions of the Charter, but rather to suggest a framework of inquiry by which basic policies may be clarified and appropriate alternatives in community action projected for their realization. In common with other consequential problems of legal policy, it seems indispensable here to seek to illuminate the relevant process of interaction by which participants seek to coerce each other, the process of claim by which participants invoke authority for minimizing resort to coercion, and the process of decision through which authoritative decision-makers respond to the claims. Each of these distinctive processes involves certain participants, variously characterized, seeking a variety of objectives, by management of certain base values according to a great range of coercive and persuasive strategies, utilizing differing methods of interaction, claim, and decision, attaining particular outcomes and effects, and being affected by various and changing conditions. Careful orientation in these processes will permit us to distinguish facts from legal consequences and to pose issues with the sharpness of focus necessary for effective clarification of community policies.[23] After a brief survey of these processes to illustrate the kind of details that are relevant to such clarification, we shall conclude with a brief appraisal of the more fundamental community policies.

The Process of Interaction

PARTICIPANTS

All the various participants in the world social process may be seen to engage in the use of lesser coercion that has effects across state lines.

[23] The contextual orientation offered here is adapted from that employed for analysis of policy problems arising from the exercise of major coercions in McDougal and Feliciano, *op.cit. supra* note 1, passim.

The nation-state is certainly the most important actor in this process, but other territorially organized groups, such as provinces and subordinate states in federated systems and even cities, on occasion apply a significant measure of coercion. International governmental organizations, both global and regional, engage in coercive practices, more recently on an increasing scale, as illustrated by the role of the United Nations forces in the Middle East and the Congo. The transnational political party, or order, is often responsible for violent episodes that have impacts far beyond the locale of occurrence. Private associations, especially those specialized to wealth, have been known to employ practices against each other and against other participants that impose a high degree of constraint. Even the individual human being, though of course the basic actor on behalf of every group participant, may on his own behalf control sufficient bases of power to engage in coercive strategies.

For richer indication of the type of significant detail, it is useful to survey detailed characteristics of the more important participants.

States obviously vary greatly in their total value position, especially in relative power, and it is only commonplace to note that this latter difference may alone determine the degree of coerciveness in their relationships. Variations in power position range in magnitude to such extremes that states on the lower end of the scale may command much less effective power than supposedly lesser territorially organized groups, such as cities, and less even than other types of participants, such as some private associations.

The nature of the power structure within states, particularly whether power is shared widely or concentrated in a narrowly based elite group, is sometimes regarded as an important factor affecting resort to coercive practices. Totalitarian orders, whose internal structures of authority and control exclude wide participation in the governing process, may be more likely to engage in external coercion than states whose structures permit a genuinely shared access to power. On occasion the significance of this type of internal structure has been seen in the possibility that the more democratically inclined states would resort to force for humanitarian reasons.

The wealth processes within states obviously differ greatly in the degree of industrialization and in the relative importance of mineral and agricultural productivity in the gross national product. Apart from the relation of these differences to relative power positions in an aggregate sense, obviously they also bear upon the degree of coerciveness characterizing particular interactions. Though technological innovations apparently continue to outstrip scarcity of particular resources, it need not be assumed that the overwhelming balance of strength will always be with the industrialized states as it is now.

A more complete identification in this context of the characteristics of a state would also take careful note of its alliances and affiliations with other states, more particularly those alliances which associate it with competing blocs. It may be significant to take account also of the practice of rejecting certain types of alliances with other states.

By turning to other important group participants, comparable suggestions of potential details of identification could be made. It might be fruitful to consider, in the case of international governmental organizations, the regional or global character of the group, the structures of authority within the organization and its component organs, the extent to which responsibility is shared for the consequences of a group decision, and the scope of authority and control over base values made available by members.

Transnational political groups appear to merit special attention in future inquiry. Study might fruitfully take into account, in particular, the relations of authority and control between a group and a particular state, the resources available to such groups as bases of power, and the range of their operations around the globe.

OBJECTIVES

The relationship between the objectives sought by coercion and the system of public order projected by the community is most important for policy. Coercion may be exercised in support of, or in opposition to, the decisions of the organized community, and it seems indispensable to distinguish between the two very different perspectives. The common mistake of those who label collective action under the authority of an international organization as "illegal" intervention is to ignore such a distinction.

Another method of characterizing the objectives of participants which may and should be relevant to decisions about the permissibility of the coercion exercised would consider the consequentiality of the values demanded, the degree of inclusiveness or exclusiveness, and proposed extension or conservation.

The consequentiality of the objectives sought by coercion would seem especially significant for making decisions in a community that projects a system of public order based upon fundamental policies of minimizing the use of coercion and promoting peaceful change. Relevant indexes of consequentiality include the number and importance of values affected, the degree of impact upon values, and the number of participants whose values are affected in specified intensity.

The degree of inclusiveness or exclusiveness refers to the degree of participation admitted in the sharing of the values demanded. The problem is to identify the self on behalf of whom objectives are sought by coercion. The self system may extend to the whole of mankind or to a wide range of other participants or be strictly confined to the primary self consisting of a single participant.

The characteristics of conservation or extension refer to whether the participant is seeking to conserve or defend certain values or to acquire values held by others. It may be especially important to take account of community perspectives about the reasonableness of certain value positions since determining what values are regarded as "held by others" is likely to be affected by the general consensus about the reasonableness of the value position occupied.

SITUATIONS

The situations in which coercion occurs may be described by such general characteristics as the spatial position of the actors, the timing of the events in relation to other events, the institutionalization of the arenas of interaction, and the current level of crisis. The location of events may have important consequences for the possible modes of coercion available to participants including such consequences as varying calculations of effectiveness, the base values that are available for use, the objectives that the actor seeks, and the degree of importance he attaches to these goals. Timing is indicated as an important factor to call attention to the sequence of events in the total context, since the degree of coerciveness may depend not upon the alleged coercive practice itself but upon its relation to other events. The degree of institutionalization of the arena of interaction is particularly important in terms of patterns, especially whether it is organized or unorganized. It continues to be considered important whether deprivations may be prevented or redressed by reference to collective decision through established group procedures or whether the arena is so unorganized that unilateral action might appear to be the only available remedy. The prevailing crisis level perhaps bears more heavily on policy than other situational considerations. The existence of high levels of tension and insecurity obviously influences the employment of lesser forms of coercion, perhaps both to depress and to exacerbate the tendency to resort to such forms, and, as indicated previously, this factor is accorded considerable weight in contemporary policy recommendations.

BASE VALUES

People, resources, and institutions are the fundamental components of power which all participants manage in social processes. States are, of course, usually the most powerful participants in terms of control over these bases of power, but, as mentioned above, other participants may control sufficient assets to play a role equal to or greater than that of some states. Among states the differing access to base values is a fundamental condition affecting their interaction and determining the coerciveness of their relations. The unique character of a particular asset may create possibilities in coercion not open to states generally. Location on a critical strait or waterway, for example, may give a state special advantages. In such a context actions that might otherwise have slight impact could assume a highly coercive character. Other assets that have special relevance for policy include control of nuclear weapons.

STRATEGIES

The modalities of coercion, or techniques for managing base values, are commonly employed by participants in varying combination, sequence, and mutual relation to create conditions favorable to the realization of objectives. Though each of the instruments of policy—economic, diplomatic, ideological, and military—may be applied separately, the more important conception takes all into account. The principal condition sought to be created in terms of practices of coercion is, generally, the expectation of loss and the calculation that the target will be better off by conforming to the policies of the coercer.

An inquiry into the practices of lesser coercion, in terms of the various instruments available, might reveal much of special relevance to policy. Appropriate attention would be devoted, with respect to each instrument, to participants employing it, the specific objectives sought, the targets of the coercion, the precise methods adopted, including personnel, equipment and centers and routes of operation, and the immediate outcomes and long-term effects.

Special focus on the military instrument appears justified because of its significance in the context of lesser intensities of coercion. Other instruments may of course be used to project coercion of the same degree of intensity, but the potentialities of escalation and generally increased tension seem greater in connection with active employment of military force than with other types of coercive operations.

OUTCOMES

The outcomes of the process of coercion refer to the varying types and degrees of intensity in coercion actually achieved. The range in intensity is obviously enormous. The availability of nuclear weapons, not to speak of bacteriological and chemical weapons, and the development of revolutionary new guidance systems enable certain participants to approach the extreme of making the planet virtually uninhabitable or, at the least, of destroying modern civilization. Weapons of World War II vintage continue to be employed, of course, and high levels of force are still frequently attained by their use both in more episodic situations and in those of considerable duration. At the same time increasingly refined techniques of infiltration and subversion, sophisticated measures for manipulating the flow of goods and services, and improved methods in symbol dissemination and communication permit increasingly fine, but highly effective, gradations in the application of coercion. And accompanying all these forms are the innumerable types of pressure and constraint that are an inevitable feature of a world arena whose major participants are highly unequal in both aggregate and particular value positions.

The relevance of all these varying intensities of coercion to the appraisal of the lawfulness of minor coercions is obvious. Authoritative community policies and prescriptions already provide standards for identifying major coercion, general criteria for determining the permissibility of such coercion, and procedures for coping with impermissible resort to force. But the position of minor coercions is not so clear. It is questioned, in the first place, whether such coercions ought to be considered impermissible at all. If so, it is uncertain whether contemporary policies and prescriptions provide adequate criteria for distinguishing minor coercion from the ordinary coercion associated with normal interstate behavior or establish with sufficient explicitness a satisfactory range of remedial procedures.

EFFECTS

The critical nature of the long-term consequences of resort to coercion consists, beyond the destructiveness of the particular instance, in the possibility that even the exercise of a lesser form of coercion may trigger catastrophic violence. The bases for this view lie, no doubt, in the apprehension that nuclear weapons technology will soon be within the reach of a considerable number of states, in the likelihood that more advanced delivery systems will increasingly become available beyond the small circle of states now possessing them, and in the general instability characterizing a system built upon such complex and rapidly changing technology. In light of these expectations, it is thought by some that states have much less to lose from enduring those deprivations to their interests that do not threaten important bases of power than from responding to these lesser deprivations with minor, but perhaps forceful, coercion.

A completely different set of expectations is entertained by those who contend that in the long run suppression of resort to minor coercion would tend to make comprehensive force more likely. In this view the current state of affairs is characterized by a collective security system that is not effective nor likely to be so, by a preference for peaceful change which unfortunately is not translated into techniques by which such change may be achieved, and by a set of economic and social conditions that lead to constant change and friction inflicting more or less serious deprivations, though less than the use of force, upon state interests. As a result of these factors, it is suggested, a state may suffer considerable injury that the existing system remains completely unable to remedy through collective procedures. If the individual state is also forbidden to resort to minor coercion in self-help, the accumulation of irritations and pressures may create conditions favorable to the employment of very intense forms of coercion.

CONDITIONS

Though the context in which coercion occurs obviously does not remain static, and features relevant to one instance of coercion may have no relevance with respect to another, certain conditions may be emphasized as especially important. These include the rate of population increase in certain areas, the increasing interdependence of peoples around the globe, the tendency toward a multipolar arena, and the emerging crystallization of identifications among some elites with regard to symbols of past domination. A fuller treatment would indicate the detailed relevance of these trends for expectations of coercion, but even brief consideration suggests the possibilities. The continued and growing disparity between the size of the population and productive potential in certain states creates extremely favorable conditions for resort to coercion. Increasing interdependence does not necessarily entail co-operation for securing values, since recognition of the same condition may also facilitate the imposition of deprivations. The recent deceleration of the tendency toward bipolarity and the emergence of a multipolar arena, in which several states possess the capacity to employ devastating force, may create moderating tendencies as recognition increases of the gravity of even limited coercion in such an explosive context. On the other hand, an apparent identification system incorporating newly independent states, but formed around the wholly negative rejection of historical forms of domination, may create occasions in which major powers are tempted to interfere. For example, the recently proclaimed approval by some states of the use of force to eject a "colonial" regime may have very unfortunate consequences.

The Process of Claim

Our major concern here is to achieve a categorization of probable claims and counterclaims which will help us to clarify goals, describe and project trends, identify conditions, and recommend alternative policies.

States are the major claimants invoking community authority, but other participants very frequently have resort to processes of authority to remedy the effects of alleged unlawful resort to coercion. The objective of claimants is, of course, to secure the prescription and application of authority for restraining and coping with the harm caused by the coercive practices.

Types of Claims

The initiation of coercion occasions two very different types of claims relating to major and minor coercion. The former, more important claim, with which we are not here concerned, is that the coercion employed reaches such an intensity that it threatens important bases of power of a state and both permits the use of substantial responding coercion in self-defense and authorizes the organized community to activate the processes of collective security. The counterclaim usually alleges that the coercion employed was itself in the exercise of self-defense. These claims about major coercion are usually considered in terms of "aggression" and "self-defense" and are associated with a whole cluster of derivative claims to which the law of war is a response.

The other category of claims embraces those relating to the maintenance of minimum order when minor coercion is employed. The more important claims here are (I) the claims relating to the permissibility of minor coercion and (II) the claims relating to particular sanctioning goals.

I. The claims relating to the permissibility of minor coercion

The principal claim is that certain coercion has been or is being employed which does not reach such intensity as to constitute major coercion but which is still unlawful and gives rise to certain sanctions. The complementary claim, asserted in opposition, maintains either that the coercion is not impermissible under international law and does not give rise to sanctions, or that, though otherwise impermissible, it is itself a lawful sanction in response to a prior unlawful deprivation.

The assertion that a particular minor coercion is impermissible invokes prescriptions embodied in customary international law and in the United Nations Charter. The Charter provisions relied upon include the negative prohibition in Article 2 (4) obliging members to refrain from the use of force and the positive injunction in Article 2 (3) to settle disputes by peaceful means. In customary law the familiar prescriptions, as dark in reference as they may be, are those pertaining to intervention, nonintervention, and international torts or delinquencies, including treaty violations, property deprivations, and other lesser coercive acts.

The complementary claim that resort to minor coercion is permissible may of course be that the activities in which the state engages are inevitable in the day-to-day interactions of states and do not amount in scope and intensity to prohibited coercion. Other probable claims are that the instances of permissible use of minor coercion recognized in international law before the U.N. Charter continue to be lawful and, in particular, that Articles 2 (3) and 2 (4) do not extend to complete prohibition of all forms of coercion other than that employed in individual or collective self-defense. The state is entitled, it is accordingly urged, to rely upon prescriptions of customary international law such as permissible reprisals and permissible intervention. This argument may be supplemented by the allegation that the exercise of forceful measures of self-help is fully within the community's expectations about the sanctions permissible under contemporary international law and that the United Nations Charter may be interpreted appropriately to reflect these expectations.

It seems obvious that an appropriate inquiry into these conflicting claims about permissibility cannot be organized in terms of the legal labels invoked in justification. An outline of claims that possibly would escape this ambiguity and permit performance of the necessary tasks might be of the character set forth below. The object of the outline is to permit inquiry into both the subjectivities of actors and their operations (coercive acts). A principal subjectivity is that the actor employs coercion deliberately for achieving an objective. This (hopefully) excludes inquiry into events involving unintentional deprivations, such as accidents and other unforeseeable contingencies.

A. The claims that minor coercion is impermissible

1. Minor coercion unaccompanied by allegation of prior coercion The inquiry would consider the relevance of certain factors for past decisions in terms of phases of the process of inter-action.

2. Minor coercion employed in response to prior unlawful con-duct.

B. The claim that minor coercion is permissible (Same subheadings as in previous claim.)

All the factors in the process of interaction outlined above are of course relevant in the clarification of community policy unique to each type of claim as well as in surveying previous decisions and examining the factors that have affected them.

II. Claims relating to particular sanctioning goals

The significance of the claims relating to the five sanctioning goals listed below is to facilitate the survey and assessment of the many different sanctioning practices and techniques invoked with regard to the varying intensities of coercion in different contexts. It will be observed that each of the sanctioning goals is related to a different sequence in the process of international coercion.

A. The goal of prevention

Claims about prevention concern measures to be taken in advance of any particular instance of coercion and involve practices designed to create conditions favorable to persuasive strategies.

B. The goal of deterrence

Claims about deterrence are those to invoke collective and other procedures of settlement as a method of deterring imminent use of minor coercion. The focus would be on demands for resort to international organizations, courts, and arbitral tribunals to forestall less persuasive means of settling disputes.

C. The goal of restoration

Claims to restore public order are those made to secure community intervention, or to act unilaterally, in order to repress the employment of coercion.

D. The goal of rehabilitation

After coercion is terminated, claims center upon the measures available for reparation of the values damaged or destroyed.

E. The goal of reconstruction

Claims are also directed at the longer-term objectives of modifying structures of authority in both internal and external arenas. The object is to provide arrangements for creating perspectives that facilitate the use of persuasion in seeking value changes.

The Process of Decision

DECISION-MAKERS

The officials established by the constitutive process of decision to resolve conflicting claims about the use of minor coercion are the same as for other types of claims. They include international governmental organizations, the judges of international courts and tribunals, and the officials of nation-states. The latter are, because of the nature of the arena, still the most active and important decision-makers. It perhaps bears emphasis that state officials participate in decisions irrespective of their participation or non-participation in the coercion process.

OBJECTIVES

The overriding goal for which international decision-makers are established is that of minimizing resort to coercion. The various subsidiary goals through which this major goal is sought include prevention, deterrence, restoration, rehabilitation, and reconstruction.

ARENAS

Claimants seek to invoke community authority processes in a variety of arenas, including those that are internal and external in relation to particular states, those maintained for exercising authority functions on a continuing basis and those established for dealing with specific instances of coercion, and, finally, those arenas that exhibit organized and unorganized patterns of authority. The arenas within a state are of unusual significance with respect to minor coercion since provision of opportunity for access to internal decision processes may have considerable effect upon resort to coercion in response to alleged lesser deprivations. Arenas which are both organized and in continuous operation are similarly important for the possibility they afford of resort to collective decision as a means of redress. Traditionally the international community has lacked a significant degree of organization, and this has had great impact on decisions about the permissibility of resort to minor coercion. Although the functions of authoritative decision in the world community have in the past decades become more institutionalized, there continues to be considerable decentralization in the decisions about the use of coercion. As will be seen, this lack of effective procedures for collective decision-making still bears importantly on policy.

BASE VALUES

Decision-makers differ greatly in the values at their disposal for supporting the performance of authority functions. International governmental organizations, though accorded the not inconsiderable basis of power implicit in the grant of authority from states, still depend chiefly upon the support of member states for control over consequential assets. And when all authority functions are considered, as indicated in the outline of outcomes below, the international organization wields greater aggregate bases of power than might otherwise appear to be the case. Such organizations have at their disposal, more or less unfettered, useful military forces, a great range of skills, the active loyalties of their agents, a considerable capacity for gathering intelligence, and a surprising array of channels of enlightenment.

The officials of nation-states usually, however, control base values of far greater magnitude than other decision-makers and obviously can employ them in support of unilateral, and in rejection of collective, decision. Even this preponderance of power may serve public order, of course, when these bases of power are used to sanction choices guided by criteria of common interest. Calculations about the willingness of other states to employ their assets to support community decisions about the use of minor coercion have great impact upon the willingness of one state to commit support to collective decision, and such willingness, accordingly, has significance for policy.

STRATEGIES

The methods available for managing base values in support of a decision about the use of minor coercion include all the instruments of policy—diplomatic, economic, military, and ideological. The traditional emphasis has been upon diplomatic strategies, as suggested by the reliance, unsuccessful for the most part, upon such methods of peaceful change as negotiation, conciliation, mediation, and arbitration. One of the fundamental weaknesses of the decision process is, of course, that military strategies are not frequently available to support collective decisions.

OUTCOMES

The decisions made by officials about the permissibility of minor coercion include all the policy functions, but the more visible, critical phases of the decision process are the prescription of policy, *i.e.*, the projection of general regulations, and its application, *i.e.*, the characterization of particular conduct in terms of conformity or nonconformity with a regulation.

The prescription of policies about minor coercion evolves through both the customary shaping and development of a general consensus in the community and the procedure of explicit agreement. Custom is responsible for most of the doctrines about minor coercion, though more recently, of course, community prescriptions are to be found in comprehensive agreements such as the Covenant, the Pact of Paris, and the Charter.

The application of policy, especially the employment of minor coercion as a sanction, is also associated historically with unilateral action by individual states. The fact that very recently states have sought to institutionalize the use of coercion as a sanction has, of course, created doubts about the permissibility of employing such coercion as a mode of self-help.

Though the sanctioning efforts of the United Nations have not been a spectacular success in terms of repressing violence already initiated, the organization's efforts at prevention and deterrence represent substantial, if insufficient, progress. Such progress may be measured particularly in the many international programs directed at alleviating conditions conducive to resort to coercion. States acting independently of the group are also contributing substantially to this effort, though the motivation is perhaps related more to political advantage than to sanctioning goals.

EFFECTS

The longer term consequences of the flow of decisions about minor coercion embrace not only the distribution of particular values, and not only the kind of comprehensive public order the community establishes—whether compatible with human dignity or not—but even whether any human community is permitted to survive in recognizable form. The increasing delicacy of the balance of terror by which a precarious "peace" is maintained perhaps is too fragile even to endure the multiple shocks of resort to minor coercion. There are, thus far, few signs of willingness among the officials of major states to make explicit arrangements that will strengthen the procedures for isolating and confining these episodic resorts to lesser coercion.

CONDITIONS

Among the factors not already mentioned, those that have, or may have, an important impact on decisions about permissible minor coercion, are changes in the relative strength of the various contending world public orders, the emergence of new systems of public order, changes in interdependences and in their recognition, changes in the techniques of major and minor coercions, the expectations of particular decision-makers about the probable effectiveness of their choices, and estimation of costs involved in making and enforcing a choice.

Clarification of Policy

Clarification of the community policy he recommends is the first essential step of the scholar concerned for promoting effective community action in control of coercion, just as it is indispensable for making decisions in an arena which projects the goal of maintaining a minimum public order. If minimum order is to be secured, or meaningful steps taken to this end, it is necessary to appraise particular exercises of coercion in terms of their conformity to the goals of public order and, where the coercion does not conform to such goals, to initiate sanctioning measures appropriately designed to cope with the situation. The object of the present brief statement is obviously not to achieve this clarification in detail but rather to suggest basic, overriding goals and to indicate questions which might lead to a more meaningful detailed clarification.

The basic complementary policies at stake in the regulation of minor international coercion derive from the United Nations Charter and from the unavoidable exigencies of a world community still largely without effective organization for the collective enforcement of important international policies. On the one hand the goal is to achieve effective implementation of basic Charter objectives: the promotion of change by peaceful procedures and the prohibition of resort to coercion except in self-defense. On the other hand, in an arena that is effectively decentralized in making decisions about redress of wrongful conduct whose effects do not warrant the exercise of force in self-defense, it may be necessary to regard as authorized some resort to coercion as a sanctioning measure designed to protect against harmful, if lesser, deprivations. The goals as thus conceived appear to call for prohibition of coercion, whether or not responsive to prior illegal conduct, which seems from the perspective of the disinterested observer to have a serious potential of expanding to a high intensity, as measured by the number of participants, the scale of coercion, its duration, and other factors. Impermissibility would, in short, embrace coercion of an intensity less than justifying the use of force in self-defense, *i.e.*, coercion that does not directly threaten important base values, when in the context it appears probable that more important bases of power may become targets. Minor coercion would otherwise continue to be permissible, in response to prior illegal conduct inflicting serious harm, insofar as it is reasonably necessary to secure redress and not disproportionate to the injury received. Obviously the prior illegal conduct might itself be an impermissible use of minor coercion.

The more detailed problems for policy are, initially, to consider the factors that decision-makers should take into account in appraising particular coercion in terms of these goals and, then, to consider factors relevant to the choice of remedial, sanctioning measures to be directed at nonconforming coercion.

The first of these tasks calls both for distinguishing minor coercion from major and ordinary coercion and for considering factors relevant to distinguishing between permissible and impermissible minor coercion.

The significant distinctions between minor coercion and major or ordinary coercion are identifiable in terms of certain characteristic subjectivities and operations. Major coercion, identifiable as the intent to use intense coercion to attack important bases of power (subjectivities) and the actual attack or threat of attack upon such bases (operations), is of course prohibited by the United Nations Charter, except for self-defense. Ordinary coercion is seen in the pursuit of lawful objectives (subjectivities) by means of acts which have but slight coercive impact (operations). The particular subjectivities of minor coercion may be considered to include the deliberate use of coercion against components of a target's value position other than its important bases of power, and the operations consist of acts of considerable but not high intensity of coercion.

The key variables to be taken into account in distinguishing between degrees of coercion in terms of subjectivities and operations include all phases of the process of coercion. In seeking to survey the total context of coercion, one might, for example, consider the weight to be attached to such factors as the detailed identification of participants, particularly their relative size and strength, whether the goals sought are highly valued and whether the object is to conserve or acquire new values, the characteristics of the situation in terms of location and time relation to other events, the specific base values controlled by participants, the significance of the combination of coercive instruments employed, especially the military, the specific coercive impact of the acts involved, and the long-term effects on community values.

The determination of the impermissibility of a particular minor coercion calls for assessment of the same key variables from the perspective of determining both the probable immediate and longer-term consequences of the resort to coercion and the relation of the responding coercion to the prior unlawful act. Such a survey would entail consideration of all phases of the coercive process to determine first whether attacks on important bases of power might reasonably be expected as a consequence of the initial resort to coercion. Perhaps the factor of distinctive importance here is the modality of the coercion, especially whether military force is applied in any significant measure. The grave probability of comprehensive destruction already appears too high to permit states to have recourse to substantial military violence as a means of redressing deprivations for which the community does not provide an effective remedy. Special weight might also be attached in this determination to the alliance or bloc with which a participant identifies and the public order systems brought into conflict. Clearly the nature of the objective is a critical consideration since, for example, any use of coercion for acquiring values might be considered impermissible. Whether the purpose is to use coercion to oppose or support community policies and decisions is obviously also a basic factor. Among situational factors, the location of participants, in relation to major power centers for example, may strongly affect possibilities of expanding the scope of coercion. The importance of time may be seen in the duration of the coercion or in whether the coercive acts stem from a long-term exclusive policy or represent an immediate response to events. A discrepancy in particular base values may provide a clue to the subjectivities of the actors, as in the inferences about the consequentiality of objectives that may be drawn from failure to rely upon especially potent bases of power. The outcomes of the coercive acts in terms of the kind and degree of destruction of values actually achieved may be an essential consideration in projecting consequences.

The final task in the appraisal of permissibility in resort to minor

coercion would be the consideration of the coercion as a response to the prior unlawful act. Again reference could be made to all phases of the process of coercion to determine, by reference to the total context, whether the original harm inflicted serious or inconsequential harm, whether the response was or was not proportionate, and whether alternative remedies were fully explored.

The most difficult policy problem, not treated here, is that of assessing the factors relevant to the choice of sanctioning measures in response to non-conforming coercion. All phases of the process of authoritative decision would be considered in detail in a rational choice of sanctions. The specific problem, however, is to consider and assess the detailed practices that can be employed or that may be devised for preventing outbreaks of minor coercion, for deterring imminent use of coercion, for restoring order after coercion has occurred, for rehabilitating value patterns disrupted by coercive practices, and for reconstructing the system of order in ways designed to avoid future coercion.

The U.S. and Wars of National Liberation

QUENTIN L. QUADE

Ethics and Politics

In an age when governmental policies in both domestic and foreign areas exercise an enormous influence on the lives of all, it is perhaps self-evidently worthwhile to search for the relations between ethical perception and the political order. In this search one fruitful approach is to examine a particular substantive problem in order to locate within that problem the pertinence of ethical understanding. Such an approach is a rather humble venture, for it acknowledges the importance of the concrete situation and asks if that situation can lead to ethical awareness. Wars of National Liberation in general, and Vietnam particularly, exemplify the kind of problems which demand integral analysis.

The posture of the United States *vis à vis* Wars of National Liberation, evidenced by this nation's involvement in Vietnam, is prompting ethical examination greater, perhaps, than ever before in our history. The causes of this seem reasonably clear: our engagement in Vietnam has grown gradually over an extended period of time, giving great opportunity for fully rational judgment; and the issues in Vietnam are extraordinarily complex and perplexing. Whatever may be said of Pearl Harbor, it was a dramatic instant which had the effect of muting any serious discussion about *whether* to do battle. And the immensity of the Axis challenge had the practical effect (unhappily) of silencing any prolonged discussion of *what* and *how much* to do. No such simplicity obtains today, and one result is that the nation is undergoing an unprecedentedly profound self-examination on the question of what constitutes legitimacy in foreign policy and international conflict.

One major indicator of this self-examination is the persistent plea that religion and ethics—and religionists and ethicists—must be "relevant" to the great contemporary issues such as Vietnam, and must show an increased concern with such matters. But genuine relevance consists of more than concern. An uninformed concern is irrelevant in a crucial sense and may, indeed, be destructive. Accordingly, the seminar on which this booklet is based was not an enumeration and exchange of abstractions but was, rather, an effort to bring ethical consciousness into relation with what *is*. And this booklet, therefore, is not a tract but an attempt to find the relevance of ethics to a particularly excruciating policy problem. It is naturally as much concerned with the facts as with the principles. A relevant position can proceed only from a fusion of the two: an intense concern with the principles of international conduct, and an unabashed immersion in the situation.

Wars of National Liberation:
Some Strategic Questions

Definitions of Wars of National Liberation were offered at the seminar but, as might be expected, something less than universal agreement was achieved. For this reason, this section will be not so much an attempt to define such wars in any precise sense, as an effort to illuminate the major contentions and question areas which emerged from the consideration of "what the problem is." It should be noted, however, that two things were never far removed from discussions in the seminar: first, Vietnam, which because of its obvious urgency at times almost became co-extensive with the broader category of Wars of National Liberation; and second, the ideas of Lin Piao, Minister of Defense in Communist China, as expressed in his September, 1965, article "Long Live the Victory of People's War."

A crucial part of the difficulty presented by Wars of National Liberation stems from the ubiquity of revolutionary activity in the contemporary age. No one desires the United States to be anti-revolutionary or obsessed with the *status quo,* for there is general recognition that in many turbulent areas of the world the *status quo* is unacceptable. But what happens when "natural" revolutionary impulses become intermingled with external, aggressive forces? William V. O'Brien argued that the real threat to the free world and to the aspirations of nations peacefully to determine their own future derived from such an intermingling. Wars of National Liberation, according to O'Brien, are a combination of some degree of internal revolutionary war and "indirect aggression from abroad in the form of the organization, fomenting, direction, supply and contribution of individuals, organized units and matériel to such revolutionary wars." The problem this poses for the United States is unhappily clear: if this nation chooses to combat the "indirect aggression" it will to some extent also be combatting genuine revolutionary forces aimed at the welfare of the society.

In such a mixed situation, it becomes imperative to distinguish among revolutionary circumstances, to avoid a futile and reactionary negativism. Frank N. Trager presented one method for distinguishing and discriminating, and this approach greatly influenced the subsequent deliberations of the seminar. Trager agreed that the United States must not be against turbulence or social transformation as such, for much of it is justified and inevitable. But he contended that there is a "special kind of turbulence" which reflects planning and programming in military, political, socio-economic, psychological and cultural areas by Communists since Lenin. And this is the theory by which Wars of National Liberation are motivated. According to this, Wars of National Liberation are the currently accepted device for disintegrating what Communists call imperialism, and all major Communist leaders agree on this point. They argue only over timing and the character of the tactical situation.[1] Thus, Frank Trager would reserve the term "Wars of National Liberation" for those revolutionary situations in which communism is distinctly present and attempting to fulfill its theory of conquest.

Defined in this manner, such wars are an adaptation to contemporary conditions of Lenin's prescription for world revolution. In this phase, war in the form of revolution is to be applied to any nation that is not Communist, if the social and political contingencies are favorable. Trager noted, for example, that in Asia it made little difference if the target country was under colonial control, such as was the case in French Indo-China in 1946 and thereafter; or was a country with newly won independence, as in the Philippines and Burma in 1948; or was a country which had been promised independence, as in Malaya in 1948. In each case, differences in political character notwithstanding, Communist-fomented revolution was initiated. This is the kind of warfare which Nikita Khrushchev validated in his January 6, 1961, speech on war: general war, nuclear or conventional, was now too dangerous to be employed, and Wars of National Liberation

---

[1] Arguments in this order over timing may be very meaningful, of course, for nations do in a sense define themselves as much through the proximate means they employ as through the ultimate ends they proclaim.

represent the modern vehicle for Communist expansion. In this sense, Trager said, "Wars of National Liberation are, indeed, wars but are liberating nobody."

But if the presence of communism is the distinctive and important characteristic of these wars, a number of questions arise. For example, how do the great Communist powers, the USSR and China, relate to such wars? The position of the Soviet Union is particularly difficult to understand here. Trager said that there was a high degree of congruence between Soviet and Chinese policy, and an identity of doctrine, at the very time they are carrying on their heated arguments over other matters. He did not suggest they were acting in concert, but asserted that the congruence of their action was unmistakable. They are both, for example, involved in Vietnam in significant respects. But the meaning of this involvement is far from clear. Hans Morgenthau contended, for example, that Chinese concern over Vietnam stems primarily from the proximity of that struggle to China, and that Chinese involvement necessitates Soviet action, for the Soviets will endeavor to prevent Chinese domination of Communist movements in that area. Thus, Morgenthau interprets Soviet activity as being primarily competitive and reflexive in character, and cautions against lumping together Soviet and Chinese motives.

Herbert Dinerstein extended the analysis of Sino-Soviet differences over policy for the emerging nations. According to Dinerstein, decolonization after World War II was seen by both the Soviets and Chinese as an opportunity for Communist expansion. For them to see decolonization as an opportunity meant they were accepting a second-best, for the classic Marxist-Leninist formula of revolution in advanced industrialized countries was not working. Communists expected decolonization to be very tumultuous and to create conditions quite advantageous for Communist exploitation. The ideal situation from this point of view would be one in which indigenous revolutionary forces would be pitted against colonial forces of a different race. However, relatively few clear cases, such as Algeria and Indo-China, arose with those ideal ingredients. Accordingly, the Communists had to re-define colonialism into "neo-colonialism," and "liberation" must be fought for against foreign *influence*, e.g. American imperialism, instead of foreign occupation, e.g. the French army. From the Communist perspective today, a War of National Liberation is this kind of a struggle.

Up to this point, in Dinerstein's analysis, the Soviets and the Chinese agree. But on the question of proper Communist activity in these new conditions, large areas of disagreement have developed, and these disagreements have become an important part of the more general Sino-Soviet dispute. This dispute has a variety of elements that collectively loom very large. The Soviet Union, for example, sees China as potentially more powerful than itself and is thus challenged in a rather fundamental way. Currently, the Soviets occupy some territory which was formerly Chinese, and this is a source of tension. Another problem is that the Soviets did not expect the Chinese Communists to succeed in their revolution, and the Chinese sometimes see this as the Soviets not *wanting* their success. And on top of these and other differences there is the current and very deep dispute over correct foreign policy, especially in the emerging areas.

In Dinerstein's judgment, the Soviet Union is relatively satisfied and quite effectively hemmed in, which inclines her to be basically cautious in her policies. But China's appetites are not sated and she remains expansionistic. At the very least, she covets Taiwan, and the United States blocks her path. Since she is unprepared to confront the United States directly, China seeks the collapse of American imperialism through Wars of National Liberation which will, over time, drain and exhaust American energies. For this reason, Wars of National Liberation are a very major issue for the Chinese, but of only secondary importance for the Soviets, and they have split on this issue of how far and how rapidly to push conflict and revolution in such areas as Southeast Asia.

Thus one major line of consideration in the seminar led to an identification of several large questions concerning the strategic ramifications of Wars of National Liberation. Revolution is a widespread and in many cases inevitable phenomenon. As Hans Morganthau pointed out, very many of the revolutionary movements in emerging nations will have a Communist component, and each of these will be exposed to the risk of an eventual Communist takeover. But even if the Communist elements were to triumph in a given case or series of cases, what would it represent? Would it constitute an actual addition to Communist power? And this raises a question even more fundamental: *Is* there a recognizable general phenomenon of "Communist power," or are there in fact only distinct Communist powers? More specifically, would a Communist victory in, e.g. Vietnam, actually enhance the power of the Soviet

Union and/or China, or would such a victory only add to the Balkanization of communism? If a Communist victory in such a place as Vietnam would add nothing to the power of a general Communist system, then the U.S. may be confronting an illusory threat. But if a Communist victory would in fact add to a general Communist threat —whether it be Soviet or Chinese dominated—then such wars may constitute a genuine danger to the U.S., and engagement in them may be imperative.

Wars of National Liberation: Characteristics and Problems

A quite different series of deliberations had to do with the character of such wars as they have emerged since World War II. William O'Brien noted some of the salient features of these conflicts. In his judgment, the "indirect aggressors" in these wars conceive of the nature of international and internal conflicts, and appropriate means to resolve them, in a way contrary to traditional Western values. Specifically, such aggressors incline toward "...open-ended ... destruction. First, everything must be torn down and then one sees where to go from there." Thus, the insurgents want to "disrupt, disrupt, disrupt," as a preliminary to the construction of a good society as they see it, while the government is trying to "build up, maintain, and improve" a political-social-economic situation that is already unstable and precarious. There are certain obvious advantages for the destroyers, and they can be offset only by preponderant power.

With South Vietnam as his point of reference, George Tanham provided additional insights into the difficulties encountered in Wars of National Liberation. The target countries typically have very grave problems of disease and poor dietary conditions. As in Vietnam, there are normally serious shortages of educated people and educational facilities. Typically, also, there is an under-diversification within the economic system and a problem of maldistribution of goods. And Vietnam illustrates an even more difficult problem confronting many such countries: how to develop some sense of national bond between the people and the central government, and how to cement that bond by developing leadership at all levels of society.

These problems would exist even if there were not instigated strife, and would make governance in these areas very difficult.

But Tanham pointed out that this is only one part of the trouble. For in Vietnam, for example, there is a dedicated revolutionary group which seizes on such natural problems, exploiting and accentuating them in an attempt to overthrow and supplant existing authority. Tanham argued that the Viet Cong show their real intent by trying to destroy programs that help the people, and which, accordingly, threaten the objectives of the Viet Cong. The Viet Cong, for instance, have fought the malaria eradication program by killing malaria workers and have tried to convince the people that spraying is harmful to them. They have worked against fish-stocking programs aimed at increasing protein in Vietnamese diets. They have destroyed schools, and they have killed and intimidated the very officials whose job it is to help the people.

William O'Brien described the latter terroristic practice most graphically. He said such terrorism is

. . . generally most heavily addressed to precisely those elements in the indigenous population which show the most promise for improving society and holding it together. So if you have a friend whom you met one time at an international meeting of some kind, and he looks like the coming person in the government of one of these states, . . . I think there is a really good chance you won't see him next year or the year after that. He's the kind of person who is going to wake up one morning to find his throat slit. This will happen precisely because he is efficient.

The kinds of people needed by an underdeveloped country such as Vietnam are exactly the kind they have in too short supply: educated, administratively skilled, dedicated to the country. Within Vietnam there is a continuing competition for the use of such people, one need calling them to develop the country, and another to combat the insurgent forces. At the same time, another group, the Viet Cong, is trying to stop progress and eliminate potential leaders.[2] And, unhappily but not surprisingly, revolutionary terror tactics have been the excuse for terroristic activities on the part of government forces.

There is a kind of desperation about such circumstances, clearly. George Tanham suggested another factor which was highly important in the Vietnam case. He offered a "Coral Reef" theory as

---

[2] In the February 24, 1966, issue of *The Reporter*, Douglas Pike asserts that the Viet Cong have assassinated 61,000 leaders in South Vietnam since 1958.

a partial explanation of how the Vietnamese situation became so severe in the first place. This describes the practice of the Communist insurgents to develop strength and bases within the country before taking serious overt action. The result is that by the time they begin open insurgency activities, the country is already in trouble because the whole insurgent structure is already in being.

Another pertinent point was made by Tanham in response to a question concerning the matter of "nation-building" necessities in Vietnam. He was asked to what extent the "average" Vietnamese peasant would identify himself with the present national system in Vietnam, and he responded to the effect that there would probably be little such identification. Insofar as this is true, it may represent the ultimate problem of achieving order and security in the countries under consideration: how to give the "average" some reason to want the continued existence of the system.

These characteristics of Wars of National Liberation and the kinds of societies which can be subjected to them at the very least indicate the great difficulties which stand in the way of order and stability. At the worst, they raise a question of whether it is ultimately possible to protect such societies or successfully negate such wars.

The U. S. Response:
Actions and Aims

The preceding discussion of the essential meaning of Wars of National Liberation and the lack of agreement on this question are indicative of the complexity and ambiguity of the problem such conflicts present to the United States. But the government is not absolved from responsibility for decision simply because certitude is absent. No involvement would be a decision just as truly as engagement is. Accordingly, the government does have a policy, and examination and criticism of it provided much of the stuff of the seminar.

There is, of course, a pattern in the actions undertaken by the United States government in the past year. The government has elected to meet the insurgency in South Vietnam and the infiltration from the north, in cooperation with the government of South Vietnam. It has set no limits on the level of force it will employ, as was amply demonstrated by Administration witnesses before the Senate Foreign Relations Committee in February, 1966. Secretary of State Dean Rusk stated clearly that our force levels would be determined by the activities of the insurgents and their external supporters and, indeed, the Administration does not preclude the possibility of extending the conflict outside Vietnam if the occasion should warrant it. We have committed a large land force, huge naval and air elements, and we are prepared to commit substantially more.

These are the physical elements of American policy, but of more concern for present purposes are the central judgments which underlie the physical manifestations. Essentially, the government has answered the series of strategic questions posed earlier in this booklet, and the answers arrived at constitute the bases of American policy. Most important, perhaps, the Administration has judged that victory for the Communist forces in South Vietnam would substantially strengthen the position of China and of communism in general, and would correspondingly weaken significantly the U. S. and her allies. It is in this sense that the Administration argues the inter-connectedness of things, and says that Vietnam is part of a continuing struggle which is of absolute importance.

There can be little doubt that China is the core of the problem, in the view of the government. China is seen to be belligerent, activist, and potentially destructive. Much of this activism may reflect pride in national resurgence, and traditional desires to gain control over acres which at one time or another were under Chinese influence. But all of this is fortified and transformed by Communist ideology, which is still dynamic and virile in China. Left unchecked, in this view, China presents a grim future and a desperate threat to all those around her. The current mode of Chinese aggression, dictated by her lack of strength to combat the United States directly, is Wars of National Liberation. These have been defined most clearly by Lin Piao, and his famous article is judged by the Administration to be a genuine statement of Chinese intention. In a crucial sense, it is this presumed real intention which the Administration is opposing in Vietnam, and it will be valuable to note some of the central themes of Lin Piao's argument.

Lin Piao asserts that in many of the emerging countries of Asia, Africa, and Latin America, the native peoples are being "subjected to aggression and enslavement" by the U.S.-led imperialist powers. But the imperialists control only the major cities and are unable to pacify the countryside which provides opportunity to the "revolutionaries," as happened in the communization of mainland China.

It is possible, he says, to conceive of the whole world in those categories, in which conception Western Europe and North America become the "cities" of the world, and Asia, Africa, and Latin America the "rural areas" from which will arise the revolutionaries to crush the imperialists. "In a sense, the contemporary world revolution ... presents a picture of the encirclement of cities by the rural areas." In classic dialectical terms, "the contradiction between the revolutionary peoples of Asia, Africa and Latin America and the imperialists headed by the United States is the principal contradiction in the contemporary world." And, finally, to bring the analysis into the concrete, Lin Piao states that "Vietnam is the most convincing example of a victim of aggression defeating U.S. imperialism by a people's war. The United States has made South Vietnam a testing ground for the suppression of people's wars."

The United States government bases much of its present policy on the direct reverse of this: that if Communist forces are successful in the "testing ground" of Vietnam it would encourage further aggression and weaken the position of this and other countries. For this reason perhaps more than any others—such as treaty commitments—the government has committed the country to a massive engagement in Vietnam.

In doing so, it also answered, at least implicitly, another question raised in a prior section of this paper. The government has judged that, despite the extraordinarily difficult problems presented by insurgency warfare, and the high levels of social and political instability, it is possible to undertake successfully a program of military pacification and social stabilization. It has judged, in other words, that the monumental complexities we saw above present no insuperable obstacles. As the discussion below will indicate, both these judgments are open to argument.

If these are the central premise-judgments the government has made in arriving at a policy, we need next look at the objectives, both immediate and ultimate, which the government has formulated and which guide the implementation of policy. The proximate goals of the United States in Vietnam fall into two readily identifiable categories. First, this government seeks a military pacification in that country. To achieve this, it wants, in the words of Gen. Maxwell Taylor, to "break the back of the Viet Cong main force units." Simultaneous with this, it seeks through the application of air power to help prompt North Vietnam to cease infiltration into South Vietnam. As a result of these military activities, it is hoped that conditions for negotiation can be achieved, out of which pacification would flow. And, as a corollary of this, the government conducts a multi-dimensional diplomatic effort aimed at negotiations.

The other proximate goal is the development of social, economic, and political programs which, behind the shield of military security, are expected to create conditions of political stability and viability. On this front, the objective is to immunize South Vietnam from that internal disruption and external vulnerability which was noted above. To this end are pointed the myriad economic, agricultural, health, and educational programs, and the basic civic reforms anticipated in the political action team system now being employed. It is important to recognize these activities which are pursued while war rages, for they indicate that the government is not viewing Vietnam in simply military terms, as is sometimes suggested.

But these are precisely immediate goals, which in turn must derive rationality and coherence—if they are to have such qualities—from more long-range expectations. In this regard, the "proximate-ultimate" goal of the government is to thwart the general expansionistic drives of communism in its latest phase, and particularly to frustrate China, which stands in the forefront of this expansionism. The government's policy presupposes an antithesis between Chinese aspirations on the one hand, and the welfare of Asia and the world on the other. And it judges that international and national security demand that we contain Chinese actions.

There is more to this policy than simply confronting and stopping China in concrete instances, however. It is hoped that by stopping her, this country's policies will stimulate forces of change within the Chinese government. The recent history of the USSR looms large in this view of the Chinese future. If it is true that Soviet external actions have *moderated* in recent years (since Stalin, and especially since the Cuban missile crisis); and if it is true that a partial cause of this moderation was the policy of containment employed by ourselves and our allies; then is it not possible to argue that a policy of containment directed at China will not only block her immediate aggressions but ultimately, through frustration, encourage change toward moderation?

Ironically, Lin Piao has provided as clear a description of our ultimate objectives as has any Administration spokesman. In the article quoted above, Lin Piao asserted: "It is sheer day-dreaming for anyone to think that, since our revolution has been victorious, our national construction is forging ahead, our national wealth is increasing and our living conditions are improving, we too will lose our revolutionary fighting will, *abandon the cause of world revolution* and discard Marxism-Leninism and proletarian internationalism." (Emphasis added.) But this is exactly what the United States is attempting to promote: the abandonment of the cause of world revolution. Our government judges that if Chinese external drives are checked, over time their energies will be absorbed by the needs of their own society. In practice this would mean the abandonment of doctrine as a way of life, though not necessarily as a verbal self-description. In a sense, such an objective is based on the idea that Lin Piao is whistling in the dark.

Thus, the government seeks to contain China and, by so doing, change her. In containing her, this country attempts to protect the nations proximate to China, and thus prevent Chinese domination of a major portion of the globe. And this whole proposition may be taken at least one step further. Earlier, the tension between stopping aggression and supporting natural revolutionary impulses was observed. The synthesis which the government has tried to devise in its policy is one which distinguishes between order and the *status quo*. The *status quo* is inherently tumultuous, and any attempt to freeze it would be ultimately futile if not suicidal. But the alternative to freezing is not chaos. It is rather the seeking after order which means seeking the creation of viable political entities. In such polities, the state would be at least minimally a reflection of the needs and desires of the nation. This kind of order will derive neither from Communist domination nor from the suppression of social change and propping up of illegitimate regimes. It will derive only from preventing the one and supplanting the other.

An examination of the present position of the United States on Wars of National Liberation, as exemplified in Vietnam, reveals that the American policy rests on a series of intermediate judgments which serve as the foundation stones for that policy. In the nature of the case, such a policy is highly vulnerable. It consists of many integral parts, and if any one of them proves faulty the whole structure may have to be modified—or it may even collapse. On the other hand, the parts may withstand criticism and even be perfected by it. In any case analysis and criticism of this policy and its foundations served well to identify many of the major problems presented by Wars of National Liberation and it will be useful to consider those discussions.

U. S. Policy:
Criticized and Defended

One major critical theme was developed by Hans Morgenthau. He contended that present United States policy reflected a universalistic or globalistic mentality, and that such a posture was out of tune with international realities. The alternative to globalism is not a new isolationism, but rather a more discriminating approach to the discharge of American responsibilities. The United States, Morgenthau observed, is not obliged to involve itself wherever and whenever trouble arises or whenever our help is asked. It must reserve its decision until it determines that its real interests are at stake.

In the case of Vietnam, these real interests are not at issue, in Professor Morgenthau's judgment. Rather, this country has imposed its own view and vision on Vietnam, by no apparent right. Essentially, the United States has misappraised the character and the potential repercussions of the Vietnam conflict. It has misunderstood the nature of the Soviet Union, and now China, and the relationship of those two states to Vietnam. The two great Communist countries are actually acting out the roles of great powers and, thus, American involvement in Vietnam is based on a false premise. This is that, in Vietnam, we are confronting a unified problem: communism. The real situation is quite different from this. What universalism the Soviet Union demonstrates in Southeast Asia today is largely a competitive response to China. For example, the Soviet Union feels it must look orthodox and, accordingly, endorses Wars of National Liberation.

But because of the prevailing polycentrism among Communist nations, this Soviet endorsement constitutes no real threat to the United States. Indeed, Morgenthau suggested, perhaps the United States too should support Wars of National Liberation, for the Communist regimes that might follow from them would not necessarily—or even probably—add to Soviet or Chinese power, which should be our main concern. In short, the United States can rightly oppose the enhancement of Soviet, or Chinese, power, but Wars of National Liberation such as in Vietnam would not actually enhance that power.

In Morgenthau's view, the "objective conditions" of today are revolutionary, and the United States cannot oppose this successfully. If communism happens to be an element of a given revolutionary movement—and there is likely to be some Communist presence in such movements—it does not inevitably constitute a danger to the United States. Thus, in the case of Vietnam, for example, our efforts to oppose the revolution are faulty for at least two reasons: first, we cannot stop revolution; and second, by trying to do so we actually promote solidification within communism and add to Soviet or Chinese power. If we were content to leave that situation alone, it would at worst become only another element in the present polycentric communism.

Several elements of Morgenthau's position were not disputed. That the emerging areas are in a revolutionary condition was accepted. And that there would be a Communist component in most revolutionary situations was also agreed. But beyond that, Morgenthau's contention served excellently to illuminate one fundamental area of disagreement: whether a Communist victory in Vietnam, for example, would actually add to the power of some supra-national entity which in turn threatens the vital interests of the United States.

The major response to Morgenthau's assertion sought to demonstrate that China particularly did not represent simply a traditional power seeking to establish spheres of influence in proximate areas. Two points were made. First, China is presently representative of highly dynamic ideological drives. A "traditional" Chinese attitude might be content with simple influence over contiguous areas. But China under communism seems to seek not influence but absolute control, as was evidenced by the obliteration of Tibetan autonomy. Furthermore, it is unreal to acquiesce

in Chinese establishment of spheres of influence, for such patterns
of power are out of tune with political reality today. Today, we
see legitimate national aspirations expressing themselves all around
the globe, and these aspirations fly in the face of "spheres of
influence" prescriptions. Moreover, the relative successes of such
countries as Japan, Korea, Formosa, and Thailand indicate that
political viability is possible for the emerging nations of Asia, and
that such nations should be protected from external aggressive
forces in order to develop naturally.

In this view, a non-confronted Chinese communism would seek
to dominate all of Asia, and would constitute an immediate threat
to that continent and an ultimate threat to the United States. In
engaging in Vietnam, therefore, the U.S. is not being anti-
revolutionary, but is attempting to contain one revolutionary force
which, in operation, tends to be destructive and fundamentally anti-
revolutionary. Theodore Weber presented a specification of this.
He argued that a withdrawal from Vietnam now would be unwise,
from the standpoint of international order. Contending that the
United States should aspire to promote a viable international
order, he described China in its present stance as a basically
disruptive force. In his judgment, therefore, one basic rationale
for confronting China is to minimize her negative impact on the
international order we seek.

Paul Ramsey raised a question which had the effect of further
clarifying the issues involved in American policy. He observed
that if American policy is to stop nations from interfering with
each other, that policy is undoubtedly illimitable and erroneous.
For the pre-eminent fact of international politics is that nations do
interfere with each other, and neither we nor anyone else could
prevent that condition from obtaining. It was transparently clear
that the United States has no intention to try to block all cases of
international interference, and this reinforced the understanding
that the distinctive ingredient of a given case of interference which
would prompt United States action was the ingredient of communism. Applied to Vietnam, for example, it is not the simple fact
of international interference which has caused American engagement, but the element of Communist aggrandizement judged to be
present. Does this then mean that the United States would intervene in any situation where communism was present? According
to Administration spokesmen, it precisely does not mean that.

Rather, the United States would join with indigenous forces to combat communism when there was a will to resist, and where the United States could effectively assist. Thus, for example, should a nation, e.g., Vietnam, freely choose a Communist regime, the United States would not oppose it as long as it did not become externally aggressive.

Lin Piao's article provided another focal point for appraising the importance of communism to American attitudes towards Wars of National Liberation. Broadly speaking, three dictinct interpretations of his proclamation emerged. First, along the lines of the government's position described above, Lin Piao's thesis was interpretated by some as a Chinese *Mein Kampf*, an actual blueprint for aggression. Interpreted in this manner, the "People's War" concept is an actual program, and the United States is endangered by it and should respond to it.

But others viewed Lin Piao's article as a statement of weakness. Arnold Kaufman, for example, contended that the Defense Minister's remarks were really an admission that China, though sympathetic to Wars of National Liberation, was unable and/or unwilling to support concretely the revolutionary groups in such conflicts. In this sense, the doctrine is not an expression of an unrestrained impulse to power and domination, but rather a natural expression of sympathy and a talking loudly when you do not have a big stick. Related to this was Herbert Dinerstein's evaluation that Lin Piao's statement should be seen as a new myth for Communist ideology, that it was, in other words, a rationalization of failure. The "opportunities" for communization which had been anticipated from decolonization had not materialized. Success has been scarce, the old doctrine had not been working. But you need a justification for maintaining the cause, so you develop the "country and city" thesis as a supporting myth for your system.

A third position emerged, which contradicted neither of the first two but tried to synthesize them. It suggested that whether the doctrine of "People's War" was a *Mein Kampf* or a statement of weakness and rationalization would be determined through time, as much by American action as by Chinese will and intention. From this perspective Lin Piao's statement should be seen not as a rigid, completed position, but as something yet to be specified according to prevailing circumstances. Thus for example, American actions in Vietnam should be perceived as part of fluid, not static, situation. And this action would be justified by its hoped-for impact on future policies of China, North Vietnam, even the USSR, as well as the indigenous Communist groups in, e.g., Laos, Cambodia, Thailand. The doctrine of the "People's Wars" might indeed be a *Mein Kampf* if China were not confronted, but if she is, that doctrine will probably stand as an expression of frustrated impotence.

A related, and very fundamental line of criticism was developed by Arnold Kaufman. Kaufman argued that there was a kind of imbalance between the highly decisive series of actions this country has undertaken, on the one hand, and the highly tentative character of our policy premises, on the other hand. Most specifically, he said that our policy rests on quite uncertain presumptions about the *intent* of the alleged enemies. This problem is seen as particularly acute when one reflects on the general ignorance in this country of the reality within China. Related to this, American policy presumes not only the intent of the Chinese, for example, but also it presumes that we can rationally communicate to them through the medium of our present policies. Both presumptions are, obviously, radically lacking in certitude, are highly tentative, and, indeed, can be defended only in tentative categories.

The first defense rests on the generally uncertain character of political decision-making. Actions often have to be taken on less than perfect grounds, and of course to refuse to act is a policy also. The other defense is that the record of Communist activity, while lacking the clarity of Hitler's aggressions, for example, is nonetheless substantially indicative of aggressive intent, sufficiently, at least, to indicate that action is called for.

This entire sequence of inquiries and responses was directed at the roots of American policy, and helped illuminate those roots. A different set of concerns queried various aspects of the policy in terms of its feasibility. Even if the basic problem is roughly as the government sees it, is present American policy capable of coping with the problem? The first question here relates back to a problem previously noted: the apparent advantage the destroyer-disrupter has over the builder-maintainer. Can the much-discussed "modern firepower" of the United States, for instance, be brought to bear in an effective manner against elusive insurgency forces? Can a military shield be erected behind which the political, economic, and social transformation can take place?

Frank Trager noted that the only ultimate resolution to the Vietnamese situation is to aid and win over the peasants in the countryside. This prompted the question of how bombing South Vietnam serves to "win over the countryside." Trager's answer to this essentially was that you do what must be done. The Viet Cong began the step up to massive destruction, and the Americans and South Vietnamese are obliged to respond in kind, or forfeit. If they set some *a priori* limits on the level of response to the Viet Cong, they would be inviting the Viet Cong to proceed to that limit immediately. It was Trager's judgment that the military shield could be erected successfully. He stated that "this Vietnamese peasant who makes up 85 per cent of the population wants what most people want. He wants a little elementary security so he can at least have two or three crop years free from war and with one set of taxes, . . . without the terror from which he has suffered. And that can be provided to him with our support of the other allies of Vietnam."

A similar question concerned bombing North Vietnam. Since the North Vietnamese government can, apparently, exist in rural areas if need be, how does bombing the North reduce their will to engage? The response to this, by Trager and by government spokesmen on many occasions, is that bombing in the North is done not to break their will but to make difficult their assistance to the Viet Cong and to make them perceive their vulnerability.

In the months since this seminar was held, and particularly in late February and early March of 1966, the Administration has pointed to significant indications of progress in the Vietnamese military campaign. Only time will tell whether these signs are reliable barometers of success which really foretell an end to the stalemated conditions obtaining until now. But as another line of questions in the seminar indicated, even, a "victory" in Vietnam would not be a full vindication of our policy. For even if our policy works in Vietnam, will it actually deter future repetitions, will it actually teach anyone anything so as to discourage comparable developments elsewhere? How many such wars will there be, and how many can the United States be engaged in without seriously damaging herself?

It has been said the United States stockpiles nuclear weapons precisely so nuclear weapons will never be used. Similarly, it can be said that the United States has chosen to engage in a War of

National Liberation to ensure that there will be no more wars like it. But at this point, a very interesting problem emerges. First of all, as seen above, such a policy seeks to teach, to communicate certain facts to the aggressor, presumed ultimately to be China. As we have seen, there is no guarantee that such communication is possible. Second, if Wars of National Liberation such as Vietnam should prove in the final analysis not to be concerted, not to be orchestrated by China or anyone else, but to be genuinely spontaneous movements, then the United States is teaching no one, but is only engendering antipathy and frustration.

On the other hand, if the Viet Cong with the North Vietnamese are actually serving as proxies for China, and if they are finally negated by American power, then it is possible that future prospective proxies might be hesitant to gamble everything as the Viet Cong and North Vietnam are doing.

While some questioned American policy in terms of its capacity to achieve its objectives, others criticized it for being disproportionate in its means. Present policy, however one looks at it, is tremendously destructive. The levels of force and violence are very high, and in the nature of the conflict these tools of violence cannot always be applied with discrimination. Thus, for example, as Arnold Kaufman pointed out, there is inherent in the present policy a predictable, though not intended, destruction of non-combatant life and welfare. And, in the view of some, whatever objective we might achieve in Vietnam is not worth the violence which must be expended in achieving it. A crucial aspect of this view was the question of the fate of a society which falls under Communist domination. While few praise Communist rule, is it so bad as to justify the havoc a war visits on the society in question? And, who judges it to be so horrible, the indigenous population or the United States? And, however bad Communist domination may be, is it not a sign of despair to suggest that a society which comes under Communist rule is doomed more finally than if it is torn by war? In short, is there any good to win or evil to be avoided which provides a justification for the kind of policy we are presently pursuing?

A different kind of criticism of American policy was lodged by George Tanham and is, implicitly at least, being increasingly acknowledged by policy-makers. Tanham stated that the South Vietnamese government and American forces have been insufficiently concerned with three areas of development: (a) among the peasants, which the urban-oriented government has too often ignored while the Viet Cong has concentrated its attention on this social element; (b) the youth, to which the Viet Cong offers a program and an ideology, even if only dimly perceived; (c) local political structures which have been inadequately attended to. The latter point especially needs stressing, for much of the utility of economic and social reforms may be lost if there is no vigorous and reliable political structure within which such reforms may be pursued. It was suggested that the United States has been to some extent trapped by the success of Marshall Plan aid. Forgetting that such aid was provided to politically viable nations, there has been a tendency to neglect the primacy of politics with the result that much economic aid has come to naught. Tanham suggested, for example, that the United States establish an AID-type agency for political development to aid in the creation of political structures in emerging nations.

A final very significant area of question should be noted. It concerns the effect of domestic conditions in the United States on our ability to conduct rationally the kind of war being fought in Vietnam. Deeply engaged though this country is in Vietnam, it still has very limited military aims. The United States does not want to seize and control territory as it wanted to do, for instance, in invading Europe in World War II. It does not want to obliterate an enemy—North Vietnam—for ultimately it wants stability and independence in all developing nations. The United States, for example, has refrained from bombing the dike system in North Vietnam—though it might do it in some circumstances—simply because its purpose is not to devastate the country but to discourage it from interventionist policies.

In short, the United States wants a military effort tightly controlled by and deriving its rationale from political criteria. But such an effort is very difficult to sustain in terms of the political conditions within the American society. The Administration does not want rising tides of emotionalism about the war, for that emotionalism might vent itself by calling for a policy of obliteration—send North Vietnam, and China, too, if they ask for it, "back to the Stone Age."

But without emotional development, it is very difficult to build and maintain public support for the massive commitment of men and supplies which Vietnam entails. In a situation such as this there would seem to be a large chance that wrong motives might dictate the ultimate policy. A leadership, always sensitive to political opinion, might be inclined to shorten the war by a policy of obliteration, which would negate the political achievements. Or, it might choose to "end the mess" by getting out, not because the ends were achieved or rationally changed, but because of weariness and looming political disaster. The kind of policy presently pursued by the United States has these dangers within it, and an integral part of such a policy must be to combat these dangers most directly.

It is at least interesting to note the absence within the seminar of two kinds of criticism which are frequently heard elsewhere. One such absentee was the kind of legalistic critique lodged so often by Wayne Morse, accusing the Administration of violating both international law and the United States Constitution. The other was the obliteration-type policy which has been advocated from time to time. Hopefully interpreted, the latter omission indicates that the seminar's participants were neither frustrated nor despairing; and the former omission indicates that no one there thought it possible to resolve a most complex political problem by reference to legalism.

Looking back on this section of criticism and response, it is abundantly clear that its function was to raise and clarify questions, and that it resolved none of them. But, it seems equally clear, that is purpose enough.

Wars of National Liberation and the "God Bit"

At this juncture, some would say, it is time for the "God bit," that rather embarrassing moment when, at the end of a session which has been devoted to analysis of a political problem, the religiously oriented organization pays its respects to that which distinguishes it from, e.g., the Foreign Policy Association. But that softly cynical view is patently a false one, as a reading of the preceding pages demonstrates. To talk of the wisdom of policies, as we have been doing; to talk of the "national posture" and national responsibilities, as we have been doing; indeed, to talk at all of what this nation should do in response to Wars of National Liberation or any other urgent matter is to involve oneself immediately and profoundly in the ethical order. This concluding section which seeks to distill the primary ethical considerations emerging from the seminar is, therefore, not the dutiful grafting of a homily on to the tree of "political reality." It is rather a natural outgrowth of that tree and, in a sense, its most important product.

William O'Brien put one of the prime questions of ethics and policy very clearly. Even if it is possible to win one of these wars in some militarily definable sense, he asked, "... is it still possible to remain true *more often than not* ... to the Western values for which the joint defense against international and external totalitarian forces is undertaken in the first place? There is a question of the probabilities of success, and there is also a question of the impact of participation in these wars on many of the values that we hold and are defending." One answer to O'Brien's question was given by a "senior (military) planner," quoted in *U. S. News & World Report,* February 7, 1966: "You can't fight a war with one set of rules for the enemy and another for ourselves."

This probably seemed to him, and perhaps many who read it, a rather clear statement of an obvious truth—a very practical judgment. Yet in fact it is a hugely pregnant and troubling observation, for it presents and begs the whole question of the meaning and relevance of moral commitment. Do we have an identifiable "set of rules"? If we do, how do they guide us, and are they prohibitive in some absolute sense? Or are they just advisory, and subject to abandonment "on provocation"? In what are our rules rooted? Are they just customary, developed in one context but not applicable to another? Are any of our principles actual limits of the actions we might undertake, or are all limits evaporated by the prudential situation?

Theodore Weber examined these questions quite explicitly. He observed that our traditional and present moral stance on war may be violated if we fight in the manner Wars of National Liberation seem to demand. But our present stance was itself worked out in different circumstances, and we must re-examine our basic commitments in relation to the new circumstances to see whether or not engagement in Wars of National Liberation is justifiable. We may be limited by our moral principles, but only an examination of them will tell us.

Weber asked to what extent a war such as Vietnam is a new thing, demanding a new morality, i.e., a new relating of commitments and principles to new conditions which call for new moral judgments. Its most obvious distinctiveness is in the dominant use of guerrilla tactics as the mode of combat. The problems this poses have partially been noted above, but perhaps the most acute difficulty is that with guerrilla warfare comes the inter-mingling of combatant and non-combatant, and the corresponding difficulty of applying force without massive damage to non-combatant elements of society. A part of the same problem is simply to know who the combatants are. Does this kind of condition make effective action by us morally unacceptable, or should it cause us to re-define our moral code in search of a new operative guideline?

A second element of this situation is the fact that our adversary is Asian, and specified by Communist ideology. In other words, the enemy operates on the basis of a definition of morality sharply distinguished from our traditional codes, and, as a part of this, a military ethic also different from ours. Should our codes take cognizance of this, and perhaps adjust to it? If our moral stance in fact inhibits success in the actual conflict, are we obliged to stand by it? That an individual can be self-sacrificial is clear, but that self-sacrifice can be a public virtue is markedly less obvious.

Such questions as these force consideration of what authorizes or legitimizes actions in the international order. If the common good or general welfare of society authorizes actions within a nation, what is the criterion *among* nations? Paul Ramsey pointed out that Pope John XXIII had made reference to a world common good, which presented political obligations to men and states. But Hans Morgenthau said he could not identify the substance of a world common good. The common good of the United States, for example, could conceivably contain a notion of world obligation, but there is no world community, and thus no world common good, except perhaps avoidance of nuclear war.

Arnold Kaufman, on the other hand, contended that it is an "immoral posture" to suggest that national interest is a morally sufficient ground for our policy. There are other considerations, patently moral, which bind the actions of men. These moral considerations are in some sense universal, whereas national interest or national prudence necessarily refers to particularistic maxims. To seek the welfare of all people is such an obligation, and to implement the rules of justice is likewise an obligation pertinent to policy. And these supra-national obligations become increasingly weighty as the threat to national security becomes decreasingly apparent. Thus, in Professor Kaufman's view, the lack of clarity of the Vietnamese threat to U.S. security should magnify this country's concern for obligations other than self-interest.

As Professor Morgenthau observed, there is no world community in being. But to work toward one is still possible and may in fact be obligatory in the modern circumstance. Along these lines, Theodore Weber argued that to be good, our international actions should reflect a concern for the international system. The present elements of this would include the nation-state phenonenon, the preponderance of the great powers, the present international structures, and the various ideological systems currently being espoused. But this system is undergoing change, and we have obligations to see that this change takes certain forms. Particularly, Weber said, we should strive to make the various states viable and free of external coercion; contacts among nations should be multiplied; the margins of authority of existing international organizations should be extended and conflict resolution institutionalized; and, as a corollary, the authority of the great powers should be reduced.

But the vehicle for doing such things is the state, and the state in its nature seeks the nation's interest. It is in this sense that the idea of national interest is a legitimate idea, and not only legitimate but inevitable. Weber stated, and many agreed, that any integral national interest would look to the good of the international order as one of its objectives. Arnold Kaufman said we, through the state, should seek the welfare of all and universal justice.

But whether this happens or not will, in the final analysis, depend on what kind of society we have, on whether the preponderance of society's members perceive and accept obligations to other men. There is nothing intrinsic to the state, which is in its own way a perfect and sufficient society, that demands concern for others. If society consists preponderantly of people with such a concern, then the responsive state would give witness to this in its international activities. But if society lacks this concern, the state will not have it either, will not evidence it, and, one may argue, *should* not evidence it. In a very fundamental sense, this is where the limits of politics are seen, and the domains of philosophy and theology appear.

One other thing appears too, and that is the very personal nature of responsibility in the modern polity. Democratic man is always pleased to accept the authority vacated by pre-democratic rulers, but is less anxious to shoulder the responsibility. Democratic man is a highly culpable man, and as such he needs to strive for integralness and true circumspection. He may still judge wrongly, but he will have fulfilled his responsibility.

Countering Guerrilla Attack*

WALT W. ROSTOW

WHEN the Kennedy Administration accepted the responsibility of government it faced four major crises: Cuba, the Congo, Laos, and Viet Nam. Each represented a successful Communist breaching—over the previous years—of the Cold War truce lines which had emerged from the Second World War and its aftermath. In different ways each had arisen from the efforts of the international Communist movement to exploit the inherent instabilities of the underdeveloped areas of the non-Communist world; and each had a guerrilla warfare component.

Cuba, of course, differed from the other cases. The Cuban revolution against Batista was a broad-based national insurrection. But that revolution was tragically captured from within by the Communist apparatus; and now Latin America faces the danger of Cuba's being used as the base for training, supply, and direction of guerrilla warfare in the Hemisphere.

More than that, Mr. Khrushchev, in his report to the Moscow conference of Communist parties (published January 6, 1961), had explained at great length that the Communists fully support what he called wars of national liberation and would march in the front rank with the peoples waging such struggles. The military arm of Mr. Khrushchev's January, 1961, doctrine is, clearly, guerrilla warfare.

Faced with these four crises, pressing in on the President from day to day, and faced with the candidly stated position of Mr. Khrushchev, we have, indeed, begun to take the problem of guerrilla warfare seriously.

To understand this problem, however, one must begin with the great revolutionary process that is going forward in the southern half of the world, for the guerrilla warfare problem in these regions is a product of that revolutionary process and the Communist effort and intent to exploit it.

The Old Order Changes

What is happening throughout Latin America, Africa, the Middle East and Asia is this: old societies are changing their ways in order to

* From *Army Magazine*, September, 1961. Copyright 1961 by Association of the U.S. Army and reproduced by permission. This article is drawn from an address by Dr. Rostow before the graduating class of the Counter Guerrilla course of the Army's Special Warfare Center at Fort Bragg. Of the eighty students in the class, sixty-three of them were from twenty different nations and only seventeen from the United States.

create and maintain a national personality on the world scene and to
bring to their peoples the benefits modern technology can offer. This
process is truly revolutionary. It touches every aspect of the traditional
life: economic, social and political. The introduction of modern technology brings about not merely new methods of production but a new
style of family life, new links between the villages and the cities, the
beginnings of national politics, and a new relationship to the world
outside.

Like all revolutions, the revolution of modernization is disturbing.
Individual men are torn between the commitment to the old and familiar way of life and the attractions of a modern way of life. The power
of old social groups—notably the landlord who usually dominates the
traditional society—is reduced. Power moves towards those who can
command the tools of modern technology, including modern weapons.
Men and women in the villages and the cities, feeling that the old ways
of life are shaken and that new possibilities are open to them, express
old resentments and new hopes.

This is the grand arena of revolutionary change which the Communists are exploiting with great energy. They believe that their techniques of organization—based on small disciplined cadres of conspirators—are ideally suited to grasp and to hold power in these turbulent
settings. They believe that the weak transitional governments, that one
is likely to find during this modernization process, are highly vulnerable to subversion and to guerrilla warfare. And whatever Communist
doctrines of historical inevitability may be, Communists know that
their time to seize power in the underdeveloped areas is limited. They
know that, as momentum takes hold in an underdeveloped area—and
the fundamental social problems inherited from the traditional society
are solved—their chances to seize power decline. It is on the weakest
nations—facing their most difficult transitional moments—that the
Communists concentrate their attention. They are the scavengers of
the modernization process.

Scavengers of Modernization

They believe that the techniques of political centralization under
dictatorial control—and the projected image of Soviet and Chinese
Communist economic progress—will persuade hesitant men, faced by
great transitional problems, that the Communist model should be
adopted for modernization, even at the cost of surrendering human
liberty. They believe that they can exploit effectively the resentments
built up in many of these areas against colonial rule and that they can

associate themselves effectively with the desire of the emerging nations for independence, for status on the world scene, and for material progress.

This is a formidable program, for the history of this century teaches us that communism is not the long run wave of the future towards which societies are naturally drawn. On the contrary. But it is one particular form of modern society to which a nation may fall prey during the transitional process. Communism is best understood as a disease of the transition to modernization.

What is our reply to this historical conception and strategy? What is the American purpose and the American strategy? We, too, recognize that a revolutionary process is under way. We are dedicated to the proposition that this revolutionary process of modernization shall be permitted to go forward in independence, with increasing degrees of human freedom. We seek two results: first, that truly independent nations shall emerge on the world scene; and, second, that each nation will be permitted to fashion, out of its own culture and its own ambitions, the kind of modern society it wants. The same religious and philosophical beliefs which decree that we respect the uniqueness of each individual, make it natural that we respect the uniqueness of each national society. Moreover, we Americans are confident that, if the independence of this process can be maintained over the coming years and decades, these societies will choose their own version of what we would recognize as a democratic, open society.

Commitments to Freedom and Independence

These are our commitments of policy and of faith. The United States has no interest in political satellites. Where we have military pacts we have them because governments feel directly endangered by outside military action, and we are prepared to help protect their independence against such military action. But, to use Mao Tse-tung's famous phrase, we do not seek nations which "lean to one side." We seek nations which shall stand up straight. And we do so for a reason: because we are deeply confident that nations which stand up straight will protect their independence and move in their own ways and in their own time towards human freedom and political democracy.

Thus, our central task in the underdeveloped areas, as we see it, is to protect the independence of the revolutionary process now going forward. This is our mission and it is our ultimate strength. For this is not —and cannot be—the mission of communism. And in time, through the fog of propaganda and the honest confusions of men caught up in the business of making new nations, this fundamental difference will become increasingly clear in the southern half of the world. The American interest will be served if our children live in an environment of strong, assertive, independent nations, capable, because they are strong, of assuming collective responsibility for the peace. The diffusion of power is the basis for freedom within our own society; and we have no reason to fear it on the world scene. But this outcome would be a defeat for communism—not for Russia as a national state, but for communism. Despite all the Communist talk of aiding the movements of national independence, they are driven in the end, by the nature of their system, to violate the independence of nations. Despite all the Communist talk of American imperialism, we are committed, by the nature of our system, to support the cause of national independence. And the truth will out.

The Vitals of the Victory

The victory we seek will see no ticker tape parades down Broadway —no climactic battles nor great American celebrations of victory. It is a victory which will take many years and decades of hard work and dedication—by many peoples—to bring about. This will not be a victory of the United States over the Soviet Union. It will not be a victory of capitalism over socialism. It will be a victory of men and nations which aim to stand up straight, over the forces which wish to entrap and to exploit their revolutionary aspirations of modernization. What this victory involves—in the end—is the assertion by nations of their right to independence and by men and women of their right to freedom as they understand it. And we deeply believe this victory will come—on both sides of the Iron Curtain.

If Americans do not seek victory in the usual sense, what do they seek? What is the national interest of the United States? Why do we Americans expend our treasure and assume the risks of modern war in this global struggle? For Americans the reward of victory will be, simply, this: it will permit American society to continue to develop along the old humane lines which go back to our birth as a nation— and which reach deeper into history than that—back to the Mediterranean roots of Western life. We are struggling to maintain an environment on the world scene which will permit our open society to survive and to flourish.

The Dimensions of Independence

To make this vision come true places a great burden on the United States at this phase of history. The preservation of independence has many dimensions. The United States has the primary responsibility for deterring the use of nuclear weapons in the pursuit of Communist ambitions. The United States has a major responsibility to deter the kind of overt aggression with conventional forces which was launched in June, 1950, in Korea. The United States has the primary responsibility for assisting the economies of those hard-pressed states on the periphery of the Communist bloc, which are under acute military or quasi-military pressure which they cannot bear from their own resources; for example, South Korea, Viet Nam, Taiwan, Pakistan, Iran. The United States has a special responsibility of leadership in bringing not merely its own resources, but the resources of all the Free World to bear in aiding the long-run development of those nations which are serious about modernizing their economy and their social life. And, as President Kennedy has made clear, he regards no program of his administration as more important than his program for long-term economic development, dramatized, for example, by the Alliance for Progress in Latin America. Independence cannot be maintained by military measures alone. Modern societies must be built, and we are prepared to help build them.

Finally, the United States has a role to play . . . in learning to deter guerrilla warfare, if possible, and to deal with it, if necessary.

A Battle for the Mind and Spirit of Man

I do not need to tell you that the primary responsibility for dealing with guerrilla warfare in the underdeveloped areas cannot be American. There are many ways in which we can help—and we are searching our minds and our imaginations to learn better how to help; but a guerrilla war must be fought primarily by those on the spot. This is so for a quite particular reason. A guerrilla war is an intimate affair, fought not merely with weapons but fought in the minds of the men who live in the villages and in the hills; fought by the spirit and policy of those who run the local government. An outsider cannot, by himself, win a guerrilla war; he can help create conditions in which it can be won; and he can directly assist those prepared to fight for their independence. We are determined to help destroy this international disease; that is, guerrilla war designed, initiated, and supplied, and led from outside an independent nation.

Although as leader of the Free World, the United States has special responsibilities which it accepts in this common venture of deterrence, it is important that the whole international community begin to accept its responsibility for dealing with this form of aggression. It is important that the world become clear in mind, for example, that the operation run from Hanoi against Viet Nam is as clear a form of aggression as the violation of the 38th parallel by the North Korean armies in June, 1950.

In my conversations with representatives of foreign governments, I am sometimes lectured that this or that government within the Free World is not popular; they tell me that guerrilla warfare cannot be won unless the peoples are dissatisfied. These are, at best, half truths. The truth is that guerrilla warfare, mounted from external bases—with rights of sanctuary—is a terrible burden to carry for any government in a society making its way towards modernization. As you know, it takes somewhere between 10 and 20 soldiers to control one guerrilla in an organized operation. Moreover, the guerrilla force has this advantage: its task is merely to destroy; while the government must build and protect what it is building. A guerrilla war mounted from outside a transitional nation, is a crude act of international vandalism. There will be no peace in the world if the international community accepts the outcome of a guerrilla war, mounted from outside a nation, as tantamount to a free election.

The sending of men and arms across international boundaries and the direction of guerrilla war from outside a sovereign nation is aggression; and this is a fact which the whole international community must confront and whose consequent responsibilities it must accept. Without such international action those against whom aggression is mounted will be driven inevitably to seek out and engage the ultimate source of the aggression they confront.

Alternatives to Guerrilla Aggression

I suspect that, in the end, the real meaning of the conference on Laos at Geneva will hinge on this question: it will depend on whether or not the international community is prepared to mount an International Control Commission which has the will and the capacity to control the borders it was designed to control.

In facing the problem of guerrilla war, I have one observation to make as an historian. It is now fashionable—and I daresay for you it was compulsory—to read the learned works of Mao Tse-tung and Che Guevara on guerrilla warfare. This is, indeed, proper. One should read with care and without passion into the minds of one's enemies. But it is historically inaccurate and psychologically dangerous to think that these men created the strategy and tactics of guerrilla war to which we are now responding. Guerrilla warfare is not a form of military and psychological magic created by the Communists. There is no rule or parable in the Communist texts which was not known at an earlier time in history. The operation of Marion's men in relation to the Battle of Cowpens in the American Revolution was, for example, by rules which Mao merely echoes; Che Guevara knows nothing of this business that T. E. Lawrence did not know or was not practiced, for example, in the Peninsular Campaign during the Napoleonic wars, a century earlier. The orchestration of professional troops, militia, and guerrilla fighters is an old game whose rules can be studied and learned.

My point is that we are up against a form of warfare which is powerful and effective only when we do not put our minds clearly to work on how to deal with it. I, for one, believe that, with purposeful efforts, most nations which might now be susceptible to guerrilla warfare could handle their border areas in ways which would make them very unattractive to the initiation of this ugly game. We can learn to prevent the emergence of the famous sea in which Mao Tse-tung taught his men to swim. This requires, of course, not merely a proper military program of deterrence, but programs of village development, communications, and indoctrination. The best way to fight a guerrilla war is to prevent it from happening. And this can be done.

Similarly, I am confident that we can deal with the kind of operation now under way in Viet Nam. It is an extremely dangerous operation; and it could overwhelm Viet Nam if the Vietnamese—aided by the Free World—do not deal with it. But it is an unsubtle operation, by the book, based more on murder than on political or psychological appeal. When Communists speak of wars of national liberation and of their support for "progressive forces," I think of the systematic program of assassination now going forward in which the principal victims are the health, agriculture, and education officers in the Viet Nam villages. The Viet Cong are not trying to persuade the peasants of Viet Nam that communism is good: they are trying to persuade them that their lives are insecure unless they cooperate with them. With resolution and confidence on all sides and with the assumption of international responsibility for the frontier problem, I believe we are going to bring this threat to the independence of Viet Nam under control.

Assassination of a Rising Culture

My view is, then, that we confront in guerrilla warfare in the underdeveloped areas a systematic attempt by the Communists to impose a

serious disease on those societies attempting the transition to modernization. This attempt is a present danger in Southeast Asia. It could
quickly become a major danger in Africa and Latin America. I salute
in particular those among you whose duty it is—along with others—to
prevent that disease, if possible, and to eliminate it where it is imposed.
As I understand the course you are now completing, it is designed to
impress on you this truth: you are not merely soldiers in the old sense.
Your job is not merely to accept the risks of war and to master its skills.
Your job is to work with understanding, with your fellow citizens, in
the whole creative process of modernization.

From our perspective in Washington you take your place side by
side with those others who are committed to help fashion independent,
modern societies out of the revolutionary process now going forward.
I salute you as I would a group of doctors, teachers, economic planners,
agricultural experts, civil servants, or those others who are now leading
the way in the whole southern half of the globe in fashioning new nations and societies that will stand up straight and assume in time their
rightful place of dignity and responsibility in the world community; for
this is our common mission.

Each of us must carry into his day-to-day work an equal understanding of the military and the creative dimensions of the job.

I can tell you that those with whom I have the privilege to work are
dedicated to that mission with every resource of mind and spirit at our
command.

Intervention: Three Problems of
Policy and Law

ROGER FISHER

EVERYONE recognizes that the problem of intervention involves questions both of policy and of law, but there is disagreement as to how the two are to be distinguished and how they are related. The very question of how one ought to perceive the relationship between international law and international policy is itself a matter of policy. This paper is intended to illustrate one working approach to that policy question, first by some general remarks and then by discussion of three problems.

Some international lawyers prefer to sweep all policy issues into a determination of what is lawful. They consider rules of law as handy indexes to policy considerations and to the accumulated wisdom of the past. By reviewing these in the light of an exhaustive check list of considerations, one decides what course of action is reasonable. If it is reasonable then, by definition, it is legal. Under this view, law is not regarded as a restraint on behavior, a restraint which it might sometimes be reasonable to break. At least in the international area it would never be reasonable to break the law, for if the conduct were reasonable it would be lawful.

Others of us prefer to consider policy considerations as having a dual role. Policy is taken into account in determining what is the law, but only to the extent consistent with a legal tradition reflecting well-known canons of statutory construction and judicial restraint. Under this view a judge, or anyone else deciding what the law is, behaves as though his decision were determined by objective rules interpreted in an objective way. The framing of laws should, but decisions according to law should not, take everything into account. The goddess of justice is regularly pictured as being blindfolded, representing this limitation on what should be considered. The policy benefits that follow from deciding questions with judicial restraint and by reference to objective rules are deemed to outweigh the benefits that follow from acting like Solomon and deciding each question afresh as a policy matter. When I speak of law I use the word in this non-McDougal sense. I mean rules and norms of conduct determined by methods approaching traditional legal analysis. Defining law in this way results in there being some policy considerations not embodied in the law in a particular case.

This traditional conception of law seems particularly useful in the international area, for it helps to focus attention on the gap between what a country believes the law to be and what it believes it is wise or reasonable to do. In a domestic court it is enough to persuade a judge of what the law is. Once he has been persuaded of the law he need not be given further reasons why he ought to follow it. The question, "Ought this court to follow the law?" simply does not arise. This is true of the lowest state court and of the Supreme Court of the United States. With rare exceptions, it is also true of non-judicial governmental officials. An assistant may be asked by the Postmaster General for a memorandum on his constitutional or statutory powers to seize a book. The Postmaster General does not ask for a memorandum on whether or not he should exceed his powers. If he thinks that sound policy requires that he have additional powers, he will seek to have the law changed.

In the domestic scene this is belaboring the obvious. We have a government of laws and not of men. But if we shift our sights to the international arena it is not only not obvious, it is not true. Seldom is it enough to persuade the Secretary of State or a presidential assistant that a proposed course of action would violate international law. He will want to know also whether the law should be observed. He will often accept a statement as to the rules of international law but believe that it is wise or reasonable to break the rules. As the law looks to him, and as it looks to me, there exists outside the law a policy question: "Should the law be respected?"

The rules of international law are often less precise than the rules of domestic law. There is a great deal of room for refinement and clarification, work which should, of course, take into account the conflicting substantive interests involved. But the clarification of rules does not exhaust the problem. We must also worry about that possible gap between what looks legal to a government official and what looks reasonable to him. Some may try to close the gap by telling the official that whatever he finds to be reasonable, is legal. It strikes me as wiser, and likely to be more helpful in producing international order, to start from the other end—to make an objective and traditional lawyer-like determination of what is the rule of international law, and then seek to persuade the official to follow it. In my view, legality, like honesty, has objective qualities. To persuade a decision-maker that international legality is the best policy, like trying to persuade him that honesty is the best policy, is a useful task. If successfully done it will tend to produce order. On the other hand, to try to persuade an international decision-maker that whatever is reasonable is legal, is like trying to persuade him that whatever is the best policy is honest. It is not a useful task. If successfully done it will tend to produce disorder.

Rules of law must be related not only to the policies they are designed to serve, but also to the means by which compliance with the rules is to be sought. For the foreseeable future the basic means by which compliance with international law may be obtained is through the enlightened self-interest of the various governments. If this is so, we must be prepared to argue that respect for international rules does in fact serve the interest of each government. The most fruitful perspective from which to discuss a question of international law may, therefore, be the one which seeks to persuade a government official of what a government ought to do.

Should We Intervene by Force in Response to Intervention by Force?

A central question in the conduct of international affairs is that of the use of armed force by one country within the territory of another. Although there is much room for discussion, the basic rules of international law are reasonably clear. In the United Nations Charter all members undertook to refrain in their international relations from the threat or use of force against the territorial integrity or political independence of any state. One can go beyond this. It is illegal for one country to use armed force within the territory of another against the will of its legitimate government. On the other hand, with the consent of the legitimate government, other countries may lend military assistance either to defend it against foreign attack or to help it maintain internal law and order—up to the point where it is threatened with revolution. If a government is threatened by an internal and potentially successful revolution it is the duty of other governments to stand aside.[1] Even if, as in Hungary, the existing government invites assistance from another nation, a popular revolution should be permitted to run its course without outside interference. The United States, which was established through revolution, has always recognized that right in others.

One might start with the preliminary question of whether the United States would like a world in which these rules were respected by all, or whether it would prefer a world in which force was generally used to settle disputes. In discussion of disarmament, some people appear to take a position which is fundamentally an assertion that the United

---

[1] See, e.g., Stowell, *Intervention in International Law* (1921), Hyde, *Intervention in Theory and Practice*, 9-10 (1911).

States' objectives can best be achieved—or can only be achieved—in a world in which might is right. They seem to believe that the ideas and institutions which explain our existence as a nation can make their way in the world only if they are emblazoned on regimental banners. A sufficient answer to this belief is the danger of such international anarchy in a nuclear age. A premise of this paper is that the United States would prefer a world in which all countries respected the basic rules against intervention to a world in which all countries did not.

One other premise needs to be stated. The United States cannot expect to engage in forceful intervention itself and at the same time have all other governments refrain. In isolated cases, it might be possible to carry out secretly a limited program of forceful interference in other nations' affairs. But in a democracy any continuing policy of sending significant intervening forces into other countries could not be kept secret for long. Faced with such conduct by the United States, totalitarian governments, which may more easily act in secret and more easily justify immediate actions by reference to remote goals, could be expected quickly to follow our example.

Neither of these assumptions is often challenged by government officials. The disagreement arises when we have to decide on a response to another nation's act of intervention. It is in this situation that an official is likely to murmur pointedly that our observance of the Queensberry Rules does not seem to keep our opponents from hitting below the belt, and to ask whether we should not do better to imitate them. Examining the question, the official will discover that there are alternative courses of conduct: to respond with intervention of our own or, refraining from intervention, to adhere to international law and try to bring pressure to bear on other nations to do likewise.

A policy of subversive intervention by the United States is subject to serious handicaps. It may be, as our officials seem to believe, that the officials of totalitarian governments proceed by making Machiavellian assessments of what they can get away with, without regard to moral restraints on private or national conduct. I, for one, do not believe that this is so. The human need to feel that what one is doing is somehow the right thing to do is not a uniquely American or Western trait. I think the first step toward international understanding is to realize that officials of other countries regard themselves as good people, pursuing proper ends by legitimate means. But whether this is true of all nations or not, it is clear that the conduct of the United States and other free nations is subject to both moral and political restraints. Our officials could not, even if they wished, embark on a program of political assassinations or mass terrorism of noncombatants in a time of peace. Such restraints limit the possibilities of intervention; they do not prohibit it altogether. There are ways of intervening that are open to us if the objective to be served is, or is thought to be, important enough. But it remains true that a general disregard of the obligation not to intervene will be less advantageous to the United States than to nations which, by our standards, are less squeamish.

More generally, the international situation which presently confronts us is not one in which a United States policy of intervention is likely to be successful. In the West, such a policy might conceivably extend the reach of democracy. Forceful subversion might enable us occasionally to replace a dictatorship with a democratic regime. But attempts to give illegal support to revolutionary movements in Spain, Portugal, and Latin America, for example, would be immediately and seriously disruptive of existing arrangements for military and economic co-operation. The certain loss in these areas is not recovered in a possibility, tenuous at best, of revolutionary success. Moreover, even if that possibility were realized, the questions would remain whether the establishment of democracy would be permanent and, if it were, what our relations would be with a new government anxious to test its strength. Even if these doubts could be overcome, we should be left with the dilemma of separating governments which are "satisfactory" from those which are not and, with respect to the latter, of choosing among rival revolutionary groups.

In the Communist world, subversive intervention offers even less promise of success. Covert action by the United States within the Soviet Union or the countries within its orbit appears more likely to solidify resistance to change than to bring about a counter-revolution. Even in Cuba, beyond the reach of Soviet ground forces, the possibility of undermining the Castro regime by giving subversive support to Cuban rebels is remote. Attempts in that direction will, in the long run, probably seem comparable to giving support to Chiang's dream of recapturing the Chinese mainland. Internal change in nations where communism is now established depends almost entirely on the attitude of the people there. It depends on their national goals and on what we can tell them about our part of the world, not on the necessarily sporadic support which we might give to underground movements. To be sure, in a particular case, such support might have marginal utility in pushing back the iron curtain, but this possibility must be considered with the greatest skepticism.

Active participation in subversive movements by the United States would remove whatever inhibitions the Communist nations now feel against engaging in subversive conduct. We would, in effect, be discarding the rules altogether because our opponents observe them less fully than do we. But if it is true that we are up against "bad men" who seize every opportunity to achieve their objectives, this is like throwing Br'er Rabbit into the briar patch.

The situation which I have pictured is a discouraging and frustrating one. Communist governments engage in subversive activities and make some gains. If we respond in kind we gain little and increase the possibility of further intervention—and further gains—on their side.

Such considerations cannot demonstrate that seeking to counter subversive intervention by engaging in it ourselves will in fact do more harm than good. They do suggest that a policy of responding with counter-subversion has comparatively little to offer and runs the risk of causing the United States to suffer a net loss. The second alternative, a policy of adhering to international law and trying to cause other nations to do likewise, may well offer greater hope of success.

Simply to refrain from intervention ourselves is not likely to produce restraint in other governments. Our bad example will surely be followed; our good example, by itself, will not. A successful policy must not only avoid providing an excuse for forceful intervention; it must tend to induce other nations to lessen their subversive activities. It must decrease the possibility of gain from subversion and increase the cost of the gamble. In such a policy, international law can play a central role.

Efforts to frustrate foreign subversion by supporting a local government are legal under international law, unless the government is faced with a genuine local revolution—which, by definition, is not a problem of foreign intervention. At the invitation of the local government, as is the case of the United States in South Vietnam, almost all means which the United States might use within South Vietnam to counter intervention are permitted by international law. Not only military but intelligence personnel may be made available to friendly governments to help them deter or track down and capture saboteurs, assassins, and others who may be operating within their borders on behalf of a foreign government.

But such direct measures designed to decrease the gains of subversion should be accompanied by clarification of the rules of international law if we are to increase the political cost to other nations of engaging in illegal subversive intervention. This requires clarification of the rules and the facts.

One significant feature of governments is that they feel compelled to justify what they do according to principle. We should make the most of this. We should also recognize that any government that spends vast amounts on propaganda is one which considers public opinion important and is likely to recognize that public actions speak louder than words. A major aspect of the present contest between East and West is the struggle for popular support among politically active people throughout the rest of the world. It costs a country some of its support every time it becomes obvious that it is breaking the rules it professes.

World public opinion is not all-important. It can certainly be outweighed by other considerations. Even more relevant to our problem is the fact that there can be a great deal of difference between one kind of adverse public opinion and another. On some occasions, for example, an adverse reaction simply reflects a general wish that the action had not been taken. This may have been true with respect to the neutral reaction to the Soviet resumption of nuclear testing in the fall of 1961. On other occasions, however, an adverse reaction reveals a radical change of beliefs and attitudes by a particularly significant group. It may reflect complete dismay at the Communist system or a rude awakening as to what a Communist government is really like. This was the kind of reaction which followed the brutal Russian suppression of the Hungarian revolution. That action caused many members of the Communist party in various countries to resign from the party. The Soviet Union paid a heavy and meaningful price for its intervention, a price it will not want to pay often.

If we are to expect such a price for noncompliance with the international law of intervention, we shall have to clarify the rules beyond the basic propositions stated above. We must sharpen our theory of what the law ought to be. If, as here urged, we conclude that the best policy is to respect the rules even though others do not, we should do what we can to develop an international consensus to that effect. We should develop criteria for distinguishing between a revolutionary group that has some outside support and foreign subversion that has some domestic support. We should be able to state how far assistance to a friendly government is compatible with the recognition of the right to revolt. The formulation of at least tentative answers to questions such as these is a pressing task facing us if we are to develop a policy guided by rules of international law. And in order to make it understood that this is our policy, we must state clearly what rules we ourselves are following.

The next step is to make every attempt to raise the rules which we propose, or these rules as modified by the proposals of other nations, to a position of general acceptance among the nations of the world. Our adherence to law will be such in name only unless we are prepared to recognize the views of others entitled to an equal voice in developing these rules.

In his April 22, 1961, message to President Kennedy concerning the American role in the attack on Cuba, Premier Khrushchev said: "We consider that any interference by one state in the affairs of another, especially armed interference, is a violation of all international laws."[2] It is easy to find other statements by Russian and Chinese Communists proclaiming the importance of non-intervention and their respect for international law. One is tempted to dismiss these words as merely words, confident that they are camouflage for acts of intervention over the globe. But although skepticism about Russian sincerity is justified, we should not forget that the lack of any standards for defining intervention makes it hard for us as well as for them to know how to characterize a situation. In any event, we should use the pronouncements of the Russians and Chinese, sincere or not, to emphasize the law of intervention, and as a basis for clarifying it. There are so many different situations around the world—from Eastern Europe to Africa to Latin America—that it might be possible to articulate some genuinely neutral principles of law. Even if not, the attempt to do so would bring into sharper focus the fact that some involvements in the affairs of other nations are lawful and some are not, and thereby put pressure on every nation to state in each case the general principle to which it adheres which justifies its conduct.

In addition to clarifying the law, every attempt should be made to ascertain and publicize the facts in situations where one side or another is accused of unlawful intervention. In many cases, international fact-finding bodies have proved an effective means to this end. Where this device is impractical, the United States should consider the discovery and publication of documented facts a primary objective. A well-prepared White Paper can have an impact far beyond that of bare assertions of intervention no matter how true they may be.

Let me illustrate the central policy role which the clarification of law and facts might play with the present situation in Vietnam. In South Vietnam, as elsewhere, the United States is attempting to reduce the effect of subversive Communist intervention by assisting broad programs of economic and social reform. We provide technical and military assistance directed specifically at the problem of subversion. Such measures are an important part of our foreign policy. They significantly reduce the possibility of gain from subversive intervention. But unless

2 *N.Y. Times*, April 23, 1961, p. 25.

we can distinguish both for ourselves and for others our intervention in support of the Vietnamese government from the activities of the Viet Cong in South Vietnam, showing the former to be lawful and the latter not, we expose ourselves to charges of colonialism and domination,[3] and make it easier for the Viet Cong to increase its activities. Assuming that South and North Vietnam are now to be regarded as separate nations, we should, as an essential element of even our military measures to frustrate Communist intervention in South Vietnam, expose and publicize the distinction between our activities, solicited by the Vietnamese government, and the infiltration of Communist forces from the north.

Like the United States, the Communist nations are heavily engaged in an attempt to win the support of the uncommitted nations. They are concerned to cement loose ties which they now have with other nations and to weaken ties which different, and often the same, nations have with the United States. In this contest it is important that the United States exact the full price in loss of popular support for Communist acts of illegal intervention. The reaction may not often be comparable to the aftermath of Hungary, but this does not mean that the price for lesser intervention is insignificant. That the Communists do not regard it as insignificant is attested by statements like that of the Chinese foreign ministry, charging the United States with "intervention and aggression"[4] in South Vietnam. The success of our lawful activities in opposition to Communist subversion depends in large measure on our ability to forestall such propaganda by making clear the facts of each situation and the rule of international law which applies. On such ability depends also the prevention of unlawful Communist activity, or at least a lessening of the net gains which can be achieved from it. If we cannot make lawlessness so costly as to yield a net loss, we surely can reduce the profit significantly.

By such a blending of law and policy I would hope to persuade officials of our government that the United States should not intervene by force in violation of existing international law even though other governments do. In the harsh reality of today's world we have few enough weapons. Law, and the deference to principle which governments necessarily profess, are weapons which we should use with skill and understanding.

[3] *The New York Times*, for example, referred to "the Communist propaganda line already being dinned that the Americans have simply taken the place of the French rulers of Vietnam" (April 1, 1962, § 4, p. 5).

[4] *N. Y. Times*, February 25, 1962, p. 17.

Should We Decide for Ourselves Which Rule of Intervention Applies?

A second big problem in the law of intervention is that of characterizing the factual situation. Even if countries agree on the rules, there remains the difficult question of applying the rules to the facts. As a policy matter, what method should the United States use for deciding whether a particular situation is a revolution, a case of foreign aggression, or a case of internal disorder?

In South Vietnam, both sides are receiving support from other nations. To the extent that the legitimacy of external support for one side depends on the fact that the other side receives such support, the possibility of an escalating situation in which nations give an increasing amount of what they regard as lawful assistance to their favored contender can be avoided only if it is clear which is *the* legitimate government in South Vietnam. Similarly, the lawfulness of support for one side or another may depend on where you start. Should the Viet Cong guerrillas who remained in South Vietnam after the Geneva settlement of 1954 be considered as invaders from North Vietnam, or are they now to be regarded as South Vietnamese, attempting to reform their government? Is Katanga a part of the Congo or an independent state with the right of self-determination? At the root of the difficulty is the problem of recognition.

In recent years, the United States has taken the position that recognition of a government or state is a political act within the unlimited discretion of each government. We have steadfastly refused to recognize the government of China, continuing to operate as if Chiang and his officials on Taiwan constituted that government. So long as we reserve the right to base international legal relationships on a policy of recognition that ignores reality, we must accept the assertion of the same right by other nations. But this permits the Soviet Union to recognize a Communist Viet Cong government as the legitimate government of South Vietnam, which it could then lawfully assist in resisting the government which we recognize and support. Bluntly, all the rules about intervention are meaningless if every nation can decide for itself which governments are legitimate and how to characterize particular limited conflict. Unless we are prepared to continue a situation in which the legality of intervention will often depend on which side of the fence you are on, and in which, therefore, our policy necessarily becomes one of countering force with force, we must be willing to refer questions of recognition and characterization of a disorder to some authority other than ourselves. The United Nations is the most likely candidate for this role.

We should not expect Charter revision in the immediate future. But imaginative use of the existing United Nations machinery could probably meet the problem. The recognition problem could be resolved by U.N. admission procedures, combined with the question of credentials. Most of the world is in the United Nations. The question of the legitimacy of a government can in these circumstances usually be answered by its status in the U.N. For this to be effective, however, the United States must reverse its current position that recognition is a political decision which each government can take unilaterally. We should shift to the position that the existence of a state or the existence of a government is a community decision, to be taken in the light of the facts. Such recognition need not signify approval of the regime any more than the *de facto* recognition of a corporation connotes government approval of its products.

The United States might be prepared to accept recommendations to member states by a two-thirds vote of the General Assembly that a particular government be accepted as the government of a designated territory. This could be our standard. The example of Katanga suggests that the General Assembly will not always come out on the side of independence for every unit that may seek self-determination. To be sure, there is merit in the current American position that recognition is a political question. The difficulty lies in the consequences of different governments reaching different decisions. Like the United States, the General Assembly may make a political decision as to which government ought to be recognized. But the decision would be nonetheless useful for being political.

In addition to the problem of characterizing governments there is the problem of characterizing conflicts. Is it a domestic revolution, requiring other governments to stay out, or is it a case of internal lawlessness or foreign attack, in which all governments may help the recognized government and none may help the insurgents? Here, again, the General Assembly by resolution could recommend the appropriate action.

The suggestion that the United States refer such questions to the United Nations and follow the decision of the General Assembly meets a number of fundamental criticisms. Strong voices in the Senate have recently renewed the complaint that the United States is deferring too often to the views of the United Nations. In answering such criticisms international lawyers and government officials should have a clear conception of what our basic international policies are, where these will be furthered by seeking and accepting United Nations determinations, as, I think, is the case with determinations of status, and where they will not.

At the present time the United States is prepared to fight for the principle that countries should not suffer from what the United States considers to be aggression. It is a good and honorable principle. It is not unlike the principle that within this country both the federal and state governments will act to see that the people do not suffer from unconstitutional conduct. But within this country it has been found wise to institutionalize the process for deciding what is unconstitutional. In fact, an institutionalized decision is essential if we are to avoid a head-on conflict between governments which view the situation differently, each defending the principle as it sees it. For the state of Louisiana or the executive branch of the federal government to defend the Constitution as it is interpreted by others is not to abandon principled behavior. Similarly, to defer to the United Nations on such questions as which is the legitimate government of a country is not to abandon principle. On the contrary, it is to accept the principle that the legitimate government of a country may better be deemed to be that government which is thought to be so by two-thirds of the countries of the world than that which is thought to be so by the United States.

But, some will say, the United Nations might determine that South Vietnam was subject to an internal revolution and that the United States should withhold all assistance. To accept such a United Nations determination might mean the loss of one more country to communism. It might. But one cannot repeat too often that the United States is not fighting to subject South Vietnam to American control. We are engaged in carrying out a painful and unpleasant duty, and one which we may not be able to carry out successfully. We are fighting to defend the rules of decent conduct toward people. We can do more to maintain those rules by not insisting that we should be the judge in every case.

This does not mean that we should refer every decision to the United Nations or follow their recommendation on every issue. But in the determination of which is the legitimate government and in the characterization of limited conflict we have more to gain by accepting and urging others to accept a United Nations decision than by reaching an individual decision. If the General Assembly recommends that the United States disarm or refrain from particular action, we should not feel bound by it. The United States ought not to determine its foreign policy by deciding what would make the United Nations happy. Far from it. But where particular questions of status require a uniform decision throughout the world, we should appreciate the virtue of having an institution make the decision. Rather than insist upon defending the international community against aggression as defined by us, we can seek to defend it against aggression as defined by the clear majority of that community—a policy which should equally well defend us, which might have more chance of success, and which should lessen the critical problem of plausibly legitimate intervention on both sides of a local war.

What Restraints Should We Respect on the Use of Pressure Short of Force?

Talk of the general problem of the use of coercion by one government against another tends to confuse two drastically different questions under the single label "intervention." At the very time that the government of South Vietnam requested thousands of American soldiers to come into its country to help defend the regime, it objected to the United States' meddling in its "internal" affairs. South Vietnam obviously considered the two questions separable. So did the United States. It was reported that the United States decision to step up military intervention was coupled with a decision "de-emphasizing the necessity for the reform of President Diem's autocratic and often capricious regime."[5] What are the international guidelines with respect to one government's concerning itself with the domestic affairs of another?

Much attention in the past has been devoted to the degree of "domesticity" of the question in which the foreign government is interested, but such a test can hardly determine the propriety of action by other governments. Internal matters are sometimes of legitimate concern to other countries. On the other hand some international matters, such as a vote at the United Nations, should probably be free from foreign coercion. Certainly a boycott by a major power designed to bring about a particular vote in the Security Council by a smaller country would be highly objectionable. Further, neither the kind nor the intensity of coercion (short of armed force, or threats of force) automatically makes it subject to legitimate criticism.

There appears to be little law to date in this area. Most of the issues are ones of reason and politics. The United States is not required by international law to aid a particular country, or to allow American citizens to travel there, or to buy goods from that country; it would seem

[5] *Id.*, April 1, 1962, § 4, p. 5.

that any of these might legally be conditioned upon any decision of the pressured country. The pressure might not be effective, but there is no law against trying. Nonetheless, there are strong considerations relating to the development of an international order which bear both on the objectives sought and the means used.

In looking for criteria as to which pressures are appropriate and which are not, we may profit from the experience of individuals. When my neighbor asked my consent to build a carport nearer to our boundary than permitted by a building restriction, I conditioned my consent on his building a fence to hide the cars. As an alternative I might have conditioned my consent on his designating me as executor under his will. Although the first condition would cost him more money, it probably struck him as far more reasonable and less offensive than would have been the case with the second. The fence and the carport are directly and immediately related. Discussions between us were limited in scope to such things as the height, length, and type of fence. If I had suggested a price that had no relationship to the action sought other than that it involved the same person, I would have opened up every issue between us for possible inclusion in the bargain. I would also have appeared arbitrary and unreasonable, and for this reason my condition would be less easy to accept.

Such personal analogies suggest a general criterion where one country is seeking to bring pressure on another: the more direct and immediate the relationship between the pressure adopted and the end sought the better. This is not an either/or standard, but rather a matter of degree. In international relations it is desirable that coercion be in a form which is obviously relevant to the end sought. The more apparent and immediate the relevance, the less disruptive the pressure. The degree of relevance may, to be sure, be subject to intuitive judgment rather than measurement, but the general proposition can be illustrated. Perhaps with study it can be refined. The United States, for example, might appear to have no legitimate interest in what color another government painted its public buildings. For the United States to threaten to embargo all goods to that country unless it painted its public buildings green would seem to be unwise, and a gross meddling in the affairs of another country. Also, it might well prove to be ineffective, since it is politically difficult for governments to yield to pressure of that kind. On the other hand, if the United States had a surplus of green paint and offered to supply free paint for the public buildings of the other government provided that it decided to paint them green, there could be no possible objection. The rightness or wrongness of the pressure relates neither to the ends nor to the means but to the directness of the relationship between the two.

In any one transaction the United States has its immediate short-run objective of getting results and its long-run objective of fostering an orderly pattern for handling questions arising among nations. Relating the pressure used directly to the ends sought will on some occasions aid in the accomplishment of the immediate objective by lessening resistance on the part of the coerced government. If coercion is immediately connected with the result sought, it seems fairer, it usually involves fewer officials (who are often in one minor part of the government), and acceding may not require a broad governmental decision.

On most occasions, however, the way to get quick results may be to use all available pressure no matter how remote from or unrelated to the action sought. In these cases the short-run interest of getting results must be weighed against the long-run interest which, I suggest, is promoted by trying to deal with each problem in terms of what is directly relevant to that particular problem. In one sense, so long as the world consists of national units, every event occurring within a country can be attributed to the government and identified as national action. In this way, any action with respect to a nation can be considered as relevant to any other action with respect to the same nation. For example a starving child, whom American Quakers would like to help, and a Communist editorial writer who attacks "Wall Street Capitalists" may both be in China. The United States might thus say that so long as "you" criticize "us" in that way "we" will not give "you" wheat. Conduct within each country is attributed to the country as a whole, and all issues between people in the two countries are thus deemed interrelated. It is in this respect that the cold war is truly like a war. All events are related to a single national contest of wills. A commercial aviation agreement with the Soviet Union becomes relevant to a dispute over the status of East Germany.[6]

A wiser way to handle international conflict is illustrated by President Kennedy's response to the 1962 expropriation of American-owned property in Brazil. Members of Congress had introduced legislation to cut off all economic assistance to nations in which American assets had been expropriated without compensation. President Kennedy, pointing out that the property had been taken by the governor of a province, said: "I can think of nothing more unwise than to attempt to pass a resolution at this time which puts us in a position not of disagreement with

6 *Id.*, August 22, 1962, p. 1.

a governor of a state who is not particularly our friend, but instead, really, with the whole Brazilian nation. . . ."[7]

In domestic law we have learned that it is useful to try to settle disputes on their merits rather than on an *ad hominem* basis. It may be useful to try to cope with international problems on their merits rather than on an *ad nationem* basis. Overall leverage may be appropriate in cases where one country is truly interested in the overall conduct of another country, as a psychiatrist is interested in the whole man. Where foreign aid is given because one country is interested in the economic development of another, the leverage need not be limited to the disposition of the particular products bought with the aid given. But as we have seen in the case of the proposal to deny welfare funds to mothers of illegitimate children, leverage is likely to be deemed harsh and will probably be unsuccessful unless its relevance to the conduct is apparent. Cutting off all economic aid to Laos as a means of putting pressure on the right-wing government to enter talks to form a coalition government encountered an initial reaction of defiance.[8]

Although there appears now to be no international law requiring non-forceful coercion to be reasonably related to the ends sought, international law does recognize that a country's absolute right to deny a benefit does not include the right to restrict it arbitrarily. A country may exclude all aliens if it wishes, but if it grants them permission to come in it must treat them according to certain minimum standards. In considering the development of the international law of peaceful coercion such precedents may be more relevant than those of forceful intervention which have been used in the past to support charges of "economic aggression."

These three problems in the field of intervention involve a great deal of policy and some international law. We international lawyers who seek a community governed by law must be prepared as part of our task to persuade governments to take steps in that direction. Most of such steps, from the point of view of a government official, depend on questions of policy, not of law. In arguing policy, however, we should not limit ourselves to the policy issues as they are seen by others. We must also try to present, in persuasive fashion, the arguments in favor of that all-important policy, the policy of resolving international questions according to principle and according to law.

7 *Id.*, March 8, 1962, p. 14.
8 *Id.*, March 6, 1962, p. 30.

Intervention, Civil War and the Role
of International Law

WOLFGANG FRIEDMANN

I should like to state at the outset that, on the question of intervention and indirect aggression, I generally agree with the observations of Professor Henkin, made here in 1963,[1] and on the question of intervention in civil wars, with Professor Wright's comments made in 1959.[2] I do not wish to add to the innumerable definitions of aggression [3] nor to the voluminous discussion whether or not a definition of aggression is possible and desirable; nor do I wish to spend much time on the spate of statements of principle and definitions that have emanated from the Special Committee on Principles of International Law Concerning Friendly Relations and Co-operation among States (Mexico, 1964). I consider these essentially as an exercise in political maneuvering, indispensable because no state can let another get away unchallenged with protestations of unblemished virtue without protesting its own superior virtue. But I find it difficult to see how this new exercise has advanced or even clarified such international law as exists in the field under discussion.

I believe that some further discussion is needed on the question of the rôle of international law in civil wars, in the light of the events of the last few years in such strife-torn areas as the Congo, Cyprus and Viet-Nam.

In order to see the problem of the interrelations between intervention, recognition, civil war and international law in proper perspective, it may be necessary to restate briefly certain theoretical foundations:

1. The most basic principle of international law is the equal claim to integrity of all states, regardless of their political or social ideology.[4] Without such an assumption, it is impossible to maintain even a minimum of universal international order. Contemporary international society is built upon a foundation of legally sovereign states which are entitled to the same degree of respect and recognition. This means the rejection of any differentiation according to their ideology, be it Communism, Fascism, imperialism, capitalism or social democracy. It also implies the rejection of the subtler discrimination made by some international lawyers between those who defend the "values of human dignity" and those who threaten

---

[1] 1963 Proceedings, American Society of International Law 147–162.

[2] 1959 ibid. 145–153.

[3] E.g., the drafts presented to the U.N. General Assembly Special Committee, 1956. See 1956 Report of Special Committee, Doc. A/3574 (General Assembly, 11th Sess.).

[4] Cf. Jessup, The International Problem in Governing Mankind (1947): "We resent and oppose any attempt by the Soviet Union to impose their concept of democracy upon us or to instil it into our midst by undercover propaganda. We cannot deny their right to resent and oppose any attempt of ours to impose or to instil our concept of democracy upon them. . . . The international problem is not one of securing throughout the world an ideological uniformity which has never existed." (p. 38.)

them. When it is said, for example,[5] that "it is not the particular physical modality of destruction that is relevant to law and policy, but rather the purposes and the effect of the destruction and the relation of these purposes and effects to the value of a free world society," it follows with dangerous ease that the defenders of the "values of a free world society," *i.e.*, principally the United States, may be justified in using preventive force and other forms of forceful intervention—*e.g.*, against a pro-Communist regime in Cuba—when in their own unchecked judgment they consider such action necessary to counter a threat to the "values of human dignity." Such doctrines are, in essence, the counterpart of the Communist doctrine that aggression and intervention are justified in pursuit of wars of "liberation" from "colonialism" or "imperialism."

It is possible to reject the relevance of international law to the question of intervention in the affairs of other states, and to regard this whole matter entirely as a question of balance of interests in which "ethical restraint," including the restraints imposed by international law, are at most one factor in the balance.[6] But as long as we talk in terms of international law, there can be no retreat from the view that a political or social system as such does not put a state outside the protection of international law. Once this is abandoned, there can only be strife between competing international orders, each led by one of the world's three giants (a situation foreshadowed in George Orwell's "1984"). We must regard the Soviet Union, Castro's Cuba, both Chinas, Franco's Spain— or even East Germany and North Viet-Nam, insofar as general customary international law implies their *de jure* or *de facto* recognition as sovereign states—as within the reach of that law.

2. Intervention: The report of the Special Committee on Principles of International Law Concerning Friendly Relations and Co-operation among States,[7] contains a typical restatement of the official Communist view on intervention, as formulated, for example, in the proposal by Czechoslovakia:

> States shall refrain from any direct or indirect intervention under any pretext in the internal or external affairs of another state. In particular, any interference or pressure by one State or group of States for the purpose of changing the social or political order in another State shall be prohibited.

Neither the proposer nor any other state will take this formulation as a serious description of state practice. As it is put, more realistically, in the statement by the United Kingdom:

> . . . it should be recognized that in an interdependent world, it is inevitable and desirable that states will be concerned with and seek to influence the actions and policies of other states, and the objective of international law is not to prevent such activity, but rather to ensure that it is compatible with the sovereign equality of states and self-determination of their peoples.

[5] McDougal and Schlei, Studies in World Public Order 817 (1960).
[6] Thus, Dean Acheson in 1963 Proceedings, *op. cit.* 13.
[7] A/5746, Nov. 16, 1964, 19th Session.

It is of the very essence of international politics that states should seek to influence the actions of other states in a multitude of ways. Information centers and cultural exchanges are a relatively mild way of doing so, although they may easily come to be regarded as centers of intelligence and propaganda, rather than of information. A whole scale of economic measures, from discriminatory tariffs or import quotas to economic boycott, are designed to affect the position of the country concerned. In the post-war period, economic aid has been an important means of "intervention." The granting or withholding of economic assistance is used, sometimes in conjunction with bilateral trade agreements, to create a favorable political posture. How far such policies have been effective is another question.

The relevant question for the international lawyer is at what point the manifold forms and degrees of intervention may be said to amount to an act of unlawful interference with the sovereignty of another country. Certain acts of intervention, permissible by international law, may do far greater harm to another country than direct acts of interference that impair the sovereignty, and are forbidden by international law. The U. S. military inspection flights over Cuban territory, while perhaps more easily tolerated than they would otherwise be, because they are an aftermath of the missile crisis of October, 1962, are an infringement of sovereignty over airspace. But they are far less damaging to Cuba than the U. S. economic boycott, which removes the United States as Cuba's most important buyer of sugar and limits and prohibits the use of U. S. port facilities to ships of other nations trading with Cuba. Absent international agreements or organizations which limit national sovereignty, any national measures that affect another nation's economic life are legitimate, even though they may starve it to death. The slightest act of physical violation of sovereignty is not. There would probably be little disagreement that any organized activity designed to overthrow an incumbent government, or perhaps to destroy the independence of the state concerned, e.g., the setting up of political action centers or the installation of compact military units designed to assist rebel movements, is illegal. This would apply to the present U. S. establishment in South Viet-Nam if a new South Vietnamese government asked the United States to leave, and its military apparatus nevertheless remained. Nor could the United States or any other government make the "democratic" constitution of the new government the criterion, since it has acquiesced in the non-democratic procedures by which all governments have, since 1954, been constituted in Viet-Nam, both North and South.

The paradox is that while a state may regard such and many other limited organized acts of interference by a foreign state as illegal, it is at liberty to renounce its sovereignty altogether, for example, by consenting to the absorption of the country by another state. International law does not prohibit Castro's Cuba from becoming a republic of the U.S.S.R. any more than it could have objected to the fusion of Britain and France, which Winston Churchill offered in the hour of despair in the summer of 1940. Apart from the Monroe Doctrine, which is not part of general international law but a unilateral American declaration of policy, the United States could not have objected to such action in the name of international law but only on the grounds of overriding national policy considerations.

The borderlines between the many customary and tolerated degrees of interference in the affairs of another state, and illegitimate intervention, must always remain fluid. The only proper way out is the strengthening of international co-operative agreements. This applies to such fields as economic strangulation or boycott, as well as broadcasting. It is not the techniques of international law that are deficient, but the state of political relations. Thus, it would at any time be possible to revive and enlarge the abortive International Broadcasting Convention of 1936, which was designed to eliminate the use of broadcasting as a means of political propaganda with the purpose of undermining the government of another state. The Spanish Non-Intervention Pact of the same time did not fail because of any inability of the participating Powers to control the flow of arms, but because of the political unwillingness, especially on the part of Germany and Italy, to make it work.

Civil War, Recognition and Intervention

The rôle of international law in civil wars has become a matter of even more pressing importance in recent years. This is largely due to three factors: the first is the phenomenal increase in the number of unstable new states. The instability is sometimes the result of long-standing racial and ethical tensions, and sometimes the result of political and ideological divisions. The former factor clearly predominates in the strife between Greeks and Turks in Cyprus, although this conflict has, because of the Zurich Pact of 1959, international implications which directly involve Britain, Greece and Turkey. It is predominant in the threat of a disintegration of the Nigeria Federation into three or more racially antagonistic parts. Racial and religious antagonism threatens to disrupt the Sudan whose Southern population—Negro, pagan and economically underdeveloped—has no links with the dominant northern part which is Arab and Moslem. In the Congo, racial and political factors are now mixed, since tensions between different tribes intersect with the struggle between the relatively conservative Tshombe government and the Communist-led forces of the rebels. In Yemen, where Saudi Arabia supports the royalists and Egypt the Republicans, and in Viet-Nam, where North and South Viet-Nam may, since the agreement of 1954, be considered as *de facto* separate states, the civil war aspects of the conflict are purely political and to some extent religious, but not racial.

The second reason for the increased importance of civil war for international law is the intertwining of civil and international conflict. In all of the major internal conflicts of recent years which have provoked international tension and intervention, notably in the Congo, Cyprus, Yemen and Viet-Nam, there have been genuine and major elements of internal rebellion reflecting the deep social and political turmoil, but they have been obscured and distorted by outside interventions and counter-interventions dictated by strategic and political reasons. The secession movement of Katanga, as well as the present Communist rebellion in the Congo, spring from genuine tribal and social antagonisms. Greeks and Turks in Cyprus are deeply and tragically split by ethnical and religious tensions. Even the most ardent foe of Communism must admit that, until a short time ago, the Viet-Cong movement in South Viet-Nam represented a genuine political and social revolution against a government which itself is split between Buddhist and Catholic factions, between authoritarian and democratic elements. In the absence of an impartial fact-finding body and an effective international conciliation and peacekeeping machinery, outside states, concerned with the outcome of the struggle for strategic or ideological reasons, may choose to emphasize the civil war or the international factors in the conflict.

The importance of this vast measure of discretion as to the "right" of intervention in civil war conflicts with international implications—sometimes euphemistically described as "the decentralized structure of desion making in the international community"[8]—has increased further through the claim that intervention against what the intervening state judges to be outside support for an internal rebellion, is legitimated as an act of "collective self-defense" permitted by Article 51 of the U.N. Charter. It is claimed[9] that a state which, in response to the request of a government, gives it military assistance against revolutionary forces which, in the judgment of the assisting state, are directed and master-minded by an outside Power, acts in self-defense against aggression.

Third, the elasticity of international intervention in internal conflicts is increased by the very wide measure of discretion in the speed and manner in which any individual state may recognize insurgents in another state, either as belligerents or as the legitimate government. The absence of any international recognition procedure, *e.g.*, through United Nations resolution, leaves a wide margin of discretion to the individual states with regard to the recognition of insurgent movements or new states. While the general standards of recognition are broadly accepted, each state judges for itself how to apply them. In some cases, such as the continued refusal by the United States to recognize the Communist regime as the Government of China, despite the now overwhelming evidence of 16 years of its continuity and stability, it is clearly a matter of policy prevailing over the legal standards of recognition. In referring to legal standards, I do not wish to endorse the controversial doctrine (Lauterpacht) which regards recognition strictly as a matter of law. What I believe to be beyond controversy is the *negative* aspect of the legal standards of recognition. Without the presence of these minimum standards (territory, population, substantial control) recognition is unlawful. When they are present, a

---

[8] See, *e.g.*, McDougal and Feliciano, Law and Minimum World Public Order 40 (1961).

[9] For the most recent authoritative exposition of this view, see the speech made by Secretary of State Dean Rusk at the Annual Dinner of this Society on April 23, 1965, below, p. 247.

wide measure of discretion exists as to the time and manner of recognition. A foreign state has, therefore, a great deal of freedom of maneuver in deciding whether to intervene in a civil war. It has much discretion in choosing whether to recognize insurgents as belligerents or even as the legitimate government of the country. At most, it may be said that in extreme cases of foreign assistance to rebels, their immediate recognition as the legitimate government at a time when they had no substantial control of the country, as was notably the case in the almost immediate recognition of the Franco Government by Germany and Italy after the rebellion, is a thinly disguised interference in the affairs of another state, utterly at variance with established principles of recognition.

The enormous degree of elasticity thus left by customary international law to the manner and modality of intervention, calls for a reappraisal of the rights of the contending sides with regard to outside assistance in a civil war. What is probably still the prevailing view is that the incumbent government, but not insurgents, has the right to ask for assistance from foreign governments, at least as long as insurgents are not recognized as "belligerents" or "insurgents."[10] The traditional view is stated by Oppenheim[11] as follows: "a foreign state commits an international delinquency by assisting insurgents in spite of being at peace with the legitimate government." This view has been invoked, for example, by the Soviet Government in justification of its intervention in Hungary in 1956 in support of the Kadar government; by the United States for its intervention in Lebanon in 1958 and, from 1960 onwards in Viet-Nam, and by Great Britain in justification of its military assistance to the Jordanian government in 1958. In one of the most fateful of modern civil wars, the Spanish Civil War of 1936 to 1939, the Western governments chose, however, to treat the Franco rebellion as on a par with the government by signing the abortive Non-Intervention Pact, which was immediately and completely dishonored by Germany and Italy, which supported Franco as "the legitimate" Government of Spain, and, to a lesser and far more justifiable extent, by the Soviet Union, which supported the incumbent Republican government, in response to the German/Italian intervention. Nor did the United States choose to invoke the distinction between incumbent government and rebels, with regard to its intervention in Guatemala in 1954, or in its recent policies towards Castro's Cuba. The Communist states accord themselves an even greater liberty of action by justifying wars of "national liberation," which means that they will support insurgent movements or incumbent governments according to their political ideology. So deep are the political conflicts leading to intervention and counter-intervention, that in this writer's submission, the distinction between the rights of incumbent governments and of substantial movement of rebellion has lost all meaning. In none of the important recent internal-

---

[10] R. A. Falk, in International Aspects of Civil Strife at 194 (Rosenau ed., 1964), distinguishes between "rebellion" (purely domestic internal war), "insurgency" (partially internationalized conflict) and "belligerency" (fully internationalized conflict).

[11] 2 International Law 60 (6th ed., Lauterpacht, 1952).

international conflicts have the contending outside states even bothered to accord the status of "insurgents" or "belligerents" to the other side.

In these circumstances there is much justification for the view expressed by a number of authoritative writers that no meaningful legal distinction can be made with regard to claims for outside assistance, as between the incumbent government and insurgents.

The case for neutrality rather than intervention on the side of the incumbent government in civil war situations has been well stated by Hall: [12]

> . . . Supposing the intervention to be directed against the existing government, independence is violated by an attempt to prevent the regular organs of the state from managing the state affairs in its own way. Supposing it, on the other hand, to be directed against rebels, the fact that it has been necessary to call in foreign help is enough to show that the issue of the conflict would without it be uncertain, and consequently that there is a doubt as to which side would ultimately establish itself as the legal representative of the state. . . .

The same point of view has been vigorously restated more recently by Quincy Wright in many writings.[13] The most recent writer on this subject[14] has also criticized the traditional doctrine in the following words:

> Aid may be given to the government on the basis of the right assumed to exist in customary law of aiding a legitimate government. This form of action has a less secure legal basis than appears at first sight and there are certain objections to it based on considerations of principle (the principles of self-determination and non-interference in internal affairs) and of policy (the danger of making an internal conflict international).

Most contemporary civil war situations—to witness Cyprus, the Congo, Yemen or Viet-Nam—have too many international implications not to lead to some intervention on the one or the other side. Indeed, the history of recent civil war conflicts with international implications shows that intervention by a foreign state on behalf of one side has invariably produced counter-intervention by some other state in favor of the other side.[15] In these moves and counter-moves, legal considerations have played a minimal part. The state that happens to favor the incumbent government will evoke, in support of its action, the theory that support for the government in power is justified by international law, whereas support for the rebels is not. But if its political interests lie the other way, it will forget

[12] A Treatise on International Law 347 (8th ed., 1924).

[13] See in particular his article, "United States Intervention in the Lebanon," 53 A.J.I.L. 112, 121 et seq. (1959).

[14] Brownlie, International Law and the Use of Force by States 327 (1963).

[15] R. A. Falk (in International Aspects of Civil Strife 185, 207 ff. (Rosenau ed., 1964)) sees the main causes of such intervention in the revolutionary ideology of China and the Soviet bloc and the anti-colonial commitments of the Afro-Asian nations. He deduces from this a counter-balancing right of counter-intervention (rule of mutuality). Kaplan (ibid. 92 ff.) sees civil war intervention, more impartially, as a result of the "loose bipolar period" (choosing as examples Soviet intervention in Hungary and U. S. intervention in Lebanon).

about this doctrine. In the balance of international politics, the distinction between support for government as distinct from rebel movements, has become almost meaningless. The alternatives are either isolation of the conflict by neutrality, or intervention and counter-intervention with all the dangers illustrated by the gradual escalation of the Viet-Nam war. This points to the alternative of organized action by the international community. While the legal power of the United Nations to intervene in situations which threaten international peace and security is not circumscribed (Article 24), the exercise of this power must be a matter of careful balance of considerations, a policy decision, not one of automatic application of legal principles. Generally, such policy considerations should counsel caution with regard to intervention in internal social or political conflict, whether the assistance of the United Nations is invoked by the incumbent government or not. United Nations intervention has proved conspicuously more successful when it has served as a buffer force betweeen hostile nations, than when it has sought to intervene in a social conflict. UNEF has for eight years succeeded in keeping Israel and Egypt from getting at each other's throat in the Gaza Strip. But even if financial resources had permitted the U.N. Forces to stay longer in the Congo, it is highly doubtful whether it could have solved—as distinct from delayed—the deep-seated social, political and racial tensions within that unhappy country. Again, in the Cyprus conflict, where the tensions between the Greek and Turkish elements of the population are part of an international conflict which deeply involves Greece and Turkey, the United Nations serves the vital function of providing a cooling-down period for possible settlement, and of giving some justification to the antagonistic states (Greece and Turkey) for postponing, if not renouncing, military intervention.

In sum, international law has never been equipped to intervene in civil war situations. While today the United Nations does have some reserve function in this area where international peace is concerned, this is more than countered by the increased turbulence of a multitude of unsettled international conditions in an increasing number of countries. The powers granted to the United Nations, especially by Article 24 of the Charter, should, therefore, be used only in exceptional circumstances, generally in situations which imply *national* rather than *social* conflict and where the intervention of the United Nations can help in the cooling down of the national conflicts involved. Any intervention of the United Nations in essentially ideological and political conflicts is likely to split it beyond repair and to destroy the already fragile political and financial support on which it depends.

Conclusions

In this perturbing and dangerous situation, the international lawyer does a better service to the cause of international law by acknowledging that, in the absence of a functioning international peacekeeping and order machinery, it is policy, not law, that determines the actions of states with regard to intervention in civil wars and with respect to ''indirect aggression." This is, in fact, the position taken by Mr. Dean Acheson in his analysis of the Cuban crisis of 1962. While this position is deeply unsatisfactory if it is meant to be a final appraisal of the minimum requirements of an international order of peace, it is a realistic assessment of the motivations of states in the actual conduct of international affairs. Until there is an effective international organization, the only slender hope for peace lies in the balance of force, intervention and restraint used by the major antagonists in the interest of survival. The alternative attempt, which leads international lawyers to vindicate the actions of their own governments, whatever they are,[16] can only lead down the slippery path of intellectual subservience. The self-immolation of an independent intellectual and professional class, characterized more than a generation ago by the French writer, Julien Benda, as *"la trahison des clercs,"* has been one of the principal grounds for the moral rot of totalitarian regimes of the right and of the left. The lawyer becomes the manipulator. Not the least of the values for which the United States and its allies have stood through two World Wars has been the right of independent criticism. The maintenance of this intellectual integrity is no less important a weapon in the fight against totalitarianism than armies and bombs.

[16] *Cf.* R. A. Falk, "Contemporary Theories of International Law," 50 Virginia Law Review 234, with reference to the position taken by most American commentators on the Cuban quarantine: "The authors instead appear to mobilize legal arguments in support of a national position in a period of crisis. This is an appropriate perspective for an American official or perhaps a citizen, but it is inappropriate for international lawyers concerned with appraising legality from a global perspective in such a way that the nation of a scholar's origin is a factor of diminishing importance. The one-sided nature of the various analyses was particularly striking for authors who used the rhetoric of a world community perspective but limited themselves to the arguments favorable to the United States' (regional) interpretation of law."

II. LEGAL PERSPECTIVES

An Approach to
Issues of International Law Raised
by United States Actions in Vietnam

ELIOT D. HAWKINS

Introduction

THE legality of the United States military involvement in Vietnam has been the subject of sharp and continuing debate directed toward the ultimate question of whether or not this country's presence is lawful. Marked attention and substantial efforts have rightfully been directed to this inquiry, but at the same time many of the legal conclusions expressed in the debate depend on vigorously disputed versions of the facts. This paper does not attempt to weigh conflicting factual claims and accordingly does not reach the ultimate question of legality.

Nevertheless it seems important to clarify if possible the points which are in dispute. Issues raised generally by the United States involvement should be examined to determine which are presently capable of resolution and which cannot be resolved without choosing between conflicting versions of the facts or competing legal theories. Some legal arguments advanced in the debate appear not to be supportable and deserve comment. In addition, little has been said about the impact of United States actions on the future state of international law. The debate, it is submitted, should focus more sharply on the effect of American military measures as precedents in other conflicts involving different political and foreign policy considerations. This paper will attempt to develop these suggestions as a framework for further inquiry.

Issues

The states or entities involved in the Vietnam conflict have decided unilaterally what the facts are and how they should be legally characterized. The United States Government and those who consider the American involvement lawful assert that South Vietnam has been attacked and that this country and others are acting with it in collective self-defense under Article 51 of the United Nations Charter.[1] Some

[1] The Government's chief legal memorandum is Dept. of State (Legal Adviser), *The Legality of United States Participation in the Defense of Viet-Nam* (March 4, 1966), reprinted at 112 *Cong. Rec.* 5274 (daily ed. March 10, 1966) and at 60 *Am. J. Int'l. L.* 565 (1966) [hereinafter cited as Legal Adviser's *Memorandum*]. An earlier and much shorter memorandum, *Legal Basis for United States Actions Against North Viet-Nam* (March

opponents claim that United States forces instead have intervened in a civil war and have committed aggression against North Vietnam, in violation of the Charter and the 1954 Geneva Accords.[2] Among the legal issues raised are the scope of rights of collective self-defense under the Charter, the bearing of the SEATO Treaty, the status of the two Vietnams and of the 1954 Accords, the existence of an armed attack on South Vietnam, the significance of the 1962 Geneva Accords, and the application of the principle that military measures taken in self-defense should be proportional or reasonably necessary in view of the threat presented.

Issues Which Can Be Resolved

Some questions of international law developed in the debate appear to be answerable. These concern (1) the application of Articles 51 and 53 of the United Nations Charter; (2) the bearing of the SEATO Treaty on the American involvement; and (3) the present international status of North and South Vietnam. The use of force by the United States is entirely consistent with Articles 51 and 53 if it is accepted that an armed attack has been made on South Vietnam. Yet even if there has been such an attack the SEATO Treaty, while not requiring agreement by all parties before one of them may respond with force, does not commit the United States as a matter of legal obligation to take military measures in the absence of a collective decision specifying such action. Apart from the Treaty, however, measures of collective self-defense taken in response to an armed attack are legitimate under Article 51. Finally, whatever the status of North and South Vietnam

---

8, 1965) is reprinted at Staff of Senate Comm. on Foreign Relations, 89th Cong., 2d Sess., *Background Information Relating to Southeast Asia and Vietnam* 199 (Comm. Print 2d rev. ed. 1966) [hereinafter cited as *Background Information*]. See in support of the legality of United States actions Professors Bishop, Baxter, McDougal, Sohn, and Alford, Letter to President Johnson dated Feb. 14, 1966, in 112 *Cong. Rec.* 3694 (daily ed. Feb. 23, 1966); Moore, Underwood, and McDougal, *The Lawfulness of United States Assistance to the Republic of Viet Nam* (unpublished monograph, May 1966); Moore, *The Lawfulness of Military Assistance to the Republic of Viet-Nam*, 61 *Am. J. Int'l. L.* 1 (1967).

2 See, e.g., Lawyers Committee on American Policy Toward Vietnam, *American Policy Vis-a-Vis Vietnam, Memorandum of Law*, in 112 *Cong. Rec.* 2552 (daily ed. Feb. 9, 1966); Standard, *United States Intervention in Vietnam is Not Legal*, 52 *A.B.A.J.* 627 (July 1966); Commager, "Our Vietnamese Commitment," *Diplomat* (June 1966), in 112 *Cong. Rec.* 11174 (daily ed. May 27, 1966); 112 *Cong. Rec.* 1975 (daily ed. Feb. 3, 1966, remarks of Senator Morse). For a summary of the two sides' views by an authority critical of the U.S. involvement see Wright, "Legal Aspects of the Viet-Nam Situation," 60 *Am. J. Int'l. L.* 750-53 (1966).

prior to or as a result of the signing of the Geneva Accords in 1954, it would seem that owing to the events which have occurred since then both Vietnams are now *de facto* states.

1. ARTICLES 51 AND 53 OF THE CHARTER

Certain critics of the use of force in Vietnam by the United States have argued that in order to act in collective self-defense under Article 51 states must be members of regional systems and that such use of force is illegal unless previously authorized by the Security Council as provided in Article 53.[3] In addition, Article 51 is said not to permit the United States actions in any event because it refers to an attack occurring against a member of the United Nations, and South Vietnam is not a member.[4] This analysis is incorrect.

Article 51 deals with self-defense, individual and collective, and recognizes an exception to the general prohibition in Article 2 (4) of the Charter against the use of force by member states individually. The text of Article 51 is as follows:

> Nothing in the present Charter shall impair the inherent right of individual or collective self-defense if an armed attack occurs against a Member of the United Nations, until the Security Council has taken the measures necessary to maintain international peace and security. Measures taken by Members in the exercise of this right of self-defense shall be immediately reported to the Security Council and shall not in any way affect the authority and responsibility of the Security Council under the present Charter to take at any time such action as it deems necessary in order to maintain or restore international peace and security.[5]

Article 53 deals with enforcement measures by members under regional arrangements of the character referred to in Article 52. Authorization from the Security Council is required for any such action. The Article provides:

> 1. The Security Council shall, where appropriate, utilize such regional arrangements or agencies for enforcement action under its authority. But no enforcement action shall be taken under regional arrangements or by regional agencies without the authorization of the

[3] Lawyers Committee *Memorandum, supra,* at 2554, 2557; Standard, *supra,* at 633; Commager, *supra,* at 11175; remarks of Senator Morse, *supra,* at 1975.

[4] Lawyers Committee *Memorandum, supra,* at 2553-54; Standard, *supra,* at 628.

[5] 59 Stat. 1031, 1044-45 (1945), T.I.A.S. No. 993.

Security Council, with the exception of measures against any enemy state, as defined in paragraph 2 of this Article, provided for pursuant to Article 107 or in regional arrangements directed against renewal of aggressive policy on the part of any such state, until such time as the Organization may, on request of the Governments concerned, be charged with the responsibility for preventing further aggression by such a state.

2. The term enemy state as used in paragraph 1 of this Article applies to any state which during the Second World War has been an enemy of any signatory of the present Charter.[6]

The first error in the critics' analysis summarized above is the contention that action under Article 51 necessarily brings Article 53 into play. Instead under the Charter collective self-defense is a separate matter from regional enforcement action. Article 51 deals with forcible responses which in certain circumstances are permitted to states *until* the Security Council takes action. The rationale is self-preservation. This right would be compromised and the Article rendered meaningless if it were read with Article 53 to require that the Council approve in advance measures intended to be effective only in the absence of Council action. Rather than lending itself to this interpretation Article 51 states that "Nothing in the present Charter"—which would include Article 53—"shall impair the inherent right of . . . self-defense." And there would be no reason for the separate and urgent reporting requirement in Article 51 if the Council had already approved the measures in question and would receive reports under Article 54.[7]

Moreover, Articles 51 and 53 are in different chapters of the Charter. The significance of this fact is pointed up by the legislative history of Article 51, which in draft form appeared with the present Article 53 in Chapter VIII, entitled "Regional Arrangements."[8] In the final version of the Charter, however, Article 51 appears in Chapter VII, entitled "Action With Respect to Threats to the Peace, Breaches of the Peace, and Acts of Aggression." It follows that limitations put on regional enforcement action do not apply to measures of collective self-defense

[6] 59 Stat. 1045.

[7] Article 54 appears in Chapter VIII of the Charter and provides: "The Security Council shall at all times be kept fully informed of activities undertaken or in contemplation under regional arrangements or by regional agencies for the maintenance of international peace and security." 59 Stat. 1031, 1045 (1945).

[8] Lawyers Committee *Memorandum, supra,* at 2554-55 n. 13; 5 Whiteman, *Digest of International Law* 1061 (Dept. State Pub. 7873 [1965], quoting from Professor Waldock in 81 *Recueil Des Cours* [1952, II] 451, 503-05).

even though the states taking such measures happen to belong to a regional arrangement.[9]

The second error in the critics' analysis concerns the alleged restrictive quality of certain language in Article 51. The reference in that Article to attacks on member states should not be interpreted as a ban on participation by members in the collective self-defense of non-members. The Article itself does not affirmatively assert a rule but rather recognizes that certain established rights regarding the use of force continue to exist pending action by the Security Council. Clearly Article 51 could not deprive states outside the United Nations of their rights under preexisting international law, and the right of self-defense could have little practical value in the decentralized international system if one of the relatively few non-member states could not ask members for assistance. There is no suggestion in the Article either that members may call only on other members for collective self-defense. Indeed the assertion that Article 51 has in any sense a "limiting" nature is open to considerable question. Even the language "if an armed attack *occurs*" has been said not to be restrictive. The French text refers to self-defense when a member is "l'objet d'une agression armée," possibly a broader test,[10] and a number of authorities hold that Article 51 does not rule out responses to threats of attack in exercise of the right of preventive self-defense.[11]

In any event it appears to be generally accepted by governments that under Article 51 members of the United Nations may join in the collective self-defense of non-members. This has certainly been the understanding of the United States since the NATO defense structure was formed.[12] At that time Italy and Portugal were not members, and West Germany is in the same category today. Again in the Korean War the first American military actions were taken before the Security Council

[9] Moore, *supra* note 1, at 16-17 (and see authorities cited in nn. 37, 39); Professors Bishop et al., Letter, *supra* note 1; Brierly, *The Law of Nations* 395-96 (6th ed. Waldock 1963).

[10] 5 Whiteman, *supra*, at 987 (quoting from Thomas and Thomas, *Non-Intervention* 123-24 [1956]); Brierly, *supra*, at 418-20. See also the references in these works to other non-English versions of the text of Article 51.

[11] See the quotations from writings both for and against this broad interpretation of the right of self-defense collected in 5 Whiteman, *supra*, at 981-91. See also in support of a possible broad interpretation, with the conclusion that the scope of the right is at least uncertain, Brierly, *supra*, at 419-20. *Contra*, Henkin, *Force, Intervention, and Neutrality in Contemporary International Law*, 1963 Proc. Am. Soc'y. Int'l. L. 147.

[12] This view is expressed in a memorandum by the Legal Adviser of the Department of State dated April 13, 1949. 5 Whiteman, *supra*, at 1079-81.

had called for forcible resistance to the North Korean attack.[13] The British Government also considered that Article 51 would not have prevented participation in the defense of South Korea, a non-member, in the absence of action by the Council.[14] Other mutual security arrangements concluded by members of both major blocs (see, e.g., the Warsaw Treaty of 1955)[15] operate on the same principle.

In short the alleged restrictive interpretation of Article 51 is not supported by the practice and expectations of states. As one commentator has put it (in Moore, *supra* note 1, at 16), this interpretation would mean

> . . . that today, East Germany, West Germany, North Korea, South Korea, Switzerland and the People's Republic of China as well as the R.V.N. and the D.R.V. [South and North Vietnam] could not be collectively assisted by Members of the United Nations if subjected to attack.

In addition, many authorities agree that under Article 51 member states may lawfully assist non-members.[16] The fact that South Vietnam does not belong to the United Nations is thus by itself no bar to the United States military measures.

2. THE BEARING OF THE SEATO TREATY

Opponents of American actions in Vietnam have asserted that we are acting illegally under the Treaty because it requires agreement by all eight parties before military measures can be taken,[17] and that even were there such unanimity Article 53 of the Charter would prohibit resort to force unless this step had been authorized by the Security Council.[18] In contrast the United States Government contends at least that unanimous agreement is not required and that we are authorized

---

[13] This was the basis of a Soviet complaint. Spanier, *The Truman-MacArthur Controversy and the Korean War* 37 (Cambridge 1959) .

[14] Speech by Prime Minister Attlee in the House of Commons on July 5, 1950, in Spanier, *supra*, at 38.

[15] 5 Whiteman, *supra*, at 1102.

[16] Moore, *supra* note 1, at 13-16; Wright, *supra* note 2, at 751; Moore, Underwood, and McDougal, *supra* note 1, at 57-59; Professors Bishop et al., Letter, *supra* note 1; 5 Whiteman, *supra* note 8, at 1060-81; Brierly, *supra* note 9, at 394 n. 1, 419.

[17] Lawyers Committee *Memorandum, supra* note 2, at 2556-57; 112 *Cong. Rec.* 1974 (daily ed. Feb. 3, 1966, remarks of Senator Morse) ; Standard, *supra* note 2, at 632. This may be the French interpretation of the Treaty, which has been described as stressing a "rule of unanimity" (*N.Y. Times*, March 26, 1967, at 5) . The statement could also reflect a view, however, that the only Treaty provision applicable to the situation in Vietnam is Article IV (2) , which requires consultation.

[18] See note 3.

under Article IV (1) of the Treaty to respond with force if there is a Communist attack in the stated area.[19] Some statements by Government officials have also been interpreted as a claim that the Treaty legally commits us so to respond.[20] Neither the critics' view stated above nor such a claim of legal obligation appears to be warranted, however, by the instrument or by international law.

The Southeast Asia Collective Defense Treaty and a Protocol to it were signed on September 8, 1954 and entered into force on February 19, 1955. By the Protocol the parties extended the military and economic measures of Articles IV and III, respectively, to Cambodia, Laos and "the free territory under the jurisdiction of the State of Vietnam."[21] The military protection thus extended to South Vietnam is found in the provisions of Article IV:

1. Each Party recognizes that aggression by means of armed attack in the treaty area against any of the Parties or against any State or

[19] The Government clearly argues that United States military measures in Vietnam do not violate the Treaty. Legal Adviser's *Memorandum*, 60 *Am. J. Int'l. L.* 573-75.

[20] A key word in some official statements of our position has been "commitment," rather than "authorization." See, for example, the Legal Adviser's *Memorandum* in which the heading of a sub-point discussing the effect of the Treaty under a general heading mentioning American "commitments" states: "The United States Undertook an International Obligation to Defend South Viet-Nam in the SEATO Treaty" (60 *Am. J. Int'l. L.* 573). Later in this sub-point it is also said that "the United States has a commitment under article IV, paragraph 1, in the event of armed attack" (*id.*, at 574). The question whether the Treaty obligation to defend South Vietnam requires the use of force if other forms of assistance prove unsuccessful is not specifically discussed, however, in the *Memorandum*, although in Point IV (B) the position appears to be that the President is authorized but not obliged to take such a step.

The word "commitment" has also been used often in the context of American forces being in Vietnam. And statements that the United States is "committed" to what it is doing there have been made at times long after the bombing of North Vietnam and the full-scale use of ground troops started in 1965. See, e.g., President Johnson, "Remarks Upon Receiving the National Freedom Award in N.Y.C.," Feb. 23, 1966, in *Background Information*, 285, 287; Secretary Rusk in *The Vietnam Hearings*, 11-12, 50-51, 233-34, 253-55, 259-64 (Vintage ed. 1966). Secretary Rusk's statements at the Senate hearings in 1966 were made in the context of questions as to whether the United States was entitled or obliged under the Treaty to do what it was doing in Vietnam, and in the context also of some statements describing the Government's position as being that we were legally bound so to act. Commentators who have interpreted the Government's position as being one of legal commitment to use force under the Treaty and who have criticized any such claim include Krock, "The Sudden Rediscovery of SEATO," *N.Y. Times*, March 6, 1966, at E 11, and Goodwin, *Reflections on Vietnam*, at 112 *Cong. Rec.* 8902 (daily ed. April 28, 1966).

[21] The SEATO Treaty ([1955] 1 U.S.T. 81; T.I.A.S. No. 3170) is reprinted in *Background Information* 70. The signatories were Australia, France, New Zealand, Pakistan, the Philippines, Thailand, Britain, and the United States. Cambodia and Laos withdrew from the coverage of the Protocol in 1956 and 1962, respectively (*id.*, at 4, 100-101).

territory which the Parties by unanimous agreement may hereafter designate, would endanger its own peace and safety, and agrees that it will in that event act to meet the common danger in accordance with its constitutional processes. Measures taken under this paragraph shall be immediately reported to the Security Council of the United Nations.

2. If, in the opinion of any of the Parties, the inviolability or the integrity of the territory or the sovereignty or political independence of any Party in the treaty area or of any other State or territory to which the provisions of paragraph 1 of this Article from time to time apply is threatened in any way other than by armed attack or is affected or threatened by any fact or situation which might endanger the peace of the area, the Parties shall consult immediately in order to agree on the measures which should be taken for the common defense.

3. It is understood that no action on the territory of any State designated by unanimous agreement under paragraph 1 of this Article or on any territory so designated shall be taken except at the invitation or with the consent of the government concerned.[22]

This language is inconsistent with the claimed prerequisite of unanimity. In a case of "aggression by means of armed attack," which the United States asserts has occurred, Article IV (1) specifies that *each* signatory will "act to meet the common danger." The obligation is several as well as joint.[23] It clearly differs from the duty to consult provided in Article IV (2) for situations not involving an attack. Paragraph (1) does mention "unanimous agreement" but in the context only of designating territories rather than determining whether measures are to be taken under the paragraph. Again in its "Understanding" appended to the Treaty the United States indicated that in the event of "communist aggression" it accepted under Article IV (1) an obligation to do more than consult with the other parties.

To contend that the use of force in collective self-defense under Para-

---

[22] *Background Information* 71. In an "Understanding" (*id.*, at 73) appended to the Treaty the United States declared that it interpreted Article IV (1) to apply only to Communist aggression and armed attack.

[23] A former U.S. Ambassador to Thailand has viewed Article IV as permitting individual or collective action and has stated that it is understood all parties must agree to collective action. He indicates, however, that the U.S. saw SEATO as a collective organization until the Laotian crisis of 1961, and that thereafter the U.S. and Thailand agreed that individual action could be taken without a unanimous decision. Young, *The Southeast Asia Crisis*, 1965 Hammarskjöld Forum 48, 57-59.

graph (1) would be subject to Article 53 of the Charter is equally incorrect.[24] Members of regional systems may take such measures under Article 51 without following the procedure of Article 53.

... [I]t is clear that the parties to a regional arrangement are entitled to combine together in measures of collective self-defence without the prior authorization of the Council, although the Soviet Union contended the contrary with reference to the North Atlantic Treaty Organization; the right of collective self-defence is governed by Article 51 and is entirely independent of the provisions regarding regional arrangements.[25]

The assertion that United States actions violate the SEATO agreement therefore requires a conclusion that an attack has not occurred or that on some separate ground the actions violate principles of international law reiterated in the Treaty.

It by no means follows, however, that the American military involvement is a mandatory response under Article IV (1). While the Treaty represents a deliberate statement of this country's purpose to resist Communist armed attacks, the means are not specified. The question whether our policy requires the use of armed force is separate from the question of duties established by the Treaty. In the absence of a collective decision by the parties as to the measures required, assistance in some form other than armed force would satisfy the duty to "act" stated in Article IV (1).[26]

Indeed if this were not so the United States would be unable lawfully to withhold the commitment of its forces upon the occurrence of any Communist attack in the Treaty and Protocol area. And if the view of mandatory response were accepted, it has been pointed out that a conflict between two SEATO members or covered states could present the other parties (although perhaps not the United States owing to its "Understanding" about Communist aggression) with the

[24] See note 9.

[25] Brierly, *supra* note 9, at 395-96.

[26] This is the British view (*N.Y. Times*, April 20, 1967 at 6). The Secretary General of SEATO, Lt. Gen. Jesus Vargas, stated a similar view at a SEATO Council meeting in Australia on June 27, 1966:

In relation to SEATO in particular, Viet-Nam is incontrovertible proof of the wide latitude of freedom open to individual members of the alliance to choose the manner and degree of assistance to be rendered, or even for any one member to withhold assistance or keep the matter under consideration for as long as it pleases.

As we all know, assistance under the Manila Pact may be collective or individual (quoted in 113 *Cong. Rec.* S 2657 [daily ed. Feb. 27, 1967]).

impossible duty of militarily assisting each state claiming to have been attacked.[27]

A comparison of Article IV (1) with Article 5[28] of the NATO Treaty shows significant differences. The latter provision states that an attack on one party is an attack on all, mentions the possible use of armed force, and looks to restoring or maintaining the security of the treaty area. Comparable provisions do not appear in Article IV (1) of the SEATO Treaty. There is in addition legislative history that the design was "to distinguish SEATO from the alleged NATO principle of automatic military response to an armed attack."[29]

Nor can it be said that the SEATO Treaty has been generally interpreted as requiring such an automatic response. The Governments of France, Britain, and Pakistan do not share this view. And in some instances United States officials have expressed the opinion that the Treaty does not legally oblige us to take the military measures which have been taken in Vietnam. For example, in a colloquy with Senator Fulbright during hearings in 1966 Secretary Rusk stated that our obligation was

> . . . an obligation of policy. It is rooted in the policy of the Treaty. I am not now saying if we had decided we would not lift a finger about Southeast Asia that we could be sued in a court and be convicted of breaking a treaty. This is not the point I want to talk about.[30]

A Congressional research committee has also interpreted the Treaty as not mandating the use of force.[31] Accordingly, for the reasons discussed

---

27 Falk, "International Law and the United States Role in the Viet Nam War," 75 *Yale L. J.* 1122, 1151 (1966).

28 63 Stat. 2241, 2244 (1949), T.I.A.S. No. 1964. Article 5 provides:

> The Parties agree that an armed attack against one or more of them in Europe or North America shall be considered an attack against them all; and consequently they agree that, if such an armed attack occurs, each of them, in exercise of the right of individual or collective self-defense recognized by Article 51 of the Charter of the United Nations, will assist the Party or Parties so attacked by taking forthwith, individually and in concert with the other Parties, such action as it deems necessary, including the use of armed force, to restore and maintain the security of the North Atlantic area.
>
> Any such armed attack and all measures taken as a result thereof shall immediately be reported to the Security Council. Such measures shall be terminated when the Security Council has taken the measures necessary to restore and maintain international peace and security.

29 Moore, Underwood, and McDougal, *supra* note 1, at 98 and nn. 311, 312; Standard, *supra* note 2, at 632.

30 *The Vietnam Hearings, supra* note 20, at 35-36.

31 In a 1966 report the Committee on Planning and Research of the House Republican Conference stated that the decision to use American troops in combat ". . . was not forced

above the parties to the SEATO Treaty cannot be considered legally obliged to respond with force in the event of an armed attack in the Treaty area.

3. THE INTERNATIONAL STATUS OF NORTH AND SOUTH VIETNAM

One of the paramount issues in the debate is whether or not the war in Vietnam is a struggle between two separate states. On this point the United States Government and those who believe the American involvement to be lawful contend that South Vietnam is such a state,[32] that it has asked our assistance, and that under Article 51 of the Charter we are helping it to defend against an attack from another country. In opposition it is said that North and South are merely zones and that we have intervened in a civil war, in violation of international law.[33] While there are some international aspects resulting from alleged violations of borders with Laos and Cambodia,[34] critics of United States actions see the war as occurring substantially within the jurisdiction of a single state of Vietnam or within the southern zone (except for the bombing of the North) of that state. The critics argue that North and South Vietnam cannot have separate international standing because that would contradict the Geneva Accords of July 1954.

---

upon [the President] by the SEATO Treaty or by any other obligation entered into by an earlier administration." Conference Comm. *supra, The United States and the War in Vietnam,* in 112 *Cong. Rec.* at 22377 (daily ed. Sept. 20, 1966).

[32] Legal Adviser's *Memorandum,* 60 *Am. J. Int'l. L.* at 565; Moore, Underwood, and Mc-Dougal, *supra* note 1, at 5-7, 23-29; Moore, *supra* note 1, at 3; Professors Bishop et al., Letter *supra* note 1, at 3694-95. United States officials have often referred to the Republic of Vietnam as a "country" or "nation" and have spoken of its "political independence." See, e.g., the statement by President Eisenhower in a joint announcement with President Diem in May 1957 (*Background Information* 82), the statement by Vice-President Johnson in a joint communiqué with President Diem in May 1961 (*id.,* at 86), statements by Secretary Rusk in news conferences in 1961-1965 (*id.,* at 90, 96, 113, 116, 141, 162-64, 168, 171), statements by President Kennedy in a letter to President Diem dated December 14, 1961 (*id.,* at 92), statements by Secretary McNamara in 1964 and 1965 (*id.,* at 119-21, 223), statements by President Johnson in 1964-1966 (*id.,* at 131, 155, 203, 206, 226, 227, 263), and a statement by Ambassador Goldberg in a letter to the President of the Security Council dated July 30, 1965 (*id.,* at 245). *But see* Partan, "Legal Aspects of the Vietnam Conflict," 46 *B.U.L. Rev.* 281, 297 n. 54 (1966) and *Background Information* 83 for some contradictory United States statements referring to Vietnam as a divided country.

[33] Lawyers Committee *Memorandum, supra* note 2, at 2555-56; Standard, *supra* note 2, at 630; Wright, *supra* note 2, at 756-59.

[34] Alleged violations of the Laotian border are discussed below. Alleged activity in Cambodia in support of the Vietcong is reported in a letter from a soldier and in news articles in 113 *Cong. Rec.* H 4875-76 (daily ed. May 1, 1967), and 112 *Cong. Rec.* 10355-57 (daily ed. May 17, 1966). On May 26, 1964 in the Security Council Ambassador Stevenson discussed instances of claimed Vietcong activity in Cambodia during the period from 1961 to 1964 (50 Dept. State Bull. 939-40 [1964]).

These Accords are made up of Agreements on the Cessation of Hostilities in each of Vietnam, Cambodia and Laos, and an unsigned Final Declaration.[35] While there are references to the "Democratic Republic of Viet-Nam" and a reference to another entity termed the "State of Viet-Nam"[36] in the Accords, the instruments generally speak of "regrouping" (or "Northern" and "Southern") "zones" and refer to "Viet-Nam" in the singular. The military demarcation line between the zones, in the words of Paragraph 6 of the Final Declaration, is "provisional and should not in any way be interpreted as constituting a political or territorial boundary."

The military Agreement for Vietnam refers in Article 14 to pending elections "which will bring about the unification of Viet-Nam," and Paragraph 7 of the Declaration directs that elections be held in July 1956. In Paragraphs 11 and 12 the Declaration again emphasizes the "unity and territorial integrity" of "Viet-Nam." Other significant features of the Agreement for Vietnam include the undertakings in Article 14 to refrain from reprisals, to guarantee "democratic liberties," and to permit civilians to change zones, the provisions in Articles 16 and 17 prohibiting the introduction into Vietnam of additional military personnel or equipment except for certain replacements of men and material, the provisions in Articles 18 and 19 banning new military bases, bases controlled by foreign states, adherence by either zone to a military alliance and the use of either zone "for the resumption of hostilities or to further an aggressive policy," and the provisions in Chapter VI creating a Joint Commission and International Commission for Supervision and Control. The Final Declaration notes and reiterates the chief obligations specified in the three Agreements.

If the Accords are considered by themselves, North and South Vietnam would not be separate countries but merely temporarily divided parts of a single state. It has been argued, however, that the State of

[35] The instruments are reprinted in *Background Information* 36-68. Neither the United States nor the "State of Viet-Nam" joined in the Declaration. The United States declared separately that in accordance with Article 2 (4) of the Charter it would not threaten or use force to disturb the Accords and that it would view with concern "any renewal of the aggression in violation of the . . . agreements" (*id.*, at 69). The State of Viet-Nam accepted the cease-fire but protested the other provisions of the settlement. Moore, Underwood, and McDougal, *supra* note 1, at 12, 81-85. See also President Diem's letter of December 7, 1961 to President Kennedy (*Background Information* 93).

[36] The D.R.V. is mentioned in Art. 14 (b) of the Agreement for Vietnam as the party to take over the civil administration of Hanoi and Haiphong (*Background Information* 40). Each of the Agreements was signed by the D.R.V.'s Vice-Minister of National Defense (*id.*, at 48, 57; Moore, Underwood, and McDougal, *supra*, n. 44). Both the D.R.V. and the State of Viet-Nam appear in the Final Declaration's list of countries participating in the Geneva Conference (*Background Information* 66).

Viet-Nam (as predecessor to the present Republic of Vietnam) became a fully independent state before execution of the Accords by reason of treaties concluded with France in June 1954,[37] and that even prior to this date the State of Viet-Nam had received considerable international recognition (including that of the General Assembly in 1952), as had the Democratic Republic of Viet-Nam.[38] It is argued further that both these states participated as such in the Geneva Conference, that the French representatives clearly stated they could not commit the State of Viet-Nam, and that no participant intended the language about "zones" to "undercut the existing credentials of statehood" belonging to the government which it favored.[39]

> The participants at the Conference each wanted to avoid recognizing the government championed by the other side as a lawful government of any part of Viet Nam and each wanted to preserve the claims to sovereignty over all of Viet Nam of the government that they recognized. . . .[40]

On the other hand it is argued that the Geneva settlement was reached by France acting as well for South Vietnam, which was not fully independent. South Vietnam would therefore be bound by the Accords as successor to France.[41]

Whatever the status of South and North Vietnam in 1954, events since then have been said to generate "substantial expectations within the international community that [they] are separate and independent states under international law."[42] South Vietnam has been recognized by about 25 nations in addition to those states (approximately 35) which recognized the State of Viet-Nam prior to the 1954 Accords. Since then South Vietnam has also joined a number of additional international organizations and specialized agencies of the United Nations. North Vietnam has been recognized by about 24 countries, an

[37] Moore, Underwood, and McDougal, *supra*, at 10; Young, *supra* note 23, at 118; Crozier, *South-East Asia in Turmoil* 93 (Penguin Books 1965). On the other hand, these treaties are said not to have come into effect by Partan, *supra* note 32, at 289, citing 1 Whiteman, *supra* note 8, at 289 (1963).

[38] Moore, Underwood, and McDougal, *supra*, at 8-11.

[39] That this was the intent of the British Government, for example, is said to be shown by a 1956 Command Paper in which the Government reaffirmed its policy to be that of " '. . . recognising, in accordance with [its] obligations under Article 12 of the Final Declaration of the Geneva Conference, the Government of the Republic of Vietnam as the only legal Government of Vietnam' " (*id.*, at 16 and n. 63).

[40] Moore, Underwood, and McDougal, *supra* note 1, at 13 (and see generally at 11-17).

[41] Partan, *supra* note 32, at 291-92; Lawyers Committee *Memorandum*, supra note 2, at 2555-56; Wright, *supra* note 2, at 762.

[42] Moore, Underwood, and McDougal, *supra*, at 29.

increase of perhaps 15 over the comparable figure in 1954.[43] Laos appears to have relations with both North and South Vietnam, and several authorities have concluded that they are *de facto* separate countries.[44]

In 1957 during debates in the General Assembly over resolutions for the admission of "Viet-Nam" or for the admission of both Vietnams and both Koreas, and during debates in the Security Council on resolutions for the admission of "Viet-Nam," a number of delegates expressed the view that South Vietnam was an independent country. Different Soviet delegates also stated on several occasions in the Assembly that there were two independent countries in each of Vietnam and Korea.[45] In addition delegations from both South and North Vietnam participated as separate "Governments" in the 1961-1962 Geneva Conference and in the Accords establishing the neutrality of Laos.[46]

The leaders of both Vietnams have also described the entities controlled by them as sovereign states. Governments in South Vietnam have maintained that it was an independent state prior to the 1954 Accords and that it has remained so.[47] President Ho Chi Minh in his letter of February 15, 1967 to President Johnson,[48] and a party and government delegation of North Vietnam in a joint statement made on April 17, 1965 with a corresponding Soviet delegation,[49] declared variously that North Vietnam was "independent and sovereign" and "one Socialist country."[50]

[43] Details of these actions are given in Moore, Underwood, and McDougal, *supra*, at 8, 10, 11, 28, 29 and nn. 23, 24, 32, 36, 39, 40, 105-07, 114, 116.

[44] *Id.*, at 29 and nn. 116, 119; Moore, *supra* note 1, at 4 and n. 8; Crozier, *supra* note 37, at 134-35. See also Brierly, *supra* note 9, at 155, where the opinion is expressed that the "constitutional changes" in Vietnam produced states which were "new legal persons" needing specific votes of admission for membership in the United Nations.

[45] Moore, Underwood, and McDougal, *supra*, at 24-27. The Assembly Resolution recalled its 1952 resolution "finding Viet-Nam qualified for membership," noted that "Viet-Nam" was excluded owing to the opposition of one permanent Council member, and reaffirmed its determination that "Viet-Nam" was "fully qualified." During 1957 and 1958 the U.S.S.R. vetoed action on two Assembly resolutions calling for the admission of "Viet-Nam," and the United States opposed the Soviet "package deal" resolution (Wright, *supra* note 2, at 758 n. 19). Both North and South Vietnam apparently have applications for membership on file. Moore, Underwood, and McDougal, *supra*, at 27 n. 104.

[46] The Accords consist of a Declaration and a Protocol. Paragraph 5 of the Declaration provides that it and the Laotian Government's statement of neutrality "shall be regarded as constituting an international agreement." *Background Information* 101.

[47] Moore, Underwood, and McDougal, *supra*, at 85.

[48] The letter is reprinted at 113 *Cong. Rec.* S 4215 (daily ed. March 22, 1967).

[49] Raskin and Fall, *The Vietnam Reader*, at 365-66 (Vintage ed. 1965).

[50] See also Secretary General U Thant's stated understanding, expressed in an explanation of the North Vietnamese attitude toward American bombing and a possible reciprocal

In some instances, however, each government has inconsistently asserted both its own area's sovereignty and the continuing indivisibility of Vietnam. Thus Premier Pham Van Dong on April 13, 1965 stated that the United States must "cease all encroachments on the territory and sovereignty of the DRV," and also that pending the peaceful reunification of Vietnam the two zones must respect the military provisions of the 1954 Accords.[51] Similarly, South Vietnam's new Constitution[52] proclaims in Article 1.1 that "Viet-Nam is a territorially indivisible, unified and independent republic." Yet it subsequently also provides in Article 4.1 that the "Republic of Viet-Nam" will abide by such international law rules as "are not contrary to its national sovereignty and the principle of equality between nations."

It is submitted that the actions taken within the international community toward and by North and South Vietnam at least since 1956 show substantial acceptance of a status of *de facto* statehood for both entities and have displaced the provisions of the 1954 Accords which bear on statehood. As some commentators have put it, "The signatories to the Geneva Accords could have had no competence forever to preclude others from recognizing South Vietnam as a state."[53] North Vietnam would be in the same position. The elections specified in the Accords were not held, and both regimes continued thereafter to administer their respective areas. Each government had charge of a defined territory, controlled the population, and engaged in foreign relations. Such actions have been treated as establishing that an entity is a state.[54] Moreover, these developments appear to parallel events in Germany and Korea. There arrangements for unification were never put into effect, and separate regimes came into being which did not accept each other's independence but nevertheless controlled their own territories and became active in international affairs.

The extent of the South Vietnamese Government's control after the earlier years of the conflict has been questioned, but if the United States

---

response in the event of cessation, that the North considers itself an independent country: ". . . the other side maintains a totally different approach from that of, for instance, the United States. They maintain that . . . there are questions of principle involved. They maintain that the United States has no right to bomb an independent, sovereign country." *N.Y. Times*, Jan. 11, 1967, at 4.

[51] *Background Information* 295.

[52] The Constitution of the Republic of Viet-Nam approved by the National Constituent Assembly on March 18, 1967 and promulgated on April 1, 1967 is reprinted at 113 *Cong. Rec.* S 7733 (daily ed. June 6, 1967).

[53] Professors Bishop et al., Letter *supra*, note 1, at 3694.

[54] Restatement, Second, Foreign Relations Law of the United States §4, *State Defined* (1965).

position that North Vietnam has attacked the South is accepted, any such diminishing control would certainly not deprive the victim of its international standing. Even if the United States position is rejected, the extent of the Saigon Government's control would bear not on the separate standing of South Vietnam vis-à-vis North Vietnam but on whether or not the rebelling element may properly be recognized as having the status of either a belligerent or an insurgent.[55] The fact that there is a contest for the control of a particular entity does not cause it to cease being a state. Indeed a state's recognition of a regime rebelling against the established government of another state violates the latter state's rights under international law if the actual authority and prospects of the revolutionary regime do not meet certain requirements.[56]

North and South Vietnam have each received substantial recognition only from countries belonging to one of the major blocs. This fact does not amount, however, to a denial of statehood. Under the more generally accepted view, the act of recognition is "declaratory" rather than "constitutive":

> A state may exist without being recognized, and if it does exist in fact, then, whether or not it has been formally recognized by other states, it has a right to be treated by them *as* a state.[57] (italics in original)

None of East and West Germany and North and South Korea, for example, enjoys widespread recognition from states in both blocs, but there can be no doubt that each is itself a state.

Questions of Fact and Law

While as has been discussed some issues appear capable of resolution,

[55] See *id.*, §94, Comment e, *Recognition of belligerency and insurgency*, and §101, *Minimum Requirements for Recognition of Revolutionary Regime*; Brierly, *supra* note 9, at 141-43.

It could be argued that in the same way as North and South Vietnam have become factually separate states, the National Liberation Front has become entitled to recognition as a belligerent or an insurgent. The argument would focus on the control exercised by the N.L.F. in some instances and its diplomatic activities such as maintaining representatives in a number of foreign countries. Questions arise, however, regarding the degree of the N.L.F.'s control of territory and population and its non-observance of the laws of war (see on these points the Restatement and Brierly, *supra*). Another basic issue in this matter is whether the N.L.F. can be considered a development indigenous to South Vietnam (see Moore, Underwood, and McDougal, *supra* note 1, at 28 and n. 111; Pike, *Viet Cong—The Organization and Techniques of the National Liberation Front of South Vietnam*, 307-08, 315-16, 321 [M.I.T. 1966]).

[56] Restatement, *supra*, at §100, *Minimum Requirements for Recognition of New State*, and §101.

[57] Brierly, *supra* note 9, at 139.

others lead to a part of the debate over legality in which the facts and some propositions of law are much disputed. Among such major questions are (1) whether or not there was an armed attack within the meaning of Article 51 of the Charter, (2) the possible application of that Article even if the two Vietnams are not separate states, (3) the present status of the 1954 Geneva Accords, (4) the significance for the war in Vietnam of the 1962 Geneva Accords, and (5) the application of the rule of proportionality or reasonable necessity to measures of collective self-defense. All of these issues—apart from the second one if it is accepted that North and South Vietnam are *de facto* states—have an important bearing on the ultimate question of legality.

1. HAS AN ARMED ATTACK OCCURRED?

United States actions are based on the claim that we have responded to an armed attack by North Vietnam upon South Vietnam. Whatever may have occurred since American bombing raids began in February 1965, however, there was prior to that time no open mass movement by North Vietnamese troops across an international demarcation line, as there was by North Korean troops in 1950 in Korea. What other actions can be said to come within the legal definition of "armed attack"? As long as it is feasible to use force "against the territorial integrity or political independence" of a state[58] without resorting to the obvious and direct form of invasion, there would be no justification for limiting "armed attack" to the familiar model. That a country's use of force in fomenting and assisting armed revolutionary activity in another state would constitute an attack has been accepted as a matter of law by some authorities[59] and has been asserted in a number of instances. These include the support given by various Balkan countries to guerrillas in Greece in 1946, charges by Lebanon against the United Arab Republic in 1958, the French bombing in 1958 of a point in Tunisia through which men and arms were being supplied to Algerian rebels, Venezuelan charges against Cuba in 1963 and currently, and recent charges reportedly made by the United Arab Republic against

[58] Such action is prohibited by Article 2 (4) of the Charter of the United Nations, which provides: "All Members shall refrain in their international relations from the threat or use of force against the territorial integrity or political independence of any state, or in any other manner inconsistent with the Purposes of the United Nations." 59 Stat. 1031, 1037 (1945).

[59] Moore, *supra* note 1, at 12 and the authorities there cited. See also General Assembly Resolution 380-V (1950) condemning as aggression the fomenting of civil strife in another state, quoted in part in Moore, Underwood, and McDougal, *supra* note 1, at 43.

Saudi Arabia.[60] In 1948 the General Assembly of the United Nations noted in Resolution 193 the conclusions of a Special Committee that the Balkan çountries' actions threatened Greek independence and territorial integrity, and it called on the countries to cease their activities.[61]

In the context of Vietnam the United States takes the position that there has been an armed attack. The Administration considers that prior to 1965 North Vietnam, by developing "a covert political-military organization in South Viet-Nam"[62] and by infiltrating men, had contributed "the critical military element of the insurgency"[63] in the South. The facts are in dispute. Some observers report a significant degree of North Vietnamese control and military presence in the conflict;[64] others consider it basically a civil war between the South Vietnamese Government and indigenous rebels.[65] Thus one commentator has noted:

> To the extent that one accepts the factual conclusions drawn in its favor by the United States on the one hand, or by the Democratic Republic of Vietnam on the other, . . . there is today little doubt that the legal conclusions sought to be drawn are accurate.[66]

Differences between various infiltration figures help to show the difficulty of establishing the critical facts. A majority of the International Control Commission created by the 1954 Accords found in June 1962

[60] The earlier examples are discussed in Thomas and Thomas, *The Dominican Republic Crisis 1965—Legal Aspects*, 1966 Hammarskjöld Forum 27-28. The recent Venezuelan charges are reported in *N.Y. Times*, May 13 and 17, 1967, at 1 and 10, respectively. See also the examples discussed in 5 Whiteman, *supra* note 8, at 1108-09, 1162-64. The statement that U.A.R. planes had bombed towns in Saudi Arabia because they were "bases of aggression" against the Republic of Yemen was recently attributed to the commander of the U.A.R. force. *N.Y. Times*, May 17, 1967, at 9.

[61] Quotations from the text of Resolution 193 are given in Moore, Underwood, and McDougal, *supra*, at 43-44.

[62] Legal Adviser's *Memorandum*, 60 *Am. J. Int'l. L.* 565.

[63] *Id.*, at 566.

[64] See Crozier, *supra* note 37, at 134-35, 137-43, and the articles by Neil Sheehan (*N.Y. Times*, May 2, 1966, at 1) and Takashi Oka (*N.Y. Times*, July 31, 1966 [Magazine], at 9, 46) discussed in Moore, *supra* note 1, at 9-10 n. 22. See also the alleged quotation from President Ho Chi Minh in the Belgian publication *Red Flag* of July 10, 1959: "we are building socialism in Vietnam, but we are building it in only one part of the country, while in the other part we still have to direct and bring to a close the middle-class democratic and anti-imperialist revolution." *Background Information* 5; Crozier, *supra*, at 137.

[65] Wright, *supra* note 2, at 758, 762 n. 32; Kahin and Lewis, *The United States in Vietnam*, Ch. V, "The Origins of the Civil War" (Delta 1967); Devillers, "The Struggle for Unification of Vietnam," in *Vietnam, History, Documents, and Opinions on a Major World Crisis* 230 (M. Gettleman ed. 1965).

[66] Partan, *supra* note 32, at 304.

that "in specific instances . . . armed and unarmed personnel" and supplies had been sent from North to South Vietnam to carry out "hostile activities, including armed attacks," but the Commission did not report on the numbers involved.[67] As to the year 1964, for example, the State Department in its report of February 1965 estimated on the information then available that infiltrators under the "military discipline of . . . Hanoi" amounted to 7,400 or more (including at least 3,300 native North Vietnamese). Some specific details allegedly obtained from captured North Vietnamese soldiers were given in the report. The Defense Department's statistics as of the end of 1966 put the 1964 figures at 12,400 without distinguishing between native Northerners and any other category.[68] On the other hand, Senators Mansfield and Hatfield have stated that only 400 North Vietnamese soldiers went into South Vietnam during 1964, and Senator Hatfield has said that in June 1966 the Pentagon confirmed Senator Mansfield's figures.[69] In short while it seems clear that infiltration has taken place, there is disagreement as to its amount and nature and as to its significance in determining the character of the conflict prior to 1965.[70]

[67] The Commission's Special Report dated June 2, 1962 is reprinted in full at 113 *Cong. Rec.* S 4086 (daily ed., March 20, 1967), and the language quoted in the text appears at S 4087. For further discussion of this Report, which found violations of the 1954 Accords on the part of both North and South Vietnam, see below.

[68] State Dept. Report, *Aggression from the North* (Feb. 27, 1965) in *Background Information* 173, 181-82. The Defense Dept. figures appear at 113 *Cong. Rec.* S 2665 (daily ed. Feb. 27, 1967).

[69] See speeches by Sen. Mansfield in 1966 (112 *Cong. Rec.* 12857 [daily ed. June 16, 1966]) and by Sen. Hatfield in 1967 (113 *Cong. Rec.* S 6040 [daily ed. April 28, 1967]). Professor Arthur Schlesinger, Jr., has also stated recently that according to the Department of Defense there were only 400 North Vietnamese regular troops in South Vietnam in March 1965. Schlesinger, *Vietnam and the 1968 Elections*, at 113 *Cong. Rec.* S 14454 (daily ed. Oct. 9, 1967).

[70] In February 1965 the Canadian member of the Commission, dissenting from its majority finding that reports of air strikes on North Vietnam showed violations of the 1954 Accords, stated that these events had resulted from the North's increased efforts ". . . to incite, encourage, and support hostile activities in South Vietnam, aimed at the overthrow of the South Vietnamese administration. These activities are in direct and grave violation of the Geneva Agreement and constitute the root cause of general instability in Vietnam. . . ." (Moore, Underwood, and McDougal, *supra* note 1, at 35; see also note 87 below regarding the apparent absence of Commission status for committee conclusions cited by the Canadian member.) Similar statements were made by Hon. Paul Martin, the Canadian Foreign Minister, when he presented a report on Vietnam to a Committee of the Canadian House of Commons on June 10, 1965 (see 113 *Cong. Rec.* S 14408-11 [daily ed. Oct. 9, 1967]).

On the other hand, Professor Bernard Fall considered in 1965 that despite Northern assistance the Vietcong were not controlled by Hanoi. See Fall, "Viet-Cong—The Unseen Enemy in Viet-Nam," in Raskin and Fall, *supra* note 49, at 252-61. And for the view that the State Department's 1965 Report demonstrates relatively little North Vietnamese sup-

2. MAY THE UNITED STATES ACT IN COLLECTIVE SELF-DEFENSE WITH SOUTH VIETNAM IF THE LATTER IS NOT A SEPARATE STATE?

The view that North and South Vietnam are *de facto* states has been advanced above. If South Vietnam has been attacked, the use of force by it and other states in individual and collective self-defense would be legitimate under Article 51 of the Charter. Even if the two Vietnams are not regarded as independent countries, however, the United States Government and others who consider this country's involvement lawful have urged that the rules relating to an "armed attack" still apply.

Their position is that whatever South Vietnam's qualifications for statehood, it must be considered an international entity when the issue is the legality of initiating the use of force across the 1954 demarcation line.[71] Otherwise a fundamental purpose of the Charter and international law generally, to prohibit force unless used in self-defense or authorized by a collective decision in the United Nations, would be frustrated. Similarly, a major aim of the 1954 Accords, to end and prevent the resumption of hostilities (see Article 19 of the Military Agreement for Vietnam and Paragraph 5 of the Final Declaration), would be defeated. The experience of the international community with various recognized and continued demarcation lines is said to show that hostilities crossing them become international and justify defense measures.[72] Underlying this experience is said to be the rule that political grievances do not permit the use of force: ". . . the breach of a treaty is not in itself an 'armed attack' within the meaning of Article 51 of the Charter."[73]

---

port for the guerrillas in South Vietnam see Stone, "A Reply to the White Paper," in *Vietnam* (M. Gettleman ed.), *supra* note 65, at 317. The estimate of at least 40,000 for aggregate personnel infiltrated from North Vietnam during the period from 1959 through 1964 (Legal Adviser's *Memorandum*, 60 *Am. J. Int'l. L.* 565) is relatively small in comparison with the Defense Department's 1966 estimates of the combined Vietcong and North Vietnamese forces at the end of each year from 1960 through 1964. These figures are 36,000, 63,000, 79,000, 92,000 and 126,000, respectively (113 *Cong. Rec.* S 2665 [daily ed. Feb. 27, 1967]). Nevertheless comparative numbers would not necessarily be the test of military direction or assistance. Nor would they dispose of the question whether or not the guerrilla war began on orders from North Vietnam (on this point contrast the authorities cited in note 64 with those cited in note 65).

71 Legal Adviser's *Memorandum*, 60 *Am. J. Int'l. L.* 569-70; Moore, Underwood, and McDougal, *supra* note 1, at 5 and nn. 53, 249; Moore, *supra* note 1, at 1-2, 4-6.

72 Moore, *supra*, at 2, 5, and see the passages there quoted from McDougal and Feliciano, *Law and Minimum World Public Order* 221 (1961) and Wright, *International Law and Civil Strife*, 1959 *Proc. Am. Soc'y. Int'l. L.* 145, 151.

73 McNair, *Law of Treaties*, 577 n. 1 (1961), cited in Moore, *supra*, at 5, and in Moore, Underwood, and McDougal, *supra*, at 88-89 and n. 281.

The view that South Vietnam is an international entity for this purpose is disputed as a matter of law. It is urged that Vietnam differs from other cases of divided countries. The 1954 Accords followed a "colonial" war between France and the Vietminh won militarily by the latter and settled politically at Geneva. The settlement was intended to encompass the entire territory and is to be distinguished from political solutions in other cases because it was one of unity rather than continued division. As France's successor South Vietnam was bound by the Accords. Accordingly, under this view, South Vietnam with United States assistance repudiated the settlement, and North Vietnam thereupon became entitled to consider the demarcation line inoperative and to wage what amounted to a civil war.[74] Disregard of the cease-fire line is said to be justified by the principle that a material breach of a multilateral treaty entitles an affected party to suspend operation of the treaty, at least in part, between it and the defaulting state (see Article 57 of Draft Articles on the Law of Treaties drawn up by the International Law Commission).[75]

3. WHAT IS THE PRESENT STATUS OF THE 1954 GENEVA ACCORDS?

Both regimes in Vietnam have been charged with numerous violations of the Accords. Yet neither the North nor the South has repudiated the 1954 agreements as a whole with the notification specified, for example, in the recent Draft Articles on the Law of Treaties.[76] Instead both parties (even though South Vietnam has maintained since 1954 that the Accords do not bind it) continue to allege violations of at least the prohibition on hostilities.[77] North Vietnam also invokes the Ac-

[74] Wright, *supra* note 2, at 756-58; Falk, *supra* note 27, at 1125, 1129, 1137, 1153-54.

[75] *Reports of the International Law Commission*, 21 U.N. GAOR Supp. 9, at 82, U.N. Doc. A/6309/ Rev. 1 (1966).

[76] See Article 62 (*id.*, at 89).

[77] North Vietnam submitted a formal complaint to the International Control Commission when bombing of targets in the North started in February 1965, and South Vietnam did the same regarding alleged attacks by the North (Moore, Underwood, and McDougal, *supra*, at n. 70). North Vietnam lodged complaints again when U.S. ships shelled coastal targets in the North (*N.Y. Times*, Feb. 27, 1967, at 3) and U.S. field artillery began shelling across the demarcation line from positions in South Vietnam (*id.*, Feb. 26, 1967, at 2). In February 1967 South Vietnam made a protest to the Commission over alleged military operations by Northern forces in the demilitarized zone (*id.*, May 20, 1967, at 2), and in March North Vietnam protested an air strike on an iron and steel complex (*id.*, March 12, 1967, at 1). When American forces undertook ground operations in the demilitarized zone, officials in the North termed this a violation of the Accords (although not an invasion), but they apparently did not submit a complaint to the Commission (*id.*, May 20 and May 22, 1967, at 1, 2 and 14).

That the demarcation line still has importance generally is shown by the distinction

cords, as interpreted by it, as the basis for settlement and the reason why United Nations involvement would be inappropriate.[78] In addition, the Foreign Minister of South Vietnam recently proposed that the provisions of the 1954 armistice be reinstated. His major points were reported as renewed recognition of the 17th Parallel as the demarcation line between the two Vietnams, another exchange of population between South and North, and the creation of a new international commission to supervise the armistice.[79]

For the period prior to the United States bombing raids begun in February 1965 the major violations charged against South Vietnam include repudiation of the provisions for elections in 1956,[80] political reprisals and repressing popular expression, insufficient compliance with the provisions for inspections by the International Control Commission,[81] importing and permitting the introduction of American military equipment and personnel, and entering into a military alliance with the United States.[82] North Vietnam has been charged with vastly enlarging its army by early 1956 with the help of equipment and men from China,[83] interfering with civilians trying to leave its zone,[84] re-

---

drawn by Hanoi and others between bombing of North and South Vietnam (see the Soviet condemnation of American strikes on the North as "bombing raids on the territory of a third country" in Moore, Underwood, and McDougal, *supra*, at n. 119) and by the widely held view that an invasion of the North would be extremely serious (*N.Y. Times*, May 22, 1967, at 10; and see *id.*, May 22 and Jan. 16, 1967 at 8 and 1 for reports of a communication between Communist China and the U.S. to the effect that the former would intervene if there were an invasion of North Vietnam). North Vietnam has also thus far denied that its troops are present in the South (Moore, Underwood, and McDougal, *supra*, at n. 72).

[78] *Id.*, at nn. 70, 233; Moore, *supra* note 1, at 6 and n. 15; see also Wright, *supra* note 2, at 753 n. 8.

[79] *N.Y. Times*, May 30, 1967, at 6.

[80] The U.S. Government's position is that even if South Vietnam were bound by the Accords, conditions in North Vietnam made it impossible to have free elections by secret ballot as stipulated in Paragraph 7 of the 1954 Final Declaration (Legal Adviser's *Memorandum*, 60 *Am. J. Int'l. L.* 578). See also Young, *supra* note 23, at 109-14. Critics have replied that the Accords called for elections in 1956 in any event as a fundamental part of the settlement (Wright, *supra*, at 759-60; Falk, *supra* note 27, at 1152-53). The British Government in a Note given to the U.S.S.R. in April 1956 took the position that the free elections provided in the Accords were desirable but that South Vietnam was not legally obliged to participate (Moore, Underwood, and McDougal, *supra*, n. 278).

[81] As to reprisals and instances of non-compliance see the article by Devillers and extracts from I.C.C. reports in *Vietnam* (M. Gettleman ed.), *supra* note 65, at 222-24, 172, 176, 179-80; see also Fall, "How the French Got Out of Viet-Nam," in Raskin and Fall, *supra* note 49, at 90-92.

[82] As to equipment, men, and the alliance see the 1962 I.C.C. report discussed below.

[83] Speech of June 1, 1956 by Asst. Sec. of State Robertson, citing a British Note given to the U.S.S.R. in April 1956, in *Background Information* 80. See also Young, *supra* note 23, at 107, 113-14.

[84] Fall, *supra* note 81, at 91.

pressing popular expression,[85] moving men and equipment across the demarcation line to engage in hostilities, and insufficient compliance (after earlier years) with the provisions for Commission inspections.[86] Since February 1965 it appears that both Vietnamese regimes have taken actions which, by themselves, would constitute very substantial violations of the Accords.[87]

Perhaps the central question of fact arising from these allegations is which of the pre-1965 military violations (if the charges are accurate) occurred in response to prior violations by the other regime. Insofar as the military provisions of the Accords are concerned, North Vietnam protested to the International Control Commission at least as early as April 1960 against an alleged "formidable" increase in American personnel,[88] although United States figures are that such personnel increased only from 327 to around 770 or 800 by the end of 1960.[89] South Vietnam protested to the Commission at least as early as November 1960 that regular army forces from the North had infiltrated through Laos and attacked in the Kontum-Pleiku area.[90] By a 2 to 1 majority the Commission, adopting a report of its Legal Committee, found in June 1962 that "in specific instances" North Vietnam had sent men and equipment to the South in order to carry out "hostile activities, including armed attacks," and that the North's zone had been "used for inciting, encouraging and supporting hostile activities in the Zone

---

[85] Wright, *supra* note 2, at 755 n. 15; Devillers, *supra* note 65, at 220.

[86] As to movement across the line see the discussion below and the 1962 I.C.C. Report, which is reprinted in full at 113 *Cong. Rec.* S 4086 (daily ed. March 20, 1967). Denial of cooperation by both parties was also charged by the I.C.C. in 1962 (*id.*, at S 4088). In 1961 it had similarly noted non-cooperation by both parties and had stated that the number of formal citations of non-compliance did not measure the degree of cooperation of either side (Moore, Underwood, and McDougal, *supra* note 1, at n. 285).

[87] See the I.C.C.'s majority report of February 13, 1965, which recites reports from North Vietnam of the bombing raids on its territory and states that these "indicate violations of the Geneva Agreement" (*Vietnam* [M. Gettleman ed.], *supra* note 65, at 190). The Canadian member, dissenting, stated that the events had resulted from North Vietnam's intensification of its "aggressive policy" in violation of the Agreement and quoted what he called conclusions of the Legal Committee in detailed support. The Indian member denied that the quoted information had the sanction of the Commission or its Committees (Moore, Underwood, and McDougal, *supra*, at 33-35; the authors sought more information on the above contradiction but were unsuccessful [*id.*, at n. 135]). As the United States in 1954 pledged only not to disturb the Accords with force in accordance with the U.N. Charter (*Background Information* 69), its actions now, if legitimate under the Charter, would not violate its declaration.

[88] *Background Information* 6.

[89] *Ibid.*; see also the statistics at 113 *Cong. Rec.* S 2665 (daily ed. Feb. 27, 1967) and 112 *Cong. Rec.* 24855 (daily ed. Oct. 10, 1966). If there were any U.S. military personnel operating covertly, as has been charged, they would presumably not be included in these figures.

[90] *Background Information* 7.

in the South, aimed at the overthrow of the Administration. . . ."[91]
The Commission also found that South Vietnam had unlawfully received increased military aid from the United States and, in the creation of a U.S. Military Command (February 1962) and the increase of personnel beyond the stated Advisory Group strength, had entered a prohibited "factual military alliance."[92] Authorities disagree, however, on the significance of these findings and other factual assertions. Some conclude that the American build-up occurred in response to North Vietnam's actions.[93] Others find increases in violations by both sides in the conflict after 1958 and suggest that in any event the effect of the demarcation line with its restraints on hostilities had lapsed.[94]

One commentator considers that as the various claims cannot be disposed of in the present state of international fact-finding procedures

> . . . the best that can be done is to attempt to preserve as much of contested agreements as possible in situations in which parties raise and dispute material breach claims. It is suggested that in the Vietnam context this might be done by noting past and present claims of material breaches of the Geneva Agreements, but regarding both sides as continuing to be bound by these Agreements as far as may be possible today and in the future.[95]

Although both sides may agree that the 1954 Accords still have some force, this has little practical significance, since there is substantial disagreement at present on what the Accords mean.

4. WHAT IS THE SIGNIFICANCE OF THE 1962 GENEVA ACCORDS FOR THE WAR IN VIETNAM?

Following approximately a year of hostilities in Laos between government forces and the Pathet Lao a conference was held from May 1961 to July 1962 between all parties to the earlier Accords (including

---

91 113 *Cong. Rec.* S 4087 (daily ed. March 20, 1967).

92 *Id.*, at S 4087-88.

93 Moore, *supra* note 1, at 11; Moore, Underwood, and McDougal, *supra*, note 1, at 30-31 and n. 124, citing a statement in 1965 by the British Secretary of State for Foreign Affairs that "the action from the North preceded the arrival of United States forces in any considerable degree in the South."

94 Wright, *supra* note 2, at 764-67; Falk, *supra* note 27, at 1153-54. The 1966 report of the group headed by Senator Mansfield stated that the Vietcong "counter response" in 1965 to the U.S. troop build-up was to increase their force by recruitment and infiltration of Northern troops, and that prior to late 1964 mainly cadres and military leadership had been infiltrated. Report to Senate Comm. on Foreign Relations, 89th Cong., 2d Sess., *The Vietnam Conflict: The Substance and The Shadow* 1, 3 (Comm. Print Jan. 1966).

95 Partan, *supra* note 32, at 296.

both North and South Vietnam), together with the countries comprising the existing International Control Commission and Burma, Thailand and the United States. A Declaration on the Neutrality of Laos and a Protocol thereto were signed.[96] A proposal by South Vietnam[97] resulted in a provision in Paragraph 2 (i) of the Declaration that the parties would not use Laotian territory "for interference in the internal affairs of other countries." In other provisions of the Declaration the parties agreed not to bring foreign troops into Laos, not to establish any foreign military installation there, and not to "facilitate or connive at" any such acts. Article 2 of the Protocol directed that all foreign military personnel be withdrawn from Laos as soon as possible and in any case within 30 days after the Commission's teams were ready to supervise the withdrawal. Article 4 again prohibited the introduction of foreign troops into Laos (except French military instructors if requested). All war material except such conventional armaments as the Laotian Government might need for national defense was banned by Article 6.

While the conference and the Accords dealt with Laos, it seems evident that the provisions just discussed also affected the conflict in Vietnam and that this must have been appreciated by the parties.[98] At least since 1960 South Vietnam and the United States had claimed that some of the principal routes for infiltration from the North to the South crossed Laotian territory. Clearly any introduction of troops or war material into Laos by either side in the Vietnam conflict for purposes related to that conflict would violate the 1962 Accords.

The factual history of the parties' observance or non-observance of these instruments is difficult to determine. Prince Souvanna Phouma, the Laotian Premier, stated recently that his government cannot control or halt the movement of North Vietnamese troops through the country to South Vietnam, and that he estimates 30,000 such troops are in Laos.[99] In 1966 the International Control Commission published a

[96] The Accords are reprinted in *Background Information* 99-107 and are discussed generally in Czyzak and Salans, "The International Conference on the Settlement of the Laotian Question and the Geneva Agreements of 1962," 57 *Am. J. Int'l. L.* 300 (1963).

[97] Czyzak and Salans, *supra*, at 308.

[98] In answer to a question about the increasing use of Laos as a Communist base in violation of pledges that it would be neutral, Secretary Rusk stated at a news conference on November 17, 1961: *"This is one of the subjects which have been discussed at Geneva,* and certainly if there is to be any substance whatever in the notion of a neutral and independent Laos, then any arrangements for Laos must insure that Laos not itself be used as a route of penetration and infiltration and subversion against south Viet-Nam." *Background Information* 88 (italics added).

[99] *N.Y. Times*, April 7, 1967, at 8. The leader of the Pathet Lao side, Prince Souphan-

majority report which is said to document the operations of North Vietnamese forces in Laos.[100] There are conflicting reports on the presence or absence of United States soldiers,[101] and United States planes are said to be engaged in active operations against the infiltration routes.[102]

In the view of the United States Government it complied substantially with the 1962 Accords whereas North Vietnam did not.[103] This may be true regarding the withdrawal of forces and the use of Laotian infiltration routes, but the roles of parties to the Treaty regarding the supply of war material and other forms of assistance to Laotian factions are harder to determine. It has been said that both sides in the conflict are violating the Accords at present.[104] The activity of either side in aiding local forces in Laos is a different matter, however, from the use of Laos in connection with the war in Vietnam. Unless the United States and South Vietnam have interfered in Laos in order either to strike at North Vietnam or to facilitate the conduct of hostilities in the South, there would appear to be no justification by way of the principle of material breach of a treaty for North Vietnam's continuing, resuming, or starting (as the case may be) the use of Laotian infiltration routes. In any event, whatever the status of the two Vietnams under the 1954 Accords, both of them undertook in the 1962 Geneva Agreement separate international obligations which had a bearing on the war in Vietnam.[105]

---

ouvong, has been reported as charging the Premier with inviting the Pathet Lao to take part in elections designed to improve the rightists' position so that U.S. troops could be used against North Vietnam's supply routes to South Vietnam (id., Nov. 19, 1966, at 4).

100 Id., Aug. 23, 1966, at 9, and July 25, 1966, at 2. The Polish member abstained.

101 The use of special patrols has been reported by Seymour Topping (N.Y. Times, June 17, 1966, at 4). In contrast Tom Wicker has reported that no U.S. troops are fighting in Laos (id., Feb. 13, 1967, at 6).

102 Topping, supra; Legislative Reference Service, U.S. Policy Toward the Far East: Chronology of Significant Events, 1844 Through July 30, 1966, in 112 Cong. Rec. 26751, 26758 (daily ed. Oct. 19, 1966), where it is said that U.S. planes have bombed routes in Laos since December 1964.

103 See, e.g., statements by Secretary Rusk during 1966 in The Vietnam Hearings, supra note 20, at 51-52, 278-80.

104 For a short summary of current interference in Laos, see study prepared for Senate Comm. on Foreign Relations, 89th Cong., 2d Sess., Neutralization in Southeast Asia: Problems and Prospects at 29 (Comm. Print Oct. 1966).

105 It could be argued that the infiltrations across the Laotian border, if accurately reported, constitute a major expansionist element in the war, and that if the border were closed in accordance with the 1962 Accords it would be far simpler to defend against other alleged infiltrations without striking directly at North Vietnam. See, e.g., reports on the feasibility of constructing a barrier to seal off the demilitarized zone (N.Y. Times, July 21, 1967, at 2; New Republic [July 8, 1967], reprinted at 113 Cong. Rec. A 3576 [daily ed. July 17, 1967]; and Christian Science Monitor, Jan. 24, 1967, reprinted at 113

5. HOW DOES THE RULE OF PROPORTIONALITY OR REASONABLE NECESSITY APPLY?

As a general matter the legality of the use of force by the United States directly against North Vietnam depends on the disputed charge that an armed attack has occurred. If this is correct, military action against the attacker on its territory, as occurred in Korea in the 1950's, would be legitimate. Yet such use of force is subject to a requirement of proportionality under the "customary law" of self-defense.[106] This restriction is not, however, a mechanical limitation permitting defenders to use only the same numbers and kinds of weapons as those of the attackers[107] but rather ". . . a requirement that defensive action should not involve greater coercion than is reasonably necessary for the defense of the fundamental values under attack."[108] And under a related principle force must be used in self-defense rather than as a reprisal for a prior injury.[109] The United States military involvement as a whole has been criticized under the rule of proportionality, and specific actions have been termed reprisals.

The first alleged reprisal is the bombing of torpedo boats and their facilities in North Vietnam following the incidents in the Gulf of Tonkin in 1964. In his report of August 5, 1964[110] to the Security Council Ambassador Stevenson stated that one United States destroyer had been attacked on August 2 when 30 miles off the North Vietnamese coast and had returned the attackers' fire, that on August 3 the United States "took steps to convey" to Hanoi a note warning of the "grave consequences" which would follow further unprovoked assaults, that on August 4 two destroyers were attacked when 65 miles from shore, and that thereafter the air strikes were made. He also stated that the de-

---

Cong. Rec. A 823 [daily ed. Feb. 22, 1967]) and on the effectiveness of naval patrolling against infiltration by the coast (*Newsweek* [July 31, 1967], at 26).

[106] McDougal and Feliciano, *supra* note 72, at 217.

[107] *Id.*, at 218, 241-44.

[108] Moore, *supra* note 1, at 18. Professor Moore also quotes the following definition from McDougal and Feliciano, *supra*, at 242-43: " 'Proportionality in coercion constitutes a requirement that responding coercion be limited in intensity and magnitude to what is reasonably necessary promptly to secure the permissible objectives of self-defense. For present purposes, these objectives may be most comprehensively generalized as the conserving of important values by compelling the opposing participant to terminate the condition which necessitates responsive coercion. . . . Thus articulated, the principle of proportionality is seen as but one specific form of the more general principle of economy in coercion and as a logical corollary of the fundamental community policy against change by destructive modes.' " (Moore, *supra*, at 18 n. 41.)

[109] Wright, *supra* note 2, at 764, 767.

[110] *Background Information* 132-35.

stroyers had not taken any belligerent action before being attacked, although from testimony given later before the Senate Foreign Relations Committee it appears that on July 31 both ships had been within the twelve-mile territorial limit claimed by North Vietnam and in the general area of (although not protecting) South Vietnamese ships which were shelling islands off the coast of the North.[111]

The destroyers' position on July 31 has been called a provocation, although not a justification for the North Vietnamese action.[112] The ships' location on this date could in no event be characterized, however, as provoking the second North Vietnamese attack made on August 4 when the ships were 65 miles from shore and in the absence of a peaceful answer to the United States note. On the facts as described above the North Vietnamese attacks were illegal because the destroyers had not taken hostile action. Clearly the United States was entitled to protect its ships and to resist illegal interference with their passage through international waters.[113]

Nevertheless there remains a question whether the two incidents were sufficient grounds for the military action taken against North Vietnamese territory.[114] The Government has claimed that in fact these incidents were part of a larger and long-standing pattern of illegal use of force by North Vietnam in violation of international agreements. The attacks on the destroyers have been connected with North Vietnam's asserted use of terror and infiltration tactics in South Vietnam, and with its alleged combat operations in Laos, including attacks in May 1964 on United States reconnaissance planes seeking—at the request of the Laotian Government—to determine the situation in areas of Laos where Communist forces had blocked inspection by the International Control Commission under the 1962 Accords.[115] On the other hand, if protection of United States ships and free passage alone are considered, it would appear that these goals were achieved by means short of the air strike.

The second alleged reprisal is the bombing of military targets in North Vietnam on February 7, 1965, following attacks on United

111 Stone, "International Law and The Tonkin Bay Incidents," in Raskin and Fall, *supra* note 49, at 310-11.

112 Remarks of Senator Morse, as reported in Stone, *supra*, at 310.

113 Brierly, *supra* note 9, at 424 (discussing the *Corfu Channel* case [1949] I.C.J. 4) . A "police action" is distinguished at *id.*, 425.

114 Whether the United States could properly have reacted as it did to a continuing series of illegal attacks on its ships is still another question. Repetition of this kind would present a more serious threat.

115 See, e.g., statements by President Johnson on August 5, 1964 and April 27, 1965 (*Background Information* 131, 227) , and by Ambassador Stevenson to the Security Council on August 5, 1964 and February 7, 1965 (*id.*, at 134, 158) .

States bases in South Vietnam. These strikes were described in a White House statement as "retaliatory attacks" and "appropriate reprisal action" for "a more aggressive course of action" ordered by Hanoi and "made possible by the continuing infiltration of personnel and equipment from North Viet-Nam."[116] It is generally acknowledged, however, that South Vietnam's military position was extremely perilous at this time,[117] and one observer has described the February attacks as evidence that the South was nearly cut in two.

> The real significance of the Pleiku and Qui Nhon actions was less the calculated selection of American targets than the *fait accompli* of partition. As government forces quickly discovered, the Vietcong had seized control of the . . . strategic highway supplying the Second Corps headquarters and all of the northern part of the High Plateau. . . . The war, it was clear, was entering its final phase.[118]

If the general claim of an armed attack by North Vietnam is accepted, an increase in the measure of defensive force used would be a reasonably necessary response to the very serious military threat then presented.

It is difficult to apply a test of proportionality or reasonable necessity to the United States involvement as a whole because of the character of the guerrilla war in the South and the nature of the bombing targets in the North. The Government claims that its measures are aimed only against North Vietnam's capacity for infiltration and its immediate defenses against the air strike. There is dispute over the degree of restraint exercised by American forces and over the question whether civilian casualties have been sought or recklessly incurred. If direction of or assistance to insurgents can amount to an armed attack so as to permit collective self-defense, however, permissible measures must relate to the military realities. Thus it would not be unreasonable to oppose guerrillas with forces considerably larger than their own numbers (and larger also than the forces which might be necessary for conventional warfare) in order to offset the advantages accruing to combatants who cannot be identified readily and whose means of attack include terror and sabotage.[119]

---

[116] *Background Information* 154-55.

[117] Mansfield report, *supra* note 94, at 1.

[118] Denis Warner, "Vietnam," *The Reporter* (March 25, 1965), at 28.

[119] In the case of guerrillas quite a high ratio of defensive forces would seem to be legitimate under the test of reasonable necessity. Professor Bernard Fall, writing in *Viet-Nam Witness*, has stated that the ratios of pacification forces to insurgents in Malaya, Cyprus and Algeria were 50 to 1, 110 to 1, and 10 to 1, respectively. See the quotation at Falk, *supra* note 27, 1132 n. 41.

Strict application of the minimum defensive forces thought necessary to end an opponent's coercion could perpetuate a stalemate.[120] Yet if activities constituting the asserted armed attack continue even though they do not increase in intensity, it would seem that the United States and South Vietnam could reasonably raise the level of force used in order to end the attack. To the extent that a serious threat persists over time it would make a greater response necessary. A limiting consideration would be the danger in the nuclear age of taking steps to increase levels of violence.

It could be argued that the possibility of a drawn-out conflict requires the rule of proportionality or reasonable necessity to be interpreted as also forbidding the use of just enough defensive force to prevent military victory by the other side without ending the conflict. Such a rule would appear to be dangerous, however, in the nuclear age. Despite the possibility of a protracted war, it seems that in any event the rule should not be interpreted as contemplating immediate commitment, upon resisting an attack, of forces supposed to be clearly decisive. Such a test would spur rapid build-ups by both parties to a conflict without necessarily resulting in a quick solution.

The question whether the American response in South Vietnam has been proportionate or reasonably necessary in view of the threat thus appears to depend not on the immediacy of its success but on the relation of legitimate military effects to civilian casualties and to other damage resulting from the use of force. This would turn on the factual implementation of United States policies for clearing some sectors of civilians[121] and limiting combat operations in areas where civilians may be present.[122] The test for strikes against North Vietnam would focus on the relation of targets to the North's alleged military efforts[123] and on the principle that measures of self-defense may not attack the North's "territorial and political integrity."[124] As thus stated, however, and particularly in the context of a war fought for the control not of

120 See Falk, *supra*, at 1144.

121 Civilians have been moved, for example, from a cleared area south of the demilitarized zone. *N.Y. Times*, July 21, 1967, at 2.

122 For an outline of the latter policy see General Westmoreland's speech to a meeting of the Associated Press in 113 *Cong. Rec.* S 5857 (daily ed. April 25, 1967).

123 See Secretary McNamara's discussion of targets and their selection in a news conference of April 26, 1965. *Background Information* 218-20.

124 Moore, *supra* note 1, at 19. During hearings before the Senate Foreign Relations Committee in 1966 Secretary Rusk stated: ". . . we do not seek to destroy the Hanoi regime or to force the people of North Vietnam to accept any other form of government." *The Vietnam Hearings, supra* note 20, at 241.

land but of people[125] who often remain in the battle area, the rule of proportionality or reasonable necessity, even if followed, seems in fact to be a relatively minor restraint on the level of destruction.

For the reasons discussed the five questions just considered cannot be readily answered. A major obstacle is the difficulty of determining the facts. There is sharp disagreement over the allegations of armed attack by North Vietnam and over the timing and interrelation of the violations of the 1954 Geneva Accords with which each side has charged the other. There is disagreement also as to the relevant legal principles if the separate statehood of the two Vietnams is not accepted. In addition, while it seems clear as a matter of principle that under the 1962 Accords both regimes undertook an obligation not to bring forces into Laotian territory, and that military measures taken in collective self-defense are subject to the requirement of reasonable necessity in relation to the values attacked, the application of these rules is in some doubt. As to the use of Laos, the timing and the present extent of violations of the 1962 Accords are unclear, but even if the position of the United States is accepted, North Vietnam's breach of this obligation would not seem to affect any rights it might assert to use force in the South other than by way of Laos. As to reasonable necessity, the nature of the targets being struck in North Vietnam and the effects of American operations in South Vietnam are again subjects of dispute. While the above questions by no means become unimportant because they have not been answered, in these circumstances the legality or illegality of the United States involvement as a whole cannot be decided. To do so would require resolution of these issues, apart from the second one if *de facto* statehood is accepted, and this in turn involves choosing between conflicting versions of the facts.

United States Actions as Precedents

The legal debate, it is submitted, should focus more sharply upon the possible effect of United States actions on the future state of international law. The international legal system is a decentralized one.

---

[125] During the 1966 hearings General Taylor defined one American military objective as "securing a high proportion of the population": "We are in Vietnam to safeguard the people who are the real target of the enemy. Terrain has little meaning except insofar as it supports people. Thus the extent of control and protection of population is the true measure of progress rather than control of territory." *The Vietnam Hearings, supra,* at 173. See also the definition of "revolutionary war" in Crozier, *supra* note 37, at 60: "Revolutionary war is in fact a struggle for the minds and bodies of the people among whom the irregulars live and fight."

Unilateral actions of states, particularly if they are major powers, can serve as precedents and may eventually create rules. As the United States has taken steps which affect basic aims of international law, the future implications of this country's course of action should be examined.

One such subject for consideration involves possible restraints on the initiation of military measures of collective self-defense.[126] If North Vietnam and South Vietnam are considered separate states or international entities, it seems to be the first time that the United States has used such force directly against the territory of a country whose alleged "armed attack" was not an open assault across a border. While the legal characterization of "armed attack" has been applied in a number of instances to uses of force other than direct invasions,[127] the answering measures, if any, have generally been confined to the attacked territory. This was true, for example, in Greece in 1946. In some cases of alleged foreign participation in insurgencies the use of force in response has not been confined to the attacked territory. Examples include the French strike against an area in Tunisia in 1958, a British raid in 1964 against a fort in Yemen claimed to be a center for assistance to terrorists in Aden, and the Egyptian bombing of towns in Saudi Arabia in connection with the war in Yemen.[128] The French and British responses were single raids, however, and none of these measures approaches the systematic and sustained nature of the American bombing of North Vietnam.

These actions taken by France, Britain and the United Arab Republic have brought protests.[129] To the extent that any of these strikes can be validly characterized as a reprisal, it would be legally distinguishable from the United States bombing, granting a prior armed

126 Another subject for consideration involves possible precedents limiting the duration and destructiveness of measures taken in collective self-defense. The United States has used force in claimed collective self-defense under Article 51 of the Charter and has submitted the dispute to the Security Council, but the Council has not acted. As has been discussed, the principle of proportionality or reasonable necessity appears to have been but a relatively minor restriction on the level of destruction accompanying the use of defensive force. It would seem important to consider whether other restraints could not be developed. One major difficulty, however, is the need for action in this area on the part of both adversaries. Neither side, certainly, would accept a unilateral restraint which rendered its military efforts ineffectual.

127 See Question 1 above and note 60.

128 For the French and Egyptian raids see note 60. The British raid is discussed in Wright, *supra* note 2, at 767 n. 57. The French and British raids are also discussed in Stone, *supra* note 111, at 307-08.

129 As to the French and British bombings see Wright and Stone, *supra*. The United States has deplored the Egyptian raids, as is discussed in the text.

attack by North Vietnam. Yet the reported rationale for the Egyptian air strikes did not mention retaliation but charged Saudi Arabia with aggression against Yemen.[130] And the bombing was treated as a serious step by the United States Government in misgivings publicly expressed. In the words of the State Department spokesman, "There have reportedly been civilian casualties and, to say the obvious, we are deeply concerned about this escalation of tension between Arab states."[131]

It has been pointed out that such actions against the territory of a third state help to erase the distinction between civil and international war.[132] If enlarging the area in which force is to be used becomes necessary in defending a country against attack by infiltration (as distinct from an open invasion across a border) and is legitimate in a decentralized legal system, a precedent involving the procedural restraint, at least, of prior resort to international bodies or other arrangements for settling disputes without force would help to preserve something of the peacekeeping aspect of the Charter. Indeed members of the United Nations have a general duty under Article 33 (1) to seek peaceful resolution of disputes "first of all."[133] Although it has been said that the related Charter ". . . requirement that Members 'settle their disputes by peaceful means' has not achieved significance as an independent legal obligation,"[134] a course of action complying with the limited direction that peaceful resolution be attempted would set a useful precedent for world order. The example of such a prior effort might serve to prevent or lessen conflict in the future.

Thus while Article 33 (1) is not connected in terms to Article 51, it is necessarily affected by any resort to force on the part of member states. The United States has given aid to South Vietnam since at least 1954 and has operated a Military Assistance Command there since February 1962. Hostilities between North and South Vietnam via infiltration from the North have been alleged to be in progress

---

[130] See note 60.

[131] N.Y. Times, May 17, 1967 at 9.

[132] Falk, supra note 27, at 1133.

[133] Article 33 provides:

1. The parties to any dispute, the continuance of which is likely to endanger the maintenance of international peace and security, shall, first of all, seek a solution by negotiation, enquiry, mediation, conciliation, arbitration, judicial settlement, resort to regional agencies or arrangements, or other peaceful means of their own choice.

2. The Security Council shall, when it deems necessary, call upon the parties to settle their dispute by such means. 59 Stat. 1031, 1042 (1945).

[134] Henkin, supra note 11, at 148. The reference is to Article 2 (3) of the Charter, which provides: "All Members shall settle their international disputes by peaceful means in such a manner that international peace and security, and justice, are not endangered." 59 Stat. 1031, 1037 (1945).

since at least 1959,[135] and yet the United States did not submit the Vietnam dispute to the Security Council until January 31, 1966,[136] approximately a year after the start of the bombing. And the first American report to the Council occurred only in August 1964.[137]

That the United States did make efforts to find a peaceful settlement before using force directly against North Vietnam is demonstrated by its participation in the Laotian Conference of 1961-1962 and in the 1962 Accords. Although these Accords were not directed in terms at the war in Vietnam their provisions clearly affected it, and they were counted on to lessen the conflict in the course of neutralizing Laos.[138] Secretary Rusk has also stated that between early 1961 and 1965 the United States engaged in repeated diplomatic consultations about the problems of Vietnam and Laos. As summarized by the Secretary these include the meeting between President Kennedy and Chairman Khrushchev in June 1961, other bilateral talks with Russia, talks with Communist China, indirect contacts with Hanoi, private discussions generally in the United Nations and support for the Soviet-initiated but unsuccessful invitation to Hanoi to attend the Security Council deliberations following the 1964 incidents in the Gulf of Tonkin, an attempt to use the machinery established under the 1962 Accords for another conference on Laos, and many discussions with other interested governments.[139]

The question remains, however, whether more could have been done. For example, no formal resort was had to the United Nations prior to the United States bombing of North Vietnam.[140] It is likely that had this effort been made there would have been substantial obstacles in

135 Legal Adviser's *Memorandum*, 60 *Am. J. Int'l. L.* 565.

136 For the text of Ambassador Goldberg's letters to the President of the Council and the text of an American draft resolution see *Background Information* 271-73. See also Partan, *supra* note 32, at 303 n. 72.

137 See note 110.

138 See note 103.

139 See Secretary Rusk's summary at a news conference on June 18, 1965 of his review for the Cabinet of efforts to settle problems in Southeast Asia peacefully. 53 Dept. State Bull. 5-9 (1965). See also his statements at news conferences of February 25, 1965, and November 26, 1965 (*Background Information* 162-64, 258-60) and during hearings before the Senate Foreign Relations Committee in 1966 (*The Vietnam Hearings, supra* note 20, at 51-52).

140 For example, in answer to a question about taking the situation in South Vietnam to the United Nations as a threat to the peace, Secretary Rusk stated at a news conference on November 17, 1961: "I think there is a possibility that this question will come to the United Nations at some stage. I think at the present time we believe that the consultations with other governments in which we are now engaged and our consultations with the Government of south Viet-Nam would be the most immediate steps to be taken up." *Background Information* 90.

the way of full consideration of the Vietnam dispute. From mid-1960 through 1962 the United Nations was beset by the problems of the Congo and Katanga.[141] Subsequently there developed the budget and voting crises stemming from the costs of established peacekeeping operations.[142] Moreover, in the case of Laos, when the factions in the Laotian Government were at odds in 1959 and it was charged that North Vietnam had intervened across the border to support pro-Communist forces, the United Nations achieved only limited results. Against strong Soviet opposition the Security Council first dispatched an investigating subcommittee, and Secretary General Hammarskjöld later sent out a personal representative to report on developments.[143] But when civil war followed in 1960-1961 with increasing foreign participation, the United Nations' involvement proved ineffective,[144] and progress toward neutrality in the form of the 1962 Geneva Accords seems to have come from an understanding reached directly between President Kennedy and Chairman Khrushchev.[145]

The United States appears to have considered that formal resort to the United Nations would be unavailing. The likelihood of a Soviet veto, the opposition expressed by North Vietnam and Communist China to any so-called meddling by the United Nations in Vietnam, and the feeling of some members, at least, that the appropriate machinery was that of the Geneva Conference have all been cited as reasons why the dispute was not brought up officially.[146] In addition there seems to have been doubt whether the process of debate would be conducive to a settlement.[147]

[141] See the discussion in Boyd, *United Nations: Piety, Myth and Truth* 121-59 (Penguin Books 1964).

[142] *Id.*, at 183-84.

[143] *Id.*, at 113-15.

[144] Young, *supra* note 23, at 73.

[145] See statements by Secretary Rusk in 1965 (e.g., *Background Information* 258, 260; 53 Dept. State Bull. 6) and in 1966 (*The Vietnam Hearings, supra* note 20, at 51, 262-63). The Secretary also stated that in contrast to Laos, no understanding was reached on Vietnam.

[146] See statements by Secretary Rusk at news conferences in 1965 and during the 1966 hearings (53 Dept. State Bull. 9, 1011 [1965]; *The Vietnam Hearings, supra*, at 257-58). See also North Vietnam's denial of Security Council jurisdiction to consider the incidents in the Gulf of Tonkin in 1964 (Moore, Underwood, and McDougal, *supra* note 1, at 68), and Secretary General U Thant's statement, at a news conference on February 24, 1965, of the North Vietnamese and Chinese positions against action by the United Nations regarding Vietnam (*id.*, at 69).

[147] In a news conference on December 9, 1965 Secretary Rusk was asked about putting North Vietnam's aggression before the United Nations. He answered the question, in part, as follows:

. . . there is the question as to whether debate contributes toward a settlement. The

Despite these difficulties, however, there is no reason to conclude that an effort to bring the conflict to the United Nations would have had worse results. Certainly formal submission cannot guarantee progress, but the organization's lack of achievement to date regarding Vietnam is not necessarily a test of what might have happened if it had been called on before the bombing of North Vietnam started. When the United States moved on January 31, 1966 to submit the matter to the Security Council, our position was that as the possibilities offered by private consultation had been explored intensively during the bombing pause just ended, a barrier to formal discussion had been overcome. As Secretary Rusk put it at a news conference on January 31:

> . . . the principal problem was, can quiet diplomacy proceed more effectively than can be achieved through public debate? Now, that quiet diplomacy has been tested fully in the past several weeks. It will not be abandoned. But, nevertheless, there is not the same obstacle to a full discussion in the Security Council as was apparent, say, 4 or 5 weeks ago.[148]

It does appear that similar considerations could have brought submission of the dispute before 1965. At least since General Taylor's report of November 1961 the Government had given attention to the possible necessity of taking defensive measures directly against North Vietnam.[149] At some point during the intervening three years it would

---

theory of the United Nations Charter in article 33 is that debate is a drastic remedy. Positions get frozen. Public positions have to be taken that may get in the way of an exploration of a settlement.

Now, we don't object at all to this matter being considered in the United Nations. We don't object to any agency or instrument of the United Nations trying to find some way to bring this matter to a solution. But, as this matter has been discussed among delegates in New York, it seems to be their feeling that simply a harsh debate without any result at the end of it would not contribute toward a settlement of the problem. And that has always been the difficulty about taking it to the United Nations. 53 Dept. State Bull. 1011-12 (1965).

148 *Vietnam: The 38th Day* (Dept. of State Publication 8050, Far Eastern Series 144. reprinted from Dept. State Bull., Feb. 14, 1966).

149 During the 1966 hearings General Taylor quoted a portion of his 1961 report when testifying before the Senate Foreign Relations Committee about "the critical decisions in 1965 to introduce United States ground forces and to initiate the bombing campaign against military targets in the North":

Both of these courses of action had been under consideration at least since November, 1961, when I presented my report to President Kennedy following a visit to Saigon to appraise the growing criticality of the situation there.

We did not take either action at that time but my report contained the following comment with regard to the possible necessity of using air power against the source of the Viet Cong support in North Vietnam: I quote: "While we feel that the program

seem that public debate could have been sought in the United Nations without harming any private initiatives for settlement. And this approach would have been an alternative to ones which the United States rejected, such as General de Gaulle's proposal in 1963 for a neutral Vietnam,[150] a French call in 1964 for reconvening the Geneva Conference on Laos,[151] and a suggestion from Secretary General U Thant in 1964 for a secret meeting in Burma between representatives of North Vietnam and the United States.[152] In addition, settlement proposals put forward as a matter of public record at the United Nations could have dispelled various charges, based on comments of United States officials,[153] that the real aim of American policy was a military victory.

Events in Vietnam and elsewhere[154] demonstrate the need for prior

---

recommended represents those measures which should be taken now, I would not suggest that it is the final word. If the Hanoi decision is to continue the irregular war declared on South Vietnam in 1959 with continued infiltration and covert support of guerrilla bands in the territory of our ally, we will then have to decide whether to accept as legitimate the continued guidance, training, and support of a guerrilla war across an international boundary.

"Can we admit the establishment of the common law that the party attacked and his friends are denied the right to strike the source of the aggression after the fact that external aggression is clearly established?" *The Vietnam Hearings, supra* note 20, at 171-72.

[150] *Background Information* 14.

[151] *Id.,* at 16. The proposal was endorsed by the Soviet Union, Poland, Cambodia, India, and Communist China and was rejected by the United States and Britain.

[152] Staff of Senate Republican Policy Committee, *The War in Vietnam,* in 113 *Cong. Rec.* H 5242, H 5250 (daily ed. May 9, 1967). A proposal for negotiations by the Secretary General in March 1965 was at first rejected by the United States (*Background Information* 19), but it later changed its position. Subsequent efforts by Britain, Canada, the United States, and a number of non-aligned countries to bring about negotiations in 1965 were rejected by North Vietnam and Communist China (see the extracts from the British Government's publication, *Recent Exchanges Concerning Attempts to Promote a Negotiated Settlement of the Conflict in Viet-Nam* [Viet-Nam No. 3 [1965], Command Paper 2756], quoted in Moore, Underwood, and McDougal, *supra* note 1, at 194-203 n. 232).

[153] See statements of Secretary McNamara during the period 1962-1964 quoted in the House Republican Conference Committee report, *supra* note 31, at 22383-84, a White House statement on October 2, 1963 summarizing a report by Secretary McNamara and General Taylor (*Background Information* 110), a statement by General Harkins in the service newspaper *Stars and Stripes* on November 1, 1963, as quoted in the Senate Republican Committee report, *supra* note 152, at H 5248, and a message from President Johnson to General Minh dated December 31, 1963 (*Background Information* 114-15).

[154] In addition to charges by the U.A.R. against Saudi Arabia (*supra* note 60), recent news reports and commentaries have frequently mentioned alleged guerrilla forces in various countries which are said to be assisted or controlled by foreign states. Among the countries or territories involved are Venezuela, Bolivia, Colombia, Guatemala, Ethiopia, Kenya, Aden, Mexico, Burma, and South Korea. The foreign state charged in the first five instances is Cuba, together with the Sudan in the case of Ethiopia. See, e.g., *N.Y. Times*

efforts under Article 33 (1) before one state takes military measures against another allegedly controlling or assisting an insurgency in a third state. In such cases it would seem most desirable that resort to force in collective self-defense under Article 51, particularly when the conflict has developed over a period of years, be preceded by a history of maximum effort to resolve the problem peacefully through all available international arrangements, including the United Nations. A precedent of this sort would make Article 33 more effective.

(1967) Aug. 2, at 13; July 31, at 7; July 28, at 30; July 21, at 9; July 6, at 34; June 26, at 9; April 10, at 34; and regarding Ethiopia, *id.*, July 4, at 5; March 3, at 3. Kenya has blamed Somalia and the latter's alleged aid from the U.A.R. and the U.S.S.R. In this connection Kenya has circulated a warning to Somalia in the United Nations and in the Organization of African Unity (*N.Y. Times*, May 3 and 2, 1967, at 1 and 15, respectively). The British in Aden and elsewhere in the Federation of South Arabia have blamed revolutionaries from Yemen, with Egyptian support (see, e.g., *N.Y. Times*, May 14, 1967, at 2E). The People's Republic of China has been charged with aid to subversives in Mexico (*N.Y. Times*, July 23 and 20, 1967, at 8E and 1, respectively) and is said to be feared by the Burmese Government as a possible source of assistance to Burmese insurgents (*id.*, July 9, 1967, at 3E). North Korea is said to be attempting to create guerrilla warfare in South Korea (*N.Y. Times* [1967] July 5, at 1 and September 14, at 21).

Legal Aspects of the
Vietnam Conflict

DANIEL G. PARTAN*

Perhaps it is inevitable at this stage in history that governments of nation-states will formulate policy in areas perceived as vital to the national interest with little or no attention to the existing conception of international law or to the impact that their action will have on the development of international law. This may be the present reality, but it is not the only reality. It is also becoming apparent that human survival will require the subordination of short-range advantages by particular nation-states to the achievement of world order based on law. If this goal is to be reached, closer attention must be paid to the legal aspects of policy decisions especially as they relate to the formation of law for the future. In this spirit this paper explores what appear to the author to be the central international legal questions presented by the Vietnam conflict.

I. A Brief Look at History

The present conflict in Vietnam has its origins in over fifty years of French colonial rule in Indochina, and in the events that followed the close of the Second World War in Asia.

French control over the Indochinese peninsula began with military conquest which was initiated in the 1850's and was gradually extended over half a century to include all of what is now Laos, Cambodia and Vietnam.[1] In 1899 the French organized the area as the French Indo-Chinese Union, consisting of the French Protectorates of Laos and Cambodia, the French colony of Cochin-China in the Mekong Delta in southern Vietnam, and the French Protectorates of Annam in central Vietnam and Tonkin in northern Vietnam.[2] French rule was supplanted by the Japanese conquest in the 1940's, which ended only with the capitulation of the Japanese forces in 1945.

Meeting at the Potsdam Conference in 1945, the Big Three Powers, the United States, Great Britain and the Soviet Union, gave the task of receiving the Indochina territories from the defeated Japanese to Great Britain for the areas south of the 16th parallel and to the Republic of China for the areas north of that parallel. Meanwhile, the Vietminh (the "Viet Nam Doc-Lap Dong Minh Hoi," or League for

---

* Associate Professor of Law, Boston University, and Research Associate, Rule of Law Research Center, Duke University; LL.B., Harvard, 1958; LL.M., Harvard, 1961.

[1] See, e.g., Jumper & Normand, Vietnam, in Government and Politics of Southeast Asia 375 (2d ed. Kahin 1964).

[2] The constitutional history of the State of Vietnam is briefly stated in 1 Whiteman, Digest of International Law 284-91 (1963), and 2 id. at 234-38 (1963).

the Independence of Vietnam), led by Ho Chi Minh, proclaimed the independence of the Democratic Republic of Vietnam and established a government for all of Vietnam with its seat at Hanoi.[3]

The British, who had received control over southern Vietnam from the Japanese, rearmed the French and relinquished authority over the area to them. The Chinese, however, retained military control over the north and permitted the Vietminh to function as a de facto civil regime. On March 6, 1946, the French Government recognized the Republic of Vietnam "as a free state," but not as an independent state, and agreed with the Vietminh Government to enter into "friendly and frank negotiations" on the future status of Indochina.[4] The March 6 agreement provides that: "The French Government recognizes the Republic of Vietnam as a free state, having its Government, its Parliament, its army, and its finances, and forming part of the Indochinese Federation and the French Union."[5] Subsequent attempts to give particular content to the March 6 agreement through negotiations between the Vietminh regime and the French authorities were without success, the major barriers to agreement being the incorporation of the French colony of Cochin-China into the Republic of Vietnam and the degree of independence to be granted the Republic of Vietnam within the framework of the French Union.[6] By December 1946, major open hostilities had broken out and the French Indochinese War had begun, a war that was destined to end in military defeat for the French Union Forces at Dienbienphu and in political capitulation at the Geneva Conference of 1954.

Despite the continued conflict with the Vietminh, and despite their earlier agreement with the Vietminh, the French Government agreed on June 5, 1948, to recognize an independent "State of Vietnam" within the French Union with former Emperor Bao Dai as its head.[7] The State of Vietnam, consisting of the entire area of the former Tonkin and Annam Protectorates and the former Cochin-China colony, was recognized by

---

[3] See Declaration of Independence of the Democratic Republic of Vietnam, Sept. 2, 1945, 3 Ho Chi Minh, Selected Works 17-21 (1962), in Vietnam: History, Documents, and Opinions on a Major World Crisis 57-59 (Gettleman ed. 1965).

[4] See New Cycle in Asia: Selected Documents on Major International Developments in the Far East, 1943-1947, 169 (Isaacs ed. 1947).

[5] Ibid.

[6] See, e.g., Hammer, Indochina, in The State of Asia: A Contemporary Survey 240-67 (Rossinger & Associates eds. 1951) reprinted in Gettleman, op. cit. supra note 3, at 63-86.

[7] See 1 Whiteman, op. cit. supra note 2, at 284-86. Emperor Bao Dai had proclaimed the independence of Vietnam on March 11, 1942, during the Japanese occupation, id. at 284, but this proclamation was apparently superseded by the resumption of French control over South Vietnam and the French recognition of the Vietminh "Republic of Vietnam" on March 6, 1946. The June 5, 1948 Agreement between France and the "State of Vietnam" provided that France recognized "the independence of Viet-Nam, whose responsibility it will be to realize freely its unity." Id. at 285.

France as an independent state within the French Union by an agreement signed on March 8, 1949, by President Auriol for France and by Emperor Bao Dai for the State of Vietnam.[8] Thus constituted, the State of Vietnam was recognized by the United States on February 7, 1950, along with the Kingdoms of Laos and Cambodia, "as independent states within the French Union."[9] The United Kingdom issued a similar statement on the same day.[10] The Soviet Union recognized the Vietminh regime in North Vietnam as the Democratic Republic of Vietnam during the same year.[11] Each regime, that of Bao Dai's "State of Vietnam" in the south, and Ho Chi Minh's "Democratic Republic of Vietnam" in the north, claimed authority over the whole of Vietnam.

Emperor Bao Dai's government sought full independence for the State of Vietnam, however, and Franco-Vietnamese talks toward this end were begun at Paris in March 1954, just prior to the opening of the Indochina phase of the Geneva Conference. Basic French opposition to independence for Vietnam was overcome by the need for unity at the Geneva Conference, and on June 4, 1954, France and the State of Vietnam initialed two treaties intended to resolve the question of future relations between the State of Vietnam and the French Union. One treaty was to establish the State of Vietnam as a "fully independent and sovereign State," while the second was to transfer certain policy-making functions to the High Council of the French Union, "on a basis of sovereign equality."[12] These treaties were never signed, and consequently never entered into force. The State of Vietnam thus continued as an "independent state within the French Union" until agreements concluded after the close of the Geneva Conference transferred full sovereignty to an independent Vietnam thereafter termed the Republic of Vietnam.[13]

II. THE GENEVA AGREEMENTS

The armed conflict between the French Union forces and the Vietminh continued and broadened throughout the early 1950's. Each side

---

[8] Id. at 285-88. The agreement of March 8, 1949, embodied in an exchange of letters between Emperor Bao Dai and President Auriol, provided in part that: "The foreign policy of the French Union, within the framework of which Viet-Nam shall exercise its rights through its delegates to the High Council . . . shall be examined and coordinated under the direction and responsibility of the Government of the French Republic, by the High Council of the Union, on which the Government of Viet-Nam will be represented by delegates freely chosen by it." Id. at 286. See also Royal Institute of International Affairs, Documents on International Affairs, 1949-50, 596-608 (1953).

[9] 2 Whiteman, op. cit. supra note 2, at 235-36.

[10] Id. at 236

[11] See Gettleman, op. cit. supra note 3, at 50 n.6.

[12] Fall, Viet-Nam Witness 54 (1966). See 1 Whiteman, op. cit. supra note 2, at 289; 2 id. at 237.

[13] See note 27 infra.

sought and obtained money and arms from outside of Vietnam. The Vietminh, the Democratic Republic of Vietnam, received substantial support from the Communist Chinese after the defeat of the Republic of China and the expulsion of Chiang Kai-shek from mainland China.[14] The French Union forces and the State of Vietnam received over one billion dollars in military and economic aid from the United States during the same period.[15]

In February 1954, the Foreign Ministers of the United States, France, the United Kingdom and the Soviet Union met at Berlin and agreed to convene a conference at Geneva for the dual purpose of "reaching a peaceful settlement of the Korean question" and discussing "the problem of restoring peace in Indochina."[16] The Indochina phase of the Geneva Conference convened on May 8, 1954, the day after a key French military fortress at Dienbienphu had fallen to the Vietminh. In addition to the four major powers that had convened the conference, Laos, Cambodia, the Democratic Republic of Vietnam, the State of Vietnam, and the People's Republic of China were represented at this phase of the Geneva Conference.

The Geneva Conference concluded an Agreement on the Cessation of Hostilities in Vietnam, signed on July 20, 1954, on behalf of the Commander-in-Chief of the French Union Forces in Indochina for France and on behalf of the Commander-in-Chief of the People's Army in Vietnam for the Democratic Republic of Vietnam.[17] No other member of the Conference signed the Agreement on the Cessation of Hostilities in Vietnam.

The Geneva Conference also adopted a Final Declaration endorsing the main points of the Agreement on the Cessation of Hostilities in Vietnam.[18] The Final Declaration was not signed, but was accepted orally by Britain, France, the Soviet Union, the Chinese People's Republic and the Democratic Republic of Vietnam. The Final Declaration was not accepted by the United States or by the State of Vietnam. Instead, the United States made a unilateral declaration taking note of the Agreement and the Final Declaration and promising that, in accordance with its obligations under Article 2(4) of the United Na-

---

14 See, e.g., Address by Secretary of State Dulles before the Overseas Press Club, March 29, 1954, in 2 Dep't of State, American Foreign Policy, 1950-1955, 2373 (1957) (hereinafter cited as American Foreign Policy).

15 See Report of Senators Mansfield, Boggs, Pell and Smith to the Senate Foreign Relations Committee, 88th Cong. 1st Sess., Viet Nam and Southeast Asia (Comm. Print 1963). The Report states that "estimates of U.S. aid of all kinds to French Indochina through 1954 place the figure at about $1.2 billion." Id. at 3.

16 Plans for the Geneva Conference on Korea and Indochina: Quadripartite Communique of the Berlin Conference, Feb. 18, 1954, in 2 American Foreign Policy, note 14 supra, at 2372, 2373.

17 1 id. at 750-67. The agreement entered into force on July 22, 1954.

18 Id. at 785-87. The Final Declaration was adopted on July 21, 1954.

tions Charter, the United States would not use or threaten force "to disturb" these agreements, and declaring that the United States "would view any renewal of the aggression in violation of the aforesaid agreements with grave concern and as seriously threatening international peace and security."[19] The State of Vietnam refused to accept the Final Declaration, but declared that it would not use force to resist the cease-fire, and that it would "make and support every effort to re-establish a real and lasting peace in Vietnam."[20]

The key provisions of the Agreement on the Cessation of Hostilities in Vietnam, endorsed in the Final Declaration of the Geneva Conference, were as follows:[21]

1. The Agreement declares a complete and simultaneous cessation of hostilities throughout Vietnam, and a withdrawal of the opposing forces to either side of a "provisional military demarcation line," roughly fixed at the 17th parallel. (Agreement Arts. 1-15, Final Declaration paras. 1-2.) Article 1 provides that the French Union Forces "shall be regrouped" to the south of the provisional military demarcation line, and that the forces of the People's Army of Vietnam shall be regrouped to the north of that line.

2. The Agreement provides that no troop reinforcements or additional military personnel, or arms, munitions or war material may be introduced into either military regrouping zone in Vietnam. (Agreement Arts. 16-17, Final Declaration para. 4.)

3. The Agreement provides that no new military bases and no military base under the control of a foreign state may be established in either military regrouping zone in Vietnam. (Agreement Arts. 18-19, Final Declaration para. 5.)

4. The Agreement provides that neither of the two military regrouping zones shall adhere to any military alliance, and that neither shall be "used for the resumption of hostilities or to further an aggressive policy." (Agreement Art. 19, Final Declaration para. 5.)

5. An International Commission for Supervision and Control in Vietnam, consisting of Canada, India, and Poland, is established by the Agreement "for the control and supervision of the application of the provisions of the agreement. . . ." (Agreement

[19] Id. at 787-88. The United States declaration, as well as the cease-fire agreements and the Final Declaration of the Geneva Conference, are reprinted in Senate Foreign Relations Comm., 89th Cong. 1st Sess., Background Information Relating to Southeast Asia and Vietnam (Comm. Print 1965).

[20] The oral declarations by Britain, France, the Soviet Union, the Chinese People's Republic and the Democratic Republic of Vietnam accepting the Final Declaration, and by the United States and the State of Vietnam refusing to do so, are printed in Further Documents Relating to the Discussion of Indochina at the Geneva Conference, Cmd. No. 9239, Misc. no. 20 (1954) reprinted in Gettleman, op. cit. supra note 3, at 154-59.

[21] The quotations in the following paragraphs are taken from the text of the Agreement and the Final Declaration as printed in 1 American Foreign Policy, note 14 supra, at 750-67 and id. at 785-87.

Art. 34.) The parties shall give the International Commission "all possible assistance and cooperation." (Agreement Art. 25.)

6. "Pending the general elections which will bring about the unification of Viet-Nam, the conduct of civil administration in each regrouping zone shall be in the hands of the party whose forces are to be regrouped there in virtue of the present Agreement." (Agreement Art. 14(a), endorsed by the Final Declaration in para. 7.)

The Final Declaration of the Geneva Conference also explicitly recognized what was implicit in the establishment of military regrouping zones in the Agreement on the Cessation of Hostilities in Vietnam. Paragraph 6 of the Final Declaration states that:

The Conference recognizes that the essential purpose of the agreement relating to Viet-Nam is to settle military questions with a view to ending hostilities and that the military demarcation line is provisional and should not in any way be interpreted as constituting a political or territorial boundary.

In addition, with regard to free elections, paragraph 7 of the Final Declaration states that:

The Conference declares that, so far as Viet-Nam is concerned, the settlement of political problems, effected on the basis of respect for the principles of independence, unity and territorial integrity, shall permit the Viet-Namese people to enjoy the fundamental freedoms, guaranteed by democratic institutions established as a result of free general elections by secret ballot. In order to ensure that sufficient progress in the restoration of peace has been made, and that all the necessary conditions obtain for free expression of the national will, general elections shall be held in July 1956, under the supervision of an international commission composed of representatives of the Member States of the International Supervisory Commission, referred to in the agreement on the cessation of hostilities. Consultations will be held on this subject between the competent representative authorities of the two zones from 20 July 1955 onwards.

For their own part, the states adhering to the Final Declaration of the Geneva Conference undertook in paragraph 12 "to respect the sovereignty, the independence, the unity and the territorial integrity" of Vietnam as a whole, and to refrain from interfering in the internal affairs of Vietnam.

A subsequent "Geneva Agreement," the 1962 Declaration and Protocol on the Neutrality of Laos, is sometimes also referred to as part of the Geneva Agreements on Vietnam. The 1962 agreement was concluded at an International Conference on the Settlement of the Laotian Question, at which all of the Geneva Conference members, including both the Democratic Republic of Vietnam and the Republic of Vietnam, were represented, along with Burma, Thailand, and India, Canada and Poland as members of the International Commission for Supervision and Control in Laos, an entity that had been created by the 1954 Geneva Agreement on the Cessation of Hostilities in Laos parallel to the Commission created by the Agreement on the Cessation of Hostilities in Vietnam. Each of these governments signed the Declaration on the Neutrality of Laos, in which they pledged not to introduce troops or military personnel into Laos, and not to use Laotian territory for interference in the internal affairs of other countries. These obligations relate to the Vietnam conflict in view of the charges that North Vietnam continues to use the Ho Chi Minh trail through Laos to aid the National Liberation Front in South Vietnam, but of course that act would violate North Vietnamese obligations under the 1954 Geneva Agreements as well.

III. Violations of the Geneva Agreements

The agreements concluded at Geneva relating to Vietnam are, first, the Agreement on the Cessation of Hostilities in Vietnam, a treaty signed on behalf of the Commanders-in-Chief of the French Union forces and of the army of the Democratic Republic of Vietnam, and second, the Final Declaration of the Geneva Conference, a document that was not signed, but was accepted orally by representatives of all the members of the Geneva Conference except the United States and the State of Vietnam. The unilateral statements made by representatives of the latter two members have been quoted in the preceding section.

There is no longer any doubt that the events that have taken place in both North and South Vietnam would, when viewed apart from legal arguments that may be raised as to the effect of the Geneva Agreements, make out serious violations of those agreements on both sides of the "provisional military demarcation line." The territory in each "regrouping zone" is certainly being "used for the resumption of hostilities" against the other zone in violation of Article 19 of the Agreement on the Cessation of Hostilities in Vietnam. Substantial numbers of additional military personnel and amounts of arms, munitions and war material have been received in both North and South Vietnam contrary to Articles 16, 17 and 19 of the Agreement. In addition, free general elections have not been held to settle the future of all of Vietnam, as contemplated in Article 14(a) of the Agreement and in paragraph 7 of the Final Declaration. Furthermore, the present authorities in each zone, the "Democratic Republic of Vietnam" in the north and the "Republic of Vietnam" in the south, have each charged the other with "aggression" in violation of Article 19 of the Agreement.

The facts charged to constitute violations of the Geneva Agreements on both sides of the demarcation line are supported by the reports issued by the International Commission for Supervision and Control in Vietnam established by the Agreement on the Cessation of Hostilities in Vietnam. Although the Commission, which consists of representatives of India, Canada and Poland, has frequently been prevented from observing suspicious activities on the scene, it has been able to see enough over the past twelve years to come to firm conclusions as to violations in some instances.[22] In its 1962 report, the Commission stated:

> The Legal Committee [of the Commission] . . . with the Polish Member dissenting . . . has come to the conclusion that in specific instances there is evidence to show that armed and unarmed personnel, arms, munitions, and other supplies have been sent from the zone in the North to the zone in the South with the object of supporting, organizing, and carrying out hostile activities, including armed attacks, directed against the Armed Forces and Administration of the zone in the South. . . . [and that] there is evidence to show that the P.A.V. [People's Army of Vietnam] has allowed the zone in the North to be used for inciting, encouraging, and supporting hostile activities in the zone in the South, aimed at the overthrow of the Administration in the South. [These acts and activities are] in violation of Articles [10,] 19, 24, and 27 of the Agreement on the Cessation of Hostilities in Vietnam. . . .
>
> Taking all the facts into consideration, and basing itself on its own observations and authorized statements made in the United States of America and the Republic of Vietnam, the Commission concludes that the Republic of Vietnam has violated Articles 16 and 17 of the Geneva Agreement in receiving the increased military aid from the United States of America in the absence of any established credit in its favor. The Commission is also of the view that, though there may not be any formal military alliance between the Governments of the United States of America and the Republic of Vietnam, the establishment of a U.S. Military Assistance Command in South Vietnam, as well as the introduction of a large number of U.S. military personnel beyond the stated strength of the MAAG (Military Assistance Advisory Group), amounts to a factual military alliance, which is prohibited under Article 19 of the Geneva Agreement. . . .[23]

For the purpose of discussing the relevant legal issues in the sections that follow, the facts found by the International Commission for Supervision and Control in Vietnam, and certain other charges made by the parties to the Vietnam conflict, will be assumed to be accurate.

---

[22] The reports of the International Commission for Supervision and Control in Vietnam are regularly published by Great Britain in the Command Paper series. Very brief excerpts are reprinted in Gettleman, op. cit. supra note 3, at 166-90.

[23] 1962 Special Report of the International Commission for Supervision and Control in Vietnam, Vietnam no. 1, Cmnd. No. 1755. The quoted portions are from paras. 9 and 20, reprinted in Gettleman, op. cit. supra note 3, at 187-88.

IV. EFFECT OF VIOLATIONS OF THE GENEVA AGREEMENTS

Considering that the Republic of Vietnam is not a party to the Agreement on the Cessation of Hostilities in Vietnam, and did not accept the Final Declaration of the Geneva Conference, can the Republic of Vietnam be held to the obligations of these documents?

Article 27 of the Agreement is relevant here. That Article provides in part: "The signatories of the present Agreement and their successors in their functions shall be responsible for ensuring the observance and enforcement of the terms and provisions thereof."[24]

At the time of the Geneva Conference, the "State of Vietnam" existed under the 1949 agreement with France as an independent state within the French Union.[25] Along with the other "Associated States" of Laos and Cambodia, the State of Vietnam enjoyed considerable sovereign power over internal affairs, but was subject in foreign affairs to decisions of the High Council of the French Union. In other words, the final power of decision as to the international obligations of the State of Vietnam was the responsibility of the French Union rather than solely of the Government of the State of Vietnam.[26]

Subsequent to the Geneva Agreements, the French withdrew from Vietnam and transferred full control over the affairs of the State of Vietnam to that entity, which became the "Republic of Vietnam" on October 26, 1955.[27] This ultimate transfer was contemplated in the Geneva Agreements. The Final Declaration of the Geneva Conference took note of a French declaration that France "is ready to withdraw its troops from the territory of Cambodia, Laos and Viet-Nam, at the

---

[24] 1 American Foreign Policy, note 14 supra, at 761.

[25] See note 8 supra and accompanying text.

[26] Referring to the 1949 agreements between France and the State of Vietnam, quoted at note 8 supra, U.S. Assistant Legal Adviser Meeker wrote in 1950 that: "The foreign policy of Viet-Nam, it appears, is to be determined ultimately in the High Council of the French Union. The Government of Viet-Nam shall be represented in the High Council, but the agreement does not state in what manner the Council shall reach its decisions. Examination of the English and French texts of the March 8 agreement discloses that the Government of the French Republic will play a very important and perhaps predominant role in the operations of the High Council." 1 Whiteman, op. cit. supra note 2, at 287.

[27] France and the State of Vietnam initialed a pair of Franco-Vietnamese Treaties of Independence and Association on June 4, 1954, but these treaties were never signed and are not in force. Id. at 289. Later in the same year, after the adoption of the Geneva Agreements, France met with Cambodia, Laos and the State of Vietnam in a Quadripartite Conference at Paris, and concluded thirteen quadripartite agreements on Dec. 29, 1954, which were interpreted by the French delegation as making "the independence promised" to Cambodia, Laos and Vietnam "a reality." Id. at 290. In its brochure, Viet-Nam: The Struggle for Freedom (1964), the U.S. Department of State notes that "complete independence from France did not come to South Viet-Nam until well after the [Geneva] conference." Id. at 8. The State of Vietnam was proclaimed the Republic of Vietnam on Oct. 26, 1955, by President Ngo Dinh Diem following a referendum that deposed Bao Dai. See Senate Foreign Relations Comm., 89th Cong. 1st Sess., Background Information Relating to Southeast Asia and Vietnam 69 (Comm. Print 1965).

request of the governments concerned . . ." and that "the principle of respect for the independence and sovereignty, unity and territorial integrity of Cambodia, Laos and Viet-Nam" will guide France in efforts to achieve peace in the area.[28]

The Republic of Vietnam is now fully independent of France. Does this independence carry with it the responsibility of accepting and implementing the Geneva Agreements in South Vietnam, a responsibility that had been accepted for the area by France at a time when the French Union held ultimate responsibility for the international relations of the State of Vietnam?

There is no agreement on the extent to which a newly independent state, such as the Republic of Vietnam, must be regarded as bound by obligations accepted prior to independence by the state responsible for the conduct of its foreign relations. While it appears to be accepted that a successor state does not necessarily succeed to all the rights and duties of the predecessor state, Oppenheim's *International Law* comments that it would be "equally wrong to maintain that no succession whatever occurs," and concludes that "no general rule can be laid down concerning all the cases in which a succession takes place."[29] Lord McNair notes that there is very little judicial or arbitral authority, and that accordingly "we must rely to a greater extent than usual upon practice, and bear in mind that, while State practice is one of the main sources of international law . . . , it is only after a reasonably uniform practice of considerable duration that rules of law crystallize out."[30] McNair comments that:

> In this transitional period when new States are emerging every few months by reason of the fragmentation, peaceful or revolutionary, of old States, it is not possible, apart from the case of local obligations adhering to the territory passing from one sovereignty to another, to state with certitude that this or that rule of customary law has been evolved. . . .[31]

Thus, although treatise writers most often seek to express the results of their research in terms of general rules of international law in this area as in others, such statements must be regarded as less secure with respect to the law of state succession than may be true of other areas in international law.[32] Each case must be judged on its own merits and with full appreciation of all relevant interests.

---

28 Final Declaration of the Geneva Conference, paras. 10, 11, in 1 American Foreign Policy, note 14 supra, at 787.
29 1 Oppenheim, International Law 158 (8th ed. H. Lauterpacht 1955).
30 McNair, The Law of Treaties 591 (1961).
31 Id. at 591 n.1.
32 McNair, for example, comments that: "In spite of some evidence to the contrary, . . . it is submitted that the general principle is that newly established States

In the case of the Geneva Agreements, three points seem reasonably beyond controversy.[33] First, the provisions quoted from the Agreement on the Cessation of Hostilities in Vietnam and from the Final Declaration of the Geneva Conference demonstrate that the Conference understood that the French would be leaving Vietnam, and apparently contemplated that the provisions of these agreements could be carried out in South Vietnam by the successors to the French authorities. Second, the unilateral declaration by the State of Vietnam demonstrates that although the Saigon Government did not wish to accept the letter of the Geneva Agreements, it intended to accept the cease-fire and to cooperate with efforts to achieve a peaceful settlement.[34] Third, assuming that at the time of the Geneva Conference the French had the authority under international law to determine the international relations of the State of Vietnam,[35] the objections expressed by the Saigon Government ought not to suffice to relieve it of whatever obligation it might now have as a successor state to carry out arrangements made by the French. If protest alone could avoid responsibility, there would be little reality to the obligations of a successor state under international law.

The available records of the Geneva Conference contain no direct indications that France or the other members of the Conference intended to dictate terms to the Saigon Government, and in this sense it might be said that France was not acting explicitly to bind the State of Vietnam when it accepted the Geneva Agreements. The fact remains, however, that certain obligations assumed by France related to its conduct of the external relations of the State of Vietnam, and it is these

---

which do not result from a political dismemberment and cannot fairly be said to involve political continuity with any predecessor, start with a clean slate in the matter of treaty obligations. . . ." Id. at 601. See also O'Connell, The Law of State Succession 32 (1956), where it is said that: "A State which begins its life by breaking off from an older international person does so, speaking generally, unencumbered by treaty provisions, and with unfettered freedom to enter into whatever international agreements it considers appropriate. . . ."

[33] The comments made below apply equally to the Agreement on the Cessation of Hostilities in Vietnam and to the Final Declaration of the Geneva Conference. Although the latter was not signed, it was embodied in a written statement accepted orally for France by Mendes-France, then Prime Minister of France. As noted by the International Law Commission in its Commentary to Article 1 of its Draft Articles on the Law of Treaties, international law relating to validity, operation and effect of international agreements applies to all classes of agreements however embodied, and such juridical differences as exist "spring neither from the form, the appellation, nor any other outward characteristic of the instrument in which they are embodied: they spring exclusively from the content of the agreement, whatever its form." Report of the International Law Commission, U.N. Gen. Assem. Off. Rec. 17th Sess., Supp. No. 9, at 5 (A/5209) (1962).

[34] The statement by the representative of the State of Vietnam is cited at note 20 supra. See id. and accompanying text.

[35] The basis for this assumption is detailed in notes 8, 24 and 25 supra.

obligations that might be regarded as having passed to the Republic of Vietnam on its accession to full independence.

Considering that the purpose of the Geneva Agreements was to bring an end to hostilities so that the political future of the area could be decided by a process of self-determination through general elections, and that this purpose is in accord with the aims of the world community as expressed in the United Nations Charter,[36] it would make better sense to regard the obligations of the Geneva Agreements as the type of obligations that devolve upon successor states than to permit a successor state to avoid these obligations because it was not a party to the agreements. Under less compelling circumstances the International Court of Justice has indicated general agreement with the proposition that states emerging into independence are bound by treaty obligations undertaken on their behalf prior to independence.[37] There is no firm guidepost for predicting what an international tribunal might decide as to the obligation of the Republic of Vietnam to observe the Geneva Agreements, but the better view from the standpoint of world peace would be to regard a successor state in the position of the Republic of Vietnam as bound by arrangements of the type achieved at the Geneva Conference.

On the assumption that both the Democratic Republic of Vietnam and the Republic of Vietnam are bound by the Agreement on the Cessation of Hostilities in Vietnam and by the Final Declaration of the Geneva Conference, may either or both avoid their responsibilities under these agreements as a result of violations by the other side?

The draft articles on the law of treaties under preparation by the International Law Commission provide in Article 42(1) that: "A material breach of a bilateral treaty by one party entitles the other to invoke the breach as a ground for terminating the treaty or suspending its operation in whole or in part."[38] The concept of a "material breach" is defined in Article 42(3)(b) as the "violation of a provision which is essential to the effective execution of any of the objects or purposes of the treaty."[39]

Certainly many of the violations of the Geneva Agreements that

---

[36] See U.N. Charter art. 1, paras. 1, 2; art. 2, paras. 3, 4, 6.

[37] Case concerning Rights of Nationals of the United States of America in Morocco (France v. U.S.A.), [1952] I.C.J. Reports 176, 193, 217.

[38] Report of the International Law Commission, U.N. Gen. Assem. Off. Rec. 18th Sess., Supp. No. 9, at 16-17 (A/5509) (1963) (hereinafter cited as 1963 ILC Report). With regard to a "material breach" of a multilateral treaty, Draft Art. 42(2) would permit any other party to suspend the treaty in relations between itself and the defaulting state, but not to terminate the treaty unless all the other parties agree to take that step. Ibid.

[39] Id. at 17. The "unfounded repudiation of the treaty" is also a "material breach." Art. 42(3)(a). Ibid.

have taken place on both sides of the military demarcation line are "material breaches" in the sense described, but neither side has elected in terms to terminate the Agreements or to suspend their operation.[40] Article 51(1) of the International Law Commission's draft provides that a party alleging a ground for terminating or suspending the operation of a treaty "shall be bound to notify the other party or parties of its claim."[41] The notice required under Article 51(1) must indicate the grounds relied upon, the action contemplated, and a specified reasonable period for reply. If the claim is contested, the parties must seek a peaceful solution "through the means indicated in Article 33 of the Charter of the United Nations."[42] Article 51(5) provides, however, that the failure to give notice does not prevent a party from relying upon an alleged material breach "in answer to a demand for the performance of the treaty or to a complaint alleging a violation of the treaty."[43] The only relevant exception is the Article 47(b) provision that a party loses its right to rely upon an asserted material breach if after knowledge of the facts constituting the breach it so conducts itself "as to be debarred from denying that it has elected . . . to consider the treaty as unaffected by the material breach. . . ."[44]

The numerous statements made by both North and South Vietnam, and the acts engaged in by those governments, no doubt establish that neither party considers the Geneva Agreements "as unaffected" by the material breaches at least so far as temporary partial suspension of the terms of the agreements is concerned, but the statements do not appear to go so far as to claim suspension or termination of the agreements in their entirety.[45] In these circumstances perhaps the parties

---

[40] The Government of the Republic of Vietnam has stated that it "does not consider itself bound in any way by the Geneva Agreements which it did not sign." Embassy of Vietnam, Press and Information Service Vol. 1, no. 20, Aug. 19, 1955, in Gettleman, op. cit. supra note 3, at 194. In practice the Government of the Republic of Vietnam has carried out some of the obligations of the Geneva Agreements. For example, that government has co-operated to some extent with the International Commission for Supervision and Control in Vietnam. See, e.g., the Commission's Seventh Interim Report, Vietnam no. 2, Cmnd. No. 335 (1957). On Dec. 7, 1961, in a letter to President Kennedy, President Diem said South Vietnam had "honored the 1954 Geneva Agreements even though they resulted in the partition of our country" and had "publicly pledged that we will not violate the demarcation line . . . [and are prepared] to reunify Viet-Nam on the basis of democratic and truly free elections." 46 Dep't State Bull. 13-14 (No. 1175, Jan. 1, 1962).
[41] 1963 ILC Report, note 38 supra, at 26.
[42] U.N. Charter art. 33, para. 1 provides as follows: "The parties to any dispute, the continuance of which is likely to endanger the maintenance of international peace and security, shall, first of all, seek a solution by negotiation, enquiry, mediation, conciliation, arbitration, judicial settlement, resort to regional agencies or arrangements, or other peaceful means of their own choice."
[43] 1963 ILC Report, note 38 supra, at 26.
[44] Id. at 24.
[45] See, e.g., the statement cited in note 34 supra.

might be considered as debarred from electing at this date to rely upon the alleged breaches as justifying suspension or termination of the Geneva Agreements for the future. In this sense the parties might still be regarded as bound by the Geneva Agreements even though they would remain entitled to defend against particular claims relating to past conduct on the basis of material breaches alleged to have been committed by the other side.

This result is not explicitly called for by the International Law Commission's draft, but it would add to the salvage value of treaties like the Geneva Agreements when beset with claims and counterclaims of material breaches. The approach suggested here is also consistent with the claims presently made in the Vietnam situation. In its 1965 memorandum on the "Legal Basis for United States Actions Against North Vietnam" the United States commented that "a material breach of a treaty by one party entitles other parties at least to withhold compliance with an equivalent, corresponding or related provision until the other party is prepared to observe its obligations," and that:

> The extensive North Vietnamese violations [of the Geneva Agreements] certainly justify South Viet-Nam at least to withhold compliance with those provisions of the Accords which limit its ability to protect its very existence. Both South Viet-Nam and the United States have made clear that the actions which they have taken will no longer be necessary if North Viet-Nam would comply with the Accords.[46]

The International Law Commission has recognized that its draft could not deprive a party of the right to rely upon a material breach even though that party had failed to give notice of its claim as required by Article 51(1), but it also considered that:

> Some of the grounds upon which treaties may be considered invalid or terminated . . . if allowed to be arbitrarily asserted in the face of objection from the other party, would involve real danger for the security of treaties. These dangers were . . . particularly serious in regard to claims to denounce or withdraw from a treaty by reason of an alleged breach by the other party. . . . In order to minimize these dangers the Commission has sought to define as precisely and as objectively as possible the conditions under which the various grounds may be invoked. But whenever a party to a treaty invokes one of these grounds, the question whether or not its claim is justified will nearly always turn upon facts . . . which may be controversial. Accordingly, the Commission considered it essential

---

[46] The United States memorandum, issued by the Department of State on March 8, 1965, is reprinted in Senate Foreign Relations Comm., 89th Cong. 1st Sess., Background Information Relating to Southeast Asia and Vietnam 191 (Comm. Print 1965) (hereinafter cited as 1965 Legal Basis Memorandum). The quoted portions are from page 194.

that the present articles should contain procedural safeguards against the possibility that the nullity or termination of a treaty may be arbitrarily asserted . . . as a mere pretext for getting rid of an inconvenient obligation.[47]

In the Vietnam conflict, no doubt in common with any serious conflict involving the use of force, reciprocal claims of material breaches of relevant treaty provisions quite clearly "turn upon facts," which, to use the Commission's phrase, are highly controversial. For example, the United States has charged that:

> From the very beginning, the North Vietnamese violated the 1954 Geneva accords. Communist military forces and supplies were left in the South in violation of the accords. Other Communist guerrillas were moved north for further training and then were infiltrated into the South in violation of the accords. . . . As the Communist aggression intensified during 1961, . . . the United States found it necessary in late 1961 to increase substantially the numbers of our military personnel and the amounts and types of equipment introduced by this country into South Viet-Nam. . . . [T]he systematic violation of the Geneva accords by North Viet-Nam justified South Viet-Nam in suspending compliance with the provision controlling entry of foreign military personnel and military equipment.[48]

For its part, North Vietnam charges South Vietnam with an early material breach of the agreements in its refusal to consult with the North Vietnamese on the subject of general elections and to hold general elections in July 1956, as required by paragraph 7 of the Final Declaration of the Geneva Conference.[49] South Vietnam and the United States have responded to this claim by asserting that South Vietnam's actions "involved no breach of obligation" in that the "conditions in North Viet-Nam during that period were such as to make impossible any free and meaningful expression of popular will."[50]

Clearly no outside observer is equipped to decide between competing claims of this nature, and in the present state of the world community there is no regular means of securing an impartial judgment or of enforcing that judgment should it be rendered. There may be present possibilities for creating new international fact-finding procedures and

---

[47] 1963 ILC Report, note 38 supra, at 27 (Commentary to Article 51).

[48] U.S. Dep't of State, The Legality of United States Participation in the Defense of Viet-Nam, 54 Dep't State Bull. 474, 482-83 (No. 1396, March 28, 1966) (memorandum submitted to the Senate Committee on Foreign Relations, March 8, 1966, hereinafter cited as 1966 Legality Memorandum).

[49] Paragraph 7 of the Final Declaration is quoted in the text following note 21 supra.

[50] 1966 Legality Memorandum, note 48 supra, at 483. See, e.g., Preside t Diem's statement on elections in Vietnam, July 16, 1955, in Gettleman, note 3 supra, at 193-94.

institutions through the United Nations,[51] but until this development becomes a reality, the best that can be done is to attempt to preserve as much of contested agreements as possible in situations in which parties raise and dispute material breach claims. It is suggested that in the Vietnam context this might be done by noting past and present claims of material breaches of the Geneva Agreements, but regarding both sides as continuing to be bound by those agreements as far as may be possible today and in the future.

V. VIETNAM: TWO "STATES" OR ONE?

The Geneva Agreements clearly indicate that the separation of Vietnam into two military regrouping zones was intended to be temporary. Article 1 of the Agreement on the Cessation of Hostilities in Vietnam speaks of a "provisional military demarcation line" as the dividing line between North and South Vietnam. Article 14(a) entrusts the "civil administration in each regrouping zone" to "the party whose forces are to be regrouped there" pending "the general elections which will bring about the unification of Viet-Nam." Paragraphs 6 and 7 of the Final Declaration of the Geneva Conference, quoted in Part II above, endorse and strengthen this arrangement. Paragraph 6 states explicitly that "the military demarcation line is provisional and should not in any way be interpreted as constituting a political or territorial boundary." In paragraphs 11 and 12 of the Final Declaration the countries adhering to that Declaration specifically pledge to respect "the sovereignty, the independence, the *unity* and the territorial integrity" of the State of Vietnam considered explicitly as a single state.[52]

The United States did not endorse the Geneva Agreements, but it did pledge not to use force to disturb these agreements, and in making that declaration nothing was said to indicate that the United States rejected the Conference view that Vietnam consisted of a single state temporarily divided. In fact, the United States referred to Vietnam as one of the several "nations now divided against their will," as to which the United States would "continue to seek to achieve unity through free elections supervised by the United Nations."[53] Most recently, the

---

[51] See General Assembly Resolution 2104 (XX), adopted Dec. 20, 1965, on the question of methods of fact-finding; and the Secretary-General's study on Methods of Fact-Finding with respect to the execution of International Agreements, U.N. Doc. No. A/6228 (1966); see also Partan, Peaceful Settlement and the Cold War, 34 U. Cinc. L. Rev. 293, 321-24 (1965), reprinted as World Rule of Law Booklet No. 36.

[52] The Agreement on the Cessation of Hostilities in Vietnam and the Final Declaration of the Geneva Conference are quoted from 1 American Foreign Policy, note 14 supra, at 750-67, 785-87. The emphasis on "unity" in para. 12 of the Final Declaration is added.

[53] Id. at 788. The reference to elections supervised by the United Nations implicitly rejects the concept of para. 7 of the Final Declaration, which called for elec-

United States has in effect affirmed this view by stating that the Geneva Agreements "are an adequate basis for peace in Southeast Asia," and that the "question of reunification of Viet Nam should be determined by the Vietnamese through their own free decision."[54]

As to the Republic of Vietnam, the Saigon Government has not sought to repudiate the view that the entire area of Vietnam constitutes one state rather than two. To do so would mean a recognition of the partition, which the Saigon Government refused to do at Geneva, and at least an implicit recognition of the authority of Hanoi as the government of a separate state of North Vietnam. To the contrary, the position of the Republic of Vietnam has been that Hanoi is at most a de facto regime exercising control over North Vietnam by force, and that Vietnam remains a single state divided against its will.[55]

---

tions "under the supervision of an international commission composed of representatives of the Member States of the International Supervisory Commission" established by the Agreement on the Cessation of Hostilities in Vietnam, namely Canada, India and Poland. Id. at 786. The United States language was drawn from the "Potomac Charter" of June 29, 1954, in which the American President and the British Prime Minister stated "Common Principles of Anglo-American Policy" of world-wide application. Id. at 1707.

[54] Fourteen Points for Peace in Southeast Asia, Dep't of State, Press Release No. 4, Jan. 7, 1966, in 54 Dep't State Bull. 225 (No. 1390, Feb. 14, 1966). The statement was repeated by Secretary Rusk on Feb. 18, 1966, in his testimony before the Senate Foreign Relations Committee, in 54 Dep't State Bull. 346, 353-54 (No. 1393, March 7, 1966). The Secretary also spoke of the "systematic aggression by Hanoi against the people of South Vietnam" as being an "effort by a Communist regime in one half of a divided country to take over the people of the other half at the point of a gun and against their will." Id. at 352. Some United States statements appear to diverge from this view. For example, the State Department's 1965 "White Paper" entitled "Aggression from the North" charges Hanoi with setting out "deliberately to conquer a sovereign people in a neighboring state." Dep't of State, Aggression from the North 1 (1965). The Department's March 8, 1965 memorandum on the "Legal Basis for United States Actions Against North Viet-Nam," however, is careful to refer to Hanoi's "aggression . . . carried out across the internationally agreed demarcation line of 1954 between North and South Viet-Nam, and across international frontiers between Viet-Nam and Laos." 1965 Legal Basis Memorandum, note 46 supra, at 192-93. Note that the latter half of this statement clearly refers to "Viet-Nam" as a single state. The State Department's 1966 Legality Memorandum, note 48 supra, appears to move toward the top of the fence on this issue. The opening sentence asserts that U.S. action has been in response to requests from the Government of South Vietnam to assist "that country in defending itself against armed attack from the Communist North." Id. at 474. The Memorandum goes on to argue that "The right of Individual and Collective Self-Defense Applies Whether or Not South Viet-Nam Is Regarded as an Independent Sovereign State." Id. at 477-78. Referring to the "provisional military demarcation line" established at the 17th parallel by the Geneva Agreements, the Memorandum notes that this line "was intended to be temporary." Id. at 477. The Memorandum also points out that the Republic of Vietnam "has been recognized as a separate international entity by approximately 60 governments the world over," but draws no conclusion as to whether South Vietnam must now be regarded as an independent sovereign state. Ibid.

[55] See, e.g., the Saigon Government's 1955 statement that it hoped to achieve unity and freedom "by every means at its disposal resulting from the independence and sovereignty solemnly recognized by France toward the State of Vietnam which is the only legal State." Embassy of Vietnam, Press and Information Service Vol. 1, no. 20, Aug. 19, 1955, in Gettleman, op. cit. supra note 3, at 195.

The passage of time or the total repudiation of the Geneva Agreements might result in acceptance of two separate independent sovereign states in Vietnam, just as a change in the juridical view taken of the division of Germany, Korea or China would produce a similar result, but clearly more ought to be required to achieve this end than occasional, possibly ill-considered, remarks on the legal status of the two Vietnams.[56] If the balance of the Geneva Agreements is regarded as binding on both Vietnams as suggested in the preceding section, however, the choice between one independent sovereign state in Vietnam and two appears to have no significant legal impact on the self-defense argument discussed in Part VII below.

VI. STATUS OF THE NATIONAL LIBERATION FRONT

The origin, composition, direction and control of the Vietcong forces, or the National Liberation Front (NLF), is at the heart of the controversy between the Republic of Vietnam and the Democratic Republic of Vietnam. The United States has charged that:

> The North Vietnamese regime in Hanoi systematically created the Viet Cong Forces; it provides their equipment; it mounted the guerrilla war — and it controls that war from Hanoi on a day-to-day basis. . . .
> The National Liberation Front is not a political entity expressing the will of the people of South Viet-Nam—or any substantial element of the South Vietnamese population. It is a facade fabricated by the Hanoi regime to confuse the issue and elaborate the myth of an indigenous revolt. . . .
> To be sure the Viet Cong military forces include a number of indigenous Southerners under Northern control. Neither the United States nor the South Vietnamese government has ever questioned that fact. But the composition of the Viet Cong military forces is not the issue when one discusses the role of the Front. The issue is whether the Front has any color of claim as a political entity to represent these indigenous elements.
> The evidence makes clear that it does not. It is purely and simply a factitious organization created by Hanoi to reinforce a fiction. . . .[57]

No doubt the acts charged against Hanoi by the United States would constitute a violation of the Geneva Agreements.[58] Article 19 of the Agreement on the Cessation of Hostilities in Vietnam provides that neither zone in Vietnam shall be "used for the resumption of hostilities

---

[56] See note 54 supra. The sixty governments that have recognized South Vietnam "as a separate international entity" certainly cannot be said to have done so with intent to establish two separate independent sovereign states in Vietnam. The ambiguities and contradictions in United States statements illustrate the point.

[57] Address by United States Under Secretary of State Ball, The Issue in Viet-Nam, delivered at Northwestern University, Jan. 30, 1966, in 54 Dep't State Bull. 239, 241-43 (No. 1390, Feb. 14, 1966).

[58] See, e.g., note 23 supra and accompanying text.

or to further an aggressive policy."[59] The Democratic Republic of Vietnam has charged the Saigon Government with numerous violations of the Geneva Agreements, and in particular with a failure to implement the provisions relating to elections. It has also charged that the United States assistance to South Vietnam constitutes "aggression," but Hanoi has not sought to suspend or to terminate the Geneva Agreements on this basis. As explained in Part IV above, Hanoi must therefore still be regarded as bound by these agreements. If the United States charges are accurate, therefore, there is reason to consider that the National Liberation Front, having been created by Hanoi in violation of the Geneva Agreements, is an illegal organization that ought to be accorded no standing in international law.

If, on the other hand, the National Liberation Front is in truth an indigenous South Vietnamese group, established, directed and controlled by South Vietnamese rebels, what would be its standing in international law? There is no doubt that, whatever the origin of the National Liberation Front, it has received and is receiving tangible military assistance from North Vietnam. There is also no doubt that any aid of this kind would violate the Geneva Agreements, but the mere existence of illegal outside assistance, and consequently of violations of the Geneva Agreements by North Vietnam, would not deprive the National Liberation Front of whatever standing it might otherwise have in international law.

Considering the National Liberation Front as indigenous to South Vietnam, the conflict in South Vietnam would then clearly be a civil war between the NLF and the Saigon Government. This would be true whether Vietnam is considered as a single state temporarily divided against its will, as suggested in Part V above, or as two separate states. If Vietnam is a unitary state, the civil war consists in a battle between opposing South Vietnamese factions for control of the southern regrouping zone; if Vietnam has become two distinct states, the civil war is simply a battle for control of one of them. In either case, however, the Geneva Agreements would bar aid by North Vietnam to the National Liberation Front. So long as the Geneva Agreements remain in force, Article 24 of the Agreement on the Cessation of Hostilities in Vietnam clearly forbids such intervention through its provision directing that the "armed forces of each party shall respect . . . the territory under the military control of the other party, and shall commit no act and undertake no operation against the other party. . . ."[60]

Considered as an indigenous rebel group fighting a civil war in South

---

[59] 1 American Foreign Policy, note 14 supra, at 759.
[60] Id. at 761.

Vietnam, the National Liberation Front might be recognized as a "belligerent" in international law. Oppenheim's *International Law* states:

> The principles governing recognition of belligerency are essentially the same as those relating to the recognition of States and Governments. Certain conditions of fact, not stigmatised as unlawful by International Law—the Law of Nations does not treat civil war as illegal—create for other States the right and the duty to grant recognition of belligerency. These conditions of fact are: the existence of a civil war accompanied by a state of general hostilities; occupation and a measure of orderly administration of a substantial part of national territory by the insurgents; observance of the rules of warfare on the part of the insurgent forces acting under a responsible authority; the practical necessity for third States to define their attitude to the civil war.[61]

There is no unanimity as to whether the status of a rebel group as "belligerents" must be recognized if the above conditions are satisfied. Oppenheim comments that refusal to recognize belligerent status under these conditions "must be deemed contrary to sound principle and precedent,"[62] but it is acknowledged that many writers consider the recognition of belligerency in relation to insurgents to be "an act of unfettered political discretion."[63] In accord with the latter view, no government would be obliged to recognize the National Liberation Front as a belligerent no matter how solid its credentials under the quoted criteria.

Even if the National Liberation Front were to be recognized as a belligerent by some governments, as for example by Hanoi, Peking and Moscow, the fact of such recognition would not alter the restrictions on intervention accepted by Hanoi in the Geneva Agreements. Recognition of belligerency would no doubt be regarded by the Saigon Government as an unfriendly and hostile act, but so long as the conditions of such recognition are satisfied, Saigon would have no basis for protest.

The broader question of a duty not to intervene in civil wars, discussed in the next section, is not affected by recognition of belligerency. Belligerents in war have traditionally been regarded as having certain rights and duties derived from their status as belligerents,[64] rights and duties that do not arise until a rebellion is acknowledged to satisfy the

---

[61] 2 Oppenheim, International Law 249 (7th ed. H. Lauterpacht 1952) (footnotes omitted). The "practical necessity" referred to in the quoted language means that third-party states may not act until the civil war has a direct impact on them requiring them to take some official view of it, as where rebel vessels seek to interfere with shipping. Oppenheim comments that without this requirement, "recognition of belligerency might be open to abuse for the purpose of a gratuitous manifestation of sympathy with the cause of the insurgents." Id. at 249-50.

[62] Id. at 250 (footnotes omitted).

[63] Id. at 250 n.2.

[64] See, e.g., id. at 673-84.

requirements set out above. Prior to recognition as belligerents, however, a rebel group that satisfies the factual criteria set out above is generally classed as an "insurgent" group entitled to demand that outside states refrain from assisting the incumbent government. Insofar as it applies to the Vietnam conflict, the rule against intervention would also bar aid to the NLF considered as a rebel group, regardless of whether the NLF is classed as an "insurgent" or as a "belligerent."

VII. External Assistance:
"Aggression" or "Collective Self-Defense"?

There is no longer any doubt that each of the immediate parties to the conflict in South Vietnam, the National Liberation Front and the Government of South Vietnam, is receiving substantial military assistance in men, money and arms from outside of South Vietnam. There is also no doubt that considered alone, the acts of giving and of receiving such assistance would violate the Geneva Agreements in so far as they apply to the Democratic Republic of Vietnam and to the Republic of Vietnam.

North Vietnam has argued, however, that the National Liberation Front is the "sole genuine representative of the people of South Vietnam" and that the Saigon Government is but the "creation" and the "lackey" of the United States.[65] North Vietnam's position, therefore, appears to be that any aid given by it to the National Liberation Front is aid to the legitimate authority in South Vietnam, and that by this token the aid would not amount to a resumption of hostilities in violation of the Geneva Agreements. Furthermore, Hanoi argues that the United States is guilty of "aggression" against the Vietnamese people by its aid to South Vietnam. Hanoi has stated:

Vietnam is one, the Vietnamese people are one. The U.S. imperialists having encroached on the territory of the Vietnamese Fatherland, every Vietnamese is duty bound to fight against them for national salvation. . . . [The U.S. authorities] have seriously violated the 1954 Geneva Agreements on Vietnam, grossly trampled underfoot international law, and committed monstrous crimes against the Vietnamese people.[66]

Perhaps North Vietnam might claim on the basis of the asserted violations of the Geneva Agreements in the south, including the central charge against the Saigon Government that it prevented the free elections called for by the Geneva Agreements, that the violations were

---

[65] See, e.g., Memorandum of the Democratic Republic of Vietnam, Sept. 1965, in 1 Viet-Report, no. 3, Oct. 1965, p. 13. The quoted language is from p. 13, col. 2, and p. 14, col. 3.

[66] Id. at p. 13, cols. 2-3. Compare the claim made by the Saigon Government quoted in note 55 supra.

material violations which entitle Hanoi to suspend or terminate the Geneva Agreements. Hanoi does not appear to have raised this argument, however. In the same document quoted above, Hanoi goes on to state that the "1954 Geneva Agreements are an international legal document which all participants must respect and correctly implement."[67] Not having sought to avoid the effects of the Geneva Agreements, Hanoi remains bound by them,[68] and the question is presented of whether the charges levied by Hanoi as to "aggression" by the United States and as to the character of the Saigon Government would, if true, entitle the Hanoi Government to come to the assistance of the National Liberation Front.

An identical question is presented when the Vietnam conflict is viewed from the other side. As has been noted, Saigon and the United States charge that the National Liberation Front is organized, directed and controlled by Hanoi.[69] In other words, to use Hanoi's language, the charge is that the NLF is the "creation" and the "lackey" of the Democratic Republic of Vietnam. In addition, the United States and South Vietnam charge Hanoi with "aggression." The United States "White Paper" published in 1965, entitled *Aggression from the North: The Record of North Viet-Nam's Campaign To Conquer South Viet-Nam,* states:

> South Viet-Nam is fighting for its life against a brutal campaign of terror and armed attack inspired, directed, supplied, and controlled by the Communist regime in Hanoi. This flagrant aggression has been going on for years. . . .
> Above all, the war in Viet-Nam is *not* a spontaneous and local rebellion against the established government. . . .
> In Viet-Nam a Communist government has set out deliberately to conquer a sovereign people in a neighboring state. And to achieve its end, it has used every resource of its own government to carry out its carefully planned program of concealed aggression.[70]

The parallel charges of "aggression" and creation of puppet regimes levied by each side against the other each present the same basic question of the extent to which an outside government is entitled to come to the aid of its ally, termed the "legitimate" authority in South Vietnam, against the illegal intervention by the other side. As with the controversy over the facts underlying charges of violations of the Geneva Agreements, there presently exists no institution competent to resolve these inconsistent claims, and the most that can be done is to consider the impact

---

[67] Id. at p. 14, col. 3.
[68] See Part IV supra.
[69] See Part VI supra.
[70] U.S. Dep't of State, Aggression from the North 1 (1965) (emphasis in the original). See also note 54 supra.

of the view of international law implicit in the claims that have been made.

The United States has argued that international law permits a victim of armed aggression "to defend itself and to organize a collective self-defense effort in which others who are willing may join."[71] This right, in the United States' view, is recognized in Article 51 of the United Nations Charter, which provides that:

> Nothing in the present Charter shall impair the inherent right of individual or collective self-defense if an armed attack occurs against a Member of the United Nations, until the Security Council has taken measures necessary to maintain international peace and security.

Consistent with its view that U.S. assistance to South Vietnam is part of a collective self-defense effort, the United States has, from time to time, reported to the Security Council on the measures taken for the defense of South Vietnam as required by the second sentence of Article 51.[72] Most recently the United States has requested the Security Council to meet to consider the situation in Vietnam and has submitted a draft resolution to the Council, but no action has been taken by the Council.[73]

In contrast to Article 51 of the Charter, Article 2(4) provides as follows: "All Members shall refrain in their international relations from the threat or use of force against the territorial integrity or political independence of any state, or in any other manner inconsistent with the Purposes of the United Nations." In the United States' view, Article 2(4) is not a barrier to United States assistance to South Vietnam for the following reasons:

> In the first place, it is plain that the use of force against territorial integrity and political independence has been initiated by North Viet-Nam and not by anyone else. Secondly, paragraph 4 of Article 2 of the Charter does not place an absolute prohibition on the use of force. It permits the use of force in a manner consistent

---

[71] 1965 Legal Basis Memorandum, note 46 supra, at 193. The 1966 Legality Memorandum, note 48 supra, is founded on much the same point, asserting at the outset that: "International law has long recognized the right of individual and collective self-defense against armed attack. South Viet-Nam and the United States are engaging in such collective self-defense consistently with international law and with United States obligations under the United Nations Charter." Id. at 474.

[72] See, e.g., Statement by the United States Ambassador in the Security Council, Aug. 5, 1964, in 51 Dep't State Bull. 272 (No. 1313, Aug. 24, 1964) (relating to the measures taken by the United States in response to attacks on U.S. vessels in the Gulf of Tonkin); Letter from the U.S. Ambassador to the President of the Security Council, Feb. 7, 1965, in 52 Dep't State Bull. 240 (No. 1339, Feb. 22, 1965) (relating to United States and South Vietnamese air action against North Vietnam).

[73] See Letters from the U.S. Ambassador to the President of the Security Council, Jan. 31, 1966, in 54 Dep't State Bull. 229, 231 (No. 1390, Feb. 14, 1966); see also Part IX infra.

with the purposes and principles of the Charter. Moreover, the Charter itself specifically provides for the use of force in certain circumstances—action through the United Nations itself, action through regional arrangements, and action in self-defense. The actions of the United States and the Republic of Viet-Nam, being defensive in character and designed to resist armed aggression, are wholly consistent with the purposes and principles of the Charter and specifically with Article 2, paragraph 4.[74]

To the extent that one accepts the factual conclusions drawn in its favor by the United States on the one hand, or by the Democratic Republic of Vietnam on the other, namely that the aid given by each to its ally in South Vietnam is aid to a legitimate government to assist it in self-defense against armed aggression from outside of South Vietnam, there is today little doubt that the legal conclusions sought to be drawn are accurate.

Some have argued that Article 51 of the United Nations Charter defines the right to use force in self-defense in the post-charter world in the sense of limiting that right to cases of "armed attack."[75] Even accepting that concept, the accuracy of which is far from clear,[76] the test certainly has been satisfied in South Vietnam on the facts as stated by either the United States or by the Democratic Republic of Vietnam. Whatever "armed attack" might mean under other circumstances, it

---

[74] 1965 Legal Basis Memorandum, note 46 supra, at 193. The 1966 Legality Memorandum, note 48 supra, being focused on the claim that United States participation is based on the right of collective self-defense against armed attack, simply points out that U.N. Charter art. 51 expressly states that the remaining provisions of the Charter "in no way diminish the inherent right of self-defense against armed attack." Id. at 475. The 1966 Legality Memorandum also asserts that "action taken in defense against armed attack cannot be characterized as falling within" the proscription of art. 2, para. 4, because the record of the San Francisco Conference at which the U.N. Charter was drafted makes clear that the provision "was not intended to restrict the right of self-defense against armed attack." Id. at 477. In support of this proposition, the memorandum cites the Report of Rapporteur of Committee 1 to Commission I of the San Francisco Conference, 6 U.N. Conf. Int'l Org. Docs. 446, 459 (1945), in which it is stated that despite art. 2, para. 4, "the use of arms in legitimate self-defense remains admitted and unimpaired."

[75] See, e.g., Henkin, Force, Intervention, and Neutrality in Contemporary International Law, 1963 Proceedings of the Am. Soc. of Int'l Law 147, 150-52; Jessup, A Modern Law of Nations 165-67 (1947). Even if art. 51 is to operate as a definition of the post-Charter right to use force in self-defense, that right might more accurately be cast in terms of "armed aggression," which is the phrase used in the equally authentic French text of the Charter, than in terms of "armed attack." See Partan, The Cuban Quarantine: Some Implications of Self-Defense, 1963 Duke L.J. 696, 698 n.8, reprinted as World Rule of Law Booklet No. 24.

[76] The 1966 Legality Memorandum, note 48 supra, for example, in common with many other official United States statements, speaks of art. 51 as referring to, rather than defining, the inherent right of self-defense. The memorandum notes that "article 51 restates and preserves, for member states in the situations covered by the article, a long-recognized principle of international law," id. at 475, and that "article 51 does not impose restrictions or cut down the otherwise available rights of United Nations members." Id. at 476. See also Partan, note 75 supra, at 696-700.

certainly ought to include open military assault on a legitimate government on its own territory by large numbers of foreign troops regardless of whether the foreign troops cross openly or clandestinely into that territory, and regardless of whether the foreign troops cross an international boundary or a military demarcation line.[77] In South Vietnam each side charges the other with a continuing program of armed aggression involving armed attack against the legitimate authority in South Vietnam; in these circumstances the right to use force in self-defense turns on the accuracy of the factual allegations rather than the accuracy of the legal conclusions.[78]

On the assumption that the facts alleged on either side establish the right to use force in self-defense, it has also been argued that nevertheless this right does not justify receipt of aid from the outside unless both the recipient and the donor are properly members of a regional collective security pact within the meaning of Chapter VIII of the United Nations Charter.[79] As applied to U.N. Members, it is difficult to agree that by accepting the Charter by implication they relinquished this aspect of their international law right to use force in self-defense;[80]

---

[77] The 1965 Legal Basis Memorandum, note 46 supra, argues that "what began as covert and indirect aggression has become open armed aggression" and that this "adds up to open armed attack within the meaning of Article 51." Id. at 192-93. The 1966 Legality Memorandum, note 48 supra, charges that "by the end of 1964, North Viet-Nam may well have moved over 40,000 armed and unarmed guerrillas into South Viet-Nam," id. at 474, and that more recently "Hanoi has begun to infiltrate elements of the North Vietnamese army" into South Vietnam, and that "there is evidence that nine regiments of regular North Vietnamese forces are fighting in organized units in the South." Id. at 475. The memorandum then concludes that: "In these circumstances, an 'armed attack' is not as easily fixed by date and hour as in the case of traditional warfare. However, the infiltration of thousands of armed men clearly constitutes an 'armed attack' under any reasonable definition." Ibid.

[78] As regards Hanoi, the "aggression" would be unlawful under the Geneva Agreements and also under the United Nations Charter. U.N. Charter art. 2, para. 6 provides that the U.N. "shall ensure that states which are not Members of the United Nations act in accordance with these [United Nations] Principles so far as may be necessary for the maintenance of international peace and security." Even if, as has been argued, Vietnam constitutes one state rather than two, so that the border between the north and the south remains a military demarcation line rather than an international boundary, Hanoi's violation of that line would threaten international peace due to the concern that the member states of the Geneva Conference have in the stability of the settlement reached at that conference. The word "states" in art. 2, para. 6 should no doubt receive a broad enough interpretation so as to effectuate the purpose of the article in the case of states now divided against their will, and would no doubt include both North and South Vietnam for this purpose, without disturbing the general understanding that Vietnam is a unitary state. As regards the United States, the "aggression" charged would of course be contrary to U.N. Charter art. 2, para. 4, quoted in the text above.

[79] See Memorandum of Law Prepared by the Lawyers Committee on American Policy Towards Vietnam, entitled American Policy vis-à-vis Vietnam, at 6-7. See also Part VIII infra.

[80] The 1966 Legality Memorandum, note 48 supra, points out that the argument that collective self-defense may be exercised only by Chapter VIII organizations

but as applied to non-Members, such as Vietnam, there can be no basis for the argument. Article 2(6) of the Charter is an effort to apply Charter principles, including the principle stated in Article 2(4), to non-Members, but nothing in the Charter purports to apply the asserted limits under Chapter VIII to non-Members.[81]

The discussion up to this point has rested on the assumption that the facts as charged by Hanoi, or alternatively, the facts as charged by Saigon and by the United States, are accurate. The conclusion on these facts is that "self-defense" is an adequate basis for receipt of aid from the outside.[82] This conclusion of course rests upon the corresponding assumption that in each case the government supplying men, money and arms to its puppet government in South Vietnam is guilty of "armed aggression," which would violate the United Nations Charter and the Geneva Agreements in the case of Hanoi, and the United Nations Charter in the case of the United States.[83]

There is a third possibility. The truth may be that the National Liberation Front is neither the "sole genuine representative of the people of South Vietnam" as maintained by Hanoi, nor "a factitious organization created by Hanoi to reinforce a fiction" as charged by the

---

"ignores the structure of the charter and the practice followed in the more than 20 years since the founding of the United Nations." Id. at 478. Although the "practice" referred to is controversial, in that not all U.N. Members have accepted the concept of NATO and SEATO being "collective self-defense organizations" under art. 51 rather than regional organizations under Chapter VIII, the fact remains that by its terms and in the understanding of most U.N. Members art. 51 is a "savings clause" rather than an affirmative definition of the right to use force in self-defense. See id. at 475; note 76 supra.

[81] U.N. Charter art. 2, para. 6 is quoted in note 78 supra. The Lawyers Committee memorandum, note 79 supra, also argues that since Saigon is not a Member of the United Nations, and since "South Vietnam is merely a temporary zone not even qualifying politically as a state . . . , even if it be assumed that an 'armed attack' . . . has occurred against South Vietnam . . . neither the right of individual self-defense nor the right of collective self-defense can become operative." Id. at 5. The assumption that only "states" that are Members of the United Nations are entitled in international law to defend themselves against outside armed aggression could not possibly be founded on U.N. Charter art. 2, para. 6 which relates only to maintaining international peace by imposing U.N. principles on non-Members. Such a principle could certainly also not be part of customary international law, which is based on the equality of states. As to the status of South Vietnam, as contemplated by the Geneva Agreements, it is not a "state" but it is still a defined and recognized zone with rights and obligations under the Geneva Agreements. One of these rights, derived at least from the duty of North Vietnam to commit no act against the south under Article 24 of the Agreement on the Cessation of Hostilities in Vietnam, is certainly to protect its character as an independent zone against outside armed aggression. Certainly nothing in either the U.N. Charter or the Geneva Agreements would deny this right. See also the 1966 Legality Memorandum, note 48 supra, at 476-78.

[82] The right to receive aid from the outside in self-defense against armed aggression from the outside would be limited by the general international law limit on the use of force in self-defense that the force used be necessary in the circumstances and proportional to the danger. These limits are discussed at the close of this section.

[83] See note 78 supra.

United States.[84] The NLF may be a truly indigenous South Vietnamese rebel group seeking to overthrow the Government of South Vietnam. On this assumption, would aid either by Hanoi to the NLF or by the United States to Saigon be lawful?

As has been argued,[85] Hanoi remains bound by the Geneva Agreements despite their asserted violation by the Saigon Government. The Saigon Government also remains bound by these agreements, so that on the basis of the Geneva Agreements both the grant of aid by Hanoi to the NLF and the receipt of aid by Saigon from the United States would be unlawful.[86]

As to the "self-defense" argument, would either Saigon or the NLF be entitled to receive outside assistance in defense either against its opponent or against the aid illegally received by its opponent from the outside?

It has frequently been asserted that bona fide civil war situations result in a duty of non-intervention for third-party states.[87] Civil war is not unlawful under the Charter of the United Nations, but civil wars may threaten international peace through pressure for external intervention on both sides.[88] In these circumstances the United Nations would have the authority to intervene under Chapter VII of the Charter,[89] but Article 2(4) would condemn unilateral intervention by any individual state.[90]

Given unlawful intervention on behalf of one side in a civil war, however, may the other side then seek external aid in self-defense? This should certainly be true on the part of the government which would then

---

[84] See notes 57 and 65 supra and accompanying text.

[85] See Part IV supra.

[86] The legal limits as regards the United States derive from the U.N. Charter since the United States cannot be held to the Geneva Agreements.

[87] Falk comments that under traditional international law: "A presumption in favor of stability in the world allows foreign states to intervene on behalf of the incumbent in the situation of mere rebellion. However, if the intrastate conflict is sustained in time and place, it becomes interventionary, according to the traditional theory, to help either faction." Falk, Janus Tormented: The International Law of Internal War, in International Aspects of Civil Strife 185, 206 (Rosenau ed. 1964). See also notes 61 and 64 supra and accompanying text.

[88] One recent example is the breakdown of law and order in the Republic of the Congo, illustrating both the potential and the problems of meeting the threat to international peace of foreign involvement in civil wars through United Nations intervention. See, e.g., Gordon, The United Nations in the Congo (1962); The Role of the United Nations in the Congo (Tondel ed. 1963).

[89] See, e.g., Partan, supra note 51, at 332-34.

[90] General Assembly Resolution 2131 (XX), adopted on Dec. 21, 1965, by 109 votes in favor, to none against, with only the United Kingdom abstaining, states that "direct intervention, subversion, as well as all forms of indirect intervention are contrary" to United Nations principles and are, "consequently, a violation of the Charter." The Assembly therefore declared that "no State shall organize, assist, foment, finance, incite or tolerate subversive, terrorist or armed activities directed to the violent overthrow of the regime of another State, or interfere in civil strife in another State. . . ."

be faced in some measure with an "armed attack" from the outside.[91] It should also be true for the rebel group, at least once it attains the status of an "insurgent" or of a "belligerent" in international law, for it would then be, in effect, a government exercising control over people and territory just as any other government.[92] Any other rule would, in effect, tend to outlaw civil war by weighting the scales in favor of the incumbent government.

Where outside intervention has occurred in a bona fide civil war, however, it will be almost impossible in practice to separate the "unlawful intervention" from the "legitimate collective self-defense." The better result if it were possible, therefore, would be to regard both interventions as unlawful. Under the United Nations Charter as it now stands, however, it would not be possible to reach this result for it would involve an additional restriction on the right to use effective force in self-defense.

Acknowledging the right of legitimate governments to receive outside aid to defend against outside armed aggression, or the right both of the incumbent government and the bona fide rebel group to receive outside aid in a civil war situation to defend against outside aid illegally given to its opponent, there remains the question of limits on such aid viewed in the context of self-defense. There is general agreement that even when force may be used in self-defense under international law, the force actually used must be limited to the force necessary to accomplish the lawful result.[93] In the case of outside aid to defend against unlawful assistance to one side in a civil war, presumably the lawful aid must be limited to that found necessary to offset the unlawful aid. Since in cases such as the Vietnam conflict each side will be claiming that the other's aid is unlawful, however, there is no objective stopping point, and there is no longer any reality to the hope that rules of law will effectively determine the actions of the governments involved.

In these circumstances, little would be added by attempting to determine whether United States bombing of North Vietnam,[94] or North

---

[91] See notes 75 and 76 supra.

[92] See notes 61 and 64 supra and accompanying text.

[93] See, e.g., Brierly, The Law of Nations 406 (6th ed. Waldock 1963), quoting Webster's famous comment in the Caroline case, 2 Moore, Digest of International Law 412 (1906), that the "necessity of self-defense" must be "instant, overwhelming, leaving no choice of means and no moment for deliberation" and that the action taken must not be "unreasonable or excessive, since the act justified by the necessity of self-defense must be limited by that necessity and kept clearly within it."

[94] Secretary Rusk spoke of the bombing as follows: "In resisting the aggression against it, the Republic of Viet-Nam is exercising its right of self-defense. It called upon us and other states for assistance. And in the exercise of the right of collective self-defense under the United Nations Charter, we and other nations are providing such assistance. . . . Our assistance has been increased because the aggression from the North has been augmented. Our assistance now encompasses the bombing of North Viet-Nam. The bombing is designed to interdict, as far as possible, and to inhibit, as far as may be necessary, continued aggression against the Republic of Viet-Nam. When that aggression ceases, collective mea-

Vietnamese intervention with increasing numbers of regular army troops, can be "justified" as "proportional" to the alleged acts defended against. Unless made by a competent international agency, such as the United Nations Security Council, the only effective judgment as to the proportionality of a response asserted to be in self-defense will be the judgment reached by the government taking the action. There is at present no international institution competent to review that action and thereby to evolve standards as to what force is proportional when the right to use force in self-defense is properly invoked. Since clearly developed standards do not exist, and since each side in the Vietnam conflict attaches a high priority to avoiding defeat, if not to achieving victory, there is no present possibility for effectively limiting allegedly defensive responses to a theoretical legal standard of necessity and proportionality. The double misfortune of the Vietnam conflict, however, is that the acts of force claimed to be taken in self-defense will not build standards of proportionality and necessity that might serve to limit future conflicts. Each act, such as the use of napalm or the progressive bombing of North Vietnam, is only a step along the road to total war that is implicitly threatened by the announced determination to do whatever is necessary to end the "aggression" by the other side. Where that is the objective, and where this objective is mirrored on the other side, the concepts of "necessity" and "proportionality" can have no observable limits when applied by each side unilaterally without review through an international institution.

The present discussion has been concerned with the character or level of participation in the Vietnam conflict, rather than with the related question of observance of the rules governing the conduct of the participants. In this latter area, what are termed the "laws and customs of warfare" stand in large measure on a firmer footing than the international law standards of "necessity" and "proportionality" in self-defense, and can therefore be expected to yield greater content in the Vietnam context. Even in this relatively stable area, however, charges have been traded as to the ill-treatment of prisoners, resort to terrorism, and use of poison chemicals or gasses. If supported by the facts, these changes further illustrate the inadequacy of unilaterally applied legal standards as a means of controlling conduct in the Vietnam conflict.

VIII. SEATO and the Vietnam Conflict

On September 8, 1954, less than two months after the close of the Geneva Conference, Australia, France, New Zealand, Pakistan, the Philippines, Thailand, the United Kingdom and the United States signed

---

sures in defense against it will cease." Address by Secretary Rusk, The Control of Force in International Relations, before the American Society of International Law, April 23, 1965, in 52 Dep't State Bull. 694, 698 (No. 1350, May 10, 1965).

the Southeast Asia Collective Defense Treaty at Manila in the Philippines.[95] That treaty provides in Article IV, paragraph 1, as follows:

> Each Party recognizes that aggression by means of armed attack in the treaty area against any of the Parties or against any State or territory which the Parties by unanimous agreement may hereafter designate, would endanger its own peace and safety, and agrees that it will in that event act to meet the common danger in accordance with its constitutional processes. Measures taken under this paragraph shall be immediately reported to the Security Council of the United Nations.[96]

The Republic of Vietnam did not become a party to the SEATO treaty, which would clearly be prohibited by the express terms of Article 19 of the Agreement on Cessation of Hostilities in Vietnam, but at the Manila Conference the parties to the SEATO treaty also accepted a protocol in which they unanimously designated "the free territory under the jurisdiction of the State of Vietnam" as falling within the area protected under Article IV of the SEATO treaty.[97]

Speaking of the impact of the SEATO treaty in the Vietnam conflict, Secretary of State Rusk recently stated:

> The language of this treaty is worth careful attention. The obligation it imposes is not only joint but several. The finding that an armed attack has occurred does not have to be made by a collective determination before the obligation of each member becomes operative. Nor does the treaty require a collective decision on actions to be taken to meet the common danger. If the United States determines that an armed attack has occurred against any nation to whom the protection of the treaty applies, then it is obligated to "act to meet the common danger" without regard to the views or actions of any other treaty member.[98]

Although as interpreted by the United States the quoted language of Article IV of the SEATO treaty obliges each party to "act to meet the common danger" whenever an armed attack occurs even though SEATO itself has taken no action, in these circumstances each party must still decide for itself whether an "armed attack" has in fact occurred, and what action it will take to meet what it perceives as the "common danger."[99] The United States considers that the term "armed attack"

---

[95] 6 U.S. Treaties & Other Int'l Agreements 81, T.I.A.S. No. 3170 (1955). The treaty entered into force on Feb. 19, 1955.
[96] 1 American Foreign Policy, note 14 supra, at 913.
[97] Id. at 916.
[98] Statement before the Senate Foreign Relations Committee, Feb. 18, 1966, in 54 Dep't State Bull. 346, 349 (No. 1393, March 7, 1966). The Secretary also said that "It is this fundamental SEATO obligation that has from the outset guided our actions in South Viet-Nam." Ibid. The SEATO agreement is not mentioned in the State Department's 1965 Legal Basis Memorandum, but is discussed extensively in the 1966 Legality Memorandum.
[99] In transmitting the SEATO treaty to President Eisenhower in 1954, Secre-

has the same meaning in the SEATO treaty as in the United Nations Charter,[100] and an "armed attack" having been acknowledged to have occurred against South Vietnam, the United States considers that it therefore has an obligation to act to meet the common danger presented by that attack.[101]

The SEATO treaty contains no procedures for collective action to meet a common danger presented by an armed attack. Article V establishes a Council "to consider matters concerning the implementation" of the treaty, but the treaty does not provide any specific powers for the SEATO Council save that it "shall provide for consultation" on such military and other planning as may be required.[102] Article IV, paragraph 2, provides for immediate consultation when peace is threatened "in any way other than by armed attack," but the stated purpose of this consultation is only to "agree on the measures which should [not shall] be taken for the common defense."[103]

The SEATO Council has discussed the Vietnam conflict at its annual meetings and has expressed its "grave concern about the continuing Communist aggression against the Republic of Vietnam," and its judgment that the "evidence continues to show that this organized campaign is directed, supplied and supported by the Communist regime in North Vietnam, in flagrant violation of the Geneva accords of 1954 and 1962."[104] As far as action is concerned, however, the most that the SEATO Council has done is to note the support that the Republic of

---

tary of State Dulles pointed out that the commitment in art. IV, para. 1, "leaves to the judgment of each country the type of action to be taken in the event an armed attack occurs." 1966 Legality Memorandum, note 48 supra, at 481.

[100] Ibid.

[101] When the United States signed the SEATO treaty, it did so with the "understanding that its recognition of the effect of aggression and armed attack and its agreement with reference thereto in Article IV, paragraph 1, apply only to communist aggression. . . ." 1 American Foreign Policy, note 14 supra, at 915. The 1966 Legality Memorandum, note 48 supra, describes the purpose of the SEATO treaty as "to give the assurance of United States assistance to any party or protocol state that might suffer a Communist armed attack, regardless of the views or actions of other parties." Id. at 481.

[102] 1 American Foreign Policy, note 14 supra, at 914.

[103] Id. at 913-14. The treaty contains no provision relating to voting in the SEATO Council save that each SEATO member shall be represented on the Council.

[104] Communique adopted by the SEATO Council at its Ninth Meeting, Manila, April 15, 1964, in 50 Dep't State Bull. 692 (No. 1297, May 4, 1964). The quoted portions are from paragraph 6 of the communique; paragraph 10 records the dissent of the French member, who "stated that under the present serious circumstances it was wise to abstain from any declaration." The 1964 communique was reaffirmed in 1965, noting that "substantial assistance and reinforcement have been given during the past year by certain member governments in order to assist South Viet-Nam in resisting aggression from the North." 52 Dep't State Bull. 923, 924 (No. 1354, June 7, 1965). The French were represented only by an observer, who stated that, "as he had not participated in preparing this communique, the French Government does not consider itself to be committed by it." Id. at 926.

Vietnam "is receiving from member nations of SEATO and from other nations in the free world,"[105] and to agree that:

> [T]he members of SEATO should remain prepared, if necessary, to take further concrete steps within their respective capabilities in fulfillment of their obligations under the treaty. . . . [and that] the defeat of the Communist campaign is essential not only to the security of the Republic of Vietnam, but to that of South-East Asia.[106]

In addition to the United States, several members of SEATO have contributed military assistance to the Saigon Government, as have some states that are not members of SEATO,[107] but this aid, said to be delivered in a collective self-defense effort, is aid carried on outside of the SEATO framework.

There have been, therefore, no international law problems relating to the activities of SEATO with respect to the Vietnam conflict. The major relevance of SEATO and the SEATO treaty have been in the domestic controversy within the United States over the authority of the President to order United States troops into action in Vietnam without specific prior congressional authorization.[108] Thus the administration, referring to the provision of the United States Constitution that treaties are "the supreme Law of the Land,"[109] argues that "Article IV, paragraph 1, of the SEATO treaty establishes as a matter of law that a Communist armed attack against South Viet-Nam endangers the peace and safety of the United States," and that under the U.S. Constitution "it is the President who must decide when an armed attack has occurred" and who has "the constitutional responsibility for determining what measures of defense are required."[110] Even if this reading of the Constitution is accepted, however, the resulting clear constitutional authority

---

105 50 Dep't State Bull. 692 (No. 1297, May 4, 1964) (1964 Communique, para. 7).

106 Ibid. (paras. 8 and 9).

107 Among SEATO members, as of March 1, 1966, only Australia and New Zealand have contributed combat forces; outside of SEATO, South Korea has contributed a substantial number of combat troops. See The New Republic, March 5, 1966, p. 6.

108 See the 1966 Legality Memorandum, note 48 supra, at 484-85. The memorandum also relies heavily on the joint resolution adopted by Congress on Aug. 10, 1964, following the attacks in the Gulf of Tonkin on United States vessels. Id. at 485-88. That resolution declares that "the Congress approves and supports the determination of the President, as Commander in Chief, to take all necessary measures to repel any armed attack against the forces of the United States and to prevent further aggression," and that in accordance with its obligations under the SEATO treaty the U.S. is prepared, "as the President determines," to take all necessary steps to assist any SEATO protocol state requesting assistance in defense of its freedom. Act of Aug. 10, 1964, 78 Stat. 384.

109 U.S. Const. art. VI, para. 2.

110 1966 Legality Memorandum, note 48 supra, at 485. A contrary view of the U.S. Constitution is stated at length in the Memorandum of Law prepared by the Lawyers Committee on American Policy Towards Vietnam, note 79 supra, at 17-24.

for the President to act in the Vietnam conflict does not add to the arguments that may be raised to justify United States action under international law and the Charter of the United Nations.

IX. THE ROLE OF THE UNITED NATIONS

As has been mentioned, the United States has from time to time reported its assistance to South Vietnam to the Security Council as required by Article 51 of the United Nations Charter.[111] In addition, on January 31, 1966, the United States formally requested a meeting of the Security Council "to consider the situation in Vietnam" and submitted to the Council a draft resolution by which the Security Council would note its concern at the continuation of hostilities in Vietnam and call for "immediate discussions without preconditions . . . among the appropriate interested governments to arrange a conference looking toward the application of the Geneva Accords of 1954 and 1962 and the establishment of a durable peace in Southeast Asia."[112] The Council agreed by a vote of nine in favor to two against (Bulgaria and the Soviet Union), with four abstentions (France, Mali, Nigeria and Uganda), to place the question of Vietnam on its agenda, but it has not yet met to consider that question.[113]

The range of action open to the Security Council under Chapter VII of the Charter is certainly broad enough to encompass whatever might be necessary to keep the peace in South Vietnam while a peaceful settlement is worked out between the parties. The precedents available range from a United Nations truce supervision organization created to observe compliance with truce agreements, as in Yemen and along Israel's borders, and a United Nations border patrol created to assist in preventing subversive border crossings, as in Greece and Lebanon, to a more powerful United Nations Force charged with direct functions in maintaining law and order within a state while a more permanent settlement is negotiated, as in Cyprus and the Congo.[114] The feasibility of any one of these approaches depends upon the willingness of the parties, and of other interested states, to achieve a peaceful settlement, rather than upon the authority of the United Nations to assist the parties in the ways suggested once that basic agreement has been achieved.[115]

---

[111] See note 72 supra.

[112] Letters from the U.S. Ambassador to the President of the Security Council, Jan. 31, 1966, in 54 Dep't State Bull. 229, 231 (No. 1390, Feb. 14, 1966).

[113] Id. at 239 n.9. The Council's vote was taken on Feb. 2, 1966.

[114] For a brief review of permissible United Nations action, see Larson, Questions and Answers on the United Nations 5-22 (3d ed. 1964); Partan, note 89 supra, at 293-340. See also the five part program for United Nations action in Vietnam proposed by Don and Arthur Larson in Vietnam and Beyond: A New American Foreign Policy and Program 34-40 (1965).

[115] The United Nations action contemplated here is action by the Security Council. Under certain circumstances, when Security Council action is blocked by

In the present circumstances there are good reasons to doubt that any form of United Nations involvement would be acceptable to both sides. First, a majority of the governments directly and vitally affected by the Vietnam conflict are not represented at the United Nations.[116] There is of course no barrier to *ad hoc* participation by non-Members in discussions of the Vietnam issue in the Security Council or other appropriate United Nations organ,[117] but this form of participation has apparently been rejected by the Democratic Republic of Vietnam, by the National Liberation Front, and by the People's Republic of China.[118] The second and more important reason to doubt the utility of United Nations involvement at present, however, is that both the United States and the Democratic Republic of Vietnam apparently continue to regard their respective national security interests in South Vietnam as basically incompatible.[119] So long as this is true, there is no common ground

the veto, the General Assembly would have authority under the Uniting-for-Peace Resolution to act to maintain international peace and security. See, e.g., Halderman, Legal Basis for United Nations Armed Forces, 56 Am. J. Int'l L. 971 (1962), reprinted as World Rule of Law Booklet No. 16. If, therefore, substantial agreement could be achieved between the immediate parties to the conflict in South Vietnam, and their active allies, on a United Nations facilitated or enforced solution, the organization could lend its hand despite a veto in the Security Council.

[116] Of the four immediate participants, Saigon, Hanoi, the United States and the National Liberation Front, only one, the United States, is a member of the United Nations. In addition, of the states contiguous to Vietnam, Cambodia, Laos and the People's Republic of China, the former two are U.N. Members, while the latter is not.

[117] U.N. Charter art. 32 provides in part that "any state which is not a Member of the United Nations, if it is a party to a dispute under consideration by the Security Council, shall be invited to participate, without vote, in the discussion relating to the dispute." Following the Gulf of Tonkin incident in August 1964, both North and South Vietnam were invited to participate in Security Council discussion. See 1964-1965 Report of the Security Council, U.N. Gen. Ass. Off. Rec. 20th Sess., Supp. No. 2, at 3-4 (A/6002) (1965). North Vietnam responded that the problem lay within the competence of the Geneva Conference on Indo-China, and not of the Security Council. Id. at 6-7.

[118] When the United States requested on Jan. 31, 1966, that the Security Council consider the situation in Vietnam, note 112 supra, Hanoi responded that the Security Council had no right to deal with the Vietnam question and that any resolution it might adopt "intervening in the Vietnam question would be null and void." N.Y. Times, Feb. 2, 1966, p. 1, col. 7. Hanoi reiterated that the question fell within the competence of the Geneva Conference and not of the Security Council. See note 117 supra.

[119] At present both the United States and North Vietnam appear to regard as the only acceptable settlement one in which the other side would withdraw totally its support for its ally in South Vietnam, and in which that ally would be excluded from control over the process by which South Vietnam would decide its future. The United States supports "free elections in South Viet Nam to give the South Vietnamese a government of their own choice," Statement by Secretary Rusk before the Senate Committee on Foreign Relations, Feb. 18, 1966, in 54 Dep't State Bull. 346, 354 (No. 1393, March 7, 1966) (hereinafter cited as Rusk Statement), but apparently would exclude the National Liberation Front as the puppet of North Vietnam from any role in preparing for or conducting these elections. See id. at 350-53. South Vietnam's projected September 1966 elections will exclude Vietcong participation; indeed, Saigon's law would punish "moves which weaken the national anti-Communist effort" and "plots and actions under the false name

between the governments that have intervened in the conflict in South Vietnam upon which United Nations action can be founded, and any United Nations intervention would appear to favor one side over the other.

This, it is submitted, accounts for the reluctance of many members of the Security Council to discuss the Vietnam conflict, or even to include that item on the agenda of the Security Council.[120] Certainly most United Nations Members are becoming increasingly concerned at the threats of escalation of the Vietnam conflict, yet they recognize that United Nations action can be effective only if it is acceptable to the governments directly involved in the fighting in South Vietnam.

The most that can be done through the United Nations at present, therefore, is to continue to search for alternatives to present policies. Secretary-General U Thant has taken the initiative in this process by publicly urging the parties to make concrete proposals on "such practical questions as what type of government in South Viet-Nam, representative, as far as possible, of all the sections of the South Vietnamese people, could take over the responsibility of organizing the exercise by the people of their right to decide their own affairs."[121] U Thant has also suggested to the parties "that peace can only be restored by a return to the Geneva Agreements, and that, as a preparatory measure, it would be necessary to start scaling down military operations, and to agree to discussions which include the actual combatants,"[122] not merely other interested governments.[123] If the parties were to accept some of these

---

of peace and neutrality." Fall, Vietnam's Twelve Elections, The New Republic, May 14, 1966, p. 14. Hanoi's position is that the "internal affairs of South Viet-Nam must be settled by the South Vietnamese people themselves in accordance with the program of the National Liberation Front," Rusk Statement, supra, at 354, but the NLF program calls for the overthrow of the Saigon Government as the puppet of the United States. Id. at 355-56. Hanoi has also stated that "so long as United States imperialists pursue their war of aggression in Vietnam . . . the people in both zones of Vietnam . . . are determined . . . to inflict total defeat on United States imperialist aggressors." N.Y. Times, Feb. 2, 1966, p. 15, col. 5.

[120] See note 113 supra. See also Letter from Ambassador Matsui of Japan to the Members of the Security Council, U.N. Doc. No. S/7168 (1966), in which the Ambassador, who served as President of the Security Council for February 1966, notes that differences of views as to the usefulness of Security Council discussion of the Vietnam conflict have "given rise to a general feeling that it would be inopportune for the Council to hold further debate at this time." Ibid.

[121] Press Conference of the Secretary-General, Jan. 20, 1966, in U.N. Monthly Chronicle, Feb. 1966, p. 34.

[122] Address by the Secretary-General at Atlantic City, New Jersey, May 24, 1966, in N.Y. Times, May 25, 1966, p. 5, col. 2. The Secretary-General noted that he did not wish "to pronounce any judgments as to where right or wrong, responsibility or culpability, reality or myth, may lie in what is a tragic situation for all the peoples and governments involved." Ibid.

[123] The United States has declared that: "The Viet Cong would not have difficulty being represented and having their views represented if for a moment Hanoi decided she wanted to cease aggression." Rusk Statement, note 119 supra, at 354. This formulation is derived verbatim from President Johnson's extemporaneous

suggestions, and to act on that acceptance, the way would be open toward more effective United Nations participation in the search for a peaceful settlement.

At this writing the logic of military force threatens catastrophic expansion of the Vietnam conflict.[124] As Secretary-General U Thant recently commented:

> The world has been watching the inexorable escalation of the war in Vietnam with increasing anxiety. Little by little, larger forces and more powerful armaments have been introduced, until an anguished and perplexed world has suddenly found that a limited and local conflict is threatening to turn into a major confrontation. And though the fear of a much larger conflict may still have a restraining influence upon the demands of military strategy, the temptation to win a military success may still prove stronger than the more prudent call to reason.[125]

That call to reason, and the tools to implement it if heeded, can be provided by the United Nations. As President Kennedy once said, the United Nations is "our last best hope in an age where the instruments of war have far outpaced the instruments of peace."[126]

---

response to a question on direct negotiations with the Vietcong at a News Conference on July 25, 1965. 1 Weekly Compilation of Presidential Documents 15, 18 (1965). Prior to that comment the administration always spoke of negotiations with "governments"; since then administration spokesmen have frequently quoted the Johnson language, as did Secretary Rusk, but their intent in doing so has been far from clear. See, e.g., Senator Mansfield's statement calling for a Vietnam peace conference, N.Y. Times, April 19, 1966, p. 8, col. 4.

124 The New York Times reported on June 10, 1966, p. 3, col. 4, that recent public opinion polls showed that President Johnson's popularity had declined to its lowest point since he took office, a decline that was attributed by the administration "to an increase in the number of Americans who think he should step up the war in Vietnam to win a quick victory." Walter Lippmann comments that this pressure might induce the President to "appease the Hawks by bombing closer to Hanoi and Haiphong." Boston Globe, June 14, 1966, p. 12, col. 6. An all-out effort against the North, according to Lippmann, however, "will arrive at a point where China will intervene and not, most probably, without some support from the Soviet Union." Ibid. Hans Morgenthau has commented that neither China nor the Soviet Union "can afford to watch the destruction of a 'fraternal Socialist country' without giving aid commensurate with the threat." Morgenthau, Johnson's Dilemma: The Alternatives Now in Vietnam, The New Republic, May 28, 1966, pp. 12, 13.

125 Address at Atlantic City, May 24, 1966, note 122 supra, at cols. 2-3. The Secretary-General concluded that: "The solution lies in the hands of those who have the power, and the responsibility, to decide. If they seek a peaceful solution, the United Nations and many of its members stand ready to help them in all possible ways." Id. at col. 5.

126 President Kennedy's Inaugural Address, Jan. 20, 1961, in Public Papers of the Presidents of the United States: John F. Kennedy, 1961, at 1, 2 (1962).

The Lawfulness of Military Assistance to the Republic of Viet-Nam*

JOHN NORTON MOORE

The major thrust of contemporary international law is to restrict coercion in international relations as a modality of major change. The use of force as an instrument of change has always been wasteful, disruptive, and tragic. In the nuclear era the renunciation of force as a method of settlement of disputes has become an imperative. These necessities have resulted in a widely accepted distinction between lawful and unlawful uses of force in international relations which is embodied in the United Nations Charter. Force pursuant to the right of individual or collective defense or expressly authorized by the centralized peacekeeping machinery of the United Nations is lawful. Essentially all other major uses of force in international relations are unlawful.[1] These fundamental proscriptions are designed to protect self-determination of the peoples of the world and to achieve at least minimum world public order. As such, they reflect the basic expectations of the international community. Since they are aimed at prohibiting the unilateral use of force as a modality of major change, they have consistently authorized the use of force in individual or collective defense at least "until the Security Council has taken the measures necessary to maintain international peace and security." This defensive right is, at least at the present level of effectiveness of international peacekeeping machinery, necessary to the prevention of unilateral use of force as an instrument of change. The fundamental distinction between unlawful unilateral force to achieve major change and lawful force in individual or collective defense against such coercion is the structural steel for assessment of the lawfulness of the present military assistance to the Republic of Viet-Nam.

---

* This article draws heavily on a more comprehensive paper entitled "The Lawfulness of United States Assistance to the Republic of Viet Nam," written by the author and James L. Underwood in collaboration with Myres S. McDougal, and distributed to Congress by the American Bar Association. This joint study is summarized by Senator Javits at 112 Cong. Rec. 13232-33 (daily ed., June 22, 1966), and is reprinted in full at 112 Cong. Rec. 14943 (daily ed., July 14, 1966), and —— Philippine Int. Law J. —— (1967). The joint study also includes an analysis of the lawfulness of United States assistance under internal constitutional processes.

For different perspectives on the problem treated in this article, see Standard, "United States Intervention in Vietnam Is Not Legal," 52 A.B.A.J. 627 (1966); Wright, "Legal Aspects of the Viet-Nam Situation," 60 A.J.I.L. 750 (1966). See generally Finman and Macaulay, "Freedom to Dissent: The Vietnam Protests and the Words of Public Officials," 1966 Wis. Law Rev. 632.

[1] See generally McDougal and Feliciano, Law and Minimum World Public Order 121–260 (1961).

Assessed against this fundamental structure, defensive assistance to the Republic of Viet-Nam is lawful under the most widely accepted principles of customary international law and the United Nations Charter. The unilateral use of coercion by the Democratic Republic of Viet-Nam (the D.R.V.)—North Viet-Nam, against the territorial and political integrity of the Republic of Viet-Nam (the R.V.N.) is unlawful. Analysis placing principal emphasis on minimum world public order and genuine self-determination as basic community policies indicates that, for purposes of assessing the lawfulness of the use of force, the Republic of Viet-Nam and the Democratic Republic of Viet-Nam are separate international entities, that there is an unlawful armed attack on the R.V.N. by the D.R.V., that third states may lawfully assist in the collective defense of the R.V.N., and that the response of the R.V.N., the United States and other assisting nations is reasonably necessary to the defense of the R.V.N.

I. FOR PURPOSES OF ASSESSING THE LAWFULNESS OF THE USE OF FORCE THE REPUBLIC OF VIET-NAM AND THE DEMOCRATIC REPUBLIC OF VIET-NAM ARE SEPARATE INTERNATIONAL ENTITIES

It is often asserted that the Viet-Nam conflict is merely a civil war between North and South Viet-Nam, with the implication that North Viet-Nam may lawfully use the military instrument against South Viet-Nam and that defensive assistance to the R.V.N. is intervention in a civil war. Such arguments are not new. Similar assertions were made by the U.S.S.R. during the Korean conflict.[2] Although, as in Korea, there are a number of similarities between the Viet-Nam conflict and a civil war, for the purpose of assessing the lawfulness of the use of force by the D.R.V. against the R.V.N. and the lawfulness of responding defensive military assistance to the R.V.N. there can be no question but that the R.V.N. is a separate international entity. McDougal and Feliciano point out in their treatise *Law and Minimum World Public Order:*

> The decisions reached by the United Nations in the Palestine and Korean cases suggest that conflicts involving a newly organized territorial body politic, or conflicts between two distinct territorial units which the community expects to be relatively permanent, are, for purposes of policy about coercion, to be treated as conflicts between established states. Thus, the applicability of basic community policy about minimum public order in the world arena and competence to defend against unlawful violence are not dependent upon formal recognition of the technical statehood of the claimant-group by the opposing participant. . . .[3]
> Our emphasis here is merely that rational community policy must be directed to the coercive interactions of territorially organized communities of consequential size, whatever the "lawfulness" of their origin and whatever the prior niceties in the presence or absence of the ceremony of recognition.[4]

[2] Kelsen, The Law of the United Nations 930, note 6 (1964); McDougal and Feliciano, *op. cit.* note 1 above, at 221.

[3] McDougal and Feliciano, *op. cit.* note 1 above, at 221.

[4] *Ibid.,* note 222.

Since disputes about the legality of the origin of territorial entities or exercises of authority over territory are common, it would greatly undermine the basic prohibition on unilateral use of force in international relations to allow unilateral resort to force to change a continuing *de facto* exercise of authority. The R.V.N. and the D.R.V. have at least been separate *de facto* international entities for the more than twelve-year period since the Geneva Accords of 1954. Professor Friedmann points out this reality when he says: "It may be conceded that North and South Viet-Nam are today *de facto* separate states, even though the Geneva Agreement of 1954 spoke of 'two zones.' " [5] In fact, the evidence indicates that the R.V.N. is a state under international law and that today there are substantial expectations that the D.R.V. and the R.V.N. are separate and independent states under international law.[6] On three separate occasions, once prior to the Accords, and twice since then, the General Assembly of the United Nations has found that the R.V.N. or its predecessor, the state of Viet-Nam, is a state entitled to admission to the United Nations. On each occasion the "veto" of the U.S.S.R. has defeated the Security Council resolution calling for admission.

The status of the R.V.N. as a state under international law is confirmed by the recognition presently accorded it by about 60 nations. It is also presently a member of at least 30 international organizations including 12 specialized agencies of the United Nations, has a permanent observer at the United Nations, and has participated in a large number of international conferences. The R.V.N. is a member of as many specialized agencies of the United Nations as is the Republic of Korea and is a member of more such agencies than are Albania, Cambodia, Cuba, Czechoslovakia, and the U.S.S.R., among others. With respect to the D.R.V., its claims to statehood are strengthened by the recognition presently accorded it by about 24 nations, and its participation in a number of international conferences. The substantial expectations that the D.R.V. and the R.V.N. are separate and independent states under international law are also evidenced by the package-deal proposal of the U.S.S.R. in 1957 to admit the D.R.V., the R.V.N. and both Koreas to the United Nations as four separate states.[7]

---

[5] Friedmann, "United States Policy and the Crisis of International Law," 59 A.J.I.L. 857, at 866 (1965).

[6] For more detailed treatment of the evidence, see McDougal, Moore and Underwood, "The Lawfulness of United States Assistance to the Republic of Viet Nam," 112 Cong. Rec. 14943, 14944-48 (daily ed., July 14, 1966).

[7] During the debates on this and the other draft resolutions calling for the admission of the R.V.N., the three Soviet delegates said between them:

"[B]oth in Korea and in Viet-Nam two separate States existed, which differed from one another in political and economic structure. . . .

"The fact was that there were two States in Korea and two States in Viet-Nam. . . .

"The realistic approach was to admit that there were two States with conflicting political systems in both Korea and Viet-Nam. In the circumstances, the only possible solution was the simultaneous admission of the four countries constituting Korea and Viet-Nam. . . .

"[T]wo completely separate and independent States had been established in each

Today, more than twelve years after the Geneva Accords of 1954, it denies reality to assert that there are not at least two continuing *de facto* international entities in Viet-Nam.[8] The D.R.V. and the R.V.N. unmistakably function as separate entities in the international arena. They have separate governments, separate international representation, separate constitutions, separate territories, separate populations, separate armies, and have developed for a substantial period of time along separate ideological lines. Whether or not the D.R.V. and the R.V.N. are full-fledged *de jure* states under international law, and there are substantial expectations that they are, they are at least separate international entities with respect to the lawfulness of the use of force. In these circumstances the D.R.V. may not unilaterally resort to force against the R.V.N. consistent with the vital expectations of the peoples of the world about the preservation of minimum world public order and the minimization of destructive modes of change.

A favorite argument of those who characterize the Viet-Nam conflict as a civil war is to invoke the language of the Accords to the effect that "the military demarcation line is provisional and should not in any way be interpreted as constituting a political or territorial boundary."[9] Under the Geneva Accords a principal purpose of the agreements was a military cease-fire making the use of force by one zone against the other unlawful. If nothing else, the two zones were at least intended as separate international entities with respect to the lawfulness of the use of force. To get

---

of those countries, [Korea and Viet Nam] with different political, social and economic systems." *Ibid.* at 14947.

[8] Professor Lauterpacht listed both Viet-Minh and Viet-Nam as separate states under international law apparently even prior to the Accords. Under the heading "States At Present International Persons," Professor Lauterpacht listed among others "Viet-minh, Vietnam, North Korea and South Korea." 1 Oppenheim, International Law 255–258 (8th ed., Lauterpacht, 1955). See also Murti, Vietnam Divided 171–172, 172, note 7 (1964).

As Dr. B. S. N. Murti, an Indian scholar who was actively associated with the International Commission For Supervision and Control in Viet-Nam, has written in 1964: "Two independent sovereign States, claiming sovereignty over the whole country, came into existence in Viet Nam and the division of the country seems permanent. . . ." *Ibid.* at 7. "Both the States are completely independent with full-fledged Governments of their own owing no allegiance to the other." *Ibid.* at 176.

[9] William Standard, in a recent article in the American Bar Association Journal invokes this language to indicate that "It cannot be asserted that South Vietnam is a separate 'country' so far as North Vietnam is concerned." Standard, "United States Intervention in Vietnam Is Not Legal," 52 A.B.A.J. 627, 630 (1966). The group known as the "Lawyers Committee on American Policy Toward Vietnam," of which Standard is Chairman, make much the same point. "Memorandum of Law of the Lawyers Committee on American Policy Toward Vietnam," 112 Cong. Rec. 2552, 2555–56 (daily ed., Feb. 9, 1966).

Aside from the very considerable uncertainties as to whom the Geneva Accords bound and the reasonable expectations of the participants with respect to the Geneva settlement, Standard and the Lawyers Committee miss the point. The issue is not whether North and South Viet-Nam are separate countries, although there are substantial expectations today that they are, despite this language, but whether they are separate international entities for purposes of assessing the lawfulness of the use of force.

comfort from the Accords for the proposition that force by the D.R.V. against the R.V.N. is not unlawful is to stand the agreements on their head. The Geneva Accords of 1954 affirm for Viet-Nam the norm of customary international law that force by one international entity against another is unlawful as a method of settlement of political disputes. Clearly, the use of force as an instrument of political settlement across an international cease-fire line is not civil strife for purposes of assessing its lawfulness under international law.[10]

It is also not tenable to suggest that the use of force by the D.R.V. against the R.V.N. is civil strife on the theory that the Accords ceased to have legal validity when elections were not held in 1956. Regardless of the failure to hold elections in 1956, and whether or not the Accords have continuing validity, in reality there are two, at least *de facto*, separate international entities in Viet-Nam. If the major framework of contemporary international law as reflected in the United Nations Charter is to have efficacy, one such entity cannot resort to unilateral use of force to achieve settlement of a political dispute against another, regardless of asserted unlawfulness of its origin or continuation. The argument made by some, that the Accords ceased to function when elections were not held and that the D.R.V. could then lawfully employ force against the R.V.N., sanctions unilateral determination to resort to force against another at least *de facto* international entity to remedy an asserted political grievance or breach of treaty. As Lord McNair points out, a breach of treaty as such can never amount to an "armed attack" justifying the resort to force.[11] The argument also seems to assume that, if the Accords ceased to have legal validity, the situation would revert to the pre-Accords state. In view of the separate reality of two functioning international entities after—and to some extent even prior to—the Accords, it is at least equally credible to assume that cessation of legal validity of the Accords would sanction the *status quo* and provide yet another indication of two separate *de jure* states in Viet-Nam.

In any event, the evidence strongly indicates that the military demarcation line in Viet-Nam *is* of continuing validity despite the failure to hold elections in Viet-Nam in 1956. There is no provision in the

[10] As Professor Quincy Wright pointed out in the 1959 Proceedings of the American Society of International Law:

"Another complication may result from the protracted functioning of a cease-fire or armistice line within the territory of a state. While hostilities across such a line by the government in control of one side, claiming title to rule the entire state, seems on its face to be civil strife, if such lines have been long continued and widely recognized, as have those in Germany, Palestine, Kashmir, Korea, Viet Nam and the Straits of Formosa, they assume the character of international boundaries. Hostilities across them immediately constitute breaches of *international* peace, and justify "collective defense" measures by allies or friends of the attacked government, or "collective security" measures by the United Nations. If this were not so, armistice and cease-fire lines would have no meaning at all. . . ." Wright, "International Law and Civil Strife," 1959 Proceedings, American Society of International Law 145, 151.

[11] McNair, Law of Treaties 577, note 1 (1961). See also Bowett, Self-Defence in International Law 189 (1958).

Accords which indicates that the military cease-fire line would cease to have validity should the elections not be held. In fact, the continued functioning of the International Control Commission (I.C.C.) after 1956 and the official messages of the Co-Chairmen of the Conference suggest that the failure to hold elections did not affect the continuing legal validity of the international cease-fire line in Viet Nam.[12] Moreover, there is evidence that both the D.R.V. and the R.V.N. regard the Accords as having continuing legal validity, as their continuing complaints to the International Control Commission indicate.[13] As the "Four Point" proposals[14] of the D.R.V. aptly demonstrate, assertions that the Accords ceased to have legal validity when the 1956 elections were not held would seem to be more rationalization than accurate reflection of the D.R.V. attitude toward the Accords or of contemporary community expectations.[15]

To allow the D.R.V. to make the unilateral determination that the Accords are no longer in effect and that it may use force to aggressively achieve its objectives in a non-defense situation is a negation of the principal structure of contemporary international law as embodied in the United Nations Charter. The fundamental proscription prohibiting unilateral force as a modality of major change prohibits such use despite any number of political grievances, whether they be legitimate or illegitimate. Any justification of unilateral action because of asserted political grievances would substantially destroy the present structure of world public

[12] See McDougal, Moore and Underwood, note 6 above, at 14971, note 71. In an official message from the British and Soviet Co-Chairmen, which adverted to the possibility of non-implementation of the election provisions, the Co-Chairmen said: "Pending the holding of free general elections for the reunification of Viet-Nam, the two Co-Chairmen attach great importance to the maintenance of the cease-fire under the continued supervision of the International Commission for Viet-Nam." Documents relating to British Involvement in the Indo-China Conflict (Misc. No. 25 [1965], Command Paper 2834) 96–99, at 97.

[13] See McDougal, Moore and Underwood, note 6 above, at 14971, note 70. "The commission receives an average of one note daily from North Vietnam protesting alleged violations of the Geneva agreements. . . ." New York Times, Aug. 6, 1966, p. 3, col. 6 (city ed.).

[14] The "Four Points" state the public position of the D.R.V. with respect to negotiation of the Viet-Nam conflict. They rest heavily on unilateral U. S. compliance with the Geneva Accords of 1954 as interpreted by Hanoi. See the April 8, 1965, speech by Mr. Pham Van Dong excerpted in Recent Exchanges Concerning Attempts to Promote a Negotiated Settlement of the Conflict in Viet-Nam (Viet-Nam No. 3 [1965], Command Paper 2756), at 51.

[15] For the stress that the D.R.V. places on the Accords, see McDougal, Moore and Underwood, note 6 above, at 14978. Hanoi also invokes the Geneva Accords as the principal reason why United Nations "intervention" is inappropriate. Ibid. The D.R.V. position on whether Viet-Nam is one or two international entities is not the simple "civil war after elections were not held" argument put forward by some. By way of example, Ho Chi Minh's letter to heads of state on January 28, 1966, said: "U.S. imperialists have massively increased the strength of the U.S. expeditionary corps and sent in troops from a number of their satellites to wage direct aggression in South Vietnam. They have also launched air attacks on the D.R.V., Democratic Republic of Vietnam, an independent and sovereign country, and a member of the Socialist camp." New York Times, Jan. 29, 1966, p. K, col. 5 (city ed.).

order. The only condition for lawful unilateral use of force—and then only "until the Security Council has taken the measures necessary to maintain international peace and security"—is individual or collective defense. If that condition is absent, unilateral force by the D.R.V. against the territorial and political integrity of the R.V.N. is unlawful and an armed attack gives rise to appropriate defensive rights in the R.V.N. to meet that illegality. If there is an armed attack on the R.V.N. by the D.R.V., the R.V.N. may lawfully take measures to defend itself consistent with the right of individual or collective defense recognized under contemporary international law and the United Nations Charter.

II. THERE IS AN UNLAWFUL ARMED ATTACK ON THE REPUBLIC OF VIET-NAM BY THE DEMOCRATIC REPUBLIC OF VIET-NAM

In addition to the fundamental community proscription that unilateral resort to coercion is unlawful as an instrument of major change, the strong community interest in restricting coercion limits the right to use intense coercion in individual or collective defense to, generally speaking, very serious situations in which there is no reasonable alternative to the use of force for the protection of major values. This community policy is reflected in the famous "necessity" test of the *Caroline* case, and in the language of Article 51 of the United Nations Charter, which expressly reserves the right of individual and collective self-defense if there is an "armed attack." By such verbal tests, contemporary international law expresses the judgment that minor encroachments on sovereignty, political disputes, frontier incidents, the use of non-coercive modalities of interference, and generally aggression which does not threaten fundamental values, such as political and territorial integrity, may not be defended against by major resort to force against another entity. These tests are simply representative of the community interest in restricting intense responding coercion in individual or collective defense to those situations where fundamental values are seriously threatened by coercion. Such tests have few magic qualities for making these determinations, and decision must depend on the context. As McDougal and Feliciano indicate:

> [T]he coercion characterized as "permissible" and authorized by the general community in the cause of "self-defense," should be limited to responses to initiating coercion that is so intense as to have created in the target state reasonable expectations, as those expectations may be reviewed by others, that a military reaction was indispensably necessary to protect such consequential bases of power as "territorial integrity" and "political independence". . . .[16]

This is the real issue in making the characterization as to whether there is an "armed attack" on the R.V.N. by the D.R.V. or whether the responding coercion was "necessary."

In arguing that there is no "armed attack" against the R.V.N. justifying a defensive response by the R.V.N., William Standard and the group known

[16] McDougal and Feliciano, *op. cit.* note 1 above, at 259.

as the "Lawyers Committee on American Policy Toward Vietnam" apparently assume that the only right of defense under the United Nations Charter is spelled out in Article 51 and is limited by the "armed attack" test, presumably a somewhat more restrictive test.[17]   There is a substantial body of opinion among international legal scholars, however, that the Charter was not intended to restrict the right to initially take defensive action in any way, and that Article 51, drafted for the purpose of accommodating regional security organizations, did not restrict that right, whether by an "armed attack" requirement or any other.[18]   Even if the restrictive interpretation of the Charter is accepted, accurate characterization of the evidence with reference to the policy of this language indicates that there is unquestionably an "armed attack" by the D.R.V. against the R.V.N.   Among other evidence of this "armed attack":

On June 2, 1962, the International Control Commission, composed of representatives from India, Canada and Poland and established pursuant to the Geneva Accords, issued a Special Report which considered allegations of aggression and subversion on the part of the D.R.V. against the R.V.N.   In this Special Report, the first report so designated since the commencement of the I.C.C.'s reporting in 1954, the Commission, with the Polish representative dissenting, adopted the following findings of the Legal Committee:

> Having examined the complaints and the supporting material sent by the South Vietnamese Mission, the Committee has come to the conclusion that in specific instances there is evidence to show that armed and unarmed personnel, arms, munitions and other supplies have been sent from the Zone in the North to the Zone in the South with the object of supporting, organizing and carrying out hostile activities, including armed attacks, directed against the Armed Forces and Administration of the Zone in the South.   These acts are in violation of Articles 10, 19, 24 and 27 of the Agreement on the Cessation of Hostilities in Viet-Nam.
>
> In examining the complaints and the supporting material, in particular documentary material sent by the South Vietnamese Mission, the Committee has come to the further conclusion that there is evidence to show that the PAVN [The People's Army of Viet Nam—the Army

17 See references in note 9 above.

18 See, *e.g.*, Bowett, Self-Defence in International Law 184–193 (1958); McDougal and Feliciano, *op. cit.* note 1 above, at 233–241; Stone, Aggression and World Order 92–101 (1958).   The restrictive interpretation advocated by some scholars that the right of defense under the U.N. Charter is limited by the language of Art. 51 differs principally in practical effect from the above interpretation in assessing the lawfulness of anticipated defense and the lawfulness of response to attacks not involving the use of the military instrument.   Since the D.R.V. aggression against the R.V.N. utilizes the military instrument as the principal strategy and since the response of the R.V.N. and the United States does not even remotely raise questions of anticipatory defense, there would seem to be little doubt that an "armed attack" has taken place even under this more restrictive view of the Charter.   For scholars advocating the more restrictive view see, *e.g.*, Jessup, A Modern Law of Nations 165–167 (1948); Wright, "International Law and Civil Strife," 1959 Proceedings, American Society of International Law 145, 148, 152.

of the D.R.V.] has allowed the Zone in the North to be used for inciting, encouraging and supporting hostile activities in the Zone in the South, aimed at the overthrow of the Administration in the South. The use of the Zone in the North for such activities is in violation of Articles 19, 24, and 27 of the Agreement on the Cessation of Hostilities in Viet-Nam. . . .[19]

In adopting these findings of the Legal Committee, the Commission said: "The Commission accepts the conclusions reached by the Legal Committee that there is *sufficient evidence to show beyond reasonable doubt* that the PAVN has violated Articles 10, 19, 24 and 27 in specific instances." [20]

In a February, 1965, report, the Canadian representative to the I.C.C. said in a dissenting statement:

It is the considered view of the Canadian Delegation that the events which have taken place in both North and South Vietnam since February 7 are the direct result of the intensification of the aggressive policy of the Government of North Vietnam. In the opinion of the Canadian Delegation, therefore, it should be the chief obligation of this Commission to focus all possible attention on the continuing fact that North Vietnam has increased its efforts to incite, encourage, and support hostile activities in South Vietnam, aimed at the overthrow of the South Vietnamese administration. These activities are in direct and grave violation of the Geneva Agreement and constitute the root cause of general instability in Vietnam, of which events since February 7 should be seen as dangerous manifestations. The cessation of hostile activities by North Vietnam is a prerequisite to the restoration of peace in Vietnam as foreseen by the participants in the Geneva Conference of 1954.[21]

A number of leading journalists have reported in the *New York Times* that the evidence indicates a high degree of initiation and control of the conflict from Hanoi. They also report that since late 1964 North Vietnamese regular army units have been moving into the R.V.N., a movement which has intensified since then and which has resulted in North Vietnamese regular army troops making up a substantial proportion of those fighting in the R.V.N.[22] According to the United States Department of State:

[19] Special Report to the Co-Chairmen of the Geneva Conference on Indo-China (Vietnam No. 1 [1962], Command Paper 1755). Great Britain Parliamentary Sessional Papers, XXXIX (1961/62), at 6–7.

[20] *Ibid.* at 7 (emphasis added). The Commission also found after recording this armed aggression from the D.R.V. that the R.V.N. had violated Arts. 16, 17 and 19 of the Geneva Agreements by receiving military assistance. *Ibid.* at 10. It is erroneous to merely "balance" the violations recorded against both sides in this report. The kinds of violations recorded against the two sides are crucially different. For a fuller exploration of this point and a discussion placing the Commission findings in the broader context of the Geneva settlements and the norms regulating the use of coercion, see the discussion in Section VI below.

[21] Special Report to the Co-Chairmen of the Geneva Conference on Indo-China, February 13, 1965 (Vietnam No. 1 [1965], Command Paper 2609), at 14–15.

[22] New York Times correspondent Neil Sheehan, in an article in the May 2, 1966, New York Times, points out that:

In the three-year period from 1959–1961, North Viet Nam infiltrated an estimated 10,700 men into South Viet Nam. . . . The aggression by Hanoi became substantial in 1959 and had intensified to dangerous proportions by late 1961. . . .

It is now estimated that by the end of 1964 North Viet Nam had infiltrated over 40,000 men into South Viet Nam. Most of these men were infiltrated through the territory of Laos in plain violation of the

---

"The available evidence strongly indicates that the war was actually initiated on orders from Hanoi. . . . The instrument for the renewal of guerrilla warfare was the clandestine organization that had been deliberately left behind when the bulk of the Communist-led Vietminh troops, who fought the French and were the predecessors of the Vietcong, were withdrawn to the North in 1954.

"The existence of such a clandestine Communist party organization in the South has been documented. In this regard, analysts also point out a fact often little understood in the West, that there is only one Communist party in Vietnam and that its organizational tentacles extend throughout both the North and the South. At no time since the mid-nineteen-forties, when the struggle against the Japanese, and then the French began, has the politburo of the party lost control over its branch in the South. . . .

"By 1960, the evidence indicates, Hanoi decided that some instrument was necessary to lend an aura of legitimacy and to disguise Communist control over the guerrilla warfare its cadres had fostered in the South [leading to a call for the formation of the N.L.F.]. . . .

"[T]he Liberation Front does not control the Vietcong armed forces, despite its claims to the contrary. Documentary evidence, interrogation of prisoners and other intelligence data indicate that the guerrilla units are directed by an organization known as the Central Office for South Vietnam, or Cosvin as it is commonly called here.

"Cosvin is believed to be the senior Communist headquarters in the South, reporting directly to the reunification department of the Communist party in Hanoi and thus to the politburo. Through its military affairs department, Cosvin acts as a high command for the Vietcong guerrilla units. . . ." New York Times, May 2, 1966, p. 1, col. 2 (city ed.).

Similarly, Takashi Oka, a former Far East correspondent for the Christian Science Monitor, who has been in Viet-Nam for the past two years, wrote recently in the New York Times Magazine:

"Ho Chi Minh's Laodong party, with the intense, single-minded Le Duan as secretary general, was the Communist party for all of Vietnam until the Geneva Accords of 1954 divided the country into Communist North and non-Communist South. It retained its clandestine network in the South, and began expanding party membership there in earnest soon after the Third Party Congress (Hanoi, September, 1960), which decided on the 'liberation' of South Vietnam. When it changed its name in the South to People's Revolutionary party, it was following the Communist scenario of an insurrection independent of Hanoi. . . .

"The Communist chain of command begins in Hanoi, where the Laodong party's central committee openly maintains a reunification department headed by Maj. Gen. Nguyen Van Vinh. Analysts in Saigon believe that the reunification department is an agency for transmitting orders from the Laodong politburo to the South. Policy-making is the sole prerogative of the politburo, with Le Duan himself probably playing a major role.

"From the reunification department in Hanoi, orders go out to C.O.S.V.N., which is at the same time the central committee of the People's Revolutionary party." Takashi Oka, "The Other Regime in South Vietnam," New York Times Magazine, July 31, 1966, p. 9, at 46.

In a recent article about General Vo Nguyen Giap, Commander of the North Vietnamese Army, the New York Times reported: "Late in 1964 General Giap ap-

1962 Geneva Agreement on the Neutrality of Laos. Native North Vietnamese began to appear in South Viet Nam in large numbers in early 1964, and in December 1964 full units of the regular North Vietnamese Army began to enter the South. The latest evidence indicates that elements of the 325th PAVN division began to prepare for the move south in April 1964. . . .[23]

Although there is certainly evidence that the conflict in the R.V.N. also has internal support, the totality of evidence—whether or not the above evidence is accepted in its entirety—strongly indicates that the campaign to overthrow the recognized government of the R.V.N. by intense coercion receives at least substantial military assistance and direction from the D.R.V. and suggests that prior to any significant increase in United States assistance, D.R.V. initiative was a critical element in the conflict. There can be little doubt from the evidence that this was so prior to the commencement of bombing of military targets in the D.R.V. in February, 1965, and the introduction of United States combat units in the spring of 1965. This use of the military instrument by the D.R.V. against the R.V.N. is not a minor aggression nor one effectuated by non-coercive means such as propaganda. It is not a mere political dispute and it is not a minor frontier incident. Nor does the attack raise questions of the right to prevent an armed attack before it occurs. Instead, the attack, whether initiated and controlled by the D.R.V. or merely substantially assisted by the D.R.V., is a serious, sustained and determined

---

parently decided, with the concurrence of party leaders, to move to phase three [mobile warfare] in the war in South Vietnam. So he began moving North Vietnamese regular army units down the Ho Chi Minh Trail." New York Times, July 31, 1966, p. 2, col. 5 (city ed). According to the Mansfield Report, "Infiltration of men from North Vietnam through Laos has been going on for many years. It was confined primarily to political cadres and military leadership until about the end of 1964 when North Vietnam Regular Army troops began to enter South Vietnam by this route." Mansfield, Muskie, Inouye, Aiken and Boggs, The Vietnam Conflict: The Substance and the Shadow—Report to the Senate Committee on Foreign Relations, 112 Cong. Rec. 140, 141 (daily ed., Jan. 13, 1966). Times Saigon correspondent, Charles Mohr, recently reported that according to informed sources the latest intelligence estimates indicated that "of the 177 enemy combat battalions in South Vietnam, 81, or 46 per cent, are now North Vietnamese. . . ." New York Times, Aug. 10, 1966, p. 1, col. 4, at p. 5, col. 5 (city ed.).

These figures are not far from those released by General William Westmoreland at a press conference on Aug. 14, 1966, when he indicated that:

"At the present time there are approximately 280,000 Vietcong. This consists of about 110,000 main-force North Vietnamese regular army troops; approximately 112,000 militia or guerrilla forces; approximately 40,000 political cadre, and approximately 20,000 support troops. Regular troops have been, in recent months, moving down from North Vietnam to South Vietnam in great numbers.

"Since the first of the year, we estimate that at least 30,000 regular troops have moved down, and perhaps as many as 50,000. You are well aware that several weeks ago a regular army North Vietnamese division crossed the demilitarized zone. This is the latest intrusion." New York Times, Aug. 15, 1966, p. 2, col. 4, at col. 7 (city ed.).

[23] The Basis for United States Actions in Viet Nam Under International Law 5 (Mimeograph, U. S. Dept. of State).

attack on the territorial and political integrity of the R.V.N. The totality of the context, characterized by use of military force as the principal strategy, constitutes intense coercion creating in the target state reasonable expectations that it must use the military instrument to preserve its fundamental values.

Whether or not the "armed attack" language of Article 51 of the Charter places restrictions on the right of individual or collective self-defense, the intense and sustained attack aimed at the political and territorial integrity of the R.V.N. and employing the military instrument as the predominant strategy unquestionably gives rise to rights of individual and collective defense. As an analysis of the purpose of this "armed attack" language indicates, an "armed attack" is not limited to the overt Korean type of invasion. Professor Kelsen points out:

> Since the Charter of the United Nations does not define the term "armed attack" used in Article 51, the members of the United Nations in exercising their right of individual or collective self-defense may interpret "armed attack" to mean not only an action in which a state uses its own armed force but also a revolutionary movement which takes place in one state but which is initiated or supported by another state. In this case, the members could come to the assistance of the legitimate government against which the revolutionary movement is directed.[24]

And Professor Brownlie writes:

> [I]t might be argued that "armed attack" in Article 51 of the Charter refers to a trespass, a direct invasion, and not to activities described by some jurists as "indirect aggression." But providing there is a control by the principal, the aggressor state, and an actual use of force by its agents, there is an "armed attack."[25]

The evidence suggests that D.R.V. initiative in the use of the military instrument goes significantly beyond such descriptions.

This armed attack by the D.R.V. against the R.V.N. is unlawful. The actions of the D.R.V. are neither pursuant to authority of the United Nations nor individual or collective defense. A study of the I.C.C. reports with respect to the grievances asserted by the D.R.V. demonstrates that the D.R.V. has no legitimate claim to justify its aggression against the R.V.N. as defense. The principal D.R.V. allegations of R.V.N. breach of the Accords are failure to consult on the holding of elections in 1956, reprisals against resistance leaders, inadequate co-operation with I.C.C. controls, and entering into a military alliance with and receiving military assistance from the United States. Since none of these principal asserted grievances of the D.R.V. constitute a legitimate defense situation, even if all of these grievances were legally justified and the R.V.N. were bound by the applicable provisions of the Geneva Accords, the D.R.V. in its attack on the R.V.N. would still be acting contrary to the fundamental com-

24 Kelsen, "Collective Security under International Law," 49 International Law Studies 88 (1956).

25 Brownlie, International Law and the Use of Force By States 373 (1963).

munity norms on the regulation of coercion. Its activities constitute unilateral use of force as an instrument of political change and as such are unlawful.

In the perspective of the community framework for the regulation of coercion in international relations, the unilateral armed attack by the D.R.V. on the political and territorial integrity of the R.V.N. is unlawful and gives rise to the right of individual and collective self-defense.

III. THE UNITED STATES MAY LAWFULLY ASSIST IN THE COLLECTIVE DEFENSE OF THE REPUBLIC OF VIET-NAM

The right of collective defense is recognized under both customary international law and the United Nations Charter. That right is the right to assist or be assisted by another state on invitation of a state which is subjected to unlawful attack. In a world with only limited expectations as to the effective competence of the existing centralized peacekeeping machinery, such a right has been regarded as necessary to prevent weaker states from becoming the victims of more powerful states. Moreover, in a global era in which we may accurately speak of a "world community," interdependencies among states suggest real interests, defense and otherwise, in what transpires in other parts of the globe. Article 51 of the Charter recognizes these factors when it refers to "the inherent right of individual and collective self-defense."

The fundamental community interest in restricting coercion has qualified the right of individual or collective defense by establishing an overriding competence in the centralized peacekeeping machinery of the United Nations to deal with the situation as it sees fit in the interest of world peace and security. But since the United Nations Security Council may be delayed in its response, may be paralyzed by the "veto" or may otherwise be unable to act for political reasons, the Charter clearly contemplates that the right of individual or collective defense exists in the first instance until qualified by the Security Council acting in a particular case. The language of Article 51 of the Charter reflects this understanding when it says "until the Security Council has taken the measures necessary to maintain international peace and security." In effect the structure of the Charter reaffirms the right of individual or collective defense but makes it subject to possible later community review by the existing, but unfortunately imperfect, centralized peacekeeping machinery. The initial determination as to when an attack justifies responsive measures in individual or collective defense has always been left for individual determination and nothing in the Charter was intended to or does vary this necessity.[26] Specifically, such defensive measures are not predicated on a

[26] Bowett, Self-Defence in International Law 193, 195 (1958); Brierly, The Law of Nations 319-320 (5th ed., 1955); Jessup, A Modern Law of Nations 164-165, 202 (1948); Kelsen, The Law of the United Nations 800, 804, 804, note 5 (1964); Kelsen, "Collective Security under International Law," 49 International Law Studies 61-62 (1956); McDougal and Feliciano, Law and Minimum World Public Order 218-219 (1961); Stone, Legal Controls of International Conflict 244 (1954); Thomas and Thomas,

finding by the Security Council of a breach of the peace or aggression or armed attack under Article 39 or 51 or any other provision of the Charter. The argument of William Standard and the Lawyers Committee that some such United Nations action is required before the United States may lawfully assist the R.V.N. is erroneous.[27] Neither the R.V.N., the D.R.V. nor the United States has the right to be final judge in its own case. But this is not the issue. Their action, of course, is properly subject to community review. But it is lawful for the United States to assist in the collective defense of the R.V.N. at least until, in the language of Article 51, "the Security Council has taken the measures necessary to maintain international peace and security." To date the Security Council has not taken the measures necessary to maintain international peace and security in Viet-Nam. In the absence of such measures, the right of the United States to participate in the collective defense of the R.V.N. continues unimpaired.

With major emphasis, Standard and the Lawyers Committee assert that, because Article 51 speaks of "an armed attack against a member of the United Nations," the United States may not lawfully assist in the collective defense of the R.V.N., a non-Member of the United Nations.[28] As has been pointed out, there is a substantial body of opinion among international legal scholars that the United Nations Charter was not intended to restrict the right to initially take defensive action in any way, and that Article 51 did not restrict that right. In any event, the above restrictive interpretation of Article 51 with respect to non-Members has been almost universally rejected by legal scholars. Professor Kelsen says that ". . . according to an almost generally accepted interpretation of Article 51, the right of collective self-defense may also be exercised in case of an armed attack against a non-member state."[29] Professor Brownlie points out:

> It has been suggested by some writers that a literal interpretation of Article 51 would permit members to act in collective defence only when another member state has been attacked. This hypothesis is of

---

Non-Intervention 171 (1956); Kelsen, "Collective Security and Collective Self-Defense under the Charter of the United Nations," 42 A.J.I.L. 783, 791–795 (1948).

[27] Professor Kelsen indicates the correct doctrine when he says:

"Since within a more or less centralized system of international security the exercise of the right of individual and collective self-defense must be permitted because the central organ of the organization cannot interfere immediately after an illegal use of armed force has taken place, the question of whether or not the use of armed force which has actually taken place is illegal must be decided by the state which claims to be exercising the right of individual or collective self-defense. However, this is true only as long as the central organ of the security organization does not interfere. As soon as it does, this central organ must decide that question, and it may decide that question in another way than the state which claims to be exercising its right of self-defense." Kelsen, "Collective Security under International Law," loc. cit. note 24 above, at 61–62 (1956).

[28] Standard, loc. cit. note 9 above, at 628.

[29] Kelsen, "Collective Security under International Law," loc. cit. note 24 above, at 88.

doubtful validity for several reasons. There is no evidence that this was the intended effect of the Charter provisions and many members of the United Nations have participated and still participate in mutual security pacts which include non-members. Kelsen asserts that such restriction of collective defence is inconsistent with Article 2, paragraph 6. Finally, the Security Council resolutions of - 25 and 27 June and 7 July relating to the Korean hostilities employ wording reminiscent of Article 51 in the context of recommending states to give assistance to a non-member.[30]

Most, if not all, legal scholars who have answered this question have agreed that the United Nations Charter does not restrict a Member from participating in the collective defense of a non-Member.[31] Article 51 was drafted largely to reassure the Latin American delegates that collective defense pursuant to regional arrangements would not be disturbed. Since the principal concern was that of the Latin American states worried about the status of their right to receive collective defense under the Act of Chapultepec if they were to join the United Nations, the language of Article 51 quite naturally was concerned with preserving the rights of Members to receive collective defense protection. Nothing in the history of the article suggests that it was intended to restrict the rights of Members to collectively assist non-Members.[32]

[30] Brownlie, note 25 above, at 331.

[31] In addition to the discussion by Professors Kelsen and Brownlie cited in notes 29 and 30 above, see Bowett, op. cit. note 26 above, at 193–195; Brierly, Law of Nations 305 (6th ed., Waldock, 1963); Heindel, Kalijarvi and Wilcox, "The North Atlantic Treaty in the United States Senate," 43 A.J.I.L. 633, 657–658 (1949). See also McDougal and Feliciano, op. cit. note 26 above, at 233–241; Pompe, Aggressive War An International Crime 66 (1953); Thomas and Thomas, op. cit. note 26 above, at 171.

Scholars indicating in the context of the Viet-Nam debate that the U.N. Charter does not restrict a Member from participating in the collective defense of a non-Member include Professor Myres S. McDougal, Sterling Professor of Law at Yale, Professor Louis B. Sohn, Bemis Professor of International Law at Harvard, and Professor Quincy Wright, Professor of International Law at the University of Virginia.

The only authority cited by Standard and the Lawyer's Committee for the proposition that U.N. Members may not assist in the collective defense of non-Members is an excerpt from Stone, op. cit. note 26 above, at 244 to the effect that "the license of Article 51 does not apparently cover even an 'armed attack' against a non-Member." Standard has not done his homework. Professor Stone is one of the scholars taking the position that the right of individual and collective defense under customary international law is not impaired by Art. 51. Although, as the quotation by Standard illustrates, Professor Stone does take a narrow view of the right of Members to assist in the collective defense of non-Members when acting under the license of Art. 51, he does not take the position, necessary for Standard's argument, that the U.N. Charter restricts a Member from participating in the collective defense of a non-Member. In fact, in his more recent book, Aggression and World Order, Professor Stone indicates that a consequence of the extreme restrictive interpretation of the U.N. Charter would be that a Member could not assist in the collective defense of a non-Member, and terms such a result an absurdity and injustice. He clearly opts against what he terms this "extreme" view. See Stone, Aggression and World Order 92–98, at 97 (1958). Professor Stone's interpretation of Art. 51 seems to be based solely on the literal text and is also open to the criticism discussed above.

[32] See, generally, McDougal and Feliciano, op. cit. note 26 above, at 235; Russell and Muther, A History of the United Nations Charter 688–712 (1958).

It should also be pointed out that such a restrictive interpretation of Article 51 is merely one interpretation, and is not logically required by the text of that article. If Article 51 is to be interpreted to prohibit the right of a Member state to assist a non-Member state, the phrase "if an armed attack occurs against a member of the United Nations" must be interpreted as meaning "if *and only if* an armed attack occurs against a member of the United Nations." Syntactically these interpretations are quite different. No plausible policy rationale has as yet been offered—much less any policies offered by the framers of Article 51—as to why Members should be permitted to assist in the collective defense of other Members but not of non-Members. The distinction is specious. It would mean, for example, that today, East Germany, West Germany, North Korea, South Korea, Switzerland and the People's Republic of China as well as the R.V.N. and the D.R.V. could not be collectively assisted by Members of the United Nations if subjected to attack. And in the past it would have raised doubts about collective assistance to Indonesia or Israel for example. Such an interpretation is unlikely to have wide appeal to any ideological grouping, as the practice of both East and West in concluding regional defense treaties with non-Members indicates. Since the major purpose of Article 51 was essentially to reaffirm the right of individual and collective defense, the verbal quibble restricting that right is contrary to the major purpose of the article. This argument, a favorite in the attack on the lawfulness of United States assistance to the R.V.N., is reminiscent of what Judge Jerome Frank called preoccupation with "word magic."[33] It cannot be taken seriously.

Collective defense, whether pursuant to Article 51 or not, does not require a pre-existing regional defense agreement.[34] This means that the United States may lawfully assist in the collective defense of the R.V.N. whether or not that action is taken by virtue of the SEATO Treaty. As has been discussed, collective defense under either customary international law or the United Nations Charter does not require prior United Nations authorization of any kind. This is so regardless of whether the collective defense measures are pursuant to a regional defense arrangement or not. Standard, however, asserts that "the United States actions also violate Article 53 of the United Nations Charter, quoted above, which unequivocally prohibits enforcement action under regional arrangements except with *previous* Security Council authorization."[35] The Lawyers Committee makes the same argument.[36] This argument, for which they cite no authority, is erroneous when applied to the Viet-Nam context. Although international legal scholars differ as to whether particular col-

[33] Frank, Law and the Modern Mind 24–82 (Anchor Book ed., 1963).

[34] See Kelsen, The Law of the United Nations 795–796 (1950); Pompe, Aggressive War An International Crime 66 (1953); Thomas and Thomas, Non-Intervention 172 (1956); Kunz, "Individual and Collective Self-Defense in Article 51 of the Charter of the United Nations," 41 A.J.I.L. 872, 874 (1947).

[35] Standard, note 9 above, at 633.

[36] Memorandum of Law, note 9 above, at 2557.

lective defense treaties are "regional arrangements" within Chapter VIII of the Charter, they are in agreement that collective defense activities, whether termed pursuant to a regional arrangement, a collective defense treaty or something else, are not subject to the prior authorization and reporting requirements of Articles 53 and 54 of the Charter.[37] For the very purpose of Article 51 was principally to preserve the right of individual and collective defense when the Latin American countries were concerned lest the major Power "veto" in the Security Council would deprive them of that right. The clear understanding of the framers of the Charter was that action in individual or collective defense, whether pursuant to a regional arrangement or not, would not be subjected to a requirement of prior approval from the Security Council, although such action would be subject to later review by the United Nations. This understanding is evidenced not only in Western defense treaties such as NATO and SEATO, but also in the 1955 Warsaw Treaty of Friendship, Cooperation and Mutual Assistance between the Soviet Union and Communist East European nations, and the 1950 Joint Defense and Economic Cooperation Treaty of the Arab League. Senator Mansfield, a member of the United States Delegation to the conference which established SEATO, evidenced the relation of SEATO to Article 51 when he told the Senate:

> The Southeast Asia Collective Defense Treaty is consistent with the provisions of the United Nations Charter. The treaty would come under the provisions of Article 51, providing that nothing contained in the United Nations Charter shall deprive one of the states from the individual or collective right of self-defense.[38]

Senator Mansfield further noted in the same speech that measures taken under Article 51 "do not need prior approval of the Security Council. . . ."[39]

The United States at the request of the R.V.N. is assisting in the collective defense of the R.V.N. against armed attack. That assistance is lawful, whether taken by virtue of the SEATO Treaty or not. The actions of the United States, the R.V.N. and the D.R.V. are subject to later community

---

[37] See Jessup, A Modern Law of Nations 208 (1948); Kelsen, The Law of the United Nations 792–795, 921–927 (1950); Kelsen, "Collective Security under International Law," 49 International Law Studies 264 (1956); McDougal and Feliciano, Law and Minimum World Public Order 245 (1961); Stone, Legal Controls of International Conflict 248–251 (1954); Thomas and Thomas, Non-Intervention 187 (1956); Heindel, Kalijarvi and Wilcox, "The North Atlantic Treaty in the United States Senate," 43 A.J.I.L. 633, 639 (1949); Kelsen, "Is the North Atlantic Treaty a Regional Arrangement?", 45 A.J.I.L. 164–166 (1951).

[38] 101 Cong. Rec. 1055 (1955).

[39] Ibid. Ruth Lawson has summarized this understanding:

"The relationship of contemporary regional and global organizations is worthy of special comment. The collective defense organizations based on the North Atlantic Treaty and the Rio, Manila, Baghdad, and Warsaw pacts are ultimately grounded in Article 51 of the United Nations Charter, which with notable prescience legitimized collective defense against armed attack without Security Council authorization." Lawson, International Regional Organization vi (1962).

review by the Security Council, which may take "measures necessary to maintain international peace and security" as it sees fit. The efforts of the United States and the R.V.N. to secure such review have to date been unsuccessful. They have been consistently opposed by the D.R.V. and the People's Republic of China, which continue to maintain that the United Nations has no right to examine the question.[40]

IV. THE RESPONSE OF THE UNITED STATES AND THE REPUBLIC OF VIET-NAM IS REASONABLY NECESSARY TO THE DEFENSE OF THE REPUBLIC OF VIET-NAM

The fundamental community interest in restricting coercion as a modality of change carries with it a requirement that defensive action should not involve greater coercion than is reasonably necessary for the defense of the fundamental values under attack. This is the issue often subsumed under the "proportionality" test.[41] Disciplined answer to whether a particular responsive coercion is reasonably necessary to the preservation of the fundamental values under attack will not be provided by a simple comparison of types of coercion used by both sides, or counting of units committed to the field by the opposing participants. Nor will it be solved by the verbal magic of the *Caroline* or "proportionality" tests. Instead, meaningful characterization must depend on all of the relevant features of the context, including the scope and intensity of the attack as well as the response.

There is little doubt that the scope and intensity of the attack on the R.V.N. has presented a grave threat to its territorial and political integrity. That attack has been characterized by widespread terror and assassination, guerrilla raids and sabotage, and more recently by mobile warfare involving large-size regular army units of the D.R.V. In its early stages it was principally characterized by infiltration of armed and unarmed personnel in support of guerrilla activities, and from about late 1964 it involved the use of regular PAVN army units in large-unit "mobile warfare." According to the Mansfield Report, by early 1965 the situation had become so serious that the R.V.N. was in imminent danger of total collapse.[42] Militarily, the situation had deteriorated to the point where there was serious concern that the R.V.N. would be cut in two.

The United States and R.V.N. response to this attack has been reasonable under the circumstances. That response divides imperfectly but most use-

---

[40] See McDougal, Moore and Underwood, note 6 above, at 14955–56, 14977–79.

[41] As McDougal and Feliciano indicate:
"Proportionality in coercion constitutes a requirement that responding coercion be limited in intensity and magnitude to what is reasonably necessary promptly to secure the permissible objectives of self-defense. For present purposes, these objectives may be most comprehensively generalized as the conserving of important values by compelling the opposing participant to terminate the condition which necessitates responsive coercion. . . . Thus articulated, the principle of proportionality is seen as but one specific form of the more general principle of economy in coercion and as a logical corollary of the fundamental community policy against change by destructive modes." *Op. cit.* note 37 above, at 242–243.

[42] Mansfield, Muskie, Inouye, Aiken and Boggs, note 22 above, at 140.

fully into three major periods: prior to 1961, from mid-1961 to February, 1965, and from February, 1965, to the present.[43] Prior to 1961 the United States had no military casualties and had only a very limited Military Assistance Advisory Group in the R.V.N.—probably not more than about 800–900, with figures somewhat lower in earlier years. Infiltration and military assistance from the D.R.V. apparently were initiated as a significant factor during the latter part of this period. Beginning about mid-1961, in response to increased infiltration from the D.R.V., the United States began a moderate buildup of United States military advisory personnel, reaching roughly 12,000 by mid-1962 and about 23,000 by January 1965. An indication of the relatively minor combat exposure of United States advisory personnel during much of this period is evidenced by the fact that as late as September 2, 1963, President Kennedy indicated that as few as forty-seven Americans had been killed in combat in Viet-Nam. It was not until after the D.R.V. had significantly stepped up infiltration and other assistance and had begun the introduction of their regular army units into the R.V.N. pursuant to the escalation of the conflict to the third "mobile warfare" phase of guerrilla strategy, and after the R.V.N. had reached the stage of imminent collapse, that the United States and the R.V.N. in February, 1965, began regular air strikes against military objectives in the D.R.V., and that the United States in the spring of 1965 began an introduction of regular combat units.[44] Since then, both the attack and the response have intensified.

The air strikes against the D.R.V. have been focused on interdicting the use of the military instrument by the D.R.V. against the R.V.N. Air strikes have been narrowly limited to certain objectives chosen for their high military effect, principally transportation facilities, petroleum storage areas and facilities, military barracks, ammunition dumps, and anti-aircraft emplacements. Such strikes have been carefully controlled to minimize civilian casualties and are reasonably related to the permissible objective of interdicting the flow of arms and combat units into the R.V.N. They result in few civilian casualties and little unnecessary property destruction in relation to their military effect. The limited nature of the air strikes against the D.R.V. and the absence of other United States and R.V.N. defensive measures such as a commitment of ground forces to the D.R.V. strongly support the contention of the United States that it seeks only to interdict the D.R.V. attack on the R.V.N., that it seeks no wider war, that it is not attacking the territorial and political integrity of the D.R.V., and that it does not seek to punish the D.R.V. by militarily unnecessary or remote destruction. The air strikes have taken place in a context of two bombing pauses and a continuing United States position calling for unconditional negotiations, with the first order of business a stop to the hostilities.

[43] See McDougal, Moore and Underwood, note 6 above, at 14974, note 124.
[44] According to the Mansfield Report, as late as May, 1965, U. S. regular combat units were still not engaged on the ground. Mansfield, Muskie, Inouye, Aiken and Boggs, note 22 above, at 141.

Operations within the R.V.N. and most supporting air strikes have been carried out carefully and have been relevant to reasonably necessary military objectives. Air strikes on populated areas resulting in civilian casualties should not be undertaken in contexts in which civilian casualties may be out of proportion to the legitimate and reasonably proximate military effect. Some such incidents have occurred and every effort should be made to prevent them from recurring.

With respect to the use of the military instrument by the D.R.V.-Viet-Cong, the evidence suggests that the scope and intensity of the attack on the R.V.N. have increased and that the use of the military instrument is not primarily related to reasonably necessary defensive measures. The use of coercion by the D.R.V.-Viet-Cong has also been characterized by deliberate terrorism against civilian and political targets. In this context, the United States and R.V.N. response has been measured and reasonable. That response is necessitated by the continuing intense attack on the political and territorial integrity of the R.V.N. It has been gradual, limited and reasonably necessary to the permissible objective of the defense of the R.V.N.

V. VIET-NAM AND THE REQUIREMENTS OF MINIMUM WORLD PUBLIC ORDER

In the welter of charges and countercharges growing out of the Viet-Nam conflict it is easy to lose sight of fundamentals in a preoccupation with legalistic arguments or the ambiguities of the situation. Some are surprised and dismayed to learn that both sides assert grievances. It is easy to take another step and assume that both sides are responsible for initiating and continuing the use of the military instrument, or that the conflict is a just one because of the existence of grievances, or that questions of lawfulness are irrelevant. But probably most conflicts are fought over grievances which the parties consider just. The existence of asserted grievances, whether just or unjust, is not surprising and is not the point. The central issue facing the international community is the regulation of coercion. That issue has resulted in the outlawing of unilateral coercion as a modality of major change, regardless of asserted grievances. The policies behind this legal norm, the minimization of destructive modes of change, are fundamental to orderly relations in the international community and are by no means irrelevant to the Viet-Nam conflict. In fact, the dangers inherent in that conflict re-enforce the conviction that these norms for the maintenance of at least minimum world public order are the crucial policies in the situation. The principal inquiry for assessment of lawfulness must be appraisal of the activities of both sides in the light of the basic contemporary legal norms that force, pursuant to the right of individual or collective defense or expressly authorized by the centralized peacekeeping machinery of the United Nations, is lawful, and that essentially all other major uses of force in international relations are unlawful. These contemporary norms, also embodied in the United Nations Charter, are binding alike on Members and non-Members of the United Nations.[45] Meaningful discussion of the lawfulness of United States assistance must relate to these fundamental expectations of the world community as to the lawfulness of the use of force.

Claims by the participants that their actions are lawful defensive actions and those of the opponents unlawful and aggressive must be evaluated by appraisal of the total context. Relevant features include the strategies employed, the arena of the conflict, and particularly the outcomes sought and objectives of the participants. So appraised, United States assistance is lawful and the attack of the D.R.V. is unlawful.

Any reasonably impartial analysis of the context must conclude that a major objective of the D.R.V. use of the military instrument against the R.V.N. is fundamental change of the existing and at least *de facto* situation in Viet-Nam. The context strongly suggests that the unilateral D.R.V. resort to force is aimed at the political and territorial integrity of the R.V.N. Principal D.R.V. objectives, sought through coercion, seem to be settlement of political disputes with the R.V.N., change in the political form of government in the R.V.N. in favor of one similar and closely related to, if not controlled by, the D.R.V., and probably also eventual if not immediate unification of Viet-Nam under the Communist government of Ho Chi Minh. In the process it seeks United States withdrawal from the R.V.N. The conflict was unmistakably not precipitated by any real threat to the political or territorial integrity of the D.R.V. D.R.V. use of the military instrument against the R.V.N. evidences this in that it does not have as its principal object interdiction of the use of the military instrument against the D.R.V. This use by the D.R.V. of military force as a modality of major change in Viet-Nam is the central feature of the conflict. It is evidenced by the South and not the North as the principal arena of the fighting, the stated objectives of the parties and their conditions of settlement, and the continuing aggressive, not defensive, strategies in the use of the military instrument by the D.R.V. This D.R.V. attempt at forceful extension of its values is neither defensive nor pursuant to United Nations authorization. Such a resort to coercion as a modality of major change is unlawful.

On the other hand, judged by the same framework, the United States response is not aimed at the territorial and political integrity of the D.R.V. The use of coercion against the D.R.V. is of a limited nature and designed to interdict the D.R.V. attack against the R.V.N. An acceptable outcome would leave the D.R.V. as a viable and continuing entity. In fact, assistance has even been offered for the economic development of the D.R.V. The United States does not seek to change by force the existing state of affairs in Viet-Nam and Southeast Asia. Its emphasis is on conservation, not extension, of values in its use of military force in that area. Such defensive action is lawful.

---

[45] See McDougal, Moore and Underwood, note 6 above, at 14980, note 248; Jessup, *op. cit.* note 37 above, at 167–168.

Because of the great community interest in restricting coercion, a particularly relevant feature of the total context is the stress placed by the participants on removing the conflict from the battlefield to the negotiating table. The emphasis on settlement of disputes by pacific means is a corollary of the community interest in restricting coercion and is incorporated in Chapter VI of the United Nations Charter. The context of the Viet-Nam conflict indicates a substantial dichotomy between the positions of the opposing participants with respect to willingness to adopt more rational procedures for conflict resolution. The United States, Britain, Canada, India, the R.V.N., seventeen non-aligned nations, and recently Thailand, Malaysia and the Philippines have called for unconditional negotiations or a reconvening of the Geneva or other peace conference on Southeast Asia .[46] These extensive efforts to achieve a peaceful solution pursuant to Article 33 of the Charter through negotiation, the machinery of the Geneva Accords and the machinery of the United Nations have been consistently refused by the D.R.V., the U.S.S.R., and the People's Republic of China.[47] Most recently, the efforts of Prime Minister Wilson of Great Britain, Prime Minister Indira Gandhi of India, and United Nations Secretary General U Thant to obtain a reconvening of the Geneva Conference on Viet-Nam have been rebuffed by the U.S.S.R.,[48] and the efforts of Thailand, Malaysia, and the Philippines to invoke an Asian peace conference have been rebuffed by Peking and Hanoi.[49] Two United States bombing pauses have underscored the United States search for peace but have been met by no announced interest in negotiation or reduction in hostilities by the D.R.V. In the face of this largely one-sided refusal to negotiate or substitute peaceful and more rational procedures for settlement of the Viet-Nam conflict, principal responsibility for the continuation of the conflict must rest with those opposing peaceful procedures and who seem determined to continue reliance on the use of force to achieve their objectives.

VI. NEW MYTHS AND OLD REALITIES

The Ambiguous Geneva Settlement

The election arguments from the text of the 1954 Geneva Accords are high on the list of aphorisms offering false certainty. Critics of United

---

[46] See McDougal, Moore and Underwood, note 6 above, at 14977–79, note 233; New York Times, Aug. 19, 1966, p. 2, col. 7 (city ed.); Aug. 7, 1966, p. 10, col. 1; Aug. 4, 1966, p. 4, col. 3 (city ed.).

[47] *Ibid.* See also *ibid.*, July 25, 1966, p. 3, col. 5 (city ed.). But U. N. Secretary General U Thant has indicated that in 1964 and early 1965 Hanoi may have had more interest in negotiations.

[48] *Ibid.*, July 31, 1966, p. 3, col. 5 (city ed.). British Foreign Secretary George Brown was equally unsuccessful in his efforts to convince the Soviets to convene a peace conference. See the New York Times, Nov. 26, 1966, p. 6, col. 4 (city ed.).

There have recently been some hints that the Soviet attitude on the Viet-Nam issue is thawing.

[49] See New York Times, Aug. 19, 1966, p. 2, col. 7 (city ed.); Aug. 11, 1966, p. 2, col. 4 (city ed.); Aug. 9, 1966, p. 2, col. 4 (city ed.).

States assistance point to the language of the Final Declaration with respect to the elections which were to be held in 1956 to indicate that the D.R.V. has been justly aggrieved by R.V.N. non-cooperation on such elections, and by implication that D.R.V. use of force against the R.V.N. is thereby justified. And they assert that the R.V.N. has widely violated the Accords by receiving military assistance from the United States, again with the implication that D.R.V. use of force is thereby justified. Although the use of force by the D.R.V. certainly does not follow, even if the D.R.V. were justly aggrieved on these issues, such assertions mask false certainty and largely ignore the totality of the Geneva settlement and its context in favor of a verbalistic microcosm. Similar difficulties arise in the invocation by all major participants of the Geneva Accords as the basis for settlement. Although such joint invocation would normally lead to expectations of immediate settlement, the positions of the major participants in the conflict are not close. The invocation of the Geneva Accords has masked fundamentally different objectives. The cause of all this obscurity is that the Geneva Accords themselves reflect a highly ambiguous settlement and conceal a number of fundamental problems with which the Conference—perhaps intentionally—did not come to grips. For example, although the Accords adverted briefly to elections to be held in 1956, they did not devote major attention to implementing unification and there is some evidence that at least some of the participants actually intended a semi-permanent partition of Viet-Nam at least until such time as there might be a *rapprochement* between the D.R.V. and the state of Viet-Nam, the predecessor government of the R.V.N.[50] Anthony Eden,

[50] For documentation with respect to the discussion in this section see McDougal, Moore and Underwood, ''The Lawfulness of United States Assistance to the Republic of Viet-Nam,'' 112 Cong. Rec. 14943, 14972, notes 74 and 75 (daily ed., July 14, 1966). In a recent article in The Reporter, Victor Bator makes many of these same points with respect to the ambiguities of the 1954 Geneva settlement. See Bator, ''Geneva, 1954: The Broken Mold,'' The Reporter 15 (June 30, 1966). According to Bator:

''The primary motivation of the Vietminh was to consolidate their rule somewhere, anywhere, in Vietnam. To accomplish this, Ho Chi Minh was willing to make political concessions from his militarily superior position. So it came about that, on May 25, the head of the Vietminh delegation first mentioned partition. It was to be based on a regrouping of forces on either side of a line of demarcation that would give both parties an area with a sufficiently large population to exist independently. . . .

''The contradictions and the equivocations in the documents that emerged from the Geneva Conference gain added emphasis by the procedure by which they were reached. As narrated in memoirs such as those of Anthony Eden, who presided at Geneva, or in the detailed accounts of Bernard B. Fall, Jean Lacouture, and Philippe Devillers, partition—so ambiguously treated in the documents—was the most important subject of bargaining, both in principle and in its geographical application. It was discussed continually, if confidentially, within each delegation, but for a time was carefully ignored when the delegations met.

''When at last partition was openly breached by the Vietminh, the French and British were elated. From that moment the location of the dividing line became the principal hurdle blocking the road to a settlement. Secretary of State Dulles, in order to underscore his insistence that it be drawn on the 17th parallel and to demonstrate western unity on this point, flew from Washington to Paris to meet with Eden and Premier Pierre Mendès-France. There were discussions even about the viability of the

who was apparently a chief proponent of partition, seems to have had more than merely provisional partition in mind, and President Eisenhower indicated that the settlement implied nothing else but partition.   The state of Viet-Nam protested against the partition in the settlement and some of the provisions of the settlement, such as those for the transfer of civilians between zones, suggest longer-term partition was adverted to.   Although it is likely that there will continue to be a dispute as to the "real" intention of the participants at Geneva, if in fact they shared any common intention, the fact was that the central feature of the settlement was the division of Viet-Nam between two essentially economically viable and at least *de facto* international entities.   The election provisions, which obviously would be the key to unification, received only rather airy treatment.

Major difficulties were also papered over with respect to the position of the state of Viet-Nam, certainly a necessary participant in any future unification.[51]   For the state of Viet-Nam objected and refused to be bound by the agreements prior to Geneva, at Geneva, and after Geneva, a position which was certainly clear to all of the participants at the Conference.   Although the state of Viet-Nam indicated at the Conference that it would not use force to resist the cease-fire, it made it clear that it reserved to itself complete freedom of action.   Since the French had to a substantial degree granted independence to the state of Viet-Nam prior to the signing of the Accords, and had in any event entered into a series of independence agreements with the state of Viet-Nam which would, under generally accepted principles of international law, take precedence over later inconsistent treaty obligations, there was at least substantial question whether France had capacity to bind the state of Viet-Nam.   Moreover, there is little indication that France intended to bind the state of Viet-Nam by the Accords, and both the separate presence of the state of Viet-Nam at the Conference and the statements of the French delegates at the Conference suggest that France neither intended to bind nor felt itself legally capable of binding the state of Viet-Nam.   As background to all of this, by the time of the Conference the state of Viet-Nam had been recognized by more than 30 states, was a member of a number of specialized agencies of the United Nations, and for the past two years had been endorsed by the General Assembly of the United Nations as a state qualified for membership.   These factors greatly strengthen the consistent position of the R.V.N. that it was not bound by the provisions of the Accords other than to refrain from disturbing the cease-fire by force, and specifically lend credence to its position that it was not bound by the election provisions of the Accords.   That the Conference tolerated such an independent po-

---

two parts.   It is hard to believe that all this activity could have been devoted to the location of a temporary military demarcation line, a kind of billeting arrangement that would shortly disappear.   The innocent-sounding text of the final agreement must have signified something of greater import."   *Ibid.* at 17.

[51] For documentation with respect to discussion of this point, see McDougal, Moore and Underwood, note 50 above, at 14944–48, 14956–58, 14969–71, notes 22, 23, 24, 33, 34, 36, 37, 41, 44 and 49; 14980–82, notes 251, 252, 254, 261, 262, 267, 270, 274, 275, 276, and 278.

sition with respect to a major participant was a surprising failing of the hard-headed diplomats at the Conference, unless, of course, they adverted to semi-permanent partition as a possible basis for settlement, recognizing the fact that an unambiguous settlement was politically impossible at the time.

In addition to these major ambiguities in the Geneva settlement, the Accords were seriously lacking in provisions for an effectively policed cease-fire, and their military restrictions, which seemed to have a significantly greater impact on the state of Viet-Nam, were inadequate to ensure meaningful demilitarization or military supervision of both North and South. The principal military restriction in the Accords, other than the core provision making unlawful the use of force by one zone against the other, was a ban on *introduction* of troop reinforcements, additional military personnel, and reinforcements of armaments and munitions. Contrary to popular interpretations, the Accords did not prohibit build-up of indigenous forces, and as such the effectiveness of the Accords was reduced.[52] The Accords also prohibited military alliances. Since it was the state of Viet-Nam which depended most heavily upon outside assistance for its defense, these provisions of the Accords, while only doubtfully ensuring effective demilitarization of North and South Viet-Nam, seemed to fall most heavily on the defensive ability of the state of Viet-Nam, an entity that had expressly refused to accept the Accords except to respect the cease-fire. Moreover, the International Commission for Supervision and Control (the International Control Commission), which was composed of representatives of India, Canada, and Poland, had little real power, no real peacekeeping force, was chronically underfinanced, and was hampered by a requirement of unanimous action for most major decisions. It was also reduced in effectiveness by the consistent and understandable position of the R.V.N. that it was not bound by the agreements, although it would co-operate in maintaining the cease-fire. Under the circumstances, when the participants perceived non-co-operation as in their interest, the I.C.C. could do little but issue reports. Recent proposals to strengthen I.C.C. control over the Cambodian border and the demilitarized zone have been supported by the United States and the R.V.N.

There are in the ambiguous Viet-Nam context also arguments that the R.V.N. was bound by the Accords,[53] and evidence that the participants

---

[52] See McDougal, Moore and Underwood, note 50 above, at 14970, note 46.

[53] The principal argument seems to be based on Art. 27 of the Agreement on the Cessation of Hostilities, which says that: "The signatories of the present Agreement and their successors in their functions shall be responsible for ensuring the observance and enforcement of the terms and provisions thereof. . . ." It is argued that the R.V.N. succeeded to the obligations of the French Union Forces. But if the R.V.N. is not otherwise bound by the Agreement, there is little reason to suggest that it is bound by Art. 27. In light of the evidence suggesting that France considered the state of Viet-Nam independent prior to the signing of the Accords, that France did not intend to bind the state of Viet-Nam and that the state of Viet-Nam expressly refused to be bound by the Agreements, this argument from the text of Art. 27 is not persuasive. There remain among others the questions of whether France had legally granted independence to the state of Viet-Nam prior to the signing of the Accords and,

expected elections to be held in 1956. Limited military control was fairly effectively achieved by the Commission, at least in the early years. But the point is, though the separation of Viet-Nam between the D.R.V. and the R.V.N. is the central feature of the present context and the starting point for any settlement in Viet-Nam, the 1954 settlement in its totality always has been seriously ambiguous and inadequate. The text of the "agreements" concealed continuing serious *disagreements* among the people of Viet-Nam as well as between and among major East-West Powers. Provisions for implementation avoided the difficulties. The nebulous legal status of the unsigned Final Declaration of the Conference reflected them. Had it been otherwise, there would probably be no Viet-Nam conflict today. It is not helpful, then, that the D.R.V., while refusing to negotiate, can nevertheless righteously invoke immediate implementation of the text of the Accords—as interpreted by the D.R.V., of course, and ignoring D.R.V. encroachments of the text—as a precondition for negotiations.

It should also be pointed out that the United States is not bound by the Geneva Accords of 1954 other than to refrain from disturbing the agreements by force in accordance with pre-existing obligations under the United Nations Charter. Bedell Smith, the United States delegate to the Geneva Conference made it evident to all concerned that the United States would not be bound by the Agreement on the Cessation of Hostilities or the Final Declaration of the Conference. President Eisenhower, in a statement issued the day of the Final Declaration of the Conference, also affirmed that the United States was not a "party to or bound by the decisions taken by the Conference." [54] Nothing in the United States assistance is inconsistent with its unilateral declaration at Geneva, which pointed out that "it would view any renewal of the aggression in violation of the . . . agreements with grave concern and as seriously threatening international peace and security."

Perhaps most importantly, the legal relevance of the Accords to the present conflict must be analyzed in the context of community norms with respect to the lawfulness of the use of force. Wide publication of I.C.C. reports indicating "violations" of the Accords against both sides and indicating R.V.N. objections to the "agreements" has been popularly interpreted as proof that the United States position is unlawful. These reports, like any others, must be viewed in their total context; that means awareness of the ambiguities and limitations of the Geneva settlement,

---

even if not, whether the independence agreements entered into by France with the state of Viet-Nam prior to the Accords would take precedence over any later inconsistent agreements entered into by France. Moreover, it is not clear from this provision that the parties adverted to the R.V.N. as a successor "in their functions"; for example, it is also open to the interpretation that they were referring to successive Commanders-in-Chief of the PAVN and French Union Forces. Nor would this argument solve the question of whether the R.V.N. was bound by the Final Declaration. Attempts to find certainty in the basic outline of the Geneva settlement, whether from the language of Art. 27 \or any other, oversimplify the case.

[54] Background Information Relating to Southeast Asia and Vietnam, Committee on Foreign Relations, United States Senate (Rev. ed., Comm. Print, June 16, 1965), at 60.

the broader context of fundamental community norms as to the lawfulness of the use of force, and the rôle and function of the International Control Commission. The I.C.C., established pursuant to the Agreement on the Cessation of Hostilities, was given the task of supervising application "of the provisions of the agreement." [55] As such, it has been principally concerned with certain control tasks assigned to it, and with investigation and report on implementation of the text of the Accords. Because of this emphasis on application "of the provisions of the agreement," the I.C.C. reports are a useful indication of factual breaches of that text by both sides, and of interpretation of the text. But the I.C.C. has not reconciled the fundamental ambiguities in the Geneva settlement and has quite naturally concentrated on textual "violations." Consequently, in the context of the evidence suggesting that the R.V.N. was not bound by the Accords and their continuing refusal to be bound other than to respect the cease-fire, I.C.C. criticism of R.V.N. objections is hardly surprising. Moreover, the I.C.C. is not an international tribunal which either has authority, or which has attempted, to evaluate the over-all lawfulness of the actions of the participants in the Viet-Nam conflict. It has been principally concerned with securing implementation of the Accords and to that end has been interested in pointing out "violations" of the text without effectively relating the actions of the parties to asserted justifications or attempting to assess the lawfulness of those claims by reference to fundamental community proscriptions. Even this function has been carried out with restraint and concern lest the Commission jeopardize its usefulness as a neutral body. An example of this approach is the 1962 Special Report of the Commission, which cautiously reported "violations" by the D.R.V. for its use of force against the R.V.N. and then continued to record "violations" by the R.V.N. for its receiving defensive military assistance from the United States. The Polish delegate even dissented from these cautious conclusions, feeling that it emphasized D.R.V. violations too much rather than receipt of assistance by the R.V.N. This dissent and others suggest, perhaps not surprisingly, that not all the members of the I.C.C. can be said to be truly disinterested participants. But as a factual report and an interpretation of the text of the Accords, the 1962 Special Report is authoritative. The D.R.V. *was* using force against the R.V.N., the United States *was* providing defensive assistance to meet that attack, and both actions *were* interpreted by the Commission as "violations" of the text of the Accords. Meaningful assessment of the lawfulness of United States assistance to the R.V.N., however, must relate these actions to the broader community norms with respect to the lawfulness of the use of force. Judged in this total context, the D.R.V. attack on a separate international entity documented in this report was unlawful, and the defensive response of the United States indicated by this report was entirely lawful and justified departure from the text, even if the United States and the R.V.N. were bound by the agreement. Judged by com-

[55] Arts. 34 and 36 of the Agreement on the Cessation of Hostilities.

munity standards as to the lawfulness of the use of force, there are profound differences between the aggressive "violations" recorded against the D.R.V. and the defensive "violations" recorded against the R.V.N., and these aggressive actions of the D.R.V. justify the responding defensive assistance. There is no question but that such defensive assistance does not justify the aggressive actions of the D.R.V. This application of the fundamental community norms with respect to the use of force in international relations to the facts of the situation in Viet-Nam is the central task in ascertaining the lawfulness of United States assistance and is one with which the I.C.C. was *not* concerned. That the United States defensive assistance is lawful is also supported in this context by the conventional legal norm that material breach of agreement permits suspension of any corresponding obligations.[56]

An examination of the major ambiguities and limitations of the Geneva settlement re-enforces for the Viet-Nam context the importance of the fundamental community expectation that asserted breach of agreement or political grievances which do not present defense situations do not justify resort to unilateral coercion. The progress of implementation of those Accords must be viewed in the total context of the Geneva settlement and the community norms relating to the lawfulness of the use of force. The inherent ambiguities of the Geneva settlement cast doubt on the reasonableness of asserted D.R.V. expectations with respect to short-range unification of Viet-Nam. The use of force to assert such D.R.V. interpretations is unequivocally unlawful. Any other conclusion sanctions unilateral determination to resort to force as an instrument of major change and, as has been aptly demonstrated in the Viet-Nam conflict, endangers minimum world public order.

Civil War and "Intervention"—The Sound and the Fury

Popularly the Viet-Nam conflict is often referred to as a civil war, and critics of United States assistance argue that by assisting the R.V.N. the United States has unlawfully "intervened" in a civil war. The Lawyer's Committee even sees a close analogy to the United States Civil War.[57] Interestingly, critics differ as to whether they view the conflict as a civil war within the R.V.N. or as a civil war between the R.V.N. and the D.R.V. Although they may characterize the Viet-Nam conflict a civil war in either of these two senses, and sometimes shift back and forth between them, such characterizations mask the real issues at stake, which are the lawfulness of the use of force by the D.R.V. against the R.V.N. and the lawfulness of responding United States assistance. Characterization of the Viet-Nam conflict as a civil war in either of these senses for the purpose of assessing the lawfulness of the use of force and the lawfulness of responding defensive assistance is misleading. For, although the Viet-

---

[56] See authorities cited in McDougal, Moore and Underwood, note 50 above, at 14959, 14982, notes 289 and 290.

[57] Memorandum of Law of Lawyers Committee on American Policy Toward Vietnam, reprinted in 112 Cong. Rec. 2552, at 2554 (daily ed. Feb. 9, 1966).

Nam conflict does have some features of a civil war, the context is substantially different for purposes of assessing the lawfulness of the use of force. Features such as an international military demarcation line between the D.R.V. and the R.V.N., substantial international recognition of both entities, prolonged separate development, division between major contending ideological systems of the world, and substantial outside influence and assistance to the rebels in the R.V.N., set the Viet-Nam conflict apart. In this context, as discussed in section I, force by the D.R.V. against the R.V.N. as a modality of major change is unlawful. The use of force by one such entity against the other is too disruptive of minimum world public order. In these circumstances, it is perfectly lawful for the R.V.N. to receive defensive assistance for the purpose of preserving its territorial and political integrity against unlawful armed attack from the D.R.V.

Similarly, for purposes of assessing the lawfulness of the use of force, it is misleading, or at least obscures the issue, to characterize the conflict *within* the R.V.N. as a civil war. For whether or not the Viet-Cong are militarily controlled by Hanoi, and whether or not the major conflict was precipitated by Hanoi, there can be little doubt that substantial military assistance and direction is supplied by Hanoi. Such assistance and direction, which is in violation of the international cease-fire line separating the D.R.V. and the R.V.N., is unlawful. In its totality it unmistakably constitutes an armed attack aimed at the political and territorial integrity of the R.V.N. In these circumstances it is entirely lawful for the R.V.N. to receive defensive assistance for the purpose of preserving its integrity against unlawful armed attack. Invocation of authorities concerned with civil wars and talk of intervention substantially miss the point in the complex context of the Viet-Nam conflict. Discussion in this context of norms governing the right to assist one or another of the parties in a context characterized by unaided indigenous revolt, while fascinating, is not very helpful. In fact, even in the classic civil war of an essentially indigenous revolt unaided significantly by outside assistance, the prevailing expectation, although controversial, seems to be that the recognized government may receive assistance but the insurgents may not.[58] A principal policy with respect to such norms is the ensuring of self-determination to the peoples of the entity in question. When the insurgents are at least significantly aided by third parties, as in the Viet-Nam conflict, it is difficult to see how self-determination can be invoked to prohibit offsetting defensive assistance to the recognized government. Not surprisingly, the authorities are essentially unanimous in recognizing the right of assistance to the recognized government to offset unlawful outside assistance to the rebels.[59] The direction and assistance from the D.R.V. is at least substantial enough

[58] See, *e.g.*, authorities collected in McDougal, Moore and Underwood, note 50 above, at 14975–76, notes 176 and 179. But see, *e.g.*, Wright, ''International Law and Civil Strife,'' 1959 Proceedings, American Society of International Law 145, 149.

[59] *Ibid.* Also see Brownlie, International Law and the Use of Force by States 327 (1963).

to create grave doubt that, if offsetting United States assistance were not provided to the recognized government, the resulting outcome would reflect majority sentiment within the R.V.N. And even in the absence of a military nose-count or weapons-count with respect to D.R.V. control and assistance of the insurgency in the R.V.N., the evidence that the D.R.V. has always exercised substantial control of the Communist Party apparatus within the R.V.N. casts serious doubt on assertions that the N.L.F. and Viet-Cong apparatus are meaningfully representative of indigenous senti-ment. Even in the absence of such aid, direction or initiation, there is little reason to accept the seemingly neutral absolute advanced by some that self-determination requires that outside assistance never be given to any faction in another international entity. The judgment that self-determination requires that neither the recognized government nor in-surgents can ever be aided disarmingly conceals the naïve assumption that whatever takes place within the confines of a territorial entity is pursuant to genuine self-determination of peoples and that outside "intervention" is necessarily disruptive of self-determination. One suspects that advocates of this "neutral principle" confuse self-determination of entities with genuine self-determination of peoples. As the reapportionment decisions should remind us, people, not territory, are the relevant standard.[60] As-sistance to the recognized government is a prominent feature of the con-temporary international scene and such assistance need not be contrary to genuine self-determination. Professor Sohn has pointed out a number of such examples:

> [S]ince the early days of the United Nations the practice has de-veloped that military assistance to a recognized government is per-mitted, even if its purpose is to assist in suppressing civil strife. . . . When objections were raised in 1946 to the presence of British troops in Indonesia and Greece, the defense that they were there on invitation was accepted by a majority of the Security Council. . . . When military revolts tried to overthrow the Governments of Kenya, Uganda and Tanganyika in 1964, these Governments asked for British as-sistance and no objection was raised by anybody to it, though attempts were made later to replace the British troops with African troops. . . . Similarly, when revolts started in Gabon and other French-speaking West African States in 1964, French troops were invited to restore peace.[61]

Assistance to a recognized government to prevent take-over by an armed minority employing terrorist tactics is not inconsistent with a meaningful

---

60 The frequent emphasis on Viet-Cong control of territory in the popular literature also evidences this misconception. Although it is questionable what "control" means in this context, and whether military "control" is a particularly relevant standard in any sense, if "control" of people is looked to rather than trees or acres, the Saigon government has substantially better credentials than the N.L.F.-Viet-Cong. According to the Mansfield Report the Saigon government controls about 60% of the population compared with only 22% for the rebels. The remainder is disputed. See Mansfield, Muskie, Inouye, Aiken and Boggs, note 22 above, at 142.

61 Letter from Louis B. Sohn, Bemis Professor of International Law, Harvard, to John Norton Moore, April 21, 1966.

right of self-determination. Nothing in the United Nations Charter requires license for armed minority take-over in the name of an all-encompassing right to revolution nor guarantees recognized governments the right to oppress their peoples. Lawfulness of assistance to either faction must be determined in reference to genuine self-determination and the requirements of minimum world public order, not in blind reliance on black-letter rules as to which side, if any, can be aided in a civil war and sometimes suggesting an Alice-in-Wonderland search for neutral principles. The truth of the matter is that outside assistance to one or another faction may or may not be in the interest of genuine self-determination. The only answer to whether it is or not is careful analysis of the relevant features of the context, particularly the objectives of the participants. Self-determination, of course, is not the only important policy in deciding the lawfulness of such assistance. The requirements of minimum world public order are also vital policies at stake and may sometimes reflect more important values than self-determination. The requirements of minimum world public order, that is, the avoidance of unilateral coercion as a modality of major change, would in most contexts seem more strongly applicable to assistance to insurgent groups than to assistance to the recognized government. Perhaps it is not surprising, then, that prevailing international law seems to permit assistance to the recognized government but not to the insurgents. It is precisely by slighting these fundamental requirements of minimum world public order, as well as by self-serving characterizations of self-determination that the Communist concept of just wars of national liberation is deficient. Such slogans, whether intended to be "neutral principles" or to foster a particular ideology, dangerously obfuscate meaningful appraisal of the real policies at stake. The point is that the abstract norms regarding the lawfulness of assistance to the recognized government in a civil war are not only not applicable to the VietNam conflict but are of only limited usefulness anyway. And even if the Viet-Nam conflict is simplistically characterized as a civil war, prevailing norms as to the lawfulness of assistance to the recognized government support the lawfulness of military assistance to the R.V.N. In the VietNam conflict, the principal policies for assessing lawfulness are reflected in the structure for the preservation of minimum world public order, i.e., the minimization of destructive modes of change, and the requirements of genuine self-determination. United States assistance to the R.V.N. is both consistent with fundamental community expectations respecting the lawfulness of the use of force, and with self-determination of the people of the R.V.N.

Neither polity in Viet-Nam is a happy one with respect to ideal operation of the principle of self-determination. Neither party has a government meaningfully responsive to the electorate through democratic processes. These difficulties are shared by many emerging nations and the context of a major conflict has made it particularly difficult for the R.V.N. to improve. The situation does not convince, however, that the D.R.V.-Viet-Cong offer the people of the R.V.N. a more meaningful chance for self-determination. Despite the often-quoted dictum of President Eisenhower writing in a different context about a different issue some twelve years ago,[62] the repeated assertions of most South Vietnamese leaders, including those opposing the present government, indicate that they share no illusion that the N.L.F. stands for their right of self-determination. It is extremely doubtful that a scientific observer could fairly conclude from the evidence today that the majority of the South Vietnamese feel that they are represented by the N.L.F. Even if the recognized government assisted is not the happiest example of operation of the democratic process, if lack of such assistance would result in take-over by an even more undemocratic regime which does not convince that it is representative of indigenous majority sentiment and which holds no hope for meaningful democratic processes, there is little reason to suggest that self-determination prohibits such assistance. If the unhappy fact of a non-democratically elected government prohibits assistance to prevent minority take-over by the destructive modality of wars of national liberation, much of the underdeveloped areas of the world lie vulnerable. Minimum world public order would be largely illusory. Non-democratically based governments must be encouraged to yield to more democratic and socially sensitive processes, but a requirement that they cannot be assisted against coercive take-over by even more undemocratic regimes is an overkill. Such a requirement would seriously impair minimum world public order while not enhancing genuine self-determination. Each case should depend on evaluation of the relevant features of the context, assessing the impact on self-determination and minimum world public order of the possible alternatives. In the ambiguous context of the Viet-Nam conflict, this question of the impact of the probable outcome on genuine self-determination, should defensive military assistance not be provided, is a particularly relevant question. Criticism of support to the present government must take cognizance of the effect on self-determination of effectuating an alternative which would withdraw such assistance, as well as the potentialities of the major contending systems to implement genuine self-determination in the sense of the widest possible participation in decision-making. Certainly a principal goal of the United States must be the genuine self-determination of the people of the R.V.N. and it is to be hoped that the United States will make every effort to promote alternatives which maximize the freedom of choice of the people of the R.V.N. and encourage truly democratic government. There are some indications that the present government of the R.V.N. is trying to move in this direction. But it is not unreasonable to recognize that today the people of the R.V.N. are entitled to their own self-determination free from D.R.V. or Communist coercion. That means the freedom to choose their own form of government and social institutions and to decide for themselves whether they wish unification with the North at some future time. That is the reality in Viet-Nam and one which the D.R.V. is seeking to alter by force. Such an attempt is unlawful and may properly be opposed by defensive assistance.

[62] See Eisenhower, Mandate for Change 449 (Signet ed., 1963).

VII. LAWFULNESS AND BEYOND—POLITICAL INITIATIVES
AND THE SEARCH FOR PEACE

An analysis of the principal policies underlying the relevant legal norms indicates that providing defensive military assistance to the Republic of Viet-Nam is a lawful policy alternative. That lawfulness means compliance with existing structures of international law and the United Nations.

The conflict in Viet-Nam continues because of wide differences between the objectives of the participants and the willingness of the D.R.V. aggressively to pursue its aims by force. Until that willingness is changed or unless the United States abandons the Republic of Viet-Nam, the conflict is likely to continue. In this context, proposals for a sweeping unilateral cease-fire by United States forces "to create conditions for negotiations" [63] are unrealistic. The evidence suggests that the D.R.V. objectives remain unchanged and seriously pursued. But the capacity of the situation for international expansion does indicate a strong interest of the United States and the world community in moderation in response. Limitation rather than expansion of the response against the territory of the D.R.V. would seem a surer and less hazardous path to eventual willingness of the D.R.V. to adopt more rational procedures for conflict resolution. Short of a major threat to the integrity of the D.R.V., it seems probable that, contrary to their public statements, they will not fight forever when it becomes evident that their objectives cannot be achieved by force. Their continued escalation of the attack against the R.V.N. suggests that they have not yet reached that conclusion. The point when they will is not in sight and may require increases in defensive forces within the R.V.N. But a threat to the political and territorial integrity of the D.R.V. should be avoided. Such a threat seems certain to contribute to continuation and international expansion of the conflict. Unlimited expansion to the D.R.V. or other bizarre proposals may become more popular if the conflict drags on. Such solutions are likely to be the surest path to a much longer and more serious conflict. Although perhaps the most unpopular course, the response both North and South should continue to be a measured defensive response to D.R.V.-Viet-Cong initiatives.

This unhappy prognosis underscores the tremendous importance of the search for a negotiated settlement. The search for peace in Viet-Nam must be pursued as aggressively politically as it is pressed on the battlefield. The strong United States efforts to obtain a peaceful solution to the conflict should be continued and intensified. It may be useful in this regard to continue to underscore United States willingness to achieve a peaceful solution by periodic scaledowns or bombing pauses, the continuation of which is announced to be conditioned on some reciprocal reduction of hostilities. Initiation and support of proposals for strengthening I.C.C. effectiveness should be stressed.[64] Any responsibility for failure to adopt such proposals should be assessed and publicized. The search for peace

[63] See Standard, note 9 above, at 634.
[64] See, generally, New York Times, Aug. 23, 1966, p. 1, col. 1 (city ed.).

might also be aided by greater emphasis on clarification of long-run United States goals in Viet-Nam. Such emphasis on goal clarification might be coupled with comprehensive alternative solutions which would be acceptable to the United States and the R.V.N. If specific compromise solutions are placed before the international community by the United States and the R.V.N., world opinion might contribute to greater pressure on Hanoi to negotiate a settlement. Such clarification should not mean abandonment of United States willingness to hold unconditional negotiations, which should be continually sought and stressed. Such clarification would mean offering as additional bases for negotiation specific long-run solutions to the Viet-Nam conflict which would be satisfactory to the United States and the R.V.N. without prejudice to future negotiation on alternative plans. Such alternatives should preserve the basic integrity of the R.V.N. as an entity whose peoples are entitled to self-determination. Consistent with that goal, such alternatives should also provide opportunity for elements opposed to the government of the R.V.N. to express their preferences democratically rather than militarily. Much of the uneasiness among members of the world community about United States policies in Viet-Nam is caused by their concern in the ambiguous Viet-Nam context with whether the United States actions are conducive to genuine self-determination of the people of the R.V.N. That the United States is acting in the interest of self-determination could be clarified by proposing specific plans for meaningfully supervised elections allowing participation of all factions within the R.V.N. Such plans might be conditioned on cessation of hostilities. They would affirm that the principal goal of the United States in Viet-Nam, as in the rest of the world, must be human dignity and meaningful self-determination.

There is nothing concrete nor uniquely creative about these suggestions. Their purpose is simply to indicate that there may be value in the United States proposing positive plans for solution to the Viet-Nam conflict in addition to maintaining its position in favor of unconditional negotiations. Should Hanoi continue to refuse publicly offered reciprocal reduction of hostilities or reject publicly proposed compromise solutions, the world must not mistake which side refuses to adopt rational procedures for conflict resolution. These and other political initiatives are an important technique for discouraging D.R.V. aggression in Viet-Nam and should continue to be pressed. The political initiatives endorsed here may or may not be practical, but the important point is that political initiatives should play a major rôle in the United States response. Such initiatives have a substantial capacity for increasing the pressure on Hanoi to seek a non-military solution. If the present D.R.V. determination to achieve its objectives by the use of force continues, such measures are unlikely to achieve a short-term settlement of the Viet-Nam conflict. But they may aid in clarifying the United States position in Viet-Nam and increase the pressure on Hanoi to limit its aggression and seek a rational solution. As such, they may hasten the day when the use of force will yield to more rational processes.

Legal Aspects of the Viet-Nam Situation

QUINCY WRIGHT

The Viet-Nam hostilities arose and have escalated because of the radically different perceptions of the situation by the principal parties.[1] A settlement might be possible if each side understood the image perceived by the other. An analysis of the interpretation of the situation which would result from an impartial application of international law, presumably reflecting the consensus of world opinion, might also be helpful.

The United States position has been repeatedly stated by the President and the Secretary of State [2] and was expounded in a fifty-two page memorandum, published on March 4, 1966, by the Legal Adviser of the Department of State, entitled "The Legality of United States Participation in the Defense of Viet-Nam." [3]

The United States holds that the cease-fire agreement of 1954 established a boundary between what became virtually independent states of North and South Viet-Nam, that North Viet-Nam, by infiltrating men and supplies to assist the Viet-Cong, was guilty of "armed attack" upon South Viet-Nam in violation of international law and the cease-fire agreement, that South Viet-Nam was justified in using force in self-defense, and that the United States was justified, under international law and Article 51 of

[1] The importance of distorted images and diverse perceptions of the situation, resulting from established stereotypes and ideologies, as well as from inconsistent desires and expectations for the future, in the initiation and development of international conflicts is emphasized in The Craigville Papers, International Conflict and Behavioral Science, Roger Fisher, ed. (N. Y., Basic Books, 1964), especially in contributions by Anatol Rapaport (p. 13), William Gamson (p. 27), Kenneth Boulding (p. 85), Morton Deutsch (p. 142), Urie Bronfenbrenner (p. 161), and Lester Grinspoon (p. 272). See also my comments in A Study of War 1116, 1503, 1562 (University of Chicago Press, 1965); Problems of Stability and Progress in International Relations 145, 165 (Berkeley, Calif., 1954); "International Conflict and the United Nations," 10 World Politics 38 ff. (1957); "The Escalation of International Conflicts," 9 Journal of Conflict Resolution 417 (1965).

[2] See Department of State, White Papers, December, 1961, and February, 1965; White House Statement, Oct. 2, 1965; and President Johnson's address at Johns Hopkins University, April 7, 1965, printed in The Vietnam Reader 123, 128, 193, 343 (Marcus Raskin and Bernard Fall, eds.) (hereafter cited as Raskin and Fall). The White Papers of February, 1965, the Johns Hopkins address of April 7, 1965, and Secretary of State Rusk's address to the American Society of International Law, April 23, 1965 are printed in Vietnam, History, Documents and Opinions 284, 323, 330 (Marvin E. Gettleman, ed.; New York, Fawcett Publications, 1965) (hereafter cited as Gettleman).

[3] Department of State, Office of the Legal Adviser, The Legality of United States Participation in the Defense of Vietnam, March 4, 1966; reprinted in 60 A.J.I.L. 565 (1966) (cited hereafter as U. S. Legal Brief).

the United Nations Charter, in assisting South Viet-Nam at its request by measures of "collective self-defense against armed attack," including the bombing of installations in North Viet-Nam. It contends, I believe correctly, that, in spite of the express limitation of Article 51 to defense against armed attack upon "a Member of the United Nations," the principle of the article, affirming a principle of customary international law, applies equally to a non-Member even if it is not a wholly independent state.[4] Furthermore, the United States points out that it reported its action to the United Nations as required by Article 51, and that organization, by failing to take any action to restore international peace and security in accord with the authority and responsibility given it by Articles 39 and 51, has tacitly approved the United States position. Express approval of the United States position was given by the SEATO Council at its meeting in Canberra, Australia, on June 29, 1966, with the French representative abstaining and the Pakistan representative reserving.[5]

The North Vietnamese Government under Ho Chi Minh has been less explicit in defining its position [6] but it seems to hold that the Democratic

[4] It has been argued that the Charter intended to permit "collective self-defense" only of "members of the United Nations" in order to prevent third-party intervention in behalf of a revolting community or colony whose independence the intervening state may have recognized. International law, however, permits defensive alliances. Art. 2, par. 4, of the Charter forbids armed attack upon any "state," and a valid cease-fire line forbids such attack upon the territory protected by it. It would, therefore, appear that a state can exercise "the inherent right of collective self-defence" (Art. 51) in behalf of any genuinely independent "state" the victim of "armed attack" in violation of Article 2, par. 4, or even an imperfectly independent state protected by an internationally valid cease-fire line. The United States assumed that it could collectively defend non-Members of the United Nations when it admitted Portugal (before it was a Member) and West Germany to NATO and when it made defensive alliances with Japan (before it was a Member) and South Korea. The Soviet Union made a similar assumption in making defensive alliances with certain of its "satellites" in Europe before they were Members.

[5] New York Times, June 30, 1966, p. 12. The International Commission to supervise the Geneva Cease-Fire in Viet-Nam considered the de facto alliance of the Southern Zone of Viet-Nam with the United States and SEATO a violation of the cease-fire agreement. See 8th Report, 1957–58, par. 30; Special Report, 1962, par. 20 (Gettleman 175, 188); and below, notes 53, 63. Endorsement of the United States position by SEATO has no weight in international law. The Harvard Research in International Law suggested that aggression could not be attributed to a state unless "duly determined by a means which that state is bound to accept" (33 A.J.I.L. Supp. 871 (1939)). While a necessity for self-defense permits a temporary unilateral determination of aggression by armed attack, such determination, whether by a state or an alliance, is not authoritative in international law because the other side is not bound to accept it. Failure of the United Nations to act cannot be assumed to indicate tacit approval of defense measures under Art. 51, unless the reasons for this failure so indicate.

[6] The statements of the South Viet-Nam National Liberation Front (Viet-Cong) of Dec. 20, 1960, and of March 22, 1965, with notes by the North Viet-Nam government; the Policy Declaration by North Viet-Nam Premier Pham Van Dong, stating four points for negotiation of peace, April 14, 1965; and the Joint Statement by North Viet-Nam and the Soviet Union, April 17, 1965, are printed in Raskin and Fall 216, 232, 342, 362. The Vietnamese Declaration of Independence, Sept. 2, 1945; the Abdica-

Republic of Viet-Nam, proclaimed in September, 1945, with Ho as its head, and recognized as a "free state" by France and Bao Dai, who had abdicated as Emperor of Annam, is one state; furthermore, that Ho, as the leader of Vietnamese nationalism, was justified by the principle of "self-determination" in resisting the French effort in 1946 to re-establish Bao Dai as head, not of an independent Viet-Nam, but of a "free state" within the French Community. It points out that after Ho's forces in a seven-year war had defeated France at Dien Bien Phu in 1954, Ho was in a position to establish his authority over the whole of Viet-Nam and that he agreed to the cease-fire line, established by the Geneva Conference of 1954, because the compromise settlement would prevent further foreign intervention and the temporary division of Viet-Nam would be terminated by an election to be held in July, 1956, which would result in union under his government.[7] On the basis of these facts, North Viet-Nam contends that the Diem Government in South Viet-Nam succeeded to the obligations of France under the Geneva Agreement (Article 27), even though Bao Dai's representative reserved on them at Geneva, and that it violated those obligations by refusing to implement the provisions concerning elections and by accepting United States military contingents in South Viet-Nam and establishing a *de facto* alliance. Ho Chi Minh is therefore convinced that these continuing violations of provisions of the Geneva Agreement which had induced him to accept it, justified him by 1958 in considering the cease-fire line suspended and in continuing his efforts, begun against France in 1946, to unite Viet-Nam by force. Ho Chi Minh, in short, contends that after he was defrauded, by a conspiracy of Diem and the United States, of the opportunity pledged by the Powers at Geneva to extend his government by peaceful means over the whole of Viet-Nam, then recognized as a single state, he became free to consider the cease-fire line suspended and to assist the Viet-Cong, his supporters in the south,

---

tion of Bao Dai as Emperor of Annam, August, 1945; the French recognition of Viet-Nam as a "free state," March, 1946; and the Viet-Minh's directive for resistance of Dec. 20, 1946, are printed in Gettleman 57, 59, 61, 87. See especially Ho Chi Minh's letter to the heads of several states printed in the Washington Post, Jan. 29, 1966, p. A 12.

[7] In this he agrees with President Eisenhower who wrote in his memoirs, Mandate for Change 372: "I am convinced that the French could not win the war because the internal political situation in Vietnam, weak and confused, badly weakened their military position. I have never talked or corresponded with a person knowledgeable in Indochinese affairs who did not agree that had elections been held as of the time of fighting, possibly 80 percent of the population would have voted for the Communist Ho Chi Minh as their leader rather than Chief of State Bao Dai. Indeed, the lack of leadership and drive on the part of Bao Dai was a factor in the feeling prevalent among Vietnamese that they had nothing to fight for." See Robert Scheer, How the United States Got Involved in Vietnam 11 (Center for the Study of Democratic Institutions, Santa Barbara, Calif., 1965). It is unlikely that this estimate, if correct for 1954, would have changed radically by 1956. In an election in South Viet-Nam in 1955, Diem proved to be much more popular than Bao Dai, but there was never a test of his relative popularity with Ho Chi Minh.

For texts of Geneva Agreements, 1954, and other relevant documents, see 60 A.J.I.L. 629-649 (1966).

in hostilities against the Diem and subsequent South Vietnamese governments which opposed the Geneva political settlement.[8] The situation was therefore, in Ho's opinion, one of "civil strife" within the domestic jurisdiction of Viet-Nam, and the United States violated international law, the United Nations Charter, and the Geneva agreements by intervening with armed force.

The United States has replied to this position by asserting that, while ultimate unification of Viet-Nam by free elections is not ruled out, the Geneva Powers could not have really intended that Viet-Nam be united by an election in 1956 because conditions for "free general elections by secret ballot" to establish "fundamental freedoms guaranteed by democratic institutions," called for by the Geneva resolutions, could not be established by that date, especially in Communist North Viet-Nam. Consequently the failure to hold the elections did not suspend the cease-fire agreement which the United States insists was violated by North Viet-Nam first. Referring to the Geneva prohibition (Articles 16, 17) of the introduction into Viet-Nam of troop reinforcements and new military equipment (except for replacement and repair) and of adherence of either zone to any military alliance, and the use of either zone for the resumption of hostilities or to "further an aggressive policy," the United States seeks to justify its establishment of forces and bases in South Viet-Nam as replacements of personnel and equipment,[9] as assistance to the South Vietnamese Government to fight Communism in its zone,[10] or as resistance to infiltration or invasion from the north in violation of the Geneva Agreement. For the latter justification it cites:

> the international law principle that a material breach of an agreement by one party entitles the other at least to withhold compliance with an equivalent, corresponding, or related provision until the defaulting party is prepared to honor its obligations.

It therefore contends that:

> the systematic violation of the Geneva Accords by North Viet-Nam justified South Viet-Nam in suspending compliance with the provision controlling entry of foreign military personnel and military equipment.[11]

[8] Premier Pham Van Dong of North Viet-Nam in his statement of April 8, 1965, indicated his willingness to go back to Geneva in a peace negotiation, provided it included the political as well as the military provisions (New York Times, April 14, 1965; Raskin and Fall 342). North Vietnamese assistance to the Viet-Cong across the cease-fire line would clearly be illegal if the cease-fire agreement were in effect, as insisted by the United States. In saying in this note "pending the peaceful unification of Vietnam . . . the military provisions of the 1954 Geneva agreement must be strictly respected," and referring to violations by the United States, he stated a bargaining position. This statement also recognized the autonomy of South Viet-Nam under the South Vietnamese Liberation Front and said "the peaceful reunion of Vietnam is to be settled by the Vietnamese people in both zones without foreign interference." (See note 20 below.)

[9] U. S. Legal Brief 29; 60 A.J.I.L. 576 (1966).

[10] International Control Commission, Special Report, 1962, par. 6, referring to joint declaration of Vice President Johnson and Premier Diem, May 13, 1961, Gettleman 186, 205.

[11] U. S. Legal Brief 30–31; 60 A.J.I.L. 577 (1966).

It has been widely believed that Ho Chi Minh's activity has been motivated less by a nationalistic policy of uniting Viet-Nam than by a policy of expanding Communism to South Viet-Nam and other states;[12] and that the United States intervention has been motivated less by love for, or obligations to, the South Vietnamese people than by the Truman doctrine of containing Communism and preventing the fall of dominoes.[13] Whatever motivations may have been influential, it is clear that international law does not recognize ideological differences, and that intervention by a state in the internal affairs of another state, even on invitation of the government which it recognizes, whether in behalf of a Communist faction to assist its "war of liberation" or in behalf of an anti-Communist faction to "contain Communism," violates traditional international law and the United Nations Charter.[14] Consequently these possible motivations have not been referred to in the legal arguments. Cold War ideologies have undoubtedly been important in the Viet-Nam hostilities, but other political motives have also played a part—both nationalism and humanitarianism. Ho Chi Minh, although a Communist, was accepted by both Communists and anti-Communist Vietnamese as the leader of Vietnamese nationalism during the struggle against Japan and France, and during the Geneva Conference the representatives of both Ho Chi Minh and Bao Dai

[12] See Ho Chi Minh, "The Path Which Led Me to Leninism," April, 1960, and "Founding of the Communist Party," February, 1930, printed in Gettleman 30, 33.

[13] The White House statement of Oct. 2, 1965, said: "The Security of South Vietnam is a major interest of the United States as other free nations. We will adhere to our policy of working with the people and government of South Vietnam to deny this country to Communism." (Raskin and Fall 128.) President Eisenhower's statement (note 7 above) suggests that this motivation influenced the United States in seeking to prevent elections until the state of opinion in Viet-Nam had radically changed. The domino theory was first stated by President Eisenhower to indicate the United States' national interest in containment of Communism in Southeast Asia. Insofar as it implies a rigid and undiscriminating application of the containment policy, it is vigorously criticized by Don R. and Arthur Larson (Vietnam and Beyond 6 ff., Duke University, 1965); Hans J. Morgenthau (Vietnam and the United States 62, 77, Washington, Public Affairs Press, 1965, reprinted in Gettleman 365); George F. Kennan, who initiated the policy of containment in 1947 (Report to subcommittee of Committee on Foreign Affairs, House of Representatives, May 14, 1965, reprinted in Raskin and Fall 15); The American Friends Service Committee (Report on Peace in Vietnam 12 ff., 65, New York, Hill and Wang, 1966); Walter Lippmann (numerous columns in the New York Herald Tribune, 1965); 28% of 525 members of the New York Council on Foreign Relations polled in 1965 (American Dilemma in Vietnam, a Report on the Views of Leading Citizens in Thirty-Three Cities 14, New York, Council on Foreign Relations, 1965); J. W. Fullbright (Ark.), Chairman, Foreign Relations Committee; Mike Mansfield (Mont.), Dem. Floor Leader; Wayne Morse (Ore.); Ernest Gruening (Alaska); Frank Church (Idaho), and other Senators (quoted, Raskin and Fall 209, 281; Gettleman 376); Quincy Wright ("Principles of Foreign Policy," World View, Council on Religion and International Affairs, February, 1965, reprinted in Raskin and Fall 7).

[14] Quincy Wright, "International Law and Ideologies," 48 A.J.I.L. 616 (1954); "International Law and Civil Strife," 1959 Proceedings, American Society of International Law 45 ff.; The Role of International Law in the Elimination of War 61 (University of Manchester Press, 1962).

claimed to be the head of a single Vietnamese national state. The United States had given extensive educational and economic aid to South Viet-Nam, establishing friendly ties especially during the Diem period, and was shocked by the reports of purges and barbarities in North Viet-Nam and the flow of refugees, mainly from the North, after the Geneva Conference.[15]

The legal issues, clarification of which might contribute to a judgment of the validity of the diverse images of the Viet-Nam situation, may be stated as follows:

1. Are the hostilities between North and South Viet-Nam international hostilities or civil strife, *i.e.*, is Viet-Nam two states or one?

2. Was the requirement for an election in 1956 dependent on the development of conditions assuring that the election would be free and fair?

3. Was the requirement concerning elections in the resolutions of the Geneva Conference such an integral part of the Cease-Fire Agreement between France and the Democratic Republic of Viet-Nam (Ho Chi Minh) as to permit suspension of the cease-fire when the elections were frustrated?

4. If it is assumed that the cease-fire line continued in operation, was North Viet-Nam guilty of "armed attacks" upon South Viet-Nam justifying the United States bombing attacks north of the cease-fire line, which began in February, 1965, as measures of "collective self-defense"?

The following issues of international law and United States Constitutional law have been discussed, but are of less importance in clarifying the different images of the situation.

5. Did the reprisals undertaken by the United States in the Gulf of Tonkin episode of August, 1964, violate international law?

6. Did the Congressional Resolution of August 7, 1964, after the Tonkin episode authorize the extensive military action ordered by the President since February, 1965?

7. Did the United States have a binding commitment to use armed force in defense of South Viet-Nam before February, 1965?

[15] Nearly a million refugees, mostly Roman Catholics and dependents of the colonial native army left North for South Viet-Nam after Geneva, and the land reform program in the North led to brutalities. General Nguyen Giap, Commander-in-Chief of North Vietnamese forces, in a speech of Oct. 31, 1956, admitted that the North Vietnamese government in this program had "executed too many honest people," resorted to "terror which became far too widespread," "failed to respect the principles of freedom of faith and worship in many areas," "attacked tribal chiefs too strongly," resorted to "disciplinary punishments and executions" instead of education, and "torture came to be regarded as a normal practice during party reorganization." These oppressions resulted in serious revolts among the peasantry which in Ho Chi Minh's home province had to be put down by the regular army. (See U. S. Legal Brief, p. 33; Bernard Fall, New York Times Magazine, July 10, 1966, p. 52.) Even worse brutalities were reported in the American press. Whether if shorn of exaggerations they were worse than in the South during the Diem regime has been controversial. See Friends Service Committee, note 13 above, p. 45; Scheer, note 7 above, pp. 26 ff., 58 ff.; Devillers, note 16 below, Gettleman 222 ff.

1. The evidence suggests that Viet-Nam is one state and that the hostilities of Ho Chi Minh's government against the Saigon Government would be civil strife within its domestic jurisdiction unless forbidden by the cease-fire Agreement.

During the hostilities between the "Democratic Republic of Viet-Nam" under Ho Chi Minh and France, supporting the "Republic of Viet-Nam" under Bao Dai from 1946 to 1954 and during the Geneva Conference, both sides regarded Viet-Nam as one state, the legal issue being whether it was an independent state or a "Free State" within the French Community.[16] When the hostilities ended with French defeat, large areas of the south were occupied by Ho Chi Minh's forces, the Viet-Minh, and areas in the north by forces of France and Bao Dai. The Cease-Fire Agreement of 1954 signed by representatives of France and the Democratic Republic of Viet-Nam provided for the withdrawal of these forces across the cease-fire line, substantially the 17th parallel, and very explicitly declared that

[16] The underlying political issue was whether it should be a state with Communist or with Western orientation, but this was overshadowed by the desire for peace by all the Powers represented, except the United States and Bao Dai. See Donald Lancaster, former official in the British Legation, Saigon, "Power Politics at the Geneva Conference, 1954," from The Emancipation of French Indochina 313 ff. (London, 1961) reprinted in Gettleman 118 ff.; see also American Friends Service Committee, note 13 above, p. 41, and General de Gaulle's news conference, July 23, 1964, quoted in Raskin and Fall 268. There seems to have been a general expectation among the participants that the compromise settlement accepted by all the representatives, except those of the United States and Bao Dai, would result in elections which would unite Viet-Nam under Ho Chi Minh. "The Conference ended amid a flurry of mutual congratulations, while Molotov, giving further proof of the unusual amiability which had distinguished Soviet behavior throughout the proceedings, paid a fulsome compliment to Eden, stressing the latter's outstanding services and rôle in the Conference, a rôle which Molotov insisted 'cannot be exaggerated'." (Lancaster, loc. cit., Gettleman 136, 159.) "The disproportion between the monolithic power of the Vietminh, armed with the halo of victory, and the almost derisory weakness of the so-called Nationalist Vietnam was such that in the summer of 1954 almost no one thought that the two years' delay won by M. Mendès-France at Geneva could be anything but a respite in which to salvage as much as possible from the wreck. At the end of the period, unity would certainly be restored, this time to the benefit of the Vietminh, the basic hypothesis then acknowledged by all being that the Geneva Agreements would definitely be implemented." (Philippe Devillers, "The Struggle for Unification of Vietnam," The China Quarterly, London, Jan.–March, 1962, p. 3; reprinted in Gettleman 211.) "The opinion of the French at the time of Geneva (and that of most Western experts) was that the Accords would simply delay the eventual Viet Minh victory, since Ho's forces would surely win the elections scheduled for July, 1956" (Robert Scheer, note 7 above, p. 20). "If Geneva and what was agreed upon there means anything at all, it means . . . Taps for the buried hopes of freedom in Southeast Asia! Taps for the newly betrayed millions of Indochinese who must now learn the awful facts of slavery from their eager Communist masters! Now the devilish techniques of brainwashing, forced confessions and rigged trials have a new locale for their exercise." (Cardinal Spellman, Speech, American Legion Convention, Aug. 31, 1954, quoted in New York Times, Sept. 1, 1954; Gettleman 239, and Robert Scheer, note 7 above, p. 21, who credits the Cardinal with much influence in inducing the United States to upset the Geneva settlement by building up Diem as head of an independent South Viet-Nam (p. 24).)

this line was not an international boundary but a "provisional military demarcation line" and that the territories at each side were not states but "zones." [17]   The final resolutions of the Conference declared that "the independence, unity and territorial integrity" of Viet-Nam should be respected, and provided that elections "shall" be held in July, 1956, to determine the government of Viet-Nam. These resolutions did not constitute a formal treaty and were not signed by any of the delegates. They were, however, accepted by all of the delegates except those of the United States and Bao Dai's Republic of Viet-Nam, both of whom made statements "noted" by the Conference. In regard to the reservation by Bao Dai's representative, the Chairman at the final session of the Conference, Anthony Eden, said:

> We can not now amend our final act, which is the statement of the Conference as a whole, but the Declaration of the Representative of the State of Vietnam will be taken note of.[18]

It seems clear that the Conference recognized Viet-Nam as one state and provided that it should be united by one government in 1956.

After the Geneva Conference and frustration of a four-year effort by Ho Chi Minh to have the elections held, the Southern Zone, now under Ngo Dinh Diem, supported by the United States, declared itself independent and was recognized by some governments, placed under the protection of SEATO, and permitted to represent Viet-Nam in some international organizations, but it was not admitted to the United Nations.[19]

[17] There was active debate at Geneva over the location of this line and the agreement put it further north than Ho's delegate wanted. The United States has argued that this indicates an opinion on both sides that the line would mark a division for a long time, probably beyond 1956, but it can also be argued that Ho gave way in spite of his strong military position because he thought the line would last for only two years. "The Vietminh was reluctant to agree to this partition, which left it slightly less than half of the territory of Vietnam despite the fact that at the time it controlled three-quarters. However, Ho Chi Minh's government was under strong Soviet and Chinese pressure to give way on this point. The concern of China and probably also the Soviet Union, was that a continuation of the war might cause the introduction of American military power—possibly atomic—in support of the French, a course of action which the United States did in fact come very close to taking. The Vietminh accepted this temporary loss because of the explicit promise in both the armistice agreement and in the Geneva Declaration that within a period of two years national elections would be held to unify the country. They had every reason to believe that these elections would take place because the agreements stipulated that France, the other party to the armistice, was to maintain control of civil administration in the South until elections were held. (Article 14a of the armistice agreement.) In effect, then, the elections and the military truce were interdependent." (Friends Service Committee, *op. cit.* note 13 above, p. 41.) This accorded with the expectation of most of the Powers at Geneva (see note 16 above).

[18] Gettleman 159.

[19] The U. S. Legal Brief (p. 12) says: "The Republic of Viet-Nam in the South has been recognized as a separate international entity by approximately 60 governments the world over. It has been admitted as a member of a number of the specialized agencies of the United Nations." Most of these sixty governments, including the United States, recognized the Republic of Viet-Nam (Bao Dai) before the Geneva division, though they accepted the Saigon Government as its representative

Ho Chi Minh, the Communist states and many unaligned states, including India, did not accept this situation. In 1956, Diem began to be actively resisted by the Viet-Cong, the name given to the Viet-Minh in the Southern Zone, and after 1958 Ho Chi Minh's government began to assist it by infiltrations of men and supplies from the Northern Zone. Diem's government, although supported by United States economic, educational and military aid, was not able to eliminate the Viet-Cong, which in 1960 organized the "South Vietnam National Liberation Front" in control of much of the Southern Zone outside of the major cities.[20] Diem became increasingly dictatorial and unpopular and was assassinated on November 1, 1963. The succession of unstable governments which have followed him have never controlled half of the territory of South Viet-Nam.

South Viet-Nam was clearly regarded as part of Viet-Nam before 1954 and as a "zone" of that state separated by a temporary cease-fire line by the Geneva Conference, and it seems not to have acquired sufficient governmental authority, stability, public support, or recognition to be-

---

after the division. A number of states recognized the Democratic Republic of Viet-Nam (Ho Chi Minh) before the Geneva separation and continue to accept the Hanoi government as its representative. Eight or nine states have missions with the National Liberation Front (Viet-Cong) in South Viet-Nam. (George A. Carver, Jr., 44 Foreign Affairs 347 at 367 (1966).) The Republic of Viet-Nam was admitted to UPU, UNESCO and WMO before Geneva, and to ILO, WHO, and FAO in 1950, and the Saigon Government has continued to represent Viet-Nam in these international organizations. These facts do not prove that South Viet-Nam is a "separate international entity" any more than the recognition by many states and the United Nations of the Republic of China, represented by the Government at Taipei (Chiang Kai-shek), proves that Taiwan is a separate political entity, though other facts may support this contention. The U. S. Legal Brief also says: "The United Nations General Assembly in 1957 voted to recommend South Viet-Nam for membership in the organization, and its admission was frustrated only by the veto of the Soviet Union in the Security Council." The brief does not notice that the Soviet Union proposed simultaneous admission of both Viet-Nams (Devillers in Gettleman 220), which the United States opposed, as it has opposed "two Chinas." The United States has also suggested that the extension of SEATO protection to South Viet-Nam soon after Geneva indicates that the Western-oriented states did not believe Viet-Nam would be united under a Communist government in 1956; but see notes 5 and 16 above.

[20] The Viet-Cong were originally the supporters of Ho in the South when he was considered the symbol of Vietnamese nationalism, and the South Vietnamese National Liberation Front, which was formed in December, 1960, includes many non-Communist elements (see Devillers, note 16 above, Gettleman 229 ff.). The United States considers it a mere arm of Ho's government which should not be independently represented at any peace conference. (See Secretary Rusk's television statement, reported in the New York Times, Dec. 8, 1965.) The Front, however, Ho himself, other Communist states and some Americans like Senators J. W. Fulbright, Robert Kennedy, and the Friends Service Committee, credit it with an autonomous status which justifies its representation at any peace negotiation. The negotiating position stated by Premier Dong on April 8, 1965, and by the Front on July 22, 1965, appears to be a recession from Ho's original position in that it recognizes that two Viet-Nams will exist until united by "the Vietnamese people themselves," and thus converges toward the United States position stated by President Johnson on April 7, 1965, and by Secretary Rusk on Aug. 3, 1965. (See note 8 above, and Friends Service Committee, note 13 above, p. 56 ff.)

come an independent state under international law since then.[21]   Consequently, apart from the Cease-Fire Agreement and American intervention, hostilities in Viet-Nam should be regarded as civil strife.

2. Diem and the United States have contended that it was understood at Geneva that the election called for by the resolutions could not be held until conditions assured that the election would be free and fair.   It is true that the resolution referred to "free general elections by secret ballot" and that General Bedell Smith, reserving for the United States on the Resolutions, said:

> In the case of nations now divided against their will, we shall continue to seek to achieve unity through free elections supervised by the United Nations to insure that they are conducted fairly.[22]

The conditions in Viet-Nam which might impair the freedom and fairness of elections were, however, well known to the members of the Geneva Conference when they provided categorically for the holding of elections in July, 1956, for their supervision by the International Control Commission, and for consultations to prepare for them beginning on July 20, 1955.   The delay of two years was "in order to ensure that sufficient progress in the restoration of peace has been made, and that all the necessary conditions obtain for free expression of the national will." [23] These political provisions resulted from compromises between the Western and Communist states represented at Geneva.   They were believed necessary to achieve agreement and peace in Southeast Asia.[24]   Failure to observe their precise terms would, therefore, jeopardize the entire agreement, as subsequent events demonstrated.

It would appear, therefore, that Ho Chi Minh was entitled to regard the holding of elections in July, 1956, as obligatory on the parties to the Cease-Fire Agreement, including France and its successor in South Viet-Nam, Diem.   The premature withdrawal from Viet-Nam of the French, who were considered responsible for preparing for the elections in the Southern Zone has been criticized, but the government of the Southern Zone clearly succeeded to this responsibility.[25]   General responsibility for

---

21 This is controversial.   The United States argues that, whatever may have been the situation in 1956, the *de facto* existence of South Viet-Nam and its wide recognition probably gave it a status of independence during the Diem period and since, but that in any case it had become a "separate international entity" which the United States could defend from aggression (Legal Brief, p. 14).   See note 19 above.

22 Gettleman 157; 60 A.J.I.L. 645 (1966).

23 Gettleman 152; 60 A.J.I.L. 644 (1966).

24 General de Gaulle, at a news conference on July 23, 1964, said: "At the time everyone seemed to desire it (an end of fighting) sincerely."   Printed in Raskin and Fall 269.   See also notes 16 above and 28 below.

25 Art. 27 of the Geneva Cease-Fire Agreement (Gettleman 146; 60 A.J.I.L. 638 (1966)).   At the same news conference (July 23, 1964) General de Gaulle referred to the "shock caused in the South by the withdrawal of our administration and our forces," which he attributed to the "determination of the Americans to take our place in Indochina" because of their assumption of an anti-Communist mission throughout the world, their aversion "to any colonial work which had not been theirs," and

carrying out the political provisions of the Geneva Conference lay with the "Co-Chairmen (Britain and the Soviet Union) and the Geneva Powers" as indicated by the International Control Commission in its tenth report in 1960.[26]

3. The evidence suggests that the provisions concerning elections in the final resolutions of the Geneva Conference were considered essential elements in the Cease-Fire Agreement. This agreement, therefore, became suspendable when the elections were frustrated by one of the parties and the other party, Ho Chi Minh, was free to consider his obligation to respect the cease-fire line suspended and to continue his long effort to unify Viet-Nam by force.

There can be little doubt but that Ho Chi Minh regarded the Geneva resolutions as a part of the settlement to which he agreed. Military unification of Viet-Nam was within his grasp after the defeat of France at Dien Bien Phu if external aggression, especially by the United States, could be avoided. It is incredible that he would have agreed to the cease-fire, even though he desired it, in the hope that it would prevent such intervention, unless he was convinced that unification would shortly be effected by the peaceful method of elections.[27] A study of the diplomacy at Geneva suggests that the principal Powers except the United States were more interested in peace than in ideologies, and recognized that the political provisions of the settlement, which would probably result in a national Communist Viet-Nam, were the price of peace, and were therefore no less important than the military provisions.[28]

---

to the "natural desire in such a powerful people to ensure themselves of new positions." Raskin and Fall 269.   [26] See note 36 below.

[27] It has been suggested that the provision requiring that elections be free and fair, and the bargaining at Geneva on the location of the cease-fire line and the length of the cooling-off period before the elections, on both of which Ho's representative receded, indicate that Ho was more interested in the cease-fire than in the elections. This argument is not convincing. Ho undoubtedly wanted a cease-fire to avoid United States intervention, for which Dulles had been pressing, but he may have attached more weight to the positive dating of the elections than to their freedom, and cared less for the location of the cease-fire line than to its prospective termination in two years. See Bernard Fall, "How the French Got Out of Vietnam," New York Times Magazine, May 2, 1965, printed in Raskin and Fall 88, and note 17 above.

[28] The British, led by Anthony Eden, who with Molotov was co-chairman of the Conference, and the French, led by Mendès-France, who had succeeded Laniel as Prime Minister during the Conference, took the lead in the negotiations and favored compromises which would assure peace, in opposition to the desire of the United States, led by Secretary of State Dulles and later by General Bedell Smith, to contain Communism by military intervention. The British and French spirit of compromise was supported by the Soviet Union, represented by co-chairman Molotov, who was anxious to induce France to reject the pending "European Defense Community," and by China, represented by Chou En-lai, who was worried about United States intervention. President Eisenhower, who had recently negotiated peace in Korea after his election as a "peace" President, moderated Dulles' Cold-War position and later wrote in his Mandate for Change that "By and large, the settlement obtained by the French Union at Geneva in 1954 was the best it could get under the circumstances." (Scheer, note 7 above, p. 18.) The United States, therefore, tolerated the compromise settlement, though it did not subscribe to it. Frustration of the election was, therefore, not

The Department of State's legal brief emphasizes the principle of international law that

> A material breach of an agreement by one party entitles the other at least to withhold compliance with an equivalent, corresponding, or related provision until the defaulting party is prepared to honor its obligations.[29]

The brief used this principle to justify its escalation of hostilities in response to North Vietnamese infiltration contrary to the cease-fire requirements, but the principle seems more in point to permit North Viet-Nam to regard the obligation to respect the cease-fire line as suspended after the provision for terminating this temporary line in 1956 was frustrated by the refusal of South Viet-Nam to co-operate in carrying out the election. Not only was the provision for elections a major factor in inducing Ho Chi Minh to accept the temporary cease-fire, but it is expressly mentioned in the Cease-Fire Agreement, which provides:

> Pending the general elections which will bring about the unification of Viet-Nam, the conduct of civil administration in each regrouping zone shall be in the hands of the party whose forces are to be regrouped there in virtue of the present Agreement.[30]

This provision of the Cease-Fire Agreement could only be interpreted by reference to the conference resolutions which provided:

> The Conference recognises that the essential purpose of the Agreement relating to Viet-Nam is to settle military questions with a view to ending hostilities and that the military demarcation line is provisional and should not in any way be interpreted as constituting a political or territorial boundary. The Conference expresses its conviction that the execution of the provisions set out in the present declaration and in the Agreement on the cessation of hostilities creates the necessary basis for the achievement in the near future of a political settlement in Viet-Nam.
>
> The Conference declares that, so far as Viet-Nam is concerned, the settlement of political problems, effected on the basis of respect for the principles of independence, unity and territorial integrity, shall permit the Vietnamese people to enjoy the fundamental freedoms, guaranteed by democratic institutions established as a result of free general elections by secret ballot. In order to ensure that sufficient progress in the restoration of peace has been made, and that all the necessary conditions obtain for free expression of the national will, general elections shall be held in July 1956, under the supervision of an international commission composed of representatives of the member states of the International Supervisory Commission, referred

---

only a breach of faith with Ho but also with the major Powers. (See Lancaster, *op. cit.* note 16 above, and Friends Service Committee *op. cit.*, note 13 above, p. 41.) Anthony Eden, while noting in his memoirs (Full Circle 143) that through the Geneva accords "the Vietnamese (*i.e.*, Bao Dai) had saved more of their country than had at one time seemed possible," expressed his "regret" a dozen years after Geneva that these accords had not been accepted by the United States and carried out (44 Foreign Affairs 230 (1966)).

29 U. S. Legal Brief, pp. 30, 31; 60 A.J.I.L. 577 (1966).

30 Art. 14 (a). See Gettleman 140; 60 A.J.I.L. 632 (1966).

to in the Agreement on the cessation of hostilities. Consultations will be held on this subject between the competent representative authorities of the two zones from 20th July, 1955, onwards.[31]

Although the Government of the Republic of Viet-Nam (Bao Dai) was not a party to these agreements, France was, and the Diem government established in the Southern Zone as successor to France was bound by them. Its failure to carry out the provisions, which were regarded as the essence of the agreement by the "Democratic Republic of Viet-Nam" (Ho Chi Minh), would relieve the latter of the obligation to respect the cease-fire line and would entitle it to continue its interrupted effort to unify Viet-Nam by force.[32]

The resistance to this effort by the Saigon Government, therefore, constituted "civil strife" within the domestic jurisdiction of Viet-Nam, and American intervention involving the use of armed force against the Viet-Cong in the south and the bombing of installations in the north was a violation of traditional international law forbidding intervention in the domestic jurisdiction of another state and prohibited even to the United Nations,[33] unless the situation constituted a threat to or breach of the peace entitling it to take measures to restore international peace and security.[34]

There is no doubt but that breach of a valid cease-fire line constitutes a violation of international law, as does violation of an international boundary. This was held in the Korean situation of 1950, as noted by the State Department's legal brief.[35] This brief does not discuss the question of whether the cease-fire line in Viet-Nam became suspendable after frustration of the conditions which induced its acceptance by one of

[31] Pars. 6, 7, Gettleman 150–151; 60 A.J.I.L. 644 (1966). These resolutions were not signed, but the P.C.I.J. recognized that oral agreements might be binding in the Eastern Greenland case (Series A/B, No. 53). See also Eberhard P. Deutsch, "The Legality of the United States Position in Vietnam," 52 American Bar Association Journal 436 at 440 (1966).

[32] "When in a civil war a military struggle for power ends on the agreed condition that the competition will be transferred to the political level, the side which repudiates the agreed conditions must expect that the military struggle will be resumed." (Friends Service Committee, op. cit. note 13 above, p. 43.) The U. S. Legal Brief (p. 33) says: "The South Vietnamese Government realized these facts [that conditions for a fair election did not exist in North Viet-Nam] and quite properly took the position that consultations for elections in 1956 as contemplated by the accords would be a useless formality." The Brief adds in a footnote: "In any event, if North Viet-Nam considered there had been a breach of obligation by the South, its remedies lay in discussion with Saigon, perhaps in an appeal to the co-Chairmen of the Geneva conference, or in a reconvening of the conference to consider the situation. Under international law, North Viet-Nam had no right to use force outside its own zone in order to secure its political objectives." No reference is made to the fact that Ho Chi Minh had attempted all these remedies for four years without results. Not until 1958 did he conclude that Diem and the Powers had buried the Geneva agreements, and begin to give assistance across the cease-fire line to the Viet-Cong, which had renewed civil strife in South Viet-Nam in 1956, after the date for the elections had passed. See Devillers, in Gettleman 216 ff.; Fall, in Raskin and Fall 90.

[33] U.N. Charter, Art. 2, par. 7.   [34] Ibid., Art. 39.

[35] U. S. Legal Brief, p. 13; 60 A.J.I.L. 570 (1966).

the parties, nor is this question discussed by the International Control Commission, which continued to examine alleged violations of the Cease-Fire Agreement up to 1965, thus suggesting that it continued to operate and to bind the parties. The Control Commission's responsibility was, however, limited to supervising the execution of the military provisions of the Geneva Agreement and did not extend to judging the effect on these provisions of non-fulfillment of the political settlement reached at Geneva. It did, however, recognize the importance of fulfillment of these provisions and the responsibility of the Geneva Powers in the matter. In its tenth report in 1960 the Commission said:

> During the period under report, there has been no progress in regard to the political settlement envisaged in the Final Declaration. The parties have not held consultations with a view to holding free nation-wide elections leading to the reunification of Vietnam and thereby facilitating early fulfillment of the tasks assigned to the Commission and the termination of its activities. The Commission is confident that this important problem is engaging the attention of the Co-Chairmen and the Geneva Powers and that they will take whatever measures they deem necessary to resolve it.[36]

The United States legal brief dismisses the contention that the hostilities were civil strife, by characterizing any analogy to the American Civil War as:

> an entire fiction disregarding the actual situation in Viet-Nam. The Hanoi regime is anything but the legitimate government of a unified country in which the South is rebelling against lawful national authority.[37]

There are undoubtedly differences in the two cases but there are also similarities. The issue of civil strife in America in 1861 and in Viet-Nam in 1965 was whether the Declaration of Independence of the United States of July 4, 1776, and the Declaration of Independence of the Democratic Republic of Viet-Nam of September 2, 1945, closely resembling it,[38] contemplated in each case a unified state as held by Lincoln and Ho Chi Minh, or permitted secession as held by Jefferson Davis and Diem. There is no doubt that a "unified country" did not exist in the United States during the period when the Confederate States of America occupied the South or in Viet-Nam when the Republic of Viet-Nam (Diem) occupied much of the southern half of that country. It is true the analogy is imperfect because the United States was a unified country for many years before 1861 and Viet-Nam has been in almost continuous strife with France or South Viet-Nam since its Declaration of Independence. Furthermore South Viet-Nam has received more recognition as a state than did the Confederate States.[39] Nevertheless the position of Ho in regard to the

---

[36] Par. 68; Gettleman 181.

[37] U. S. Legal Brief, p. 12; 60 A.J.I.L. 569 (1966).

[38] Gettleman 57.

[39] There is also the ideological difference that in Viet-Nam the South professed the doctrine of individual freedom against Communism in the North, while in the United

legal unity of Viet-Nam is similar to that of Lincoln in regard to the United States, and the position of the United States in Viet-Nam is similar to that which Great Britain would have had if it had intervened in behalf of the Confederacy as it threatened to do in 1861, giving rise to diplomatic notes by Secretary of State Seward and a resolution by Congress indicating that such a move would be an unfriendly act.[40]

Giving full consideration to the military and political provisions of the Geneva settlement, it would appear that the cease-fire had lapsed by 1958 and the situation had become one of civil strife in which outside states were forbidden by international law to intervene even on the invitation of one side.

4. Even if the cease-fire line remained legally effective, North Viet-Nam could not be accused of "aggression" against South Viet-Nam unless it had launched an unjustifiable "armed attack" upon the latter prior to the United States bombing raids across that line in February, 1965.[41] The basic American argument to justify these raids was that they were acts of "collective self-defense" permitted by Article 51 of the United Nations Charter.[42] The meaning of this article has been controversial.

It is true that traditional international law permitted military action in self-defense if there were an "instant and overwhelming necessity permitting no moment for deliberation," i.e., if hostile forces were about to attack. It seems clear, however, that the San Francisco Conference, by limiting self-defense to cases of "armed attack," intended to eliminate all preventive or pre-emptive action in order to maintain to the utmost

States the North professed this doctrine against slavery in the South. As noted above, such ideological differences are not recognized in international law except insofar as a state may have accepted covenants of human rights (note 14 above). This difference, however, probably prevented British intervention in behalf of the Confederacy after Lincoln had turned the Civil War into a war against slavery, rather than a war to preserve the Union, by the preliminary Emancipation Proclamation of September, 1862. (6 Moore, International Law Digest 7.) The difference also undoubtedly influenced U. S. intervention on the side of South Viet-Nam. Stereotypes about the offensive character of Communism and evidence of lack of respect for human rights in North Viet-Nam aroused American opinion against Ho Chi Minh, even though there was evidence of similar denials of human rights by Diem's Government, leading to his assassination, and the intervention itself resulted in increased brutalities against civilians from government and guerrilla activities on both sides and aerial bombings by the United States (see note 15 above).

[40] The British lost interest in intervention after the war became one against slavery, but France continued to urge intervention. See 6 Moore, Digest of International Law 6–10.

[41] On this assumption, these raids, if of a magnitude to constitute "armed attack" and if not justifiable as "collective self defense" measures, would constitute aggression against North Viet-Nam, justifying that country in military action in defense. See Q. Wright, The Rôle of International Law in the Elimination of War 60.

[42] The United States at first sought to justify these raids as "reprisals" in response to attacks on Pleiku and Tuy Hoa "ordered and directed by Hanoi" (White House Statement, Feb. 7, 1965). This was similar to the justification given for the Tonkin Bay action six months earlier, but legal examination indicated that the facts would not justify "reprisals" in either situation, and that in any case military reprisals are forbidden by the U.N. Charter. See notes 56–58 below.

the basic obligation of Members of the United Nations to "refrain in their international relations from the threat or use of force."[43]

Furthermore it is clear that "armed attack" implies military action. Consequently military defensive action is not permissible under the Charter in response to economic, psychological, or other forms of subversion or intervention not involving military coercion. There can be no doubt but that bodies of armed "volunteers" crossing a frontier or cease-fire line, such as the Chinese in the Korean hostilities of 1950, or ostensibly private "military expeditions" or "armed bands" leaving one country for the purpose of attacking another, as the Cuban refugees in the Bay of Pigs affair of 1961, constitute, if of considerable magnitude, an "armed attack."[44]

Finally an "armed attack" which constitutes a legitimate act of self-defense against an illegal "armed attack" cannot justify subsequent attacks by the aggressor.[45]

According to the International Control Commission[46] there were frequent violations of the Cease-Fire Agreement after 1957. In that and subsequent years it noted violations by the Southern Zone by permitting the establishment of United States military personnel and aircraft in its area and by entering into a *de facto* military alliance with SEATO and the United States.[47] The United States legal memorandum sought to justify these actions by asserting that "from the very beginning, the North Vietnamese violated the 1954 Geneva accords" by leaving Communist military forces and supplies in the South and infiltrating Communist guerrillas from the North to the South.[48] The Control Commission's report of June, 1955, however, indicated that both sides were satisfied with the manner in which withdrawals and transfers required by the agreement were effected.[49] The United States brief asserted that 23,000 men were infiltrated from the North to the South from 1957 to 1962,[50] and the Control Commission noted charges of such infiltration during this period, but not until 1962 did it assess the allegations and the evidence to support them. On that date it submitted a Special Report which called attention to the "rapid deterioration of the situation,"[51] and quoted a report of its legal committee, with the Polish member dissenting:

[43] U.N. Charter, Art. 2, par. 4. See Philip Jessup, A Modern Law of Nations 166 (N. Y., Macmillan, 1948); Ian Brownlie, International Law and the Use of Force by States 273 (London, 1963); Q. Wright, *op. cit.* note 41 above.

[44] Q. Wright, "The Cuban Quarantine," 57 A.J.I.L. 546 ff. (1963).

[45] Note 41 above.

[46] The International Control Commission established by the Cease-Fire Agreement was composed of representatives of Canada, Poland and India, with the latter presiding. Its reports are printed in British Command Papers, 1955 to 1965, and extensive extracts are printed in Gettleman 166 ff., and Raskin and Fall 273 ff. In some of its reports either Poland or Canada abstained.

[47] Note 5 above.

[48] U. S. Legal Brief, p. 29; 60 A.J.I.L. 576 (1966).

[49] Interim Report, May–June, 1955. Gettleman 167.

[50] U. S. Legal Brief, p. 2; 60 A.J.I.L. 565 (1966).

[51] Gettleman 185.

... in specific instances there is evidence to show that armed and unarmed personnel, arms, munitions and other supplies have been sent from the Zone in the North to the Zone in the South with the objective of supporting, organizing and carrying out hostile activities, including armed attacks, directed against the Armed Forces and administration of the Zone in the South. These acts are in violation of Articles 10, 19, 24, and 27 of the Agreement on the Cessation of Hostilities in Vietnam. . . . there is evidence to show that the PAV (Peoples Army of Vietnam) has allowed the Zone in the North to be used for inciting, encouraging, and supporting hostile activities in the Zone in the South, aimed at the overthrow of the Administration in the South. The use of the Zone in the North for such activities is in violation of Articles 19, 24, and 27 of the Agreement on the Cessation of Hostilities in Vietnam.[52]

In the same report the Control Commission concluded that South Viet-Nam had violated Articles 16 and 17 of the Geneva Agreement by receiving military aid from the United States and Article 19 by making a *de facto* military alliance with that country.[53]

In a Special Report of 1965 the Control Commission noted a joint communiqué of February 7, 1965, from the acting Premier of South Viet-Nam and the United States Ambassador announcing military action against military installations in North Viet-Nam in response to aggression by North Viet-Nam forces against Pleiku and Tuy Hoa; and also a communiqué of February 8, 1965, from the North Vietnamese mission protesting the bombing in North Viet-Nam on February 7 by air forces of "the United States imperialists." The Commission commented without concurrence of the Canadian member: "These documents point to the seriousness of the situation and indicate violations of the Geneva Agreement."[54]

There seems to be no evidence that organized contingents of the North Vietnamese army crossed the cease-fire line until after the United States bombing attacks began in February, 1965. Whether infiltrations before that date were of sufficient magnitude to constitute "armed attacks" and whether they could be justified as defense measures against the military activities of South Viet-Nam and the United States in violation of the Geneva agreements is controversial. The Department of State's legal brief of March 4, 1966, says:

In these circumstances an "armed attack" is not as easily fixed by date and hour as in the case of traditional warfare. However, the infiltration of thousands of armed men clearly constitutes an "armed attack" under any reasonable definition. There may be some question as to the exact date at which North Viet-Nam's aggression grew into an "armed attack," but there can be no doubt that it had occurred before February 1965.[55]

[52] Par. 9; Gettleman 187; quoted in part in U. S. Legal Brief, p. 3.
[53] Par. 20; Gettleman 188.
[54] *Ibid.* 189–190. There has been doubt whether the attack on Pleiku and Tuy Hoa actually proceeded from North Viet-Nam. It was probably made by Viet-Cong guerrillas. See Raskin and Fall 398.
[55] U. S. Legal Brief, pp. 3–4; 60 A.J.I.L. 566 (1966).

The reports of the Control Commission indicating gradual increase in violations of the Geneva cease-fire by both sides after 1958 do not permit of a clear judgment on which side began "armed attacks." The problem is in any case irrelevant if the cease-fire line had become ineffective because of the frustration of the elections and United States intervention, as suggested above. There is no evidence of any action by North Viet-Nam which could be regarded as an armed attack upon the South prior to 1958, after Ho Chi Minh had engaged in four years of fruitless effort to carry out the resolutions of the Geneva Conference. In these circumstances Ho Chi Minh's action in support of the Viet-Cong did not constitute aggression or armed attack in international relations but civil strife within the domestic jurisdiction of Viet-Nam, similar to the action of the North against the South in the American Civil War. Whether called "intervention," "reprisals" or "collective defense," the United States response by bombings in North Viet-Nam, which began in February, 1965, violated international law, the United Nations Charter, and the Geneva Agreement, if the latter were in effect.

5. Reprisals in traditional international law were permitted only to remedy an injury resulting from violation by another state of its obligations under international law, after the injured state had made formal complaint and demanded reparation, and had unsuccessfully sought to obtain a remedy by all peaceful means available, and provided the measures of reprisal did not exceed in severity the injury complained of.[56] The United States "reprisals" in the Bay of Tonkin incident of August, 1964, seem to have conformed to none of these conditions, and the same was true of the Pleiku incident of February, 1965. There were no clear proof that an injury had been received because of a violation of international law by North Viet-Nam, no formal complaint to the North Viet-Nam government, no effort to obtain a remedy by peaceful means, and the response was far in excess of any alleged injury. Furthermore, the United Nations Charter abolished the traditional right of reprisals, as declared by the Security Council in April, 1964,[57] by requiring the Members to settle their international disputes by peaceful means and to refrain from the use or threat of force in international relations except in defense against armed attack or under authority of the United Nations.

The United States relied on the obsolete doctrine of reprisals in this case rather than on the right of self-defense against armed attack. It alleged that a United States naval destroyer had been attacked by North

[56] The Naulilaa Arbitration, Portugal v. Germany, 1928, 6 Hackworth, Digest of International Law 154; William W. Bishop, Jr., International Law, Cases and Materials 747 (Boston, Little, Brown, 1962).

[57] Passed as a criticism of the British retaliatory raid during hostilities on the Yemen border. See I. F. Stone, "International Law and the Tonkin Bay Incidents," I. F. Stone Weekly, Aug. 24, 1964, reprinted in Raskin and Fall 307 ff. The Security Council had passed similar resolutions on other border incidents on Nov. 24, 1953, Jan. 19, 1956, April 9, 1962. See also The Corfu Channel Case, [1949] I.C.J. Rep. 35; and Rosalyn Higgins, The Development of International Law through the Political Organs of the United Nations 217 (London, 1963).

Vietnamese torpedo boats while patrolling beyond territorial waters on August 2 and 4, 1964, in the Bay of Tonkin. North Viet-Nam contended that the destroyers were within its territorial waters, which it had extended to twelve miles, and that surveillance of these waters was necessitated because of a South Vietnamese naval attack on its installations on July 31. The United States destroyers seem not to have been injured but the United States reprisals destroyed several North Vietnamese torpedo boats and the installations in five North Vietnamese ports. Congress endorsed this reprehensible "shooting from the hip" by passing a resolution almost unanimously on August 7 authorizing the President to take similar action in the future.[58]

6. By this resolution Congress:

> Approves and supports the determination of the President, as Commander in Chief, to take all necessary measures to repel armed attack against the forces of the United States and to prevent further aggression. . . . the United States is, therefore, prepared, as the President determines, to take all necessary steps, including the use of armed force, to assist any member or protocol state of the Southeast Asia Collective Defense Treaty requesting assistance in defense of its freedom.

The President has cited this resolution as justification for his extensive escalation of the hostilities in Viet-Nam, but it has been contended by some Senators that the action taken requires a declaration of war under the Constitution, and others have asserted that in voting for it they had in mind only limited actions such as that in the Bay of Tonkin. The text, however, goes much further. The issue seems unimportant in view of the broad Constitutional powers of the President to use armed force without Congressional support or declaration of war.

Practice and Supreme Court decisions make it clear that the President as Commander-in-Chief and under general legislation has extensive power to use the armed forces when he deems it necessary to defend American territory or citizens or to meet treaty obligations, but not as an instrument of policy. The major limitation upon such action appears to be the Congressional power to withhold appropriations.[59] In the Vietnamese situation Congress not only voted the funds requested by the President but authorized him to use armed force to assist SEATO states and states mentioned in the Protocol.

7. The United States has asserted that the SEATO Treaty and correspondence of President Eisenhower with Diem created a binding obligation to defend South Viet-Nam from armed attack. The correspondence does not seem to have involved a legal commitment to use armed force in defense of South Viet-Nam, but rather a United States policy of giving economic and military aid to build up a South Viet-Nam capable of resistance to subversion or aggression.

[58] See Raskin and Fall 396; 60 A.J.I.L. 580–581 (1966).
[59] Q. Wright, The Control of American Foreign Relations 286 ff., 294 ff., 307 (New York, Macmillan, 1922).

The SEATO agreement provides for consultation among the SEATO states in case one of them or an area covered by the treaty, such as South Viet-Nam, is in danger from action less than armed attack, and for collective defense in a case of armed attack.[60]   There has been no agreement among SEATO Powers to take any form of collective action, and none of these Powers except Australia and New Zealand,[61] which have contributed limited forces, have considered themselves under an obligation to engage in the defense of South Viet-Nam. A resolution in the SEATO meeting of June 29, 1966, endorsed the United States position but with abstention by the French representative and reservation by the Pakistan representative.[62]

No American President seems to have recognized any legal commitment to use armed force to defend South Viet-Nam prior to 1965.   The United States in signing the SEATO Treaty declared that its obligations under the treaty applied only in case of "Communist" aggression, and it stated at the Geneva Conference of 1954 that "it would view any renewal of aggression . . . with grave concern."   It appears that American military action in Viet-Nam has been in pursuit of the policy of containing Communism rather than in fulfillment of any legal obligation and, as stated by the Control Commission, South Viet-Nam's acceptance of this action has violated the Geneva Agreement.[63]

My study of the course of forty-five international conflicts since World War I indicated that the relative magnitude of national interests and present and future capabilities and vulnerabilities involved in the situation as perceived by the decision-makers, and their perceptions of the state of national and world opinion concerning the conflict, have had more influence than legal obligation or commitment in determining the escalation or settlement of these conflicts.   The Viet-Nam conflict has been no exception.   Applying the formula relating the magnitude of these factors as perceived by the parties, I concluded in the summer of 1965 that:

[60] Don and Arthur Larson, Vietnam and Beyond 17 ff. (Duke University, 1965), printed in Raskin and Fall 99 ff.; text of treaty and protocol in 60 A.J.I.L. 646 .(1966).
[61] The Philippines have discussed sending a small force.
[62] Note 5 above.   [63] Note 13 above, and Gettleman 175.

Hostilities in Vietnam are likely to escalate for a time, but eventually South Vietnam and the United States will win, unless mounting national and world opinion brings about a cease-fire, or unless entry of the Soviet Union or China, or both, initiates World War III.[64]

This conclusion seems applicable a year later.

[64] Q. Wright, "The Escalation of International Conflicts," 9 Journal of Conflict Resolution 440 (December, 1965).

Law and Politics in the Vietnamese War: A Comment

WOLFGANG FRIEDMANN

The learned articles on the legal aspects of the Viet-Nam conflict, published in the October, 1966,[1] and January, 1967,[2] issues of this JOURNAL, give rise to some fundamental reflections on the rôle of international law in a situation that deeply divides the country, and especially the scholarly community, and that stirs up deep emotions and passionate partisanship. The articles of Professor Quincy Wright and Professor John Norton Moore are both scholarly, moderately phrased and inspired by a common conviction of the importance of international law in the affairs of mankind, on the need to develop it as an effective instrument in the outlawry of aggression, on the urgency to "hasten the day when the use of force will yield to more rational processes."[3] Both writers use the documentations on the history and development of the Vietnamese war, including the reports of the International Control Commission and the briefs of the U. S. Government. Yet they arrive at opposite conclusions. Professor Wright believes "that American military action in Viet-Nam has been in pursuit of the policy of containing Communism rather than in fulfillment of any legal obligation . . ."; while certain specific actions, notably the initiation of bombings in North Viet-Nam by the United States in February, 1965, "violated international law, the United Nations Charter, and the Geneva Agreement, if the latter were in effect."[4]

Professor Moore holds, to the contrary, "that there is an unlawful armed attack on the R.V.N.[5] by the D.R.V.,[6] that third states may lawfully assist in the collective defense of the R.V.N., and that the response of the R.V.N., the United States and the other assisting nations is reasonably necessary to the defense of the R.V.N."[7]

The first, inadequate, explanation of this stark conflict of views of two legal scholars, writing as professors of international law, not as advocates of either side, would be that such discrepancies are a familiar and inevitable feature of any legal interpretations, domestic as well as international. Countless decisions of the U. S. Supreme Court are reached by a court split five to four, and often reversed in the course of a few years by the conversion of the minority into a majority. Few contemporary students of jurisprudence still maintain the belief—predominant in the 19th century—that legal decisions and interpretations are purely a matter

[1] Quincy Wright, "Legal Aspects of the Viet-Nam Situation," 60 A.J.I.L. 750 (1966).

[2] Moore, "The Lawfulness of Military Assistance to the Republic of Viet-Nam," 61 A.J.I.L. 1 (1967).

[3] Moore, *loc. cit.* at 34.   [4] *Loc. cit.* at 769, 767.

[5] Republic of Viet-Nam, *i.e.,* South Viet-Nam.

[6] Democratic Republic of Viet-Nam, *i.e.,* North Viet-Nam.

[7] *Loc. cit.* at 2.

of analytical deduction, a process of legal logic detached from value and policy considerations. Law reviews and law reports abound in conflicting decisions and discussions about the extent of a manufacturer's liability to a consumer, the policeman's right of search, the validity of confessions, or the limits of corporate or labor union autonomy.

Yet the analogy is faulty. For all the vagaries of conflicts and interpretations, the authority and the controlling function of law in domestic matters are not challenged. There is a constant interplay between legislation and judicial interpretation. The judicial process is continuous and compulsory. There is usually a hierarchy of courts in which facts, evidence, and legal conclusions can be sifted, analyzed, and revised. The *ex parte* pleadings are not the last word. Although selection and evaluation of evidence by the trial judge is a cardinal—and largely unreviewable —element in the legal process, the facts as they finally emerge in the process of trying and re-trying by trained and generally detached judges, are not often challenged. But in international conflicts such process is exceptional. The World Court, or any other international tribunal, is rarely invoked in major conflict situations. Moreover, the International Court has not yet reached the stage where the opinions of its fifteen members can be easily detached from their national positions and allegiances. For the most part, international legal disputes do not get beyond the stage of party argument, the parties being generally the governments engaged in the dispute. The United Nations provides a kind of forum— but one that is political rather than judicial in character—and the proliferation of Members, coupled with the chronic weakness of the Security Council as a decision-making organ, has tended more and more to fragment the United Nations into partisan groups, and to make authoritative resolutions on highly controversial and sensitive matters increasingly difficult.

The gravest consequence of this growing paralysis of collective decision-making by the United Nations is its frequent inability to take the decision to use force out of the hands of the individual contestants. The basic philosophy both of the League of Nations and of the United Nations is predicated on the assumption that, as long as violence cannot be banished from the conduct of international affairs altogether, a collective decision to use or authorize force, reached by constitutional procedures within a near-universal organization is legitimate and presumed to be just, where the use of force by an individual state or even by an alliance of states, acting without reference to the provisions of the Charter, is not. If it should become a predominant belief of governments and world opinion that the Members of the United Nations apply double standards, that any one state will use different criteria when judging the Russian intervention in Hungary, the Franco-British-Israeli intervention in the Suez Canal crisis, the U. S. intervention in the Dominican Republic, or the behavior of South Africa in South West Africa, the open return to the unrestrained national use of force tempered only by the balance of power will be further accelerated.

It is against this background that we must view the discrepancy between the conclusions of Professors Wright and Moore. In the present writer's opinion, there are two major and interconnected reasons for this conflict: first, there is the selection of facts, which tends to be tailored to the desired conclusions. Unlike in the domestic legal process, such selectivity can only be checked by the give and take of public discussion, not by the authoritative evaluation of an impartial judicial body. Second, and this is one of the basic unsolved questions of our generation, there are deep disagreements as to the extent to which the norms of international law should be regarded as a superior set of values, where they conflict with what the particular author regards as national interest. Under a deceptive surface allegiance to "world order" or any other formula expressing respect for a supernational order of values, there are in fact two irreconcilable approaches: one that uses the arguments of international law as rhetoric in the Aristotelian sense. It acknowledges that international law is a sufficiently important element in the conduct of international relations and in the formation of world opinion to use it as part of the armory of national policy. But this use of international law does not permit it to be employed as a restraint on national action where the two clash. A more candid expression of this approach is, in Mr. Acheson's formulation,[8] the use of "accepted legal principles of international law as a matter of ethical restraint" yielding to overriding national interest. In a less open—and in the present writer's opinion more dangerous—form, the norms of international law are professedly used as an objective and compelling standard, but in fact interpreted so as to conform, in all cases, with national policy.

The alternative approach is willing to regard international legal norms as controlling national behavior, even if it means the legal condemnation of the writer's nation. That it is possible, in this country, to do so with regard to the rights and wrongs of the Vietnamese war without being penalized or ostracized is evidence of the continued existence of an open society. But it may also be predicted that, as the war goes on and escalates, as more and more American soldiers are killed, and the resources and prestige of the country are more deeply committed, any opposition to, or doubt in, the legality of the United States action in Viet-Nam will become increasingly regarded as an unpatriotic act. For it is not only the physical and legal power of the state that—especially in situations of emergency—compels conformity; this power expresses, by and large, the deeply ingrained traditions, beliefs and convictions of the great majority of the peoples of all countries.

It is this writer's submission that Professor Wright's article represents essentially the second, and Professor Moore's article the first, approach. This belief is not due to the present writer's own preferences, or to the fact that a writer who concludes that the actions of his own country are illegal, demonstrably takes international law seriously, while one who comes to the opposite conclusion may or may not do so. The present

8 1963 A.S.I.L. Proceedings at 13.

writer does not fully agree with Professor Wright's conclusions, or with those of The Lawyers Committee on Viet-Nam. He accepts, for example, that South Viet-Nam is today a *de facto* state, whatever the origin and causes of its creation. He also believes that the refusal to accept the claim of the United States to be acting in Viet-Nam in defense of international law and the U.N. Charter does not necessarily lead to the conclusion that the United States is an aggressor. Rather is it the method of thinking, the ambiguous use of terminology and the bias in the selection of facts that in this commentator's opinion expose Professor Moore's thesis to serious criticism.

In these brief comments, it must suffice to discuss three aspects of Professor Moore's presentation: first, the selection of official statements and documents purporting to prove that North Viet-Nam but not South Viet-Nam or the United States had violated international agreements before the United States resorted to direct military action; second, the differential treatment of the North Vietnamese complaints about the violation of the Geneva Accord provisions for elections to be held in 1956, as "political grievances whether they be legitimate or illegitimate," not justifying "unilateral action," as compared with the glossed-over intervention of the United States immediately after the Geneva Accord in the establishment of a separate and fully recognized state of South Viet-Nam; third, the contention that "the requirements of minimum world public order, that is, the avoidance of unilateral coercion as a modality of major change, would in most contexts seem more strongly applicable to insurgent groups than to assistance to the recognized government." [9]

As to the selection of relevant facts, it would seem obvious that the various statements, memoranda, and briefs of the State Department and other high U. S. Government officials, like those of the North Vietnamese Government and its spokesmen, are *ex parte* statements. They are designed to persuade, and therefore select or twist facts as required for the presentation of the case, while ignoring inconvenient facts. There is no impartial forum or tribunal to assess the evidence, but the minimum requirement of "objective" scholarship is to make use of the arguments of both sides. This Professor Wright does in citing the North Vietnamese as well as the South Vietnamese and American arguments. [10] But one looks in vain for a corresponding confrontation in Professor Moore's article. The statements in the State Department's brief of March, 1966, and in other U. S. pronouncements, are taken as objective facts, whereas the North Vietnamese contentions are dismissed as "political grievances . . . legitimate or illegitimate."

Some corrective to partisan statements lies in the various reports of the International Control Commission (composed of Canadian, Indian and Polish representatives), the nearest approach to an impartial fact-finding authority that can be found in the whole Viet-Nam situation. Professor Moore does indeed quote the Commission on several occasions. The impression given by the quotations (on pages 8 and 9 of his article) is that

[9] *Loc. cit.* at 31.   [10] *Loc. cit.* at 757 ff.

the Commission allotted all or most of the blame for violations of the Geneva Accords to North Viet-Nam. A report of June 2, 1962, is quoted as confirming that there was at that time organized armed intervention by North Viet-Nam. The next quotation is from the dissent of the Canadian representative in a report of February, 1965, accusing the Government of North Viet-Nam of "intensification of the aggressive policy." But the reports of the International Control Commission, which are available in many collections, American and non-American, date from 1956, and even the most superficial study will reveal that until about 1959 the Commission, while acknowledging violations of the demilitarization provisions by both sides, attributed at least equal and more serious violations of the obligations to South Viet-Nam.[11] Until 1959 (rather than 1958, the date given by Professor Wright) even the U. S. documents do not allege organized infiltration of North Vietnamese armed forces into South Viet-Nam, although it is clear from the Control Commission's reports that North Viet-Nam did not "demilitarize." But during the same period South Viet-Nam systematically built up its military alliance with the United States, and this was the obvious reason for its refusal to permit inspection of various airports through which U. S. military supplies flowed into the country.

In the context of his highly selective quotations of the International Control Commission's reports, Professor Moore treats the Commission as an authoritative and objective organ. But when, later in his article, short reference is made to observations of the I.C.C. that diverge from the U. S. viewpoint, its status is deprecated. Professor Moore mentions, almost incidentally, that "the ICC reports are a useful indication of factual breaches of the text [i.e., the agreement on the cessation of hostilities] by both sides, and of interpretation of the text." But lest this might lead to the conclusion that North Viet-Nam had some justification for feeling no longer bound by the Geneva Accords, the I.C.C. is now described as

> not an international tribunal which either has authority, or which has attempted, to evaluate the overall lawfulness of the actions of the participants in the Viet-Nam conflict. It has been principally concerned with securing implementation of the Accords and to that end has been interested in pointing out "violations" of the text without effectively relating the actions of the parties to asserted justifications or attempting to assess the lawfulness of those claims by reference to *fundamental community prescriptions*. (Italics by the present writer.)

Yet the 1962 special report, which by several years postdates the admitted North Vietnamese intervention, is cited as authoritative proof of North Vietnamese aggression.

Fact selection is even more obvious in Professor Moore's failure to note the intervention of the United States, dating from 1954, and consisting in the establishment of, and military and economic support for, a separate and sovereign state of South Viet-Nam, as part of the Dulles policy of containment of Communism. This attitude led logically to the refusal even to

11 See, *e.g.*, the Tenth Interim Report, 1960, Cmd. 1040, London.

entertain the possibility of organizing Viet-Nam nation-wide elections in 1956, as clearly provided for in the Geneva Accords. As Professor Wright points out,[12] the refusal of South Viet-Nam, with the unconditional support of the United States, to co-operate in organizing elections in 1956, contrary to the explicit provisions of the cease-fire agreement, supply a substantial argument for the North Vietnamese contention that, after this refusal, the obligation to respect the cease-fire line was frustrated. The contention which is central to the State Department's legal brief of March, 1966— that "a material breach of an agreement by one party entitles the other at least to withhold compliance with an equivalent, corresponding, or related provision until the defaulting party is prepared to honor its obligations"[13]—could be turned against the United States. It all depends on who started violating the agreement. Even more double-edged would be the argument that neither South Viet-Nam nor the United States was bound by the agreements. This argument, which would absolve North Viet-Nam as well as South Viet-Nam, is obviously not adopted by the State Department. It is, of course, arguable whether the refusal to co-operate in even an attempt to organize nation-wide elections, however serious, was sufficient to suspend the obligations of the cease-fire agreement, just as it is possible to argue about the respective gravity of the violations of the cease-fire on both sides between 1954 and 1962. But it is indefensible, in a scholarly presentation, to select relevant facts and documents in the manner in which Professor Moore has done.

The basic philosophy underlying Professor Moore's approach is summed up in the following passage:

> Nothing in the United Nations Charter requires license for armed minority take-over in the name of an all-encompassing right to revolution nor guarantees recognized governments the right to oppress their peoples. Lawfulness of assistance to either faction must be determined in reference to genuine self-determination and the requirements of minimum world public order, not in blind reliance on black-letter rules as to which side, if any, can be aided in a civil war and sometimes suggesting an Alice-in-Wonderland search for neutral principles. The truth of the matter is that outside assistance to one or another faction may or may not be in the interest of genuine self-determination. The only answer to whether it is or not is careful analysis of the relevant features of the context, particularly the objectives of the participants. Self-determination, of course, is not the only important policy in deciding the lawfulness of such assistance. The requirements of minimum world public order are also vital policies at stake and may sometimes reflect more important values than self-determination. The requirements of minimum world public order, that is, the avoidance of unilateral coercion as a modality of major change, would in most contexts seem more strongly applicable to assistance to insurgent groups than to assistance to the recognized government. Perhaps it is not surprising, then, that prevailing international law seems to permit assistance to the recognized government but not to the insurgents.[14]

[12] *Loc. cit.* at 761.
[13] U. S. Legal Brief, pp. 30–31; also in 60 A.J.I.L. 565 at 577 (1966).
[14] *Loc. cit.* at 31.

Put in a nutshell, this means that civil wars and revolutions are instruments of change, that international law is hostile to change by force in civil as well as in international war, and that therefore governments may "in most contexts" legitimately request assistance from outside, but insurgents may not. The determining criteria are "genuine self-determination"—which may, however, have to yield to "more important values," and "minimum world public order."

The present writer has sought to demonstrate elsewhere,[15] that the application of this Metternich doctrine of legitimacy, strenuously opposed by the United States at the time of the Holy Alliance and countered by the Monroe Doctrine directed against intervention by non-American Powers in the revolutions of Latin America, is an anachronism in the turbulent world of the 1960's. Its assertion by the United States at this time would mean that it has adopted the philosophy of the Holy Alliance and is now pledged to the suppression of revolution. However, this country has never been consistent in the application of this doctrine nor presumably wishes to adhere to it when policy interests dictate otherwise. Perhaps this is implicit in Professor Moore's somewhat coy admission that assistance to insurgent groups is impermissible only "in most contexts." The legitimacy of assistance to an incumbent government and the illegitimacy of corresponding assistance to rebels have been one of the pillars of the United States' legal argument in the Viet-Nam situation. This doctrine has been invoked in support not only of U. S. military action in Viet-Nam, but also in the Lebanon crisis in 1958 and, more dubiously, in the Dominican intervention of 1965, where an urgent request was made by the U. S. Ambassador to the tottering government to request U. S. assistance! But one looks in vain for any admission by the supporters of the "legitimacy" doctrine that, on this theory, the now openly admitted U. S. interventions in Iran in 1951 or in Guatemala in 1954, which were instrumental in unseating the incumbent governments, or the abortive Bay of Pigs invasion of 1961, designed to overthrow the Castro government, were clearly illegal. It is difficult not to conclude that the supporters of the "legitimacy" doctrine are eloquent when it justifies U. S. action, but silent when it does not do so. Professor Moore does not go so far as to adopt the doctrine that any Communist government is, by virtue of its very existence, an aggressor—a doctrine which would not only be incompatible with the basic principles of international law and the United Nations, which regard the internal political and social structure of a state as irrelevant to international rights and duties, but is clearly at variance with contemporary U. S. policy, which recognizes the increasingly national and diversified character of Communist governments.

The theory of differentiation between incumbent governments and insurgents supports the assertion made by Hans Morgenthau, for example, that international law is nothing but a consolidation of the *status quo*.[16] This is a deplorable doctrine to adopt for anyone who, like Professor Moore

15 See Changing Structure of International Law 265 ff.
16 See Politics Among Nations 90 ff. (3rd ed., 1960).

and most of us, strives for the use of international law as a progressive instrument of co-operation among nations.

Time and again Professor Moore invokes "minimum world public order," a formula made familiar by Professor McDougal's many writings. This goes together with the rejection of "black letter rules," and contempt for "Alice-in-Wonderland search for neutral principles." This is ominously reminiscent of the similar formulas used by the Lord Chancellor in Britain during the Suez Canal crisis in order to justify the Franco-British intervention [17] and, almost a decade later, by the Legal Adviser of the State Department in justification of the U. S. intervention in the Dominican Republic.[18] The reference to "neutral principles," if it means anything, means that policy objectives decide what is right and wrong. And in the absence of third-party determination, "minimum world public order" means, Humpty-Dumpty-like, what the policy-maker wants it to mean, a catch-all phrase to justify whatever action the writer wishes to justify. U. S. action in Viet-Nam is in the interest of "minimum world public order," if you share all the assumptions of Professor Moore, i.e., that the United States did not intervene in violation of the Geneva Accords by the establishment of the state of South Viet-Nam and the refusal to contemplate elections; that only North Viet-Nam violated the obligations of the cease-fire agreement; that the Vietnamese conflict is not essentially a civil war; that assistance to the incumbent government is legitimate, but assistance to the rebels is not; and that the defense of the incumbent government is in the interest of such order. All these assumptions are deeply controversial and they do not become any less so by incantations of "minimum world public order" or "fundamental community prescriptions." By the same token, one could contend that continued attempts by the Governments of France, Britain, Holland and Belgium to keep their colonies under subjection, instead of letting them move to independence, would have been in the interest of "minimum world public order." If Professor Moore's legitimacy doctrine is correct, such actions and outside armed support for them would have been in accordance with international law, unless, of course, a "minimum world public order" required otherwise.

Lastly, a word about the legitimacy of U. S. action as an instrument of "collective self-defense" in implementation of the U.N. Charter. Professors Wright and Moore agree with many writers that, under Article 51 of the Charter, it is legitimate for Members of the United Nations to assist even a non-Member against aggression, and that such action need not necessarily wait for U.N. authorization, although this should be forthcoming sooner or later. That the Charter permits organized or unorganized action in self-defense, pending U.N. action, is undoubted. Increasingly, this right of self-defense is now extended to assistance given to a third country. If time and again individual action or the action of a few states, acting for political and strategic reasons, takes the place of

[17] H. L. Deb., Vol. 199, Col. 718, 1956, as quoted in 59 A.J.I.L. at 869 (1965).
[18] See Address by Leonard B. Meeker to American Foreign Law Association, June 9, 1965, as quoted in 59 A.J.I.L. at 868 (1965).

action organized or authorized by the United Nations, the principle of collective security becomes a farce, the exception becomes the rule and the alleged action in implementation of U.N. principles of collective security becomes a mere cloak for the individual use of force dictated by national political interests. Professor Bowett's formulation of the issue [19] is all the more important, as it was published well before the Viet-Nam issue became acute:

> The individual members cannot on the one hand delegate primary responsibility for the maintenance of international peace and security to the Security Council (Art. 24), and on the other claim this right of unilateral action to support any state which they consider to be acting in self-defence. This sort of freedom of alliance cannot stand together with a system of collective security as centralized as the United Nations Charter. The Charter clearly intends that the prohibition of Art. 2 (4) will admit of only the minimum exception of self-defence, strictly construed, and subject to the overriding authority of the Security Council.

* * * * *

> It is, finally, obvious that, though in the nature of things the decision to resort to self-defence rests initially with the individual state whose rights are violated, since that decision rests on a unilateral judgment on the respective legal rights of the states concerned, it cannot be final or conclusive. The decision to exercise self-defence is a preliminary decision for which the state bears full responsibility, and it cannot be maintained that its own judgment is conclusive on the question of the respective rights of the parties concerned. No one state can arrogate to itself the final right to determine unilaterally the question whether another state is in breach of established duties.

The provisions of SEATO, on which Professor Moore mercifully hardly relies, illustrate the perversion of the idea of collective security. The provisions in the treaty which permit individual action by any one member to protect the integrity, *inter alia,* of a territory enumerated in the schedule to the treaty were written in at the insistence of the United States as part of the containment policy immediately after the Geneva Accords. Between 1954 and early 1965, during which period U. S. involvement in South Viet-Nam steadily increased, nobody thought of SEATO, but since then it has become increasingly prominent in the legal arguments of the U. S. Government. It is a tenable argument only because SEATO does permit individual state intervention as determined by the intervener. Even a valid authorization by the SEATO Council as a regional organization, arguably though far from certainly, in conformity with Article 51 or 52, cannot be obtained. Two of its eight members, France and Pakistan, are strongly opposed to the U. S. intervention in Viet-Nam.

The last occasion when the restraining provisions of the U.N. Charter against the unilateral use of force were effectively invoked was in 1956, when the General Assembly, with the joint support of the United States and the U.S.S.R., stopped the Franco-British-Israeli action in the Suez

[19] Self-Defence in International Law at 218, 262 (1958).

Canal Zone.[20] Apart from this, unilateral interventions have either been tolerated or condoned by the United Nations, whether they were the Soviet intervention in Hungary, the Chinese occupation of Tibet, the Dominican intervention of the United States, or the mutual interventions in Viet-Nam. All these have been individual actions and, in the case of the Dominican intervention, the United States actively opposed any rôle of the United Nations altogether. We delude ourselves if we believe that, by the mere unilateral invocation of collective security principles, national acts of force change their character. Whether the U. S. action in Viet-Nam— assuming that it continues to observe the restraint that has generally characterized it up to the present—will eventually serve to provide an equilibrium and to substitute "rational processes" for the use of force, remains to be seen. But if it should succeed in this objective, it will have done so not by reliance on international law but by reliance on national power, opposed by countervailing national power, eventually leading to a negotiated settlement. This is not international law as embodied in the Charter; it is not "minimum world public order," except on the hypothesis that political objectives pursued by the United States are necessarily concomitant with such order because the United States stands for the proper values and its opponents do not.

The candid truth is, as Professor Wright concludes, that international law has neither motivated nor controlled the mutual interventions in Viet-Nam. The war—which is not called a war—moves in a legal vacuum. This certainly does not mean that international lawyers should ignore the whole area, especially since conflicts of mixed civil and international character may well become the principal type of armed strife in our time. The careful study of contemporary conflicts of this kind, a comparison of the state practices and of the various justifications of intervention and counter-intervention,[21] may be the prelude to the gradual elaboration of customary or treaty rules in this field, and perhaps of new types of international organization. This is the way in which international law has developed and must continue to grow. But we delude ourselves as to the degree to which international law controls the Viet-Nam type of conflict at this time, if we disguise the legal anarchy by the invocation of formulas that merely cloak the nakedness of the political and ideological struggle.

Law and Politics in the Vietnamese War: A Response to Professor Friedmann   JOHN NORTON MOORE

In the last issue of the JOURNAL [1] Professor Wolfgang Friedmann published a critique of my article on the lawfulness of military assistance to South Viet-Nam which appeared in the January, 1967, issue of the JOURNAL.[2] His reply was welcome both because continuing dialogue has proven a helpful method for clarification of the legal issues on Viet-Nam and because it was particularly gratifying, following our debate at the 1966 Annual Meeting of the Society, to have an opportunity to clarify the issues separating us. Nevertheless, Professor Friedmann's reply was disappointing: disappointing partly because of his misunderstanding of my position but principally because he failed to develop any substantive position on Viet-Nam.

Before responding to the three points which he makes to support his criticism it may be helpful to elaborate on the principal reason for disappointment at his reply and to briefly evaluate the assumptions underlying what seems to be his position on the legal issues of the Viet-Nam conflict.

Despite the fact that Professor Friedmann has debated the subject on a number of occasions, his position is unclear. Apart from short references in articles devoted to other subjects [3] he seems to have developed no analysis of his own. His earlier endorsement of the "Lawyers Committee Memorandum" [4] would lead one to conclude that he regards military assistance to Viet-Nam as unlawful, were it not for his repudiation of some (which ones and why he does not clarify) of the conclusions of the "Memorandum." [5] His reply does not say whether he regards such assistance as lawful or unlawful, and is stated in such equivocal terms as

> the refusal to accept the claim of the United States to be acting in Viet-Nam in defense of international law and the U.N. Charter does not necessarily lead to the conclusion that the United States is an aggressor.[6]

[1] Friedmann, "Law and Politics in the Vietnamese War: A Comment," 61 A.J.I.L. 776 (1967).

[2] Moore, "The Lawfulness of Military Assistance to the Republic of Viet-Nam," 61 A.J.I.L. 1 (1967).

My own views are further elaborated in "International Law and the United States Role in Viet Nam: A Reply," 76 Yale Law J. 1051 (1967), and "The Role of Law in the Viet Nam Debate," 41 Connecticut Bar J. 389 (1967). Additional background documentation supporting this view may be found in Moore and Underwood, "The Lawfulness of United States Assistance to the Republic of Viet-Nam," 112 Cong. Rec. 14943 (daily ed., July 14, 1966), reprinted in 5 Duquesne Law Rev. 235 (1967).

[3] See Friedmann, "United States Policy and the Crisis of International Law," 59 A.J.I.L. 857, 865–66 (1965); idem, "Intervention, Civil War and the Rôle of International Law," 1965 Proceedings, American Society of International Law 67.

[4] See the letter from the Lawyers Committee on American Policy Toward Vietnam to President Johnson, Jan. 25, 1966, in 112 Cong. Rec. 2551 (daily ed., Feb. 9, 1966).

[5] Friedmann, note 1 above, at 778–779. Professor Friedmann has informed me that his endorsement of the "Lawyers Committee Memorandum" was qualified but that his reservations were not published. By way of further clarification of his reservations, however, he indicates only that he does "not agree with some of their [the Lawyers Committee] statements, e.g., on U.S. aggression and the de facto status of South Vietnam."   [6] Ibid. at 779.

But other than this equivocal statement, and the statement that South Viet-Nam is today a *de facto* state,[7] one looks in vain for discussion supporting any aspect of the South Vietnamese position or questioning any aspect of the North Vietnamese resort to force—a surprising position for one who condemns as "scholarly indefensible" writers who assertedly fail to advert to both sides.

Although there is some risk of error in defining it, his position seems to be that the conflict within South Viet-Nam is primarily a "civil war," that therefore the United States is prohibited from rendering assistance to the recognized government, and that the United States intervened "in violation of the Geneva Accords by the establishment of the state of South Viet-Nam and the refusal to contemplate elections."[8]

There are a number of difficulties with this position. In the first place, it assumes as "objective fact" a simplified version of the Geneva settlement, the failure to hold elections, and the evolution of the Republic of Viet-Nam as a state, and places undue emphasis on United States support to South Viet-Nam after the "Accords," without offering any evidence or even adverting to the serious ambiguities and shortcomings of the Geneva settlement.

There is substantial evidence that the Geneva settlement was a power compromise between bitter and powerful protagonists, that it suffered from substantial ambiguity because of an inability of all of the participants to agree, and that it may have created contradictory expectations in the major participants in the negotiations. The central feature of the settlement was the division of Viet-Nam between two already existing political rivals. This division, coupled with the weakness of the political settlement provisions, suggests that the parties were aware of the possibility of an extended partition. The later Soviet attempt to admit both North and South to the United Nations re-enforces the suggestion that partition was the major reality of the settlement.

The settlement in its total context was laudatory in effectively halting the immediate fighting, but beyond that, its major outlines were contradictory and ambiguous, its peacekeeping and political settlement provisions were weak, and it is a mistake to idealize it as a starting point for condemnation of the lawfulness of United States assistance.[9] Most import-

---

[7] *Ibid.*   [8] Friedmann, note 1 above, at 783.

[9] The evidence is developed in Moore, "International Law and the United States Role in Viet Nam: A Reply," 76 Yale Law J. 1051 (1967). By way of illustration, Ellen Hammer writes that:

"In contrast to the detailed implementation provided for ending hostilities and for the *de facto* partition of the country (including the right of each Vietnamese to decide whether he wished to live north or south of the seventeenth parallel), the Final Declaration offered no long-term perspective for a definitive settlement of the Vietnamese question. The method by which the desirable conditions laid down in Article 7 were to be achieved, was not explained. . . .

"Thus, although the Franco-Vietminh war was ended at Geneva in July 1954, a political solution for Vietnam was postponed to some unspecified future date.

antly, regardless of interpretation of the Geneva settlement, the grievances of the North with respect to implementation of the "Accords" are of a qualitatively different order than Hanoi's resort to force.

Secondly, it is highly questionable, in the light of the whole background of the conflict and the relationship and objectives of the North with respect to the fighting, whether "civil war" non-intervention norms provide the most useful structure for analysis of the conflict.

Critical models of the Viet-Nam conflict which picture it as "civil war" and the White Paper models which picture it as "aggression from the North" oversimplify the reality. Real-world Viet-Nam combines some elements of civil strife (both within the South and between North and South) with elements of the cold-war divided-nation problem and "aggression from the North"; all complicated by an uncertain international settlement. North Viet-Nam is one half of an at least *de facto* divided nation rendering assistance across an international cease-fire line to an armed insurgency in the other half whose leadership is significantly interrelated with leadership in Hanoi. It is generally believed that one of the objectives of that assistance is more or less long-run unification of Viet-Nam under the hegemony of Hanoi, an objective which Hanoi says is justified by the Geneva settlement. This context suggests that the conflict is not most usefully characterized as an internal struggle for control of the South Vietnamese Government. Features which make the application of non-intervention norms particularly questionable include the acutely dangerous cold-war divided-nation element, an international cease-fire line separating North and South, the historical interrelation between Hanoi and the Viet-Minh-Viet-Cong, and the objectives of Hanoi in sustaining the conflict. In these circumstances, assistance from Hanoi is considerably more serious than third-party assistance to insurgents to influence a struggle for internal control.

Community concern about the use of force, particularly the acutely dangerous use of force across *de facto* cold-war boundaries and cease-fire lines, suggests that in this context the Charter proscription outlawing the use of force as a modality of major change is the most crucial norm for appraisal of the war.

But though Professor Friedmann acknowledges that North and South Viet-Nam are separate *de facto* states, he ignores discussion of the legal consequences flowing from this characterization and the surrounding context and fails to apply the principle of Article 2 (4) of the Charter to the relations between the two states. The facts that he stresses, such as the failure to hold the 1956 elections, United States assistance to the South after Geneva, and the range of non-forceful violations recorded by the International Control Commission against both North and South, seem to focus more on considerations suggesting the 19th-century concept of "just

---

"The agreements outlined at Geneva . . . contained few if any provisions for their long-term execution. They were a series of desires for the future, drawn up by the conference participants." Hammer, Vietnam Yesterday and Today 144, 247 (1966).

war'' than contemporary Charter proscriptions outlawing the use of force except in defense against armed attack.

Under the Charter the central focus for analysis of the lawfulness of the use of force in Viet-Nam must be whether one of the international entities that Professor Friedmann acknowledges are separate *de facto* states made an armed attack on the other. The historical process by which North and South became separate states and their non-forceful grievances against each other are no more the *central issues* than focus in the recent Arab-Israeli conflict on how Israel became a state.

Thirdly, even if it is accepted that the conflict is best characterized as a ''civil war'' within the South, and that non-intervention norms provide the best normative framework, the most reliable evidence of what has been happening in Viet-Nam, as set out in the writings of Fall, Lacouture, Schlesinger, Crozier, Warner, Zasloff, Pike and many others, some of whom are critical of United States policy, indicates that substantial North Vietnamese assistance and direction to the insurgents preceded the first significant United States increase in military assistance over pre-insurgency levels.[10]   Although scholars differ about the degree of control exercised by Hanoi, and whether in its initial stages the insurgency within the South was an indigenous reaction to the oppressive measures of the Diem regime, the evidence from all sources strongly supports the conclusion that the North was rendering substantial assistance and direction to the insurgency prior to the first major military response from the United States—which took place in late 1961 as a partial implementation of the Taylor-Rostow Report.   Though this crucial chronology has been largely overlooked, an examination of any of the scholarly treatments of the subject indicates that the United States military build-up was a reluctant response to an increasingly deteriorating military posture caused at least in part by increasing assistance and direction from Hanoi.

There is almost unanimous agreement among international law scholars that assistance provided to a widely recognized government is a lawful response to offset assistance provided to insurgents.   Since one of the major policies of the non-intervention norms is to ensure self-determination, a ''neutral non-intervention'' norm that neither side can be aided in a ''civil war'' is much too suspect as a general prophylactic rule after insurgents have begun to receive substantial external assistance.   So even if non-intervention norms did provide the best normative framework for appraisal of the conflict, the facts of the struggle in Viet-Nam would still strongly support the conclusion that assistance to South Viet-Nam is lawful.

Lastly, the ''neutral non-intervention'' norm which Professor Friedmann relies on, is itself controversial.[11]   It may be that in some contexts such a rule will better effectuate community goals, but for reasons that this writer has outlined elsewhere,[12] and which are partly developed in reply to Professor Friedmann's third point, there are some reasons for suggesting that

---

[10] The evidence is developed in Moore, note 9 above.

[11] See, for example, Farer, ''Intervention in Civil Wars: A Modest Proposal,'' 67 Columbia Law Rev. 266 (1967).   [12] See Moore, note 9 above.

a norm allowing assistance only to the widely recognized government may be more realistic in the inter-bloc conflicts such as Viet-Nam.

Professor Friedmann's own position with respect to the legal issues of the Viet-Nam conflict is not clear. The position which he seems to adopt is questionable in relying on a "model" which oversimplifies the conflict, in failing to focus on the differences between the use of force and grievances not involving use of force, in relying on a "neutral non-intervention" norm without analysis of impact on applicable community policies, and in failing to apply his own legal assumptions to a widely held view of the facts.

Though these assumptions seem to implicitly underlie much of Professor Friedmann's criticism of my article, he offers three specific aspects of the presentation to support his criticism.

He first criticizes:

> . . . the selection of official statements and documents purporting to prove that North Viet-Nam but not South Viet-Nam or the United States had violated international agreements before the United States resorted to direct military action. . . .[13]

There are a number of reasons why this criticism is unpersuasive. First, the documentation referred to was cited as *evidence of fact* that North Viet-Nam had rendered substantial military assistance and direction to the conflict within the South, and the text makes this clear. It was not offered to prove the conclusion of law "that North Viet-Nam but not South Viet-Nam or the United States had violated international agreements before the United States resorted to direct military action." As *evidence* of this use of the military instrument by the North the article relied on: the findings of the International Control Commission in its 1962 Special Report, a dissenting statement (labeled as such) of the Canadian representative in a February, 1965, I.C.C. Report, a short excerpt from a State Department memorandum, the articles of two highly regarded journalists, Neil Sheehan and Takashi Oka, one a reporter for the *New York Times* and the other a former Far East correspondent for the *Christian Science Monitor,* and the Mansfield Report, which is generally regarded as a reasonably objective treatment. The presentation of this evidence commences with the statement "among other evidence of this 'armed attack,'" and concludes with the statement that:

> Although there is certainly evidence that the conflict in the R.V.N. also has internal support, the totality of evidence—*whether or not the above evidence is accepted in its entirety*—strongly indicates that the campaign to overthrow the recognized government of the R.V.N. by intense coercion receives at least substantial military assistance and direction from the D.R.V. and suggests that prior to any significant increase in United States assistance, D.R.V. initiative was a critical element in the conflict. . . .[14]

Secondly, Professor Friedmann offers no evidence of any kind to contradict any of the factual conclusions, and contents himself with the charge

[13] Friedmann, note 1 above, at 779.
[14] See Moore, note 2 above, 8–11, at 11 (emphasis added).

that the sources are one-sided official statements and that "The statements in the State Department's brief of March, 1966, and in other U.S. pronouncements, are taken as objective facts. . . ."[15] But neither the State Department brief of March, 1966, nor the White Papers are mentioned or cited in the article. And although not developed in the article, the writings of Fall, Lacouture, Schlesinger, Warner, Crozier, Pike and Zasloff among others, provide evidence that this summary is a minimum statement of North Viet-Nam's involvement. Since the evidence has been developed in greater detail in a recent *Yale Law Journal*[16] article, there would be little point in repeating it here.

Lastly, and most importantly, Professor Friedmann's criticism suggests that he missed the major thrust of the argument regarding the fundamental limitation on the use of force as an instrument of national policy. For it is not of great significance whether North Viet-Nam or South Viet-Nam first violated the Accords. The crucial questions are what kinds of "violations" were indicated and who resorted to the military instrument as a modality of major change? The implication of Professor Friedmann's statement that the United States first resorted to "direct military action" is unsupported.

Professor Friedmann purports to show bias in fact selection in the choice of "highly selective quotations"[17] from I.C.C. Reports and in the discussion of I.C.C. findings. He states that "The impression given by the quotations (on pages 8 and 9 of his article) is that the Commission allotted all or most of the blame for violations of the Geneva Accords to North Viet-Nam,"[18] but he fails to reveal that in a note to this quotation on page nine it is said:

> . . . The Commission also found after recording this armed aggression from the D.R.V. that the R.V.N. had violated Arts. 16, 17 and 19 of the Geneva Agreements by receiving military assistance. . . . It is erroneous to merely "balance" the violations recorded against both sides in this report. The kinds of violations recorded against the two sides are crucially different. . . .[19]

Professor Friedmann does not deal with the point that the kinds of violation are crucially different but instead proceeds to take the writer to task for not including all of the I.C.C. findings of "violations" of the Accords against both sides from 1956 until about 1959. He asserts "the reports of the International Control Commission . . . date from 1956,[20] and even the most superficial study will reveal that until about 1959 the Commission, while acknowledging violations of the demilitarization provisions by both sides, attributed at least equal and more serious violations of the obligations to South Viet-Nam."[21] Professor Friedmann fails to note that my article

15 Friedmann, note 1 above, at 779.   16 See Moore, note 9 above.
17 Friedmann, note 1 above, at 780.   18 *Ibid.* at 779–780.
19 Moore, note 2 above, at 9, note 20.

20 This is inaccurate. The Commission issued in 1954 and 1955 four reports which, among other things, indicate the serious concern of the Commission with Northern implementation of Art. 14(c), the provision allowing persons to choose zones.

21 Friedmann, note 1 above, at 780.

lists all of the principal grievances of the North against the South which are evident in a complete reading of the I.C.C. Reports.[22]   They are: failure to consult on the holding of elections in 1956, reprisals against resistance leaders, inadequate co-operation with I.C.C. controls, and entering into a military alliance with and receiving military assistance from the United States.

None of these grievances constitute justification under Article 51 of the Charter for military attack on the South or for substantial military assistance to insurgents in the South across a cease-fire line.   Perhaps the major point of my article is that there is a major difference in kind between these North and South grievances under the settlement.   The South, which Professor Friedmann concedes is a *de facto* state separate from the North, did not institute a major military attack on the territorial and political integrity of North Viet-Nam.   North Viet-Nam did use the military instrument against the South, seriously threatening its political and territorial integrity.   Even if all North Viet-Nam's grievances were accepted as legally justified, an attack by North Viet-Nam against the South is a violation of Article 2 (4) of the Charter, and the South and its allies may lawfully defend against it.

At Potsdam Stalin promised that Korea would be divided only temporarily; but when temporary occupation turned into permanent communization, South Korea did not militarily attack across a major cold-war dividing line, despite United Nations support for a unified Korea.   Such an attack from South Korea, like military assistance from North Viet-Nam, could have been expected to trigger major conflict and must be regarded as outlawed by Article 2 (4).   Such disputes which do not involve major military threats to fundamental values do not justify resort to force.   This conclusion re-enforces a broad rather than a narrow interpretation of the Charter and substantially strengthens applicability of the prohibition of force as an instrument of national policy.

This is perhaps the single most crucial norm of contemporary international law—that resort may not be had to the use of the military instrument as a modality of major change or as an instrument of national policy for dispute-settlement.   Surely Professor Friedmann, who is deeply committed to strengthening international law as an effective force for peace, should recognize the fallacy of trying to justify use of the military instrument by reference to grievances which do not remotely constitute an armed attack.   That is what is meant by the reference to North Viet-Nam's grievances, which do not involve a military threat to its political and territorial integrity, as "political grievances" not justifying resort to the use of force.   Since the major issue is the lawfulness of military assistance to South Viet-Nam, it is the fundamental normative structure restricting the use of force which is most important to this determination.   Emphasis on the kinds of non-forceful "violations" indicated by the I.C.C. Reports from 1956 to 1959 is misleading.

[22] Moore, note 2 above, at 12.

A reading of the first ten Interim Reports of the I.C.C. supports Professor Friedmann's statement that the Commission attributed "more serious violations" to South Viet-Nam, but the statement fails to take into account the over-all judgment of the Commission itself expressed in its 11th Interim Report. In this Report the Commission stated:

> The Indian and Canadian Delegations are convinced that there have been many instances of non-co-operation by both Parties which have impeded the work of the Commission and its Teams. These have not in all cases reached the stage of formal citations because of evasions and lack of co-operation on the part of the Party concerned. For this reason the two Delegations agree that, in the experience of the Commission, the number of formal citations in itself is no fair measure of the degree of co-operation received from either party.[23]

Professor Friedmann's discussion also fails to note that the consistent South Vietnamese position was to deny that they were bound by other than the cease-fire provisions of the Accords and that as a result they submitted fewer formal complaints of violation than did the D.R.V.[24] And he fails to note that in 1958 the Commission found Hanoi so "incongenial" for its effective functioning that it transferred its headquarters from Hanoi to Saigon.[25]

Undoubtedly the South did not live up to the text of the Accords in a number of ways. Their record is poor, as a study of the I.C.C. Reports during the Diem period demonstrates. But these "violations," in large part procedural violations for failure to co-operate with I.C.C. controls, should be read in the broader context of the ambiguous Geneva settlement, increasing militarization of the North, an on-going insurgency in the South, and South Viet-Nam's refusal to be bound by other than the cease-fire provisions. Most importantly, a complete reading of the Commission Reports from 1954 through the Special Report of 1962 [26] indicates that no complaint of the North qualitatively approaches the complaint of the South of armed aggression by the North against the South. The major use of force is the one asserted violation by both sides that is crucially

[23] Eleventh Interim Report of the International Commission for Supervision and Control in Vietnam (Vietnam No. 1 [1961], Command Paper 1551). Great Britain Parliamentary Sessional Papers XXXIX (1961/62), at 25.

[24] See the articles from the Indian daily, The Hindustan Times, and the New Delhi periodical, Thought, discussing the operation and reports of the Commission, collected in Ngo Ton Dat, "The Geneva Partition of Vietnam and the Question of Reunification During the First Two Years," pp. 481–487, Appendix U (Unpublished Ph.D. dissertation, Cornell University, 1963). On December 16, 1961, the Hindustan Times wrote: "On the whole . . . the non-co-operation of the North seems more ominously purposeful than the non-co-operation of the South." Ibid. at 485.

[25] Ngo Ton Dat, ibid. at 419, note 4. Dat adds that "the members of the commission were constantly denied freedom of circulation and investigation by the Viet-Minh." Ibid.

[26] Citations for all of the Commission reports and a summary of the principal grievances asserted against both sides may be found in Moore and Underwood, note 2 above, at note 285 and accompanying text. See also Dai, "Canada's Role in the International Commission for Supervision and Control in Vietnam," 4 Canadian Yr. Bk. Int. Law 161 (1966).

different in kind and much more serious if the issue is the lawfulness of the use of force.

It was the use of force by the North that directly precipitated the dangerous military confrontation, and on this question of which side initiated and sustained the use of force—which was the purpose of relying on the I.C.C. Reports—there was no "fact selection." The Reports indicate a serious use of the military instrument by the North against the South but not vice versa. In short, Professor Friedmann's criticism for not placing equal emphasis on the charges and procedural violations recorded against the South from 1956 to 1959 is neither wholly informed nor responsive to the purpose in emphasis of facts most pertinent to conclusion about the lawfulness of military assistance to the South.

Professor Friedmann also charges that the I.C.C. Reports are cited as "authoritative proof of North Vietnamese aggression," [27] but when "reference is made to observations of the I.C.C. that diverge from the U.S. viewpoint, its status is deprecated." [28] Since, as has been previously pointed out, the I.C.C. Reports were cited as *evidence of fact* of North Vietnamese use of the military instrument against the South, evidence that is not contradicted elsewhere in the Reports, Professor Friedmann's statement that the article relied on it as "authoritative proof of North Vietnamese aggression," *a conclusion of law,* is inaccurate. As in Professor Wright's article, the point is made that the I.C.C. has only limited responsibility.[29] It is not "an international tribunal which either has authority, or which has attempted, to evaluate the over-all lawfulness of the actions of the participants in the Viet-Nam conflict." [30] My article indicates, however, that its Report is authoritative "as a factual report and an interpretation of the text of the Accords," and it explicitly accepts the factual findings of the I.C.C. and its interpretation of the text that "the D.R.V. *was* using force against the R.V.N., the United States *was* providing defensive assistance to meet that attack, and both actions *were* interpreted by the Commission as 'violations' of the text of the Accords." [31] There is nothing inconsistent in using the Reports as evidence of what happened but not as authoritative determinations of the lawfulness of those actions and this same standard is applied to both U.S. and North Vietnamese actions.

Professor Friedmann's second criticism is:

> . . . the differential treatment of the North Vietnamese complaints about the violation of the Geneva Accord provisions for elections to be held in 1956, as "political grievances whether they be legitimate or illegitimate," not justifying "unilateral action," as compared with the practically ignored intervention of the United States immediately after the Geneva Accord in the establishment of a separate and fully recognized state of South Viet-Nam . . .[32]

---

[27] Friedmann, note 1 above, at 780.   [28] *Ibid.*
[29] Wright, "Legal Aspects of the Viet-Nam Situation," 60 A.J.I.L. 750, 763 (1966).
[30] Moore, note 2 above, at 27.   [31] *Ibid.*
[32] Friedmann, note 1 above, at 779.

Nowhere does Professor Friedmann demonstrate more clearly his failure to deal with the major argument. The "differential treatment" of North Vietnamese actions against South Viet-Nam and U.S. action with respect to South Viet-Nam results from the fact that their actions *are* crucially different. The fundamental question is whether these indicated actions should be treated alike for purposes of community policy about restrictions on the use of force. The clear answer is no. North Viet-Nam's grievance with regard to the failure to hold elections was "political" in the sense that Article 2 (4) of the Charter outlaws the use of force except in defense against a major military attack threatening fundamental values. South Viet-Nam's grievance with respect to North Viet-Nam's use of the military instrument was not at all "political" in this sense. It constituted a serious threat to the political and territorial integrity of South Viet-Nam and could lawfully be met with the use of defensive force and military assistance from its allies. Any other result would tie the hands of South Viet-Nam while allowing North Viet-Nam to pursue its objectives by force. And if we are talking about appraisal of the lawfulness of the use of force, it is not at all anomalous in this context, as Professor Friedmann contends,[33] to assert that the norm—material breach of agreement justifies suspension of corresponding obligations—is available as a defense to the South but not to the North. The major concern, of course, is the use of force, not material breach of agreement.

It is one of the tasks of the writer to focus on differences which are crucial for the legal determinations being made and to select and develop questions which are most pertinent to decision. Such fact selection is a necessary task of decision and Professor Friedmann's failure to even note these crucial differences is a fundamental error in his position.

This second criticism also reflects Professor Friedmann's acceptance, without discussion, of a simplified version of the Geneva settlement which pictures the United States as upsetting the expectations created at Geneva. This assumption is also questionable.

The object of Professor Friedmann's third criticism is

> . . . the contention that "the requirements of minimum world public order, that is, the avoidance of unilateral coercion as a modality of major change, would in most contexts seem more strongly applicable to insurgent groups than to assistance to the recognized government."[34]

In elaborating this criticism he summarizes my analysis of the non-intervention norms as a "Metternich doctrine of legitimacy."[35] But, as was emphasized in the article, it is doubtful that "civil war" norms even provide the most useful analytic framework for appraisal of the Viet-Nam conflict. The substantial assistance provided by the North across a continuing *de facto* boundary separating the major cold-war camps, in violation of the major purpose of the 1954 Agreement on the Cessation of Hostilities, and provided with a more or less long-run objective of terri-

---

[33] *Ibid.* at 780–781.   [34] *Ibid.* at 779.
[35] *Ibid.* at 782.

torial and political absorption of the South, involves features which distinguish the Viet-Nam conflict from a "civil war." Even if the norms regarding intervention in intra-state conflict were applicable to Viet-Nam, it was pointed out that essentially all scholars are in agreement that assistance provided to a widely recognized government is at least legitimate to offset substantial assistance provided to the insurgents, as is the case in Viet-Nam. If the North is privileged to use force to aid the insurgency in the South, it is difficult to see why South Viet-Nam's allies are not privileged to assist her against this use of force.

These principal contentions do not even raise the question of non-intervention in situations of purely intra-state conflict. But Professor Friedmann does not even advert to these principal points. Instead, he proceeds to focus on the policy critique of the intervention norms themselves, characterizing my views as "Professor Moore's legitimacy doctrine." [36] This is a misnomer of my position. As even the passage which Professor Friedmann quotes makes clear, my article questions the traditional approach which lays down a single rule that only the widely recognized government can be aided or a "neutral non-intervention" rule that neither side can be aided. Neither rule is exclusively supported by state practice and there is reason to suggest that both greatly oversimplify the range of intra-state conflict and, when mechanically applied, may be counter-productive. As a preliminary alternative the article calls for examination of the policies underlying the purpose of restrictions on intervention and their application to more precisely differentiated contexts.

My analysis tentatively identified self-determination and minimum public order as the principal policies applicable (although there may be others which will more clearly emerge in other contexts), and concluded that both policies supported defensive assistance to South Viet-Nam considerably more than they supported North Viet-Nam's assistance to insurgents in the South. In the analysis of minimum public order as a policy, it was stated that

> The requirements of minimum world public order, that is, the avoidance of unilateral coercion as a modality of major change, would in most contexts seem more strongly applicable to assistance to insurgent groups than to assistance to the recognized government.[37]

It is apparently this statement on which Professor Friedmann relies as indicative of "Professor Moore's legitimacy doctrine." The statement calls attention within the over-all policy discussion to the real differences in probable consequences for minimization of coercion when military assistance is provided to insurgents rather than to a widely recognized government. Among other reasons for these differences: widely recognized governments generally control the organized military apparatus making military opposition to them likely to result in prolonged conflict;

---

[36] *Ibid.* at 783.

[37] Moore, note 2 above, at 31. This statement is part of the over-all discussion of "civil war" non-intervention norms, *ibid.* at 28–32.

recognized governments may be incorporated in a world order bloc that views their overthrow as an unacceptable impairment of bloc power or security; recognized governments may have defensive arrangements with third Powers which will be triggered by the conflict; and recognized governments as the representative of the state may be receiving continuing military assistance from external Powers commenced prior to insurgency. Analysis is incomplete which fails to take account of these and other real differences between the widely recognized government and insurgents which affect the consequences of rendering assistance to the two sides.

And although both the traditional "legitimacy doctrine" and the "neutral non-intervention" norm are questionable as absolutes, both are supported by distinguished contemporary scholars, and there is reason to suggest that, at least in the inter-bloc context, the "aid to widely recognized government only" doctrine has as much reason to support it in real-world application as the "neutral non-intervention" norm. Considerations which suggest this conclusion are the desirability of focusing on the great threat to peace in providing sustained assistance to insurgents across cold-war boundaries, the difficulty of appraising covert assistance in externally sponsored "wars of national liberation," and realism about constraints felt by opposing bloc Powers to support existing friendly regimes, as evidenced by the events in Hungary, East Germany, Malaysia, Korea, Greece, and now Viet-Nam.

Having elsewhere attempted a more detailed preliminary policy analysis with respect to non-intervention norms,[38] I will merely point out here the importance of continuing analysis of the whole non-intervention area, both with respect to the normative and process sides of the problem. The most profitable direction for study on the normative side may be careful analysis of goals to be served, greater breakdown of the diverse types of intra-state conflict with more precise recommendation for each major type, and exploration of a range of alternatives to total prohibition of assistance.[39]

Professor Friedmann's three points, which must bear the burden of his criticism, do not show that there is anything "scholarly indefensible"[40] in my analysis, and he fails to show that military assistance to South Viet-Nam is not a lawful policy alternative.

As a unifying theme, Professor Friedmann criticizes what he says is a dangerous use of international law norms professedly as objective standards

---

[38] Moore, note 9 above. See also my brief recommendation of a framework for inquiry about non-intervention norms in 1967 Proceedings, American Society of International Law 75.

[39] Professor Farer's recent suggestion of a prohibition on tactical support is the kind of alternative which breaks new ground and which should be explored. See Farer, note 11 above. Though this writer doubts that this alternative, which focuses solely on the modalities of assistance, is realistic for all contexts, for example, the inter-bloc conflict, it may be a useful alternative for some types of intra-state conflict. The important point is that alternatives other than either/or should be explored and that the modalities of assistance, objectives of the participants, arenas of fighting, and outcomes (supervised elections, perhaps), are highly relevant.

[40] Friedmann, note 1 above, at 781.

but actually as rationalizations of national policy.[41] He further implies that the differences between us with regard to the legal issues of the Viet-Nam conflict are not based on the inevitable discrepancies in legal interpretation but rather exist because he takes international law seriously while I merely rationalize government policy.

It is true that blind loyalty to one's country will neither move the world toward a more civilized state of international relations nor serve the national interest. This is true but is also largely non-controversial. This universal agreement makes it tempting to brand scholars who support the lawfulness of a particular national action as seeking only to serve a nationalistic bias. But a coincidence of national policy and the norms of international law does not prove guilt by association. And preoccupation with this theme is a form of tilting at windmills which can result in as serious an impairment of meaningful communication as the labeling and dismissing of dissenters.[42]

The most useful dialogue requires presentation of the conclusions which the author thinks correct and reply to the substantive arguments made by others. And particularly on an emotional and divisive issue such as Viet-Nam, it is imperative to keep in mind that it is an issue on which reasonable men *do* differ. Professor Friedmann's reply is disappointing in each of these respects.

The general tone of much of Professor Friedmann's critique suggests a jurisprudential ambivalence which may be partly responsible for his concern about rationalization of national policy. Though his discussion of non-intervention norms indicates a jurisprudence sensitive to policy argument, he seems uncomfortable when confronted with more explicit policy analysis. This takes the form of his damning without explanation or illustration my "method of thinking" and my "ambiguous use of terminology."[43] Later he elaborates on this theme:

> Time and again Professor Moore invokes "minimum world public order," a formula made familiar by Professor McDougal's many writings. This goes together with the rejection of "black letter rules," and contempt for "Alice-in-Wonderland search for neutral principles." This is ominously reminiscent of the similar formulas used by the Lord Chancellor in Britain during the Suez Canal crisis in order to justify the Franco-British intervention and, almost a decade later, by the Legal Adviser of the State Department in justification of the U.S. intervention in the Dominican Republic. . . . [I]n the absence of third-party determination, "minimum world public order" means, Humpty-Dumpty-like, what the policy-maker wants it to mean, a catch-all phrase to justify whatever action the writer wishes to justify. . . .[44]

No formula or approach, whether policy-oriented or the most pedantic

---

[41] *Ibid.* at 778.

[42] Professor Friedmann reiterates this theme in a debate with Professors A. J. Thomas and A. A. Berle on the Dominican Republic crisis. See The Dominican Republic Crisis 1965: The Ninth Hammarskjöld Forum 112–113 (1967).

[43] Friedmann, note 1 above, at 779.   [44] *Ibid.* at 783.

search for "black and white" rules, guarantees "correct" results in analysis of complex issues of international law or the same result when applied by different scholars. All suffer alike from the absence of third-party determination. Yet Professor Friedmann's suspicion of policy analysis suggests both that he believes that a search for "black and white" rules offers greater certainty of "correct" results and that he thinks consciously or unconsciously that policy justification is unnecessary and even dangerous. But there are strong reasons for suggesting that the available range of complementary norms of international law makes a simplistic rule application a more dangerous exercise (dangerous in the sense of ease of manipulation of result) when dealing with complex major issues than the conscious application of norms in the light of their function.

It is a mistake to read the Charter as if it were a municipal traffic ordinance. The "Lawyers Committee Memorandum" is a prime example of pseudo-scholarship anchored in this "red and green" approach. Such simplistic approaches are frequently characterized by over-concern for literal meaning such as the now discredited "non-member" argument and by single-factor analysis such as the argument that the Viet-Nam war is a "civil war" because the Geneva Accords indicated that the military demarcation line was provisional. This kind of preoccupation with a single feature fails to take into account the total manifold of events which are important for determination about the aggression-defense abstractions of the Charter.

The check on policy argument, like that on any other kind of legal argument, is scholars willing to reply to it; to point out why a particular policy is not applicable, or why there are overriding policy considerations against its application, or to show why an argument represents a personal recommendation and does not reflect existing norms. There is nothing mysterious or subject to greater abuse in such analysis. And in the long run those methods of analysis which seek not only the "identification" of norms but also the appraisal of their application by some kind of widely shared community values provide greater hope for reaching satisfactory decision. Legal scholarship must be concerned not only with rules and principles but also with purpose and values.

Norms of international law provide standards of conduct for the United States and all other national actors. But a purely "legalistic" approach to international law is as deficient as a raw *realpolitik* approach. The former emphasizes rules without consideration of function or context and ignores the problem of control in an imperfect world; and the latter ignores, among other things, the importance of perspectives of authority as an influence on international affairs. The theory of international law exhibited by both of these schools is incomplete.

International law is vital in innumerable ways, not the least of which are to provide norms of conduct for national and international decision-makers, to provide guides to the reasonable expectations of other actors in the international arena, and to clarify, through emphasis on dialogue about community common interest, a different range of policies.

Because of this relevance of international law to problems of contemporary foreign relations Professor Friedmann's seemingly realistic statement that the Viet-Nam conflict "moves in a legal vacuum"[45] is not the most useful appraisal. The question is not simply whether the decisions taken on both sides leading to the Viet-Nam conflict were "motivated" by international law, or whether international law "controls" the conflict, but is also what international law has to say about those decisions today. The structure embodied in the United Nations Charter regarding the lawfulness of the use of force has a great deal to say about them and is essential for balanced appraisal of the conflict.

The Vietnamese war is as ambiguous and difficult a conflict as this century has seen. Politically, the alternatives and the national interest are heatedly, honestly and sometimes irrationally argued. Debated are interests in credibility of commitments, containment of Communism, effects on the domestic order and the morality of the use of force. Legal dialogue adds a unique dimension to this debate—the focus on the regulation of coercion in international affairs. In this normative structure the Clausewitzian pursuit of war as an instrument of national policy and the "just war" concept have been scrapped. In their place the Charter proscribes all use of the military instrument as a modality of major change in international affairs. If this is a rigidity of international law, it is a rigidity well founded in the danger of a nuclear Dunkirk and the bitter experience of two world wars. The more recent tragedies of Korea, Kashmir, the Sino-Indian border dispute, Viet-Nam and lately Palestine, for the third time in twenty years, are testimony to the vital truth of this principle. Political disputes, black, white or grey, provide no justification for major resort to force. There *is* a South Viet-Nam and its neighbors must learn to live in peace with it.

JOHN NORTON MOORE

Viet-Nam and the International Law of Self-Defense

LEONARD C. MEEKER[1]

THROUGHOUT this land, the war in Viet-Nam weighs heavy on the minds of Americans. It is again and again the subject of our talk, under the pressing flow of news dispatches and under the thousand impacts this war has on our lives. It is never far from our thoughts.

Fighting a war is never cheap, never easy. The Viet-Nam war is a particularly difficult one. As President Johnson has said, this is a new kind of war. It is not a war of major battles to be won or lost. It calls for courage and fortitude to stick it out, over a long period of time if need be.

There are few who would not be rid of the war. It impinges directly on the lives of American young men by the tens and hundreds of thousands. Most Americans are anxious to turn our full resources to another great war—a war on poverty and hunger at home and throughout the world. Some believe the Viet-Nam war divides the world at a time when we are most impelled to seek world cooperation.

One cannot but be concerned about these problems. No one can say that debate is unnecessary—quite the contrary. We are dealing with great issues. There are risks to be weighed and roads that must be chosen.

It is my purpose, in the hour we have together this evening, to locate the Viet-Nam war in the great river of time: first, to indicate something of how it arose; then, to relate it to the existing framework of international law; finally, to consider the place of this conflict in the building of a more stable and just world order as nations move along the high-road of history.

Origins of the Viet-Nam Conflict

Viet-Nam has a very short political history under that name—one that does not go back even 20 years. Viet-Nam is made up of three areas that were included in what France called, for purposes of colonial administration, Indochina. Those areas were: Tonkin in the Red River Delta of the north, Annam along the central coast, and Cochin China in the south around Saigon. In the 19th century France ruled these areas as protectorates and colonies, along with Laos and Cambodia; all together, they made up Indochina.

[1] 1966 Louis Caplan Lecture in Law at the University of Pittsburgh Law School, Pittsburgh, Pa., on Dec. 13 (press release 292).

The colonial picture was a typical one: administrators from France to govern; French armed forces to keep order; colonists to direct agriculture and trade; native gentry and leaders who were clients of the French and profited from the relationship; finally, the Indochinese majority, who performed the labor of the country and received relatively little return for their toil.

Japan's military leaders, as part of their program of expansion and conquest, occupied Indochina in 1940. The colonial administration and the European residents of Indochina by and large collaborated with the Japanese. They hoped thereby to keep the political, economic, and social situation under control.

It was in World War II that the recent history of Viet-Nam began. Dissidents who opposed the French and the Japanese carried on a resistance movement. Ho Chi Minh was the acknowledged leader of this movement from the beginning. By 1945 the drive for independence had become a significant political force. The sense of nationalism and the ideas of self-determination were at work in Indochina, as they were elsewhere in Asia and soon came to be in Africa.

But France in the postwar period did not follow the course of independence soon taken by Britain for India, Burma, and other Commonwealth territories. France sought instead to restore and reinforce its colonial administration in Indochina. What had been wartime resistance by the Viet Minh organization continued and grew as a struggle to rid the country of colonial rule. In 1949 France sought to stem the tide by setting up indigenous governments of limited authority in Cambodia, in Laos, and in a new State of Viet-Nam. France kept control of foreign affairs, defense, and financial matters.

The guerrilla campaign of the Viet Minh grew into a major war with the French colonial forces. At the end of 5 years the battle of Dien Bien Phu had been lost by the French, and Paris had decided to seek a political settlement. This was the origin of the Geneva conference of 1954, in which the five great world powers took part, along with Cambodia, Laos, and North and South Viet-Nam—each of which by then had its own regime. The Government in the South had been created by and was alined with France. Hanoi was the seat of the rebel Viet Minh regime which had been fighting the French. Its concentration of military and political power was in the North, but it had guerrilla units operating throughout the country. The participants in the Geneva conference did not have to produce any agreement at all. They were free to continue all the existing disagreements. The French and Viet Minh military forces could have gone on with the fighting, to whatever conclusion it would yield. Since, however, they did reach a series of international agreements, we are entitled to look at them as binding legal instruments.

We will want first to see what contracts were made. We will want to see what provision was made for insuring compliance. We will want to look at what happened in fact. We will want to examine the legal rights of the parties in the circumstances of 1956 to 1966.

The Geneva Accords

The 1954 Geneva conference produced agreements on Cambodia and Laos as well as on Viet-Nam, but for present purposes we shall consider only the instruments relating to Viet-Nam.[2] The chief of these was the Agreement on the Cessation of Hostilities in Viet-Nam. It was signed on behalf of the commander in chief of the French Union forces in Indochina and on behalf of the commander in chief of the People's Army of Viet-Nam.

The very first article of the Viet-Nam cease-fire agreement fixed a demarcation line, near the 17th parallel in central Viet-Nam, "on either side of which the forces of the two parties shall be regrouped after their withdrawal, the forces of the People's Army of Viet-Nam to the north of the line and the forces of the French Union to the south." Under article 19 of the same agreement, the two parties were bound to insure that the zones assigned to them "are not used for the resumption of hostilities or to further an aggressive policy." And under article 24 each party was obligated to "commit no act and undertake no operation against the other party." Articles 16 and 17 of the agreement prohibited the introduction into Viet-Nam of additional armed forces or weapons, but permitted the rotation of troops and the replacement of worn-out or used-up materiel. Article 18 prohibited the establishment of new military bases throughout Viet-Nam territory.

In a separate document, known as the Final Declaration of the Geneva Conference,[3] the conference powers agreed that the settlement of political problems in Viet-Nam should "permit the Viet-Namese people to enjoy the fundamental freedoms, guaranteed by democratic institutions established as a result of free general elections by secret ballot." There were to be general elections in July 1956 under the supervision of the International Control Commission. Consultations on this sub-

---

[2] For texts, see *American Foreign Policy, 1950-1955, Basic Documents*, vol. I, Department of State publication 6446, p. 750.

[3] *Ibid.*, p. 785.

ject were to be held between representatives of the two zones beginning in July 1955.

Here, then, were the basic undertakings of the Geneva accords. If observed, they should have kept the peace in Viet-Nam. What was to insure that the parties would live up to these undertakings? The agreement sought to provide some machinery for international supervision.

There was to be an International Control Commission, made up of representatives of India, Canada, and Poland. The Commission was to oversee fulfillment of all the obligations of the agreement. It was to have inspection teams at its disposal and access to any and all places in both zones of Viet-Nam. Some of the Commission's decisions could be made by majority vote; others, including those dealing with violations or threats of violations which might lead to a resumption of hostilities, would require a unanimous vote of all members.

In this respect, the arrangement was flawed from the beginning. Any member of the Commission could veto a decision on a question of compliance with the agreement. On other matters, even a majority might be unobtainable because the representative of India, in carrying out his Government's policy of nonalinement, could remain aloof and equivocal on important matters. Vetoes were in fact cast, and the Indian chairman of the Commission often pursued his national policy of neutralism and nonalinement. The Commission had other difficulties, too. The zonal authorities, and particularly those in North Viet-Nam, denied access to the inspection teams of the Commission.

As a result of this state of affairs, the world has not had an effective, authoritative, and impartial reporting mechanism on the facts in Viet-Nam. There could and did arise disputes about the facts in Viet-Nam. For example, who lived up to the cease-fire agreement, and who broke it? Was the subsequent conflict indigenous and essentially a civil war, or was there the intervention of substantial and perhaps crucial external force?

Events in Viet-Nam Since 1954

Issues like these have a bearing on the international legal rights of the parties. Because they are an essential part of the legal analysis, we must try to deal with them. Since, for the most part, we do not have available authoritative findings by an impartial international body, it is necessary to work with the best evidence that can be gathered.

I should like to set out what the United States Government believes happened after July 1954 and to set these events beside the provisions of the Geneva accords. I shall, of course, discuss what the Government of South Viet-Nam and the Government of the United States did after July 1954. But because their actions were in the nature of a response to events directed from Hanoi, it seems most logical to examine first what the other side was doing.

Despite the obligation of regroupment in the cease-fire agreement, some effective Communist guerrilla units continued to operate in areas of South Viet-Nam where they had been during the hostilities with France. Large numbers of the southern Viet Minh troops who were withdrawn north of the demarcation line were retained by Hanoi in military or security units; others received further training in guerrilla warfare.

The North Vietnamese regime began to infiltrate these ethnic Southerners into South Viet-Nam as early as 1957. Up to the concluding months of 1964, approximately 40,000 infiltrators moved south, to join the guerrillas already there who had been supported with arms and supplies by Hanoi since 1956. Once in South Viet-Nam, the infiltrators were assigned to existing combat units or used to form new units, frequently in their original home provinces. All of this activity—the training, the equipping, the transporting, the assigning—was directed from Hanoi. It did not just happen within South Viet-Nam.

As the infiltration from the North continued, Hanoi began to exhaust its supply of ethnic Southerners who could be sent into the South for guerrilla warfare. Beginning in late 1964, the infiltrating units consisted essentially of North Vietnamese soldiers organized in regular army units. Upward of 80,000 of these troops have infiltrated from the North during the last 2 years. The Northerners have frequently entered in large units, rather than in small groups, and have retained their military organization. After allowing for casualties from all causes, it is estimated that there are today about 45,000 North Vietnamese army regulars in South Viet-Nam. This represents nearly half of the main force of Communist combat troops in the South—a force currently estimated at 100,000. Of the remaining 55,000, many are irregulars who earlier infiltrated from the North; almost all the rest have been recruited from Communist-held areas in the South—there has been no rallying to the Communist cause from Government-held areas.

Let us now look at what the Communists have been doing with their forces in South Viet-Nam during the last 10 years. They began their operations with terrorism and assassination aimed at local government officials. From 1957 to 1959 more than 1,000 civilians were assassinated or kidnapped by Communist guerrillas in the South. In the ensuing 2 years their attacks were intensified and began to be conducted by battalion-size units against the military and security forces of the Government in the South. The level of military activity increased progressively.

With the arrival of regular North Vietnamese army units, beginning in the concluding months of 1964, sizable military engagements have taken place almost continuously in many different parts of South Viet-Nam. Unlike Korea, where the Communists launched openly an invasion in broad daylight across an international demarcation line, the Communists in Viet-Nam have resorted to covert and clandestine tactics. This is the strategy of what Communist ideology and propaganda call the "war of national liberation."

On the basis of the evidence which has been accumulated over a period of time, it seems beyond dispute that from the beginning the conflict in South Viet-Nam has not been simply an indigenous rebellion. Much of the military manpower came from the North. So also with weapons and supplies. And, perhaps most important of all, the planning, the direction, the orders, have come from Hanoi.

International Law in Relation to the Viet-Nam Conflict

How does one apply international law to this kind of problem?

It is necessary to begin by finding out what international law is. We have a fairly clear idea of what it is not. It is not a framework of government such as our own and other democratic countries have at home. There is no international legislature to make the rules of the game for all to accept and follow. There is no system of courts. There is no police force.

What is a government to do in the face of so imperfect a world, in the face of so chaotic a scene, such as that created by large-scale violence and hostilities in Southeast Asia? Some have suggested that it is best to acknowledge there is no real law to deal with such a situation of conflict and that the proper course is to proceed with whatever practical actions will most advance the military power, the security position, and the general interests of the United States. I wonder if such a view does not beg an important question. Will this country's security be enhanced, will its interests be served, without our making an honest and determined attempt to develop international law and live by it?

We may feel the absence today of a law-giver outside national governments, who could, to our comfort and security, give and enforce law among the nations. That absence does not relieve us of moral and political obligations. It means instead that governments will have to go on working very hard if there are to be functioning and effective processes and institutions of world law in the future.

Let us remember, too, that the shape of things to come is in no small way determined by the actions of great powers. This is an aspect of the responsibility that the United States, along with other countries, bears in the modern world. I have no doubt myself that the road of pragmatism and the road of idealism run together as we consider the needs and the possibilities for developing effective world law.

INTERNATIONAL AGREEMENTS

1. There are many ways of making law. One powerful means of lawmaking available to governments is to join in making international agreements and then to act in conformity with them.

In the case of Viet-Nam we have the Geneva accords as a starting point and legal framework for dealing with the situation. Although the United States did not sign the accords, from the beginning it undertook to respect them, and President Eisenhower said that "any renewal of Communist aggression would be viewed by us as a matter of grave concern."[4]

The United States began as early as 1954 to arrange for aid to South Viet-Nam to promote its viability and development. For nearly 7 years United States forces and materiel in the South stayed within the limits set by the Geneva accords for external military assistance, despite the fact that North Viet-Nam had been violating these accords from the start and despite the gradual escalation of these violations. Not until late 1961 did the number of United States military personnel in the South rise above 900. When the United States made the decision to exceed the limits laid down by the Geneva accords, it was on the basis of a principle of international law similar to the doctrine of fundamental breach in the domestic law of contracts. North Viet-Nam had violated seriously the obligation to prevent the northern zone from being "used for the resumption of hostilities or to further an aggressive policy." In these circumstances, South Viet-Nam was relieved from the obligation to comply with the cease-fire agreement's limitations on military manpower and materiel when the South needed additional strength for its own defense against aggression from the North.

Here it is noteworthy that in June 1962 the Indian and Canadian

---

[4] For a statement made by President Eisenhower on July 21, 1954, see BULLETIN of Aug. 2, 1954, p. 163.

members of the International Control Commission found it possible to agree as follows in a report:

> . . . there is evidence to show that armed and unarmed personnel, arms, munitions and other supplies have been sent from the Zone in the North to the Zone in the South with the object of supporting, organizing and carrying out hostile activities, including armed attacks, directed against the Armed Forces and Administration of the Zone in the South. . . .
>
> . . . there is evidence to show that the PAVN [People's Army of Viet-Nam] has allowed the Zone in the North to be used for inciting, encouraging and supporting hostile activities in the Zone in the South, aimed at the overthrow of the Administration in the South.

The Commission also cited the Republic of Viet-Nam for its activities in importing military equipment and personnel above the limits imposed by the 1954 Geneva accords. However, these actions were taken by South Viet-Nam as part of its effort to defend itself against aggression and subversion from the North. And at no time did South Viet-Nam undertake to overrun the North by force.

I have mentioned this report of the International Control Commission because it shows that the international machinery set up by the Geneva accords agreed with the legal analysis of the situation made by the United States, when that machinery was able to function. But for most of the last dozen years, it has been unable to function as intended.

GOVERNMENT ACTIONS AND PRECEDENTS THEY CREATE

2. Another way in which international law is made is through the actions of governments and the precedents they create. If a government acts consistently with a series of coherent principles, it may make a contribution to the common law of nations. The United States Government has tried to do this in the case of Viet-Nam, both with respect to situations not envisioned by the Geneva accords and in giving practical interpretations and applications to the general rules laid down by the Charter of the United Nations.

Some commentators, in talking about Viet-Nam, have set up three categories of situations for their legal analysis of the problem: The first is the category of wholly indigenous rebellion. The second category is one in which there is large-scale intervention from outside short of armed attack. The third is the category of armed attack, in which one country employs its regular military forces to gain control of another country.

The evidence does not allow for the conclusion that the war in Viet-Nam was ever a simple category-one situation. It was probably, for quite some period of time, a category-two situation. By the end of 1964, however, it had become very clearly a category-three situation.

Critics of United States Government policy have argued that, if there was North Vietnamese intervention in the South, any United States assistance to South Viet-Nam that might be justified would have to be confined geographically to South Viet-Nam. Even if one were to concede that such a rule applies in the case of a category-two situation, it certainly does not apply to a case of armed attack. Legitimate defense includes military action against the aggressor wherever such action is needed to halt the attack.

During the decade after Geneva, the United States did confine its assistance to South Viet-Nam to military personnel, supplies, and activities in the South. The United States took no action against the source of aggression in the North. Then, in late 1964, as I have already indicated, North Viet-Nam moved into a new phase of its aggression and began dispatching southward whole units of its regular armed forces. The tempo of the war had increased by early 1965, and additional measures of defense were required.

INFILTRATION—CURRENT MODE OF "ARMED ATTACK"

3. I have heard and read arguments by some that Viet-Nam does not present a situation of "armed attack" because invading armies were not massed at a border and did not march across it in broad daylight. To be sure, that is the way armed attacks occurred in 1914, at the beginning of World War II, and even in Korea. But strategies and tactics have changed. The current mode of armed aggression in Viet-Nam is by the infiltration of military units and the weapons of war under cover of darkness, through jungle areas, and across the territory of a neighboring state—Laos.

The law, if it is to be a living and working force, must concern itself with the substance and the reality of what is going on. The answer to a question of law cannot properly turn on the mere form or appearance that a protagonist may give to its action. The judgment whether North Viet-Nam has engaged in "armed attack" against the South cannot depend on the form or appearance of its conduct. The crucial consideration is that North Viet-Nam has marshaled the resources of the state and has sent instrumentalities of the state, including units of its regular armed forces, into South Viet-Nam to achieve state objectives by force—in this case to subject the South to its rule.

MEASURES OF COLLECTIVE DEFENSE

4. United States and South Vietnamese airstrikes and other military actions against North Viet-Nam have been based on the legal proposition that they are measures of collective defense against armed attack from the North. I would like to take up some of the arguments that have been made against this proposition. First, it has been argued that, while the United States says South Viet-Nam is under armed attack, no international body, such as the United Nations, has made such a finding. The United States Government regrets that neither the Security Council nor the General Assembly of the United Nations has been able or seen fit to express itself on Viet-Nam. But ought we to adopt the view that if the United Nations makes no finding, there is therefore no armed attack and the aggressor must accordingly be permitted to pursue his ambitions without being subjected to effective countermeasures?

Certainly the United Nations Charter does *not* say this. Article 51 of the charter, dealing with armed attack, says that "the inherent right of individual or collective self-defense" may be exercised "until the Security Council has taken the measures necessary to maintain international peace and security." Thus it is for a defender to claim and assert that armed attack has taken place, justifying measures of defense. The defender does not have to await action by the Security Council. His duty, as is made clear by the remainder of article 51, is to report to the Council. Then the Council will, in the end, decide what has happened, who is right, and what measures must be taken.

The United States has several times reported to the Council in the last 2 years on military actions in Viet-Nam. The Council has taken no action. In January and February 1966 the Council elected not to debate the situation in Viet-Nam, although the United States had once again raised the whole question. In September of this year Ambassador [Arthur J.] Goldberg made a full presentation to the General Assembly on Viet-Nam.[5] The subject was a central topic in the month-long general debate that was held in New York during October. Again, no United Nations action was taken.

[5] *Ibid.*, Oct. 10, 1966, p. 518.

INTERNATIONAL LINES OF DEMARCATION

5. Another argument made against the United States legal position on collective self-defense is that Viet-Nam is a single country and that the regime in the North is not legally precluded from taking steps, including the use of force, to unify North and South Viet-Nam under a single Communist regime. Any such argument ignores the plain provisions of the Geneva accords of 1954. It also suggests a view of international law that would operate to undermine peace and security in many parts of the world.

The Geneva accords are very clear in drawing a demarcation line between North and South Viet-Nam. This line was to be respected by the opposing armed forces, including all elements—regular or irregular —under their control. It divided Viet-Nam into two zones which would be administered by different authorities. The line was set by an international agreement negotiated at a conference in Geneva of the principal powers concerned.

The fact that the demarcation line was not intended as a permanent boundary surely did not give either side license to disregard it. The very purpose of the line was to end hostilities and separate the fighting forces. Moving troops from one zone to the other to engage them in hostilities was clearly in breach of the international agreement reached at Geneva in 1954.

It was also true in the Korea of 1950 that the 38th parallel was not a permanent boundary but instead an international demarcation line established at the end of World War II. Like the line in Viet-Nam, the line in Korea was not intended to last; it was hoped that the country could be unified. But all of this made the North Korean invasion of that year no less an armed attack under international law.

The importance of respecting international lines of demarcation is evident in Europe also. The lines of demarcation between East and West Germany and around West Berlin have never been intended as permanent boundaries. However, they are lines of great importance, and any moves to disregard them would have the gravest consequences.

QUESTION OF "FREE ELECTIONS"

6. Still another argument has been advanced by some to justify the actions of Hanoi. It runs as follows: The Geneva accords looked forward to a political settlement as the result of which Viet-Nam would be unified; elections were to be held in the summer of 1956, and during the preceding year consultations were to be held between the authorities of North and South concerning the elections; South Viet-Nam declined

to take part in consultations, and there have been no elections; hence, North Viet-Nam had freedom to proceed in its own way with reunification of the country.

This argument has no merit. The elections referred to in the Geneva accords were to be *"free* general elections by secret ballot."* Even the North Vietnamese Defense Minister in effect admitted long ago that such elections would have been impossible in North Viet-Nam. Speaking at the 10th Congress of the North Vietnamese Communist Party Central Committee in October 1956 General [Vo Nguyen] Giap said:

> We have made too many deviations and executed too many honest people. We attacked on too large a front and seeing enemies everywhere, resorted to terror, which became far too widespread.

Thus it cannot properly be said that there was any breach of agreement by South Viet-Nam when it declined to proceed toward elections that could not possibly have been meaningful.

DEFENSE MEASURES PROPORTIONAL TO ATTACK

7. Before concluding this review of the United States legal position, I would like to refer to the principle that measures of defense must be proportional to the attack. The United States program of airstrikes against North Viet-Nam has been designed for the purpose of interfering with transport to the South; destroying supplies intended for shipment to the South; in short, to halt the continuing aggression by North Viet-Nam. As Ambassador Goldberg said 2 months ago:

> It is because of the attempt to upset by violence the situation in Viet-Nam, and its far-reaching implications elsewhere, that the United States and other countries have responded to appeals from South Viet-Nam for military assistance.
>
> Our aims in giving this assistance are strictly limited.
>
> We are not engaged in a "holy war" against communism.
>
> We do not seek to establish an American empire or a sphere of influence in Asia.
>
> We seek no permanent military bases, no permanent establishment of troops, no permanent alliances, no permanent American presence of any kind in South Viet-Nam.
>
> We do not seek to impose a policy of alinement on South Viet-Nam.
>
> We do not seek to overthrow the Government of North Viet-Nam.
>
> We do not seek to do any injury to mainland China nor to threaten any of its legitimate interests.

We do not ask of North Viet-Nam an unconditional surrender or indeed the surrender of anything that belongs to it.

Efforts to Find a Peaceful Settlement

I have been setting forth reasons in support of United States military actions against North Viet-Nam. Justification for these actions in no way displaces a continuing obligation we have under the United Nations Charter to seek a peaceful settlement. It has long been said that nations must try to settle their disputes by peaceful means before any resort to force. But it is no less true that the participants in armed conflict are bound to go on seeking a settlement by peaceful means even while hostilities are in progress.

Particularly in the last 2 years, the United States has made major efforts to negotiate an end to the war in Viet-Nam. In April 1965 President Johnson, in response to the appeal of 17 nonalined countries, offered to commence negotiations without precondition.[6] This was not acceptable to Hanoi. A year ago the United States conducted a concentrated peace offensive for over 5 weeks. Again there was no affirmative answer from the other side.

At the General Assembly this fall, Ambassador Goldberg summed up our aims in the following way:

> We want a political solution, not a military solution, to this conflict. By the same token, we reject the idea that North Viet-Nam has the right to impose a military solution.
>
> We seek to assure for the people of South Viet-Nam the same right of self-determination—to decide its own political destiny, free of force—that the United Nations Charter affirms for all.
>
> And we believe that reunification of Viet-Nam should be decided upon through a free choice by the peoples of both the North and the South without outside interference, the results of which choice we are fully prepared to support.
>
> . . . We are prepared to order a cessation of all bombing of North Viet-Nam the moment we are assured, privately or otherwise, that this step will be answered promptly by a corresponding and appropriate deescalation on the other side.

Prospects Into the Future

It is not given to us to foresee in what way the Viet-Nam war will end. It is possible that the protagonists will meet at the conference

---

[6] For text of President Johnson's address at Johns Hopkins University, Baltimore, Md., see *ibid.*, Apr. 26, 1965, p. 606.

table and settle the conflict by negotiation. The United States will continue to press its efforts toward peaceful settlement.

It is also possible that, over time, North Viet-Nam will gradually reduce and ultimately cease its intervention in the South, having found that force does not pay and that the relationships between North and South must be worked out on the levels of economic intercourse and political accommodation.

Other possibilities have been urged by some: for example, outright withdrawal of United States forces from Viet-Nam or withdrawal of those forces to a few coastal bases. I cannot see that any such ending to the war in Viet-Nam would be acceptable from the point of view of the world community interest in peace and justice among nations. Such an ending would gravely impair the effectiveness of the international law that we have today.

For one thing, withdrawal and abandonment of South Viet-Nam would be to sacrifice the Geneva accords and advertise for all to see that an international agreement can with impunity be treated by an aggressor as a mere scrap of paper. Moreover, withdrawal and abandonment of South Viet-Nam would undermine the faith of other countries in United States defense treaty commitments and would encourage would-be aggressors to suppose they could successfully and even freely impose on their weaker neighbors by force.

In less than 2 months after the 1954 Geneva conference on Indochina, the United States and other Pacific countries signed the Southeast Asia Collective Defense Treaty. By a unanimously agreed protocol, that treaty covers South Viet-Nam. The parties to the treaty have engaged jointly and severally to "act to meet the common danger" if there is "aggression by means of armed attack" against any of the parties or any protocol state. To disengage from this commitment could have no other effect than to undermine the assurance of all concerned that the United States will live up to its commitments. Political and military stability will not be achieved but could instead be destroyed by a policy of making agreements and then not carrying them out.

We have seen in Europe, during the two decades since World War II, the success of a policy of insisting that the integrity of international settlements not be upset by force. The strengthening of Western Europe through the Marshall Plan and the North Atlantic Treaty put an effective curb on Soviet expansionism. We have seen a favorable development in the increased maturity of Soviet conduct toward the rest of the world. With a growing stake in preserving and developing what has already been achieved at home, the Soviet Government plainly pursues a very different course from that of the younger and still more violent revolution in China.

It is an important part of the task of building a more secure and just world to weight the balances of other governments' processes of calculation, so far as we are able, in the direction of discussion and reason and away from violence and force. This is part of the meaning of the Viet-Nam war today. The use of external force to gain political ends must not turn out to be profitable.

The course of history shows that the temptation to prey upon weaker nations has often been too strong. In 1910 William James foresaw: "The war against war is going to be no holiday excursion or camping party." He emphasized the vast difficulty involved in abolishing war. "Extravagant ambitions," he wrote, "will have to be replaced by reasonable claims, and nations must make common cause against them."

This process of making common cause goes on even in the troubled world of 1966. For all the disappointments, shortcomings, and sometimes retrograde motion, the institution of the United Nations has recorded progress in the long world campaign for peace with justice. The processes and machinery of world organization will have to be strengthened and developed. Governments will have to learn and act upon the conviction that change is necessary to justice but that it must be ordered and peaceful change, without violence.

James' essay from which I quoted was directed to finding a "moral equivalent of war"—a constructive activity that could take over war's historic function of offering challenge to man's ambitions and binding peoples together against a common foe. If it is challenge we need, the world scene is abundant. There are no apparent limits to the resources and energies that nations could put into the exploration of space or into the improvement of man's condition on earth. The pressure of exploding population on food resources in the world is as threatening as any invasion from outer space could be.

The world still has time in which to adjust and redirect man's activities toward survival and growth. Will we not have the wit and the will to make this effort? It seems a necessity in this time when, as President Kennedy said: "man holds in his mortal hands the power to abolish all forms of human poverty and all forms of human life."[7]

[7] For text of President Kennedy's inaugural address, see *ibid.*, Feb. 6, 1961, p. 175.

III. WORLD ORDER PERSPECTIVES

The Control of Force in International Relations

BY THE HONORABLE DEAN RUSK

Secretary of State

When this distinguished Society was founded fifty-nine years ago, the then Secretary of State, Elihu Root, became its first President. With the passage of time, the Secretary of State has been elevated to a less demanding rôle, that of Honorary President. Secretary Root himself not only established the precedent of becoming President while Secretary of State: he also superseded it by continuing to serve as your President for eighteen years. The *Proceedings* of the first meeting indicate that Secretary Root not only presided and delivered an address, but that he also selected the menu for the dinner.

The year 1907, when the first of the Society's annual meetings was held, today appears to have been one of those moments in American history when we were concentrating upon building our American society, essentially untroubled by what took place beyond our borders. But the founders of this Society realized that the United States could not remain aloof from the world. It is one of the achievements of this Society that, from its inception, it has spread the realization that the United States cannot opt out of the community of nations—that international affairs are part of our national affairs.

Questions of war and peace occupied the Society at its first meeting. Among the subjects discussed were the possibility of the immunity of private property from belligerent seizure upon the high seas and whether trade in contraband of war was unneutral. Limitations upon recourse to force then proposed were embryonic, as is illustrated by the fact one topic for discussion related to restrictions upon the use of armed force in the collection of contract obligations. The distance between those ideas and the restrictions upon recourse to armed force contained in the

Charter of the United Nations is vast. It is to these Charter restrictions and their place in the practice and malpractice of states that I shall address much of my remarks this evening.

II

Current United States policy arouses the criticism that it is at once too legal and too tough. Time was when the criticism of American concern with the legal element in international relations was that it led to softness, to a "legalistic-moralistic" approach to foreign affairs which conformed more to the ideal than to the real. Today, critcism of American attachment to the rôle of law is that it leads not to softness, but to severity. We are criticized not for sacrificing our national interests to international interests, but for endeavoring to impose the international interest upon other nations. We are criticized for acting as if the Charter of the United Nations means what it says. We are criticized for treating the statement of the law by the International Court of Justice as authoritative. We are criticized for taking collective security seriously.

This criticism is, I think, a sign of strength—of our strength, and of the strength of international law. It is a tribute to a blending of political purpose with legal ethic.

American foreign policy is at once principled and pragmatic. Its central objective is our national safety and well-being—to "secure the blessings of liberty to ourselves and our posterity." But we know we can no longer find security and well-being in defenses and policies which are confined to North America, or the Western Hemisphere, or the North Atlantic Community. This has become a very small planet. We have to be concerned with all of it, with all of its land, waters, atmosphere, and with surrounding space. We have a deep national interest in peace, the prevention of aggression, the faithful performance of agreements, the growth of international law. Our foreign policy is rooted in the profoundly practical realization that the Purposes and Principles of the United Nations Charter must animate the behavior of states, if mankind is to prosper or is even to survive. Or at least they must animate enough states with enough will and enough resources to see to it that others do not violate those rules with impunity.

The Preamble and Articles One and Two of the Charter set forth abiding purposes of American policy. This is not surprising, since we took the lead in drafting the Charter, at a time when the biggest war in history was still raging and we and others were thinking deeply about its frightful costs and the ghastly mistakes and miscalculations which led to it. The kind of world we seek is the kind set forth in the opening sections of the Charter: a world community of independent states, each with the institutions of its own choice, but co-operating with one another to promote their mutual welfare . . . a world in which the use of force is effectively inhibited . . . a world of expanding human rights and well-being . . . a world of expanding international law . . . a world in which an agreement is a commitment and not just a tactic.

We believe that this is the sort of world a great majority of the governments of the world desire. We believe it is the sort of world man must achieve if he is not to perish. As I said on another occasion: "If once the rule of international law could be discussed with a certain condescension as a Utopian ideal, today it becomes an elementary practical necessity. *Pacta sunt servanda* now becomes the basis for survival."

Unhappily a minority of governments is committed to different ideas of the conduct and organization of human affairs. They are dedicated to the promotion of the Communist world revolution. And their doctrine justifies any technique, any ruse, any deceit, which contributes to that end. They may differ as to tactics from time to time. And the two principal Communist Powers are competitors for the leadership of the world Communist movement. But both are committed to the eventual Communization of the entire world.

The overriding issue of our time is which concepts are to prevail: those set forth in the United Nations Charter or those proclaimed in the name of a world revolution.

III

The paramount commitment of the Charter is Article 2, paragraph 4, which reads:

> All Members shall refrain in their international relations from the threat or use of force against the territorial integrity or political independence of any State, or in any other manner inconsistent with the Purposes of the United Nations.

This comprehensive limitation went beyond the Covenant of the League of Nations. This more sweeping commitment sought to apply a bitter lesson of the interwar period: that the threat or use of force, whether or not called "war," feeds on success. The indelible lesson of those years is that the time to stop aggression is at its very beginning.

The exceptions to the prohibitions on the use or threat of force were expressly set forth in the Charter. The use of force is legal: as a collective measure by the United Nations, or as action by regional agencies in accordance with Chapter VIII of the Charter, or in individual or collective self-defense.

When Article 2, paragraph 4, was written it was widely regarded as general international law, governing both Members and non-Members of the United Nations. And on the universal reach of the principle embodied in Article 2, paragraph 4, wide agreement remains. Thus, last year, a United Nations Special Committee on Principles of International Law concerning Friendly Relations and Cooperation among States met in Mexico City. All shades of United Nations opinion were represented. The Committee's purpose was to study and possibly to elaborate certain of those principles. The Committee debated much and agreed on little. But on one point, it reached swift and unanimous agreement: that all states, and not only all Members of the United Nations, are bound to refrain in their international relations from the threat or use of force against the territorial integrity or political independence of any state. Non-recognition of the statehood of a political entity was held not to affect the international application of this cardinal rule of general international law.

But at this same meeting in Mexico City, Czechoslovakia, with the warm support of the Soviet Union and some other Members, proposed formally another exemption from the limitations on use of force. Their proposal stated that: "The prohibition of the use of force shall not affect . . . self defense of nations against colonial domination in the exercise of the right of self-determination." The United States is all for self-defense. We are against colonial domination; we led the way in throwing it off. We have long favored self-determination, in practice as well as in words; indeed, we favor it for the entire world, including the peoples behind the Iron and Bamboo curtains. But we could not accept the Czech proposal. And we were pleased that the Special Committee found the Czech proposal unacceptable.

The primary reason why we opposed that attempt to rewrite the Charter —apart from the inadmissibility of rewriting the Charter at all by such means—was that we knew the meaning behind the words. We knew that, like so many statements from such sources, it used upside-down language, that it would in effect authorize a state to wage war, to use force internationally, as long as it claimed it was doing so to "liberate" somebody from "colonial domination." In short, the Czech resolution proposed to give to so-called "wars of national liberation" the same exemption from the limitation on the use of force which the Charter accords to defense against aggression.

What is a "war of national liberation"? It is, in essence, any war which furthers the Communist world revolution—what, in broader terms, the Communists have long referred to as a "just" war. The term "war of national liberation" is used not only to denote armed insurrection by people still under colonial rule—there are not many of those left outside the Communist world. It is used to denote any effort led by Communists to overthrow by force any non-Communist government. Thus the war in South Viet-Nam is called a "war of national liberation." And those who would overthrow various other non-Communist governments in Asia, Africa, and Latin America are called the "forces of national liberation."

Nobody in his right mind would deny that Venezuela is not only a truly independent nation but that it has a government chosen in a free election. But the leaders of the Communist insurgency in Venezuela are described as leaders of a fight for "national liberation," not only by themselves and by Castro and the Chinese Communists, but by the Soviet Communists. A recent editorial in *Pravda* spoke of the "peoples of Latin America . . . marching firmly along the path of struggle for their national independence" and said: "the upsurge of the national liberation movement in Latin American countries has been to a great extent a result of the activities of Communist parties." It added:

The Soviet people have regarded and still regard it as their sacred duty to give support to the peoples fighting for their independence. True to their international duty the Soviet people have been and will remain on the side of the Latin American patriots.

In Communist doctrine and practice, a non-Communist government may be labeled and denounced as "colonialist," "reactionary," or a "puppet," and any state so labeled by the Communists automatically becomes fair game; while Communist intervention by force in non-Communist states is justified as "self-defense" or part of the "struggle against colonial domination." "Self-determination" seems to mean that any Communist nation can determine by itself that any non-Communist state is a victim of colonialist domination and therefore a justifiable target for a war of "liberation."

As the risks of overt aggression, whether nuclear or with conventional forces, have become increasingly evident, the Communists have put increasing stress on the "war of national liberation." The Chinese Communists have been more militant in language and behavior than the Soviet Communists. But the Soviet Communist leadership also has consistently proclaimed its commitment in principle to support wars of national liberation. This commitment was reaffirmed as recently as Monday of this week by Mr. Kosygin.

International law does not restrict internal revolution within a state, or revolution against colonial authority. But international law does restrict what third Powers may lawfully do in support of insurrection. It is these restrictions which are challenged by the doctrine, and violated by the practice, of "wars of liberation." It is plain that acceptance of the doctrine of "wars of liberation" would amount to scuttling the modern international law of peace which the Charter prescribes. And acceptance of the practice of "wars of liberation," as defined by the Communists, would mean the breakdown of peace itself.

IV

Viet-Nam presents a clear current case of the lawful versus the unlawful use of force. I would agree with General Giap and other Communists that it is a test case for "wars of national liberation." We intend to meet that test. Were the insurgency in South Viet-Nam truly indigenous and self-sustained, international law would not be involved. But the fact is that it receives vital external support, in organization and direction, in training, in men, in weapons and other supplies. That external support is unlawful for a double reason. First, it contravenes general international law, which the United Nations Charter here expresses. Second, it contravenes particular international law: the 1954 Geneva Accords on Viet-Nam, and the 1962 Geneva Agreements on Laos.

In resisting the aggression against it, the Republic of Viet-Nam is exercising its right of self-defense. It called upon us and other states for assistance. And in the exercise of the right of collective self-defense under the United Nations Charter, we and other nations are providing such assistance. The American policy of assisting South Viet-Nam to maintain its freedom was inaugurated under President Eisenhower and continued under Presidents Kennedy and Johnson. Our assistance has been increased because the aggression from the North has been augmented. Our assistance now encompasses the bombing of North Viet-Nam. The bombing is designed to interdict, as far as possible, and to inhibit, as far as may be necessary, continued aggression against the Republic of Viet-Nam. When that aggression ceases, collective measures in defense against it will cease. As President Johnson has declared: ". . . if that aggression is stopped, the people and Government of South Viet-Nam will be free to settle their own future, and the need for supporting American military action there will end."

The fact that the demarcation line between North and South Viet-Nam was intended to be temporary does not make the assult on South Viet-Nam any less of an aggression. The demarcation lines between North and South Korea and between East and West Germany are temporary. But that did not make the North Korean invasion of South Korea a permissible use of force.

Let's not forget the salient features of the 1962 Agreements on Laos, Laos was to be independent and neutral. All foreign troops, regular or irregular, and other military personnel were to be withdrawn within 75 days, except a limited number of French instructors as requested by the Lao Government. No arms were to be introduced into Laos except at the request of that government. The signatories agreed to refrain "from all direct or indirect interference in the internal affairs" of Laos. They promised also not to use Lao territory to intervene in the internal affairs of other countries—a stipulation that plainly prohibited the passage of arms and men from North Viet-Nam to South Viet-Nam by way of Laos. An International Control Commission of three was to assure compliance with the Agreements. And all the signatories promised to support a coalition government under Prince Souvanna Phouma.

What happened? The non-Communist elements complied. The Communists did not. At no time since that agreement was signed have either the Pathet Lao or the North Viet-Nam authorities complied with it. The North Viet-Namese left several thousand troops there—the backbone of almost every Pathet Lao battalion. Use of the corridor through Laos to South Viet-Nam continued. And the Communists barred the areas under their control both to the Government of Laos and the International Control Commission.

To revert to Viet-Nam: I continue to hear and see nonsense about the nature of the struggle there. I sometimes wonder at the gullibility of educated men and the stubborn disregard of plain facts by men who are supposed to be helping our young to learn—especially to learn how to think. Hanoi has never made a secret of its designs. It publicly proclaimed in 1960 a renewal of the assault on South Viet-Nam. Quite obviously its hopes of taking over South Viet-Nam from within had withered to close to zero, and the remarkable economic and social progress of South

Viet-Nam contrasted, most disagreeably for the North Vietnamese Communists, with their own miserable economic performance.

The facts about the external involvement have been documented in White Papers and other publications of the Department of State. The International Control Commission has held that there is evidence "beyond reasonable doubt" of North Vietnamese intervention. There is no evidence that the Viet Cong has any significant popular following in South Viet-Nam. It relies heavily on terror. Most of its reinforcements in recent months have been North Vietnamese from the North Vietnamese Army.

Let us be clear about what is involved today in Southeast Asia. We are not involved with empty phrases or conceptions which ride upon the clouds. We are talking about the vital national interests of the United States in the peace of the Pacific. We are talking about the appetite for aggression—an appetite which grows upon feeding and which is proclaimed to be insatiable. We are talking about the safety of nations with which we are allied and the integrity of the American commitment to join in meeting attack. It is true that we also believe that every small state has a right to be unmolested by its neighbors, even though it is within reach of a Great Power. It is true that we are committed to general principles of law and procedure which reject the idea that men and arms can be sent freely across frontiers to absorb a neighbor. But underlying the general principles is the harsh reality that our own security is threatened by those who would embark upon a course of aggression whose announced ultimate purpose is our own destruction. Once again we hear expressed the views which cost the men of my generation a terrible price in World War II. We are told that Southeast Asia is far away, but so were Manchuria and Ethiopia. We are told that, if we insist that someone stop shooting, that is asking them for unconditional surrender. We are told that perhaps the aggressor will be content with just one more bite. We are told that, if we prove faithless on one commitment, perhaps others would believe us about other commitments in other places. We are told that, if we stop resisting, perhaps the other side will have a change of heart. We were asked to stop hitting bridges and radar sites and ammunition depots without requiring that the other side stop its slaughter of thousands of civilians and its bombings of schools and hotels and hospitals and railways and buses.

Surely we have learned over the past three decades that the acceptance of aggression leads only to a sure catastrophe. Surely we have learned that the aggressor must face the consequences of his action and be saved from the frightful miscalculation that brings all to ruin. It is the purpose of law to guide men away from such events, to establish rules of conduct which are deeply rooted in the reality of experience.

V

Before closing, I should like to turn away from the immediate difficulties and dangers of the situation in Southeast Asia and remind you of the dramatic progress that shapes and is being shaped by expanding international law.

A "common law of mankind"—to use the happy phrase of your distinguished colleague, Wilfred Jenks—is growing as the world shrinks, and as the vistas of space expand. This year is, by proclamation of the General Assembly, International Cooperation Year, a year "to direct attention to the common interests of mankind and to accelerate the joint efforts being undertaken to further them." Those common interests are enormous and intricate, and the joint efforts which further them are developing fast, although perhaps not fast enough.

In the nineteenth century, the United States attended an average of one international conference a year. Now we attend nearly 600 a year. We are party to 4,300 treaties and other international agreements in force. Three-fourths of these were signed in the last 25 years. Our interest in the observance of all of these treaties and agreements is profound, whether the issue is peace in Laos, or the payment of United Nations assessments, or the allocation of radio frequencies, or the application of airline safeguards, or the control of illicit traffic in narcotics, or any other issue which states have chosen to regulate through the lawmaking process. The writing of international co-operation into international law is meaningful only if the law is obeyed and only if the international institutions which administer and develop the law function in accordance with agreed procedures, until the procedures are changed.

Everything suggests that the rate of growth in international law—like the rate of change in almost every other field these days—is rising at a very steep angle. In recent years the law of the sea has been developed and codified, but it first evolved in a leisurely fashion over the centuries. International agreements to regulate aerial navigation had to be worked out within the period of a couple of decades. Now, within the first few years of man's adventures in outer space, we are deeply involved in the creation of international institutions, regulations, and law to govern this effort.

Already the United Nations has developed a set of legal principles to govern the use of outer space and declared celestial bodies free from national appropriation. Already nations, including the United States and the Soviet Union, have agreed not to orbit weapons of mass destruction in outer space. Already the Legal Subcommittee of the United Nations Committee on Outer Space is formulating international agreements on liability for damage caused by the re-entry of objects launched into outer space and on rescue and return of astronauts and space objects. Already the first international sounding rocket range has been established in India and is being offered for United Nations sponsorship. To make orderly space exploration possible at this stage, the International Telecommunication Union had to allocate radio frequencies for the purpose.

To take advantage of weather reporting and forecasting potential of observation satellites, married to computer technology, the World Meteorological Organization is creating a vast system of data acquisition, analysis, and distribution which depends entirely on international agreement, regulation and standards. And to start building a single global communications satellite system, we have created a novel international institution in which a private American corporation shares ownership with forty-five governments.

This is but part of the story of how the pace of discovery and invention forces us to reach out for international agreement, to build international institutions, to do things in accordance with an expanding international and transnational law. Phenomenal as the growth of treaty obligations is, the true innovation of twentieth-century international law lies more in the fact that we have nearly 80 international institutions which are capable of carrying out those obligations.

It is important that the processes and products of international co-operation be understood and appreciated; and it is important that their potential be much further developed. It is also important that the broader significance of the contributions of international co-operation to the solving of international problems of an economic, social, scientific and humanitarian character not be overestimated. For all the progress of peace could be incinerated in war.

Thus the control of force in international relations remains the paramount problem which confronts the diplomat and the lawyer—and the man in the street and the man in the rice field. Most of mankind is not in an immediate position to grapple very directly with that problem, but the problem is no less crucial. The responsibility of those, in your profession and mine, who do grapple with it is the greater. I am happy to acknowledge that this Society, in thinking and debating courageously and constructively about the conditions of peace, continues to make its unique contribution and to make it well.

For the past two days you have been discussing the rôle of international organizations and the relation of these organizations to law. Most of that family of organizations have come out of the lessons we learned from World War II. May I say in conclusion that we shall not have a chance to learn those lessons again and start afresh after World War III. What we must deeply understand is that the lessons of World War III must be learned in advance in order to prevent it, because we shall not have a chance again, and, therefore, we will celebrate this year the 20th anniversary of what might well and properly be called man's last chance to organize a decent world order and build a peace in which ordinary men and women can live in decency right around the world.

Excerpts from the Twenty-First Annual Report of the Secretary General of the United Nations, September 18, 1966

THE INTERNATIONAL political situation has not improved. The cloud over Vietnam has grown larger and more ominous. The serious open conflict between India and Pakistan over Kashmir has, with the help of the United Nations, been calmed, but tensions have been heightened and violence has erupted elsewhere. Nuclear as well as conventional armaments have developed apace.

Comparatively little has happened to brighten the prospects of those who occupy the two-thirds of the world where poverty, disease, ignorance and lack of opportunity are the most conspicuous facts of daily life. Frustrations have been dominant in such long-standing problems as the situations in South Africa, South-West Africa and Rhodesia and such long-standing disputes as those in Cyprus and the Middle East.

A Kind of "Holy War"

The Vietnamese people, in particular, have known no peace for a quarter of a century. Their present plight should be the first, and not the last, consideration of all concerned. Indeed, I remain convinced that the basic problem in Vietnam is not one of ideology but one of national identity and survival. I see nothing but danger in the idea, so assiduously fostered outside Vietnam, that the conflict is a kind of holy war between two powerful political ideologies.

The survival of the people of Vietnam must be seen as the real issue, and it can be resolved not by force but by patience and understanding, in the framework of a willingness to live and let live. If this approach can be accepted on all sides—and the moral influence of governments and peoples outside the immediate conflict can help to bring this about —I believe it should be possible to reach a settlement which would end the suffering in Vietnam, satisfy the conscience of the world at large and remove a formidable barrier to international cooperation.

The international situations to which I have referred, the rise of tensions and the emergence of new dangers in so many parts of the world point to the need for a stronger rather than a weaker United Nations, and one which can be relied upon to undertake peace-keeping operations wherever such action could help in the restoration of stable conditions. Unfortunately although there seems to be a measure of agreement that these operations have been effective in the past and could prove useful in the future, we are still far from agreement on basic principles.

I very much hope that, in the months to come, the general membership and in particular those members who have a special responsibility with regard to the maintenance of international peace and security may find it possible, within the charter, to agree upon the procedures to be followed in launching such operations, the responsibility of the various organs in their actual conduct and the financial arrangements by which the expenditures involved may be met.

Public Confidence Grows

I must draw attention to the fact that the peace-keeping activities of the United Nations, perhaps more than any other part of its work, have enabled the organization to gain a measure of public confidence which is in danger of being lost if the member states remain deadlocked on the constitutional and financial questions involved.

There are other causes of tension which cannot be left to resolve themselves. In particular, I feel that the United Nations must make a sustained attack on the problems which we might, because of their origin or their nature, describe as the problems of colonialism. While recognizing that substantial progress has been made, we cannot afford to forget that the process of decolonization has not been completed. A hard core of actual colonialism still exists, particularly in Africa.

It is impossible, moreover, to view some of these outstanding problems—whether it is the position of the United Nations in regard to the crisis in Southeast Asia or the lack of progress in disarmament—without relating them to the fact that the United Nations has not yet attained the goal of universality of membership.

In the long run the organization cannot be expected to function to full effect if one-fourth of the human race is not allowed to participate in its deliberations. I know that there are serious political difficulties involved in correcting this situation, but I hope that the long-term advantages may be more clearly seen and the necessary adjustments made.

Excerpts from Secretary General U Thant's Speech of May 24, 1966, to the Amalgamated Clothing Workers of America, at Atlantic City, New Jersey

IF WE can conquer the atom or outer space, it is absurd that we cannot conquer urban misery or the problem of producing and distributing an adequate food supply. These simple propositions should provide a basis on which all nations should be able to start to come to terms with the world in which we actually live.

I, for one, do not think that any government or people is likely to lose in stature or dignity or worldly advantage from an all-out effort to come to terms with such questions. On the contrary, it is highly probable that the future leaders of the world will be those who first can bring themselves to make the attempt.

There have been already, in the past 20 years, governments which had the vision and the courage to throw away the outmoded trappings of a glorious past and which have gained nothing but advantage from doing so. Let us hope that they are merely the forerunners of a more general and forward-looking movement.

The Vietnamese Problem

You will expect me, I believe, to mention one specific problem which is very much on all our minds—I refer to Vietnam.

Let me say at once that I have no answers to this problem, nor do I wish to pronounce any judgments as to where right or wrong, responsibility or culpability, reality or myth, may lie in what is a tragic situation for all the peoples and governments involved. The situation is far too serious for that.

It is more important and relevant, I believe, to search objectively and without rancor for ways to end this historic tragedy.

The world has been watching the inexorable escalation of the war in Vietnam with increasing anxiety. Little by little, larger forces and more powerful armaments have been introduced, until an anguished and perplexed world has suddenly found that a limited and local conflict is threatening to turn into a major confrontation.

And though the fear of a much larger conflict may still have a restraining influence upon the demands of military strategy the temptation to win a military success may still prove stronger than the more prudent call to reason.

As the war worsens, its justification in terms of a confrontation of ideologies is becoming more and more misleading. For democratic principles, which both sides consider to be at stake in Vietnam, are already falling a victim to the war itself.

In Vietnam there is growing evidence that the so-called "fight for democracy" is no longer relevant to the realities of the situation. Twenty years of outside intervention and the presence of a succession of foreign armies have so profoundly affected Vietnamese political life that it seems illusory to represent it as a mere contest between Communism and liberal democracy.

Indeed, events have shown that the passion for national identity, perhaps one should say national survival, is the only ideology that may be left to a growing number of Vietnamese.

Thus, the increasing intervention by outside powers in the conflict— involving their armies, their armaments and, above all, their prestige— has tended to alienate the people of Vietnam from their own destiny. And if therefore the issue in Vietnam is not a struggle between two different views of democracy, what is really at stake, unless an early end to the hostilities is brought about, is the independence, the identity and the survival of the country itself.

Apart from the loss of life, destruction and human suffering which this war is causing, the war in Vietnam has also to be judged by the halt which it has imposed on the great enterprise of cooperation and understanding.

No Such Role for the U. N.

In these grave circumstances, it would appear normal to entrust a world organization such as the United Nations with the task of bringing the parties together to negotiate.

Unfortunately, the United Nations is not, at present, so constituted that it could play this role. . . . But, although the United Nations cannot act in a conflict which is beyond its scope, nonetheless, the majority of member states is increasingly concerned by its development.

They are convinced that military methods will not restore peace in Vietnam and that this war must be stopped on the initiative of the participants lest it get out of hand.

To give effect to these convictions, and also because it represents my firm belief, I have undertaken, in my personal capacity, to make a number of suggestions to the parties. In particular I have said that peace can only be restored by a return to the Geneva agreements, and that, as a preparatory measure, it would be necessary to start scaling down military operations, and to agree to discussions which include the actual combatants.

Perhaps, under these conditions, it will still be possible to arrive at an agreement between all powers concerned, and, among them, the five major powers, including the People's Republic of China. But those who are genuinely troubled today by the great problem of war and peace should not delude themselves that action by the United Nations or its Secretary General can resolve the problem.

Why Peace Forces Must Join

The solution lies in the hands of those who have the power, and the responsibility, to decide. If they seek a peaceful solution, the United Nations and many of its members stand ready to help them in all possible ways. Of course, it must be recognized that a sincere effort to reach a diplomatic settlement is a most arduous and frustrating task.

That is why all the forces of peace must join together to make their influence felt by the leaders of the countries engaged in this war, so that they may find a way to reverse its fateful trend and to restore peace before it is too late.

May I conclude by a direct appeal to you, representatives of the labor movement in one of the most advanced countries of the world.

The labor movement in the United States, though it still has much unfinished business, is now a very weighty part of the national establishment. It is a measure of your success that your movement which within living memory was an embattled newcomer battering on the doors of the old order. is now the most powerful single organized group in the country.

I urge you now, in your great success, to devote much of your energy and your organization to new and equally vital objectives—to the great problems of establishing a world order in which peace and democratic principles really prevail, and to the application in the world community of those great ideals for which you have been and are fighting in your own country.

Peace and order in the world are not the exclusive business of statesmen, diplomats and international officials. They are the urgent personal business of all men and women who are capable of wishing for a better world for their children and their fellow men.

The Legality of American Military Involvement in Viet Nam: A Broader Perspective

NEILL H. ALFORD, JR.*

WE are forcefully reminded, from time to time, of the presence in Western tradition of an impulse for transcendence and perfection. Goals thought to support a "right" order of humanity are religiously pursued, while limits upon the means chosen to attain them are frequently ignored. Our unique American experience has reinforced this Western impulse and critics of United States policy in Viet Nam fear that we are once again resorting to violence to force our concepts of an ideal society upon others.[1]

There is an immediate need for examination of the assumptions which support current American foreign policy. This examination will be difficult. While our idealism often burgeons into the pursuit of sentimental and perhaps unattainable goals in foreign affairs, this idealism is essential to cement together the disparate elements of our nation. Only recently have we become conscious of the degree of strain within the United States and of the importance of idealism in keeping the country from bursting asunder. It is futile to consider abandoning idealism in the conduct of our foreign policy, because idealism is a cultural trait too well seated to be excised without destruction of the whole social organism.

Most critics of our policy in Viet Nam have spoken from a philosophy as idealistic as that held by supporters of that policy. Both sides in the debate appear to have in mind ideal societies; neither seems overly disturbed by the means to attain them. Thus, the debate over legal aspects of the United States policy in Viet Nam has been shunted off to the side and ignored by all except law professors, lawyers and others with an interest in international and constitutional law. It is frequently said that law "has nothing to do" with the United States action in Viet Nam or that the problem is simply too serious for legal issues to be significant. This position involves assumptions about law as erroneous as they are facile.

* Professor of Law, University of Virginia; B.A. 1940, The Citadel; LL.B. 1947, Univ. of Virginia.

1. See, *e.g.*, E. O. STILLMAN AND W. PFAFF, THE POLITICS OF HYSTERIA (1964) and POWER AND IMPOTENCE (1966).

Mr. Kennan,[2] Messrs. Stillman and Pfaff[3] and others speak of law in terms of rules for resolving conflict between individuals or communities. Mr. Kennan, in particular, finds "the legalistic-moralistic" approach to international problems "the most serious fault of our past policy formulation."[4] He deplores efforts to force patterns of conflict into legalistic categories. But these criticisms ignore the constitutive functions of law. Legal processes are orderly means by which we agree upon community goals and estimate the likelihood of their attainment. More important, legal processes can build and strengthen institutions such as the United Nations which encourage the diffraction of coercion and its projection on a verbal level.

THE ARGUMENTS OF THE STATE DEPARTMENT MEMORANDUM

The assumptions underlying the positions of Messrs. Kennan, Stillman and Pfaff may result in inattention to the State Department Memorandum on Viet Nam.[5] Yet the Memorandum is an official landmark. It develops in detail arguments based on self-defense and collective self-defense, which received little official treatment in the debates following the Cuban Quarantine of 1962.[6] An analysis of the "legal response" to the "legally puzzling" "War of National Liberation" will doubtless have an effect upon official thought in the United States similar to the effect in the early 20th century of Clark's memorandum on protecting American citizens abroad[7] and the response by

---

2. KENNAN, AMERICAN DIPLOMACY 1900-1950 95-101 (1951).

3. *E.g.*, STILLMAN AND PFAFF, POWER AND IMPOTENCE 28-30 (1966).

4. KENNAN, *supra* note 2, at 95.

5. *The Legality of United States Participation in the Defense of Viet-Nam*, 54 DEP'T STATE BULL. 474 (1966) [hereinafter cited as *Memorandum*].

6. Official or semi-official statements were made by Legal Adviser Chayes and then Deputy Legal Adviser Meeker in the debates following the Cuban Quarantine of 1962. See Chayes, *The Legal Case for U.S. Action on Cuba*, 47 DEP'T STATE BULL. 763 (1962); *Law and the Quarantine of Cuba*, 41 FOREIGN AFFAIRS 550 (1963); *Remarks*, 1963 PROC. AM. SOC. INT'L L. 10; and Meeker, *Defensive Quarantine and the Law*, 57 AM. J. INT'L L. 515 (1963). The official arguments then pivoted on collective action by virtue of the resolution of October 23, 1962 by the Council of the Organization of American States. Arguments based upon self-defense or collective self-defense were not then pressed by these spokesmen, although energetically put forward by others. *E.g.*, Mallison, *Limited Naval Blockade or Quarantine Interdiction: National and Collective Defense Claims Valid Under International Law*, 31 GEO. WASH. L. REV. 335 (1962). A glimmer of the arguments advanced by the State Department officials in the debates following the Quarantine still remains in the Memorandum of March 4, 1966, with reliance upon action under Article IV of the SEATO Treaty. See *Memorandum* 480-81.

7. CLARK, RIGHT TO PROTECT CITIZENS IN FOREIGN COUNTRIES BY LANDING FORCES (Department of State, Division of Information, Series M, No. 14, Oct. 5, 1912; reprinted in Department of State Publications, No. 5 1934).

Secretary Hay to the Wilson memorandum on *de facto* blockades by insurgents.[8]

The author of this comment is in general agreement with the points made in this Memorandum in response to criticism of the legal grounds for the policy of the United States in Viet Nam. But unfortunately the Memorandum is *responsive* to attacks based upon an extremely narrow conception of law. This, in turn, has caused the Memorandum to be narrow in conception, to stress things that perhaps should not be stressed, to de-emphasize things that probably should be emphasized. Without an attempt fully to document the counter-attack to criticism of United States policy in Viet Nam, which was well done in the Memorandum and which will be done even more completely in other articles to be published in the near future,[9] the major arguments of critics of the United States policy in Viet Nam will be considered first with observations on the State Department answers to these arguments. Thereafter a somewhat broader approach than that adopted by the State Department will be suggested.

Arguments by critics based upon customary international law and upon Articles 51 and 2(4) of the United Nations Charter require detailed attention because of uncertainties in general community policy in these areas. To the extent, however, that the critics argue that South Viet Nam is not a state, their position is wholly untenable.

It has been urged, for example, that South Viet Nam (the Republic of Viet Nam) is not a state but an insurgent area resisting its *de jure* government in Hanoi. It is unfortunate that the State Department Memorandum does not take a more positive position on this point. The Memorandum suggests that South Viet Nam might lack some of the attributes of statehood, but that United States policy is still defensible because it supports the demarcation line established in the Geneva Accords of 1954 (though violated by North Viet Nam).[10]

8. U.S. NAVAL WAR COLLEGE, INTERNATIONAL LAW SITUATIONS 79-83 (1902).

9. See Deutsch, *The Legality of the United States Position in Viet Nam*, 52 A.B.A.J. 436 (1966) and J. N. Moore & J. L. Underwood, The Lawfulness of United States Assistance to the Republic of Viet Nam (unpublished manuscript).

10. The State Department Memorandum appears to take the position that the Accords are still viable, although the "systematic violation . . . by North Viet Nam justified South Viet Nam in suspending compliance with the provision controlling entry of foreign military personnel and military equipment," and "there may be some question whether South Viet Nam was bound by . . . [the] election provisions." *Memorandum* 483. There were four interrelated documents—a cease-fire agreement for Laos, Cambodia and Viet Nam and an unsigned "Final Declaration." These documents may be found in SENATE COMM. ON FOREIGN RELATIONS, 89TH CONG., 2D SESS., BACKGROUND INFORMATION RELATING TO SOUTHEAST ASIA AND VIET NAM 36-39 (Comm. Print 1966). The legal status

As pointed out in the Memorandum, sixty states have recognized South Viet Nam (eight of these are *de facto* recognitions). The General Assembly has, on two occasions, affirmed the qualifications of South Viet Nam for admission to the United Nations.[11] In both instances the Security Council failed to recommend admission because of the veto of the Soviet Union.[12] But the Soviet Union did not suggest as a reason that South Viet Nam was not a state. Instead, the Soviet Union seemed to assume state status.

South Viet Nam is a member of and is active in more of the specialized agencies of the United Nations than the Soviet Union. It has participated in forty-eight international conferences.

Although South Viet Nam has relied on French and, currently, United States military assistance, it maintains armed forces for defensive purposes larger than those of most of the members of the United Nations. While its government has relied upon United States assistance in maintaining order, its governmental policies have been to a substantial degree free from United States influence.

The only argument which might be offered against the state status of South Viet Nam is based upon the Geneva Accords of 1954.[13] It has sometimes been assumed that these Accords require a single Vietnamese state—but nothing in the Accords suggests more than an expectation that a vote would decide this issue, and no requirement was included that the votes of both South and North Vietnamese be counted together on this question.

Although the Memorandum seems to suggest that the United States continues to regard parts of the Geneva Accords of 1954 as viable, it is difficult to ascribe to this ambiguous and ill-conceived transaction a force which would deprive a community of state status at any time in the future if this community satisfies such requirements as other states impose to determine state status. These requirements seem to be that (1) the community have a reasonable probability of permanent iden-

---

of the "Final Declaration" is quite equivocal and probably the deference to it now shown springs from the will-o-the-wisp of popular elections mentioned in detail in the declaration and casually in the cease-fire agreements. The provisional nature of those Accords relating to Viet Nam, in view of the radical changes in conditions since their dubious beginning, should be a basis for disregarding them altogether, although the State Department may still value the demarcation line and several other provisions of the Accords which it would desire respected.

11. U.N. GEN. ASS. OFF. REC. 11th Sess. 1017 B(XI) (A/PV.663) (Feb. 28, 1957); U.N. GEN. ASS. OFF. REC. 12th Sess. 1144 B(XI) (A/PV.709) (Oct. 25, 1957).

12. U.N. SECURITY COUNCIL OFF. REC. (S/PV.790) (Sept. 9, 1957); U.N. SECURITY COUNCIL OFF. REC. (S/PV.843) (Dec. 9, 1958).

13. See note 10 *supra*.

tity; (2) that it have an organized government; (3) a defined territory; and (4) sufficient independence to conduct its foreign relations.[14] Other requirements might be imposed in special contexts; but undoubtedly other states share an expectation that South Viet Nam is a state.

Since arguments that South Viet Nam is not a state have no weight, the main thrust of the critics' attack upon the United States policy has been based on Article 51 of the United Nations Charter, which preserves members' rights to self-defense in cases of "armed attack."[15] The provisions of Article 51 are ambiguous and were intentionally made ambiguous to permit states to take shelter under the cover of their collective or regional defense systems if the United Nations proved impotent as a peace enforcement institution. Views also differ concerning the precise limits of the customary doctrines of self-defense and collective self-defense. This complicates the interpretation of Article 51.

One point does seem certain. No basis exists for assuming that all defensive measures contemplated by Article 51 are keyed to "armed attacks," *or* that an "armed attack," as contemplated by Article 51, occurs only when missiles are launched or forces deployed and set in motion against an adversary. Under conditions of modern military action, an "armed attack" may be regarded as a process and not solely a single hostile offensive event.

Another certain point is that Article 51 does not deprive non-members of their right to self-defense. It is quite doubtful that the parties to the Charter could impose disabilities or obligations upon non-members. Members certainly could agree to act against non-members, as they appear to have done in Article 2(6) of the Charter, or they could impose conditions upon a non-member invoking the aid of United Nations organs, as in Article 35(2) of the Charter. But it is not accepted that parties to the Charter can impose any other restraints upon the action of non-members. The State Department Memorandum suggests international custom could be affected by the continued

---

14. See BRIERLY, THE LAW OF NATIONS 122-24 (4th ed. 1949) where these requirements are briefly and conveniently discussed.

15. Article 51:

Nothing in the present charter shall impair the inherent right of individual or collective self-defense, if an armed attack occurs against a member of the organization until the Security Council has taken the measures necessary to maintain international peace and security. Measures taken by members in the exercise of this right of self-defense shall be immediately reported to the Security Council and shall not in any way affect the authority and responsibility of the Security Council under the present charter to take at any time such action as it may deem necessary in order to maintain or restore international peace and security.

application of Charter provisions, and this custom could thus affect the obligations of non-members—however, this proposition has received no general acceptance.[16]

Thus, a non-member retains whatever rights of self-defense or collective self-defense it had prior to the Charter unless changes in international custom have actually conditioned these "rights" in new ways. Certainly a provision expressly relating to members in Article 51 should not be taken by inference to refer to non-members as well, and especially not to deny to non-members rights of self-defense or collective self-defense which members retain despite the provisions of the Article. Quite clearly, South Viet Nam can act to defend itself against attacks by neighbors from the North.

The question remains of what restraints exist under the Charter upon United States assistance. Records of Committees engaged in preparatory work on Articles 51 and 2(4) indicate they intended to retain the customary doctrine of self-defense for members without requiring an "armed attack" as a precondition.[17] The supervisory structure—the institutions developed for community judgment in the Security Council and General Assembly—could determine whether self-defense or collective self-defense was properly invoked in any given situation; and Article 51 was not expected to stand independently as the only guideline for protective action. The State Department Memorandum describes its operation correctly as a "saving clause."[18] There is an additional requirement that the defensive measures be reported to the Security Council and there is also implied recognition of "collective self-defense" arrangements that might not be regional arrangements as described in Chapter VIII.

At the time of Dumbarton Oaks and the San Francisco Conference, an "armed attack" was generally understood as a process by which a state sought the initiative by a violent exercise of physical power. Survival of an adversary under such an attack required ability on the part of the adversary to strike at the source of power of the attacker. A passive defensive posture had proven utterly futile in World War II. But a counterstrike of the type required might violate Article 2(4)

---

16. See *Memorandum* 476 n.3 for support of the proposition that "it seems entirely appropriate to appraise the actions of South Viet-Nam in relation to the legal standards set forth in the United Nations Charter."

17. 12 U.N. Conf. Int'l Org. Docs. 68-82; *Report of Committee 1 to Commission I,* 6 U.N. Conf. Int'l Org. Docs. 446, 459; *Verbatim Minutes of Fifth Meeting of Commission I,* 6 U.N. Conf. Int'l Org. Docs. 202, 204.

18. *Memorandum* 475.

and would certainly serve as a link in the chain of escalation of violence which the Security Council was designed to break.

The draftsmen of Article 51 probably intended to limit only the armed counterstrike which would otherwise be in violation of Article 2(4) and in no way to preclude other exercises of power, even though by military force, consistent with Article 2(4). In order for any organization, such as the United Nations, to perform its security functions, member states would certainly have to enjoy rights of self-defense and collective self-defense as broad as those of non-members.

The United States action in Viet Nam is directed principally to the preservation of order in South Viet Nam. No recognized spokesman for South Viet Nam has contended that the territorial integrity or political independence of South Viet Nam has been violated by the United States. The air raids against supply routes and training installations in North Viet Nam are in direct support of the South Viet Nam operations. No one has ever contended that either the United States or South Viet Nam has aspirations affecting the territorial integrity and political independence of North Viet Nam. The United States simply acts to frustrate an escalating aggression by North Viet Nam, which conflicts with the principles stated in Article 2 of the Charter. The United Nations, however, is not prepared to act to counter this aggression under Article 2(6), because of the Soviet veto in the Security Council and the difficulty of organizing action in the General Assembly where the United States lacks the backing of major Western powers who find the anti-Western features of the Vietnamese war an embarrassment in their relations with their former colonies.

Just as Article 51 of the Charter does not preclude a broad spectrum of military action so long as this action is consistent with Article 2(4), the Charter does not limit a member's participation in collective defense arrangements to "members of the club." The "regional arrangements," for example, seem clearly to embrace the participation of non-members:—indeed, like membership in the specialized agencies, participation in regional security arrangements provides an opportunity for contributions by non-members to world security when their membership is denied for reasons unrelated to the qualifications expressed in Article 4 of the Charter.

It should be observed also that there are two opportunities for collective defense in addition to the commitments undertaken by members to support action by the United Nations. These are the Regional Arrangements under Article VIII and "collective defense arrangements" implied under Article 51.[19] If there is any requirement of territorial contiguity and cultural identity for Regional Arrangements, the United States has territory in the area of SEATO and a substantial cultural identity with the people of that area. Obviously it has security interests in common with SEATO members and areas brought within the protection of SEATO that will support a "collective defense agreement" with South Viet Nam under Article 51.

When critics of the United States action feel they cannot prevail by arbitrary and unnecessarily restrictive interpretations of Article 51, they then contend that the action the United States pursues in South Viet Nam is not permitted by international legal custom. The basis of this contention is an erroneous assumption of fact—that the strife in South Viet Nam is internal (or was internal until the United States commenced its assistance). There are at least three revolutions going on in South Viet Nam. George A. Carver has recently analyzed two of them:[20] (1) a battle for power between a French-educated, foreign-oriented class and a militantly "Vietnamese" group—by which the United States periodically finds its military efforts embarrassed—basically a social revolution; and (2) a North Vietnamese directed insurgency—which is the one the United States aids in suppressing. There is a third, an anti-Western revolution, currently almost dormant in South Viet Nam, but which will certainly flare up to complicate relations between the United States and Afro-Asians in the future.

But even assuming that the strife in South Viet Nam was indigenous, which it does not appear to be, there seems little in international legal custom which would preclude the United States from acting in conjunction with a friendly government to maintain internal order. The publicists are divided on the point, most taking the position that the government can be assisted.

A BROADER PERSPECTIVE

The legal critics of American involvement in Viet Nam have neglected the broader functions of law. Regrettably the Memorandum, by attempting to meet the legal critics of American involvement head-on, have adopted their narrow perspective and neglected the broader functions of law. Why should we discuss the conflict in Viet Nam in terms of a "who did it first" analysis? That approach was meaningful to the Justices in Eyre of Edward I when dealing with a fracas between

---

19. The distinction between these possible defensive arrangements is clearly made in McDevitt, *The U.N. Charter and the Cuban Quarantine*, 72 JAG J. 71 (1963).

20. Carver, *The Faceless Viet Cong*, 44 FOREIGN AFFAIRS 347 (1966).

peasants, and helps us to analyze problems which can be solved by shifting wealth from one person to another. But the values involved in Viet Nam cannot be converted into cash equivalents. Stability must be attained in South Viet Nam so that the South Vietnamese may manage their affairs without chronic violence. Yet who wins the war in Viet Nam may have little to do with the establishment of a viable system of world order; while how and what we and others *think* about our uses of power there will have a lot to do with it. Law has an important, although not exclusive, role in defining attainable goals, shaping how we think about power and other values, coordinating action to attain goals, and emphasizing the use of persuasion rather than violence to alter or satisfy demands. The "conflict resolving" features of law are least relevant to the war in Viet Nam.

The Memorandum does not clarify what the policies of the United States may be, beyond "pushing out an invader who has attacked." This hugs rather closely the formula of Article 51 of the United Nations Charter.

One can conceive of other possible policies which support our action. Red China is being excluded, at least temporarily, from the "rice bowl of Asia"; Red Chinese armies cannot turn against Europe or the rest of Asia without added food supplies, even assuming these troops can "live off the land" more effectively than Western armies. Thanks to effective action in Viet Nam, Japan need not look for markets in a wholly communized Asia—with the shift in political perspective this would entail. And the American stand in Viet Nam is a major reason why the Indonesian military was prepared to resist a communist coup.

The problems of South Viet Nam are, in microcosm, those of the underveloped world. Western ideas—democracy and communism—clash in the minds of people whose cultures have been sapped by the intellectual imperialism of the West. It may therefore also be a United States policy to seek answers or palliatives to the problems of the South Vietnamese which have broader applications.[21]

Whether or not such policy goals exist is unclear. Apart from "pushing out the invader," the goal which the Memorandum stresses, emphasis has been given lately to insuring "self-determination" by the South Vietnamese. Critics of United States policy quote different scripture for their faith in self-determination—either Wilsonian rhetoric, Buddhist demands for a referendum, or the ill-considered and obsolete

---

21. See Lansdale, *Viet Nam: Do We Understand Revolution?*, 43 FOREIGN AFFAIRS 75 (1964) which stresses the need for imaginative civilian action, to create conditions favorable to a "true" (non-Communist) Vietnamese revolutionary cause.

provisions of the 1954 Geneva Accords—but all consider self-determination (translated as determination by ballot) basic to a "decently ordered" society. Their demands have been accommodated in United States policy statements. American action is portrayed as an effort to secure self-determination for a harassed people, who otherwise would be denied its blessings.

Unfortunately, no significant vote can be taken outside the urban areas of South Viet Nam, and the countryside, containing a popular majority, is controlled at least intermittently by the Viet Cong. A vote there, until Viet Cong control is broken, would be as unreliable a statement of opinion as the one-candidate elections of "people's democracies." To uproot the Viet Cong, the United States thus stumbles onto a platform of "enfranchisement by bombardment"—repellent to all who think about it.

The Memorandum reflects some of this emphasis on an expression of free will in South Viet Nam by relying heavily upon the continuing consent of the "Government of South Viet Nam" to our assistance. This stems in turn from the "who did it first" analysis we observed earlier. But this concession encourages the assumption that if some group claiming governmental status in Viet Nam—perhaps containing members of regimes with which we have previously dealt—asked the United States to leave, we would fold our tents and steal away. The matter is not so simple.

If we were asked to leave, we would first have to determine whether the government making the request expressed the wishes of so many South Vietnamese that our continued presence would exacerbate friction rather than promote eventual stability. Critics have argued that the present South Vietnamese government is unrepresentative. This contention is based upon factual allegations that simply cannot be determined with any accuracy until stability is restored.

In any event, withdrawal is not a subject for unilateral action by the United States. Several of our SEATO allies have forces in Viet Nam. Approximately 40,000 South Korean troops are there now. Although a decision by the United States to withdraw would cause our allied participants to withdraw also, joint participation would seem to necessitate joint consultation, and great deference to the wishes of states with immediate security interests in the outcome of the war. South Viet Nam is not "estopped" from requesting us to leave, but our military involvement there has reshaped our strategic posture. Our power to strike is more flexible than our ability to remove military resources from an area of active operations. The claims of South Vietnamese who did not wish to live under a communist regime must also receive consideration. What provision would the United States make for them?

In short, an official request for withdrawal, even if backed by unverified claims of widespread South Vietnamese support, should not necessarily result in cessation of United States military action or the delivery of all or part of South Viet Nam to communist control. Issues are involved which extend far beyond simply clearing South Viet Nam of Northern troops and Northern-sponsored insurgents. Possible alternatives might include support of a basically anti-communist South Vietnamese government in a loose federation along the lines of the former French administrative subdivisions. Or the United States might seek direct international control of the area—a regime similar to a United Nations trusteeship. The various proposals for "neutralization" of South Viet Nam might be compatible with such a regime. Otherwise, we would probably have to strengthen United States forces in South Viet Nam to prop up a wavering government and achieve whatever policies United States officials now have in view.

Apart from the difficulties invited by the Memorandum's emphasis on a continuing request for assistance, its frequent mention of an "armed attack" upon South Viet Nam bogs us down in a sterile dispute concerning unverifiable factual details. Those with information about the nature and scope of communist subversive military operations will recognize the Administration's basic statements of fact as correct.[22] There is, however, a "credibility gap," and many intelligent and influential persons have not, and will not, accept *in detail* the facts offered by the Administration. Thus by emphasizing an "armed attack" as the universal solvent of the "legality" of United States assistance, the State Department permits critics of our policy to play upon the factual doubts of the American public. Indeed, the failure to link United States policy-making *with a consistent effort to encourage and support decision-making by the general community* concerning Viet Nam allows critics to portray United States policy as essentially destructive of international order, whereas in fact the United States policy consistently supports that order. This failure stems from neglect of the constitutive function of law.

---

22. *Aggression from the North: The Record of North Viet-Nam's Campaign to Conquer South Viet-Nam*, 52 DEP'T STATE BULL. 404 (1965), appearing also in SENATE COMM. ON FOREIGN RELATIONS, 89TH CONG., 2D SESS., BACKGROUND INFORMATION RELATING TO SOUTHEAST ASIA AND VIET NAM 171 (Comm. Print 1966) (less photos, maps and appendices); Carver, *supra* note 20, which contains an excellent and apparently highly accurate statement of the degree of North Vietnamese control over the Viet Cong.

There is too little emphasis in the Memorandum, apart from the concentration upon Article 51, of the relationship of the United States action in Viet Nam to the shifting functions of the United Nations. The State Department's comments on this relationship reflect much of the Memorandum's philosophy:[23]

> . . . The conclusion is clear that the United States has in no way acted to interfere with United Nations consideration of the conflict in Viet Nam. On the contrary, the United States has requested United Nations consideration, and the Council has not seen fit to act. . . .

The United States' legal case would be stronger had we not confined ourselves to filing the required reports with the Security Council but had pressed more vigorously for United Nations participation. The United Nations position, as described by Secretary General U Thant, has been that the United Nations can do nothing because North Viet Nam and Red China will not appear before it.[24]

An advocate supporting United States policy might urge that the effective, although not formally stated, functions of the United Nations are in process of change; that membership in that Organization has never precluded *all* uses of force by members except in cases of armed attack, and that the power relationship of the United States to the United Nations Organization shifts with the functions of that Organization and the interrelationships of its members, particularly the more recent ones.

Despite the several provisions in the Charter for peace supervision and enforcement, the major function of the United Nations in the past decade has been "rheostatic" activity—the diffraction of coercive features of policy exchanges and the projection of these upon a verbal level in which persuasive features can dominate. The power of the United States, and of other countries with an interest in both stability and moderately paced change, may be utilized effectively by furnishing "interim sustaining action" until those rheostatic functions can be activated. In Viet Nam the interim sustaining military operations of the United States have been protracted because the two Asian aggressors involved are unwilling to appear before the United Nations to have their operations exposed to the view and judgment of the general community.

This is not to suggest that the United States has any "policing" functions in the general community. To suggest a broad mission such

---

23. *Memorandum* 479.
24. New York Times, April 7. 1966, p. 13, col. 1,

as this, or a mission to make the world safe for "democracy," "diversity," "experiment" or any other reflection of an American way of life to be established for others, might be to encourage the "arrogance of power" which we all seek to avoid. But states having the power to support a viable world order of which most of the people of the world approve should shape their policies to support the institutions by which this order can be maintained—in this case the various organs of the United Nations concerned with peacekeeping. The United States action in Viet Nam, when viewed as "interim sustaining action" pending mobilization of more extensive efforts, military and otherwise, by the general community, should not depend for its legitimacy upon the well-documented "armed attack" by North Viet Nam. A threat to the peace is involved which ultimately will require action by the general community, and interim action by the United States is an indispensable prerequisite to an effective international solution.

International Law and the United States Role in the Viet Nam War

RICHARD A. FALK[*]

No contemporary problem of world order is more troublesome for an international lawyer than the analysis of the international law of "internal war."[1] A war is usefully classified as internal when violence takes place primarily within a single political entity, regardless of foreign support for the contending factions.[2] The insurgents who won the American Revolution were heavily supported by French arms. Wars of national liberation are not new, nor is external support for an incumbent regime. But considerable historical experience with foreign intervention in internal wars has not been adequately incorporated into prevailing doctrines of international law. In an age of civil turbulence and nuclear risk, the requirements of world order make imperative the effort to overcome the consequent confusion.[3]

The central issue is whether an externally abetted internal war belongs in either traditional legal category of war—"civil" or "international." Four sub-inquiries are relevant. What are the legal restraints, if any, upon national discretion to treat a particular internal war as an international war? What rules and procedures are available to determine whether foreign participation in an internal war constitutes "military assistance," "intervention," "aggression," or "an armed at-

* Milbank Professor of International Law, Woodrow Wilson School of Public and International Affairs, Faculty Associate, Center of International Studies, Princeton University; B.S. 1952, Univ. of Pennsylvania; LL.B. 1955, Yale University.

1. See generally INTERNAL WAR (Eckstein ed. 1964); INTERNATIONAL ASPECTS OF CIVIL STRIFE (Rosenau ed. 1964) [hereinafter cited as ROSENAU].

2. The "internalness" of an internal war is a consequence of the objectives and arena of the violence. There are, of course, a range of different types of internal war. See Rosenau, *Internal War as an International Event*, in ROSENAU 45, at 63-64. Rosenau usefully differentiates between internal wars, in terms of whether they are fought primarily to achieve changes in the personnel of the leadership, the nature of political authority, or the socio-political structure of the society.

3. For helpful exposition see Huntington, *Patterns of Violence in World Politics*, in CHANGING PATTERNS OF MILITARY POLITICS 17 (Huntington ed. 1962); see also BLOOMFIELD, INTERNATIONAL MILITARY FORCES 24-46 (1964). See the table classifying examples of internal war in terms of "basically internal," "externally abetted internal instability," and "externally created or controlled internal instability." *Id.* at 28-30. Incidentally, Professor Bloomfield located the war in Viet Nam in the middle category as of 1964.

tack"? What responses are permissible by the victim of "aggression" or "an armed attack"? Finally, what should be the roles of national, regional, and global actors in interpreting and applying the relevant rules?

If the internal war is regarded as a "civil" war, then the legally permitted response to intervention is restricted to counter-intervention;[4] an intervening nation whose own territory is not the scene of conflict may not attack the territory of a state intervening on the other side.[5] If foreign intervention were held to convert an "internal" war into an "international" war, the intervention could be regarded as an armed attack that would justify action in self-defense proportionate to the aggression. The victim of aggression is entitled, if necessary, to attack the territory of the aggressor, expanding the arena of violence to more than a single political entity.[6] Given the commitment of international law to limiting the scope, duration, and intensity of warfare, it would appear desirable severely to restrict or perhaps to deny altogether, the discretion of nations to convert an internal war into an international war by characterizing external participation as "aggression" rather than as "intervention."[7]

The American outlook on these issues has dramatically changed in recent years. John Foster Dulles is properly associated with the expansion of American undertakings to defend foreign nations everywhere against Communist takeovers by either direct or indirect aggression. But even Dulles did not propose treating indirect aggression as the equivalent of an armed attack by one country on another. In fact, during the Congressional hearings on the Eisenhower Doctrine in 1957[8]

---

4. I have developed this position in a paper given at the 1966 Annual Meeting of the American Society of International Law under the title *The International Regulation of Internal Violence in the Developing Countries*, to be published in 1965 PROC. AM. SOC. INT'L L.

5. The assertion in the text must be qualified to the extent that the United States decision to bomb North Viet Nam is treated as a law-creating precedent (rather than as a violation).

6. If the conceptions of "aggression" and "armed attack" are so vague that nations can themselves determine their content, a self-serving legal description of the desired course of state action can be given and is not subject to criticism in a strict sense. A critic would be required to stress that an expansive definition of "armed attack," although not forbidden by prior rules of law, was an unwise legal claim because of its status as a precedent available to others and because of its tendency to expand the scope and magnify the scale of a particular conflict.

7. It is important to distinguish between the factual processes of coercion and the legal labels used to justify or protest various positions taken by the participants. Aggression is a legal conclusion about the nature of a particular pattern of coercion.

8. The critical section in The Eisenhower Doctrine (1957) is Section 2:

Dulles declared ". . . if you open the door to saying that any country which feels it is being threatened by subversive activities in another country is free to use armed force against that country, you are opening the door to a series of wars over the world, and I am confident that it would lead to a third world war."[9] In my judgment, by bombing North Viet Nam the United States is opening such a door and is setting a dramatic precedent of precisely the sort that Dulles had in mind. Our pride as a nation is now so deeply dependent upon a successful outcome in Viet Nam that our Government seems insufficiently sensitive to the serious negative consequences of the Viet Nam precedent for the future of world order.[10]

The appraisal of a claim by a national government that an act of intervention is "aggression" is a complex task even if performed with utter impartiality. It depends on assessing very confused facts as to the extent and phasing of external participation, as well as upon interpreting the intentions of the participating nations. For instance, one must distinguish in the behavior of an international rival between a program of unlimited expansion through violence and intervention to assure the fair play of political forces in a particular domestic society. In the context of contemporary international politics, a crucial assessment is whether Communism or specific Communist states propose unlimited expansion by using unlawful force or whether they rely upon persuasion and permissible levels of coercion.[11] It is difficult to obtain adequate evidence on the limits of permissible political and para-military coercion.[12] Arguably, even a program of maximum ex-

---

The President is authorized to undertake, in the general area of the Middle East, military assistance programs with any nation or group of nations of that area desiring such assistance. Furthermore, the United States regards as vital to the national interest and world peace the preservation of the independence and integrity of the nations of the Middle East. To this end, if the President determines the necessity thereof, the United States is prepared to use armed force to assist any such nation or group of nations requesting assistance against armed aggression from any country controlled by international communism: *Provided*, That such employment shall be consonant with the treaty obligations of the United States and with the Constitution of the United States.
36 DEP'T STATE BULL. 481 (1957).

9. *The President's Proposal on the Middle East, Hearings before Senate Committees on Foreign Relations and Armed Services*, 85th Cong., 1st Sess., pt. 1, at 28 (1957).

10. The role of national claims of a unilateral nature in the development of international law is examined in Falk, *Toward a Responsible Procedure for the National Assertion of Protested Claims to Use Space*, in SPACE AND SOCIETY 91 (Taubenfeld ed. 1964).

11. This is the main theme of a speech by the Secretary of State. See Rusk, *Address*, 1965 PROC. AM. SOC. INT'L L. 247, 249-51.

12. I have discussed these issues in Falk, *On Minimizing the Use of Nuclear Weapons:*

pansion should be countered by self-limiting responses aimed at neutralizing Communist influence on internal wars and at building a world order that minimizes the role of military force.[13] We must also not overlook the welfare of the society torn by internal war. The great powers tend to wage their struggles for global dominance largely at the expense of the ex-colonial peoples.[14] These considerations support a conservative approach to internal wars, an approach treating them as civil wars, and permitting a neutralizing response as a maximum counteraction. And, specifically, if efforts to neutralize Communist expansion[15] in Viet Nam can be justified at all, the appropriate role of the United States is to counter "intervention" rather than to respond to an "armed attack."

The issue of self-determination is also relevant in the setting of internal war. If Communists or Communist-oriented elites can obtain political control without significant external support, it becomes difficult to vindicate Western intervention in terms of neutralizing Communist expansion. Castro's revolution represents a Communist success that was achieved without significant external support until after political control of Cuba was fully established. Part of the objection to American intervention in the Dominican Republic in 1965 arises from the absence of prior foreign intervention. The policies of preventing war, minimizing violence, and localizing conflict seem in these contexts to outweigh the objectives of anti-Communism; the United States serves both its own interests and those of the world community by respecting the outcome of internal political struggles. Unless we respect domestic political autonomy, our adversaries have no incentive to refrain from participating on the side of their faction. The primary objective in relation to

A Comparison of Revolutionary and Reformist Perspectives, in FALK, TUCKER, & YOUNG, ON MINIMIZING THE USE OF NUCLEAR WEAPONS 1 (Research Monograph No. 23, Center of International Studies, Princeton University, March 1, 1966).

13. Everyone would agree in the abstract that it is important to reconcile policies directed at limiting the expansion of adversaries with those aimed at avoiding warfare, particularly nuclear warfare. See FALK, LAW, MORALITY, AND WAR 32-65 (1963).

14. Relative peace is obtained through mutual deterrence at "the center" of the international system. Struggles for expansion are confined to "the periphery" where the risks of nuclear war can be minimized and where the costs of conflict can be shifted from the great powers to the ex-colonial nations.

15. My own judgment, based on the analysis of the Geneva settlement in 1954, is that the war in South Viet Nam represents more an American attempt at "rollback" than a Communist attempt at "expansion." The Geneva Conference looked toward the reunification of the whole of Viet Nam under the leadership of Ho Chi Minh. The introduction into South Viet Nam of an American military presence thus appears as an effort to reverse these expectations and to deny Hanoi the full extent of its victory against the French. Cf. also LACOUTURE, VIETNAM: BETWEEN TWO TRUCES 17-68 (1966) [hereinafter cited as LACOUTURE].

internal warfare is to establish rules of the game that allow domestic processes of political conflict to proceed without creating undue risks of a major war. In addition, human welfare and democratic ideals are best served by allowing the struggle between Communist and Western approaches to development to be waged by domestic factions. Recent events in Indonesia, Algeria, and Ghana demonstrate that these internal struggles for ascendancy are not inevitably won by Communists.

Civil strife can be analyzed in terms of three different types of violent conflict.[16] A Type I conflict involves the direct and massive use of military force by one political entity across a frontier of another—Korea, or Suez.[17] To neutralize the invasion it may be necessary to act promptly and unilaterally, and it is appropriate either to use force in self-defense or to organize collective action under the auspices of a regional or global institution. A Type II conflict involves substantial military participation by one or more foreign nations in an internal struggle for control, e.g., the Spanish Civil War. To neutralize this use of military power it may be necessary, and it is appropriate, to take off-setting military action confined to the internal arena, although only after seeking unsuccessful recourse to available procedures for peaceful settlement and machinery for collective security. A third type of conflict, Type III, is an internal struggle for control of a national society, the outcome of which is virtually independent of external participation. Of course, the outcome of a Type III conflict may affect the relative power of many other countries. Hungary prior to Soviet intervention, Cuba (1958-59), and the Dominican Republic prior to United States intervention, typify this class of struggle. It is inappropriate for a foreign nation to use military power to influence the outcome. The degree of inappropriateness will vary with the extent and duration of the military power used, and also with the explicitness of the foreign nation's role.[18] Thus, the reliance on Cuban exiles to carry out the anti-Castro mission at the Bay of Pigs (1961) is somewhat less inappropriate

---

16. These "types" are analytical rather than empirical in character. In actual experience a particular occasion of violence is a mixture of types, although the nature of the mixture is what makes one classification more appropriate than another.

17. Border disputes generating limited, but overt, violence by one entity against another are a special sub-type under Type I that may or may not support a finding of "armed attack" or a defensive claim of "self-defense."

18. See the emphasis on the *covertness* of the United States role in sponsoring the Bay of Pigs invasion of 1961 as an influential factor in the decision to proceed in SCHLESINGER, JR., A THOUSAND DAYS 233-97 (1965). And note that Schlesinger's opposition to the invasion was based in large part on his belief that it would be impossible to disguise the United States' role. *Id.* at 253-54.

than the use of United States Marines. Perhaps appreciating this distinction, North Viet Nam relied almost exclusively on South Vietnamese exiles during the early years of the anti-Diem war.[19]

These three models are analytical tools designed to clarify the nature and consequences of policy choices. Reasonable men may disagree on the proper classification of a particular war, especially if they cannot agree on the facts. An understanding of the controversy over the legality of United States participation in the war in Viet Nam seems aided by keeping in mind these distinct models.

The United States is treating the war as a Type I conflict. I would argue, for reasons set out in the next section, that the war belongs in Class III. But if this position entailing non-participation is rejected, then the maximum American response is counter-intervention as is permissible in a Type II situation.

Two general issues bear on an interpretation of the rights and duties of states in regard to internal wars of either Type II or III. First, to what extent does the constituted elite—the incumbent regime—enjoy a privileged position to request outside help in suppressing internal challenges directed at its control?[20] Traditional international law permits military assistance to the incumbent regime during early stages of an internal challenge. However, once the challenging faction demonstrates its capacity to gain control and administer a substantial portion of the society, most authorities hold that a duty of neutrality or non-discrimination governs the relations of both factions to outside states.[21] A state may act in favor of the incumbent to neutralize a Type III conflict only until the challenge is validated as substantial. A crucial question is whether outside states can themselves determine the point at which the challenge is validated, or whether validation is controlled, or at least influenced, by international procedures and by objective criteria of validation. The United States legal position stresses its continuing right to discriminate in favor of the incumbent regime and to deny even the political existence of the National Liberation Front (N.L.F.), despite

---

19. See, *e.g.*, WARNER, THE LAST CONFUCIAN 155 (1963) [hereinafter cited as WARNER]; FALL, THE TWO VIET-NAMS 316-84 (rev. ed. 1964) [hereinafter cited as THE TWO VIET-NAMS].

20. See, *e.g.*, Garner, *Questions of International Law in the Spanish Civil War*, 31 AM. J. INT'L L. 66 (1937).

21. See generally THOMAS & THOMAS, NON-INTERVENTION: THE LAW AND ITS IMPACT IN THE AMERICAS 215-21 (1956); see also LAUTERPACHT, RECOGNITION IN INTERNATIONAL LAW 199-201, 227-33 (1957); Falk, *Janus Tormented: The International Law of Internal War*, in ROSENAU 185, 197-209.

the *de facto* existence of the N.L.F. over a long period and its effective control of a large portion of the disputed territory.[22]

A second question partially applicable to Viet Nam is whether it is ever permissible to discriminate in favor of the counter-elite. The Communist states and the ex-colonial states of Asia and Africa assume that there are occasions warranting external participation in support of the insurgent faction. The Afro-Asian states argue that political legitimacy is established by an international consensus expressed through the formal acts of international institutions, rather than by the mere control of the constituted government.[23] This theory of legitimacy sanctions foreign military assistance to an "anti-colonialist" struggle. The extent to which this new attitude alters traditional international law is at present unclear, as is its full relevance to the conflict in Viet Nam. The argument for applicability to Viet Nam would emphasize the continuity between the 1946-54 anti-colonial war in Viet Nam and the present conflict. It would presuppose that the diplomatic recognition of South Viet Nam by some sixty countries conferred only nominal sovereignty, and that the Saigon regime is a client government of the United States, which has succeeded to the imperialistic role of the French. This approach implies that external states such as North Viet Nam, China, and the Soviet Union have "the right" to render support to the N.L.F.

These notions of permissible discrimination in favor of the constituted elite or the challenging counter-elite complicate considerably the legal analysis of participation in a Type III conflict and blur the boundaries between Types II and III. Any adequate statement of the international law of internal war, must acknowledge this complexity, and admit along with it a certain degree of legal indeterminancy.[24]

II

The vast and competent literature on the war in South Viet Nam provides an essential factual background for an impartial approach to

---

22. For a description of the extent of the N.L.F.'s governmental control see BURCHETT, VIETNAM: INSIDE STORY OF THE GUERILLA WAR 223-26 (1965); for legal argument see LAUTERPACHT, *op. cit. supra* at 175-238.

23. The legal status of a counter-elite in a colony is certainly improved by the repeated condemnations of colonialism in the United Nations and the recent passage of formal resolutions calling for decolonialization. Factors other than claims to be the constituted government are regularly taken into account in assessing claims of legitimacy in international relations.

24. For the theoretical background on legal indeterminacy in international law see Lauterpacht, *Some Observations on the Prohibition of 'Non Liquet' and the Completeness of the Law*, in SYMBOLAE VERZIJL 196-221 (1958); Stone, Non Liquet *and the Function of Law in the International Community*, 35 BRIT. YB. INT'L L. 124 (1959).

the legal issues presented in the Memorandum of Law prepared by the State Department.[25] It is impossible to summarize all of the relevant facts, but it may be useful to indicate certain lines of reasoning that account for part of my disagreement with the official legal analysis. This disagreement reflects my interpretation of the internal war as primarily a consequence of indigenous forces. Even more, it stems from my concern for taking into account certain facts entirely excluded from the Memorandum, such as the pre-1954 war against the French and the repression of political opposition by the Diem regime.

It must be kept in mind that the present conflict in Viet Nam originated in the war fought between the French and the Vietminh for control of *the whole* of Viet Nam, which was "settled" at Geneva in 1954.[26] Although the intentions of the participants at Geneva were somewhat ambiguous, the general view at the time was that the Geneva agreements anticipated reunification under the leadership of Ho Chi Minh by 1956 to coincide with the French departure. France came to Geneva a defeated nation; the Vietminh held two-thirds or more of the country.[27] Had elections been held, it is generally agreed that reunification under Ho Chi Minh would have resulted, however one interprets the suppression of political opposition in the North or intimidation in the South.[28] Independent observers also agree that the anticipation of the prospect of peaceful reunification led Hanoi to observe the Geneva arrangements during the two years immediately following 1954. The undoubted disappointment caused by the refusal of the French and the Americans to make Saigon go through with the elections helps explain the resumption of insurrectionary violence after 1956.[29]

---

25. Among those most helpful see Lacouture; The Two Viet-Nams; Fall, Vietnam Witness 1953-66 (1966) [hereinafter cited as Vietnam Witness]; Shaplen, The Lost Revolution (rev. ed. 1966) [hereinafter cited as Shaplen]; Lancaster, The Emancipation of French Indo-China (1961) [hereinafter cited as Lancaster]; Warner.

26. The settlement was not very realistic. It failed to take into account Saigon's exclusion or the American opposition to the Geneva solution. No responsibility was imposed upon the French to assure compliance with the terms of settlement prior to their withdrawal. See Warner 142-43.

27. For a general account see Lancaster 290-358; Vietnam Witness 69-83; for the fullest account of the Geneva negotiations see Lacouture & Devillers, La fin d'une guerre (1960). And see Eisenhower, Mandate for Change 332-75 (1963) for official American thinking during this period.

28. There is agreement that an election held within the prescribed period would have been won by Ho Chi Minh. See, e.g., Shaplen xi, Warner 142-43; Lacouture 32: "The final declaration of the Geneva Conference foresaw, of course, that general election would permit the reunification of Veitnam two years later. And none doubted at the time that this would be to the benefit of the North."

29. See Lacouture 32-50.

The Vietminh did leave a cadre of 5,000 or so elite guerrillas in the South, withdrawing others, as agreed, north of the Seventeenth Parallel.[30] Those left in the South apparently went "underground," hiding weapons for possible future use. This action seems no more than a reasonable precaution on the part of Hanoi in light of Saigon's continuing objection to the Geneva terms, and in view of Washington's evident willingness from 1954 onward to give Saigon political and military support. Given the terms of conflict and the balance of forces in Viet Nam prior to the Geneva Conference, French acceptance of a Viet Nam-wide defeat, American reluctance to affirm the results of Geneva, and Saigon's repudiation of the settlement, it seems quite reasonable for Hanoi to regard a resumption of the civil war as a distinct contingency. Although a decade of *de facto* independence (affirmed by diplomatic recognition) now gives South Viet Nam a strong claim to existence as a political entity, Hanoi certainly had no obligation in 1954 to respect claims of an independent political status for Saigon.[31] To clarify the diplomatic context in Geneva, it is well to recall that the Vietminh was the sole negotiator on behalf of Vietnamese interests at Geneva in 1954.

Later in 1954 the Saigon regime under Premier Diem ruthlessly suppressed all political opposition.[32] Observers agree that organization of an underground was an inevitable reaction to this suppression, and that the N.L.F. at its inception included many non-Communist elements.[33] It also appears that Saigon was unwilling to negotiate, or even consult, on questions affecting reunification, and was unwilling to normalize economic relations with Hanoi. The great economic strain imposed on North Viet Nam forced it to use scarce foreign exchange to obtain part of its food supply from other countries.[34]

Furthermore, the French military presence soon was replaced by an American military presence prior to the scheduled elections on reunification.[35] The evolution of an American "commitment" to Saigon's

---

30. *Id.* at 32-68; *cf.* Vietnam Witness 169-89.

31. Hanoi was "entitled" to prevent Saigon from establishing itself as a political entity with independent claims to diplomatic status as a sovereign state. A separation of Viet Nam into two states was not contemplated by the participants at Geneva.

32. See Warner 107-24; Lacouture 17-31.

33. Fall, *Viet-Cong—The Unseen Enemy in Viet-Nam*, in The Viet-Nam Reader (Raskin & Fall eds. 1965) [hereinafter cited as Viet-Nam Reader].

34. Lacouture 34-35, 68.

35. This is the major thesis of Lacouture, *Vietnam: The Lessons of War*, reprinted from the New York Reveiw of Books, March 3, 1966, p. 1, in *Hearings on S.2793 Before the Senate Committee on Foreign Relations*, 89th Cong., 2d Sess. 655-61 (1966) [hereinafter cited as Vietnam Hearings].

permanence and legitimacy contrasts radically with both the expectations created at Geneva in 1954 and the subsequent attitudes of the French. United States involvement in the politics of South Viet Nam increased constantly; it was no secret that the Diem government largely was constituted and sustained in its early months by the United States.[36]

Despite the escalating American political, military, and economic assistance, the Saigon regime proved incapable of achieving political stability. Numerous regimes have come and gone. None has commanded the respect and allegiance of any significant segment of the population. Often in situations of civil war diverse factions are able to establish an expedient working unity during the period of common national emergency. The N.L.F. seems to maintain substantial control over its heterogeneous followers while one Saigon regime after another collapses or totters on the brink. The United States recognized at an early stage that the Saigon regime had to transform its own feudal social structure before it could provide the basis for viable government in South Viet Nam.[37] This is a most unusual demand by an external ally; it bears witness to the fragile and dubious claim of each successive Saigon regime to govern even the parts of South Viet Nam not held by the Vietcong.

In addition, Saigon and the United States seem to have neglected repeated opportunities for negotiations with Hanoi during earlier stages of the war.[38] As late as February, 1965, the United States government rebuked U Thant for engaging in unauthorized negotiations. Until the prospects for a military solution favorable to Saigon diminished to the vanishing point, the United States made no attempt to negotiate a peaceful settlement or to entrust responsibility for settlement to either the Security Council or the Co-Chairmen of the Geneva

---

36. For an account of the *covert* dimension of the United States role in the domestic affairs of South Viet Nam see WISE & ROSS, THE INVISIBLE GOVERNMENT 155-64 (1964). There are also references to the exercise of covert influence by the United States in LACOUTURE, SHAPLEN, and WARNER. American strategies of covert influence in foreign countries are analyzed and described in BLACKSTOCK, THE STRATEGY OF SUBVERSION (1964).

37. *Cf.* letter of President Eisenhower to Premier Diem on October 23, 1954, SENATE COMMITTEE ON FOREIGN RELATIONS, 89TH CONG., 1ST SESS., BACKGROUND INFORMATION RELATING TO SOUTHEAST ASIA AND VIETNAM (Comm. Print 1965) [hereinafter cited as BACKGROUND INFORMATION]. For a recent reiteration, see *U.S. and South Vietnamese Leaders Meet at Honolulu*, 54 DEP'T STATE BULL. 302-07 (Feb. 28, 1966).

38. The American approach to a negotiated settlement is recounted and criticized in AMERICAN FRIENDS SERVICE COMMITTEE, PEACE IN VIET NAM 50-67 (1966). Among other observations, this report points out that "a careful reading of the *New York Times* shows that the United States has rejected no fewer than seven efforts to negotiate an end to the war." *Id.* at 51. See also the article by Flora Lewis, in VIETNAM HEARINGS, 323-34.

Conference.[39] This reluctance, when added to the political losses suffered by Hanoi at Geneva in 1954, makes it easier to comprehend Hanoi's reluctance to negotiate now.[40]

All of these considerations lead me to regard the war in South Vietnam primarily as a Type III conflict, in which the United States ought not to have participated. Because of Hanoi's increasing participation on behalf of the Vietcong, it is arguable, although rather unpersuasive, that this war is properly categorized as an example of Type II, so that the United States could legitimately give military assistance to Saigon, but is obligated to limit the arena of violence to the territory of South Viet Nam. The weakness of the Saigon regime compared to the N.L.F. renders necessary a disproportionately large military commitment by the United States to neutralize the indigenous advantages of the Vietcong and the support of Hanoi.[41] Our disproportionate commitment makes it appear that the United States rather than Hanoi is escalating the war. And this appearance undercuts any defense of our participation as necessary to offset participation on the other side, and thereby

39. For predictions of an American victory in South Viet Nam, see Raskin & Fall, *Chronology of Events in Viet-Nam and Southeast Asia,* BACKGROUND INFORMATION 377, 388-89, 390-92. As late as October 2, 1963, Secretary McNamara and General Taylor issued an official statement reporting their conclusion that "the major part of the United States military task can be completed by the end of 1965"; and on November 1, 1963 General Paul D. Harkins, U.S. military commander wrote in Stars & Stripes (Tokyo) that "Victory in the sense it would apply to this kind of war is just months away and the reduction of American advisers can begin any time now." The point of quoting these statements is to suggest that as long as a favorable military solution seemed forthcoming at a tolerable cost the United States was not interested in a negotiated settlement.

40. An important element in the background of Vietnamese history was the successful resistance movement led by Ho Chi Minh against the Japanese in the closing years of World War II. When the Japanese left French Indo-China, Ho Chi Minh was in control of the entire territory, and was induced to accept the return to power of the French colonial administration in exchange for promises of political independence that were never fulfilled. The recollection of this first phase of the Vietnamese war, when added to the post-1954 experience may deepen Hanoi's impression that its political success depends upon military effort. On negotiating with Hanoi, see also the REPORT OF THE AD HOC CONGRESSIONAL CONFERENCE ON VIETNAM, 89TH CONG., 2D SESS. 4-5 (Comm. Print 1966) [hereinafter cited as AD HOC CONGRESSIONAL CONFERENCE].

41. Bernard Fall, writing on the sort of military superiority that is required to achieve victory over an insurgency, says:

. . . in the past it [victory] has required a ratio of pacification forces versus insurgents that is simply not available in Viet-Nam today [Jan. 1965]. In Malaya, British and Malayan forces have achieved a ratio of 50 to 1; in Cyprus, British forces had achieved a 110 to 1 ratio, and in Algeria the French had reached 10 to 1. The present ratio in South Viet-Nam is 4.5 to 1, and the French ratio in the First Indochina War was an incredibly low 1.2 to 1, which (all other matters being equal) would suffice to explain France's ultimate defeat.

VIET-NAM WITNESS 291.

give "the true" balance of domestic forces a chance to control the outcome.[42] The State Department Memorandum assumes that the war is a Type I conflict, and argues that American participation is really collective self-defense in response to an armed attack by North Viet Nam upon South Viet Nam. But to characterize North Viet Nam's participation in the struggle in the South as "an armed attack" is unwise as well as incorrect. Such a contention, if accepted as an authoritative precedent, goes a long way toward abolishing the distinction between international and civil war. The war in South Viet Nam should be viewed as primarily between factions contending for control of the southern zone, whether or not the zone is considered a nation.[43] A claim of self-defense by Saigon seems misplaced, and the exercise of rights of self-defense by committing violent acts against the territory of North Viet Nam tends toward the establishment of an unfortunate precedent.[44]

III

The Memorandum of the State Department was submitted by the Legal Adviser to the Senate Committee on Foreign Relations on March 8, 1966.[45] In assessing it, we should keep in mind several considerations. First, the United States Government is the client of the Legal Adviser, and the Memorandum, as is entirely appropriate, is an adversary document. A legal adviser in Hanoi could prepare a comparable document. Adversary discourse in legal analysis should be sharply distinguished from an impartial determination of the merits of opposed positions.[46]

---

42. Official United States Government statements frequently imply that the United States must render help to the Saigon regime equivalent to the help given by Hanoi to the N.L.F. If "equivalent" is measured by the needs of the ratio, then it may be as much as 110 times as great as the aid given to the insurgents, whereas if equivalent means arithmetically equal, it will be completely ineffectual.

43. Hanoi itself takes a conflict-confining position that the war in Viet Nam is a civil war being waged to determine control of South Viet Nam rather than a civil or international war to determine control of the whole of Viet Nam. See, e.g., *Policy Declaration of Premier Pham Van Dong of North Viet-Nam, April 14, 1965*, in VIET-NAM READER 342-43 ("Hanoi's Four Points"). See also *Program of the National Liberation Front of South Viet-Nam, id.* at 216-21 (on Dec. 20, 1960).

44. But, as of July 1966, the United States has not attacked North Vietnamese centers of population and has made only limited attacks on industrial complexes (oil depots). The unjustified claim of self-defense has been noted, but it is well to appreciate the as yet restrained form of the claim.

45. An earlier, somewhat skimpy, memorandum, *The Legal Basis for U.S. Actions against North Vietnam*, was issued by the Department of State on March 8, 1965; for the text see BACKGROUND INFORMATION 191-94.

46. I have tried to urge a non-adversary role for the international lawyer on several ocasions: see Falk, *The Adequacy of Contemporary Theories of International Law—*

Second, the Legal Memorandum was evidently framed as a response to the Memorandum of Law prepared by the Lawyers Committee on American Policy Toward Viet Nam.[47] The argument of the Lawyers Committee fails to raise sharply the crucial issue—namely, the discretion of the United States to delimit its legal rights and duties by treating the conflict in South Viet Nam as an international war of aggression rather than as a civil war.[48]

Third, the Legal Adviser's Memorandum implies that both the facts of aggression and the legal rules governing self-defense are clear. This is misleading. Except in instances of overt, massive aggression across an international frontier, international law offers very *indefinite* guidance about the permissible occasions for or extent of recourse to force in self-defense. Doctrinal ambiguity is greatest with respect to internal wars with significant external participation.[49] International law offers very little authoritative guidance on the central issue of permissible assistance to the contending factions.[50] To conclude that international law is indefinite is not to suggest that it is irrelevant. On the contrary, if rules are indefinite and procedures for their interpretation unavailable, prevailing national practice sets precedents for the future. In this light, American activity in Viet Nam is particularly unfortunate for the future of doctrines aimed at limiting international violence.[51]

Gaps in Legal Thinking, 50 VA. L. REV. 231, 233-43 (1964); and a recent paper delivered at the Harris Conference on New Approaches to International Relations, at the University of Chicago, June 1966, with the title, New Approaches to the Study of International Law 3-9 (paper available in mimeographed form, to be published subsequently in conference volume).

47. See Lawyers Committee on American Policy Toward Vietnam, *American Policy Vis-à-Vis Vietnam, Memorandum of Law*, in VIETNAM HEARINGS 687-713.

48. The Spanish Civil War is a useful historical precedent for the legal treatment of large-scale foreign interventions on both sides of an internal war. For a full analysis see PADELFORD, INTERNATIONAL LAW AND DIPLOMACY IN THE SPANISH CIVIL STRIFE (1939). Another way of posing the issue would be to ask whether Cuba, after the Bay of Pigs invasion, might have been entitled to ask the Soviet Union for military assistance, including air strikes against staging areas in the United States. For a critical account of the legal status of American participation in the Bay of Pigs invasion see Falk, *American Intervention in Cuba and the Rule of Law*, 22 OHIO ST. L.J. 546 (1961).

49. I have argued to this effect, in ROSENAU 210-40.

50. By "authoritative guidance" I mean guidance of action by clear, applicable rules of international law that are congruent with community expectations about permissible behavior; the rules must be clear enough to permit identification of a violation without independent fact-finding procedures.

51. International customary law evolves as a consequence of national claims and counter-claims acquiring through time an authoritative status. States assert these claims and counter-claims to maximize policy considerations in various contexts. For a major exposition of this process see McDOUGAL & BURKE, THE PUBLIC ORDER OF THE OCEANS (1962).

In this section I propose to criticize the legal argument of the Memorandum, taking some issue with both inferences of fact and conclusions of law. I will analyze the consequences of characterizing international participation in Viet Nam as intervention and counter-intervention in an ongoing civil war. Although I will call attention to the shortcomings in the legal position of the United States, my main intention is to approach this inquiry in the spirit of scholarly detachment rather than as an adversary critic.[52] Such detachment is not value-free. I try to appraise the claims of national actors in light of the requirements of world order. My appraisal presupposes the desirability of narrowing the discretion of nations to determine for themselves the occasions on which violence is permissible or that an increase of the scale and scope of ongoing violence is appropriate. I am convinced that it is important for *any* country (including my own) to reconcile its foreign policy with the rules regulating the use of force in international affairs, and that, therefore, it does not serve *even* the national interest to accept a legal justification for our own recourse to violence that we would not be prepared to have invoked against us by other states similarly situated.[53] The international legal order, predominantly decentralized, depends for effectiveness on the acceptance by principal states of the fundamental ordering notions of symmetry, reciprocity, and national precedent-setting.[54]

In analyzing the Memorandum I will adhere to its outline of issues, concentrating on the most significant.

Collective Self-Defense. The Memorandum argues that the United States may, at Saigon's request, participate in the collective self-defense of South Viet Nam because North Viet Nam has made a prior armed attack. But may indirect aggression be treated as an armed attack without the approval of an appropriate international institution? The United States rests its case on the role of Hanoi in the period between 1954 and 1959 in setting up "a covert political-military organization" and by its infiltration of "over 40,000 armed and unarmed guerrillas

---

52. An adversary debate may be useful to clarify the legal issues, but an impartial perspective is also needed to help in the process of choosing among the adversary presentations.

53. America's relative inability to make effective legal protests against further nuclear testing on the high seas and in the atmosphere is partly a result of America's earlier legal defense of its own similar behavior. A legal precedent is created by the effective assertion of a claim to act, and this precedent may be difficult to repudiate, even if the precedent-setter has greater power than does the actor relying upon the precedent.

54. See FALK, THE ROLE OF DOMESTIC COURTS IN THE INTERNATIONAL LEGAL ORDER 21-52 (1964).

into South Viet Nam" during the subsequent five years. The Memorandum concludes that "the external aggression from the North is the critical military element of the insurgency," that "the infiltration of thousands of armed men clearly constitutes an 'armed attack' under any reasonable definition," and that although there may be doubt as to "the exact date at which North Viet Nam's aggression grew into an 'armed attack,' [it certainly] had occurred before February 1965."

This argument is questionable on its face, that is, without even criticizing its most selective presentation of the facts. Consider first the highly ideological character of prevailing attitudes toward the just use of force. The Communist countries favor support for wars of national liberation; the West—in particular, the United States—favors support for anti-Communist wars; and the Afro-Asian states favor support for anti-colonialist and anti-racist wars.[55] Consider also the importance, acknowledged by the United States in other settings,[56] of circumscribing the right of self-defense. The use of force on some other basis—for example, defensive intervention or regional security—moderates rather than escalates a conflict. But the invocation of self-defense as a rationale during a conflict previously contained within a single state tends to enlarge the arena of conflict to include states that are claiming and counter-claiming that each other's intervention in the civil strife is an armed attack. If the infiltration constitutes an armed attack, the bombing of North Viet Nam may be justified. But if North Viet Nam had operative collective defense arrangements with China and the Soviet Union it is easy to project a scenario of escalation ending in global catastrophe. If, on the other hand, infiltration is merely intervention, and appropriate responses are limited to counter-intervention, the area of violence is restricted to the territory of South Viet Nam and its magnitude is kept within more manageable limits.[57]

The argument in the Memorandum also assumes that armed help to the insurgent faction is under all circumstances a violation of international law. As mentioned earlier, at some stage in civil strife it is

---

55. Compare with these claims the prohibitions upon the use of force expressed in absolute terms in Article 2(4) of the United Nations Charter. Self-defense against a prior armed attack appears to be the only permissible national basis for the use of force (without authorization from the United Nations).

56. See, *e.g.*, avoidance of a self-defense rationale by government officials offering legal justification for the United States claims to interdict on the high seas Soviet intermediate range ballistics bound for Cuba in 1962. Meeker, *Defensive Quarantine and the Law*, 57 AM. J. INT'L L. 515 (1963); Chayes, *The Legal Case for U.S. Action on Cuba*, 47 DEP'T STATE BULL. 763 (1962).

57. For a fuller rationale see Falk, *supra* note 4.

permissible for outside states to regard the insurgent elite the equal of the incumbent regime and to render it equivalent assistance.[58] Since no collective procedures are available to determine when an insurgency has proceeded far enough to warrant this status, outside states enjoy virtually unlimited discretion to determine the comparative legitimacy of competing elites.[59] In effect, then, no rules of international law exist to distinguish clearly between permissible and impermissible intervention in civil strife.[60] To call hostile intervention not only impermissible but an instance of the most serious illegality—an armed attack—seems very unfortunate. In addition to a tendency to escalate any particular conflict, the position that interventions are armed attacks so broadens the notion of armed attack that all nations will be able to make plausible claims of self-defense in almost every situation of protracted internal war. It therefore seems desirable to confine the armed attack/self-defense rationale to the Korea-type conflict (Type I) and to deny its applicability in Viet Nam, whether the war in Viet Nam is denominated Type II or Type III. The Memorandum's argument on self-defense is also deficient in that it relies upon a very selective presentation of the facts. It ignores Saigon's consistent opposition to the terms of the Geneva settlement, thereby casting in very different light Hanoi's motives for the steps it took in South Viet Nam to assert its claims.[61] It is essential to recall that the pre-1954 conflict was waged for control of *all* of Viet Nam and that the settlement at Geneva was no more than "a cease-fire." President Diem's ruthless suppression of political opposition in South Viet Nam from 1954 onward, in violation of the ban on political reprisals included in the Geneva Agreements, is also relevant.[62]

---

58. *Cf.* the study of the international relations of the insurgent groups during the Algerian War of Independence by M. BEDJAOUI, LAW AND THE ALGERIAN REVOLUTION (1961).

59. If "the will of the international community" operates as the true basis of international law, the criteria of legitimacy shift to correspond to the values of the expanded membership in international society.

60. See LAUTERPACHT, *op. cit. supra* note 21, at 253-55.

61. If mutuality is the basic condition for the existence of a legal obligation, it is essential that both disputants accept the terms of settlement. If there is non-acceptance on one side, the other side is in a position to protect its position *as if* the settlement did not exist. In the setting of Viet Nam this would suggest that Hanoi was free to pursue its war aims on a pre-1954 basis and ignore the division of the country into two zones. It is ironic that South Viet Nam owes its original political identity entirely to the Geneva Agreements.

62. *Cf.* Article 15, *Agreement on the Cessation of Hostilities:* "Each party undertakes to refrain from any reprisals or discrimination against persons or organizations for their activities during the hostilities and also undertakes to guarantee their democratic freedoms." BACKGROUND INFORMATION 50, 53. See LACOUTURE 28-31; BURCHETT, VIETNAM—INSIDE STORY OF THE GUERILLA WAR 109-28 (1965).

Furthermore, the injection of an American political and military presence was, from the perspective of Hanoi, inconsistent with the whole spirit of Geneva.[63] The United States decision to commit itself to maintaining a Western-oriented regime in South Viet Nam upset the expectations regarding the Southeast Asian balance of power; in that respect, it was similar to the Soviet attempt to upset the Caribbean balance of power by installing intermediate-range missiles in Cuba in 1962.[64]

The Memorandum seems to concede that until 1964 the bulk of infiltrated men were South Vietnamese who had come north after the cease-fire in 1954. The use of exiles to bolster an insurgent cause appears to be on the borderline between permissible and impermissible behavior in contemporary international politics. The role of the United States Government in sponsoring the unsuccessful invasion at the Bay of Pigs in 1961 was a far more flagrant example of the use of exiles to overthrow a constituted government in a neighboring country than the early role of Hanoi in fostering an uprising in the South.[65] The claim by the United States to control political events in Cuba is far more tenuous than the claim by North Viet Nam to exercise control (or at least remove the influence of a hostile superpower) over political life in the South.[66] And Castro's regime was domestically viable in a manner that Saigon regimes have never been—suggesting that South Viet Nam presents a more genuine revolutionary situation than does contemporary Cuba. It seems more destructive of world order to help overthrow

---

63. The operative great power in the area was France. It was not in Hanoi's interest to give up a favorable battle position so that the United States could replace the French military presence. The worsening of their position in the area as a result of the negotiations at Geneva may explain, in part, their reluctance to negotiate a "settlement" and give up a favorable military position once again.

64. One influential view of the basis of international order stresses maintaining current balances and expectations. Any attempt to rely upon military means to upset these balances and expectations is perceived and treated as "aggression." The intrusion of Soviet military influence into the Western Hemisphere by attempting to emplace missiles constituted the provocative element. The same military result could have been achieved by increasing the Atlantic deployment of missile-carrying submarines. This sense of "provocative" might also describe the perception of the escalating American military commitment in Southeast Asia.

65. For an authoritative account of the United States role see SCHLESINGER, JR., A THOUSAND DAYS 206-97 (1965).

66. The strength of Hanoi's claim arises from the prior struggle to control the entire country, the military victory by the Vietminh in that struggle, the expectations created at Geneva that the elections would confirm that military victory, the delimitation of South Viet Nam as "a temporary zone," and, finally, the refusal by South Viet Nam to consult on elections or to refrain from reprisals.

a firmly established government than to assist an ongoing revolution against a regime incapable of governing.

African countries admit helping exiles overthrow governments under white control.[67] American support for Captive Nations Week is still another form of support outside of the Communist bloc for exile aspirations.[68] In short, international law neither attempts nor is able to regulate support given exile groups. The activities of Hanoi between 1954 and 1964 conform to patterns of tolerable conflict in contemporary international politics.

The Memorandum contends that subsequent to 1964, Hanoi has increasingly infiltrated regular elements of the North Vietnamese army until at present "there is evidence that nine regiments of regular North Vietnamese forces are fighting in the South." Arguably, the N.L.F. was not eligible to receive external support in the early years of strife after 1954, as its challenge to the government amounted to no more than "a rebellion." But certainly after the Vietcong gained effective control over large portions of the countryside it was *permissible* for North Viet Nam to treat the N.L.F. as a "belligerent" with a right to conduct external relations.[69] This area of international law is exceedingly vague; states have a wide range of discretion in establishing their relations with contending factions in a foreign country.[70]

The remainder of the first section of the Memorandum responds to the Lawyers Committee Memorandum of Law, but is not relevant to the solution of the critical legal questions. It is persuasive but trivial for the State Department to demonstrate that international law recognizes the right of individual and collective self-defense against an armed

---

67. In the Final Act of the Conference of Heads of States or Governments at Cairo in 1964 the following declaration was made by the foity-seven non-aligned powers assembled: "Colonized people may legitimately resort to arms to secure the full exercise of their right to self-determination."

68. For perceptive discussion of the status of "Captive Nations Week" in international law see Wright, *Subversive Intervention*, 54 AM. J. INT'L L. 521 (1960).

69. See the extent of international recognition accorded the F.L.N. in Algeria during their war against the French, BEDJAOUI, *op. cit. supra* note 58, at 110-38.

70. No clear rules of prohibition nor any required procedures exist which subject national discretion to international review. National discretion consequently governs practice.

For useful discussions stressing the survival under the United Nations Charter of a wider right of self-defense than the interpretation offered here see BOWETT, SELF-DEFENSE IN INTERNATIONAL LAW 182-99 (1958); McDOUGAL & FELICIANO, LAW AND MINIMUM WORLD PUBLIC ORDER 121-260 (1961); for a position similar to the one taken in the text see Henkin, *Force, Intervention and Neutrality in Contemporary International Law*, 1963 PROC. AM. SOC. INT'L L. 147-62.

attack; that non-members of the United Nations enjoy the same rights of self-defense as do members;[71] that South Viet Nam is a political entity entitled to claim the right of self-defense despite its origin as a "temporary zone";[72] and that the right of collective self-defense may be exercised independent of a regional arrangement organized under Chapter VIII of the United Nations Charter.[73] South Viet Nam would have had the right to act in self-defense *if an armed attack had occurred,* and the United States would then have had the right to act in collective self-defense.[74]

It is also important to determine whether the United States has complied with the reporting requirement contained in Article 51 of the United Nations Charter.[75] The United States did encourage a limited Security Council debate during August 1964 of the Gulf of Tonkin "incidents."[76] Furthermore, the United States submitted two reports to the Security Council during February 1965 concerning its recourse to bombing North Viet Nam and the general character of the war. And in January 1966 the United States submitted the Viet Nam question to the Security Council.[77] It seems reasonable to conclude that the Security Council (or, for that matter, the General Assembly) is unwilling and unable to intervene in any *overt* manner in the conflict in

71. For consideration of this question see BOWETT, *op. cit. supra* note 70, at 193-95.

72. See the first sentence of Article 6 of the Final Declaration: "The Conference recognizes that the essential purpose of the agreement relating to Viet-Nam is to settle military questions with a view to ending hostilities and that the military demarcation line is provisional and *should not in any way be interpreted as constituting a political or territorial boundary,"* BACKGROUND INFORMATION 58, 59. (Emphasis added.) For Saigon's relevant conduct see LACOUTURE 24-31.

73. For a useful analysis see BOWETT, *op. cit. supra* note 70, at 200-48; MCDOUGAL & FELICIANO, *op. cit. supra* note 70, at 244-53.

74. That is, it would conform to expectations about what constitutes a permissible claim to use force in self-defense. Despite considerable controversy about the wisdom of the United States' involvement in the defense of Korea, there was no debate whatsoever (outside of Communist countries) about the legality of a defensive claim. There was some legal discussion about the propriety of United Nations involvement. For an argument in favor of legality see McDougal & Gardner, *The Veto and the Charter: An Interpretation for Survival,* in MCDOUGAL & ASSOCIATES, STUDIES IN WORLD PUBLIC ORDER 718-60 (1960). In retrospect, however, Korea exemplifies "an armed attack" for which force in response is appropriate, even if used on the territory of the attacking state.

75. For communications sent by the United States to the United Nations and relied upon to show compliance with the reporting requirements of Article 51 see VIETNAM HEARINGS 634-40.

76. For a description of official United States views see *Promoting the Maintenance of International Peace and Security in Southeast Asia,* H.R. REP. No. 1708, 88th Cong., 2d Sess. (1964); see Ambassador Stevenson's statement to the Security Council on August 5, 1964, in BACKGROUND INFORMATION 124-28.

77. No action was taken by the United Nations and the debate was inconclusive and insignificant.

Viet Nam. This conclusion is reinforced by the hostility of the Communist states toward American proposals for a settlement.[78] On the other hand, there is no evidence of formal initiative by the members of the United Nations to question the propriety of the United States policies. The very serious *procedural* question posed is whether the failure of the United Nations to act relieves the United States of its burden to submit claims of self-defense to review by the organized international community.[79] A further question is whether any international legal limitations upon national discretion apply when the United Nations refrains from passing judgment on claims to use force in self-defense.[80]

The Security Council failed to endorse American claims in Viet Nam, and this failure was not merely a consequence of Soviet or Communist opposition. Therefore, if the burden of justification for recourse to self-defense is upon the claimant, inaction by the United Nations provides no legal comfort on the *substantive issue*—that is, the legality of proportional self-defense given "the facts" in Viet Nam. As to the *procedural issue*—that is, compliance with the reporting requirement of Article 51—the United States may be considered to have complied *pro forma*, but not in terms of the spirit of the Charter of the United Nations.

The overriding purpose of the Charter is to commit states to use force only as a last resort after the exhaustion of all other alternatives. In the early period after 1954 the United States relied heavily on its unilateral economic and military capability to protect the Saigon regime against the Vietcong. No *prior* attempt was made, in accordance with Article 33, to settle the dispute by peaceful means.[81] Yet the spirit of the

---

78. Neither China nor North Viet Nam indicate any willingness to acknowledge a role for the United Nations. Of course, the exclusion of China from representation in the United Nations may account for Chinese opposition to a U.N. solution. See also AD HOC CONGRESSIONAL CONFERENCE 5.

79. To what extent, that is, do states have residual discretion to determine the legality of claims to use force in the event of United Nations inability to reach a clear decision?

80. The nature of these restraints may be of two varieties: first, the considerations entering into the creation of a precedent; second, the restraints of customary international law requiring that minimum necessary force be used to attain belligerent objectives and requiring the maintenance of the distinction between military and non-military targets and between combatants and non-combatants. One wonders whether these latter distinctions can be maintained in a guerrilla war such as that in Viet Nam.

81. U.N. CHARTER art. 33(1):

The parties to any dispute, the continuance of which is likely to endanger the maintenance of international peace and security, shall, first of all, seek a solution by negotiation, enquiry, mediation, conciliation, arbitration, judicial settlement, resort to regional agencies or arrangements, or other peaceful means of their own choice.

Charter requires that a nation claiming to undertake military action in collective self-defense must first invoke the collective review and responsibility of the United Nations. The United States did not call for United Nations review until January 1966, that is, until a time when the prospects for a favorable military solution at tolerable costs seemed dismal, many months subsequent to bombing North Vietnamese territory. As long as a military victory was anticipated, the United States resented any attempt to question its discretion to use force or to share its responsibility for obtaining a settlement.[82] American recourse to procedures for peaceful settlement came as a last rather than a first resort. The United States had made no serious effort to complain about alleged North Vietnamese violations of the Geneva Agreements, nor to recommend a reconvening of a new Geneva Conference in the decade of escalating commitment after 1954. Saigon submitted complaints to the International Control Commission, but that body was neither constituted nor intended to deal with the resumption of a war for control of South Viet Nam that was apparently provoked by Saigon's refusal to hold elections.

Further, not until 1965 did the United States welcome the independent efforts of the Secretary-General to act as a negotiating intermediary between Washington and Hanoi.[83] Until it became evident that a military victory over the Vietcong was not forthcoming, the United States Government was hostile to suggestions emanating from either U Thant (or De Gaulle) that a negotiated settlement was both *appropriate* and *attainable*. The State Department's belated offer to negotiate must be discounted in light of its public relations overtones and our effort over the last decade to reverse the expectations of Geneva. The United States negotiating position is also made less credible by our failure to accord the N.L.F. diplomatic status as a party in conflict.[84] This failure is especially dramatic in light of the N.L.F.'s ability effectively to govern territory under its possession and Saigon's relative inability to do so.

The American approach to negotiations lends support to the conclusion that our sporadic attempts at a peaceful settlement are belated gestures, and that we seek "victory" at the negotiating table only when it becomes unattainable on the battlefield. The United States showed no willingness to subordinate national discretion to the collective will of the organized international community. In fact, Viet Nam exempli-

---

82. *Cf.* note 39 *supra.*
83. *Cf.* note 38 *supra.*
84. See the recommendations to this effect in AD HOC CONGRESSIONAL CONFERENCE 5.

fies the American global strategy of using military power whenever necessary to prevent Communist expansion and to determine these necessary occasions by national decisions. This militant anti-Communism represents the essence of unilateralism.[85]

One must conclude that the United States was determined to use its military power as it saw fit in Viet Nam in the long period from 1954 to January 1966. In 1966 at last a belated, if halfhearted, attempt to collectivize responsibility was made by appealing to the Security Council to obtain, in the words of the Memorandum, "discussions looking toward a peaceful settlement on the basis of the Geneva accords." The Memorandum goes on to observe that "Indeed, since the United States submission on January 1966, members of the Council have been notably reluctant to proceed with any consideration of the Viet-Nam question." Should this reluctance come as a surprise? Given the timing and magnitude of the American request it was inevitable that the United Nations would find itself unable to do anything constructive at that stage. United Nations inaction has deepened the awareness of the Organization's limited ability to safeguard world peace, whenever the nuclear superpowers take opposite sides of a violent conflict.[86] Disputes must be submitted *prior* to deep involvement if the United Nations is to play a significant role.[87] The war in Viet Nam presented many appropriate opportunities—the various steps up the escalation ladder—for earlier, more effective, American recourse to the United Nations. But during the entire war in Viet Nam, the United States has shown no significant disposition to limit discretionary control over its national military power by making constructive use of collective procedures of peaceful settlement.

Proportionality. Even if we grant the Memorandum's contention that North Viet Nam is guilty of aggression amounting to an armed attack and that the United States is entitled to join in the collective self-defense of South Viet Nam, important questions remain concerning

---

85. That is, it represents the claim to use force for purposes determined by the United States. The ideological quality of this unilateralism—its quality as an anti-communist crusade—is suggested by "the understanding" attached by the United States to its ratification of the SEATO treaty limiting "its recognition of the effect of aggression and armed attack . . . to communist aggression." It is very unusual to restrict the applicability of a security arrangement in terms of the ideological identity of the aggressor, rather than in terms of national identity or with reference to the character of the aggression.

86. For a generalized approach to the problems of international conflict given the structure of international society, see F. GROSS, WORLD POLITICS AND TENSION AREAS (1966).

87. In the Congo Operation the outer limits of United Nations capacity were tested, perhaps exceeded.

the quantum, ratio, and modalities of force employed. Elementary principles both of criminal and international law require that force legitimately used must be reasonably calculated to attain the objective pursued and be somewhat proportional to the provocation. As McDougal and Feliciano observe, "[U]nderlying the processes of coercion is a fundamental principle of economy."[88] This fundamental principle deriving from the restraints on violence found in the earliest version of the just war doctrine has two attributes: the effectiveness of the force employed and the avoidance of excessive force.[89]

The United States effort in Viet Nam combines ineffectual with excessive force. The level of military commitment to date seems designed to avert defeat rather than to attain victory. All observers agree that if the other side persists in its commitment, the search for a favorable military solution will be exceedingly prolonged. Since the United States has far greater military resources potentially available, our use of insufficient force violates general norms of international law.[90] At the same time, however, weapons and strategy are being employed to cause destruction and incidental civilian damage without making a proportional contribution to the military effort. This is particularly true of our reliance upon strategic area bombing against dispersed targets of small military value.[91]

The United States has at each juncture also claimed the legal right to engage in disproportionate responses to specific provocations. In August 1964 the Gulf of Tonkin incidents consisted of allegations that North Vietnamese torpedo boats had "attacked" some American warships on the high seas. Although no damage was reported the United States responded by destroying several villages in which the boats were

---

88. McDOUGAL & FELICIANO, *op. cit. supra* note 70, at 35.

89. Implicit in the notion of economy of force is the idea that an unjust and illegal use of force is a futile use. The idea of futility is related to the attainability of a permissible belligerent objective and is difficult to measure. If a negotiated settlement rather than victory is the objective, the amount of force required can only be assessed in terms of the probable intentions of the other side, and these shift in response to many factors, including their assessment of intentions.

90. Here again a reinterpretation of traditional thinking on war is needed to satisfy the requirements of the nuclear age. American restraint in Viet Nam is explained in part by concern with generating a nuclear war or, at least, provoking a wider war in Southeast Asia. But what legal consequences follow if this inhibition leads to prolonged violence in Viet Nam of an indecisive but devastating form?

91. The Conference participants were in agreement that the bombings in the north were of little military value, while the diplomatic disadvantages were very serious. Further escalation of the bombings, it was felt, could not be expected to improve the situation.
AD HOC CONGRESSIONAL CONFERENCE 4.

based.[92] This was the first occasion on which force was used directly against North Vietnamese territory and the justifications rested upon a reprisal theory that was largely disassociated from the war in South Viet Nam. Such a disproportionate ratio between action and reaction is typical of great power politics in which superior force is used to discipline a minor adversary. But this exaggerated response violates the legal requisites of equivalency and symmetry between the injury sustained and the response undertaken. Acceptance of mutuality and symmetry is basic to the whole conception of law in a sovereignty-centered social order.[93]

The bombing of North Viet Nam in February 1965 was also originally justified as a "reprisal" for a successful attack by the Vietcong upon two United States air bases, principally the one at Pleiku. Only in retrospect was the justification for attacking North Viet Nam generalized to collective self-defense of South Viet Nam.[94]

No clear legal guidelines exist to measure the proportionality of force used in self-defense. There is also some doubt whether proportionality applies to the belligerent objective pursued or the size and character of the aggression. If we assume that the appropriate quantum of military force is that needed to neutralize the Vietcong (the mere agent, in the American view, of Hanoi), then our military response (given our capability) appears to be disproportionately low. A guerrilla war can be won only by a minimum manpower ratio of 10:1, whereas the present ratio is no better than 5:1. Our present level of commitment of military forces merely prolongs the war; it does not aim to restore peace by means of victory.[95]

If on the other hand, North Viet Nam and the United States are considered as foreign nations intervening on opposite sides of an armed conflict, then in terms of money, materiel, manpower, and overtness the United States has intervened to a degree disproportion-

---

92. For a rather effective presentation of the North Vietnamese version of the Tonkin Incidents see Nguyen Nghe, Facing the Skyhawks (pamphlet printed in Hanoi, 1964). For an attack on the legality of the United States response see I. F. Stone, *International Law and the Tonkin Bay Incidents*, in VIET-NAM READER 307-15. For the U.S. position see references cited note 94 *infra*.

93. *Cf.* Kunz, *The Distinctiveness of the International Legal System*, 22 OHIO ST. L.J. 447 (1961).

94. *Cf.* the White House Statement of February 7, 1965, BACKGROUND INFORMATION 146-47; see also *id.* at 148-52 for the context used to justify extending the war to North Viet Nam. No charge is made that the attacks on United States military installations were ordered or performed by North Viet Nam personnel.

95. *Cf.* note 41 *supra*; see also General Gavin's testimony before the Senate Foreign Relations Committee, VIETNAM HEARINGS 270-71.

ately greater than has North Viet Nam.[96] In the early period of the war the Vietcong captured most of its equipment from the Saigon regime and the level of material support from the North was low.

The objective of American military strategy is apparently to destroy enough that is important to Hanoi and the N.L.F. to bring about an eventual *de facto* reduction of belligerent action or to force Hanoi to make a satisfactory offer of negotiations. Are there any legal rules that restrict such a strategy in terms of duration, intensity, or destruction? This question seems so central to the future of international law that it is regrettable, to say the least, that the Memorandum does not discuss it. That formalistic document implies that if a state claims to use force in self-defense, and supports its claim with a legal argument, and if the United Nations does not explicitly overrule that claim, international law has nothing further to contribute.[97] I would argue, in contrast, that it is crucial to determine what limiting considerations come into play at this point. It is certainly a regressive approach to international law to assume that if a state alleges "self-defense," it may in its untrammeled discretion determine what military action is reasonably necessary and proportional. The opposing belligerent strategies in Viet Nam seem to call for legal explanation, especially in view of the inability of either side to "win" or "settle" the war; the present standoff causes great destruction of life and property without progressing toward "a resolution" of the conflict.

The Relevance of Commitments to Defend South Viet Nam. The second main section of the Legal Adviser's Memorandum is devoted to establishing that the United States "has made commitments and given assurances, in various forms and at different times, to assist in the defense of South Viet-Nam." Much confusion is generated by a very misleading play on the word commitment. In one sense, commitment means a pledge to act in a specified manner. In another sense, commitment means an obligation of law to act in a specified manner.

During 1965-66 the United States clearly came to regard itself as having made a commitment qua pledge to assist in the defense of South Viet Nam. President Johnson expressed this pledge on many occasions. Two examples are illustrative:

---

96. For an account of some features of the escalation see MANSFIELD, ET AL., REPORT TO SENATE FOREIGN RELATIONS COMM., 89TH CONG., 2D SESS., THE VIETNAM CONFLICT: THE SUBSTANCE AND THE SHADOW (Comm. Print Jan. 6, 1966). See also SHAPLEN xii, xxii; VIET-NAM WITNESS 307-49.

97. A state, in effect, satisfies the requirements of international law merely by filing a brief on its own behalf.

We are in Viet Nam to fulfill one of the most solemn pledges of the American nation. Three Presidents—President Eisenhower, President Kennedy, and your present President—over 11 years have committed themselves and have promised to help defend this small and valiant nation.[98]

We are there because we have a promise to keep. Since 1954 every American President has offered support to the people of South Viet Nam. We have helped to build, and we have helped to defend. Thus, over many years, we have made a national pledge to help South Viet Nam defend its independence.[99]

The present commitment entailing a major military effort is of a very different order than the early conditional offers of economic and military assistance made by President Eisenhower.[100] American involvement in Vietnam is usually traced to a letter from President Eisenhower to Diem on October 23, 1954, in which the spirit of the undertaking was expressed in the following sentence: "The purpose of this offer is to assist the Government of Viet-Nam in developing and maintaining a strong, viable state, capable of resisting attempted subversion or aggression through military means." The letter contains no hint of a pledge. In fact, the United States conditions its offer to assist with a reciprocal expectation: "The Government of the United States expects that this aid will be met by performance on the part of the Government of Viet-Nam in undertaking needed reforms."[101] It is important to note that the letter contained no reference to SEATO despite the formation of the organization a few weeks before it was written, and that the role of the United States was premised upon satisfactory domestic progress in South Viet Nam.

As late as September 1963, President Kennedy said in a TV interview: "In the final analysis, it is their war. They are the ones who have to win it or lose it. We can help them, we can give them equipment, we can send our men out there as advisers, but they have to win it—the people of Viet Nam—against the Communists. We are prepared to continue to assist them, but I don't think that the war can be won unless the people support the effort. . . ."[102] This expression of American involvement emphasizes its discretionary and reversible character, and again implies that the continuation of American assistance is condi-

98. N.Y. Times, July 29, 1965.
99. N.Y. Times, April 8, 1965.
100. LARSON & LARSON, VIETNAM AND BEYOND 17-29 (1965).
101. BACKGROUND INFORMATION 67-68.
102. Id. at 99.

tional upon certain steps being taken by the Saigon regime. Even in 1965 Secretary Rusk in an address to the Annual Meeting of the American Society of International Law, provided a legal defense of the United States position in Viet Nam that stopped short of averring a commitment qua legal obligation. Mr. Rusk did not once refer to SEATO in his rather complete coverage of the subject. The crucial explanation of the American presence is contained in the following passage:

> In resisting the aggression against it, the Republic of Viet-Nam is exercising its right of self-defense. It called upon us and other states for assistance. And in the exercise of the right of collective self-defense under the United Nations Charter, we and other nations are providing such assistance. The American policy of assisting South Viet-Nam to maintain its freedom was inaugurated under President Eisenhower and continued under Presidents Kennedy and Johnson.[103]

Each successive increase in the level of American military involvement has been accompanied by an intensification of rhetoric supporting our presence in Viet Nam. By 1965 President Johnson was, as we observed, referring to Viet Nam as "one of the most solemn national pledges." It is disconcerting to realize that the United States has at each stage offset a deteriorating situation in South Viet Nam by increasing both its military and rhetorical commitment. This process discloses a gathering momentum; at a certain point, policy becomes virtually irreversible. President Johnson's use of the rhetoric of commitment communicates the irreversibility of this policy and conveys a sense of the futility and irrelevance of criticism. If we have a commitment of honor, contrary considerations of prudence and cost are of no concern.[104]

But no commitment qua pledge has the capacity to generate a commitment qua legal obligation. The Administration seems to want simultaneously to invoke both senses of the notion of commitment in order to blunt and confuse criticism. A commitment qua legal obligation is, by definition, illegal to renounce. To speak of commitment in a legal memorandum is particularly misleading. To the extent that we have *any* commitment it is a *pledge of policy*.

Secretary Rusk has injected a further confusion into the debate by his stress on "the SEATO commitment" in the course of his testimony

---

103. Rusk, *Address*, 1965 PROC. AM. SOC. INT'L L. 251-52.

104. For this reason the Administration is hostile to domestic criticism. It is, above all, unresponsive to this qualitative aspect of our presence in Viet Nam. *Cf.* President Johnson's speech at Johns Hopkins University on April 7, 1965, in VIETNAM HEARINGS 640-44.

before the Senate Foreign Relations Committee in the early months of 1966.[105] He said, for instance, in his prepared statement: "It is this fundamental SEATO obligation that has from the outset guided our actions in Vietnam."[106] The notion of the obligation is derived from Article IV (1) of the SEATO treaty which says that "each party recognizes that aggression by means of armed attack . . . would endanger its own peace and safety, and agrees that it will in that event act to meet the common danger in accordance with its constitutional processes." It is somewhat doubtful that Article IV(1) can be properly invoked at all in Viet Nam because of the difficulty of establishing "an armed attack."[107] Secretary Rusk contends, however, that this provision not only *authorizes* but *obliges* the United States to act in the defense of South Viet Nam.[108]

Ambiguity again abounds. If the commitment to act in Viet Nam is incorporated in a treaty, the United States is legally bound. Such an interpretation of Article IV(1) would apply equally to other states that have ratified the SEATO treaty. None of the other SEATO signatories acknowledge such "a commitment" to fulfill a duty of collective self-defense, nor does the United States contend they have one. France and Pakistan oppose altogether any military effort on behalf of the Saigon regime undertaken by outside states.

Secretary Rusk later softened his insistence that Article IV(1) imposed a legal commitment qua obligation upon the United States. In an exchange with Senator Fulbright during Senate hearings on Viet Nam, Mr. Rusk offered the following explanation:

> The Chairman. . . . do you maintain that we had an obligation under the Southeastern Asian Treaty to come to the assistance, all-out assistance of South Vietnam? Is that very clear?
> Secretary Rusk. It seems clear to me, sir, that this was an obligation—

---

105. *Id.* at 567. Secretary Rusk explains to the Senate Foreign Relations Committee that "the language of this treaty is worth careful attention. The obligation it imposes is not only joint but several. That is not only collective but individual.

"The finding that an armed attack has occurred does not have to be made by a collective determination before the obligation of each member becomes operative." *Cf.* the shifting views of SEATO obligation recounted in Young, *The Southeast Asia Crisis*, 1963 Hammarskjold Forum 54. Even Mr. Young, a staunch defender of administration policy, notes that "Until the crisis in Laos in 1961, the United States looked upon SEATO as a collective organization which would take military action, with all eight members participating in the actions as well as the decision." *Id.* at 59.

106. Vietnam Hearings 567; note the absence of reference to SEATO in Rusk, *supra* note 103, and in the 1965 legal memorandum, *supra* note 45.

107. See generally SEATO, 3-45, 87-163 (Modelski ed. 1962).

108. Vietnam Hearings 567.

The Chairman. Unilateral.

Secretary Rusk. An obligation of policy. It is rooted in the policy of the treaty. I am not now saying if we had decided we would not lift a finger about Southeast Asia that we could be sued in a court and be convicted of breaking a treaty.[109]

It seems evident if an armed attack has been established, the treaty imposes a legal obligation to engage in collective self-defense of the victim. But in the absence of a collective determination by the SEATO membership that an armed attack has taken place, it is difficult to maintain that Article IV(1) does more than authorize discretionary action in appropriate circumstances.

The Memorandum argues that "the treaty does not require a collective determination that an armed attack has occurred in order that the obligation of Article IV(1) become operative. Nor does the provision require collective decision on actions to be taken to meet the common danger."[110] This interpretation of Article IV(1) is a blatant endorsement of extreme unilateralism, made more insidious by its pretense of "obligation" and its invocation of the multilateral or regional scaffolding of SEATO. Here the legal position of the State Department displays maximum cynicism, resorting to international law to obscure the national character of military action. In essence, the United States claims that it is under an obligation to determine for itself when an armed attack has occurred, and that once this determination is made there arises a further obligation to act in response. This justification for recourse to force is reminiscent of the international law of war prior to World War I, when states were free to decide for themselves when to go to war.[111] The regressive tendency of this position is further intensified by applying it in a situation where there was a background of civil war and where the alleged aggression was low-scale, extended over time, and covert. Under "the Rusk Doctrine" a country alleging "armed attack" seems free to act in self-defense whenever it wishes. The rhetoric of commitment seems connected with the effort to make the policy of support for Saigon irreversible in domestic arenas and credible in external arenas, especially in Saigon and Hanoi, but it has little to do with an appreciation of the relevance of international law to United States action in Viet Nam.

The important underlying question is whether it is permissible to

---

109. *Id.* at 45; see also *id.* at 7-8.

110. *Id.* at 567.

111. For a general survey of progressive attempts to regulate recourse to war see WRIGHT, THE ROLE OF INTERNATIONAL LAW IN THE ELIMINATION OF WAR (1961).

construe an occurrence of "an armed attack" in the circumstances of the internal war in South Viet Nam. If an armed attack can be held to have occurred, then both self-defense and collective self-defense are permissible. The legal status of a claim of collective self-defense is not improved by embedding the claim in a collective defense arrangement. In fact, the collective nature of an arrangement such as SEATO might imply some obligation to attempt recourse to consultative and collective procedures before acting, at least to determine whether an armed attack has occurred and by whom. Under Secretary Rusk's interpretation of the treaty, SEATO members with opposing views on the issue of which side committed an armed attack could become "obligated" to act in "collective self-defense" against one another.[112] Surely this is the *reductio ad absurdum* of collective self-defense.

In terms of both world order and the original understanding of SEATO, the conflict in Viet Nam calls for action, if at all, under Article IV(2).[113] To categorize the conflict under Article IV(1) would seem to require a unanimous collective determination that the assistance given by Hanoi to the Vietcong amounted to an armed attack. Once that determination had been made, it might seem plausible to maintain that the obligation to act in collective self-defense exists on a joint and several basis, and that the United States might join in the defense of the victim of the armed attack without further collective authorization. Unlike the State Department position, the approach outlined in this paragraph requires that a multilateral determination of the facts precede acts of commitment. The United States might help build a more peaceful world by taking seriously the collective procedures governing the use of force which it has taken such an active role in creating.

The Geneva Accords of 1954. The agreements at Geneva were cast in the form of a cease-fire arrangement and a declaration of an agreed procedure for achieving a post-war settlement. The parties to the first war in Viet Nam were the French and the Vietminh, and the agreements were between their respective military commanders. The other powers at Geneva were mere sureties. At Ho Chi Minh's insistence the Saigon regime did not participate; Saigon was evidently dissatisfied from the outset with the terms of settlement.[114] The United States

---

112. *E.g.*, suppose Laos and Thailand became involved in a conflict in which each state accused the other of being an aggressor—and this is not impossible.

113. *Cf.* SEATO *op. cit. supra* note 107, at xiv. It is made clear both that internal conflicts abetted by subversion were to be treated under Article IV(2) and that this provision required consultation as a prerequisite to action and had become "a dead letter."

114. See VIET-NAM WITNESS 74-83. Jean Lacouture has written recently that France

Government was also reluctant to regard the Geneva settlement as binding.[115]

The Final Declaration required elections to be held in July of 1956 "under the supervision of an international commission composed of representatives of the Member States of the International Supervisory Commission."[116] The Memorandum points out that South Viet Nam "did not sign the cease-fire agreement of 1954, nor did it adhere to the Final Declaration of the Geneva Conference" and adds that "the South Vietnamese Government at that time gave notice of its objection in particular to the election provisions of the accords." At the time of the Geneva proceedings, the Saigon regime exerted control over certain areas in the South, and this awkward fact made it unrealistic to suppose that the Geneva terms of settlement would ever be voluntarily carried out. When Diem came to power and the United States moved in to fill the place left vacant by the departure of the French, it became clear, especially in view of the nation-wide popularity of Ho Chi Minh, that the contemplated elections would never be held.[117] In a sense it was naive of Hanoi to accept the Geneva arrangement or to rely upon its implementation.[118]

Saigon objected to the election provisions from the outset because it hoped for a permanent partition of Viet Nam. But permanent partition was so deeply incompatible with the objective sought by the Vietminh in the war against the French that it is hardly reasonable to expect Hanoi to acquiesce. In a sense, Hanoi's willingness to cooperate with the Geneva arrangement until 1956 is more surprising than is its later effort to revive the war in Viet Nam.

The Memorandum says that even assuming the election provisions were binding on South Viet Nam, there was no breach of obligation arising from Saigon's failure "to engage in consultations in 1955, with a view to holding elections in 1956." The justification offered for Saigon's action is that "the conditions in North Viet Nam during that period were such as to make impossible any free and meaningful expression of popular will." But the election provision in the Final Decla-

---

bears a heavy responsibility for its failure to secure full implementation of the Geneva "solution" before withdrawing from Viet Nam; in Lacouture's view France's premature withdrawal created a political vacuum immediately filled by the United States. LACOUTURE 657.

115. VIET-NAM WITNESS 69-83; see LANCASTER 313-58 for a general account of the Geneva settlement.

116. See Article 7, *Final Declaration of Geneva Conference, July 21, 1954,* BACKGROUND INFORMATION 58, 59.

117. LANCASTER 315-16.

118. *Id.* at 313-37.

ration stated no preconditions about the form of interim government in the two zones, and the type of governmental control existing in the North could have been and presumably was anticipated by those who drew up the Final Declaration. The meaning of "free elections" in Communist countries was well known to all countries including the United States, and the conditions prevailing in South Viet Nam were no more conducive to popular expressions of will.[119] The real objection to the elections was a simple one—namely, the assurance that Ho Chi Minh would win.[120] The Memorandum offers only a self-serving endorsement of Saigon's refusal to go along with the terms of settlement, although they had been endorsed by the United States representative, Bedell Smith.[121]

The Memorandum suggests in footnote 10, that North Viet Nam's remedies, had there been "a breach of obligation by the South, lay in discussion with Saigon, perhaps in an appeal to the co-chairmen of the Geneva conference, or in a reconvening of the conference to consider the situation." In light of the failure of the United States to make use of international remedies which it argues are obligatory for Hanoi, this statement is a shocking instance of legal doubletalk. Footnote 10 ends by saying that "Under international law, North Viet Nam had no right to use force outside its own zone in order to secure its political objectives." This again is misleading. No authoritative rules govern the action of the parties in the event that a settlement of internal war breaks down. Certainly if the settlement is not binding on *all* the parties, no one of them is bound by its constraints. In the absence of the Geneva Accords, Saigon would not exist as a political entity. If Saigon repudiates the Accords, Hanoi would seem to be legally free to resume the pursuit of its political objectives and to ignore the creation of a temporary zone in the South. The principle of mutuality of obligation makes it inappropriate to argue that Saigon is free to ignore the Geneva machinery but that Hanoi is bound to observe it.

Furthermore, international law does not forbid the use of force within a single state. If Hanoi may regard Viet Nam as a single country between 1954 and 1956, its recourse to force in pursuit of political objectives is not prohibited even assuming that its "guidance" and "direction" of the Vietcong constitute "a use" of force by North Viet Nam.

The Memorandum misleadingly implies that the International Con-

---

119. On the conduct of elections in Viet Nam see Fall, *Vietnam's Twelve Elections,* The New Republic, May 14, 1966, pp. 12-15.

120. WARNER 84-106, 142-43; *cf.* VIETNAM 191-94, 210-35 (Gettleman ed.).

121. For text of Smith's statement see BACKGROUND INFORMATION 61.

trol Commission (ICC) endorsed the action of the United States and Saigon and condemned the action of North Viet Nam. Both sides were criticized severely by the ICC for violating provisions of the Geneva Accords.[122] It would appear that the massive military aid given to Saigon by the United States was the most overt and disrupting violation, directly contravening the prohibition on the entry of foreign military forces and new military equipment.[123] According to the reasoning of footnote 10, North Viet Nam's remedy lay in discussion and the Geneva machinery. But a quite different line of legal reasoning is taken to justify American activity:[124] action otherwise prohibited by the Geneva Accords is "justified by the international law principle that a material breach of an agreement by one party entitles the other at least to withhold compliance with an equivalent, corresponding, or related provision until the defaulting party is prepared to honor its obligations." One wonders why this "international law principle" is not equally available to North Viet Nam after Saigon's refusal even to consult about holding elections. Why is Hanoi bound by the reasoning of footnote 10 and Washington entitled to the reasoning of reciprocal breach? The self-serving argument of the Memorandum confers competence upon the United States and Saigon to find that a breach has taken place and to select a suitable remedy, but permits Hanoi only to *allege* a breach, and forbids it to take countervailing action until the breach has been impartially verified.

The Authority of the President under the Constitution. I agree with the Legal Adviser's analysis that the President possesses the constitutional authority to use American military forces in Viet Nam without a declaration of war. Past practice and present policy support this conclusion. To declare war against North Viet Nam would further rigidify our own expectations about an acceptable outcome and it would almost certainly escalate the conflict. It might activate dormant collective defense arrangements between North Viet Nam and its allies.

But the Constitution is relevant in another way not discussed by the Memorandum. The President is bound to act in accordance with governing law, including international law. The customary and treaty norms of international law enjoy the status of "the law of the land" and the President has no discretion to violate these norms in the course

---

122. For a representative sample see VIETNAM, *op. cit. supra* note 120, at 160-90.

123. *Cf.* Articles 17, 18, *Agreement on the Cessation of Hostilities in Vietnam*, BACKGROUND INFORMATION 28, 34-35.

124. *Cf.* Department of State White Paper, *Aggression from the North*, in VIET-NAM READER 143-55; for criticism see Stone, *A Reply to White Paper*, in VIET-NAM READER 155-62.

of pursuing objectives of foreign policy. An impartial determination of the compatibility of our action in Viet Nam with international law is highly relevant to the constitutionality of the exercise of Presidential authority in Viet Nam.

The President has the constitutional authority to commit our armed services to the defense of South Viet Nam without a declaration of war *provided* that such "a commitment" is otherwise in accord with international law. Whether all or part of the United States action violates international law is also a constitutional question. International law offers no authoritative guidance as to the use of force *within* South Viet Nam, but the bombing of North Viet Nam appears to be an unconstitutional use of Presidential authority as well as a violation of international law.

IV

It is appropriate to reflect on the role of the international lawyer in a legal controversy of the sort generated by our role in Viet Nam. The rather keen interest in this controversy about international law results mostly from intense disagreement about the overall wisdom of our foreign policy rather than curiosity about the content of the law on the subject. International law has therefore been used as an instrument of persuasion by those who oppose or favor our Viet Nam policy on political grounds. In such a debate we assume that the United States strives to be law-abiding and that, therefore, it is important for partisans of existing policy to demonstrate the compatibility between law and policy and for opponents of the policy to demonstrate the opposite.

This use of international law to bolster or bludgeon foreign policy positions is unfortunate. It creates the impression that international law serves to inflame debate rather than to guide or shape public policy—an impression fostered by the State Department Memorandum. After a decade of fighting in Viet Nam, the Memorandum was issued in response to legal criticisms made by private groups and echoed by a few dissident members of Congress. It blandly whitewashed the existing government position. The tone is self-assured, the method legalistic, and the contribution to an informed understanding of the issues, minimal. None of the difficult questions of legal analysis are considered. In this intellectual context international lawyers with an independent voice need to be heard.

An international lawyer writing about an ongoing war cannot hope to reach clear conclusions about all the legal issues involved. It is virtually impossible to unravel conflicting facts underlying conflicting legal claims. Of course, we can hope that a legal commentator will acknowledge the uncertainties about the facts and that he will offer explicit reasons for resolving ambiguities in the way and to the extent that he does.[125]

Would it not be better, one is tempted to insist, for international lawyers to avoid so controversial and indeterminate a subject as the legal status of American participation in the war in Viet Nam? I think it important openly to raise this question of propriety, but clearly to answer it in the negative. The scholar has the crucial task of demonstrating the intractability of many, although not of all, the legal issues. Such an undertaking defeats, or calls into serious question, the dogmatic over-clarification of legal issues that arises in the more popular discussions of foreign policy questions. The international lawyer writing in the spirit of scholarly inquiry may have more to contribute by raising the appropriate questions than by purporting to give authoritative answers. He may enable public debate to adopt a more constructive and sophisticated approach to the legal issues.

And, finally, an international lawyer not employed by a government can help modify a distorted nationalistic perspective. An international lawyer is, of course, a citizen with strong views on national policy, but his outlook is universalized by the realization that the function of law in world affairs is to reconcile inconsistent national goals. The international lawyer seeks a legal solution that is based upon an appreciation, although not always an acceptance, of the position of "the other side" in an international dispute. His goal is a system of world order in which all nations are constrained for the common good by rules and by procedures for their interpretation and enforcement. This implies a new kind of patriotism, one that is convinced that to succeed, the nation must act within the law in its foreign as well as its domestic undertakings.

But are there occasions upon which it would be proper for a nation to violate international law? It may be contended that the United States must act as it does in Viet Nam because the international procedures of Geneva, the United Nations, and SEATO offer no protection to a victim of aggression such as South Viet Nam. The United States is acting, in this view, to fill a vacuum created by the failures of inter-

---

125. *Cf.* the inscription attributed to "An Old Jew of Galicia" in MILOSZ, THE CAPTIVE MIND 2 (1953):

When someone is honestly 55% right, that's very good and there's no use wrangling. And if someone is 60% right, it's wonderful, and let him thank God. But what's to be said about 75% right? Wise people say this is suspicious. Well, and what about 100% right? Whoever says he's 100% right is a fanatic, a thug, and the worst kind of rascal.

national regulatory machinery. In fact, it is often suggested, the refusal of the United States to act would tempt potential aggressors. Those who emphasize the obligations and ambiguities of power often talk in this vein and warn of the sterility of legalism in foreign affairs.[126] In general terms, this warning is sound, but its very generality is no guide to specific action, especially in the nuclear age. It remains essential to vindicate as explicitly as possible the reasons that might justify violating legal expectations about the use of military power in each instance by documented reference to overriding policies; slogans about peace, security, and freedom are not enough. The analysis must be so conditioned by the specific circumstances that it will not always justify the use of force. I do not believe that such an argument can convincingly be made with respect to Viet Nam, and therefore I affirm the relevance of legal criteria of limitation. If an argument in favor of military intervention is offered, then it should stress the limits and weaknesses of law or the priority of national over international concerns.[127] We would then gain a better understanding of what law can and cannot do than is acquired by the manipulative straining of legal rules into contrived coincidence with national policies.[128]

V

The foregoing analysis points to the following set of conclusions:

1) The United States insistence upon treating North Vietnamese assistance to the Vietcong as "an armed attack" justifying recourse to "self-defense" goes a long way toward abolishing the legal significance of the distinction between civil war and international war. Without this distinction, we weaken a principal constraint upon the scope and scale of violence in international affairs—the confinement of violence associated with internal wars to the territory of a single political unit.[129] Another adverse consequence of permitting "self-defense" in response to covert aggression is to entrust nations with very wide discretion to determine for themselves the occasions upon which recourse to *overt*

---

126. See generally the writings of the critical legalists. *E.g.*, KENNAN, AMERICAN DIPLOMACY 1900-1950, 95, 96 and 100; MORGENTHAU, IN DEFENSE OF THE NATIONAL INTEREST (1951).

127. Little systematic attention has been given to the rationale and logic for rejecting the claims of law under certain circumstances in human affairs. The consequence is to lead perceptions into naive over-assertions or cynical denials of the relevance of law to behavior.

128. There is a role for adversary presentation, but there is a more important need to seek bases upon which to appraise adversary claims.

129. One can emphasize the refusal to permit external sanctuary for actors supporting an internal war as a constructive precedent, but its reciprocal operation creates dangers of unrestrained violence. See generally HALPERN, LIMITED WAR IN THE NUCLEAR AGE (1963).

violence across international boundaries is permissible.[130] An extension of the doctrine of self-defense would defeat a principal purpose of the United Nations Charter—the delineation of fixed, narrow limits upon the use of overt violence by states in dispute with one another.

2) The United States made no serious attempt to exhaust international remedies prior to recourse to unilateral military power. The gradual unfolding of the conflict provided a long period during which attempts at negotiated settlement could have taken place. Only belatedly and in a *pro forma* fashion did the United States refer the dispute to the United Nations. The United States made no attempt to comply with "the international law principle" alleged by footnote 10 of the Memorandum to govern the action of North Viet Nam. Nor did it attempt during the early phases of the war to subordinate its discretion to the Geneva machinery. No use was made even of the consultative framework of SEATO, an organization inspired by United States initiative for the specific purpose of inhibiting Communist aggression in Southeast Asia.[131] Policies of force were unilaterally adopted and put into execution; no account was taken of the procedural devices created to give a collective quality to decisions about the use of force. Yet the prospect for controlling violence in world affairs depends upon the growth of limiting procedural rules and principles.

3) By extending the scope of violence beyond the territory of South Viet Nam the United States has created an unfortunate precedent in international affairs. Where international institutions fail to provide clear guidance as to the character of permissible action, national actions create quasi-legislative precedents. In view of the background of the conflict in Viet Nam (including the expectation that South Viet Nam would be incorporated into a unified Viet Nam under the control of Hanoi after the French departure), the American decision to bomb North Viet Nam sets an unfortunate precedent. If North Viet Nam and its allies had the will and capability to employ equivalent military force, the precedent would even allow them to claim the right to bomb United States territory in reprisal.

4) The widespread domestic instability in the Afro-Asian world points up the need for an approach to internal war that aims above all to insulate this class of conflict from intervention by the great powers. The early use of peace observation forces, border control machinery, restraints on the introduction of foreign military personnel, and standby

---

130. *Cf.* Henkin, *supra* note 70.

131. On the creation of SEATO see SEATO, *op. cit. supra* note 107, introduction, xiii-xix.

mediation appears possible and beneficial. Responses to allegations of "aggression" should be verified prior to the unilateral use of defensive force, especially when time is available. Claims of covert aggression might then be verified with sufficient authority and speed to mobilize support for community security actions.

5) In the last analysis, powerful nations have a responsibility to use defensive force to frustrate aggression when international machinery is paralyzed. Viet Nam, however, does not provide a good illustration of the proper discharge of this responsibility. North Viet Nam's action does not seem to constitute "aggression." Available international machinery was not used in a proper fashion. The domestic conditions prevailing in South Viet Nam were themselves so inconsistent with prevailing ideals of welfare, progress, and freedom that it is difficult to claim that the society would be better off as a result of a Saigon victory. The massive American presence has proved to be a net detriment, greatly escalating the war, tearing apart the fabric of Vietnamese society, and yet not likely to alter significantly the political outcome. The balance of domestic and area forces seems so favorable to the Vietcong that it is unlikely that the N.L.F. can be kept forever from political control. The sacrifice of lives and property merely postpones what appears to be an inevitable result. The United States voluntarily assumed a political responsibility for the defense of South Viet Nam that has been gradually converted into a political commitment and a self-proclaimed test of our devotion to the concept of collective self-defense. This responsibility is inconsistent with the requirements of world order to the extent that it depends upon unilateral prerogatives to use military power. The national interest of the United States would be better served by the embrace of *cosmopolitan isolationism*—either we act in conjunction with others or we withdraw. We are the most powerful nation in world history. It is hubris to suppose, however, that we are the policemen of the world.[132] Our wasted efforts in Viet Nam suggest the futility and frustration of the politics of over-commitment. We are not the only country in the world concerned with containing Communism. If we cannot find cooperative bases for action

---

132. Even Secretary Rusk has pointed out the limitations upon American power in emphatic terms: "We do not regard ourselves as the policeman of the universe. . . . If other governments, other institutions, or other regional organizations can find solutions to the quarrels which disturb this present scene, we are anxious to have this occur." VIETNAM HEARINGS 563; and Secretary McNamara stated in an address to the American Society of Newspaper Editors delivered at Montreal on May 18, 1966: ". . . neither conscience nor sanity itself suggests that the United States is, should, or could be the global gendarme." N.Y. Times, May 19, 1966, p. 11.

we will dissipate our moral and material energies in a series of Viet Nams. The tragedy of Viet Nam provides an occasion for rethinking the complex problems of use of military power in world affairs and calls for an examination of the increasingly imperial role of the United States in international society. Perhaps we will discover the relevance of international law to the *planning* and *execution* of foreign policy as well as to its *justification*. Certainly the talents of the State Department's Legal Adviser are wasted if he is to be merely an official apologist summoned long after our President has proclaimed "a solemn national commitment."

International Law and the United States Role in
Viet Nam: A Reply†

JOHN NORTON MOORE*

In a recent issue of the *Yale Law Journal* Professor Richard Falk
raises a number of questions about the lawfulness of the United States
role in Viet Nam.[1] The importance of some of these questions for the
direction of contemporary international law as well as for the appraisal
of the United States role in Viet Nam calls for continuing dialogue.

In analyzing the United States role in Viet Nam, Professor Falk
focuses on the problem of the international law of "internal war."[2] He
indicates that "the central issue is whether an externally abetted internal war belongs in either of the traditional legal categories of war—
'civil' or 'international.'"[3] In answering this question and the sub-

† Prof. Moore's article is a response to the arguments made by Prof. Richard Falk in
International Law and the United States Role in the Viet Nam War, 75 YALE L.J. 1122
(1966). Prof. Falk's response to this article appears *infra* at 1095. Limitations of time required that we give Prof. Falk the last word.—eds.
* Associate Professor of Law, University of Virginia; B.A. 1959, Drew University; LL.B.
1962, Duke Law School; LL.M. 1965, Univ. of Illinois. Graduate Fellow, Yale Law School,
1965-66.
1. Falk, *International Law and the United States Role in the Viet Nam War*, 75 YALE
L.J. 1122 (1966).
A condensation of Professor Falk's views carries some risk of distortion. The reader is
urged to consult Professor Falk's article before reading this reply.
My own views are elaborated and further documented in Moore, *The Lawfulness of
Military Assistance to the Republic of Viet-Nam*, 61 AM. J. INT'L L. 1 (1967). Additional
background documentation supporting this view may be found in Moore & Underwood,
The Lawfulness of United States Assistance to the Republic of Viet Nam, 112 CONG. REC.
14,943 (daily ed. July 14, 1966), reprinted in 5 DUQUESNE L. REV. 235 (1967).
See also Alford, *The Legality of American Military Involvement in Viet Nam: A Broader
Perspective*, 75 YALE L.J. 1109 (1966); Partan, *Legal Aspects of the Vietnam Conflict*, 46
B.U.L. REV. 281 (1966); Wright, *Legal Aspects of the Viet-Nam Situation*, 60 AM. J. INT'L
L. 750 (1966).
2. Falk, *supra* note 1, at 1122.
3. *Id.*

sidiary questions it poses Falk constructs a framework focused on assistance in the context of civil strife. Analytically, as a tool for clarifying policy choices, he divides violent conflict into Type I conflict, involving "the direct and massive use of military force by one political entity across a frontier of another,"[4] Type II conflict, involving "substantial military participation by one or more foreign nations in an internal struggle for control,"[5] and Type III conflict, involving "internal struggle for control of a national society, the outcome of which is virtually independent of external participation."[6] He postulates that while it is appropriate "to use force in self-defense"[7] in Type I conflict, in Type II conflict it is only "appropriate . . . to take off-setting military action confined to the internal arena,"[8] and in Type III conflict "it is inappropriate for a foreign nation to use military power to influence the outcome."[9] Professor Falk then characterizes the Viet Nam conflict as Type III,[10] but "if this position entailing non-participation is rejected,"[11] it follows, according to Falk's view, that international law prohibits United States participation in the Viet Nam conflict or at least limits the maximum response to Type II counter-intervention within the internal arena of South Viet Nam.[12]

Although his critique is both scholarly and creative, the framework proposed by Professor Falk is over-simplified for use in clarifying Viet Nam policy choices. His resulting conclusions about the illegality of the United States role in Viet Nam are unsound. The Viet Nam conflict is highly ambiguous and it begs the question to analyze it in a framework for "civil strife."[13] Although generalization is a useful tool for decision, a generalization that the Viet Nam conflict is either Type II or Type III "civil strife" ignores features of the total context which are crucial in any assessment of long run community common interest. Viet Nam, while evidencing features of "civil strife," also evidences features of the divided nation problem and raises questions of per-

---

4. *Id.* 1126.
5. *Id.*
6. *Id.*
7. *Id.*
8. *Id.*
9. *Id.*
10. *Id.* 1127.
11. *Id.*
12. *Id.* Professor Falk seems to retreat from the non-participation argument when he later asserts: "International law offers no authoritative guidance as to the use of force *within* South Viet Nam, but the bombing of North Viet Nam appears to be . . . a violation of international law." *Id.* 1155.
13. Professor Falk begins to beg the question in his second sentence when he says: "A war is usefully classified as internal when violence takes places primarily within a single political entity, regardless of foreign support for the contending factions." *Id.* 1122.

missible use of force across de facto boundaries and cease-fire lines. Analysis of the lawfulness of the United States role must consider this total context in the light of the major community policies at stake.

Real-World Viet Nam: An Ambiguous Context

Both sides in the Viet Nam debate characteristically select from the highly ambiguous context those features which reinforce their perceptions of the conflict. The "White Papers"[14] issued by the State Department in 1961 and 1965 painted too one-sided a picture of the conflict in not recognizing the extent of indigenous support for the Viet Cong within South Viet Nam and in proclaiming a homespun view of the failure to implement the election provisions of the Geneva Accords. As a result, the White Paper model of "aggression from the North" has never captured the complex reality of the Viet Nam problem. But similarly, critics of Viet Nam policy have also engaged in this "model building." In characterizing the conflict as a "civil war" and the United States role as "intervention," they focus on the features of the context pointing to Vietnamese national unity, the ill-fated unity and election provisions in the Accords, and the instability of governments in the South. In building this "civil war-intervention" model critics characteristically do not focus on the very real ambiguities in the Geneva settlement, the more than twelve year territorial, political and ideological separation of the North and South, the existence of a cease-fire line dividing North and South, and the close relations between Hanoi and the Viet Cong. Professor Falk's model essentially reflects the critics' one-sided focus.[15] As a result his first choice characterization of the conflict as "an internal struggle for control of a national society, the outcome of which is virtually independent of external participation [Type III conflict]," is misleading for purposes of evaluating the permissibility of United States assistance. The issues in Viet Nam are not nearly so neat and tidy and no amount of "model

---

14. U.S. DEP'T OF STATE, A THREAT TO THE PEACE: NORTH VIET-NAM'S EFFORT TO CONQUER SOUTH VIET-NAM (1961); U.S. DEP'T OF STATE, AGGRESSION FROM THE NORTH, THE RECORD OF NORTH VIET-NAM'S CAMPAIGN TO CONQUER SOUTH VIET-NAM (1965) (reprinted in 52 DEP'T STATE BULL. 404).

15. Professor Quincy Wright relies on a similar substantially one-sided fact selection in building a "model" of the conflict as civil strife between Hanoi and Saigon. See Wright, supra note 1, at 756-59.

It is somewhat uncertain whether Professor Falk's Type III characterization refers to "civil strife" within the South, "civil strife" between North and South, or both. Although he indicates that he regards "the war in South Vietnam primarily as a Type III conflict," much of the evidence which he relies on for this characterization seems to argue more for a North-South characterization. See Falk, supra note 1, at 1128-32. See also the North-South arguments, id. at 1138 and 1153 and notes 45, 48 and 67 infra.

building" will make them so. Real-world Viet Nam combines some elements of civil strife (both within the South and between North and South) with elements of the cold war divided nation problem and "aggression from the North," all complicated by an uncertain international settlement. Because of the complexity of this total context, neither the official nor critical models provides a sufficiently sensitive analytic tool for clarifying policy choices in the conflict. The starting point for selection of important contextual features must be analysis of the principal community values at stake.

A prominent feature of contemporary international law is the prohibition of coercion in international relations as a strategy of major change. The most widely accepted understanding of the requirements of both customary international law and the United Nations Charter is that force pursuant to the right of individual or collective defense or expressly authorized by the centralized peacekeeping machinery of the United Nations is lawful. Essentially all other major uses of force are unlawful.[16] These norms reflect awareness both of the great destructiveness of war and of the necessity for the maintenance of defensive rights in a world divided between competing public order systems and with only limited expectations toward the success of existing centralized peace-keeping machinery. At a lower level of generality customary international law and the United Nations Charter outlaw major use of military force to redress grievances, however deeply felt, in the absence of major military attack on fundamental values such as political and territorial integrity. In the nuclear age it is usually better that international disputes not be settled than that they be settled by unilateral military strategies. And this is particularly true of disputes between the major contending public order sytems, with their almost unlimited potential for escalation and destruction. These community norms also reflect the judgment, evident as well in national law, that when centralized peace-keeping machinery is not effectively available it is necessary to preserve the right of defense to those attacked. In a world in which power plays a large role in international affairs, this right of defense is a major source of control and sanction against aggression.[17] As such, it may be crucial to conflict minimization that this defensive right be maintained.

---

16. *See* M. McDougal & F. Feliciano, Law and Minimum World Public Order 121-260 (1961). *See also* McDougal & Lasswell, *The Identification and Appraisal of Diverse Systems of Public Order*, 53 Am. J. Int'l L. 1 (1959).
17. *See generally* H. Hart, The Concept of Law 208-31 (1963); H. Morgenthau, Politics Among Nations 293-96 (3d ed. 1966).

In light of the critical values of world order at stake, conflict between contending governments of a nation at least de facto divided into continuing international entities and paying allegiance to contending public order systems presents a problem of major international concern. "Rational community policy must be directed to the coercive interactions of territorially organized communities of consequential size, whatever the 'lawfulness' of their origin."[18] And this is particularly true of boundaries separating major contending public order systems. The balance of power makes the use of the military instrument across such boundaries particularly hazardous, as both Korea and Viet Nam have demonstrated. For the purposes of assessing the lawfulness of coercion across such boundaries and the lawfulness of extending assistance to the entity attacked, these real-world boundaries must be recognized as such. The label "civil strife" must not be allowed to obscure this major problem in conflict minimization. If we believe that long-run community common interest in minimization of coercion is against unilateral coercion across continuing de facto international boundaries and cease-fire lines, particularly when such boundaries separate the major cold war camps, then for purposes of policy clarification about the lawfulness of force, conflict between North and South Viet Nam is not "civil strife" regardless of other features of the context evidencing similarity with "civil strife." The ambiguous 1954 Geneva settlement certainly differentiates Viet Nam from the other divided nations of China, Germany and Korea, but the continuing and at least de facto division of Viet Nam has a substantial parallel to the cold war divided nation problem when analyzed with regard to the vital policies of minimum world public order. It is in the long run common interest not to permit change of existing and relatively permanent international divisions by unilateral military coercion however unjust the existence of the condition may seem to the protagonist of change. The Kashmir and Palestine disputes present additional contemporary examples of the importance of this principle.

As applied to Viet Nam, there is substantial evidence of the at least de facto separateness of North and South, regardless of one's view of the effect of the Geneva settlement. Thus, the State of Viet Nam (the predecessor government of South Viet Nam) and the Democratic Republic of Viet Nam (North Viet Nam) were to some extent separate de facto states even prior to the Accords of 1954,[19] and subsequent to the Ac-

---

18. M. McDougal & F. Feliciano, *supra* note 16, at 221 n.222.
19. For discussion on this point see Moore & Underwood, *supra* note 1, 112 Cong. Rec. at 14,944.

cords their real separateness became much stronger. Prior to the Accords each government was recognized by a number of states as the government of Viet Nam and each carried on separate international activities.[20] Although nations had differing expectations from the Geneva settlement, the major effect of the settlement was to consolidate territorially the existing division of Viet Nam between the two rival governments. South Viet Nam is now recognized by about 60 nations and North Viet Nam by about 24, a recognition pattern closely approximating that of North and South Korea.[21] The substantial expectations of the separateness of North and South Viet Nam after the Accords is indicated by the January, 1957 draft resolution of the U.S.S.R., a Co-Chairman of the Geneva Conference, calling for the simultaneous admission to the United Nations of North Viet Nam, South Viet Nam, North Korea and South Korea as four separate "states."[22] Both North and South have clearly functioned for twelve years since the Accords as separate international entities with governmental institutions of their own operating along different ideological lines. Both have long maintained separate foreign embassies and diplomatic representation, and have administered separate territories and populations. That the contending governments claim sovereignty to all of Viet Nam can hardly be decisive for purposes of conflict minimization, as the situation is parallel in this respect to that in Korea, China and Germany. Under the circumstances, this at least de facto

---

20. The State of Viet Nam had been recognized by about 30 to 35 states prior to the Geneva settlement. *See* DOCUMENTS RELATING TO THE DISCUSSION OF KOREA AND INDO-CHINA AT THE GENEVA CONFERENCE (Misc. No. 16) CMD No. 9186 (1964); 31 PARL. SESSIONAL PAPERS 109, 133 (1953-54); U.S. DEP'T OF STATE, AMERICAN FOREIGN POLICY—CURRENT DOCUMENTS 121 n.3 (1958).

The Democratic Republic of Viet Nam had been recognized by the People's Republic of China, the Soviet Union and a number of East European Nations. *See* B. MURTI, VIETNAM DIVIDED 171 (1964). *See also* ROYAL INSTITUTE OF INTERNATIONAL AFFAIRS, SURVEY OF INTERNATIONAL AFFAIRS 1949-50 429-30 (1953).

21. *See* U.S. DEP'T OF STATE, LEGAL STATUS OF SOUTH VIET-NAM (4/31b-865BT).

South Korea has full relations with about 64 nations while North Korea is recognized by about 25. *Id.*

22. *See* 11 U.N. GAOR Annexes, Agenda Item No. 25, at 5-7 U.N. Doc. A/SPC/L.9 (1957).

During the debates on this and other draft resolutions calling for the admission of the Republic of Viet Nam, the three Soviet delegates said between them:

[B]oth in Korea and in Viet-Nam two separate States existed, which differed from one another in political and economic structure. . . .

The fact was that there were two States in Korea and two States in Viet-Nam. . . .

The realistic approach was to admit that there were two States with conflicting political systems in both Korea and Viet-Nam. In the circumstances, the only possible solution was the simultaneous admission of the four countries constituting Korea and Viet-Nam. . . .

[T]wo completely separate and independent States had been established in each of those countries, [Korea and Viet Nam] with different political, social and economic systems.

11 U.N. GAOR Spec. Pol. Comm. 79, 81, 87, 101 (1957).

separation can not be ignored for meaningful clarification of policy alternatives.

In addition to the continuing real-world division of Viet Nam, a factor which exists as a crucial contextual feature regardless of any interpretation of the Geneva settlement, North and South are also divided by a military cease-fire line created by that settlement. In a Special Report in 1962 the International Commission for Supervision and Control in Viet Nam found that North Vietnamese military activity across that line was a specific violation of the Accords.[23] Some critics reply by pointing out that the Commission also found that South Viet Nam violated the Accords by accepting American defensive aid. But this neutral reporting proves little. The crucial question is whether these indicated breaches should be treated alike for purposes of community policy about maintenance of world public order. The clear answer is no. When put in context of community norms proscribing the use of force for settlement of disputes, the indicated breach of the North is exactly that kind of aggressive coercion proscribed, whereas the indicated breach of the South is permitted defensive response to such coercion. It is not at all anomalous in this context to assert that the norm, material breach of agreement justifies suspension of corresponding obligations, is available as a defense to the South but not the North.[24] For even if the South did breach the election provisions of the Accords, and there are serious questions here as to the legal position of the South with respect to these provisions of the Accords,[25] aggressive military strategies by the North are not a permitted response to such breach. The point is that there is a major difference in character of the indicated breaches North and South which is crucial for community policies of maintenance of minimum order and which is inherent in overriding community norms as to the lawfulness of the use of force. Failure to recognize this distinction is failure to grasp the essential community policies against unilateral coercive change embodied in the United Nations Charter. Rational community policy concerned with conflict minimization must be concerned with coercion across such international cease-fire lines. This is true regardless of the

23. SPECIAL REPORT TO THE CO-CHAIRMEN OF THE GENEVA CONFERENCE ON INDO-CHINA, CMD. NO. 1755 (1962); 39 PARL. SESSIONAL PAPERS 6-7 (1961-62).

24. Professor Falk fails to meet this point. In criticizing the State Department's "breach of agreement" argument he says: "One wonders why this 'international law principle' is not equally available to North Viet Nam after Saigon's refusal even to consult about holding elections. Why is Hanoi bound by the reasoning of footnote 10 and Washington entitled to the reasoning of reciprocal breach?" Falk, *supra* note 1, at 1154.

25. For discussion of these questions see Moore, *The Lawfulness of Military Assistance to the Republic of Viet Nam, supra* note 1.

merits of the dispute between North and South with respect to the Accords. Even if the underlying agreement created expectations denied by one of the participants, community policies against force as a strategy of change militate against resumption of hostilities. The existence of such an international cease-fire line in Viet Nam is another particular feature casting doubt on the utility of characterization of the conflict as an "internal struggle for control of a national society, the outcome of which is virtually independent of external participation."

It is one of the paradoxes of the Viet Nam dialogue that both sides rely on the 1954 Geneva settlement. In characterizing the Viet Nam conflict as a Type III conflict, Professor Falk relies heavily on a model of the Geneva settlement which he pictures as basically creating expectations of short run unification of Viet Nam under the government of Ho Chi Minh, although he admits "the intentions of the participants at Geneva were somewhat ambiguous."[26] The subsequent United States role in assisting the South, according to this model, "contrasts radically" with "the expectations created at Geneva."[27] There are factors in the manifold of events constituting the Geneva settlement that point to such a conclusion. Chief among them are Articles 6 and 7, the "no boundary" and "election" provisions of the Final Declaration. These provisions suggest that at least those participants agreeing to the Final Declaration expected that Viet Nam would be united by elections in 1956 and that the division was to be temporary. But the language of the Final Declaration is not the only source for ascertaining the genuine expectations of all the participants and in this case may be unreliable. There are at least equally important factors in the context of the Geneva settlement that cast serious doubt on the legiti-

---

26. Falk, *supra* note 1, at 1129. This theme runs all through Professor Falk's critique and constitutes one of his major assumptions. By way of some representative statements:

My own judgment, based on the analysis of the Geneva settlement in 1954, is that the war in South Viet Nam represents more an American attempt at "rollback" than a Communist attempt at "expansion." The Geneva Conference looked toward the reunification of the whole of Viet Nam under the leadership of Ho Chi Minh. The introduction into South Viet Nam of an American military presence thus appears as an effort to reverse these expectations and to deny Hanoi the full extent of its victory against the French. *Id.* 1125 n.15.

Hanoi was "entitled" to prevent Saigon from establishing itself as a political entity with independent claims to diplomatic status as a sovereign state. A separation of Viet Nam into two states was not contemplated by the participants at Geneva. *Id.* at 1130 n.31.

[T]he injection of an American political and military presence was, from the perspective of Hanoi, inconsistent with the whole spirit of Geneva. The United States decision to commit itself to maintaining a Western-oriented regime in South Viet Nam upset the expectations regarding the Southeast Asian balance of power . . . . *Id.* 1138.

The strength of Hanoi's claim [to exercise control over the South] arises from . . . the expectations created at Geneva that the elections would confirm that military victory . . . . *Id.* 1138 n.66.

27. *Id.* 1131.

macy of placing major reliance on alleged short run expectations of Hanoi with respect to unification of Viet Nam. These are factors to which Falk does not advert in constructing his model.

The memoirs of Anthony Eden[28] and the preliminary seven point program agreed to by the United States and the United Kingdom and apparently supported by French Prime Minister Mendes-France[29] strongly suggest that the real core of the settlement, at least from a Western standpoint, was partition of Viet Nam between the two major contending public order systems, a division to some extent shared by the Vietnamese people. In fact, Eden, the individual Chairman of the Conference, was a chief proponent of partition although Eisenhower indicated concern because of the loss *of the North* to "Communist enslavement."[30] Nowhere does Eden indicate that he felt he had failed to set up a permanent barrier between Ho Chi Minh and Malaya, one of his chief concerns.[31] *The Survey of International Affairs 1954*, published by the British Royal Institute of International Affairs, has this account of the Viet Minh position at the Conference:

> On 25 May the Viet Minh Foreign Minister, Mr. Dong, put forward a detailed plan, which was clearly in the nature of a first ap-

---

28. A. EDEN, FULL CIRCLE (1960). Eden writes that prior to the conference "it . . . seemed inevitable that large parts of the country would fall under Communist control, and the best hope of a lasting solution lay in some form of partition." *Id.* 117. And "I felt that the Chinese might yet be constrained to come to an arrangement which would . . . allow a free life to some part of Vietnam . . . ." *Id.* 137. And "I decided to persevere at our next meeting [with Chou En-lai] with my plan for what I called the 'protective pad.' Many countries had an interest in this and, if I could once get the conception established, the position might hold, perhaps for years. . . . It would be best if communism could be . . . halted as far north as possible in Vietnam." *Id.* 138. And Eden writes that after the Conference "The Vietnamese had saved more of their country than had at one time seemed possible. . . . In the months ahead the United States would be playing a greater part in all their [Viet Nam, Cambodia and Laos] destinies." *Id.* 160-61. *See also id.* 97, 101-02, 148-49, 156-57.

29. *See id.* 149, 156-57. Under the terms of this program the United States and the United Kingdom agreed "to respect an armistice agreement on Indo-China which:
. . .
2. Preserves at least the southern half of Vietnam, and if possible an enclave in the delta . . . .
3. Does not impose on . . . retained Vietnam any restrictions materially impairing . . . [its] capacity to maintain [a] stable non-Communist regime . . . .
4. Does not contain political provisions which would risk loss of the retained area to Communist control. . . .
Id. 149. According to Eden, M. Mendes-France supported this program. Eden writes that Mendes-France "described to us his negotiations with the Vietminh on the question of the demarcation line in Vietnam and effectively demonstrated that at no point had his position diverged from the minimum terms which had been defined by the Americans and ourselves." *Id.* 156.

30. "To me these French proposals . . . implied nothing else but partition. We knew, from experience in Korea, that this would probably lead to Communist enslavement of millions in the northern partitioned area." D. EISENHOWER, MANDATE FOR CHANGE 432 (Signet ed. 1963).

31. A. EDEN, FULL CIRCLE 97 (1960).

proximation to the "accepting price" of the insurgents . . . . This plan was, clearly, rather more than a proposal for a regroupment of forces; if put into effect it would in fact provide something like a *de facto* military partition of the country, and one that, with its provision that the two areas chosen should be economically viable, seemed to be envisaged as lasting for some time.[32]

The public record indicates that the South Vietnamese government opposed partition and supported provisional control by the United Nations of all of Viet Nam pending free elections.[33] Their refusal to agree to the political provisions of the settlement is consistent with expectations on their part that those provisions would be unworkable from their standpoint and that the agreement would actually result in de facto partition. Moreover, France had entered into a series of independence agreements with the State of Viet Nam, the predecessor government of South Viet Nam, prior to the conclusion of the Indo-China phase of the Geneva Conference[34] and French Foreign Minister Bidault indicated at the Conference that the State of Viet Nam was independent and that it was "fully and solely competent to commit Viet Nam."[35] Both the separate presence of the State of Viet Nam and these statements of the French delegate at the Conference suggest that

---

32.   ROYAL INSTITUTE OF INTERNATIONAL AFFAIRS, SURVEY OF INTERNATIONAL AFFAIRS 1954 48 (1957). And see DO VANG LY, AGGRESSIONS BY CHINA 151 (2d ed. 1960).
    The actual proposal made by the Vietminh Chief Delegate, Mr. Dong, on May 24 was:
    The readjustment is made on the basis of *an exchange of territory*, the following elements to be taken into consideration: area, population, political and economic interests so as to accord each party *zones all of a piece*, relatively widespread and offering facilities for economic activities and administrative control respectively within each zone. The demarcation line between these zones should as much as possible not create communication and transport difficulties within the respective zones.
Ngo Ton Dat, The Geneva Partition of Vietnam and the Question of Reunification During the First Two Years 163 (1963) (unpublished Ph.D. dissertation, Cornell Univ.). The author accompanied the Vietnamese Prime Minister to the Geneva negotiations. He sums up this Vietminh proposal as: "Clearly Mr. Dong's declaration could only mean one thing: the partition of Vietnam." *Id.*
    33.   *See* "The News In Review," *United Nations Review* 2 (Vol. 1, July 1954). Moore & Underwood, *supra* note 1, 112 CONG. REC. at 14981 n.267.
    34.   *See* Moore & Underwood, *supra* note 1, 112 CONG. REC. 14,969-70 nn.22, 23, 33, 36, 41. Like most of the context surrounding the Conference, these agreements were ambiguous and seem not in fact to have effectuated complete independence to the State of Viet Nam prior to the conclusion of the Conference. But taken together these agreements did provide some status to the State of Viet Nam as an international entity in its own right. For a restrictive interpretation of the effect of the agreement initialed on June 4, 1954 see Weinstein, Vietnam's Unheld Elections 12-14 (1966) (Data Paper No. 60, Southeast Asia Program, Cornell Univ.).
    Ngo Ton Dat seems to conclude that the State of Viet Nam was not bound by the Accords since the Commander-in-Chief of the French Union Forces did not have a sufficient delegation of power from the State of Viet Nam to conclude a "general armistice of vital importance." *See* Ngo Ton Dat, *supra* note 32, at 303-10.
    35.   DOCUMENTS RELATING TO THE DISCUSSION OF KOREA AND INDO-CHINA AT THE GENEVA CONFERENCE (Misc. No. 16) CMD. No. 9186 (1954); 31 PARL. SESSIONAL PAPERS 108-09, 132-34 (1953-54).

France did not intend to bind the State of Viet Nam by the political provisions of the Final Declaration. In the face of this French position at the Conference and the clear refusal of the State of Viet Nam to adhere to the political provisions of the agreements,[36] the experienced diplomats at the Conference must have been aware of the possibility that few provisions other than cease-fire and partition would be carried out.[37] In this regard it is significant that even prior to the Conference the State of Viet Nam was recognized by about thirty states and had been endorsed by the General Assembly of the United Nations as a state qualified for membership.[38] Professor Falk himself somewhat inconsistently points out that "at the time of the Geneva proceedings, the Saigon regime exerted control over certain areas in the South, and this awkward fact made it unrealistic to suppose that the Geneva terms of settlement would ever be voluntarily carried out."[39]

Some of the terms of the settlement and the fact that the Final Declaration of the Conference which contained the political settlement provisions was unsigned also suggest that the real settlement was partition or at least that the parties were never really agreed on much but a territorial division and cease-fire. The key to unification would clearly be the election provisions, which were surprisingly vague for so important a question. The only reference to elections in the signed Agreement on the Cessation of Hostilities appears in Article 14(a) and reads in full: "Pending the general elections which will bring about the unification of Viet Nam . . . ." The *unsigned* Final Declaration of the Conference adverts to the election problem only in the three sentences of paragraph seven.[40] The first two sentences are unclear and add little

---

36. *See* COUNCIL ON FOREIGN RELATIONS, THE UNITED STATES IN WORLD AFFAIRS 1954 252-53 (1956).

37. According to P. J. Honey of the University of London:
In signing the agreements they [the Vietnamese Communists] were forced to bow to strong Soviet pressure, a fact that robbed them of much prestige at home, and the only face-saving concession made to them was the unsigned "Declaration of Intention," which prescribed national elections for the reunification of Vietnam, to be held not later than July 1956. The worthlessness of this concession can be seen in a remark made by the Communist North Vietnam (DRV) Prime Minister, Pham Van Dong, to one of my Vietnamese friends immediately after the signing of the agreements. When asked which side he thought would win the elections, Dong replied, "You know as well as I do that there won't be any elections."
P. HONEY, COMMUNISM IN NORTH VIETNAM: ITS ROLE IN THE SINO-SOVIET DISPUTE 5-6 (1966). *See also id.* 67. *But see* Weinstein, *supra* note 34, at 17-18 n.71.

38. 7 U.N. GAOR Annexes, Agenda Item No. 19, at 10, U.N. Doc. A/2341 & Corr. 1 (1952); 7 U.N. GAOR 410 (1952).

39. Falk, *supra* note 1, at 1152. He also writes: "In a sense it was naive of Hanoi to accept the Geneva arrangement or to rely upon its implementation." *Id.*

40. *See* FURTHER DOCUMENTS RELATING TO THE DISCUSSION OF INDO-CHINA AT THE GENEVA CONFERENCE (Misc. No. 20) CMD. NO. 9239 (1954); 31 PARL. SESSIONAL PAPERS 9-11 (1953-54); 161 BRITISH & FOREIGN STATE PAPERS 359-61 (1954).

beyond a date for elections and the general composition of a supervisory commission, and the third sentence leaves the monumental problems to be solved by future consultations between the "representative authorities of the two zones . . . ," one of which was already publicly declaring that it would refuse to be bound by these provisions. This cavalier treatment of the political settlement must be considered a major weakness of the settlement and suggests that the parties were aware of the possibility of an extended partition in Viet Nam. In contrast, the *signed* military cease-fire agreement dealt in great detail with provisions for a continuing cease-fire, and the central feature of the settlement was the division of Viet Nam between two essentially economically viable and at least de facto international entities. The major real impact of the settlement was to stop the fighting and to reinforce an already existing political division. The provisions for allowing initial transfer of civilians between zones[41] also suggest continuing partition and are difficult to reconcile with genuine expectations of short run unification by election. In large part they reflected Western concern about loss *of the North* to Communism and a desire to enable non-Communists in the North to opt for a non-communist system in the South. Victor Bator makes much the same point with respect to the ambiguities of the settlement. According to Bator:

> The contradictions and the equivocations in the documents that emerged from the Geneva Conference gain added emphasis by the procedure by which they were reached. As narrated in memoirs such as those of Anthony Eden, who presided at Geneva, or in the detailed accounts of Bernard B. Fall, Jean Lacouture, and Philippe Devillers, partition—so ambiguously treated in the documents—was the most important subject of bargaining, both in principle and in its geographical application. It was discussed continually, if confidentially within each delegation, but for a time was carefully ignored when the delegations met.
>
> When at last partition was openly breached by the Vietminh, the French and British were elated. From that moment the location of the dividing line became the principal hurdle blocking the road to a settlement. Secretary of State Dulles, in order to underscore his insistence that it be drawn on the 17th parallel and to demonstrate western unity on this point, flew from Washington to Paris to meet with Eden and Premier Pierre Mendes-France. There were discussions even about the viability of the two parts. It is hard to believe that all this activity could have been devoted

---

41. *See* Article 14(d) of the Agreement on the Cessation of Hostilities in Viet Nam, July 20, 1954, and Article 8 of the Final Declaration of the Geneva Conference, July 21, 1954, in SENATE FOREIGN RELATIONS COMM., 89TH CONG. 1ST SESS., BACKGROUND INFORMATION RELATING TO SOUTHEAST ASIA AND VIETNAM 32, 59 (rev. ed. June 16, 1965).

to the location of a temporary military demarcation line, a kind of billeting arrangement that would shortly disappear. The innocent-sounding text of the final agreement must have signified something of greater import.[42]

There is also evidence in the ambiguous context surrounding the Conference which points to the conclusion that Hanoi placed reliance on elections being held in 1956.[43] A review of the negotiations at Geneva,

---

42. Bator, *Geneva; 1954: The Broken Mold*, THE REPORTER, June 30, 1966, at 15, 17. Bator also writes:

> The primary motivation of the Vietminh was to consolidate their rule somewhere, anywhere, in Vietnam. To accomplish this, Ho Chi Minh was willing to make political concessions from his militarily superior position. So it came about that, on May 25, the head of the Vietminh delegation first mentioned partition. It was to be based on a regrouping of forces on either side of a line of demarcation that would give both parties an area with a sufficiently large population to exist independently.

Id. at 17. *See also* B. FALL, VIET-NAM WITNESS 75-76, 123 (1966); DOCUMENTS RELATING TO THE DISCUSSION OF KOREA AND INDO-CHINA AT THE GENEVA CONFERENCE (Misc. No. 16) CMD. No. 9186 (1954) (record of Conference discussions); FURTHER DOCUMENTS RELATING TO THE DISCUSSION OF INDO-CHINA AT THE GENEVA CONFERENCE (Misc. No. 20) CMD. No. 9239 (1954); 31 PARL. SESSIONAL PAPERS (1953-54).

Lacouture candidly points out:

> A great deal of confusion surrounds this Geneva settlement. It must be emphasized that the only texts signed at Geneva were the armistice agreements between the French and the Vietminh. No one at all signed the "final declaration" of the conference— both the United States and South Vietnam had reservations about it—and it carried only the force of suggestion. But apart from the North Vietnamese, the French were the only nation that formally guaranteed to carry out the Geneva accords that provided both for partition at the 17th parallel and for elections.

Lacouture, *Vietnam: The Lessons of War, Hearings on S. 2793 Before the Senate Comm. on Foreign Relations*, 89th Cong., 2d Sess., pt. 1, at 655, 656-57 (1966). Ellen Hammer says of the political settlement provisions of the "Accords":

> [a]lthough the Franco-Vietminh war was ended at Geneva in July 1954, a political solution for Vietnam was posponed to some unspecified future date.
>
> The agreements outlined at Geneva . . . contained few if any provisions for their long-term execution. They were a series of desires for the future, drawn up· by the conference participants.

E. HAMMER, VIETNAM YESTERDAY AND TODAY 247 (1966).

43. *See* Weinstein, *supra* note 34. *See also* G. KAHIN & J. LEWIS, THE UNITED STATES IN VIETNAM 43-65 (1967). These scholars argue that Hanoi placed major reliance on the election provisions and assert a model of the Geneva settlement which de-emphasizes the ambiguities in the political settlement. Interestingly, Kahin and Lewis point out that Dulles indicated in his press statement shortly after the Conference that now the United States could build up "the truly independent states of Cambodia, Laos and southern Vietnam." *Id.* 61. They concluded that SEATO "signalled the American intent to underwrite a separate state in southern Vietnam if, despite the inadmissibility of this under the Geneva Agreements, one could be established." *Id.* 63. The authors, however, fail to draw the inference that the immediate inclusion of "the free territory under the jurisdiction of the State of Vietnam" within the protection of Article IV of the SEATO Treaty, strongly indicated Western expectations that the Geneva settlement would lead to a non-communist South Viet Nam. It should be recalled that Britain and France were also parties to SEATO.

Jean Lacouture points out that Mendes-France addressed a letter to the Saigon leaders the day after the Geneva negotiations "assuring them that France would not recognize another trustee of Vietnam's sovereignty" and ending "any chance of political co-operation between Paris and Hanoi." He refers to this letter and the signing of the SEATO Treaty on the day after Geneva as the two shadows quickly darkening the Geneva Agreement. These and subsequent actions of the British, French, Soviet and United States governments support an interpretation that partition was the core of the agreements. *See* J. LACOUTURE, VIETNAM: BETWEEN TWO TRUCES 11-12 (Vintage ed. 1966).

however, suggests that the core of the settlement was the partition and cease-fire and that the major agreement came when both sides accepted partition as the basis for settlement. There was substantially less agreement on the political settlement provisions and at least the British, American and State of Viet Nam governments were opposed to these provisions, which they feared would work in practice to jeopardize maintenance of a non-communist South. The State of Viet Nam and the United States indicated to the Conference participants that they would not consider themselves bound by these provisions. In light of the major feature of the settlement—a de facto division between two contending governments—and the expressed negative attitudes toward the political settlement provisions by other major participants at the Conference, there is serious doubt about the reasonableness of placing great reliance on the election provision.

The totality of evidence suggests that the Western nations, particularly the United States and Britain, desired that the settlement would lead to a non-communist South and expected that it had some chance of doing so, that the Vietminh desired that the settlement would lead to unification under Northern control and may have expected that takeover by political settlement or military activities would be feasible if the regime in the South proved nonviable, and that the Diem government expected that the agreement would lead to de facto partition because the election provisions were unacceptable to them. Fair interpretation of the settlement should take into account not only asserted expectations of the North, but also the contrary expectations of the United States and the State of Viet Nam *at the time of the settlement* which were communicated to all participants.

The later Soviet lack of concern toward the non-implementation of the political settlement provisions and the Soviet attempt to admit both North and South Viet Nam to the United Nations reinforces the substantial evidence that partition was the core of the settlement.

The point is that there seem to have been only minimal shared expectations on the *political* settlement, and that because of this ambiguity it is particularly unreasonable to assert the "Accords" as a justification for North Vietnamese military activities when de facto partition did result.[44]

When viewed in context there is considerable doubt as to the completeness of the model of the Geneva settlement relied on by Professor

---

44. For a detailed treatment of the background of the Conference and the negotiations leading up to the settlement, see Ngo Ton Dat, *supra* note 32.

Falk in characterizing the conflict as Type III. It seems implicit in much of his argument for this characterization that North and South are one international entity.[45] But the total manifold of events surrounding the settlement suggests that partition was the real core of the settlement. And there can be little doubt that in its total context the political settlement was highly ambiguous. This very ambiguity reinforces the danger to world order inherent in the North attempting to force its asserted expectations by use of the military instrument.

It is perhaps not unimportant that the continuing division of Viet Nam between governments of conflicting ideologies significantly reflects a traumatic split among the Vietnamese people as well as between East and West. The 1954 settlement and continued division have provided an opportunity for the Vietnamese people to choose systems, an opportunity principally taken advantage of by a flood of refugees from North to South.[46] Under the circumstances it is difficult to see the inequity in treating the two divisions as entities whose peo-

---

45. Although Professor Falk's Type III characterization is in his terms a characterization of "the war in South Vietnam," most of the considerations listed by him as leading him to so regard the conflict, such as Ho Chi Minh's asserted expectations from the Geneva settlement, asserted United States neglect of opportunities to negotiate with Hanoi, and the economic strain on Hanoi when relations between the North and South were not normalized, seem implicitly to argue that the conflict is a Type III conflict between the North and South. This suggestion that Falk is in effect substantially arguing that the conflict is civil strife between North and South is reinforced by the notable lack in his stated considerations of any analysis of the degree of independence of the Viet Cong.

In the absence of any real analysis of the relationship between Hanoi and the Viet Cong, particularly of the important questions of extent of military interaction prior to the first substantial increase in United States forces in late 1961, and prior to the commencement of regular bombing of the North in February, 1965, Falk's characterization of the conflict as Type III within South Viet Nam is unconvincing. In fact, most of the considerations which he relies on seem to indicate on their face that Hanoi's role is a major one in the total picture. See Falk, *supra* note 1, at 1127-32, 1137-38, 1151-52, 1158. See *infra* notes 48, 67.

46. According to the *Fourth Interim Report* of the International Control Commission, by July 20, 1955, 892,876 had moved from the North to the South and only 4,269 had moved from the South to the North under Article 14(d). FOURTH INTERIM REPORT OF THE INTERNATIONAL COMMISSION FOR SUPERVISION AND CONTROL IN VIETNAM (Vietnam No. 3) CMD. No. 9654 (1955); 45 PARL. SESSIONAL PAPERS 30, App. IV (1955-56).

These figures seem incomplete but the ratio of civilians going South to those going North probably remained about 10 to 1. This ratio resulted despite what one scholar has termed the "co-ordinated campaign of obstruction instituted by the authorities of the Democratic Republic of Vietnam against persons wishing to move to the south." Dai, *Canada's Role in the International Commission for Supervision and Control in Vietnam,* 4 CAN. YB. INT'L L. 161, 168 (1966).

According to Anthony Eden, "There were some indications of a greater willingness in Vietnam to face partition. There was no love lost between north and south. We felt that the distress at amputation might prove more apparent than real." A. EDEN, FULL CIRCLE 101 (1960).

P. J. Honey writes:
[A]ntagonism of long standing exists between the peoples of North and South Vietnam. The halves were divided for roughly two hundred years between the end of the sixteenth and the end of the eighteenth centuries—the dividing line was remarkably close to the present one—and a state of war existed between them.
P. HONEY, *supra* note 37, at 18.

ples are entitled to freely express their own preferences in regard to governmental institutions and unification. The conclusion "civil strife" obscures serious inquiry about this question of which territorially organized communities in Viet Nam ought to have their own right to self-determination today. Harrison Salisbury's *New York Times* reports on the relation between the N.L.F. and Hanoi indicate that even North Viet Nam concedes, at least publicly, some right to short run southern self-determination.[47] The seriousness with which the South Vietnamese Constituent Assembly functions is an indication of the substantiality of these expectations within the South. The continuing territorial separation of North and South, compounded by the ideological split among the Vietnamese people, has understandably given rise to significant expectations of individualized self-determination in the North and South. Under these circumstances it is at least as reasonable to regard both North and South as entities whose peoples are now entitled to their own self-determination about political institutions and unification as to view North and South as one entity for these purposes.[48]

---

47. *See* N.Y. Times, Jan. 16, 1967, at 1, col. 1.
Brian Crozier points out that:
   [T]he circumstances of the Vietnamese drive to the south, the distance between Saigon and Hanoi, and the difficulty of pre-air age communications have all fostered separatist sentiment in the south. For about 200 years, until the close of the eighteenth century, Vietnam was divided into mutually hostile halves roughly coinciding with the present division. This, too, colours the view that the current troubles are just another civil war.
B. CROZIER, SOUTHEAST ASIA IN TURMOIL 135 (Pelican rev. ed. 1966).
   At least one Vietnamese observer wrote in 1963: "South Vietnam has a large anti-Communist majority. And if the people of South Vietnam can really cast a free vote, it is a foregone conclusion that the Vietnamese nationals will win." Ngo Ton Dat, *supra* note 32, at 385.
48. Although the evidence on which Professor Falk relies to characterize the conflict as Type III seems to argue implicitly for characterization as Type III between North and South, he somewhat inconsistently places major reliance on characterization as Type III *within* South Viet Nam. But the evidence as related at pp. 1070-73 *infra*, simply does not support characterization of the conflict as Type III within South Viet Nam. For even if the insurgency in the South was initially an indigenous reacton to the oppressive measures of the Diem government, a proposition on which scholars differ, *compare* D. PIKE, VIET CONG 53, 80, 321 (1966) *with* G. KAHIN & J. LEWIS, *supra* note 43, at 119, *and* B. FALL, VIET NAM WITNESS 130-32 (1966), the evidence indicates that the Viet Cong were receiving assistance from Hanoi prior to the first significant increase in United States forces over pre-insurgency levels. As is evident in the writings of such Viet Nam scholars as Crozier, Fall, Lacouture, Pike, Schlesinger and Warner, there is general agreement that by 1961 Hanoi had entered the war and was assisting the Viet Cong. See note 67 *infra*. Pike indicates that by conservative estimate about 1,900 NLF cadres infiltrated from the North in the period from 1954 through 1960 and that in 1961, 3,700 more entered the South. But there is also general agreement that prior to 1961 the United States had only a very limited Military Assistance Advisory Group in South Viet Nam—probably not more than about 800-900, and that the first substantial increase in United States forces began in late 1961 with the rapid buildup of military advisory personnel, as recommended by the Taylor-Rostow report. Kahin and Lewis indicate that the major increase in United States assistance over pre-insurgency levels took place in early 1962. *See* G. KAHIN & J. LEWIS, *supra* note 43, at 77-78, 137. Apparently it was also in late 1961 and early 1962

Armed Attack and Defensive Response

Professor Falk argues alternatively that at most Viet Nam is a Type II conflict involving "substantial military participation by one or more foreign nations in an internal struggle for control."[49] In this alternative characterization of the conflict he is apparently focusing the conflict as "civil strife" within the South substantially assisted by northern military participation, rather than as "civil strife" between North and South. If, of course, North and South Viet Nam could be treated as one nation for the purpose of characterizing the conflict as "civil strife," it would be inconsistent to contend that the bombing of the North is an impermissible attack on a separate assisting state. Apparently focusing on "civil strife" within the South, then, Falk contends that "the United States could legitimately give military assistance to Saigon, but is obligated to limit the arena of violence to the territory of South Viet Nam."[50] He argues that it is impermissible to treat North Vietnamese assistance to the insurgents in the South as an armed attack justifying a defensive response against the North.[51] This analysis disarmingly fails to separate the relevant intellectual task of description of past trends in decision from that of appraisal of alternatives. Although the is and the ought are both component elements of "law," intellectual clarification requires that the scholar differentiate widespread community expectations about law (whether of the is or the ought and whether evidenced by the practices of states or the writings of publicists, etc.) from his own personal policy recommendations. But though Professor Falk argues as policy recommendation that it *ought* to be the law, he cites no authority for his thesis that in what he calls a Type II conflict it *is* appropriate to take off-setting military action only if confined to the internal arena.

that the United States first began direct military support with the use of helicopter units to ferry Vietnamese troops into combat. The testimony of Secretary of State Dean Rusk before the Senate Foreign Relations Committee that the first United States military casualty in South Viet Nam occurred in December, 1961, is indicative of the relatively small military role played by the United States prior to late 1961. THE VIET NAM HEARINGS 263 (Vintage ed. 1966). A juxtaposition in time sequence of assistance rendered by both sides indicates that the United States did not significantly expand its assistance over pre-insurgency levels prior to the critical impetus given the conflict by Hanoi's increasing assistance and direction. The increase in United States forces was a *response* to the quickening pace of the war and the increasing assistance from Hanoi. To characterize the conflict as Type III within the South for the purpose of asserting the illegality of this offsetting United States response at a time when the Viet Cong were clearly receiving increasing assistance from Hanoi is meaningless.

49. Falk, *supra* note 1, at 1126, 1127, 1132.
50. *Id.* 1132.
51. *See id.* 1136, 1140, 1150-51. This argument is crucial to Professor Falk's thesis. He writes: "South Viet Nam would have had the right to act in self-defense *if an armed attack had occurred,* and the United States would then have had the right to act in collective self-defense." *Id.* 1140.

In the absence of substantial authority, his conclusion that the bombing of the North *"appears to be . . .* a violation of international law"[52] (emphasis added) is somewhat mysterious, particularly since he elsewhere qualifies this thesis by a footnote reference that this "assertion . . . must be qualified to the extent that the United States decision to bomb North Viet Nam is treated as a law-creating precedent. . . ."[53] Candor requires acknowledgment that just as the problem of external assistance to the internal arena is unclear there are no "authoritative" rules of international law prohibiting the bombing of the North. Moreover, although international law may have great gaps in this area, in the context of Viet Nam there is greater reason to believe both as a matter of the is and the ought that the bombing of the North is a permissible defensive response.

There are two principal issues with respect to the legitimacy of defensive response against externally initiated or assisted insurgency. First, the question of whether off-setting assistance within the internal arena is legitimate and second, whether response against the territory of the assisting entity is legitimate. As Falk's proposed restriction of the armed attack test indicates, the armed attack inquiry is principally responsive to the second of these. It may be that assistance may be provided to the government forces in order to off-set external military assistance provided to the insurgents even in the absence of an armed attack as long as such assistance is confined to the internal arena. This distinction seems implicit in Falk's conclusion for Type II conflicts. It would mean that the United States could provide off-setting assistance to South Viet Nam even in the absence of an armed attack and that the question of whether there has been an armed attack is only relevant with respect to interdictive attacks against the North. But if this is the principal relevance of the armed attack test to the "internal war" situation then existing authority about armed attack suggests that defensive response against the North is permissive. Professor Kelsen suggests that this is the rule when he says:

> Since the Charter of the United Nations does not define the term "armed attack" used in article 51, the members of the United Nations in exercising their right of individual or collective self-defense may interpret "armed attack" to mean not only an action

---

52. *Id.* 1155.
53. *Id.* 1123 n.5. Although Professor Falk concludes that "international law offers no authoritative guidance as to the use of force *within* South Viet Nam," strangely he does not seem to find even equal uncertainty with respect to his thesis that in Type II conflict it is appropriate to take offsetting military action only if confined to the internal arena. *See id.* 1155.

in which a state uses its own armed force but also a revolutionary movement which takes place in one state but which is initiated or supported by another state.[54]

And Professor Brownlie supports this interpretation that there need not be a "direct invasion" to constitute an armed attack.[55]

For reasons of national interest or strategy inherent in the balance of power, states may choose only rarely to reply against the territory of an entity assisting insurgents, as the Spanish Civil War demonstrated.[56] Moreover, if the assistance to insurgents is not militarily substantial (and that is frequently the case) it may not amount to an armed attack. But there is nothing inherent in the armed attack test which restricts this right of response to instances of overt invasion. Yet that would be substantially the consequence of Professor Falk's proposal.

The purpose of the armed attack requirement in Article 51 of the United Nations Charter is to restrict the right to use force in individual or collective defense to very serious situations in which there is no reasonable alternative to the use of force for the protection of major values. By such requirements, contemporary international law expresses the judgment that minor encroachments on sovereignty, political disputes, frontier incidents, the use of non-coercive strategies of interference, and generally minor aggression which does not threaten fundamental values such as political and territorial integrity, may not be defended against by major resort to force against another entity. These tests are simply representative of the community interest in restricting intense responding coercion to those situations where fundamental values are seriously threatened by coercion.[57] Such coercive

54. Kelsen, *Collective Security Under International Law*, 49 INT'L LAW STUDIES 88 (1956). Kelsen also points out that "Participation of a state, with its armed forces, in the civil war within another state on the side of the insurgents is certainly international war in the relationship between the two states concerned." H. KELSEN, RECENT TRENDS IN THE LAW OF THE UNITED NATIONS 935 (1951). *See also* H. KELSEN, THE LAW OF THE UNITED NATIONS 798 (1950).

55. I. BROWNLIE, INTERNATIONAL LAW AND THE USE OF FORCE BY STATES 373 (1963). Brownlie clearly seems to assume that foreign assistance to insurgents can constitute an "armed attack." *Id.* at 327. He seems to adopt an "agency and control" test for armed attack in the civil strife context. *Id.* at 370-73. Although he adverts to the desirability of confining defensive measures to the territory of the defending state, his discussion does not rule out response against the territory of an assisting state in the face of a major threat. *Id.* at 327, 372-73.

56. *See generally* N. PADELFORD, INTERNATIONAL LAW AND DIPLOMACY IN THE SPANISH CIVIL STRIFE (1939). *Cf.* A. THOMAS & A. THOMAS, NON-INTERVENTION 225 (1956):

Such recognition, [German and Italian recognition of the insurgents as the legitimate government] being premature, was an illegal intervention and following it the Spanish war was converted from a civil war to an international war, and it should then have been treated as such. To apply the rules of international law devised to deal with insurgency to an international war is a great misuse of the law.

57. *See* M. McDOUGAL & E. FELICIANO, LAW AND MINIMUM WORLD PUBLIC ORDER 259 (1961).

threats to fundamental values can be effectuated as realistically by covert invasion and significant military assistance to insurgents as by armies on the march.

In the Viet Nam context the evidence strongly suggests that Hanoi provided significant military leadership and assistance to the Viet Cong from about 1959-60, an assistance which has greatly increased since then. Bernard Fall's account of the beginning of the Second Indo-China war in *The Two Viet-Nams*[58] suggests that the insurgency was substantially under the control of the Communist party apparatus even in the early years and that the National Liberation Front was substantially interrelated with Hanoi. By way of some relevant observations by Fall, certainly a qualified observer:

> A last rationale for the autonomous rise of a resistance movement in South Viet-Nam, advanced notably by the French writer Philippe Devillers, is that "the insurrection existed before the Communists decided to take part, and that they were simply forced to join in" by Diem's oppressive measures. Devillers, however, advances no evidence to the effect that the movement was not taken in hand by Hanoi *later*, precisely because it had a popular character, and thus was useful.[59]
>
> The wholly artificial character of the National Liberation Front, at least during the first year of its operation, is perhaps best shown by the fact that until April 13, 1962, it had not disclosed the names of its alleged leaders . . . .[60]
>
> In order to promote the concept that the Front and the Lao-Dong Party were separate entities, Hanoi informed the world on January 20, 1962, that a "conference of representatives of Marxists-Leninists in South Viet-Nam" had taken place on December 19, 1961, in the course of which it was decided to set up the Viet-Nam People's Revolutionary Party (Dang Nhan-Dan Cach Mang), which officially came into existence on January 1, 1962. . . .
>
> [L]ike the National Liberation Front itself, the Revolutionary Party failed to announce the names of any of its founding members. According to two circulars emanating from the Lao-Dong authorities and infiltrated into South Viet-Nam, members of the Lao-Dong were notified as early as December 7, 1961 (twelve days before the founding meeting) that the new party was created merely out of tactical necessity but would remain under the overall control of the Lao-Dong. . . .
>
> In all likelihood, the establishment of a "separate" Communist organization for South Viet-Nam follows the same pattern as the

---

58. B. FALL, THE TWO VIET-NAMS (rev. ed. 1964).
59. *Id*. 358.
60. *Id*. 356.

dissolution of the old ICP in the 1940's to give the Laotian and Khmer Communist movements a semblance of national autonomy . . . .[61]

In terms of its political-administrative apparatus, the South Vietnamese insurgency operated until December, 1960, as simply an extension of the then-existing Communist underground apparatus. . . .

Inside South Viet-Nam, the Viet-Minh seems to have maintained its old administrative structure of Interzones (lien-khu) V and VI, the former covering Central Viet-Nam south of the 17th parallel, and the latter covering the Nam-Bo (the southern part, i.e., South Viet-Nam proper, or Cochinchina). . . .

On the military side, the two zone commanders are equals *and apparently get their orders directly from Hanoi*. In 1960-62, they were Brigadier General Nguyen Don for Interzone V and a "civilian" guerrilla leader, Nguyen Huu Zuyen, for the Nam-Bo.[62]

Fall speaks of "Regiment 126, reinforced by a special 600-man battalion, infiltrated into South Viet-Nam in May, 1961, and likewise operating in the mountains west of Quang-Ngai . . . ,"[63] and reports that by mid-1963 infiltration may have involved 12,000 men.[64] He also points out that Americans were authorized to "shoot first" only in February, 1963.[65]

United Nations Secretary General U Thant, although disagreeing with those categorizing the National Liberation Front as a mere "stooge" of Hanoi, nevertheless says that the N.L.F. receives "perhaps very substantial help from the North."[66] And according to Douglas Pike, whom Arthur Schlesinger describes as the most careful student of the Viet Cong,[67] Hanoi was involved in the planning and direction of

---

61. *Id.* 357-58.
62. *Id.* 355 (emphasis added).
63. *Id.* 353.
64. *Id.* 330. Fall also writes that:
  Close to 100,000 South Vietnamese of Communist obedience left the southern area for North Viet-Nam, thus providing the latter with native southerners a plenty who were given extensive training for later operations in their home areas; among them were close to 10,000 mountaineers from the Central Plateau area. At the same time, the repatriates going north included the dependents of the hard-core fighters who were ordered to go underground in the south, as well as the raw recruits with whose training and protection the southerners had been burdened until then.
Id. 358-59.
65. *Id.* at 333.
66. N.Y. Times, Jan. 11, 1967, at 4, col. 5.
67. A. SCHLESINGER, THE BITTER HERITAGE 18 (1967). Bernard Fall says of Pike: Pike's presence is one of those small illustrations of the good side of the American system. No other book is likely to demolish more completely and more seriously all the convenient myths dished out officially about the National Liberation Front (NLF), for this is the work of an "insider." In his job Pike sees more material than anyone except the Front Leaders themselves. He has read reports from captured Viet Congs,

N.L.F. activities from the very beginning of the Front in 1959 and provided from the start what the N.L.F. most needed, organizational knowhow and expertise in insurgency.[68] As Pike puts it, "By 1959 an over-all directional hand was apparent. The struggle became an imported thing."[69] By the end of 1963, there was evidence not only of the

translations of the huge quantities of captured documents . . . and publications from Hanoi or from Front sources abroad.
Fall, *The View from Vietnam,* THE NEW YORK REVIEW OF BOOKS, Feb. 9, 1967, at 13, col. 2.
    Although not all scholars agree with Douglas Pike's thesis "that the DRV was . . . the godfather of the NLF," *see* D. PIKE, VIET CONG 321 (1966), most concede that the DRV played a significant role in the development of the Front and that Hanoi provided significant military leadership and assistance from about 1959-60.
    According to Schesinger:
    The civil insurrection in South Vietnam began to gather force by 1958; it was not until September 1960 that the Communist Party of North Vietnam bestowed its formal blessing and called for the liberation of the south from American imperialism. Ho Chi Minh was now supplying the Viet Cong with training, equipment, strategic advice and even men—perhaps two thousand a year by 1960.
A. SCHLESINGER, THE BITTER HERITAGE 17 (1967).
    Bernard Fall rejects both the Lacouture-Devillers thesis that the insurgency began "simply as an internal response to the repressive nature of the Diem regime" and the "White Paper" thesis that the insurgency was instigated from the North. He adopts a middle position which seems to concede that Hanoi played a significant role. *See* B. FALL, VIET-NAM WITNESS 130-32 (1966); M. RASKIN & B. FALL, THE VIET-NAM READER 252-61 (Vintage ed. 1965). *See also* P. HONEY, *supra* note 37, at 25-26, 67-68.
    Even Lacouture gives a chronology indicating D.R.V. intervention prior to major United States expansion of forces. He writes: "[I]n 1960 the N.L.F. had been created with the authorization of Hanoi, which thus renounced its non-intervention; in 1961 the United States entered the war." J. LACOUTURE, VIETNAM: BETWEEN TWO TRUCES 61 (Vintage ed. 1966).
    Denis Warner's account of the beginning of the second Indo-China conflict indicates that Hanoi played a significant role which preceded the first substantial United States response in late 1961 and early 1962 and that prior to that time Hanoi had "abandoned any pretence that it was not behind the rising tide of violence." D. WARNER, THE LAST CONFUCIAN 162 (Penguin ed. 1964); *see also id.* 160-76.
    Brian Crozier's account strongly suggests that although the Viet Minh were a minority when the second conflict broke out at the beginning of 1958, the North was substantially directing the southern guerrillas prior to the end of 1961. He also says: "Indeed the evidence of North Vietnamese direction and control of operations in South Vietnam is overwhelming." B. CROZIER, *supra* note 47, at 137; *see also id.* 96-97, 135-43.
    Professor Zasloff wrote in 1961 prior to major buildup of United States advisers in South Viet Nam:
    Currently the government of South Viet Nam is struggling for survival against well-organized, strongly sustained guerrilla forces—the Viet Cong—inspired and supported by the Communist Vietminh government of the North, which has made no secret of its goal of crushing the southern government and uniting Viet Nam under its hegemony.
Zasloff, *Peasant Protest in South Viet Nam,* in M. KAPLAN, THE REVOLUTION IN WORLD POLITICS 192 (1966).
    68. *See* D. PIKE, VIET CONG 77-84 (1966).
    69. *Id.* 78. Pike also points out:
    [T]he creation of the National Liberation Front, . . . was premeditated, planned, organized at length and in detail, and then pushed and driven into existence and operation. Such an effort had to be the child of the North.
Id. 80.
    In differentiating the current Viet Nam conflict from the earlier Viet Minh war, Pike says:
    [T]he later struggle in the South had a distinct imported quality about it that did not characterize either the Viet Minh war or the Communist revolution in China. The alien character was not simply a matter of outside aid or leadership. The struggle was in essence an expansionist drive by the North Vietnamese who asserted, and

presence of two North Vietnamese generals in the South[70] but northern trained cadres were being captured in numbers.[71] When the Viet Cong buildup in mid-1964 made increased material support necessary, Hanoi sent anti-aircraft and heavier weapons south.[72] And according to Pike, by the end of 1965 the N.L.F. was taken over by cadres from North Viet Nam, even down to the village level, a regularizing process which began in mid-1963.[73] There is evidence that regular units of the Army of North Viet Nam were moving into the South[74] prior to commencement of regular bombing of the North, and subsequent to 1965 it is clear that such regular units were substantially engaged in the South.[75] The seriousness of this military threat is indicated by the Mansfield Report which reported that at the time regular bombing of the North began, South Viet Nam was in imminent danger of total collapse.[76] This Viet Cong-North Viet Nam attack is the kind of serious and sustained attack threatening political and territorial integrity which justifies assistance to the South and an interdictive defensive response against the territory of the North.

As a matter of policy preference, Professor Falk argues that in a Type II conflict off-setting military assistance must be confined to the internal arena as an alternative for limiting violence.[77] This rationale

---

truly believed, that their goal of reunification was legally and morally justified. *Id.* 53.

70. *Id.* 102.

71. *Id.* 323. In what he describes as a conservative estimate, accurrate within plus or minus 10%, Pike sets out the following figures on infiltrators:

NLF Cadres from the North, 1954-1965

Year	Number
1954 through 1960	1,900
1961	3,700
1962	5,800
1963	4,000
1964	6,500 (at least a third Northerners)
1965	11,000 (almost all Northerners)
	32,900

Id. 324.

72. *Id.* 321, 325.

73. *Id.* 116

74. *See* MANSFIELD, MUSKIE, INOUYO, AIKEN & BOGGS, THE VIETNAM CONFLICT: THE SUBSTANCE AND THE SHADOW—REPORT TO THE SENATE COMMITTEE ON FOREIGN RELATIONS, 112 CONG. REC. 140, 141 (daily ed. Jan. 13, 1966); N.Y. Times, July 31, 1966, at 2, col. 5. *See also* D. PIKE, VIET CONG 164 (1966).

75. N.Y. Times correspondent Charles Mohr reported in August, 1966, that according to informed sources the latest intelligence estimates indicated that ". . . of the 177 enemy combat battalions in South Vietnam, 81, or 46 per cent, are now North Vietnamese . . . ." N.Y. Times, Aug. 10, 1966, at 1. col. 4, at 5, col. 5.

76. *See* MANSFIELD *et al., supra* note 74, at 140.

77. *See* Falk, *International Law and the United States Role in the Viet Nam War*, 75 YALE L.J. 1122, 1123 (1966).

is suspect as a blanket proposition and is especially weak as applied to Viet Nam. North Viet Nam is not simply a third party state providing assistance to a completely independent insurgency in "an internal struggle for control" of another state. Falk's implicit characterization of the conflict between North and South as "civil strife" or at least much of the evidence that he relies on to characterize the conflict as Type III[78] suggests the obvious weakness of simply treating North Viet Nam as a third party rendering assistance to an independent insurgency. But in making the alternative Type II characterization of the conflict he swings to the other extreme of minimizing the very important relationships between North and South—particularly the significant interrelation between the National Liberation Front and the Communist party apparatus of North Viet Nam. North Viet Nam is one half of an at least de facto divided nation rendering assistance across an international cease-fire line to an armed insurgency in the other half whose leadership is significantly interrelated with leadership in Hanoi. It is generally believed that a more or less long run objective of that assistance is to unify Viet Nam under the leadship of the Communist party of Viet Nam, largely dominated by the North.[79] North Vietnamese Premier Pham Van Dong's reiterated goals of "freedom and independence" cannot be meaningfully interpreted as applying only to North Viet Nam. Given the continuation of the struggle, they can only be interpreted as signifying a wider intention encompassing South Viet Nam as well. To assert that the war "should be viewed as primarily between factions contending for control of the southern zone," is to minimize this important relationship and objective of North Viet Nam and indeed the whole background of the conflict. Real-world Viet Nam will not fit either Falk's Type II or Type III paradigms, and certainly cannot be both at once. Although the assistance from the territorially adjacent North is covert and is supported by a substantial network of indigenous guerrillas, the long run objectives of the North have significant similarity with those of North Korea in the overt invasion of South Korea. They are not simply those of a third party assisting state such as the territorially remote assisting participants in the Spanish

---

78.   See notes 15 & 45 supra.

79.   According to Harrison Salisbury: "Both the Northern regime and the Liberation Front are committed to reunification and the creation of a single Vietnamese state." N.Y. Times, Jan. 16, 1967, at 1, col. 1, at 10, col. 3. But according to Wilfred Burchett: "Reunification is a long-range project realizable only in the far distant future, which Vietnamese leaders in the North and Liberation Front leaders in the South privately agree may be 10 or 20 years away." Charlottesville Daily Progress, Feb. 10, 1967, at 1, cols. 1-2. See also D. PIKE, VIET CONG 367-71 (1966); A. EDEN, TOWARD PEACE IN INDO-CHINA 21-22 (1966); P. HONEY, supra note 37, at 168-71.

Civil War. Although, of course, there are many differences, the analogy to the Korean War is for this reason alone closer than Professor Falk's analogy to the Spanish Civil War.[80] In determining permissibility of defensive measures against the territory of an assisting participant the objectives of the participant in rendering assistance and its relationship to the insurgency are highly relevant. North Viet Nam is not simply assisting in a struggle for "internal control" of the South but is substantially tied up with the military and political leadership of the insurgency in the South and has as a major, although possibly long term objective, unification with the South. This is not to argue the extent of the military assistance Hanoi was providing in the early years. The importance of the amount of that early assistance whether small or large has been greatly oversold.[81] But it is to indicate that prior to regular interdictive attacks against the North, Hanoi was so involved in the conflict in terms of its objectives in rendering assistance and its interaction with the Viet Cong that it is anomalous to speak of it as just a third party assisting state.

It should also be pointed out that there is conflicting evidence on the extent to which Hanoi was the moving party in the effective insurgency and that Professor Falk's model, which relies heavily on the controversial Lacouture-Devillers thesis, is one which minimizes Hanoi's role.[82] If a third state substantially initiates an insurgency instead of simply rendering assistance to an on-going insurgency it would seem anomalous to treat it as within Falk's Type II conflict. If the reality is that the *effective military insurgency* in South Viet Nam was substantially initiated and is substantially supported and directed by the Communist party of Viet Nam largely controlled from Hanoi, Falk's view applied to Viet Nam would simply immunize states invading covertly.

Further, even in a Type II paradigm, to restrict defensive response to the internal arena may be an undesirable restriction of the right of defense in the absence of a more effective peace-keeping machinery. It

---

80. See Falk, *supra* note 77, at 1126.
81. I share Schlesinger's judgment that the same is true of the failure to hold the 1956 elections. See A. SCHLESINGER, *supra* note 67, at 15.
82. Douglas Pike's overall thesis seems to assign a substantial role to Hanoi in the creation of the effective military insurgency in the South, *see* D. PIKE, *supra* note 79, in contrast to Professor Falk's "interpretation of the internal war as primarily a consequence of indigenous forces." Falk, *supra* note 77, at 1129. The Canadian representative to the I.C.C. concluded in a minority statement to the February 13, 1965, Special Report that North Vietnamese activities "aimed at the overthrow of the South Vietnamese administration . . . constitute the root cause of general instability in Vietnam . . . ." SPECIAL REPORT TO THE CO-CHAIRMEN OF THE GENEVA CONFERENCE ON INDO-CHINA, FEBRUARY 13, 1965 (Vietnam No. 1) CMND. No. 2609, at 14-15 (1965). For discussion of this 1965 Special Report which was prompted by the commencement of regular bombing of the North see Dai, *supra* note 46, at 171-72.

would mean, in effect, that a state might have to endure interminable outside intervention with little hope of ending the conflict by appropriate defensive actions. Presumably under this thesis even a widely recognized government could not defend its territory from massive external military assistance to insurgent factions, because if it could it would seem that assisting states participating in collective defense with the state attacked should have the same defensive rights. Although Falk's proposed rule might theoretically minimize international escalation, it might also maximize destruction within the unfortunate internal arena that gets trappped as the battleground and it might encourage external intervention in general. The Spanish Civil War does show the great internal destructiveness of a territorially restricted conflict in the absence of an effective sanction against intervention. In a world relying heavily on power the right of *effective* defense is a major deterrent to outside intervention in internal conflicts. Providing immunity to the real bases of power of the attackers both fails to provide an effective sanction against third party assistance and drastically undermines defensive rights. In doing so it closes out an option which may in some situations be the most effective method of conflict resolution at least cost to all participants. In the final analysis that is the real question and one not convincingly answered by Professor Falk's *a priori* "geographic" rule. For a number of reasons, then, there is considerable question whether the proposal to immunize the territories of intervening nations would in the long run reduce conflict or whether it would increase conflict by encouraging intervention and prolongation of conflict. Moreover, as the interdictive response against North Viet Nam illustrates, the alternatives in proceeding against an aggressively assisting external power are considerably greater than an either-or, all or nothing response. It might be that enlightened community policy would rule impermissible all out attack against the territorial and political integrity of such an assisting entity while allowing necessary limited defensive measures against resources closely related to the assistance. This alternative, which is the one being pursued in Viet Nam, stops short of ultimate escalation of the conflict while providing some sanction against unlawful military intervention.

There are sound reasons for suggesting, just as there are for doubting, that the limited bombing of the North may be an option leading to termination of conflict in the shortest period of time at least cost to all participants. Without the interdictive attacks against the North there might be less reason for the North ever to stop rendering assistance to the insurgents or to seek a negotiated settlement. The cost of guerrilla attack is by the lopsided arithmetic of such conflict much less than the cost of defense. The interdictive attacks both substantially raise the cost of assistance to the insurgents in the South, and impede assistance reaching the insurgents. They were initiated in close support of the struggle in the South in terms of supply, morale and settlement factors and do lend support to the defensive effort in these respects. To balance the picture, though, it should be pointed out that as a strategy choice, the effect of the bombing is difficult to assess and it has some serious weaknesses. For example, it is unable to prevent a substantial flow of assistance from reaching the South, it increases the risk of international escalation, it may harden the attitude of the citizenry of the North, and it has a strong negative effect on world opinion. In view of the question marks connected with it, the limited bombing of the North may or may not be the best strategy for pursuing legitimate defense objectives in Viet Nam, but it is within the range of reasonable responses, allowing for supportable differences of opinion as to the effectiveness of a particular strategy for conflict termination.

At one point Professor Falk contends that "since the United States has far greater military resources potentially available, our use of insufficient force violates general norms of international law."[83] But surely it does not violate international law to take into account the risk of escalation and of generating a nuclear war if the objective is widened from limited defensive aims. His combined argument, then, seems to be that given some United States response, international law may require a greater military commitment in the South with no hope of proceeding against the major resources in the North which are facilitating continuation of the struggle. By this observation Falk seems to have put his finger on a major difficulty with his proposal for limiting permissible response to the internal arena in Type II conflict. Since international law does seek conflict minimization by a requirement of effective force, shouldn't such force be applied against military resources whether within or without the internal arena, if a determination is reasonably made that such response is necessary to end the conflict with minimum destructiveness on all sides? This determination must, of course, include assessment of the risk of conflict escalation under each alternative and must be reasonable under all the circumstances, allowing some leeway for reasonable differences of opinion as to the effectiveness of a particular strategy. But Falk's proposed terri-

83. *See* Falk, *supra* note 77, at 1144.

torial limitation on responding defensive measures cuts down on a series of options which may well lead to conflict resolution with minimum destructiveness for all participants. The determination of what course of action will end the conflict with minimum destructiveness and risk is, of course, the real question and one which in the terribly difficult Viet Nam context is not served by the sterile accusation that "our use of insufficient force violates general norms of international law."

In view of Professor Falk's concern with conflict minimization evident in his proposal to limit responding coercion to the internal arena of a Type II conflict, it would also seem important to stress the danger to world order in providing assistance to insurgents across an international cease-fire line in a country at least de facto divided between the major contending public order systems. With respect to these activities of the North, however, he merely says "international law neither attempts nor is able to regulate support given exile groups. The activities of Hanoi between 1954 and 1964 conform to patterns of tolerable conflict in contemporary international politics."[84] And he concludes: "North Viet Nam's action does not seem to constitute 'aggression.' "[85] As a description of power processes these statements may be accurate, but as statements of contemporary international law and policies of conflict minimization they are not the most useful picture.

The United Nations has repeatedly condemned the creation or support of civil strife by external elites using internal agents. Thus the General Assembly said in condemning external assistance to the Communist guerrillas in Greece:

---

84. *Id.* 1139.

This statement is also misleading in failing to advert to Hanoi's activities with respect to Laos during this period. North Vietnamese intervention in Laos has been on a substantial scale, has not been confined to supporting exile groups and has been in flagrant disregard of the Geneva Accords of 1962. Yet this intervention in Laos is in close support of Hanoi's activities against South Viet Nam.

John Hughes, staff correspondent of The Christian Science Monitor, writes from Laos that:

> Though Laos is technically neutralized by the Geneva agreement of 1962, it in fact harbors what Premier Souvanna Phouma estimates to be 60,000 North Vietnamese troops, who of course have no right to be on Laotian soil. In part they are stiffening pro-Communist Pathet Lao units, but mainly they are support and garrison troops down the length of the Ho Chi Minh Trail, ensuring the continued passage through Laos to South Vietnam of North Vietnamese infiltrators.

Christian Science Monitor, May 3, 1967, at 1, col. 4. Some scholars indicate that Hanoi's military intervention in South Viet Nam should be placed in a larger temporal and geographical context of Viet Minh aggression against Laos and Cambodia and the drive for an all Indo-China Communist party dominated by Hanoi. *See* P. HONEY, *supra* note 37, at 168-71; B. CROZIER, *supra* note 47, at 114-33.

There is also evidence that North Viet Nam is providing training and assistance to insurgents operating in Thailand. *See* Christian Science Monitor, May 12, 1967, at 1, col. 2.

85. Falk, *supra* note 77, at 1159.

The General Assembly . . . condemning the intervention of a state in the internal affairs of another state for the purpose of changing its government by the threat or use of force,

Solemnly reaffirms that whatever the weapons used, any aggression, whether committed openly or by fomenting civil strife in the interest of a foreign power, or otherwise is the gravest of all crimes against peace and security throughout the world.[86]

And the International Law Commission Draft of a Code of Offenses Against the Peace and Security of Mankind condemned:

The organization, or encouragement of the organization, by the authorities of a state, of armed bands within its territory or any other territory for incursions into the territory of another state; or the toleration of the organization of such armed bands in its own territory, or the toleration of the use by such armed bands of its territory as a base of operation or as a point of departure for incursions into the territory of another state as well as direct participation in or support of such incursions.[87]

And as recently as December, 1966, the General Assembly "condemned all forms of intervention in the domestic affairs of States, and urged all States to refrain from armed intervention, subversion, terrorism, or other indirect forms of intervention for the purpose of changing the existing system of another State or interfering in civil strife in another State."[88] These representative pronouncements reflect the substantial community expectation that inciting or assisting civil strife is not only aggression, but is aggression presenting a particularly grave threat to minimum order in today's world. In postulating that external military assistance is inappropriate to influence the outcome in a Type III conflict, Falk seems to be concurring in this judgment although he later somewhat inconsistently asserts that "international law offers no authoritative guidance as to the use of force *within* South Viet Nam . . . ."[89] The policy of conflict minimization strongly suggests the illegitimacy of military assistance to an insurgency sustained at a high level of coercion across de facto boundaries separating major contending public order systems.[90] Should the West Germans or Nationalist Chi-

---

86. G.A. Res. 380 (v), 5 U.N. GAOR Supp. 20, at 13, 17, U.N. Doc. A/1775 (1950). *See also* A. Thomas & A. Thomas, Non-Intervention 226-29 (1956).

87. International Law Comm'n, Report, 9 GAOR, Supp. 9 at 10, 11 U.N. Doc. A/2693 (1954).

88. U.N. Weekly News Summary, Press Release WS/273, at 6 (December 22, 1966).

It is peripheral but perhaps useful to point out that the recognition of contending public order systems does not depend on acceptance of dogma about "monolithic communism."

89. Falk, *supra* note 77, at 1155. *See also id.* 1137.

90. The interesting thesis of Robert Ardrey would to some extent seem to reinforce

nese provide sustained high levels of military assistance to insurgents in East Germany or mainland China, ultimately fielding regular army units, the threat to world order would be obvious. And if the analogies are not on all fours with Viet Nam, events in Viet Nam prove them relevant if not as obvious with respect to consequences for public order when such assistance is provided. In seeking to effectuate community policies of conflict minimization, it may be more effective to focus attention on the illegality of aggressive coercive strategies across de facto international boundaries rather than attempting to further restrict the right of defense against such aggressive strategies.

External Participation in Intra-State Conflict: A Policy Inquiry

Even though Professor Falk's "civil strife" framework does not seem sufficiently sensitive to crucial features of the total Viet Nam context to provide a valid analytic base for conclusion about that conflict, his framework is a creative contribution to stimulation of general policy inquiry with respect to external participation in intra-state conflict. Since his own conclusions about Viet Nam are based on this framework it may be helpful to attempt further clarification of the major policies applicable to external participation in intra-state conflict. This discussion is intended only to air some doubts about suggested norms for Type III conflict and is not intended to offer a definitive rule if, indeed, any is possible or desirable. In fact, preliminary inquiry suggests that "Type III conflict" may encompass too wide a variety of contexts to generalize meaningfully and that more sensitive contextual clarification may be desirable.

The principal policies relevant to decision about the permissibility of external participation in intra-state conflict seem to be self-determination and maintenance of minimum public order. Self-determination, the right of peoples within an entity to choose their own institutions and form of government, is a basic community policy reflected in community condemnation of intervention and colonialism. The striking thing about self-determination as a touchstone of permissibility is that realistically it may cut for as well as against outside intervention in an internal arena and it may cut for or against assistance to either insurgents or de facto government. In the colonial war

de facto control of territory as the important standard for purposes of conflict minimization. *See generally* R. ARDREY, THE TERRITORIAL IMPERATIVE (1966).

Brownlie indicates that "the right of self-defence should be based upon peaceful possession and *de facto* exercise of authority." I. BROWNLIE, INTERNATIONAL LAW AND THE USE OF FORCE BY STATES 382 (1963).

in Algeria in 1960 self-determination may have been served by assistance to insurgents whereas in the Congo in 1961, in Greece in 1948, in Kenya, Uganda and Tanganyika in 1964, and possibly at the beginning of the Spanish Civil War in 1936, self-determination may have been better served by assistance to the government. A simplistic version of self-determination espoused by Hall[91] and advocated by some, however, identifies self-determination with anything that happens in an entity. According to this view, states should be left alone in all circumstances to work out their own form of government. If aid to the recognized government were legitimate then it would impair the right to revolution and if aid to the insurgents were legitimate it would violate independence by interfering with the regular organ of the state. This judgment that self-determination requires that neither the recognized government nor insurgents can ever be aided conceals the naive assumption that whatever takes place within the confines of a territorial entity is pursuant to genuine self-determination of peoples and that outside "intervention" is necessarily disruptive of self-determination. Such simplistic deductive notions that territorial entities should be left alone to work out their own self-determination at all costs and by any modalities ignores the twin reality that today ruthless governments in control of the total resources of a society can suppress their peoples and that minorities can through terror, sabotage and the control of the military establishment capture control of governmental machinery. The Hall view seems to adopt a kind of Darwinian definition of self-determination as survival of the fittest within the national boundaries, even if fittest means most adept in the use of force.

It may be that proscribing unilateral outside assistance to either faction will in fact result more often in genuine self-determination than allowing such assistance to either side. And the difficulty of appraising objectives of the assisting participants and determining where self-determination really lies may militate for this solution. If these assumptions really underlie a neutral rule of nonintervention in Type III conflicts, then we ought to recognize it as such and reflect both on the accuracy of the assumptions and on whether it is necessary to have this broad a prophylactic rule. Some relevant questions might be: What is the aggregate contemporary experience as to whether self-determination is aided or hindered by assistance to insurgents, by assistance to recognized governments, or by both? In what cases would a

---

91. See W. HALL, INTERNATIONAL LAW 287 (6th ed. 1909); W. HALL, INTERNATIONAL LAW 347 (8th ed. 1924).

broad prophylactic rule cut against self-determination and might we find recurring features which would signal an exception to the rule in those cases? In light of the great variety of situations presenting the problem, what is the criterion for "civil strife" triggering the rule? What functions do recognized governments serve that might make any such rule as to them more difficult or unworkable? Might legitimacy of aid to either faction be conditioned on holding free elections or on some other indicia of genuine self-determination? In view of the interdependencies among states in a world divided between contending states and blocs, to what extent is a rule focused on self-determination of only one entity realistic or desirable?[92] What are the expectations that nations will observe such rules? Answers to these questions might militate for no rule, a neutral non-intervention rule or a more narrowly drawn rule aimed, for example, at assistance to insurgents. But without more the present arguments for a neutral non-intervention rule in all Type III conflicts are unpersuasive as a requirement of self-determination.

As seems implicit in the suggested norm for Type II conflict, any rule of non-intervention based on self-determination should be modified where one participant has received external assistance. Although self-determination might still cut either way, the rule is much too suspect to operate as a prophylactic rule against external intervention after there has already been intervention on one side.

A second major policy in analyzing the permissibility of external participation in intra-state conflict is the maintenance of minimum public order. An hypothesis for inquiry with respect to public order consequences is that external assistance to insurgent groups and the fomenting of civil strife by external elites is more often seriously disruptive of minimum public order than assistance to recognized governments. Assistance to insurgents often involves high risk of prolonged conflict with entrenched elites as well as high risk of expansion of the conflict through external support for the recognized government. Recognized governments may be incorporated in a world order bloc that views their overthrow as an unacceptable impairment of bloc power or security or they may have defensive arrangements with third powers which will be triggered by assistance to insurgents. It is one of the functions of government to preserve stability and maintain inter-

---

92. Professor Falk adverts to this question in pointing out that "the outcome of a Type III conflict may affect the relative power of many other countries." Falk, *supra* note 77, at 1126.

nal order and it is to be expected that ruling elites will resist change sought through force and will call on their established international partners to help them. Recognized governments usually control greater resources than insurgents and frequently control the organized military. These conditions make insurgent attacks employing guerrilla armies and terrorist tactics likely to be prolonged costly struggles. Compare, for example, such diverse situations as Hungary and the Dominican Republic with Algeria and Viet Nam. Moreover, fomenting an insurgency, or providing assistance to it in early stages, can be simply a sophisticated form of attack. Such attacks are particularly pernicious in that they are difficult to prove and are frequently couched in rhetoric about self-determination and social reform which may or may not be the principal objectives of the attacker.

As a rule to prevent outside powers from becoming involved with one another, there is little reason to believe that a "neutral" norm would be more effective than a rule prohibiting external assistance to insurgencies only. In fact, in the cold war context there is good reason to believe that it is particularly unrealistic to ask that military aid be withheld from continuing de facto governments. Soviet assistance to the regimes in Hungary and East Germany and United States assistance to Greece and South Viet Nam indicate that realistic projections militate against attempting to proscribe assistance to entrenched governments. In contrast, expectations of violence are particularly acute when assistance is rendered to insurgent elements across cold war boundaries. Determined United States assistance to Hungarian freedom fighters would have involved high risk of acute conflict with Russia. North Vietnamese assistance to insurgents in South Viet Nam has fueled a major conflict. And substantial military assistance by Formosa to mainland insurgents would seem to carry an especially grave risk of major war. It is an observable cold war phenomenon that major powers tend to support regimes threatened by military actions initiated or supported by opposing bloc powers. In light of this practice there is certainly a strong community interest in not attempting coercive change across such boundaries.

In contrast, public order consequences are not as acute in situations of less direct cold war confrontation. For example, in newly independent African countries intervention by a former colonial power on either side may not provide the same risk of protracted and escalating conflict although the risk of extended conflict is still significant and would usually be greater if intervention were on the side of the insurgents. Where the risk of major conflict is slight, grave and continuing denial of self-determination may outweigh dangers of the use of coercive strategies of change. But where such risk is grave, minimum public order may be the most important consideration.

It may be argued that since both sides may recognize separate elite groups as the lawful representative of the state, if any rule is to be effective in preventing outside powers from confronting each other on separate sides of a civil war, the rule must proscribe assistance to both government and insurgents. But although states can always prematurely recognize one or another group as the legal representative of a state, there is usually no doubt as to which side is the government and which the insurgents despite such opposing recognition. In Greece, Algeria, Spain, the Congo, South Viet Nam, Venezuela, Cuba, Colombia and Thailand, to name a few past and present trouble spots, there can be little doubt which authority was the real-world government. The situation of contending governments without territorial separation and both with approximately equal credentials in terms of past legitimacy, de facto governmental control and international recognition doesn't seem to be the major "civil strife" problem. Even if this were a problem one criterion for assistance to a government should be that it is the only widely recognized de facto or de jure government.[93]

A rule of no assistance to either faction also runs into the problem that it is a not uncommon practice to enter into treaty arrangements with a widely recognized government to assist it in maintaining the existing form of government against external attack or internal subversion. This practice reflects the real interdependencies felt among nations. Query whether assistance to a recognized government should be impermissible if pursuant to such a pre-existing treaty of guarantee or assistance or whether failure to honor such a treaty would itself amount to intervention? A major difference between the insurgents and government is that the government is the internationally authorized agency to receive external assistance. To prohibit such assistance is more difficult than proscribing assistance to insurgents. There are at least two other reasons for this greater difficulty in addition to the problem of pre-existing treaties. First, since the recognized government

---

93. A related question is to what extent assistance to exile groups such as the Bay-of-Pigs exiles or the South Vietnamese that had gone North in 1954 is legitimate in situations where assistance to insurgents would be otherwise illegitimate. Although this circumstance may somewhat strengthen claims from the standpoint of self-determination, it is hardly decisive of genuine self-determination and has only peripheral relevance with respect to the policy of minimum public order.

is the international agency of the state entitled to receive assistance, it is legitimate even under a "neutral" norm to render assistance *prior* to "civil strife." Under this norm, then, a difficult fact determination must be made as to when "the outcome is uncertain"[94] or "civil strife" or "belligerency" or "insurgency" or some such cabalistic point has been reached before assistance becomes impermissible. By that point an assisting state may already feel committed. It is probably unrealistic to assume that assistance will often be stopped after once being legitimately begun, particularly if the facts are at all hazy, as they usually are. Moreover, could levels of assistance provided prior to "civil strife" be continued as, for example, the Military Assistance Advisory Group in Viet Nam? Must they be, on the theory that a reduction amounts to intervention on the side of the insurgents? And if some level of assistance is permissible or mandatory, is it realistic to argue that it cannot be increased?

This picture is further complicated with respect to assistance to the government forces in that one of the functions of the government is to maintain order within the community. Although at some point one can philosophically argue that maintenance of order must yield to the right to revolution, until that point is reached external assistance may be consistent with internal autonomy. Because of this function of government within the internal arena, as well as its function as international representative of the state, there is likely to be great difficulty in determining when the level of "civil strife" is such that assistance is violative of internal autonomy. Secondly, since under Professor Falk's framework assistance to a recognized government becomes legitimate again after significant military assistance has been received by the insurgents, another difficult determination must be made as to when such assistance has been rendered. But because of the difficulty of proving covert assistance to the insurgents, as Viet Nam aptly demonstrates, assistance to the recognized government even if legitimately provided in a Type II situation is likely to remain shrouded in controversy and condemned as much as, or more than (because more visible) assistance to the insurgents. Query also whether Professor Falk intends that off-setting assistance to insurgents would be permissible as a Type II conflict after the recognized government has received assistance? This would be the ultimate in "neutral" rules. Under such a rule almost any situation could become open-ended. For since the recognized govern-

---

94. *See generally* Wright, *United States Intervention in the Lebanon*, 53 AM. J. INT'L L. 112, 121-22 (1959).

ment is entitled to receive assistance prior to civil strife, external elites assisting both sides will point out that the other side's aid legitimates their own. It would seem then that an effective rule for conflict minimization must at least proscribe counter-intervention (legitimate in Type II conflict) on behalf of insurgents.

Because of the real functions of recognized governments any attempt to fashion "neutral" rules treating the government and insurgents alike is suspect. There are some reasons for suggesting that a rule preventing assistance to insurgents only might be a more realistic and no less efficacious rule in many contexts than a rule preventing assistance to both factions. Such a rule might also desirably focus attention on the probably greater threat of providing assistance to foment civil strife as compared with assistance to a widely recognized government.

Although scholars are divided on the permissibility of assistance to the two sides in Professor Falk's Type III conflict, the area of disagreement significantly reflects the greater danger to world order of providing assistance to insurgents rather than to a widely recognized government. There are a number of writers who take the position that international law does not prohibit assistance to a recognized government in a Type III conflict, and there are substantial community expectations that such assistance is permitted even if its purpose is to assist in suppressing civil strife.[95] There is, on the other hand, wider agreement that assistance to insurgents is impermissible.[96]

Although exploration of the role of international law in dealing with "civil strife" will not by itself result in valid answers for Viet Nam, such exploration is relevant to the Viet Nam problem. A preliminary attempt to clarify community policies most relevant to contexts of "civil strife" indicates that the "civil strife" structures relied on to condemn United States policy in Viet Nam are over-simplified —even if Viet Nam could be treated as "civil strife". Professor Falk's Type III conflict encompasses a range of different contexts from colonial wars to "wars of national liberation" and it may be preferable that

---

95. See the authorities collected in Moore & Underwood, *The Lawfulness of United States Assistance to the Republic of Viet Nam,* 112 CONG. REC. 14,943, 14,975-76 n.179 (daily ed. July 14, 1966), and the discussion in Moore, *The Lawfulness of Military Assistance to the Republic of Viet-Nam,* 61 AM. J. INT'L L. 1, 28-32 (1967).

96. See the authorities cited in note 95, *supra.*

In the context of Viet Nam, whatever assistance to insurgents might otherwise be permissible is clearly prohibited by the express provisions of Articles 19 and 24 of the Agreement on the Cessation of Hostilities. In its 1962 Special Report, the International Control Commission found that "there is sufficient evidence to show beyond reasonable doubt" that North Viet Nam had violated these provisions. SPECIAL REPORT TO THE CO-CHAIRMEN OF THE GENEVA CONFERENCE ON INDO-CHINA (Vietnam No. 1), CMND. No. 1755 (1962). 31 PARL. SESSIONAL PAPERS 7 (1961-62).

resulting norms be more contextually discriminating. That genuine self-determination requires in situations of "civil strife" that assistance never be provided either insurgents or the government is questionable. With respect to the policy of minimum order, assistance to insurgents seems considerably more dangerous than assistance to a widely recognized government. This difference and realism about cold war expectations suggest that at least in inter-bloc contexts it may be preferable to have a norm condemning unilateral assistance to insurgents and thereby focusing attention on the greater threat rather than attempting to prohibit assistance to both widely recognized governments and insurgents. Community expectations more clearly condemning such assistance to insurgents and problems implicit in the functions of the recognized government also militate for distinguishing between assistance to insurgents and widely recognized governments. Whatever the ultimate solution, if any in terms of such rules, the assistance of the United States to South Viet Nam would seem to be a permissive defensive response to at least off-set substantial military assistance provided to the Viet Cong. North Vietnamese assistance to the Viet Cong, however, exceeds tolerable levels of inter-bloc coercion and is an impermissive strategy of attempted change.

In appraising the role of international law in intra-state conflict, clarification of the process side—the international machinery and procedures to control conflict—is as deserving of attention as normative clarification. Substantial progress toward the rule of law in large measure depends on more effective centralized or regional peacekeeping machinery. Effective regional organizations able to make authoritative fact determinations and to authorize collective action to keep the peace would go far to alleviate the problem of regulating external participation in intra-state conflict. The United Nations Congo and Cyprus operations show that in some contexts (principally characterized by an absence of high order conflict between the major competing ideological systems) the United Nations can be an effective participant in controlling such conflict. It is important that these hopeful precedents be strengthened and it is tragic that the United Nations has been unable to significantly moderate the Viet Nam conflict. Certainly every effort should continue to be made to strengthen its role. But emphasis on the process side, however necessary for achieving more effective control of international coercion, should not obscure fundamental differences in attitudes of major participants regarding existing peacekeeping machinery. Although the United States has formally placed before the Security Council a draft resolution calling for immediate negotiations without preconditions and indicating willingness to achieve the purpose of the resolution by arbitration or mediation,[97] Hanoi and Peking have consistently rejected any role for the United Nations in settling the Viet Nam war.[98] Similarly, emphasis on the process side should not downgrade the relevance of the existing normative structure. We have not yet attained an ideal world and in the absence of a more effective peacekeeping process the existing normative structure condemning force as a strategy of major international change and preserving the right of defense against major military attack remains the principal framework for appraisal of the Viet Nam war.

The State Department Brief in Context

One of the principal strengths of an approach to foreign relations which inquires of "international law" as opposed to the neo-realist

---

97. *See* N.Y. Times, Feb. 1, 1966, at 12, cols. 2-6.

98. Secretary General U Thant said at a news conference on February 24, 1965:

The government of North Viet-Nam has all along maintained that the United Nations is not competent to deal with the question of Viet-Nam since, in its view, there is already in existence an international machinery established in 1954 in Geneva. They have all along maintained that position and, as you all know, it is a position also maintained by the Peoples Republic of China. As far as the United Nations is concerned, I think the greatest impediment to the discussion of the question of Viet-Nam in one of the principal organs of the United Nations is the fact that more than two parties directly concerned in the question are not members of this organization. I therefore do not see any immediate prospect of useful discussion in the Security Council . . . .

Press Conference, Feb. 24, 1965, quoted in M. RASKIN & B. FALL, THE VIET-NAM READER 263, at 267 (Vintage ed. 1965).

As stated by Pham Van Dong, the North Vietnamese position is:

The Government of the Democratic Republic of Vietnam declares that . . . any approach tending to secure a U.N. intervention in the Vietnam situation is also inappropriate because such approaches are basically at variance with the 1954 Geneva Agreements on Vietnam.

RECENT EXCHANGES CONCERNING ATTEMPTS TO PROMOTE A NEGOTIATED SETTLEMENT OF THE CONFLICT IN VIET-NAM (Viet-Nam No. 3) CMND. No. 2756, at 51 (1965). Hanoi reiterated this stand by way of public reply to the March 14th peace proposals of Secretary General U Thant. The public statement of Hanoi asserted:

[I]t is necessary to underline once again the views of the Government of Hanoi, which has pointed out that the Viet-Nam problem has no concern with the United Nations and the United Nations has absolutely no right to interfere in any way in the Viet-Nam question.

56 DEP'T STATE BULL. 618 (1967).

Peking militantly declares:

The United Nations has never taken a just stand on the Viet Nam question. It has absolutely no say concerning a settlement of the South Viet Nam question. . . . U.N. intervention in affairs of Indo-China cannot be tolerated. . . .

We would like to advise U Thant: save yourself the trouble. There is nothing for the United Nations to do in Viet Nam, neither is it qualified to do anything there.

Extract from an article in the Peking Peoples' Daily "Serious Advice for U Thant" contained in RECENT EXCHANGES, *supra*, 54-55.

It might also be noted that Hanoi refused to submit the Tonkin Gulf incident to Security Council investigation despite a South Viet Nam request and offer to send a delegation to the Security Council to participate in debates on the incident. *See* Moore & Underwood, *The Lawfulness of United States Assistance to the Republic of Viet Nam,* 112 CONG. REC. 14,943 (daily ed. July 14, 1966), reprinted in DUQUESNE L. REV. 235 (1967), at note 228 and accompanying text.

preoccupation with "the national interest"[99] is that a balanced international law approach seems to achieve a real focus on clarification of long run community interest. The kinds of questions focused on in this legal dialogue—regulation of international use of force and regulation of external participation in internal strife—achieve a different focus from *realpolitik* discussions of the same problems and as such add an additional dimension to the policy considerations available to the national decision maker. In these inquiries policy justification is not principally short run national interest but common and long run community interest. Legal discourse can also aid in evaluating legal arguments made by the adversaries and used as the basis of attacks on or justification for national policy, for example North Viet Nam's assertion that it has a legal right to use force against South Viet Nam. A balanced international law approach, one neither unduly focusing on "legal idealism"[100] nor "naked power"[101] and not legalistically self-limiting, *is* relevant to problems such as Viet Nam. Because of this relevance, I share Professor Falk's view that inquiry of international law is an important and helpful inquiry for the national decision maker and that international law should not be used by either side solely to "bolster or bludgeon foreign policy positions . . . ."[102] Professor Falk's criticism of the State Department brief as "formalistic" and "legalistic" and as responding to irrelevant and trivial points,[103] however, is unfair without further exposition of the context in which it was written. As he points out, the State Department brief was principally written in response to arguments made in the Lawyers' Committee Memorandum[104] which had been widely circulated in the United States and to similar legal arguments which were being made by some members of Congress. Many of the legal arguments made in the Lawyers' Committee Memorandum and in Congress against the United States position, such as the arguments that a member of the United Nations can not collectively assist in defense of a non-member and that it is unconstitutional to commit United States armed forces to South Viet Nam with-

---

99. *See* H. MORGENTHAU, POLITICS AMONG NATIONS 227-33, 275-311 (3d ed. 1966); H. MORGENTHAU, IN DEFENSE OF THE NATIONAL INTEREST (1951); Morgenthau, *To Intervene or Not to Intervene*, 45 FOREIGN AFFAIRS 425 (1967).

100. This is a sound admonition from George Kennan. *See generally* G. KENNAN, AMERICAN DIPLOMACY 1900-1950 (1951).

101. *See, e.g.*, H. MORGENTHAU, *supra* note 99.

102. *See* Falk, *supra* note 77, at 1155. *See also* Meeker, *Role of Law in Political Aspects of World Affairs*, 48 DEP'T STATE BULL. 83 (1963).

103. Falk, *supra* note 77, at 1139, 1146, 1155.

104. Memorandum of Law of Lawyers' Committee on American Policy Toward Vietnam, reprinted in 112 CONG. REC. 2552-59 (daily ed. Feb. 9, 1966).

out a formal congressional declaration of war, were legalistic in the extreme. They were also inaccurate, and Falk properly repudiates them.[105] Such arguments had achieved a wide hearing, however, and were given substantial credence by many laymen and even some members of the bar. In fact, the "word magic" of the article 51 collective defense argument was still a major tenet of arguments against lawfulness made by the Chairman of the Lawyers' Committee in an article in the *American Bar Association Journal* as late as July, 1966.[106] Moreover, a number of outstanding international legal scholars, including Professor Falk, had become associated with the Lawyers' Committee efforts and by their association lent credence to these and other legalistic arguments made in the Memorandum.[107] Because of this widespread credence which the adversary arguments of the Lawyers' Committee achieved, and their use as a basis for criticizing Viet Nam policy, they needed reply if there was to be balanced appraisal of the issues. The State Department brief performed that function. And although Professor Falk emphasizes the adversary nature of the State Department brief he does not point out that the Lawyers' Committee Memorandum was at least an equally adversary document. Candor would suggest acknowledgment that both sides in the Viet Nam debate have tended to take adversary positions.[108]

---

105. *See* Falk, *supra* note 77, at 1139-40, 1154.
106. *See* Standard, *United States Intervention in Vietnam Is Not Legal*, 52 A.B.A.J. 627 (1966).
107. *See* Letter from the Lawyers' Committee to President Lyndon B. Johnson, Jan. 25, 1966, reprinted in 112 CONG. REC. 2551-52 (daily ed. Feb. 9, 1966). Professor Falk is currently Chairman of the Consultative Council of the Lawyers' Committee. The work of the Consultative Council has been somewhat better than the earlier much circulated Lawyers' Committee efforts but is still essentially a one-sided argument.
For an example, see The Military Involvement of the United States in Vietnam: A Legal Analysis (1966).
Scholars certainly have a duty to appraise the activities of their own as well as foreign governments. *See generally* Finman & Macaulay, *Freedom to Dissent: The Vietnam Protests and the Words of Public Officials*, 1966 WIS. L. REV. 632. The point is simply that the wide circulation of the Lawyers' Committee Memorandum, endorsed by leading international law scholars and accompanied by the vocal theories of some Congressmen, created public attitudes about a number of legal points which it was hardly irrelevant or trivial to rebut. The legalistic "decaration of war" and "non-member" arguments were two of the principal arguments against lawfulness held out to the public.
108. Even the latest Lawyers' Committee efforts can only be fairly described as adversary in nature. *See* The Military Involvement of the United States in Vietnam: A Legal Analysis, *supra* note 107, and the nearly full-page advertisement "U.S. Intervention in Vietnam is Illegal," N.Y. Times, Jan. 15, 1967, at E 9.
According to a 1965 report of the International Association of Democratic Lawyers, apparently circulated principally in Europe, the Lawyers' Committee Memorandum was "distributed to 250,000 American lawyers." The Return of an I.A.D.L. Delegation from Vietnam, 1965, at 9 (unpublished manuscript). An advertisement of the Lawyers' Committee puts the distribution figure at 173,000 lawyers. THE NEW REPUBLIC, June 24, 1967, at 29. The advertisement also boasts distribution of 23,000 reprints of the N.Y. Times advertisement. *Id.*

It is perhaps inevitable in any on-going national dialogue with the importance of the Viet Nam debate that both sides will appeal as adversaries to legal arguments. Perspectives about authority are important in evaluating the wisdom of policies, and both proponents and opponents characteristically invoke legalities. The administration stress on the "obligation" arising from the SEATO Treaty[109] and the critics "non-member" argument are examples of attempts to invoke authority for contending foreign policy positions. When such appeals are made, the importance of perspectives about authority in shaping national policy make it important for legal scholars and advisors to point out essential discrepancies. In doing so they should recognize that they are performing only one task of the scholar or adviser and that, to the extent possible, clarification of community policies prior to decision may be a more important task.

The Vestiges of a Constitutional Attack

Although Professor Falk rejects the early Lawyer's Committee arguments that the President has no consitutional authority to use American military forces in Viet Nam without a declaration of war,[110] he contends that:

> The President has the constitutional authority to commit our armed services to the defense of South Viet Nam without a declaration of war *provided* that such "a commitment" is otherwise in accord with international law. Whether all or part of the United States action violates international law is also a constitutional question. . . . [T]he bombing of North Viet Nam appears to be an unconstitutional use of Presidential authority as well as a violation of international law.[111]

In this watered down form, Falk's somewhat monistic argument presents no independent grounds for unconstitutionality but depends in the first instance on the establishment of an international violation. And

---

109. The real force underlying the "obligation" argument is that United States actions with respect to Viet Nam have over a period of more than twelve years created substantial and very real expectations on the part of many Vietnamese and other Asians that the United States will assist in the defense of South Viet Nam. The SEATO Treaty was one such act both embodying and creating these expectations. SEATO grew out of the defeat of the French in the first Indo-China war, and historically has been intimately associated with the Viet Nam problem. *See* A. EDEN, FULL CIRCLE 148-49, 158-63 (1960).

110. Falk, *supra* note 77, at 1154. Professor Quincy Wright seems to substantially agree with Falk. "The issue seems unimportant in view of the broad Constitutional powers of the President to use armed force without Congressional support or declaration of war." Wright, *Legal Aspects of the Viet-Nam Situation*, 60 AM. J. INT'L L. 750, 768 (1966).

111. Falk, *supra* note 77, at 1155.

in postulating that international violation is a sufficient condition for constitutional violation the argument is erroneous. The international and constitutional consequences of exercise of the foreign relations power are not identical. The Supreme Court has held that Congress may constitutionally override valid treaties by later inconsistent legislation even though the later enactment would be a violation of international law.[112] These holdings are particularly relevant in light of the congressional authorization for executive use of the armed forces in Viet Nam, making such action in fact executive-congressional action.[113] The Executive and Congress substantially exercise the foreign affairs power of the nation and it is not clear that they are *ever* acting *unconstitutionally* solely because of violation of international norms. And if there is any authority that such action is *necessarily* unconstitutional Professor Falk does not share it with us.

It is one thing to recognize that customary and treaty norms of international law are part of "the law of the land" under Article VI for the purpose of binding the states (which essentially have no independent foreign relations power), and quite another to argue, as Professor Falk must under his thesis, that this article constitutionally restricts the exercise of the foreign relations power of the United States. It may be that in some contexts or when dealing with some types of international norms Congress or the Executive should be so restricted, but Professor Falk offers no constitutional standards as to what those contexts are. Some major problems which would have to be explored before his thesis could be applied to Viet Nam, even assuming international violation, are: What is the constitutional effect of the congressional authorization of the use of armed forces in Viet Nam by the Southeast Asia Resolution and other congressional actions with respect to Viet Nam? How do the "political question" problems affect the impact of this thesis?[114] And in what circumstances is it feasible or desirable to compel judicially changes in foreign policy because of an asserted violation of international law? As it stands, Professor Falk's

---

112. *See* Chae Chan Ping v. United States, 130 U.S. 581 (1889); Whitney v. Robertson, 124 U.S. 190 (1888); Dickinson, *The Law of Nations as National Law: "Political Questions,"* 104 U. PA. L. REV. 451, 487-90 (1956). For an illustration from Great Britain, see Mortensen v. Peters, 14 Scots L.T. 227 (1906).

113. For an analysis of the lawfulness of United States assistance to South Viet Nam under internal constitutional processes and a review of congressional action authorizing and affirming United States assistance, see Moore & Underwood, *The Lawfulness of United States Assistance to the Republic of Viet Nam,* 112 CONG. REC. 14,943, 14,960-67, 14,983-89 (daily ed. July 14, 1966).

114. *See generally* Dickinson, *supra* note 112.

constitutional argument is even more unpersuasive than the earlier "declaration of war" argument which he rejects.

Conclusion

The persistence of competing models of the Viet Nam conflict suggests that the conflict cannot be meaningfully generalized in black and white terms. Real-world Viet Nam is unalterably ambiguous, and writers on both sides do not perform a service when they assume a certainty and simplicity that does not exist. Although the conflict is not solely a product of "aggression from the North," the substantial interaction between Hanoi and the Viet Cong, the historical background of the conflict, and the objectives of Hanoi in supporting the sustained attack also belie meaningful characterization as civil strife. And Hanoi's unwillingness to negotiate mutual withdrawal from the South in the face of repeated United States declarations of willingness to promulgate a time table for withdrawal does not support a model which portrays Hanoi as merely concerned with offsetting United States assistance.

If because of Viet Nam Americans are asking themselves hard questions about the use of national power and the goals of foreign policy, the North Vietnamese must ask themselves hard questions about the use of force as an instrument of major international change. At some point it seems probable that this introspection will yield to a negotiated settlement. Neither side seems to have sufficient usable military and political power to win decisive victory short of a protracted struggle at great human and material cost. Secretary General U Thant is right both in perception and in emphasis when he terms the Viet Nam war basically a political problem that can only be solved by a political settlement. This, however, is a stricture that both sides must be willing to accept and to date the North Vietnamese have shown but flickers of interest in such a settlement. Despite this hard line from Hanoi, the United States must continue to emphasize a negotiated solution to the conflict and must energetically exploit any interest in negotiated settlement shown by participants in the opposing camp. A negotiated peace is the only alternative to a prolonged and increasingly dangerous conflict.

Emphasis on negotiated settlement should not obscure the fact that the conflict did not merely arise by accident, but that it reflects major differences in objectives of the contending participants and a value structure in Hanoi which exhibits greater willingness to achieve extension of its values by force. North Vietnamese disregard of this basic proscription against unilateral change by force is central to the conflict in Viet Nam. At Potsdam Stalin promised that Korea would be divided only temporarily,[115] but when temporary occupation of the north turned into permanent communization South Korea did not militarily attack across a major cold war dividing line despite United Nations support for a unified Korea. Such an attack from South Korea, like military assistance from North Viet Nam, could have been expected to trigger major conflict. The parallel, like all foreign affairs analogy, is not exact, but the contrast accurately points up a fundamental departure by North Viet Nam and those nations supporting it from the basic principle of the United Nations Charter outlawing war as an instrument of national policy. Acceptance by all nations of that fundamental requirement of minimum public order is a crucial first step toward a world community able to set aside its differences and get on with the real task of applying its immense resources to the alleviation of poverty, ignorance, and disease.

115. S. MORISON, THE OXFORD HISTORY OF THE AMERICAN PEOPLE 1065 (1965).

International Law and the United States Role in Viet Nam: A Response to Professor Moore

RICHARD A. FALK†

In the best traditions of scholarly debate Professor John Norton Moore has taken sharp and fundamental issue with the legal analysis of the United States' role in the Viet Nam War that I outlined in a previous issue of the *Yale Law Journal*.[1] Professor Moore has not persuaded me either that my approach is "simplistic" or that its application to Viet Nam is "unsound," but he has identified weaknesses and incompletenesses in my earlier formulation.[2] In addition, he has developed an alternative legal framework for assessing foreign intervention in violent struggles for the control of a national society. My objective in responding is to clarify the contending world order positions that each of us espouses. Although Professor Moore affirms and I deny the legality of the United States' military role in Viet Nam, the main center of intellectual gravity in this debate is less passing judgment on the grand legal issue of American presence (at this stage, a legalistic exercise), than it is assessing the policy implications of the Viet Nam precedent for the future of international legal order.

Professor Moore and I agree that international law can serve as a significant source of guidance to the national policy-maker in the area of war and peace. International law implies a process of decision incorporating perspectives that tend to be left out of account when government officials develop national policies solely by considering capabilities, strategies, and current foreign policy goals that are designed to maximize the short-run "national advantage." International law contains rules and standards rooted in the cosmopolitan tradition of a community of nations, whereas foreign policy tends to be rooted in the more particularistic traditions of each state. The future of world legal order may depend to a great degree on the extent to which the decision process relied upon in principal states to form foreign policy can come increasingly to incorporate more cosmopolitan perspectives.

† Milbank Professor of International Law, Woodrow Wilson School of Public and International Affairs; Faculty Associate, Center of International Studies, Princeton University; B.S. 1952, University of Pennsylvania; LL.B. 1955, Yale University.
1. Falk, *International Law and the United States Role in the Viet Nam War*, 75 YALE L.J. 1122 (1966).
2. Pages in parentheses in this article refer to Professor Moore's article.

International law has itself evolved through a process of decision in which national policies governing the appropriate uses of military power have been clarified by the assertion of adverse national claims buttressed by supporting explanations and rationale. This process is especially germane whenever the relevance of the rules to the claims of states is challenged on a legal basis, as it has been since the outset of major United States involvement in Viet Nam. The claims of governments to use or resist coercion serve as precedents for future claims and imply commitments to develop a certain kind of international legal system deemed beneficial both to the countries directly concerned and to the wider community of all states. My disagreement with Professor Moore centers upon the degree of discretion that international law presently accords to states with respect to the use of force in an international conflict resembling the one that has unfolded in Viet Nam in the years since 1954 and extends to the sorts of considerations (and their relative weight) that should have been taken into account in the decisions that led to the American military involvement at the various stages of its increasing magnitude. I would contend that the American military involvement resulted from a series of geo-political miscalculations, as well as from a process of decision insensitive to world order considerations.

The Viet Nam conflict demonstrates the harmful consequences for the control of international violence that can arise from contradictory national interpretations of what constitutes "aggression" and what constitutes permissible acts of "defense." Given the decentralized character of international society, it becomes more important than ever, in my view, to inhibit unilateral recourse to violence arising from contradictory and subjective national interpretations of a conflict situation. The war in Viet Nam illustrates a situation in which it is "reasonable" for each side to perceive its adversary as guilty of unprovoked aggression.[3] The potential for military escalation that follows from each side doing whatever it deems necessary to uphold its vital interests is an alarming freedom to grant governments in the nuclear age. My approach to these world order issues presupposes the central importance of establishing binding quasi-objective limits upon state discretion in international

---

3.   For a persuasive account by a psychologist as to why the North Vietnamese perceive the United States' role in Viet Nam as aggression see White, *Misperception of Aggression in Vietnam*, 21 J. INT'L AFF. 123 (1967); for a more fully documented presentation of the same position by the same author see White, *Misperception and the Vietnam War*, 22 J. SOCIAL ISSUES 1 (1967). The prospect of mutually contradictory perceptions of aggression held in good faith is central to my argument against Professor Moore's approach to world order problems. He takes no account of the reality or hazard of such misperception.

situations in which such contradictory inferences of "aggression" are characteristic. I would argue, also, that the whole effort of international law in the area of war and peace since the end of World War I has been to deny sovereign states the kind of unilateral discretion to employ force in foreign affairs that the United States has exercised in Viet Nam.[4]

Professor Moore appears content to endorse virtually unfettered sovereign discretion. In the role of a disinterested observer, he purports to pass judgment on the legal status of a contested claim to use force. Professor Moore sets forth a certain conception of world order that he posits as crucial for human welfare, and then proceeds to examine whether the claim to use force in the particular situation of Viet Nam is compatible with it. Every national decision-maker is expected to engage in the same process of assessment. But no account is taken of the serious problems of auto-interpretation that arise when recourse to force is contemplated or carried out in inflamed international settings. These problems arise because each side tends toward a self-righteous vindication of its own contentions and an equally dogmatic inattention to the merits of the adversary's position. Professor Moore's approach recalls the natural law tradition in which the purported deference to the normative restraints operative upon the behavior of a Christian prince turned out in practice to be little more than a technique of *post hoc* rationalization on the part of a government and its supporters. Surely, his analysis fails to accord reciprocal empathy to the adversary's reasonable perceptions as to who is responsible for what in Viet Nam. In fact, Professor Moore's endorsement of America's military role is neither widely nor wholeheartedly shared among states normally allied with the United States.[5]

It seems plain enough that Communist-oriented observers would regard the air strikes by the United States against North Viet Nam as unprovoked "aggression." Suggestions have even been made by more militant opponents of the United States' war actions that the passive

---

4. For a concise history of these efforts see Q. WRIGHT, THE ROLE OF INTERNATIONAL LAW IN THE ELIMINATION OF WAR (1961).

5. Anthony Lewis has summarized the situation in concise and moderate terms: "To go into the reasons for West European attitudes toward Vietnam would require rehearsing all the arguments about America's role there. Suffice it to say that only the British Government has had much favorable to say about American policy in Vietnam. No European country has a single soldier there. Much of the public on the Continent, rightly or not, see the situation as that of a huge power over-reacting." Lewis, *Why Humphrey Got That Abuse in Europe,* N.Y. Times, April 16, 1967, § 4, at 4, col. 4. Even the British Government has disassociated itself through a formal statement by her Prime Minister from United States bombing in June of 1966 of oil installations in Hanoi and Haiphong. For text of Mr. Wilson's statement see BRITISH RECORD, No. 12, July 14, 1966, Supp.

role of the Soviet Union amounts to "appeasement" of the United States and that it is the Soviet Union, not the United States, that should heed the lesson of Munich.[6] Professor Moore's emphasis on the discretion of the United States to furnish military assistance to Saigon needs to be supplemented by a consideration of what military assistance it would be reasonable for the Soviet Union and China to give to Hanoi; would not North Viet Nam be entitled to act in collective self-defense in response to sustained, large-scale bombing of its territory? And what limits could be legally placed on its exercise of self-defense other than those self-imposed by prudence and incapacity?

If we examine the war in Viet Nam from the perspective of North Viet Nam and with the same deference to self-determined reasonableness that Professor Moore confers upon the United States Government then it seems clear that the failure of the war to reach global proportions has been a consequence of Soviet and Chinese restraint (or incapacity); that is, Moore's world order position seems to legalize almost unlimited escalation by adversaries that perceive an ally as a victim of "aggression," even though that perception is not vindicated by any wider community determination and even though disinterested and reasonable men disagree as to who did what to whom. My earlier classification of international conflict into three broad categories is based on the need to avoid the anarchic consequences of adversary perception by fixing arbitrary but definite legal limits upon divergent interpretations of the rights and duties of national governments that find themselves involved in Viet Nam-type situations.[7]

Perhaps my position can be clarified by showing in a preliminary way why I reject the analogy between Viet Nam and Korea, an analogy that Professor Moore invokes to argue that similar defensive measures are appropriate in the two settings.[8] If the facts in Viet Nam are as

---

6. See, e.g., a passage from an editorial appearing in the French intellectual journal Les Temps Moderne: "The lack of clarity, the prudent policy of 'wait and see' are the tombs of the Socialist and revolutionary movement; they pave the way for other disasters just as surely as nonintervention against Spanish Fascism in 1936 set the stage for 1940 and what followed. But the parallel extends beyond the Spanish Civil War; it includes the capitulations that preceded and followed the Munich Agreements.

"The United States is convinced that the Soviet Union will desist from any test of strength until the end." The editorial goes on to call for "Socialist counter-escalation" by means of Soviet rocket strikes at United States air and naval installations in the Pacific area. Affirmative: A Deliberate Risk, translated and reprinted in 12 ATLAS, Nov. 1966, at 19, 20.

7. The basic rationale is set forth in Falk, supra note 1, at 1122-28. E.g., the United States is reported to have criticized the United Arab Republic for its attacks on Saudi Arabian border towns in the course of the struggle waged between the rival Yemeni factions for control of the Yemen. See N.Y. Times, May 17, 1967, at 1, col. 7.

8. There are other significant differences, including a war ending in 1954 for control

Professor Moore and the United States Government contend, then it might be true that North Viet Nam is guilty of a *covert* equivalent of the aggression that was attempted *overtly* in 1950 by North Korea.[9] But the assessment of the facts in Viet Nam is subject to multiple interpretations by reasonable observers in a way that the facts in Korea were not. Only the Communist states argued seriously against the conclusion that North Korea was an aggressor. Her overt military attack was sufficiently clear to permit a global consensus to form in support of defensive action by South Korea. In contrast, the obscurity of the conflict in Viet Nam generates widespread disagreement outside the Communist world as to whether either side can be termed "the aggressor," and impartial observers as august as the Secretary General of the United Nations[10] and the Pope[11] have repudiated any interpretation of the war

of the entire country, election provisions to translate this military outcome into political control at a time certain (1956), and a central government in Saigon that did not offer much prospect of governing South Viet Nam in any stable fashion even apart from Communist harrassment. Part of the relevant background is the demonstrated competence of Ho Chi Minh to govern Viet Nam in an effective manner, a competence evident even in the writings of those who are hostile to Communism and opposed to reunification under Hanoi's control. The capacity to govern territorial units effectively in the areas of the world most vulnerable to domestic trauma is itself a valuable constituent of the sort of international stability that the United States aspires to achieve for the Afro-Asian world. The background of Vietnamese social and cultural history also supports strongly the inference of an autonomous Vietnamese spirit, one that above all would resist any effort at domination by the Chinese. Ho Chi Minh's reasonableness was demonstrated in the period after World War II when he co-operated successfully with non-Communist factions in Viet Nam and made notable concessions to the French in exchange for an acknowledgment of his leadership of an independent Republic of Viet Nam; the French later repudiated these negotiations and the first Indochina War was born. For the sense of background see E. HAMMER, THE STRUGGLE FOR INDO-CHINA 1940-1955 (1955); L. BODARD, THE QUICKSAND WAR (1967); J. BUTTINGER, VIETNAM: THE EMBATTLED DRAGON [hereinafter cited as BUTTINGER].

Recently these points have also been made effectively in Farer, *The Enemy—Exploring the Sources of a Foreign Policy*, COLUMBIA UNIVERSITY FORUM, Spring 1967, at 13; see especially his quotation of the remark of Walter Robertson, Assistant Secretary of State for Far Eastern Affairs (an anti-Communist of such extreme character as to antagonize Anthony Eden because of his "emotional" approach): "If only Ho Chi Minh were on our side we could do something about the situation. But unfortunately he is the enemy." *Id.* 13.

9. It is important, however, to appreciate the degree of ambiguity that necessarily inheres in the context of *covert* coercion unless the foreign state proclaims its aggressive design, as has the United Arab Republic in relation to Israel. Without such a proclamation, one never made by North Viet Nam, the attribution of motives is speculative and unconvincing, especially if the assumed motives are relied upon to justify major responsive violence. In Korea, it was North Korea that justified its recourse to *overt* coercion by vague and unsupportable allegations that South Korea was planning to attack North Korea.

Bernard Fall commenting on the assertion "that North Vietnamese infiltration into South Viet Nam is the equivalent of the North Korean invasion of the ROK" writes that the comparison "omits the embarrassing fact that anti-Diem guerrillas were active long before infiltrated North Vietnamese elements joined the fray." B. FALL, THE TWO VIET-NAMS 345 (2d rev. ed. 1967).

10. There are many indications of Thant's position on the matter. *E.g.*, N.Y. Times, June 21, 1966, at 1, col. 5.

11. *Cf.* Pope Paul's Encyclical on Peace of Sept. 19, 1966, text in N.Y. Times, Sept. 20,

in Viet Nam that identifies North Viet Nam as the aggressor. France has openly repudiated the United States' conception of the war, and neutral public opinion at home and abroad is, to say the least, sharply split.[12] This situation of dissensus sharply distinguishes Viet Nam from

1966, at 18, col. 2. For example, taking account of the tradition of indirect rhetoric, the following passage was written with obvious application to war in Viet Nam: "We cry to them in God's name to stop. Men must come together and offer concrete plans and terms in all sincerity. A settlement should be reached now, even at the expense of some inconvenience or loss, for it may have to be made later in the train of bitter slaughter and involve great loss." The following sentence also confirms the emphasis upon the non-condemnation of either side as aggressor: "Now again, therefore, we lift up our voice, 'with piercing cry and with tears' (Hebrews, v, 7), very earnestly beseeching those who have charge of the public welfare to strive with every means available to prevent the further spread of the conflagration, and even to extinguish it entirely." More recently, Pope Paul VI has specifically urged the cessation of all forms of violence throughout Viet Nam. N.Y. Times, May 25, 1967, at 4, col. 4.

12. I regard the unprecedented intensity, range, and character of the protest movement directed at the American military involvement in Viet Nam to be significantly relevant to an appraisal of the status of United States claims under international law. The standards governing the use of force in world affairs reflect moral attitudes toward those occasions upon which it is appropriate to rely upon military power. This widespread protest phenomenon reflects the moral conviction of people throughout the world that the United States is guilty of aggressive war in Viet Nam; such a moral conviction is not inconsistent with the democratically-based support for the war given by the American public, according priority to winning a war that should not have been fought rather than to accepting the need to acknowledge error. Edwin O. Reischauer, the former American Ambassador to Japan, has well stated this orientation toward the war taken by those who continue to give their support, however, grudgingly, to the American effort in Viet Nam:

> There is not much agreement in this country about the war in Vietnam, except that it is something we should have avoided. We are paying a heavy price for it—in lives, in national wealth and unity, and in international prestige and influence. The best we can hope for from the war is sufficient peace and stability to allow that small and weak country to get painfully to its feet at last; the worst is a nuclear conflict too horrible to contemplate. Reischauer, *What We Should do Next in Asia*, Look, April 4, 1967, at 21.

It may also be well to ponder the following paragraph from the editorial columns of *The New Reublic*:

> Simultaneously [with other beneficial international policies of the United States] Mr. Johnson is pushing the Vietnam war—which is a disastrous thing. It is all very well to say the country backs him, Governor Romney being the latest "me too" recruit. Yes, the polls show the public supports continued bombing, 67 percent. But a second series of polls shows only 37 percent backing Mr. Johnson's handling of the war. Reconciling these two views isn't really very difficult. The public loathes the war. It doesn't want defeat, but it wants *out*. The two moods conflict. It backs the bombing on the simplistic ground that that will end the war quickly. And it is taking out its resentment for the war dilemma consciously or unconsciously by making Mr. Johnson the scapegoat. The New Republic, April 22, 1967, at 2.

Among those aspects of the protest against participation in the war that are most legally notable have been the efforts, never made in the Korean context to nearly the same extent, to obtain a determination by domestic courts that participation in the Viet Nam war is tantamount to the commission of a war crime; the reasoning being that the German and Japanese war crimes trials conducted after World War II concluded that an individual is criminally accountable for participation in a war of aggression (i.e., an illegal war) regardless of whether or not he is carrying out the orders of his government. There are also many cases now arising for the first time of "selective conscientious objection" in which individuals subject to the draft are claiming exemption not because they are opposed to war *in general* but because they oppose the Viet Nam war *in particular* on grounds of conscience. A dramatic instance of litigation to test whether there is a legal

Korea and strongly suggests that the discretion to act "defensively" requires some source of restraint more dependable than the wisdom of the belligerent states.[13]

The presence or absence of a consensus has considerable bearing on the legal status of a contested claim to use force in international society.[14] The Charter of the United Nations purports to restrict the unilateral discretion of states to use force to resolve international conflicts.[15] In cases where a claim of self-defense is made and challenged,

---

right of conscientious objection to a particular war has been filed. Capt. Dale E. Noyd of the Air Force Academy in the Federal District Court of Colorado in Denver. N.Y. Times, April 20, 1967, at 5, col. 3; for a description of the litigation see CIVIL LIBERTIES, No. 245, April 1967, at 1, 5. For a continuing description of evidence supporting the invocation of selective conscientious objection in the Viet Nam context see the responsible reporting of the weekly British newspaper Peace News, the bi-monthly American magazine VIET REPORT, or almost any French organ of opinion (left, right, or center). For one (among many) vivid account of the horrors inflicted on Vietnamese society see McCarthy, *Report from Vietnam II: The Problems of Success*, N.Y. REVIEW OF BOOKS, May 4, 1967, at 4.

Furthermore, for the first time during a period of war a group of international lawyers have gone on record against their own government to contend that the United States military involvement in Viet Nam is "illegal," and constitutes a violation of *both* international law and the U.S. Constitution. CONSULTATIVE COUNCIL OF THE LAWYERS' COMMITTEE ON AMERICAN POLICY TOWARDS VIETNAM AND INTERNATIONAL LAW (1967) [hereinafter cited as CONSULTATIVE COUNCIL]. The members of the Consultative Council are R. J. Barnet, R. A. Falk (Chairman), John H.E. Fried (Rapporteur), John H. Herz, Stanley Hoffmann, Wallace McClure, Saul H. Mendlovitz, Richard S. Miller, Hans J. Morgenthau, William G. Rice, and Quincy Wright.

Also for the first time since World War II there has been proposed a war crime tribunal to pass judgment on the United States role in Viet Nam and on the criminal responsibility of its President. Of course, Bertrand Russell's tribunal is a juridical farce, but the fact that it is plausible to contemplate such a proceeding and to obtain for its tribunal several celebrated individuals bears witness to the general perception of the war. For Jean-Paul Sartre's explanation of why he has agreed to serve as a judge on the Russell tribunal see Sartre, *Imperialist Morality*, 41 NEW LEFT REVIEW 3 (1967).

See also SENATE REPUBLICAN POLICY COMMITTEE, BLUE BOOK ON VIET NAM (May 1, 1967); for the text of its principal conclusions questioning the entire basis of the war see excerpts from G.O.P. Paper on War, N.Y. Times, May 2, 1967, at 10, col. 3.

13. The vagueness of the justification is accentuated in consequence by the gradual evolution of "the commitment." What started off in Viet Nam as a reluctant and indirect involvement that needed no special justification was successively widened and deepened until the involvement itself became the principal justification. With over 400,000 Americans fighting in Viet Nam and with casualties continuing to mount, there is a sense that the American effort must not be in vain; the consequence is an apparently irreversible government commitment to use military means to accomplish a political objective—namely, to defeat the Vietcong insurrection, without according any governmental legitimacy to the N.L.F.

14. The relevance of an international consensus to the legality of contested national action is considered in Falk, *On the Quasi-Legislative Competence of the General Assembly*, 60 AM. J. INT'L L. 782 (1966). And see the dissenting opinion of Judge Tanaka in the South West Africa Cases for an analysis in the setting of human rights of the shift from an emphasis upon sovereign autonomy to community solidarity in determining the character of international legal obligations. Judgment in the South West Africa Cases, July 18, 1966, [1966] I.C.J. 248, 292-94.

15. For a helpful exposition of the restrictive intention of the relevant Charter provisions see Henkin, *Force, Intervention, and Neutrality in Contemporary International Law*, 1963 PROC. AM. SOC'Y INT'L L. 147; P. JESSUP, A MODERN LAW OF NATIONS 165-67 (1948); in this context it is not necessary to contend that Article 51 restricts traditional self-defense in terms of some rigid conception of "armed attack," but only that the dis-

the burden of justification is upon the claimant. It is always possible to argue that a use of force is "defensive" and that it promotes world order by inhibiting "aggression." Therefore, fairly clear community standards would be needed to assure that what is called "defensive" is defensive; in the absence of clear community standards it becomes important to allow international institutions to determine whether recourse to "defensive force" is justified by a prior "armed attack." Where there are no generally accepted objective standards and where rivals put forward contradictory factual interpretations it becomes difficult or impossible to mobilize a consensus in the international institutions entrusted with the maintenance of peace and security.[16] Viet Nam presents such a situation of uncertainty and institutional paralysis. What restraints upon sovereign discretion to use force remain relevant? The appraisals of disinterested international civil servants, especially the

cretion of states to have recourse to force in self-defense is subject to justification and review. See, e.g., D. BOWETT, SELF-DEFENCE IN INTERNATIONAL LAW 216-18, 241, 244-45, 261 (1958), emphasizing the importance of restricting discretionary recourse to self-defense, especially on a collective basis, in the Viet Nam-type situation.

16.   Even a defensive alliance such as SEATO has been unable to maintain its solidarity in the face of the disputed facts and policies generated by the Viet Nam conflict. France and Pakistan, both Members, refuse to give their assent to SEATO's endorsement of the American "interpretation" of the war in Viet Nam. It should be recalled that SEATO was a pact among anti-Communist states determined to resist the coercive spread of Asian Communism, including explicitly its spread to South Viet Nam; the non-Communist neutralist states of Asia are, without exception, even more dubious about the American "interpretation." The relevant point is that a claim to be acting in a "defensive" way when force is used against a foreign society has no legal status unless it is supported by some kind of international authorization that commands respect; otherwise it is merely a contention by an adversary determined to make unilateral use of military power against a foreign society.

A study of South Viet Nam attitudes suggest that even in the late phases of the war in Viet Nam the people of the country reject the official United States version of "defensive" action. The poll was conducted for Columbia Broadcasting Company by Opinion Research Corporation, a respected professional polling outfit, consisted of an interview of 1,545 persons living in five major cities, 55 hamlets, and was limited to civilians of voting age living in "secured areas," those not under Vietcong control. The poll took place between November 24, 1966 and February 1, 1967. When asked who was responsible for continuing the war 31 per cent blamed the Vietcong and only 12 per cent blamed the Government of North Viet Nam; when asked whether bombing should be continued against villages suspected of containing the Vietcong 46 per cent favored an end to bombing while 37 per cent wanted it continued; when asked whether to stress negotiations with North Viet Nam or to extend military operations to North Viet Nam 60 per cent favored more emphasis on negotiations whereas only about 14 per cent favored increased military action; and finally when asked whether they favored reunification after the end of the war 83 per cent were reported in favor and only 5 per cent opposed. N.Y.Times, March 22, 1967, at 10, col. 7. The remarkable thing about this poll is that among strong anti-Communist South Vietnamese (65 per cent blamed the Communist side for the continuation of the war and only 5 per cent blamed the anti-Communist side) exposed primarily to government propaganda there still appears to be a rejection of the American idea that the war is a consequence of "aggression from the North." The attitudes on reunification also sharply question the Saigon-Washington insistence on separate sovereighty for the North and the South. See the similar character of an anti-Communist, anti-American interpretation of the war by a distinguished Buddhist in South Viet Nam, T. HANH, VIETNAM LOTUS IN A SEA OF FIRE (1967).

Secretary General of the United Nations, are distinctly relevant in this setting. The Secretary General contributes an impartial perspective and can, as U Thant has chosen to do with respect to Viet Nam, delineate the character of reasonable behavior by the adversary parties.[17] Normally such an official will refrain from judging the behavior of the participants in a conflict that cannot be handled by agreement in the political organs. The persistent refusal of the United States to comply with U Thant's proposals is indicative of its unilateral approach to the determination of the legitimacy of a contested use of international force.[18] The essence of a law-oriented approach to the use of force is to

---

17. The essential aspect of a legal settlement is the search for impartial sources of decision. It is the impartial decision-maker that is in the best position to assess the relative merits of adversary positions. This does not assure correct or just decisions in any particular instance, but merely that there will be a legal quality for the decision. The Secretary General of the United Nations is the most authoritative impartial decision-maker in the international system, especially in relation to Members of the United Nations. To deny his role or to ignore his recommendation is to subordinate the process of impartial decision to the process of unilateral decision, tending thereby to rely on power rather than law to shape the outcome of controversy.

18. The opposition of the United States to the efforts of U Thant to work for a settlement are summarized in AMERICAN FRIENDS SERVICE COMMITTEE, PEACE IN VIETNAM 50-52 (1966); F. SCHURMANN, P. SCOTT, & R. ZELNIK, THE POLITICS OF ESCALATION IN VIETNAM 135-38 (1966). On June 20, 1966, U Thant made a three-point proposal for ending the war in Viet Nam:

    (1.) Unconditional cessation of bombing in North Viet Nam;
    (2.) Scaling down of military operations in South Viet Nam;
    (3.) Inclusion of the National Liberation Front in any proposed negotiations.

N.Y. Times, June 21, 1966, at 1, col. 5. The failure of the United States to accept this proposal, consisting according to U Thant of those steps that "alone can create the conditions" leading to a peaceful settlement, is indicative of its unilateral approach to the use of military power in Viet Nam. U Thant, as Secretary General, represents the voice of the international community, a voice that deserves to be heeded especially by a Great Power using its military power to overwhelm a small state. The role of the Secretary General in identifying reasonable conduct for parties in conflict is especially great when the political organs have failed to discharge their responsibility to maintain international peace and security. As in other dealings with the United Nations during the Viet Nam war the United States has made pro forma gestures indicating its acceptance of the Secretary General's role. See, e.g., Arthur J. Goldberg's letter to U Thant in which it is said that "the United States Government will cooperate fully with you in getting such discussion started promptly [on ending the war] and in bringing them to a successful completion." Text, N.Y. Times, Dec. 20, 1966, at 6, col. 4. The United States will cooperate fully provided that it does not have to alter its belligerent and political posture. U Thant is setting forth his conception of reasonable preconditions for peace talks. What does our cooperation entail if it does not lead to an acceptance of these preconditions? Our noncooperation with U Thant is heightened by the fact that the preconditions he describes are those that seem calculated to bring the war to an end and to initiate negotiations on a reasonable basis that corresponds to the domestic balance of forces. Negotiations would proceed on an unnatural basis if either the suspension of bombing was conditional—it would be a club of death suspended by a powerful state over the destinies of a weak one—or the N.L.F. was not accorded some degree of legitimacy as a political force in South Viet Nam of a character equal to that of the Saigon regime. The insistence on nonrecognition is part of the effort to negotiate as if the N.L.F. were a creature of North Viet Nam rather than a political entity with a reality of its own. President Johnson has often repeated the idea that during the negotiations "the Vietcong will have no difficulty having their views heard," but this is not a very satisfactory assurance for an insurgent faction that has fought for over a decade to control South Viet Nam. Transcript of President's

submit claims to the best available procedures for community review and to restrict force to the levels authorized.[19]

A second kind of restraint in a situation of ambiguity is to confine violence within existing international boundaries. The decision by the United States to bomb North Viet Nam and to take military action in the territory of Laos and Cambodia is further disregard for available limits upon the self-interpretation of legal rights.[20] It is true that the United States is *not* yet using all the military power at its disposal against North Viet Nam, but such restraint is itself based on the exercise of discretion rather than upon deference to community procedures or to quasi-objective standards of limitation.[21]

News Conference on the Guam Parley, N.Y. Times, March 22, 1967, at 11, col. 3. It does not make the consent of the N.L.F. an ingredient of settlement, nor does it give to the N.L.F. any of the formal prerogatives of the Saigon regime. In effect, the civil war is ended not as a stalemate, but as a victory for the government side as it remains the sole constituted political élite.

19. We associate the intervention of law in human affairs with the role of the third-party decision-maker who is entrusted with the task of sorting out adversary contentions. International society as decentralized often successfully works out the content of reasonableness through action and interaction of adversary parties, provided the issues at stake are not vital to national security or national honor. In the context of force, however, the differential of power between adversaries of unequal strength influences their degree of flexibility in responding to counter-claims; the differences between the results of adversary interaction and of impartial third-party judgment are likely to be pronounced. The substitution of law for force in any social order involves, then, the gradual replacement of the ideology of self-help by that of third-party judgment. Perhaps, the clearest jurisprudential discussion of the limits of law in a decentralized political system is contained in H. KELSEN, PRINCIPLES OF INTERNATIONAL LAW 3-87 (2d rev. ed. Tucker 1966).

20. Both sides have violated "the sovereignty" of Laos and Cambodia, but the United States has frequently bombed infiltrators and supply lines within the territory of both states, thereby expanding further the extra-national scope of violence beyond South Viet Nam. See MANSFIELD, ET AL., REPORT TO SENATE FOREIGN RELATIONS COMM., 89th Cong., 2d Sess., THE VIETNAM CONFLICT: THE SUBSTANCE AND THE SHADOW 8-10 (Comm. Print 1966) [hereinafter cited as THE MANSFIELD REPORT]. An equivalent action by North Viet Nam or the Soviet Union would be to attack the United States air bases in Thailand. Such an expansion of the arena of combat would move the conflict dramatically closer to the threshold of general warfare. It is important to emphasize that the limited scope of the war in Viet Nam is a consequence of the failure of the Soviet Union and China to take *equivalent action* on behalf of Hanoi; such a failure is especially important in view of the United States demand that Hanoi take equivalent action in exchange for an end to bombing. See note 27 *infra*.

21. The United States reserves the discretion to decide for itself the degree of military force that it requires to secure North Viet Nam's acquiescence. In this David and Goliath situation, David is on a rack of death that has been slowly tightened over the years by a process we describe as "escalation." Goliath has had and continues to have the capacity at any point to kill David, but has sought instead to inflict pain and to threaten increasing pain until David gives in to the demands of Goliath. There is no reciprocity in such a situation of inequality. To claim restraint for Goliath is to ignore the rationale for this way of proceeding by stages. Among other factors to bear in mind is that Goliath knows that David has powerful, Goliath-like friends that may enter the scene more actively. See, e.g., the report of Harry Ashmore's visit to Hanoi on behalf of the Center for the Study of Democratic Institutions in which he quotes "a Colonel of the North Vietnamese General Staff" who "answered very solemnly" a question about his estimate "of North Vietnam's capacity to resist the American troops":

We've thought about this a great deal. We think we can handle up to 2,000,000

In this respect, the mode of Type I conflict (Korea) allows proportionate defense responses including unilateral action against the attacking state,[22] whereas in a Type II or III conflict (Viet Nam), third-party military action is either prohibited altogether or its scope confined to the political entity wherein the struggle is going on. In either event, the tendency to escalate is curtailed. My categorization of international conflict is intended to guide decision-makers and observers toward a sense of what is reasonable in a particular situation. A strong element of national discretion remains. The limits on international violence are only quasi-objective restrictions upon sovereign prerogatives.[23] There

---

Americans. This assumes that you do not increase your bombing beyond its present level. I think your combat troops will concede that we are masters of guerrilla war. We should be—we've been at it for twenty-five years. We are far less dependent on heavy supplies than your army. We are accustomed to fighting in this terrain of jungle and mountains and this advantage offsets the undoubted superiority of your sophisticated weapons and planes. This is why we think we can handle up to 2,000,000 of your troops, and stay here the rest of the century if necessary. Of course, if you put in more than 2,000,000 soldiers, or if you escalate the bombing to the point where you completely destroy our communications, then we have to accept volunteers from China, from Russia, and it would be a new war. It would no longer be our war. It would be World War III.

Mr. Ashmore commented that:

I have to assume an element of propaganda in this, but I also say that I believe the Colonel meant what he said, and was consciously reflecting the considered judgment of the North Vietnamese government. Ashmore, *Pacem in Terris II: Mission to North Vietnam*, CENTER DIARY, March-April 1967, at 17.

22. Korea is not truly an example of Type I, but of Type IV, because the United States' role was authorized by the United Nations; see pp. 1106-07 *infra* for explanation of Type IV. Nevertheless, to point up the relationship between Korea and Viet Nam it is possible to pierce the cosmopolitan veil, emphasize Soviet opposition and question the propriety of an authorization obtained in the Security Council during the Soviet boycott, and thereby view the response in Korea *as if* it proceeded without benefit of United Nations approval. In that case, Korea would appear to be an instance of Type I authorizing whatever military action is needed to restore the *status quo ante* the armed attack. On this basis I believe that the defensive armies should not have proceeded beyond the 38th Parallel, although it would have been permissible to commit war acts against North Korean territory so as to restore the *status quo ante*.

23. The Legal Adviser, Leonard Meeker, finds no difficulty in reconciling my categories of analysis with United States policy in Viet Nam: "The evidence does not allow for the conclusion that the war in Viet-Nam was ever a simple category-one situation. It was probably, for quite some period of time, a category-two situation. By the end of 1964, however, it had become very clearly a category-three situation." Meeker, *Viet-Nam and the International Law of Self-Defense*, 56 DEP'T STATE BULL. 54, 59 (1967). Mr. Meeker merely characterizes the facts to support the American legal position, including the shift of the war into "the third category." (Type I) By the end of 1964, mainly over a period of four years, about 40,000 are reported to have infiltrated from North Viet Nam according to official United States statistics. Most of those infiltrated during this period were ethnic Southerners that joined up with Vietcong units. There are several factors that militate against Mr. Meeker's inference of "armed attack" (that is, category three): first, the insurgency pre-existed North Vietnamese infiltration; as Fall notes "there had been a fairly strong anti-Diem insurgent current of non-Communist origins even before the 1956 deadline on elections between the two zones went by. . . ." B. FALL, THE TWO VIET-NAMS 356 (2d rev. ed. 1967) (*cf.* map showing pattern of insurgent control as of 1962-63, p. 354); second, the Saigon regime was enabled to resist the N.L.F. in the years before 1961 only because it was given such large amounts of economic support by the United States in the years after 1954; as the first Mansfield Report observes "in matters of

is also some uncertainty as to whether a particular conflict belongs in one category rather than another. So long as the organized international community is unable to determine the limits on authorized violence, thereby placing the conflict within Type IV (see next paragraph) it remains necessary to rely upon national discretion. The objective of articulating Types I-III is to enable a more rational exercise of national discretion through the clarification of the relationship between factual patterns and legal expectations. If states would adhere in practice to these limits, *ex parte* interpretations of fact and of law on claims to use violence in international society would decline in importance.

Professor Moore's world order position, as presently stated, ignores the relevance of international institutions and of a supranational perspective to an assessment of the legal status of a controverted use of military power. To emphasize the problem of curtailing national discretion in a world of political conflict I would now add Type IV to the previous three types.[24] Type IV conflict exists whenever a competent international organization of global (IVa) or regional (IVb) dimensions

---

defense, internal stability and economic support, the Vietnamese Government has come to depend almost wholly on the United States for outside assistance. In terms of aid, the assumption of this preponderant responsibility has meant U.S. outlays of $1.4 billion for economic assistance during the period of 1955-62. This economic aid has had some effect on Vietnamese development, but its primary purpose has been to sustain the Vietnamese economy so that it, in turn, could maintain the burden of a military establishment which has been upward of 150,000 men for the past half decade. On top of the economic aid, there has also been provided large amounts of military equipment and supplies and training for the Vietnamese Army, Navy, and Air Force and for other defense purposes. For the period 1955-62 the total of aid of all kinds in Viet Nam stands at more than $2 billion. THE MANSFIELD REPORT, app. II, at 19. For tables on the degree of United States involvement since 1954, see G. KAHIN & J. LEWIS, THE UNITED STATES IN VIETNAM 73, 185 (1967) [hereinafter cited as KAHIN & LEWIS].

The point is that North Vietnamese military assistance to an ongoing insurgency was a proportionate response at all stages to the extent of United States involvement on behalf of Saigon. And when one considers that North Viet Nam had a reasonable (if not absolutely assured) expectation that the Geneva settlement would lead to unification under their control after a period of transition enabling the French to depart, then the American interposition of a powerful non-Vietnamese "presence" must also enter into an appraisal of North Viet Nam's pre-1965 role. In such a context it seems unreasonable and without legal foundation to construe North Viet Nam's military assistance to the Vietcong as becoming an attack by one country on another. Without such a premise of attack, the United States response against North Vietnamese territory would be "unprovoked aggression." Recourse to self-defense implies a prior armed attack, and that is why United States position depends on "the armed attack" taking place before bombing the North began in February 1965.

24. In my earlier article, then, Korea and Suez are not properly examples of Type I after there was authorization of defensive action by the United Nations. Type I becomes Type IV as soon as the United Nations itself acts or authorizes action. The description, then, of Type I, in Falk, *supra* note 1, at 1126, should be amended accordingly. Types II and III can also be transferred into Type IV, although the conjectural nature of the facts and the less direct connection to international peace and security makes such a transfer less likely to take place. The Indian attack upon Goa and the Chinese attack upon Tibet are examples of Type I provided the victim entities are entitled to the status of "states." Goa's defensive prerogatives are also qualified by the limited legitimacy of colonial title to territory as of 1961.

authorizes the use of force.[25] Type IVa can be illustrated by reference to United Nations actions in Korea (1950), Suez (1956), Cyprus, and the Congo (1960). The authorization or prohibition of violence by the United Nations resolves the issue of legality, even though a particular decision may be arbitrary or unjust in any given set of circumstances.[26] The point here is that Type IV entails an authoritative consensus that may be absent in Types I-III.[27] Thus, the context of my first Yale article

25. The legal status of Type IVb is more problematical than that of Type IVa. For one thing regional organizations are themselves subject to regulation by the Security Council (Article 53(1) says that "no enforcement action shall be taken under regional arrangements or by regional agencies without the authorization of the Security Council."). For another, the opposition of the Arab League to Israel, of the Organization of African Unity to South Africa, and of the Organization of American States to Castro's Cuba points to the danger of "aggression" under the legitimizing aegis of supranationalism. At the same time, the existence of regional support for recourse to coercion is a factor that alters the legal status of a controversial use of military power. It is important to distinguish a regional actor—such as the O.A.S.—from an *ex parte* defensive alliance—such as SEATO. Authorization by SEATO would not move the conflict into Type IVb, although the absence of such authorization might cast light on claims to respond within the framework of Type I.

26. This possibility leads Julius Stone, among others, to deny almost altogether the restrictive impact of the Charter system of controls upon the discretion of sovereign states. J. STONE, AGGRESSION AND WORLD ORDER 1-3, 78-103 (1958).

27. In the absence of an authoritative consensus on a global level that embodies divergent perspectives, the construction of second-order constraints upon adversary perspectives is the essential task of international law. Types I-III provide quasi-objective guidelines that tend to confine an international conflict. Departures from these guidelines could be justified legally by exceptional circumstances and for specific objectives. But the second-order system of constraint depends on a fair correlation of the conflict with the system of graduated categories. The United States insistence on viewing North Viet Nam's role as warranting a Type I response is destructive of second-order constraints as the basic categorization does not command respect from many uncommitted observers. The generalized bombing of North Viet Nam could not be easily justified as an exception to Type II. Specific attacks upon extra-territorial guerrilla sanctuaries might be justified if the conflict was otherwise contained within Type II limits. But the objectives of bombing North Viet Nam seem primarily connected with an overall effort to secure their acquiescence to our conception of the war in South Viet Nam. President Johnson's letter of March 1, 1967 to Senator Jackson gives the Government's rationale for bombing North Viet Nam in fairly complete terms; significantly, this letter ends by saying "we shall persist with our operations in the North—until those who launched this aggression are prepared to move seriously to reinstall the agreements whose violations have brought the scourge of war to Southeast Asia." Earlier the letter says that bombing will end when the other side is willing *to take equivalent action . . ."* (emphasis added). *See President Reviews U.S. Position on Bombing of North Viet-Nam,* 56 DEP'T STATE BULL. 514, 516 (1967). What is equivalent action if it is conceded that extra-territorial violence is, at best, an *extraordinary* incident of a Type II conflict? Supplying and sending troops to aid the N.L.F. is a *normal* incident of Type II conflict. To demand, as seems implied by the official United States position, the elimination of a normal claim by a third-party state in exchange for the termination of an extraordinary claim (and in Viet Nam the extraordinary nature of the claim is aggravated by its assertion in extravagant, unspecific, and accelerating form) by its third-party opponent seems highly unreasonable. It is worth recalling that the United States' original justification for bombing North Viet Nam in February 1965 was formulated in the restrictive and exception-explaining logic of Type II as a reprisal for Vietcong attacks on United States airfields in South Viet Nam; it is worth noting that the legal reflex in February 1965 was in the manner of Type II, not Type I. This is worth noting because of the subsequent official explanations that the Viet Nam war clearly belonged to Type I by the end of 1964. *Cf.* note 23 *supra; see also* The Legality of United States Participation in the Defense of Viet-Nam, Office of the

and of this reply to Moore is provided by the conflict in Viet Nam, a conflict in which the United Nations has not been able to act collectively through its main political organs.[28] This context is in the range of Types I-III.[29]

Having set forth the factors that shape my world order position, I will turn now to Professor Moore's specific criticisms of my approach. He has three main objectives:

(1) I have construed the Viet Nam facts in a one-sided manner;

(2) My system of categorization imposes arbitrary limits on a state using force for defensive purposes;

(3) My system really declares my views as to what international law *ought to be* although it pretends to be a statement of present legal obligations binding upon a state.

Professor Moore's first principal criticism pertains primarily to my argument that it would have been appropriate to regard the conflict in Viet Nam as an example of a Type III conflict, that is, as an example of civil strife internal to one country. The second and third criticisms pertain primarily to my chief argument that the conflict in Viet Nam, whatever its early history, has become an example of Type II conflict, that is, an example of civil strife in South Viet Nam with substantial intervention on behalf of the two contending factions, the Saigon regime and the National Liberation Front (N.L.F.) (these criticisms are discussed below in Section II).

Legal Adviser, Department of State, 112 CONG. REC. 5274 (daily ed. March 10, 1966). For original reliance on a reprisal theory see Falk, *supra* note 1, at 1145; for legal criticism of even the attempt to rely on a reprisal theory see CONSULTATIVE COUNCIL 53-57.

28. But the United States bears a heavy burden of responsibility for the inaction of the United Nations as a consequence of the following considerations:

(1) Non-compliance with the proposals of the Secretary General, U Thant;

(2) Non-submission of the claim to act in self-defense to the Security Council or General Assembly for serious community review;

(3) Refusal in early stages of conflict to seek a peaceful settlement through negotiations;

(4) Alienation of China from the United Nations by its continuing exclusion from the activities of the Organization;

(5) Ambiguity as to the sincerity of United States offers to negotiate, as a consequence of coupling peace moves with steps up the escalation ladder. For scholarly documentation see F. SCHURMANN, P. SCOTT, & R. ZELNIK, THE POLITICS OF ESCALATION IN VIETNAM (1966).

29. The important distinction is between the sort of legal order that exists for Types I-III and for Type IV:

Types I-III are governed by second-order constraints self-imposed by sovereign states and based upon such quasi-objective sources of guidance and limitations as past practice, public opinion, recommendation of impartial third-party actors such as the Secretary General and the Pope, and well-defined international boundaries.

Type IV conflicts are governed by first-order constraints consisting of the determinations of international institutions. First-order constraints are *procedural* out-comes on a supranational level, whereas second-order constraints are *substantive* out-comes on a national level.

I. The Rationale Restated in Support of a Type III Classification of the Viet Nam War

Let me state clearly that when large-scale military participation by the United States in the war began to take place—say 1963—it became appropriate to treat the conflict as Type II. North Vietnamese large-scale military participation on behalf of the N.L.F. accentuates this classification of the war. My principal contention denies that the *factual* basis exists to warrant treating the Viet Nam War as belonging in Type I (which would authorize extra-territorial defensive measures) and, as a correlate denies that there exists a *legal* basis for extra-territorial violence if the war is classified as Type II. However, it remains important to consider the conflict in Viet Nam also as belonging originally in Type III so as to appreciate the principal role of the United States in converting the war into Type II, such a conversion involving conduct itself seriously at variance with my conception of the requirements of world order.[30] It is also important to acknowledge that the

---

30. The transformation from Type III to Type II is a matter of *policy* rather than *law* in any normal sense; "In sum, international law has never been equipped to intervene in civil war situations." Friedmann, *Intervention, Civil War and the Rôle of International Law*, 1965 PROC. AM. SOC'Y INT'L L. 67, 74. There are no criteria that are usefully available to identify prohibited interventions, although some efforts have been recently made to prohibit overt and direct military participation. *See* Farer, *Intervention in Civil Wars: A Modest Proposal*, 67 COLUM. L. REV. 266 (1967). The real issues of policy confronting the United States are the degree to which it reacts to revolutionary events in the Afro-Asian and Latin American countries as properly hostile to its interests. For critical accounts of this aspect of foreign policy, see E. STILLMAN & W. PFAFF, POWER AND IMPOTENCE, 15-59, 184-226 (1966); H. ZINN, VIETNAM: THE LOGIC OF WITHDRAWAL 37-50 (1967); and *see* T. HANH, VIETNAM LOTUS IN A SEA OF FIRE 60-68 (1967) for the entangling of nationalism and communism in the Viet Nam setting. For a pro-Administration judgment of the American response to foreign revolutionary activity see W. Rostow, *The Great Transition: Tasks of the First and Second Postwar Generations*, 56 DEP'T STATE BULL. 491 (1967).

The transformation from Type II to Type I is regulated by international law as it implies violent conflict *between* sovereign states rather than *within* a sovereign state. Initiating recourse to international violence, as distinct from interventionary violence, requires the prior occurrence of an armed attack.

The consequences of this difference between shifting from III to II and from III or II to I are to make different kinds of legal arguments appropriate in each context. At the same time the difference in argument can be over-stated. A successful claim by a state to act in a manner not previously regarded as legal may itelf constitute authoritative state practice that can be relied upon in the future by others, thereby transforming what had once been regarded as prohibited into what comes to be regarded as permissible. In a context where legal expectations have been regarded as well-fixed policy, considerations may incline an actor to posit a legislative claim, which if effectively asserted and accepted by the wider community, tends to reshape legal expectations. In both contexts, therefore, there is an unavoidable discretionary role played by the state with the capability to act in different ways, but in the interventionary axis of decision (III-II) there is less disposition to regard the decision to intervene as a weakening of legal order than in the armed attack-self-defense axis of decision wherein legal expectation of fairly settled character had been thought to exist, especially in view of the coordinated United States-Soviet opposition to the French-British-Israeli recourse to overt violence in the Suez Campaign of 1956.

expectations of North Viet Nam and of the N.L.F. were likely formed prior to the overt, large-scale intervention by the United States—that is, when the conflict still belonged in the Type III category. Clarifying the factual and legal reasons for regarding the early stages of the war as Type III is very centrally related, in my view, to the North Vietnamese perception of what would constitute a reasonable outcome of the Viet Nam war (regardless of its subsequent Type II history).

In considering the war in Viet Nam as belonging in Type III, especially in its early (pre-1963) phases, I intended a two-pronged argument: first a civil war between the two factions in the South and second, a civil war between the Northern and Southern Zones. My argument was essentially that in either case such a conflict should be determined by the domestic balance of forces and, that, in the setting of Viet Nam under either interpretation the anti-Saigon "entity" would have prevailed but for American (that is, non-Vietnamese) military intervention. My reasoning is essentially as follows: South Viet Nam had evolved, despite the contrary intentions of the Geneva Settlement, as a separate *de facto* political entity, and the N.L.F. emerged as a sufficiently indigenous opposition movement to be deemed South Vietnamese in character rather than as an "agent" or "puppet" of North Viet Nam.[31] In this circumstance the outcome of the N.L.F.-Saigon struggle would have been an N.L.F. victory if both the United States and North Viet Nam had remained out of the conflict, and the quantum and phasing of United States and North Vietnamese aid to the contending factions was imbalanced in favor of Saigon at every stage subsequent to 1954. This interpretation of the early stages of the Vietnamese conflict seems to enjoy the support of almost all disinterested analysts.[32]

The second prong of the Type III analysis conceives of the war in

---

31. To take seriously the issue of the autonomy of the N.L.F. it would be necessary to compare its dependence on Hanoi with Saigon's dependence on Washington at the various phases of the war. *Cf.* J. LACOUTURE, VIETNAM: BETWEEN TWO TRUCES 61-119 (1966) [hereinafter cited as LACOUTURE]; KAHIN & LEWIS, esp. chapter entitled "Americanization of the War," at 151-80. The autonomy of Saigon's discretion to terminate the war on *its own terms*, as distinct from those insisted upon by Washington, is certainly as doubtful as is the autonomy of the N.L.F. to terminate the war on conditions at variance with those insisted upon by Hanoi.

As to the extent of the American role at earlier preinsurgency stages of South Viet Nam's history *see* E. HAMMER, THE STRUGGLE FOR INDO-CHINA 1940-1955 346-64 (1954-55); "However much American officials may have wished to regard southern Viet Nam as independent, the fact and the promise of substantial American aid to the Nationalist regime gave them such influence that in the fall of 1954 it was the United States, not the Vietnamese people, who decided that Ngo Dinh Diem would continue to be Prime Minister of southern Viet Nam." *Id.* 356.

32. LACOUTURE 186-90; KAHIN & LEWIS 127-206; THE MANSFIELD REPORT 11-12.

Viet Nam as a civil war between South Viet Nam and North Viet Nam waged for control of the state of Viet Nam. According to Professor Moore, such a characterization of the war overlooks the separateness as of 1960 of these two political entities, as well as the essential ambiguity of the Geneva settlement, especially with regard to reunification. Professor Moore, although sensitive to the particularities of the division of Viet Nam in 1954, closely associates the status of Viet Nam with such other divided countries as Korea, Germany, and China. Force across a partition boundary is, as he properly points out, dangerous to world peace since the *de facto* divisions express major unresolved conflicts between the Communist and non-Communist worlds. I challenge Professor Moore's analysis on two principal grounds:

(1) The division in Viet Nam is not usefully comparable on policy grounds to that of other divided countries;

(2) The defeat of the French by the Viet Minh as embodied in the Geneva Settlement of 1954, the attitude of Saigon toward the Geneva Accords, the Southern locus of the uprising, the small magnitude of Northern interference as compared to the direct and indirect military contributions of the United States Government to Saigon, the non-viability of the regime in the South, and the national popularity of Ho Chi Minh are factors that when taken into joint account make it misleading to talk of "the aggression" of the North.

The Geneva Settlement: Face-Saving or Partition

Sir Anthony Eden, introducing his discussion of the Geneva Accords of 1954 and his ideas for settling the present war in Viet Nam, has said that

> No agreement can be so drawn as to be proof against every malevolent intention. That is why the observance of international engagements is the first condition of any peaceful society. Once allow treaties to be torn up with impunity and the world is headed for trouble; violators soon have imitators.[33]

It seems to me that Professor Moore is somewhat cavalier in explaining away the United States' insistence on non-implementation of the election provision in the Final Declaration by setting it off against a Western preference for "partition" that was consistently denied both by the language of the Agreement on the Cessation of Hostilities in Viet Nam and of the Final Declaration.[34]

---

33. A. EDEN, TOWARD PEACE IN INDOCHINA 31 (1966).
34. See especially Articles 1-9, 11-15, and 27 of Agreement on the Cessation of Hostilities

Ignoring the relevance of formal international engagements Professor Moore also supports the double standard whereby North Viet Nam's alleged export of coercion through the N.L.F. is viewed as a material breach of the Geneva Accords, whereas the United States' provision of military aid to Saigon, even though it admittedly preceded North Vietnamese coercion, is approved of as a "permitted defensive response." Moore facilely circumvents the determination by the International Control Commission that both sides were guilty of violations of the Geneva Accords which were not weighted as to relative seriousness, by asserting that "this neutral reporting proves little."[35] In fact, for Professor Moore the determination of the I.C.C. proves less than does the unsupported balancing of these two violations by an interested party—namely, the United States Government. As elsewhere in his analysis Professor Moore seems to endorse the discretionary competence of sovereign states at the expense either of binding international arrangements or of the determinations of impartial machinery set up to implement these arrangements. If the United States was so convinced that its aid to Saigon was a permissible defensive response then why did it not have this conclusion confirmed by the I.C.C. or by a reconvened Geneva Conference in the course of the years since 1954? There is little doubt that from the time when the meetings were going on in Geneva in 1954 the United States was determined to use its unilateral military power to avoid the translation of the Viet Minh's military victory over the French in the First Indochina War into a corresponding political victory. Once again it is worth quoting Anthony Eden, partly because he was a principal participant at Geneva and partly because his Tory credentials are so impeccable:

> [Dulles] reiterated his fears that, in the event, France would be compelled to depart from the seven points, and the United States would then have to disassociate herself from the resulting agreement. He said that even if the settlement adhered to the seven points faithfully, the United States still could not guarantee it.[36]

> I had already been warned by Bedell Smith that the United States Government could not associate themselves with the final declara-

---

in Viet-Nam, July 20, 1954 and Articles 6 and 7 of the Final Declaration of Geneva Conference, July 21, 1954, SENATE FOREIGN RELATIONS COMM., 89th Cong. 1st Sess., BACKGROUND INFORMATION RELATING TO SOUTHEAST ASIA AND VIETNAM, 28-42, 58-60 (rev. ed. June 16, 1965) [hereinafter cited as BACKGROUND INFORMATION.]

35. For example, paragraph 84 of the Sixth Interim Report of the ICC, December 11, 1955-July 10, 1956 reads as follows: "While the Commission has experienced difficulties in North Vietnam, the major part of its difficulties has arisen in South Vietnam." 33 PARL. SESSIONAL PAPERS, CMD. No. 31, at 30 (1956-57).

36. A. EDEN, FULL CIRCLE 156 (1960).

tion. The most they could do was to issue a declaration taking note of what had been decided and undertaking not to disturb the settlement. Since Dulles had been at least as responsible as ourselves for calling the Geneva Conference, this did not seem to me reasonable.[37]

There are two points to note. First, the United States' determination from the outset not to be fully associated with the Geneva Settlement. Why is this so if Professor Moore's view of its essential understanding is correct? To answer this by saying that the United States wanted to avoid ratifying the Communist acquisition of North Viet Nam is hardly a sufficient explanation (even if it is a part of the story) in light of Dulles' overall insistence upon preserving a free hand for American action in the future. The second point, one that strikes me as legally pertinent, is why it matters whether the United States approved of the Geneva Accords or not. The parties to the conflict had full power to settle it by agreement. It is rather far-fetched to contend that the United States assent is needed to secure a formally binding arrangement reached to end a war in which the United States was not itself a direct participant.

Not everything complex is ambiguous. Professor Moore's argument that the Geneva Settlement was ambiguous on the issue of unification is unconvincing on several grounds:

(1) The election provisions of the Geneva Accords are explicit as to date, auspices, and preconditions;[38]

(2) The fact that the Geneva Declaration was unsigned does not seriously detract from its character as a binding legal instrument;[39]

---

37. *Id.* 159-60.

38. Falk, *supra* note 1, at 1129 (and authorities cited in note 31, *supra*); CONSULTATIVE COUNCIL 43-48; KAHIN & LEWIS 52-55, 80-87; 2 BUTTINGER 839-40; the most detailed support for regarding the failure to hold the elections promised by Article 7 of the Final Declaration for July 1956 as frustrating Hanoi's sincere understanding of the Geneva Settlement is contained in a well-researched monograph, Weinstein, Vietnam's Unheld Elections (1966) (Data Paper No. 60, Southeast Asia Program, Cornell Univ.); *cf.* Lacouture, *The "Face" of the Viet Cong*, WAR/PEACE REPORT, May, 1966, at 7, 8: "One cannot say . . . that the North resigned itself, with only *pro forma* protestations, to Diem's refusal to hold the elections that had been legally set for July, 1956. During his trip to New Delhi in 1955 as well as in three separate attempts at the end of 1955 and at the beginning of 1956, Pham Van Dong, the present premier of North Vietnam, attempted to implement the provisions of the Geneva agreement. He even offered to delay the elections on condition that Saigon pledge to allow them. It was the great powers—the U.S.S.R. and Peking included—who forgot the Geneva recommendations, not Hanoi, which found itself for the second time 'cheated'." For a full account of the first time Hanoi was "cheated" see HAMMER, *supra* note 31, at 148-202; a briefer account is contained in KAHIN & LEWIS 25-28.

39. *See* KAHIN & LEWIS 51 (and citations contained in note 7 therein), including reference to Article 3(b) and commentary thereto as contained in U.N. Doc. A/16309 (1966). The fact that the United States withheld its oral assent from the Final Declaration and attached a Declaration somewhat at variance with Article 7 does not alter the legal

(3) The refusal of the Saigon regime to accept the Geneva Accords does not relieve it of the obligation to comply as France had the capacity that it explicitly sought to exercise, to bind its "successor";[40]

(4) Experienced and impartial observers generally agree that (a) unification by means of elections was part of the Geneva Settlement and (b) elections, if held, would have resulted in the consolidation of Viet Nam under the control of Hanoi;[41]

(5) The United States was from the beginning manifestly discontented with the Geneva solution, refused to endorse the outcome as a party, and set about almost immediately thereafter to undo the fulfillment of its terms.[42]

Moore advises analysts to consider the total context of Geneva and yet he neglects these critical factors. He is correct in pointing to a certain aura of ambiguity connected with securing the compliance of Saigon with a settlement that was expected to extinguish its sphere of influence. It is also appropriate, as Moore suggests, to acknowledge the subsequent *de facto* sovereignty of both North and South Viet Nam, regardless of the intentions at Geneva in 1954.[43]

---

expectations created among the real parties in interest—the French and the Viet Minh. For text of the United States Declaration, see BACKGROUND INFORMATION, 61: "In connection with the statement in the declaration concerning free elections in Viet-Nam my Government wishes to make clear its position which it has expressed in a declaration made in Washington on June 29, 1954, as follows:

In the case of nations now divided against their will, we shall continue to seek to achieve unity through free elections supervised by the United Nations to insure that they are conducted fairly.

With respect to the statement made by the representative of the State of Viet-Nam [Bao Dai], the United States reiterates its traditional position that peoples are entitled to determine their own future and that it will not join in an arrangement which would hinder this. Nothing in its declaration just made is intended to or does indicate any departure from its traditional position."

It is obvious that the United States alters the terms of Article 7 by the conspicuous omission of a definite date upon which elections should be held in Viet Nam and by the call for United Nations supervision. It is also clear that the refusal to give oral assent to the Final Declaration and the reference in the United States Statement to its refusal "to join in an arrangement" which "would hinder" its election policy indicates the serious intention of the other participants to take seriously the terms of Article 7. It is one thing for the United States and the Bao Dai regime to disassociate themselves from the Final Declaration, it is quite another to contend that the enforceability and centrality of the election provision was in any respect reduced thereby.

40. This conclusion appears to be persuasively established in Partan, *Legal Aspects of the Vietnam Conflict*, 46 B.U.L. REV. 281, 289-92 (1966).

41. See the authorities cited at note 38 *supra* for relevant references, especially Weinstein. A typical comment is in B. FALL, THE TWO VIET-NAMS (2d rev. ed. 1967), at 231, who writes that "On the grounds of its nonsignature, South Viet-Nam refused to hold elections by July 1956, since this would have meant handing over control of the South to Ho Chi Minh."

42. *Cf.* B. FALL THE TWO VIET-NAMS 229-33 (2d rev. ed. 1967); KAHIN & LEWIS 57-63; 2 BUTTINGER 834-42.

43. The expectations created as of 1954 remain relevant to the perception by North Viet Nam of what constitutes a reasonable outcome of the Second Indochina War, and influences the formulation of minimum negotiating demands.

It would consume too much space to refute Moore's interpretation of the Geneva Accords on a point-to-point basis especially as this task has already been done effectively by other authors.[44] I would, however, suggest the weakness of Moore's position by reference to the long passage he approvingly quotes from a book by Victor Bator. In this passage Bator argues that the Geneva Accords really intended "partition" and that this position is borne out by "the detailed accounts of Bernard B. Fall, Jean Lacouture, and Philippe Devillers."[45] Here is what Devillers actually thought about the Geneva Settlement:

> *The demarcation line was to be purely provisional; the principle of Vietnamese unity was not questioned, and the idea of partition was officially rejected with indignation by both sides.* . . .
>
> The disproportion between the monolithic power of the Vietminh, armed and with the halo of victory, and the almost derisory weakness of the so-called Nationalist Viet Nam was such that in the summer of 1954 almost no one thought that the two years' delay won by M. Mendes-France at Geneva could be anything but a respite in which to salvage as much as possible from the wreck. *At the end of the period, unity would certainly be restored, this time to the benefit of the Vietminh, the basic hypothesis then acknowledged by all being that the Geneva Agreements would definitely be implemented* (emphasis supplied).[46]

Devillers' position has recently been reaffirmed by Professors Kahin and Lewis in their careful and fully documented account of the Geneva Conference. These authors describe Geneva as the event that "officially registered France's defeat by the Vietminh and provided her with a face-saving means of disengagement."[47] In this regard Kahin and Lewis aver that it was the "promise of elections that constituted an essential condition insisted upon by the Vietminh at Geneva." Their reasoning is well worth quoting:

---

44. *See* KAHIN & LEWIS 43-65; also relevant on many points is D. LANCASTER, THE EMANCIPATION OF FRENCH INDOCHINA 313-58 (1961).

45. In a long and significant scholarly review article, itself not hostile to the United States' role in Viet Nam, John T. McAlister says of Bator's longer interpretation of the Geneva Conference in V. BATOR, VIET NAM: A DIPLOMATIC TRAGEDY (1965) that it "is an emotional and polemical book making no claims to be a scholarly work." McAlister, *The Possibilities for Diplomacy in Southeast Asia* 19 WORLD POLITICS 258, 269 (1967); Bator's article from *The Reporter* has been reprinted along with a series of other strongly pro-Administration articles drawn from the magazine and reflecting its partisan editorial slant in Viet Nam—VIETNAM: WHY—A COLLECTION OF REPORTS AND COMMENTS FROM THE REPORTER (1966). It is, hence, strange to rely upon an occasional piece by Bator, were it not the case that the more trustworthy commentators in the Geneva Conference all cast doubt upon "the partition" hypothesis.

46. Devillers, *The Struggle for Unification of Vietnam*, THE CHINA QUARTERLY, Jan.-March 1962, 2-3.

47. KAHIN & LEWIS 43.

France was prepared to pay the political price of that condition in order to get the armistice that she so urgently wanted. Her successor [in Saigon] would be obliged to abide by that condition or face the certain resumption of hostilities. The reason for this is patent: when a military struggle for power ends on the agreed condition that the competition will be transferred to the political plane, the side that violates the agreed condition cannot legitimately expect that the military struggle will not be resumed.[48]

Professor Moore relies upon the memoirs of Anthony Eden to establish "that the real core of the settlement, at least from a Western standpoint, was partition of Viet Nam. . . ." (1059) These memoirs are too imprecise to clarify legal analysis and are internally inconsistent,[49] although they do provide considerable insight into the divergence of the American position from that of the other Western powers at Geneva in 1954. Eden, who holds very intense anti-Communist views, is especially convincing in his account of the effort that he made to discourage the United States from undermining the whole project of a conference to end the first Indochina war.[50] The United States was lobbying at Geneva in support of a collective Western intervention in support of the French, support that the French no longer desired. Eden indicates that he was distressed to learn from a French diplomat about an official document in which the United States secretly proposed to the French that military intervention in Indochina occur "either after the failure of Geneva, *or earlier if the French so desired, and he emphasized that the American preference had been clearly expressed for the earlier date*" (emphasis supplied).[51] It seems to me that a fair-

48. *Id.* 57.
49. Anthony Eden seems primarily concerned with obtaining a Western negotiating consensus that would enable the war in Indochina to be brought to an end. There is no detailed interpretation given by the terms of the Geneva settlement and there is every indication that Eden thought that the election provisions would be carried out, despite the intra-Allied discussion in terms of "partition." A. EDEN, FULL CIRCLE 158-59 (1960). It is very strange to argue that the negotiating hopes of the United States, which were not to any degree reflected in the language or terms of the Accords themselves, should be given any weight in construing treaty-type obligations that are unambiguous on their face. It is an elementary rule of treaty interpretation that one consults the context of the agreement only to the extent that the provisions themselves are unclear. Even if the Accords do not qualify as treaties in the strict sense their content was affirmed in a solemn and formal manner. In any event, although the rhetoric of partition does imply a permanent separation of Viet Nam into two separate states, it is quite consistent with a temporary period of partition followed by elections seeking reunification. Only such an interpretation brings consistency into the Eden accounting. For the most persuasive skeptical view of the Geneva Accords—one that puts a curse on both houses—see 2 BUTTINGER 978-81.
50. A. EDEN, FULL CIRCLE 120-63 (1960).
51. *Id.* 134; *cf. id.* 93, 103, 117, 126-27 (for a sense of Eden's perception of American attitudes toward the Geneva Conference). Buttinger's account of the American attempts to rally support for military intervention is one of the most complete and

minded reading of the Eden memoirs would emphasize the degree to which talk of "partition" may have been designed to mollify the United States apprehensions about the Conference. In any event, if "partition" was the bargain, it was nowhere reflected in the Geneva Accords that resulted from the Conference. Why not?

The partition hypothesis also does not reconcile easily with Eden's evident feeling that the election provision in the Final Declaration was to be taken seriously:

> The Communists insisted that elections should be held during 1955 in Vietnam, whereas the French maintained, I thought rightly, that it would take at least two years for the country to be restored to a condition in which elections would be possible.[52]

I conclude that (1) partition was not written into the Geneva Accords and that (2) unification by elections in July, 1956 was the essential political bargain struck at Geneva in exchange for a regroupment of the fighting forces into two zones and the withdrawal to the North of the Vietminh armies. This interpretation of the Geneva Accords is crucial for an interpretation of the relevance of the post-1954 events, especially of the extent to which one emphasizes or disregards the non-implementation of the election provision. My principal contention is that once it became clear that the election provision would not be carried out recourse to coercion by Hanoi was both predictable and permissible in either of the two Type III variants—the N.L.F. versus Saigon or North Viet Nam versus South Viet Nam. On this basis I find it highly misleading and false to analogize the evidence of North Vietnamese support for the insurgency in the South with the massive attack by North Korea on South Korea in 1950. It is false even if (which is hardly possible) one accepts the State Department's "white papers" as accurate descriptions of the North Vietnamese role in the early stage of the conflict in South Viet Nam. Among other considerations distinguishing Korea are the following: the effort of Hanoi proceeded against a quite opposite political background, it was based on much more ambiguous evidence of coercion, and the coercion was of a such small scale that it could not have resulted in any substantial disturbance had not a revolutionary potential preexisted in South Viet Nam.[53]

accurate, 2 BUTTINGER 797-844; he writes that "the moves that Radford, Dulles, and Nixon made during April 1954, to stop Communism in Indochina are among the saddest chapters of U.S. diplomacy." Id. 819.

52. Id. 158, 159; see also A. EDEN, TOWARD PEACE IN INDOCHINA 38 (1966).

53. E.g., Feldman, Violence and Volatility: The Likelihood of Revolution, in H. ECKSTEIN, ed., INTERNAL WAR 111-29 (1964).

Viet Nam cannot be regarded as relevantly similar to the other divided countries of China,[54] Korea, or Germany. Although Korea and Germany differ significantly from one another as divided countries, the political "settlement" in each case consisted of a reciprocal acceptance of partition, at least until a more satisfactory political settlement could be agreed upon as to reunification. Until such a second or new political settlement emerges, if ever, the use of coercion in any form to achieve a favorable military settlement of the reunification issue is, as Professor Moore properly indicates, a dangerous disturbance of world order, a disturbance that entitles the victim entity to claim full defensive rights and one that entails the gravest consequences; the Korean War illustrates and vindicates the principle that frontiers within divided states enjoy at least the same sanctity as frontiers between undivided states. The Saigon regime cannot invoke the sanctity of the seventeenth parallel in the same persuasive manner as the Seoul regime invoked the sanctity of the thirty-eighth parallel. The political settlement at Geneva in 1954 provided a formula for the nullification (rather than one for the maintenance) of the division. In Viet Nam Saigon's establishment, rather than the subsequent attempt at its removal, of a political frontier at the seventeenth parallel represented the coercive challenge to world order.[55]

In this spirit it is worth reexamining Professor Moore's central policy test in the Viet Nam setting—namely, the prohibition by international law of coercion as a strategy of major change. On one level such a policy is an essential ingredient of minimum world order in the nuclear age. But peace cannot be divorced from minimum expectations of fair play on related matters. The Geneva Conference confirmed the results of a long anti-colonial war won at great cost to Vietnamese society by the armies of Ho Chi Minh.[56] The achievement of national independence is a goal of such importance in the Afro-Asian world that it clearly takes precedence for these countries over generalized prohibi-

---

54. It can be persuasively argued, I think, that Formosa is wrongly conceived of as an integral part of China. Therefore, China is not "a divided country" at all, but there are two countries each of which is entitled to sovereign status. For a complete argument to this effect see L. CHEN & H. LASSWELL, FORMOSA, CHINA, AND THE UNITED NATIONS: FORMOSA'S PLACE IN THE WORLD COMMUNITY (to be published in 1967).

55. See B. FALL, THE TWO VIET-NAMS 231-32 (2d rev. ed. 1967); the effort to build-up the military strength of the Saigon regime was coupled with its refusal to allow the election provision of the Geneva settlement to be carried out. To defend the seventeenth parallel as if it were an international boundary was itself tantamount to an illegal effort at splitting a state into two parts, an effort frequently productive of severe civil strife. It is only necessary to recall the American Civil War or the post-1960 efforts of Katanga to split off from the Congo.

56. See HAMMER, supra note 31.

tions on force or rules about non-intervention.[57] The Geneva Accords are not just an international agreement about which a dispute arose, but a formalized acknowledgment of a political outcome that it is reasonable to suppose could have been attained legitimately by the Vietminh in 1954 through military means.[58] In effect, the Accords were a political bargain struck by the French as an alternative to continuing the appalling destruction of lives and property. To cast aside this political bargain is to undermine severely the security of solemn international agreements and to put in jeopardy collective procedures for pacific settlement.[59]

My conclusion, then, is that Professor Moore has not persuasively demonstrated that the use of coercion across the seventeenth parallel by North Viet Nam should have been regarded as coercion across an international boundary. I wish to argue only that it was reasonable for Hanoi, given the stakes and outcome of the first Indochina war, to regard Saigon's intransigence on the issue of elections as a material breach of the Accords allowing it to act on the basis of the *status quo ante* 1954: in my terms choosing this option would result in an example of Type III conflict, a situation of internal conflict for control of all of Viet Nam in which outside participation on behalf of either faction is "intervention," at least in the sense of interfering with the process of self-determination.[60]

Despite its plausibility from the perspective of law, there are three problems with this interpretation:

(1) Hanoi has not really contended that the action of Saigon nullifies the Geneva Accords; on the contrary, Hanoi continues to urge implementation and compliance;

---

57. For example, the African states overtly proclaim their intention to resort to force against the countries of Southern Africa to end colonialism and racism. The legal status of this claim is considered in Falk, *The New States and International Order*, 118 RECUEIL DES COURS (1966).

58. After Den Bien Phu the only way to prevent a total Vietminh victory would have been a massive United States military intervention, that included combat troops; as it was, even Anthony Eden points out that the French were the recipients of at least nine times as much foreign support from the United States as the Vietminh received from China. A. EDEN, FULL CIRCLE 126-27 (1960).

59. The refusal of the United States to take the Geneva Accords of 1954 more seriously as the terms of settlement may help partly to account for the reluctance of Hanoi to negotiate with the United States. Of course, there are independent reasons to suppose that the United States may not be sincere about its various offers to negotiate an end to the Viet Nam war. *See* Draper, *Vietnam: How Not to Negotiate*, NEW YORK REVIEW OF BOOKS, May 4, 1967, at 17; Draper's criticism of the Government is so impressive because of his earlier support of the United States' anti-Castro foreign policy. T. DRAPER, CASTROISM THEORY AND PRACTICE (1965). *Cf.* KAHIN & LEWIS 207-37.

60. Quincy Wright has been a consistent advocate of this position. *See* Wright, *Legal Aspects of the Viet-Nam Situation*, 60 AM. J. INT'L L. 750 (1966); Wright, *United States Intervention in the Lebanon*, 53 AM. J. INT'L L. 112 (1959).

(2) South Viet Nam has existed as a separate political entity for more than twelve years and has been accorded diplomatic recognition by many foreign governments; the consequence is a condition of statehood with all of the normal defensive prerogatives;

(3) During the last five years third-powers have become increasingly involved on both sides in the Viet Nam War; South Korea, Thailand, Australia, New Zealand, the Philippines, the Soviet Union, and China are the principal third-party participants as of April, 1967.

As I have indicated at the outset of this section the war in Viet Nam now belongs in Type II; the functions of clarifying the argument that it was originally an example of Type III and that the United States should have left it that way are to indicate the reasonable basis of a settlement and to emphasize the unilateral role of the United States in shifting the war to an internationally more serious category of conflict.[61]

II. The Rationale Restated in Support of a Type II Classification of the Viet Nam War

To classify the Viet Nam war as a Type II conflict implies considering the war as a variety of civil strife in which two domestic factions, each of which receives substantial assistance from foreign states, are struggling for control of a sovereign state. I maintain that international law then requires that belligerent conduct remain within the territorial limits of South Viet Nam. The United States Government officially repudiates this interpretation of the war and insists that the violent conflict is properly viewed as "an armed attack" by North Viet Nam upon South Viet Nam. South Viet Nam is thus entitled to act in self-defense, including, to the extent necessary, the commission of acts of war in North Viet Nam. In my terms, the United States Government has inappropriately characterized "the facts" as vindicating a Type I classification.[62]

---

61. As a conflict moves from Type III toward Type II it tends to become more dangerous to international peace and security; as it proceeds from Type II to Type I it tends to become even more dangerous other things being equal. Therefore, the United States' role in transforming the conflict from Type III to Type I without seriously attempting at a Type IV classification is to follow a path destructive of world order in relation to the civil strife-revolution phenomena occurring throughout the Afro-Asian world.

62. The objective of establishing two categories of internationl conflict, Type I and Type II, is to underline the importance in policy and in law to distinguish between the Korea-type situation and the Viet Nam-type situation. Analytic categories are ideal types; there is no comparable clarity in real-world situations. Nevertheless, the ambi-

Professor Moore agrees with the Government that the war in Viet Nam belongs in Type I, but he goes further by arguing that even if the facts warrant a Type II classification there are no legal restrictions that necessarily confine the war to territorial boundaries and that, in the context of Viet Nam, the air and sea strikes against North Vietnamese territory have been legally reasonable. There are thus two broad sets of questions to which Professor Moore and I give different answers:

(1) Is North Viet Nam "intervening" in "civil strife" going on in South Viet Nam or is North Viet Nam "attacking" South Viet Nam? Who decides, by what criteria, and subject to what conditions?

(2) If North Viet Nam is regarded as merely "intervening" in civil strife, does international law prohibit South Viet Nam and states allied with her from committing war acts against the territory of North Viet Nam?

As Professor Moore effectively argues, South Viet Nam's *de facto* sovereignty makes it important to analyze the legal rights of the Saigon regime on the assumption that South Viet Nam is a sovereign state, as entitled as any other to act in self-defense and to receive military assistance. Moore's interpretation of North Viet Nam's role depends on two sets of assertions; neither of which I accept as to fact or law:

(1) The nature of North Viet Nam's military assistance to the N.L.F. and the political objectives motivating it constitute "an armed attack" upon South Viet Nam;

(2) The United States assistance to the Saigon regime, including bombing North Viet Nam, is a reasonable and lawful exercise of the right of self-defense.

My argument as formulated in the first article is that the conflict in South Viet Nam closely resembles other instances of prolonged civil strife in which substantial intervention by foreign countries on behalf of both the insurgent and the incumbent faction has taken place. I regard two assertions as legally determinative of the argument being made by Professor Moore:

(1) Covert assistance, even of a substantial nature, to an insurgent faction does not constitute an armed attack;

(2) Counter-intervention on behalf of an incumbent faction may not extend the conflict beyond its existing territorial boundaries.

---

guities and antagonistic misperceptions that are likely to accompany a conflict of the Viet Nam variety make it very important for states to limit their involvement to the boundaries of the society wherein the violence is located.

This reasoning seemed directly applicable to the situation in Viet Nam with the consequence that the extension of the war to the territory of North Viet Nam by the United States is deemed to be a violation of international law.

Professor Moore, if I understand him correctly, argues:

(1) My Type II paradigm confuses what the rules of international law ought to be with what the rules actually are;

(2) The weight of legal authority supports Saigon's discretion to treat North Viet Nam's aid to the N.L.F. as an armed attack and thereby authorizes defensive measures undertaken against North Vietnamese territory;

(3) Bombing North Viet Nam has been a reasonable defensive measure for the United States to undertake on behalf of South Viet Nam in view of the facts of attack and the law authorizing a proportionate response to it;

(4) The policy interests at stake are more consistent with such discretion than with the territorial limitations embodied in the Type II paradigm. Thus Professor Moore concludes there is "greater reason [than not] to believe both as a matter of the is and the ought that the bombing of the North is a permissible defensive response."

The Distinction between "Is" and "Ought" in the Context of Viet Nam: The Doctrinal Level of Discourse

I find it peculiar that Professor Moore argues, on the one hand, that the ambiguity of the legal and factual setting in Viet Nam makes it essential to assess the respective rights and duties of the parties by reference to the world order policies at stake, and on the other that my major line of legal analysis confuses what the law ought to be with what the law is. It is peculiar that Professor Moore should rely on Hans Kelsen, an arch-positivist, to support a critique that is explicitly couched in terms of the sociological jurisprudence of Myres McDougal, especially when Kelsen is invoked to show what is meant by the phrase "armed attack" as it appears in Article 51 of the Charter. Of course, Kelsen stresses the dichotomy between the "is" and the "ought," but it is this stress that seems quite contrary to Moore's assertion, one that I share, that international law is above all a process whereby actors clarify through their conduct the world order policies that each deems decisive in a particular context. For sake of clarity of discussion I shall try, despite this jurisprudential ambivalence that I detect in Professor Moore's critique, to respond directly to his analysis.

Does Type II Embody a Preference About What International Law Ought to Be?

Type II acknowledges the indeterminacy of international law with respect to intervention and counter-intervention. There is no weight of legal authority that can be crystallized in terms of rules commanding universal, or even widespread respect. In fact, respectable and responsible international jurists disagree as to whether international law:

(1) allows discrimination in favor of the incumbent;[63]

(2) requires impartiality as between the incumbent and the insurgent;[64]

(3) allows discrimination in favor of the just side.[65]

In face of this indeterminacy it seems useful to acknowledge the extent of sovereign discretion as to participating in a foreign civil war. International law does not provide authoritative rules of restraint, or stated more accurately, it provides contradictory rules of restraint of approximately equal standing. To invoke international law in this international setting, then, is to argue about desirable policy or to communicate in precise form what a particular state intends to claim; international law does not, however, postulate rules of order the transgression of which is illegal.

One of the authorities relied upon by Moore, Ian Brownlie, an international lawyer in the strict positivist sense, gives the following support to insisting upon the applicability of territorial restriction in a Type II situation:

> When foreign assistance is given to the rebels, aid to the government threatened is now generally assumed to be legal. Whether

63. *E.g.*, Professor Moore (1080-93) and Garner, *Questions of International Law in the Spanish Civil War*, 31 AM. J. INT'L. L. 66 (1937); *see also* Borchard, *"Neutrality" and Civil Wars*, 31 AM. J. INT'L. L. 304 (1937).

64. *E.g.*, Wright, *supra* note 60, and W. HALL, INTERNATIONAL LAW 347 (8th ed. 1924).

65. This position has been enunciated in its classical form by E. VATTEL, THE LAW OF NATIONS, Bk. II, § 56, 131 (1916). Although positive international law promotes either discrimination in favor of the incumbent or impartiality, the practice of states increasingly vindicates giving help to the side deemed "just." From the perspective of world order it is crucial to develop community procedures to identify which side is "just." Such procedures seem to work for those situations in which the principal rival states have apparently converging interests, as with the unresolved problems of bringing independence and racial equality to Rhodesia, South West Africa, Angola, Mozambique, and South Africa. But where rival principal states disagree, as when civil strife between "radical" and "conservative" elites occurs in the developing countries, then the determination of which side is "just" is likely to generate competitive interventions if the contradictory perceptions are acted upon. The Communist ideas of support for wars of national liberation are in conflict with American thinking on the legitimacy of helping any anti-Communist regime sustain itself against Communist opposition. In a world of antagonistic ideologies it is dangerous to maintain complete discretion on the national level to identify which faction is "just"; but, equally, in a world of insistent legislative demands it is dangerous to preclude discrimination in favor of an insurgency that is deemed just by the overwhelming consensus of international society. One approach for Cold War issues and another for Southern African issues seems imperative at this point.

this is permitted in relation to minor disturbances caused by foreign propaganda or other forms of interference is an open question. It is also uncertain as to whether the foreign assistance must be a decisive element in the imminent and serious threat to the existing government or whether it is sufficient if foreign assistance is a contributory cause. Finally, *foreign assistance to the government will be confined to measures on the territory of the requesting state unless the foreign aid to the rebels amounts in fact and law to an "armed attack"* (emphasis supplied).[66]

It is worth noticing that Brownlie attributes uncertainty to the positive law in this area, but more immediately, it is important to take account of his reliance upon territoriality as a limiting criterion. Brownlie reinforces the quoted passage in the course of his discussion of claims to use force in self-defense against alleged aggression:

It is suggested that so far as possible defensive measures should be confined to the territory of the defending state and the hostile forces themselves unless there is clear evidence of a major invasion across a frontier which calls for extensive military operations which may not be confined merely to protecting the frontier line. The precise difficulty in the case of indirect aggression is to avoid major breaches of the peace of wide territorial extent arising from defensive measures based on vague evidence of foreign complicity.[67]

It seems reasonable to regard Brownlie's discussion as a generalization of past state practice that reflects international law. My Type II boundary rule places an outer limit on the discretion of the sovereign state and is precisely the kind of quasi-objective limit that is so crucial for the maintenance of world order.

It is correct, as Professor Moore argues, that if the insurgent faction is the "agent" of the outside state then it is permissible for the victim state to respond at the source by regarding the apparent insurgency as an armed attack. But such a response requires a real demonstration of

---

66. I. BROWNLIE, INTERNATIONAL LAW AND THE USE OF FORCE BY STATES 327 (1963). *See also* Pinto, *Les Règles du Droit International Concernant la Guerre Civile*, RECUEIL DES COURS 451, 544-48 (1965).

67. *Id.* 373, "Indirect aggression and the incursions of armed bands can be countered by measures of defence which do not involve military operations across frontiers." *Id.* at 279. A recent Western visitor to North Viet Nam confirms the distinction between intervention in the South and bombing of the North as vital to the North Vietnamese perception of themselves as victims of United States aggression:

Their [North Viet Nam] position is that the bombing of the North is a separate act of aggression from fighting in the South. While they might understand and tolerate, although disapprove, American intervention in the South on behalf of the Saigon government, they regard the bombing of the North as an unconscionable act of aggression against a sovereign nation.

Ashmore, *supra* note 21, at 17, 12, 14.

instigation and control, as distinct from either a mere allegation or evidence of some assistance to a faction that appears to possess an independent character and objectives.

International law is not really indefinite on this subject. A state is not permitted to use sustained military force against a foreign country unless the justification is overwhelmingly clear.[68] It is difficult to establish unilaterally that covert uses of force by an external enemy can ever constitute an ample justification. It is difficult to distinguish a pretext from a justification, especially as the status of assistance to either side in an ongoing civil war seems legally equivalent. That is, one side may discriminate in favor of the incumbent, whereas the other side may discriminate in favor of "the just" faction, and both possess an equal legal basis.[69] In such a situation any serious concern with the policies of conflict minimization would insist, at least, that neither side has the discretion to extend the war to foreign territory.

The dynamics of internal war are such that both sides must, as the war progresses, almost certainly seek increasing external support to maintain their position in the struggle; if the scene of the internal war is a minor country then it is increasingly likely that both factions will become dependent for their political leadership upon a larger external ally.[70] Insurgent dependence on external support is not by itself proof of an aggressive design on the part of the supporter state. This dependence on an external ally is normally only an expression of the changing ratios of influence between the benefactor and recipient of military

68. Action and reaction sequences involving "incidents" have not been regulated in any very clear and definite way by international law. States interact by claim and counterclaim and the degree of legality is very largely dependent on the general impression of the reasonableness of the action undertaken by the contending states. The Gulf of Tonkin incident was a characteristic illustration of this process. The legality of the United States response depends primarily on (a) the reality of the provocation and (b) the proportionality of the response. For useful background as to practice, policy, and law in this kind of setting of sporadic violence see F. GROB, THE RELATIVITY OF WAR AND PEACE: A STUDY IN LAW, HISTORY, AND POLITICS (1949).

69. This flexibility of international law is confirmed by the discretion states possess to accord or withhold recognition from a partially successful insurgency. L. CHEN, THE INTERNATIONAL LAW OF RECOGNITION (Green ed. 1951). It is not necessary for recognition to be accorded in an express or formal manner. De facto recognition arising out of intercourse between the third-party state and the anti-government faction is sufficient provided the facts of the civil war justify the inference of dual sovereignty; i.e., each faction governs a portion of the society and this situation is likely to continue for a considerable period of time. As Lauterpacht concludes, "It is not contrary to international law to recognize the insurgents as a government exercising de facto authority over the territory under its control." H. LAUTERPACHT, RECOGNITION IN INTERNATIONAL LAW 294 (1947). See generally id. 279-94.

70. The process by which an internal war is internationalized is well-depicted in Modelski, The International Relations of Internal War, in INTERNATIONAL ASPECTS OF CIVIL STRIFE 14-44 (J. Rosenau ed. 1964).

assistance on both sides as the conflict progresses to higher magnitudes. It would be detrimental to world order to treat such ratios as equivalent to an armed attack by one state on another and prior to the war in Viet Nam there had been neither serious juridical support nor diplomatic practice that would justify treating assistance to an insurgent as an armed attack. In fact, for world order purposes, bombing North Viet Nam has to be appraised as if it were seeking to establish a new legal precedent upon which other states could and should subsequently rely.[71]

Professor Moore regards as "mysterious" my assertion that bombing North Viet Nam is simultaneously both

(1) a violation of international law and

(2) a law-creating precedent.

It may be mysterious, but it is a mystery locked into the international legal process. As a consequence of the absence of a legislature in international society, the assertion of a claim by a state to act in a certain way, if supported by an appeal to the policies and rules of law and if effectively asserted in practice, is both a violation of law as measured by prior expectations about what was permissible in a given situation and a precedent that can be subsequently invoked to legitimate future conduct of a similar sort. This can be stated more concretely by asking about whether *prior* to the war in Viet Nam a response against the territory of the state assisting an insurgent faction was regarded to be as permissible as it might be in some *subsequent* war of the Viet Nam variety.[72] Certainly, the precedent of Viet Nam will provide valuable support for any victim state that attacks foreign territory on

---

71. The international law applicable to Type II situations is subject to "legislative" modification by principal states asserting new claims in an effective fashion and defending their assertion by an appeal to international law. It would be very difficult for the United States to oppose the legal argument it has developed to support its claim to bomb North Viet Nam. In this respect, my criticism of the Meeker legal rationale for "self-defense" in Viet Nam is more that it constitutes bad "legislation" than that it is "a violation." *But cf.* Meeker, *supra* note 23. Often a precedent established for one context can be successfully invoked for different objectives in a series of subsequent contexts. This general process is very ably depicted in connection with the activities of the International Labor Organization by Ernst Haas. *See* E. HAAS, BEYOND THE NATION-STATE, esp. 381-425 (1964) (describing precedent-creation in a cold war context later being invoked in anti-colonial and anti-racist contexts with regard to "freedom of association").

72. The United States has not even restricted bombing to certain specific objectives related directly to the Vietcong war effort—for instance, the specific interdiction of supplies and infiltrators or destruction of staging areas. President Johnson explicitly includes punishment as one of three principal objectives of bombing North Viet Nam: "[W]e sought to impose on North Viet Nam a cost for violating its international agreements." *President Reviews U.S. Position on Bombing of North Viet-Nam*, 56 DEP'T STATE BULL. 514, 515 (1967). For a description of the impact of bombing on North Viet Nam see H. SALISBURY, BEHIND THE LINES—HANOI DECEMBER 23-JANUARY 7 (1967).

the ground that it was substantially assisting the insurgent. Other international settings in which a legally dubious claim was converted by its successful assertion into a legally authoritative precedent can be mentioned—for instance, testing nuclear weapons on the high seas, orbiting reconnaissance satellites, and imposing criminal responsibility upon individuals who lead their country in an aggressive war. Professor Moore once again appears hesitant to accept the full jurisprudential implications of the McDougalian orientation that he advocates: if there is a process of law-creation at work in international society, then the distinction between a violation and a law-creating precedent is one of perspective and prediction, but not logic.[73]

Is North Viet Nam's Assistance to the N.L.F. "an Armed Attack?" The Factual Level of Discourse

Only if North Viet Nam's assistance to the N.L.F. can be considered an armed attack, is proportionate self-defense available to Saigon and its allies.

Professor Moore argues that North Viet Nam is guilty of an armed attack on South Viet Nam for the following principal reasons:

(1) A substantial body of scholarly opinion holds that Hanoi actually *initiated*, as well as *assisted*, the insurgency;

(2) Hanoi exercises control over the activities of the N.L.F.;

(3) Hanoi's principal objective is to reunify Viet Nam under its control; therefore, its assistance is, in effect, a project for the territorial expansion of North Viet Nam at the expense of South Viet Nam.

These issues concern the quality, quantity, and phasing of Hanoi's role. Reasonable men disagree about the facts. Many observers, especially in the United States, regard the resolution of these factual questions as critical to their assessment of whether the United States has responded in a lawful manner. For purposes of my own analysis I would argue that *even if* the facts are accepted in the form that Professor Moore presents them the conflict in Viet Nam is appropriately treated as Type II. I would additionally argue, however, that Professor

---

73. This process is summarized in part by the maxim *ex factis jus oritur;* without legislative organs and without a general conference procedure, the growth of international law reflects the process by which claims and counter-claims interact, especially if principal states are participants.

It is, of course, possible to distinguish an arbitrary recommendation of a particular author as to preferred regulatory schemes from a reasoned application of pre-existing community legal policies to a controversial fact situation. In the former case one is dealing with *a criticism* of the legal order, whereas in the latter one is concerned with *an application* of law, albeit an application that interprets obligations in light of policy preference.

Moore's construction of the facts relies on the reporting of biased observers. Furthermore, I would contend that it is inappropriate to appraise Hanoi's connection with the N.L.F. without taking into account Washington's connection with the Saigon regime, especially after the insurgency had succeeded in establishing itself as the government for many areas of South Viet Nam.

Construing the Controverted Facts

The ambiguity of the facts in a situation in which civil strife has been allegedly abetted by external assistance is one reason why it is important to regulate the scope of conflict by objective limits. It is obviously easy for any interested state to manipulate the evidence to vindicate any response. The gradual emergence of a serious struggle for the control of South Viet Nam gave the Saigon regime and the United States an adequate opportunity to establish the facts by impartial procedures and to have recourse to international institutions to vindicate the legal inferences of "aggression," and later, "armed attack," that were drawn from the facts. It is important to realize that the United States made very little effort to secure wider community support for its preferred course of action in the decade after the Geneva settlement of 1954.[74]

Furthermore, recourse to self-defense was not prompted by any sudden necessity. It was decided upon in February, 1965, with considerable deliberateness after consideration over a period of months, if not years.[75] In this circumstance, the burden of justification seems to fall heavily on the United States for the following reasons:

(1) the essential ambiguity of the alleged aggression, especially in view of the refusal of the Saigon regime to implement the election provisions and its suppression of all political opposition;

(2) the non-recourse to the organs of the United Nations, despite the time available and the refusal to adopt the war-terminating suggestions of the Secretary General;[76]

(3) the absence of a clear showing of necessity and justification required in contemporary international law to validate the exercise of the right of self-defense;

74. CONSULTATIVE COUNCIL 71-76.
75. See the original official explanations for bombing North Viet Nam in BACKGROUND INFORMATION 148-52, and the more recent explanation in 56 DEP'T STATE BULL. supra note 72.
76. Compare Falk, supra note 1, at 1140-43, with text of Goldberg's Letter to the Secretary General on December 19, 1966, N.Y. Times, Dec. 20, 1966, at 6, col. 4, and excerpts from U Thant's introduction to the annual report on the work of the United Nations, Sept. 19, 1966, at 18, col. 5.

(4) the consistent previous international practice of confining civil strife, even in cases where the insurgent faction was aided and abetted by outside powers, to territorial limits;

(5) the locus of conflict being outside the immediate security sphere of the United States, thereby distinguishing the protective role exhibited by United States diplomacy in Latin America.[77]

These factors in the Viet Nam context are mentioned to indicate the legal background. Such a background seems to require, at minimum, a clear demonstration that the facts are as the United States contends. The so-called "white papers" issued by the State Department[78] are considered to be too one-sided even for Professor Moore. Instead he relies heavily upon Douglas Pike, author of a detailed study entitled *Viet Cong*, written at the M.I.T. Center for International Studies, during a one-year leave of absence from his role as an official of the United States Information Agency;[79] Mr. Pike had spent the preceding six years serving in Viet Nam, during which period the research was done. One need not be an editor of *Ramparts* to note that M.I.T.'s Center has long been subsidized by the C.I.A. and has given consistent guidance and support for United States foreign policy, especially with regard to the containment of communism; a list of Center publications indicates a consistent pro-Administration outlook. Mr. Pike's analysis certainly deserves careful reading, and is to some degree endorsed by Bernard Fall's interpretations, but the prospects of bias must be noted and his conclusions must be carefully tested against those reached by neutral observers.[80] In responding to Professor Moore,

77. There are broad deferences accorded to principal sovereign states to prevent hostile political changes in countries located within a traditional sphere of influence; these interferences, although vigorously controversial, do not generally endanger international peace and security because a principal state is reluctant to use force in a rival sphere of influence. Such geo-political toleration is not intended to serve as a juridical vindication for unilateral interventionary practices that have been solemnly renounced. For a legal critique of intervention carried on within a sphere of influence see Falk, *American Intervention in Cuba and the Rule of Law*, 22 OHIO ST. L.J. 546 (1961); this analysis applies *a fortiori* to the 1965 intervention in the Dominican Republic.

78. U.S. DEP'T OF STATE, A THREAT TO THE PEACE: NORTH VIET-NAM'S EFFORT TO CONQUER SOUTH VIET-NAM (1961); U.S. DEP'T OF STATE, AGGRESSION FROM THE NORTH: THE RECORD OF NORTH VIET-NAM'S CAMPAIGN TO CONQUER SOUTH VIET-NAM (1965), (reprinted in 52 DEP'T STATE BULL. 404).

79. D. PIKE, VIETCONG: THE ORGANIZATION AND TECHNIQUES OF THE NATIONAL LIBERATION FRONT OF SOUTH VIETNAM (1966) [hereinafter cited as PIKE]; see also the apparent deception in an earlier attempt to show that Hanoi dominated the N.L.F., wherein the author's C.I.A. affiliation was disguised by presenting him as "a student of political theory and Asian affairs . . . former officer in U.S. AID Mission in Saigon; author of 'Aesthetics and the Problem of Meaning.'" Carver, Jr., *The Faceless Vietcong*, 44 FOREIGN AFFAIRS 347 (1966).

80. Among other unintended conclusions that emerge from Pike's study is the clear sense that the National Liberation Front possesses the organizational efficiency, cohesion, and talent to govern South Viet Nam in a manner never achieved by the Saigon regime.

I would argue that by relying as heavily on Mr. Pike (without taking serious account of the significantly different interpretations of Jean Lacouture, George Kahin and John Lewis, and Bernard Fall) he bases his conclusions of fact on *ex parte* presentations which, due to an appearance of academic impartiality, are more misleading than "the White Papers" he dismissed as "one-sided."[81]

Space permits me only to give two illustrations of why, aside from his vested vocational outlook, I find it difficult to regard Mr. Pike as a trustworthy guide to the facts in Viet Nam. The Preface ends with this rather emotional statement of Pike's personal commitment to the United States role in Viet Nam:

> The plight of the Vietnamese people is not an abstraction to me, and I have no patience with those who treat it as such. Victory by the Communists would mean consigning thousands of Vietnamese, many of them of course my friends, to death, prison, or permanent exile. . . . My heart goes out to the Vietnamese people—who have been sold out again and again, whose long history could be written in terms of betrayal and who, based on this long and bitter experience, can only expect that eventually America too will sell them out. If America betrays the Vietnamese people by abandoning them, she betrays her own heritage.[82]

What is striking about this passage is its identification of "the Vietnamese people" with the American support of the Saigon regime. Does not Mr. Pike think that if Marshal Ky prevails "thousands of Vietnamese" would be consigned "to death, prison, or permanent exile"?[83] This is what happened to the anti-Diem opposition in the South after 1954 (and, incidentally, to the anti-Ho opposition in the North), and it is a common, if tragic, sequel to a bitter civil war. To associate the prospect of such oppression exclusively with an N.L.F. victory, as Pike does, is to endorse the most naive and sentimental American

---

From the perspective of international order the capacity to govern is certainly an element in claiming political legitimacy. A second unintended conclusion is the extent to which Hanoi's increasing influence upon the N.L.F. has been a direct consequence of the American entry into combat operations. This increase in influence has, according to Mr. Pike, temporarily at least submerged real differences in outlook and objectives between the N.L.F. and Hanoi, differences that belie the more general hypothesis that the N.L.F. is a creation and creature of Hanoi's conjuring.

81. *See, e.g.*, Max F. Millikan's Foreword in which he stresses the academic and disinterested character of the Center for International Studies and its sponsorship of Mr. Pike's inquiry. PIKE, v-vi.

82. *Id.* at xi-xii.

83. *Cf.* R. W. Apple, Jr., N.Y. Times, May 17, 1967, at 3, col. 2, describing the activities of Miss Cao Ngoc Phuong in organizing a non-Communist, Buddhist opposition to the Saigon regime's war policy and the harassment to which she has been subjected by Premier Ky's police officials while trying to carry on her activities.

propaganda. Also Pike's passage indicates the emotional character of his commitment to "the American mission," a commitment that is unqualified by any reference to the doubtful claims to rulership possessed by the present Saigon leadership.[84]

When Pike explains the creation of the N.L.F. his bias appears in the form of the following undocumented conjecture:

> The creation of the N.L.F. was an accomplishment of such skill, precision, and refinement that when one thinks of who the master planner must be, only one name comes to mind: Vietnam's organizational genius, Ho Chi Minh.[85]

Even Pike suggests that prior to the emergence of the N.L.F. in 1960 there had been sustained resistance to the Diem government by "Communists, the religious sects, and other groups."[86] The point is that even a biased accounting of the facts is compelled to take account of the pre-Communist and non-Communist role in the early years of the insurgency.[87]

---

84. Consider, for instance, the inconsistency between the claims of a democratic society in South Viet Nam and the Constitution approved by the Constituent Assembly in 1967. *See, e.g.,* Article 5: "1. The Republic of Viet-Nam opposes communism in every form. 2. Every activity designed to propagandize or carry out communism is prohibited"; Article 81(2): "The Supreme Court is empowered to decide on the dissolution of a political party whose policy and activities oppose the republican regime." For the text of the Constitution, see the *Congressional Record* (daily ed.) for June 6, 1967, S 7733-37. For a full account of the terror that commenced in 1954, see 2 BUTTINGER 893-916.

85. PIKE 76.

86. *Id.* 75. This non-Communist resistance to Saigon has also been emphasized by Bernard Fall's accounts of the early phases of the insurgency. And as recently as May 1967, Miss Cao Ngoc Phuong, who according to R. W. Apple, Jr., of the New York Times, "is regarded as a heroine by peace-oriented intellectuals in South Vietnam," is quoted as saying:

Many of my friends seem to have joined the Vietcong. We are losing the élite of our country. These people know the National Liberation Front is closely allied, with the Communists and we don't like Communism. But they see no future in this [the Ky] Government.

N.Y. Times, May 17, 1967, at 3, col. 2.

87. 2 BUTTINGER 972-92 contains a very balanced account (but one written from an anti-Communist perspective) of the origins of the Second Indochina War during the Diem regime. Buttinger writes that "The Diem Government itself created the conditions that pushed the population to the brink of open rebellion, and this convinced the Communist leadership that the South could be conquered by force," *id.* 977. Buttinger believes the "concerted effort to overthrow the Diem regime and its successor by force, was organized by the Communists, and while it would have made little headway without wide popular support, neither would it have had its amazing success without guidance and assistance from the North.

"But the Saigon-Washington version of these events, which had been reduced to the flat assertion that 'the Vietnam war is the result of external aggression' strays even farther from historical truth. Neither the strenuous efforts of Saigon nor those of Washington have produced evidence that anti-Diem terror and guerrilla warfare started as a result of infiltration of combatants and weapons from the North. No significant infiltration occurred before 1960, and very little during the next three years." *Id.* at 981-82. Even according the North as substantial a role as Buttinger does, great doubt is still cast on the American inference of "external aggression," without which Professor Moore's entire legal edifice is without proper foundation.

But if one turns to disinterested observers the situation looks significantly less supportive of the official American factual account. Jean Lacouture[88] wrote in May, 1966:

In the beginning most people in the National Liberation Front (N.L.F.) were not Communist, although more are becoming Communist day by day. . . . Until 1963, at least, the Communists were a minority in the N.L.F., and if they found it necessary one year before to create the People's Revolutionary Party (P.R.P.) within the heart of the N.L.F., it was precisely to bolster their inadequate influence.[89]

Lacouture also shows that the evidence of Hanoi's influence on the N.L.F. is very tenuous as a consequence of differences in the style and contents of its texts relevant to the war.[90]

It would appear, then, that impartial interpretations of the role of Hanoi in aiding the N.L.F. do not significantly support Professor Moore's factual inferences.[91] At best, the factual situation in Viet Nam is ambiguous with respect to the relations between North Viet Nam and the N.L.F.[92] Each side resolves the ambiguity to suit the image of the war that it seeks to rely upon. I am convinced that the facts, although ambiguous in some particulars, do not support *equally* convincing interpretations by the supporters of Saigon and by the supporters of Hanoi; I am convinced that the weight of the evidence and the burden of impartial commentary lends far closer support to Hanoi's version of "the facts" than it does to Saigon's version. But, for sake of analysis, let's assume that the ambiguity supports equally convincing, if mutually inconsistent, accounts of the role of Hanoi in the creation, control, and outlook of the N.L.F. Even so, neither legal precedent, nor legal commentary, nor sound policy analysis, supports the

---

88. Jean Lacouture is a distinguished correspondent for *Le Monde* who has written extensively on Viet Nam for more than a decade, and holds a strongly anti-Communist position.

89. Lacouture, *The "Face" of the Viet Cong*, WAR/PEACE REPORT, May 1966, 7 (written as a reply to Mr. Carver's article in FOREIGN AFFAIRS, *supra* note 79); *cf.* KAHIN AND LEWIS 109-16, especially at 109: "When the deadline for the promised election passed in July 1956, Hanoi Radio continued to counsel moderation and peaceful tactics to its Southern-based supporters.

"For the next two years revolts against Diem emanated primarily from non-Vietminh quarters."

90. Lacouture, *The "Face" of the Viet Cong*, WAR/PEACE REPORT, May 1966, at 8.

91. KAHIN & LEWIS 110-16.

92. It is not only the *facts* as such, but their *interpretation* that is subject to disagreement. The interpretation of the Vietcong's character depends on the orientation of the interpreter toward such related matters in the Viet Nam setting as Afro-Asian nationalism, the Saigon regime, the effects of American involvement, and the kind of society that would evolve from the various alternative lines of development open to South Viet Nam (including reunification with the North).

United States' contention, as of February, 1965, that North Viet Nam had committed "an armed attack." Such a claim to strike back virtually eliminates all legal restraint upon the discretion of a state or its allies to transform an internal war into an international war. As such, it repudiates the entire effort of twentieth century international law to fetter discretionary recourse to force by a sovereign state. In addition, in a situation of ambiguity the burden of asserting the right to use military power against the territory of a foreign country should be placed upon the claimant state. This burden is especially difficult to sustain when the claim to use force is generalized rather than being justified as a proportionate response to some specific provocation or being directed at some specific external target relevant to the internal war, such as a sanctuary or infiltration route. The United States has increasingly claimed for itself the right to bomb whatever it deems appropriate without restraint as to time, target, or magnitude.

Oppression by Saigon as a Causative Agent

Professor Moore's contextual account is strangely devoid of any reference to the effects of Premier Ngo Dinh Diem's reign of terror in the 1956-57 period in South Viet Nam. Bernard Fall, among others, points out that the uprising of peasants against Saigon arose as a consequence of Diem's policies that pre-existed the formation of the Vietcong and was accomplished without any interference on the part of Hanoi.[93] It is difficult to establish causal connections in the Viet Nam setting, but any account of how the violence started in South Viet Nam should call attention to the priority in time, as well as to the oppressiveness and social backwardness of the Diem regime.

It seems worth considering the account given by Joseph Buttinger, an ardent anti-Communist and the most knowledgeable narrator of the relevant historical period (World War II to the assassination of Diem in 1963).[94] Buttinger calls "[t]he manhunt against the Vietminh [the coalition of Vietnamese forces that had fought against French colonialism] an almost incomprehensible violation of common sense, and one of the major contributions to the success of the later Communist-led insurrection."[95] In addition to spreading terror throughout South Viet Nam there were "an unending series of sermons about the

---

93. B. Fall, The Two Viet-Nams (1st ed. 1963) 272: "the countryside largely went Communist in 1958-60," *i.e.*, before the Vietcong came into existence. [Quoted in 2 Buttinger 977.]
94. 2 Buttinger 974-81.
95. *Id.* 975.

evils of Communism, delivered in compulsory meetings by officials whom the peasants had every reason to despise."[96] The victims of Diem's oppression included many non-Communists; "[e]fficiency took the form of brutality and a total disregard for the difference between determined foes and potential friends."[97] Death, preceded by torture, was the form of governmental action in this pre-Vietcong period in the South when there was only an apprehension about a Communist-led insurrection, but no action. Buttinger gives an explanation of why Diem's reign of terror did not provoke official American protest that exposes the root of the Viet Nam tragedy: "The American public, which a little later was told of the many Diem officials murdered by the so-called Vietcong, learned nothing at all about these earlier events, not so much because of Saigon's censorship but rather because of *the West's reluctance openly to condemn crimes committed in the name of anti-Communism*."[98] It is this ideological biasing of perception that has led the United States Government and its supporters to believe in the rationalization of the war in Viet Nam as defense against aggression. To give Diem and his successors the kind of backing that we have given him can only be explained as part of a global crusade against the spread of Communist influence.[99]

The Relevance of United States Aid to the Incumbent Regime

The inference of "armed attack" must include an examination of the overall relevant context. But Professor Moore ignores altogether the relevance of the United States connection with the Saigon regime to an appraisal of Hanoi's role. The assistance to the N.L.F. given by Hanoi takes on a very different character if interpreted as neutralizing the assistance given by the United States to the other side in an ongoing civil struggle.[100] International law does not prohibit discrimination

---

96. *Id.*
97. *Id.* 976.
98. *Id.* (emphasis added).
99. This understanding of the American commitment must have prompted U Thant in the Introduction to the Annual Report on the work of the United Nations in 1966 to say: "I see nothing but danger in this idea, so assiduously fostered outside Vietnam, that the conflict is a kind of holy war between two powerful political ideologies." N.Y. Times, Sept. 19, 1966, at 18, col. 5. Stillman and Pfaff write in a similar vein in the course of a major analysis of U.S. foreign policy: "Our dominating impulse in Vietnam is ideological; the conventional political and strategic justifications for the American involvement in Vietnam seem peripheral, and even doubtful." E. STILLMAN & W. PFAFF, POWER AND IMPOTENCE 171 (1966).
100. Consider the relevance of these words of John Stuart Mill:
But the case of a people struggling against a foreign yoke, or *against a native tyranny upheld by foreign arms*, illustrates the reasons for non-intervention in an opposite way; for in this case the reasons themselves do not exist. . . . To assist a people thus

in favor of an insurgent, especially one that has already enjoyed a degree of success, who is deemed to be "just" nor does it prohibit counter-interventionary efforts designed to offset intervention on behalf of the incumbent.[101] The policies of self-determination at stake are best served by an attitude of impartiality. The coercive apparatus of the modern state is able to suppress even very widely based popular uprisings; the evolution of social control increasingly favors the government in a domestic struggle. The advantages of the domestic government are accentuated by its *normal* intercourse with foreign states, including its option to continue to receive foreign aid. If peaceful domestic opposition is disallowed and a coercive government is aided by a powerful external ally, then the sole possibility of approximating the ideas of self-determination is to accord equivalent rights to insurgent or anti-incumbent groups that solicit aid from foreign countries.

If the insurgency succeeds in establishing itself as the *de facto* government of a substantial portion of the territory in controversy, then foreign states are legally as entitled to deal with the insurgent faction as with the constituted government. Such discretion, expressed in traditional international law by the shifting of insurgent status from "rebellion" to "insurgency" to "belligerency," embodies a sound compromise between according respect to the constituted government as the source of domestic stability and avoiding interferences with the way in which contending groups in a national society work out a domestic balance of forces. This reasoning is applicable to the situation in South Viet Nam. As of 1961, at the latest, the National Liberation Front was in effective control of a substantial portion of South Viet · Nam and often was exercising its authority in areas under its control with more success than was the constituted regime in Saigon.[102] At such a stage in

---

kept down, is not to disturb the balance of forces on which the permanent maintenance of freedom in a country depends, but to redress that balance when it is already unfairly and violently disturbed. . . . Intervention to enforce non-intervention is always rightful, always moral, if not alwyas prudent (emphasis added).

J. S. MILL, ESSAYS ON POLITICS AND CULTURE 412 (G. Himmelfarb ed. 1962).

101. See notes 62-64 *supra* and pp. 1120-23.

102. *Cf., e.g.,* W. BURCHETT, VIETNAM: INSIDE STORY OF THE GUERRILLA WAR (1965). No friend of the N.L.F., Bernard Fall nevertheless writes that "on the local level, American sources have privately stated matter-of-factly that the local NLF administration clearly outperformed the GVN's on every count until the heavy bombardments of 1965-66 made orderly government impossible. It was an established fact that in most areas the NLF did proceed with local elections that were by and large unfettered—Communist control would exist in the form of a *can-bo* (a cadre) detached to the village chief for his paperwork—and produced more effective and more popularly supported local government than the country had enjoyed since its loss of independence in the 1860's." B. FALL, THE TWO VIET-NAMS 365 (2d rev. ed. 1967).

civil strife international law fully allows third-parties to treat the society in question as exhibiting a condition of *dual sovereignty*. In these circumstances North Viet Nam's assistance to the N.L.F. enjoys the same legal status as does the United States' assistance to the Saigon regime.[103] Such an interpretation bears centrally on any contention that North Viet Nam committed an armed attack on South Viet Nam subsequent to whatever critical date is chosen to affirm substantial *de facto* sovereignty by the N.L.F.[104] The argument of the State Department, then, that the level of support given to the N.L.F. up through 1965 establishes "aggression" of such magnitude as to be "an armed attack" is unresponsive to the basic legal issues at stake. Even accepting as accurate the conclusion that "by the end of 1964, North Viet Nam might well have moved over 40,000 armed and unarmed guerrillas into South Viet Nam" there is no consideration given to the critical fact that as of 1962 the N.L.F. enjoyed enough *de facto* sovereignty in South Viet Nam to allow North Viet Nam to furnish military assistance on the same legal premises as relied upon by the United States vis-à-vis Saigon.[105] The whole legal tradition of third-party relationships to contending factions in a civil war is to distinguish the degrees to which a revolutionary struggle has succeeded in establishing itself as a partial "government." Neither the State Department nor Professor Moore take this essential contextual factor into account to any extent in characterizing North Viet Nam's role as "an armed attack."

Given a post-1962 assumption of *de facto* dual sovereignty in South Viet Nam, third powers are entitled to neutralize and offset external

---

103. *See generally* A. THOMAS & A. THOMAS, NON-INTERVENTION: THE LAW AND ITS IMPORT IN THE AMERICAS 215-21 (1956); Falk, *The International Regulation of Internal Violence in the Developing Countries,* 1966 PROC. AM. SOC. INT'L L. at 58; for the reality and extent of N.L.F. control as of mid-1965 see B. FALL, THE TWO VIET NAMS 381, 388 (2d rev. ed. 1967).

104. See especially the basis of argument in the State Department's Memorandum of Law in its opening section vindicating recourse to collective self-defense because of a prior armed attack. CONSULTATIVE COUNCIL 113-14. There is obviously no "armed attack" if the foreign assistance is being given lawfully to one governmental unit in a situation of civil strife in which the adversary unit is receiving a much larger quantity of foreign assistance.

105. That is, the notion of neutrality was supposed to guide third-powers in the event of an ongoing civil war. *See, e.g.,* A. THOMAS & A. THOMAS, *supra* note 103, at 219:
A neutral power is always at liberty to decide whether it will permit or will prohibit aid to the disrupted state; its main duty as a neutral is that it must treat both sides equally.
An obvious corollary of this norm is that when a neutral favors one side, then this advantage can be offset by discrimination in favor of the other side. Depending on the phasing of intervention with the existence of a conflict pronounced enough to qualify as a civil war, both the United States and North Viet Nam could reasonably perceive their roles to be one of offsetting or neutralizing the intervention or non-neutrality of the other side. *Cf.* White, *supra* note 3.

assistance to the other side. Certainly, then, North Viet Nam's military assistance to the N.L.F. seems proportionate to the United States' military assistance to the Saigon regime. Even more certainly, it is unreasonable to characterize North Viet Nam's role after 1962 as "an armed attack" and the United States' role as "lawful assistance." It is also relevant to note that no American official contended that the pre-1962 role of North Viet Nam deserved to be regarded as "an armed attack"; even during the debates on the American claims of "reprisal" arising out of the Gulf of Tonkin incident in August, 1964, there was no intimation that North Viet Nam's role in South Viet Nam was of the extraordinary character justifying recourse to "self-defense." It seems clear and significant to conclude that the post-1965 contention of "armed attack" besides being unconvincing on their merits is also an example of arguing *post hoc, ergo propter hoc.*

In the months immediately after the Geneva Conference in 1954 it was widely believed that the Diem regime would collapse from its own dead weight because of its unpopularity and inefficiency. The United States gave substantial economic and indirect military support to the Saigon government from the beginning of its existence. This support included training, guiding, and paying the main units of Saigon's military establishment.[106] The United States also played an increasingly significant role in influencing the composition and outlook of Saigon's government, so significant that by the time serious civil strife broke out there was hardly any prospect of resolution being reached by the domestic balance of forces.

As the American military participation on the side of Saigon grew more overt and massive it became clearer that it was Washington and not Saigon that was the main adversary of the N.L.F.[107] As Hanoi acted to offset this American military presence in South Viet Nam it was naturally drawn into ever more substantial and overt military participation on the side of the N.L.F.[108] And certainly since 1963 the United States' control of Saigon's war effort and war aims appears to be much more explicit and decisive than does Hanoi's control over the N.L.F.'s war effort and war aims. Given the ratio of external participation on the two sides of the Viet Nam war it seems contrary both to

---

106. KAHIN & LEWIS 77-80; THE MANSFIELD REPORT 20.
107. Increasingly, it became clear that the United States, and not South Viet Nam, was determining the course of the war and the conditions for its settlement.
108. But can one imagine a conference of the N.L.F. allies summoned under the auspices of North Viet Nam in the manner of the 1965-66 conferences at Honolulu, Manila, and Guam? For comparative statistics on foreign involvement in the war in Viet Nam see KAHIN & LEWIS 185; B. FALL, THE TWO VIET-NAMS 358 (2d rev. ed. 1967).

the perceptions of common sense and to the dictates of international law to regard North Viet Nam as guilty of an armed attack. The total context suggests that the phasing and extent of the United States participation in the war has had a much greater impact upon its course than has the North Vietnamese participation, and that neither side enjoys a privileged legal status so far as the principles of either self-defense or non-intervention are concerned, at least once it became clear that the insurgent challenge was a serious and prolonged one. In fact, the legal status of Hanoi's role in assisting the insurgency is according to conventional approaches of international law dependent upon the extent to which it is reasonable to regard the insurgent faction as a counter-government in effective political control over portions of the contested territory.[109] If Professor Moore stresses the *de facto* sovereignty of South Viet Nam (regardless of the terms at Geneva), then it seems essential to acknowledge all relevant *de facto* circumstances including those that benefit the legal contentions of North Viet Nam. In the first Mansfield Report it was acknowledged that "[b]y 1961 it was apparent that the prospects for a total collapse in South Viet Nam had begun to come dangerously close."[110]

In the context of Viet Nam, however, the normal legal situation is even less favorable to the incumbent regime than it might otherwise be. Chapter III of the Cease-Fire Agreement contains a series of provisions that disallows the incumbent regime its normal freedom to receive military assistance.[111] Article 4 of the Final Declaration "takes note of the clauses in the agreement on the cessation of hostilities in Viet Nam prohibiting the introduction into Viet Nam of foreign troops and military personnel as well as of all kinds of arms and munitions."[112] Therefore, it is arguable that without the authorization of the International Control Commission it was illegal to give any direct military assistance to the Saigon regime; it is also arguable that the United States immediately fostered the violation of the spirit of the Accords by the extension of SEATO to cover South Viet Nam and by the extension of economic aid of such a character that freed Saigon to develop and modernize its military capability as directed by a growing number of United States military advisers. It is difficult to read the Geneva Accords without receiving the strong impression that one of the

---

109. *Cf.* note 102 *supra* and 1135.
110. THE MANSFIELD REPORT 21.
111. Articles 16-18; convenient text of Final Declaration, CONSULTATIVE COUNCIL 148-50, FURTHER DOCUMENTS RELATING TO THE DISCUSSION OF INDOCHINA AT THE GENEVA CONFERENCE (Misc. No. 20) CMD. No. 9239 (1954).
112. Convenient text of Final Declaration, CONSULTATIVE COUNCIL 148.

principal purposes was to prohibit post-1954 Great Power intervention in Vietnamese affairs, and given the United States' attempt to mobilize support for a Great Power intervention as an alternative to the Geneva Settlement it is difficult to avoid the conclusion that the provisions on foreign military intervention were directed, above all, at the United States.

Professor Moore suggests that the belligerent objective of North Viet Nam is reunification under Hanoi's control, and he contends that this objective is the functional equivalent of territorial conquest. Such reasoning leads Moore to conclude that Hanoi's assistance to the N.L.F. is more suitably treated as equivalent to North Korea's attack on South Korea than it is to Germany's aid to the Franco insurgency during the Spanish Civil War. I find Professor Moore's conclusion on this point, also, to rest upon a selective interpretation of the relevant context for the following reasons:

(1) Hanoi's pursuit of unification by limited, low-order coercion needs to be understood in light of the outcome of the first Indochina War and the terms of the Geneva Settlement; from the perspective of law North Viet Nam must be accorded a reciprocal discretion in interpreting post-1954 events as is claimed for South Viet Nam;

(2) The evidence advanced by Professor Moore to show that North Viet Nam is seeking reunification is largely hypothetical and speculative;

(3) Both Hanoi and the N.L.F. disavow reunification as an objective of their war effort.[113]

On this basis it seems unconvincing to equate North Korea's sudden and massive overt attack upon South Korea with North Viet Nam's slow build-up of support for the N.L.F. through covert assistance to an insurgent effort against a hostile neighboring regime allied with a hostile superpower. The United States' ill-fated support for the Bay of Pigs venture in 1961 was not so long ago.[114] We went to considerable lengths to disguise our sponsorship of the Cuban exiles intent on overthrowing Castro. Why? Precisely because different world order consequences attach to covert rather than to overt sponsorship of insurrectionary activity in a foreign country.[115] And what of the role of the C.I.A.

---

113. *Both* sides evidently avow peaceful reunification. South Viet Nam goes so far as to incorporate the following two provisions into its new Constitution: Article 1(1): "Viet-Nam is a territorially, indivisible, unified and independent republic." Article 107: "Article 1 of the constitution and this Article may not be amended or deleted." May not North Viet Nam espouse a comparable objective? *See generally* Draper, *Vietnam: How Not to Negotiate,* N.Y. REVIEW OF BOOKS, May 4, 1967, at 17.

114. *See* Falk, *supra* note 77.

115. *See* Falk, *supra* note 1, at 1126, n.18.

in the overthrow of an allegedly pro-Communist regime in Guatemala in 1954?[116] I mention these examples of covert interference not to defend this pattern of practice, but to suggest that when the United States has been an active party in support of insurrection a great effort has been made to keep its role as covert as possible for as long as possible. Likewise it was the overtness of our interference with domestic events in the Dominican Republic in 1965 that provoked such intense criticism of our action; it was probably less interventionary than the covert role in Guatemala.[117] Thus it is not accurate to analogize the covert pursuit of an interventionary policy in a foreign society with its overt pursuit in terms either of its perceived or actual world order consequences, even assuming for the sake of argument that the two modes of interference are equally effective. And therefore, and this is critical for my approach, a unilateral defensive extra-territorial response to covert coercion cannot possibly acquire the same legitimacy as would such a response if made to overt coercion. For these reasons I find it inappropriate to rely upon the Korea analogy; the Spanish Civil War I continue to regard as a helpful precedent because there was no counter-intervention undertaken against the territory of intervening states despite substantial foreign assistance to the insurgent faction.

Type II Geographical Restrictions upon "Defensive" Measures Promotes World Order. The Normative Level of Discourse

Professor Moore argues that the restrictions imposed upon the incumbent regime in a Type II situation are arbitrary and that in a particular situation defensive measures against the territory of a state supporting an insurgent *ought* to be permitted. I would agree with Professor Moore that in a *particular* war it can be argued that extra-territorial military measures may minimize the extent and duration of destruction. Relevant rules of restraint, however, must be devised with a generality of instances in mind. In the context of a Viet Nam-type war I would maintain that Type II restrictions are, *in general*, desirable. First of all, the appreciation of whether a measure is "defensive" or "offensive" cannot be reliably achieved by interested parties. Second, to the extent that extra-territorial "defensive" measures are justified by the specific characteristics of foreign support, then a

---

116.   D. WISE AND T. ROSS, THE INVISIBLE GOVERNMENT (1964). For a relevant account of Guatemala events, see D. HOROWITZ, FROM YALTA TO VIETNAM 160-61 (1965).

117.   For an account critical of the United States intervention in the Dominican Republic, see J. FULBRIGHT, THE ARROGANCE OF POWER (1966).

precise claim to use extra-territorial force should be explained in terms of particular military necessities. For example, an air strike directed against extra-territorial insurgent sanctuaries would be more easily justifiable in the context of normal Type II restraints if these sanctuaries bore a significant specific relationship to the conduct of the war. But bombing North Viet Nam has not been justified in terms of specific, limited military objectives requiring exceptional action; in fact, the American rationale for bombing North Viet Nam has changed character from time to time and the scope and intensity of the bombing action appear disproportionate to the military justification. In addition, independent, non-Communist world public opinion almost universally condemns the continuation of bombing by the United States and the Secretary General of the United Nations has repeatedly called upon the United States to stop bombing on a unilateral and unconditional basis. Hanoi, too, has insisted that the unconditional termination of bombing is the essential precondition for peace talks. The United States' effort to negotiate a reciprocal de-escalation by North Viet Nam in exchange for a halt in bombing overlooks both the general attitude in opposition of the bombing and the inequality in bargaining power that exists between the greatest military colossus in world history and a tiny war-torn and unmodernized state.

Third, the frequency of patterns of intervention and counter-intervention in civil strife throughout international society underlines the danger of spreading violence beyond its original national locus. Greece and Turkey in Cyprus and the United Arab Republic and Saudi Arabia in the Yemen are two examples of civil struggles that could grow much worse if the external sponsor of the incumbent regime felt entitled and did, in fact, attack the territory of the insurgent's external sponsor.[118] It docs not require much knowledge of fire-fighting to conclude that confining the spatial scope of a fire is one way to restrict its damaging impact.

If the coercion is sustained and substantial then the prospects of dealing with it by community procedures are improved. Because of the ambiguity of the facts and the tendency to interpret them in a self-justifying fashion in the Viet Nam setting it is important to restrict

---

118. In fact, one would imagine a serious regional war emerging if either side transgressed the limits that I argue are embodied in a Type II conflict. Only the mutual forbearance of both sides, despite their recriminations about each other's aggression, keeps the conflict at its present level. It is only because the United States is a superpower and North Viet Nam a minor state that the war in Viet Nam has not escalated to much higher levels; it is the power differential that encouraged the United States to transgress Type II restrictions in the spirit of relative prudence.

responses to the limits of Type II unless a sufficient consensus can be mobilized to shift the conflict into the Type IV category. If it qualifies as a Type IV conflict then the organized international community authorizes the response that is deemed appropriate. *Community author-ization* takes the place of overtness as the key factor vindicating a defensive response against foreign territory. I have already indicated why covert forms of coercion are so difficult to construe, especially in a mixed-up political setting. It follows from this assessment that the resources of world order should be built up to facilitate the authorita-tive community identification of covert coercion as "aggression." For this reason it would be desirable to establish border-control, fact-finding machinery, and peace observation groups in those sectors of the world containing target societies that are highly vulnerable to covert coercion. The objective of these devices is to make covert forms of coercion more *visible* to impartial observers, facilitating a consensus, legitimating a decisive defensive response, and discouraging recourse to such coercion as a means to resolve international disputes.

My overall approach to Viet Nam-type conflicts has been altered in response to Professor Moore's criticisms in several important re-spects:

(1) The creation of Type IV to establish an analytic contrast with Types I-III and to permit "self-defense" in the Viet Nam-type setting provided a suitable prior community authorization has been given.[119]

(2) The realization that aggressive designs can be effectively carried out at present by covert forms of international coercion and that it would be desirable to discourage such coercion by making it more *visible*; the eventual world order goal would be to treat *covert* coercion as we now treat *overt* coercion. The effect would be to make Type II conflicts more easily transferable into the Type IV category or more susceptible to Type I treatment. However, in international society as now constituted it seems clearly preferable to deny the victim state unilateral discretion to treat what it perceives to be "aggression" by covert means as justifying its recourse to "self-defense."[120] In a sense this legal conclusion merely restates the adverse judgment rendered by the international community on several occasions when Israel has

---

119. A defensive alliance, such as SEATO, only multi-lateralizes decisions to use force to a very slight degree; "the community" must be defined in wide enough terms to include principal divergent elements.

120. This denial is especially justifiable since (a) legitimate defensive interests can be upheld within the terms of Type II, and special exceptions thereto; and (b) shift to Type I tends both to increase the obstruction of international peace and to increase the role of military power differentials in achieving a settlement of an international dispute.

had recourse to *overt* military force in retaliation for damage that it has suffered from *semi-covert* coercion. The rejection of Israel's claim is impressive because Israel has a much more convincing security rationale than does South Viet Nam for striking back overtly and because the Arab states surrounding Israel are avowedly committed to its destruction.[121] One may argue against the fairness of such constraints upon Israel's discretion in these circumstances, but it is essentially an extra-legal appeal as the organs of the United Nations have the procedural capacity to authorize or prohibit specific uses of force, and it is the exercise of this capacity that most clearly distinguishes what is "legal" from what is "illegal" with regard to the use of force in international society. Legality depends more upon the *identity* of the authorizing decision-maker than upon the *facts of the coercion*. With respect to Viet Nam, if a principal organ of the United Nations authorized the United States' bombing of North Viet Nam, then it would be legal (unless an argument could be successfully made that the decision was "unconstitutional").[122]

Professor Moore also usefully singles out "divided" country problems for separate treatments. He is correct in pointing out that world order is especially endangered by attempts to alter coercively the *status quo* prevailing in a divided country. In this respect the tragic consequences in Viet Nam can be understood as foredestined as soon as Saigon, with the backing of the United States, acted to locate Viet Nam in the divided country category.[123] The uncertainty as to whether Viet Nam is properly classified as "divided" in Professor Moore's sense involves an interpretation of the Geneva Accords. The classification of Viet Nam as a divided country also appears to have been imprudent in view of the logistic difficulties of securing South Viet Nam against attack and in view of the inability to evolve a tolerable regime in Saigon that could provide South Viet Nam with effective government without a huge American military and economic commitment.[124] Even without

121. Israel's responses have seemed to conform much more closely to the requirements of proportionality than has the United States-South Viet Nam response, even if its allegations of coercion are taken at face value.
122. To be legal in the last analysis is to be authorized by the appropriate decision-maker; one can seek to correct "the mistake" attributed to the decision-maker, but the capacity to confer legality persists so long as the legal order is a valid one.
123. The seeds of conflict seem to have been sown by the contradictory interpretations of what was "settled" at Geneva in 1954 with regard to the terms and timing of reunification; although there is room for some misunderstanding, my orientation is heavily influenced by regarding Hanoi's interpretation of the settlement as far more reasonable than Saigon's or Washington's.
124. See the critique advanced by E. STILLMAN & W. PFAFF, POWER AND IMPOTENCE 169-74. The opportunity costs of the Viet Nam war are enormous both with respect to the pursuit of international security goals and with regard to domestic welfare goals.

a hostile North Viet Nam embittered by a sense of being cheated by the non-implementation of the Geneva Accords, there is reason to suspect that without American backing the Saigon regime would have been unable to govern South Viet Nam with any success. Predictions of imminent collapse were widespread until the American military presence assumed major proportions in 1965.[125] In addition, there was only minimal and grudging alliance support, much less community support, for regarding South Viet Nam as an inviolable sovereign entity of the same sort as West Germany or South Korea, or even Formosa. For these reasons I do not find it convincing, independent of the issue of ambiguous facts, to analogize Viet Nam to other divided country problems.

III. Comments on Professor Moore's Policy Inquiry vis-à-vis Type III Conflict

Professor Moore's perceptive discussion of the considerations that bear on the international management of intra-state conflict deserves careful study. His stress in the setting of Type III upon the policies of self-determination and minimum world public order points up the difficulty that results from the sort of over-generalization that is implicit in the kind of categorization of international conflict situations that I have proposed. I accept his criticism that my original formulation of Type III rules is "simplistic" if applied mechanically to a large variety of greatly varying international contexts. A complete response to Professor Moore's critique cannot be undertaken within the compass of this article, but will be attempted on another occasion.[126] I will restrict myself here to a few general comments on Professor Moore's approach to suggest wherein my policy emphasis differs from his with regard to the regulation of third-party participation in intra-state conflict.

Let me say in my own intellectual defense that the division of international conflict situations into three broad categories (now four)[127]

---

125. KAHIN & LEWIS 66-87.
126. For instance, Types I-IV should be appropriately sub-divided to take account of recurrent contexts that can be grouped together within each broader category. Thus in Type III there is a difference between the legislative contexts relevant to uprisings in the five countries of southern Africa, the humanitarian context of slaughter that followed after the generals' counter-coup in Indonesia (1965-66), the anarchy that has been threatened from time to time in the Congo and Nigeria from prolonged civil strife, and the hegemonial context that exists when one superpower has claimed over time special geopolitical prerogatives, acquiesced in by other states, in relation to a region.
127. See pp. 1106-08 for explanation.

was intended primarily to facilitate and organize thought about the management of all forms of international violence through a preliminary sorting out of relevant contexts and by explicating the decisive legal consequences of each. Once this preliminary task of classification has been accomplished, then it is appropriate to question whether there need to be more specific subcategories and whether rules stating exceptions should not also be included.[128] On this level, then, my response to Professor Moore is to accept his criticism, but to suggest that the attempt to categorize international conflict appears to add greater focus to policy inquiry than is possible by either an *ad hoc* response to a specific conflict (Viet Nam) or by a generalized description of the policies bearing most heavily on the legal regulation of recourse to international violence.

On a more fundamental level of policy Professor Moore, as the result of a very sophisticated analysis, appears to conclude that given the conditions of the modern world it is more desirable to endorse an approach to civil strife that authorizes discrimination in favor of the incumbent faction, especially in cold war settings, and prohibits assistance to the insurgent faction.

I am persuaded by Professor Moore's analysis to modify my original formulations to a certain extent. A neutral rule of impartiality does not preclude the continuation of (or even the moderate increase in) the level of assistance furnished a constituted government prior to the outbreak of civil strife. There are, however, restraints upon the scope and form of discriminatory external participation.[129] For one thing, foreign assistance should not include direct participation in combat operations. For another, it should not attempt to bear more than a fairly small percentage, certainly under 50 per cent, of the increased military requirements created by the domestic uprising. And finally, the external assistance should not be conditioned upon increased influences in the process of decision-making within the recipient country. In the event that the restraints sketched above are ignored, then the conflict is shifted from Type III into the Type II category, the shift itself reflecting "the violation" committed by a third-party state. If the restraints are respected with respect to aid furnished to the incumbent, then substantial aid to instigate or sustain an insurgency is a vio-

128. Note the development of international law governing the use of the oceans as depicted by M. McDougal and W. Burke in *The Public Order of the Oceans.*
129. For a creative effort at emphasizing limits on the character of intervention rather upon its occurrence see Farer, *Intervention in Civil Wars: A Modest Proposal,* 67 COLUM. L. REV. 266 (1967).

lation of Type III restraints that shifts the conflict into the Type II category as a consequence of the illegal conduct of the third party.

In the event, however, that the uprising succeeds in establishing control over a substantial portion of the area and population of the country, then a condition of *de facto* dual sovereignty exists such that third-parties can furnish assistance to the insurgent on the same basis as to the incumbent. If substantial assistance is accorded to one or both sides subsequent to *de facto* dual sovereignty the conflict is necessarily shifted into Type II, but there is no violation of international law committed by third powers. The internal situation generated a shift from Type III to Type II, as distinct from a shift coming about through interventionary roles by foreign states on either side of a Type III conflict.

If the United States had chosen to give military assistance to the Batista regime in its struggle against the Castro insurgency in Cuba, then this would be permissible unless the United States entered Cuba in the last stages of the war with its independent military capability so as to foreclose the outcome that would have resulted from the domestic balance of forces. The Soviet intervention in Hungary (1956) definitely succeeded in reversing the outcome of a domestic struggle, and was appropriately condemned by the political organs of the United Nations; the United States intervention in the Dominican Republic in 1965 designed to displace the incumbent regime was given presumably an even more objectionable form of decisive external assistance as it was directed against the incumbent faction.[130]

Professor Moore is also correct to suggest that in cold war contexts rules supporting the stability of existing regimes are probably desirable. It may be helpful to restrict pure Type III analysis to the Afro-Asian world wherein the geo-political context is of different order. In effect, Professor Moore is pointing out that the rival superpowers— the United States and the Soviet Union—provide their own form of conflict management within those segments of international society regarded as belonging to their respective spheres of influence or adhering to their respective security communities. In this regard it may be helpful to consider that concentric security zones surround each superpower and affect the actual treatment of Type III conflicts to a considerable degree:

I. *Primary Security Zone:* The United States, the Soviet Union, and

---

130. For a sympathetic account of the legal basis of the Dominican intervention, see A. THOMAS & A. THOMAS, *supra* note 103.

possibly mainland China and the principal states of Western Europe, as sovereign states in relation to their own national security;

II. *Secondary Security Zones:* Groups of countries that are traditionally subject to the influence of one superpower or the other and whose security interests are governed by the political preference of the superpower;[131]

III. *Tertiary Security Zones:* The Afro-Asian world of recently independent states in which policies of non-alignment and non-intervention are affirmed.

These security zones describe the geo-political condition in the world as of 1967. It is a complex world order issue to interrelate these political realities with the role of law in establishing common standards of restraint and interaction. It is generally true that in the Secondary Security Zones the dominant actor is able to exercise control over the outcome of Type III conflicts, although Hungary in 1956 and the Dominican Republic in 1965 were governed by interventions that did not accord generally with permissible uses of military power, at least as understood by general community expectations.[132]

Viet Nam has become such a sustained and major war because the United States has converted a Type III conflict into Type I conflict without the legitimizing benefit of an overt armed attack and without the geo-political tolerance accorded to superpower diplomacy that is confined within its own Secondary Zone. Therefore, the extra-legal categorization of security zones may help to identify those situations in which external military assistance that is carried beyond a certain threshold is likely to trigger a major off-setting military action by a principal adversary. It is now commonplace to note that the most severe forms of international violence since World War II have been the result of competing superpower interferences in the Tertiary Security Zone, especially in those circumstances, such as Viet Nam, where it is unclear whether the territory in dispute belongs in the Secondary Zone, and if so on which side, or in the Tertiary Zone.

Professor Moore's discussion is strangely devoid of any reference to the role of international institutions or to the relevance of the will of the organized international community with respect to the relative

---

131. *E.g.,* Latin America, East Europe; one might argue that the problems in Asian affairs arise out of China's attempt to establish a Secondary Security Zone on its periphery and the United States resistance to this attempt.

132. *I.e.,* there is a geo-political level of practice that exists in a state of tension with a moral-legal level of commitment; both levels converge in the policy-making process relevant to international decisions.

merits of contending factions in a Type III situation.[133] It seems to me that many of the problems that Professor Moore points out, that arise in discriminating between various Type III contexts can be resolved by according regional and global international institutions the competence to identify which faction is entitled to benefit from external assistance. Thus in the context of Southern Africa the decisive expression of the will of the international community would appear to legitimize discrimination in favor of the insurgent faction in the event that a Type III situation should arise at some future occasion;[134] such discrimination has been stridently endorsed in the African context by the Organization of African Unity.[135] Types I-III are residual categories that exist only when there is no consensus formally reached by a competent international institution.

A residual rule of impartiality does seem to minimize the role of both extra-national and domestic violence in situations where no international consensus exists. The absence of consensus is itself indicative of a potentiality for major conflict, disclosing seriously opposed interpretations of the appropriate external attitude toward the intra-state conflict. Therefore, in a Type III situation it would seem generally desirable to promote adherence to Hall's view that neither incumbent nor insurgent should be the beneficiary of discrimination.[136] What level of support for the incumbent constitutes "discrimination" and at what point a civil disturbance is properly regarded as belonging in Type III are complex determinations of fact and law for which no definite answer can here be provided.

Professor Moore, in my judgment, underrates once again the detrimental consequences of affirming the discretion of sovereign states to project their military power into foreign political conflicts. It is true that covert forms of coercion can subject a society to an "attack" that jeopardizes its political independence and territorial sovereignty, but it is also true that "the defense" of that society may involve its destruction and manipulation. To allow discrimination in favor of the incumbent to increase without limit in a situation of civil strife is to

---

133. *Cf.* Falk, *The New States and International Legal Order*, 118 RECUEIL DES COURS —— (forthcoming).

134. On jurisprudential basis see Falk, *On the Quasi-Legislative Competence of the General Assembly*, 60 AM. J. INT'L L. 782 (1966).

135. For some consideration of the difficulties that attend regional authorization of the use of force see Falk, *Janus Tormented: The International Law of Internal War*, in INTERNATIONAL ASPECTS OF CIVIL STRIFE 185, 242-46 (J. Rosenau ed. 1964).

136. On the assumption, of course, of some *de facto* control and some substantial prospect of eventual success, and subject to the geo-political qualifications of the three-zone analysis.

defeat altogether the ideals of self-determination without promoting the kind of world order premised upon the ordering capacities of territorially based sovereign states. To insulate Type III conflicts it is as important to restrict discrimination in favor of the incumbent as it is to improve the process of detecting covert assistance to the insurgent by making it more visible. To do one without the other is to invite Viet Nam-type confrontations throughout the Tertiary Security Zone. I would espouse a foreign policy of Cosmopolitan Isolationism as most suited to the attainment of world order in the Tertiary Security Zone: national military power should be brought to bear, if at all, only after formal authorization by the organized international community.[137] In my revised system of categorization, then, external assistance beyond *status quo* levels is only permissible if the intra-state conflict can be shifted from Type III to Type IV.

IV. The State Department Brief: A Further Comment

Professor Moore explains that the State Department Memorandum of Law was written mainly to deal with the public debate initiated by a widely circulated (and now redrafted) brief of the Lawyers' Committee on American Policy Towards Viet Nam.[138] As such, it should not be appraised as the full statement of the Government's position. This is undoubtedly true, but it is nevertheless disappointing that when the Department's Legal Adviser enters the public debate, he does so in such an unconvincing manner. Certainly, it does not clarify the discussion to over-clarify the facts or to make complex legal questions appear self-evident. A citizens' white paper in opposition to Government policy is primarily a call for an impartial accounting, it is intentionally and appropriately one-sided; especially in the security area it is impossible to proffer criticism in effective form unless the issues are somewhat overstated.[139] It is true, as Professor Moore writes, that the Lawyers' Committee first Memorandum emphasized many of the "wrong" issues or stated the "right" issues in the "wrong" way, but it did provoke the Government after a decade of involvement in Viet Nam to make its first serious effort to reconcile United States foreign

---

137. I have developed this viewpoint in an essay to appear in ADEPT, a literary journal published in Houston, Texas.

138. CONSULTATIVE COUNCIL 19-111.

139. Citizens do not have access to classified information, national news coverage is slanted toward affirming foreign policy in periods of crisis, and only clear conclusions will receive attention in press or government; the more balanced scholarly critique will be ignored except, perhaps, by other scholars, but it will not influence the public debate.

policy in Viet Nam with our proclaimed commitment to a law-ordered international society. That serious effort was impaired, in my judgment, by defining the issues and maintaining the adversary spirit of the Lawyers' Committee document. In a second round of public debate the Lawyers' Committee has prepared under the auspices of a Consultative Council composed of academicians a reply to the Government's Memorandum. This reply does focus more directly on the world order issues at stake and does provide the Government with a new intellectual context within which to respond. It is a sign of health for a democratic polity to engage in this sort of a dialogue during the course of a major war; it may be almost unprecedented for citizens to call their own government to account by an appeal to the constraints and institutional procedures of international law. The outcome of this dialogue, as well as its more scholarly analogues, may well shape our perceptions of the requirements of world order so as either to endorse or inhibit American involvements in a series of Viet Nam-type wars in the decades ahead.

V. On the Constitutionality of Violating International Law

Professor Moore suggests that there is no legal authority to support a view that the Executive has a Constitutional obligation to obey international law. What is more, he accuses me of advancing a "somewhat monistic argument." I acknowledge my guilt. It appears to me that the Constitution embodies the legal framework within which the Government is entitled to act. The condemnation of aggressive war and the United States' endorsement of the Principles of the Nuremberg Judgment seem to make adherence to international law a matter of Constitutional necessity. True, there is no established legal doctrine to this effect, but the question is open enough that is seems reasonable to contend that this is the way the Constitution ought to be authoritatively construed. As in domestic affairs, so in foreign affairs, we should remember that it is a Constitution that we are expounding; as the organic law of the society it must be constantly readapted to the needs of nation and its citizenry. No need is more paramount at the present time than to develop a Constitutional tradition of restraint upon the Executive's virtually discretionary power to commit the nation to war of any scope and duration. To insist on Constitutional sources of legal restraint is a part of the wider global need to erode the prerogatives of the sovereign state in the area of war and peace. So long as international society remains decentralized the most effective legal restraints are likely to be self-restraints, those that are applied from *within* rather than from *without* the sovereign state. For this reason we cannot neglect the Constitutional dimension of an allegedly illegal participation by the United States in the Viet Nam War. And for this reason it seems appropriate for domestic courts to pronounce upon, rather than to evade, such legal challenges as have been presented in the selective service context.[140]

VI. A Comment on Professor Moore's Conclusion

Professor Moore concludes his article by affirming "that the conflict cannot be meaningfully generalized in black and white terms" and yet proceeds to do so. He acknowledges that "[i]f because of Viet Nam Americans must ask themselves hard questions about the use of national power and the proper goals of foreign policy, the North Vietnamese must ask themselves equally hard questions about the use of force as an instrument of major international change." These two sets of questions as formulated by Professor Moore are not equally hard, nor are they, it is well to add, impartial in tone or content. As expressed throughout Professor Moore's article the United States' failure in his view, may at most involve errors of judgment and lapses of prudence, whereas North Viet Nam's failure consists of committing the most serious possible international delinquency—waging a war of aggression. Such a construction of the adversary positions greatly falsifies, in my judgment, the true situation. An objective interpretation of the war, as sympathetic with the United States contentions as the fact seem to permit, would acknowledge that the conflict in Viet Nam is one in which both sides sincerely, and even reasonably, perceive the other side as the aggressor. Most disinterested interpretations would, in all probability, tend to regard the United States as the sole aggressor, at least with regard to carrying the war into North Vietnamese territory.

The way in which responsibility for the war is distributed is vitally connected with what sorts of steps taken by which side are reasonable preconditions to achieve a negotiated settlement. In this regard when Professor Moore invokes U Thant to support the conclusion that "the Viet Nam was [is] basically a political problem that can only be solved by a political settlement", it seems only reasonable to add that the Secretary General has laid most of the blame upon the United States for prolonging and intensifying the war. In fact, U Thant's precondi-

---

140. See the important dissenting opinion of Mr. Justice Douglas in the decision by the Supreme Court to deny a petition for a writ of certiorari in Mitchell v. United States, 35 U.S.L.W. 3330 (1967).

tions for a negotiated settlement include the prior termination of war acts by the United States against North Vietnamese territory.

A second point of disagreement. Professor Moore writes as if the United States and North Viet Nam are in a position of bargaining parity. Such a predisposition not only overlooks the enormous disparity in scale between the two countries, but also overlooks the fact that the United States is fighting the war at a safe distance from its own society, whereas the destructive impact of the conflict is now focused directly upon the North Vietnamese homeland. This bargaining inequality is directly relevant to Profesosr Moore's comments about the "hard line from Hanoi." To advise the United States that it "must continue to emphasize a negotiated settlement" is to write as if no credibility gap existed as to the sincerity and diligence of prior American peace efforts. Such a statement also ignores the extent to which the American emphasis on negotiations has been expressed more through threatened and actual escalations than by realistic offers to end the war on some basis that preserves Hanoi's stake in the outcome to the same extent as it preserves Washington's stake.

It is not possible to consider here the basis for a negotiated settlement. I share Professor Moore's emphasis upon search for compromise in Viet Nam and for a way eventually to give effect to the principle of self-determination for the foresaken Vietnamese population. There are, however, very serious problems with a negotiated settlement that explain, perhaps, why neither side can envision any middle ground between surrender and victory. Among these serious problems the following can be mentioned:

(1) A coalition government in South Viet Nam seems unworkable that either (a) excludes both Premier Ky and the N.L.F., (b) includes Premier Ky but excludes the N.L.F., (c) includes the N.L.F. but excludes Premier Ky, or (d) includes both Premier Ky and the N.L.F. These four alternative patterns exhaust the logical possibilities, and yet no one of them seems to be a plausible basis for a stable South Viet Nam if the war is ended without prior victory by either side;

(2) The negotiating dialogue has stressed bargaining between North Viet Nam and the United States without any close attention being accorded to the more immediately concerned adversaries, namely, the N.L.F. and Saigon. There is no strong basis to believe either that the two external actors can completely impose their will upon the two internal factions or that the two external actors espouse views identical with those held by the two internal factors. Therefore, bargaining toward peace should be broadened at least conceptually to examine the

positions and leverage of all four major participants in the Viet Nam conflict. An obstacle to this position is the United States' insistence, contrary to widespread neutral and expert interpretation, that the N.L.F. has no identity separate from Hanoi;

(3) The administration of a peaceful settlement in South Viet Nam must find a way to define what constitutes "infiltration" and what constitutes foreign military intervention. These conceptions are even hard to define and even harder to administer effectively. Is an ethnic "Southerner" an infiltrator when he returns unarmed from North to South Viet Nam? By what criteria? Can the regime in Saigon purchase or receive military equipment from outside states as it wishes? Can the government in Hanoi? What criteria can be developed to limit foreign participation in a post-cease-fire environment in Viet Nam? Can a means be found to apply these criteria on a non-political basis? The Geneva machinery of 1954, with its International Control Commission, operates on a troika principle (Poland, Canada, and India) with each rival ideological orientation holding a veto. Would either side be willing to eliminate its own veto or to allow a veto to its adversary? If not, can a mutually acceptable basis for impartial administration be agreed upon?

These are some of the tough questions that beset the search for a negotiated settlement. Their answer is obviously worth seeking. A solution may rely upon substituting an all-Asian presence, possibly under Japanese initiative, for the Western presence that has dominated Vietnamese society since the Nineteenth Century (except for the equally tragic interlude during World War II).

VII. A Concluding Unscientific Postscript

The extra-legal setting of the United States involvement in Viet Nam is essential if a serious attempt is to be made to rethink the foreign policy premises that have led to this long and painful involvement. If it is correct that we have been led into a costly and unjust war in Viet Nam by ignoring our real interests in world affairs, then it is important to explain how this came about. In the context of a discussion of the relevance of international law, the main contention is that a fair-minded attention to the restraints and procedures of the international legal order would have served and continue to serve the real interests of the United States to a far greater extent than do policies arrived at by calculating short-term national advantage purely in terms of maximizing national power, wealth, and prestige. In Viet Nam, the American attempt to control the political outcome to accord with its geo-political preferences (regardless of world order consequences) requires an altogether disproportionate commitment even if one approves of the objective sought.

Such a disproportionality suggests that our policy-making process is not being rationally focused upon our "real national interests" in world affairs. This lack of focus seems to arise from a sort of rigidity that comes from endorsing an ideological interpretation of contemporary international conflict. This endorsement takes precedence over world order considerations in American foreign policy and is likely to lead us into future Viet Nams unless it is repudiated. Ideological opposition to Communism and Communist influence as the main premise for military commitment is more dangerous than discredited foreign policies based on the pursuit of wealth and power. At least the policies of conquest left the victor with tangible gains and the prospect of tangible gain allowed for a rational calculation of the proportionality of means and ends. But in the circumstances of a Viet Nam, precisely because the putative gains are intangible—even sacrificial—there is no way to conclude that it costs too much. To question this reasoning it is necessary to be explicit about its relevance. Therefore, to convey my own sense about bringing United States foreign policy into a closer appreciation of its real interests, including a greater deference to the constraints and procedures of international law, it seems useful to carry the legal analysis beyond the boundaries of law and world order. Hence, an unscientific postscript that is at once an explication of the wider orientation of United States foreign policy and a plea for its reorientation.

The United States Government contends that it has no selfish motives in Viet Nam. As President Johnson explained:

> We're not trying to wipe out North Vietnam. We're not trying to change their government. We're not trying to establish permanent bases in South Vietnam. And we're not trying to gain one inch of new territory for America.[141]

This absence of selfish motives does not establish the beneficial quality of the American involvement in Viet Nam. The United States pursues its military course in Viet Nam because it is determined to defeat a Communist-led insurgency that sprung up years ago in South Viet Nam as a consequence of many domestic and international factors, only one of which was encouragement from and support by North Viet Nam.

---

141. President Johnson's Address to the American Alumni Council, N.Y. Times, July 13, 1966, at 2, col. 3.

The United States acts *as if* the war in South Viet Nam was a consequence solely of aggression from the North.

In actuality, the war in South Viet Nam is being waged in a complex post-colonial setting wherein pressures for national self-assertion interact with ideological movements. Many Vietnamese are concerned with attaining their nationhood unencumbered by foreign domination. The United States is opposing revolutionary nationalism, as well as Communism, in South Viet Nam. And the United States is fighting on behalf of a native regime dominated by a reactionary military elite; Premier Ky was a mercenary pilot for the French in both the Algerian War of Independence and the First Indochina War and identifies himself with the politics of military dictatorship.

To wage war for or against an idea is no less destructive than to embark upon conquest for territory or for treasure. Over a century ago John Stuart Mill warned about the use of military power in the service of an idea:

> We have heard something lately about being willing to go to war for an idea. To go to war for an idea, if the war is aggressive, not defensive is as criminal as to go to war for territory or revenue.[142]

Ideological motivation may indeed be intense. Its roots are often hidden in the past. We embarked upon a program to resist Communism in 1947 with the formulation of the Truman Doctrine.[143] Such a program, at that time, was closely and sensibly related to certain geopolitical realities. The Soviet Union was ruled by a military dictator and it maintained tight control over Communist states and parties elsewhere. Western Europe was still weak from World War II. The colonial system was in its early stages of disintegration. Global Communism was a reality to be resisted and feared, although the Communist adversary was cautious, itself badly stunned and damaged by World War II. Since 1947 many changes have taken place, not least of which is the development of nuclear weapons and their deployment in a posture of mutual deterrence. The Soviet Union has followed an increasingly conservative foreign policy and its domestic society has been the scene of progressive liberalization. The Communist group of states has fallen into conflict, and many rather disjoined national varieties of Communism have emerged. Communism is today often a species of nationalism, not internationalism. Western Europe has recovered fully. Its main states are prosperous and stable.

---

142. J. S. MILL, ESSAYS ON POLITICS AND CULTURE 405 (G. Himmelfarb ed. 1962).
143. For a persuasive comprehensive analysis of the evolution of the United States foreign policy response to Communism, see D. HOROWITZ, FROM YALTA TO VIETNAM (1965).

Despite these changes in the international setting the United States has not significantly altered its dogmatic opposition to Communism. In Viet Nam President Johnson is carrying forward the basic policies of prior Administrations.[144] These policies center upon the assumption that it is always adverse to United States interests to allow a society to become identified as "Communist." To call a movement "Communist" that can also draw upon the revolutionary nationalism of a society, as both the Vietcong and Hanoi can, is to overlook one real base of political potency. Viet Nam, unlike other Asian states, is a country where Communist leadership under Ho Chi Minh has for several decades commanded almost all of the forces of anti-colonialism and nationalism. To resist these forces is to become allied with reactionary elements in the society. Unaided, these reactionary elements would have no prospect of prevailing over a popularly based nationalist movement, whether or not it is Communist led. To defeat such a nationalist movement, if at all, presupposes an enormous foreign effort on behalf of the reactionary faction, an effort of the sort the United States has been making on behalf of successive reactionary regimes in Saigon. The result for South Viet Nam is, at best, a dependence that entails a new subservience to an alien Western power. Certainly the United States has introduced more military might into Viet Nam than the French ever used to dominate the country during the colonial period. To have allowed a Vietcong victory and a possible subsequent reunification of Viet Nam under Hanoi's auspices would have merely ratified the process of self-determination internal to Viet Nam that evolved since the early efforts against the French. Such a nationalist solution even if Communist in form would not have posed any serious danger to Western interests and certainly not to direct United States security interests. Viet Nam has a long tradition of fearing and resisting Chinese domination, and there is every reason to suppose that this tradition would persist in a Communist era. The non-Communist neighbors of Viet Nam have, with the possible exception of Laos, stable governments and strong capabilities to maintain internal security.

---

144. "There *is* an American consensus on foreign affairs, and the Johnson Administration may legitimately argue that its programs carry out in action what the country demands in principle. . . . Mr. Johnson escalated the war in Vietnam, but so did Mr. Kennedy when he altered the American commitment in that country from one of assistance and counsel to the South Vietnamese government to direct, if still limited, military engagement with the Vietnamese insurgents. So did Mr. Eisenhower 'escalate,' or more properly, inaugurate, the American involvement when, in 1954, he stepped into the role the exhausted French abandoned and chose to sponsor and sustain a noncommunist government in Saigon that would prevent the country's unification under the communist Viet Minh movement which had led the war to expel the French." E. STILLMAN & W. PFAFF, *supra* note 99, at 4.

The United States has made an utterly unconvincing appeal to principles of world order; it purports to be resisting aggression in South Viet Nam. Such a contention is without any firm factual base, but its allegation in a circumstance of ambiguity allows the United States Government to maintain its war effort without admitting its true motivation, thereby confusing its supporters and angering its opponents. As Ralph K. White, an American psychologist who has made an unemotional study of the basis for perceiving aggression in Viet Nam writes: "There has been no aggression on either side—at least not in the sense of a cold-blooded, Hitler-like act of conquest. The analogies of Hitler's march into Prague, Stalin's takeover of Eastern Europe, and the North Korean attack on South Korea are false analogies." White also documents his conclusion that "aggression by us seems as obvious to them as aggression by them seems to us."[145]

One trouble with fighting for an idea is that there is no way to measure how much sacrifice its defense is worth. An absolutism sets in. The image of the enemy that justifies his destruction is held secure against prudence, reason, and morality. Only clear inferences of Communism, of aggression, and of good intentions vindicate the death and destruction inflicted upon Viet Nam. The United States can maintain these clear inferences only by denying reality or by testing reality in the same primitive way that the Aztecs justified their belief that the corn on which their civilization depended would not grow unless there were human sacrifices. "The fact that the corn did grow was probably considered solid evidence for such a view; and in those years when the harvest was bad, it was doubtless argued that the gods were angry because the sacrifices had been insufficient. A little greater military effort would result, a few more hearts would be torn from their quivering bodies, and the following year it was highly probable that the harvest would be better and the image consequently confirmed."[146] Kenneth Boulding regards primitive reasoning of this kind as the way we sustain our commitment in Viet Nam—that is "by appeals to analogy, self-evidence, and to the principle that if at first you don't succeed try more of the same until you do."[147] We are entrapped in a dangerous, self-destructive myth in Viet Nam, the elimination of which can only be sought after the relief of peace, if then. Now we can only justify the sacrifices we have already made by increasing them to the point where

---

145. White, *Misperception of Aggression in Vietnam*, 21 J. INT'L AFFAIRS 123, 125 (1967).
146. Boulding, *The Learning and Reality-Testing Process in the International System*, 21 J. INT'L AFFAIRS 1 (1967).
147. *Id.* 2.

we hope its objective will be reached, regardless of the cost to ourselves and to Viet Nam.

Finally, there is "the credibility gap." Not only is the inference of aggression needed to enable the use of a rhetoric of legitimacy in describing the American efforts in Viet Nam, but the objective of these efforts is disguised. We proclaim over and over again our search for a negotiated settlement, the sincerity of which Professor Moore endorses, and yet we accompany this search by ever-higher escalation and by pre-conditions that by mid-1967 must be interpreted to entail surrender by the adversary. President Johnson writes to Ho Chi Minh that he is "prepared to order a cessation of bombing against your country and the further augmentation of United States forces in South Viet Nam as soon as I am assured that infiltration into South Viet Nam by land and by sea has stopped."[148] How could the Vietcong maintain itself at this stage without supplies and equipment from the North? The effect of Johnson's proposal is to suggest that United States military effort in the South cannot be matched by Northern aid to the N.L.F.: it is to compel the other side to act as if it had been the aggressor. Ho Chi Minh's rejection of such an offer had to be expected. Only a combined disposition by Hanoi and the N.L.F. to call off the insurgency would seem acceptable, only a victory for American power and a defeat for its adversary made militarily possible, if at all, because we are *not* fighting against Communism, but only against the relatively beleaguered small Communist state of North Viet Nam.

This note in conclusion is an attempt to provide a political setting for the world order claims that the United States has made on behalf of its action in Viet Nam. Without a sense of this setting any appraisal of the legal issues at stake is ultimately without its proper context. Since it is "we" who are perceiving the aggression in Viet Nam, it is essential to know why our understanding of the war is not shared by people elsewhere. Only after making an ideological jail-break and thereafter rediscovering our real values and our interests at home and abroad can we avoid future Viet Nams. I am convinced that we will look back upon the war in Viet Nam as the greatest tragedy ever in American foreign policy, as a deviation from American political traditions that will appear comprehensible in retrospect only because, in Mill's phrase, we were "willing to go to war for an idea."

148. For the texts of President Johnson's letter (dated Feb. 2, 1967) and President Ho Chi Minh's reply (dated Feb. 15, 1967), see N.Y. Times, March 22, 1966, at 10, col. 2.

Intervention in Civil Wars:
A Modest Proposal

TOM FARER*

In a recent essay on the theoretical and substantive aspects of revolution, the political scientist George Pettee observes:

> From the time of the American and French Revolutions to about 1940 it would seem fair to say that the general opinion in the West was that revolution is good when needed, and that the conditions in which it is needed can occur fairly often. There were voices to the contrary, of course, but they were at least seemingly outnumbered.[1]

In fact, it is not altogether easy to demonstrate that the men who actually make American foreign policy have at any time in the past century regarded violent social revolutions with a particularly benign eye. As a nation, we have encouraged revolutions which advanced our national interest in tangible ways. We enjoyed seeing the European powers expelled from Latin America. The generally small, often ineffectual, states that emerged have to this day proved rather malleable allies. We encouraged, indeed supervised, the severence of ties between Colombia and its northernmost province. But these were far more political than social revolutions. The Mexican revolution, a genuine class convulsion, was, I think it fair to say, more tolerated than admired. The Russian revolution was regarded with both popular and official rancor for at least a decade.

With respect to form, however, Pettee is right. Particularly in the past two decades, both the men who shape our foreign policy and the intellectuals from whom they seek advice and expect justification have jettisoned the old rhetoric. Revolution is out. There are innumerable examples of this evident fact but few more apposite than the primary public justification of The Alliance for Progress: we must jimmy social reform and economic growth out of the hands of Latin American mandarins in order to outmaneuver indigenous "radicals" who contemplate the physical elimination, rather than the moral regeneration, of the economic elite. Actually, regardless of the continent concerned, our aid program is defended roughly in these terms, though we normally denominate the leftist revolutionary threat as "indirect aggression" on the theory that it is manipulated from abroad.[2]

* Assistant Professor of Law, Columbia University. A.B., Princeton University, 1957; LL.B., Harvard University, 1961.

1. G. Pettee, *Revolution—Typology and Process*, in REVOLUTION 10, 29 (C. Friedrich ed. 1966) [hereinafter cited as REVOLUTION].

2. "The independent countries of Asia, Africa, and Latin America continue to be threatened by indirect aggression—by subversion, selective terror and foreign-controlled 'wars of national liberation' .... In the long run, the best counter to indirect aggression is broad-based social and economic progress of the kind supported by AID whenever possible." U.S. AGENCY FOR INTERNATIONAL DEVELOPMENT, PROPOSED ECONOMIC ASSIS-

In addition to the formal differences, there have been substantive changes in our approach to other peoples' revolutions. The principal change is that we are actively concerned about—and are attempting to prevent—them in remote corners of the globe. Moreover, we now see each revolution as a potential or actual battle in an immense, world-wide struggle against Communism. Thus, the significance of every revolutionary civil war is grotesquely magnified, with the ultimate consequence that because we have decided that left-wing revolution is a threat to us, we guarantee that it will be a threat to the peace.

For purposes of useful analysis, the phenomenon of great power intervention in the revolutionary civil wars which erupt periodically in the southern regions of the world must be placed within the larger context of the "political, social, and scientific facts that challenge and transform the prevailing bases of international order."[3] The dominating scientific fact, of course, is the existence of nuclear weapons which provide a cataclysmic backdrop to even the most minor collision between the super-powers. Aside from the vast multiplication of independent political entities with large hopes and marginal resources, the overriding political innovation is that all the players in the international system no longer accept each other's legitimacy. At least theoretically, therefore, nations are now concerned with threats to the existence of their entire social order, rather than the risk of losing the odd province or colony.

While the ability of the United States and the Soviet Union to devastate each other regardless of who strikes first has had the beneficient effect of deterring aggression by one super-power against the other or a principal ally, it has also encouraged the belief that the system can tolerate a substantial amount of violence under the nuclear threshold. The Chinese have been

---

TANCE PROGRAMS FY 1967—SUMMARY PRESENTATION TO THE CONGRESS 7-8 (1966). *Cf.* the responses of Secretary of State Rusk to questions of Senator Church at the Vietnam hearings conducted by the Senate Foreign Relations Committee:

> SENATOR CHURCH: [A]s I have listened to your explanations this morning, I gather that wherever a revolution occurs against an established government, and that revolution, as most will doubtlessly be, is infiltrated by Communists, that the United States will intervene, if necessary to prevent a Communist success.
>
> This, at least, has been the policy we followed in the Dominican Republic and in Vietnam. I wonder whether this is going to continue to be the policy as we face new guerilla wars in the future?
>
> SECRETARY RUSK: Senator, I think it is very important that the different kinds of revolutions be distinguished. We are in no sense committed against change. As a matter of fact, we are stimulating, ourselves, very sweeping revolutions in a good many places. *The whole weight and effort of the Alliance for Progress is to bring about far-reaching social, economic changes.*
>
> SENATOR CHURCH: That is change, Mr. Secretary, without violence. History shows that the most significant change has been accompanied by violence.
>
> Do you think that with our foreign aid program we are going to be able, with our money, to avert serious uprisings in all of these destitute countries in future years?
>
> SECRETARY RUSK: Not necessarily all of them. . . .

Hearings on S. 2793 Before the Senate Committee on Foreign Relations, 89th Cong., 2d Sess. 74-75 (1966) (emphasis added) [hereinafter cited as *Hearings*].

3. R. Falk, *World Revolution and International Order*, in REVOLUTION 154. My debt to the catalyst of Professor Falk's writings is very great indeed.

insistent advocates of this thesis. In fact, a radically different assessment of the risks as well as the consequences of nuclear war may have played a major role in splitting the Sino-Soviet alliance.[4]

During the past twenty-four months, there have been increasing signs that some segment of official thought in Washington also is decidedly sanguine about the dangers of stumbling into a nuclear exchange. The critical escalation of the Vietnamese War, apparent trial balloons concerning a possible invasion of North Vietnam,[5] and the increasing intransigence of most official rhetoric (if the war is in fact a selfless resistance to naked aggression, how can we negotiate out?) all attest either to a sturdy confidence about Chinese and Russian acquiescence or the dubious belief that an extended conflict with either can be fought at the sub-nuclear level—a grim enough prospect for those who, unlike some of our more dispassionate strategists, still boggle at the idea of a few million deaths. Or perhaps we have subtly evolved to the point where a nuclear threshold no longer seems critical as it did only a very short time ago, at least for most civilian planners in the Pentagon. Thus men as disparate in their political philosophies as former President Eisenhower[6] and Senator Douglas[7] are reported to have expressed the view that we should not automatically preclude the use of nuclear weapons to end the war in Vietnam. And

---

4. The Khrushchev revisionists maintain that a single spark in any part of the globe may touch off a world nuclear conflagration and bring destruction to mankind. If this were true, our planet would have been destroyed time and time again. There have been wars of national liberation throughout the twenty years since World War II. But has any single one of them developed into a world war?
Lin Piao, *Long Live the Victory of People's War!*, PEKING REVIEW, Sept. 3, 1965, at 27.
5. At Secretary of State Rusk's news conference on August 5, 1966, the following colloquy occurred:
Q. Is there a policy inhibition on the possible use of American ground forces in the demilitarized zone if the North Vietnamese continue to use it?
A. We have not wanted to go into the zone or cross the 17th Parallel. Our attitude has been that we don't want any shooting by anybody at anyone, and that we would be glad to see all of the shooting come to an end straightaway. We have no desire to destroy the regime in North Vietnam; we have no desire to drop any bombs on North Vietnam.
[At the time this statement was made, we were, of course, engaged in dropping bombs on North Vietnam. Not surprisingly, the juxtaposition of bombing and destroying the regime was thought by some to be suggestive.]
Q. Do we draw any policy distinction between possible use of ground troops in the southern part of the demilitarized zone and moving troops over into North Vietnam?
A. I think that this is a matter that is for the future, and would turn on events.
Excerpts from State Department's transcript of Secretary of State Dean Rusk's news conference, published in N.Y. Times, Aug. 6, 1966, at 2, col. 3. *Cf. Escalation: The Back-Room Talk*, NEWSWEEK, Sept. 12, 1966, at 42:
[I]ncreasingly, there were public reflections of back-room talk about the possibility of a ground invasion of North Vietnam. . . .
[A] number of men in the Pentagon privately argue that by substantially beefing up its ground forces in Vietnam, the U.S. would be able in a single stroke to intensify its offensive operations, cut over-all casualties in the long run and bring the war to a quicker conclusion. And some of them also feel strongly that an invasion of North Vietnam would serve to shock President Ho Chi Minh out of his evident conviction that, if only he holds on long enough, domestic political pressures will force the U.S. to withdraw from Vietnam.
6. *See* N.Y. Times, Oct. 4, 1966, at 9, col. 1.
7. *See* 221 THE ECONOMIST 470 (1966).

recently one of the leading academic strategists, Bernard Brodie, has in a more general way urged increased reliance on tactical nuclear weapons.[8]

The atmospheric change has undoubtedly been produced in large measure by the apparently geometric increase in animosity between Communist China and the Soviet Union. The prevailing inclination is to believe that the breakdown of Sino-Soviet relations is impelling the Russians to seek a genuine *détente* with the United States at the expense of "wars of national liberation." This plausible assumption has an insidious tendency to encourage miscalculation. It now does seem improbable that the Russians will incur any significant risk of confrontation with the United States in order to save the Viet Cong. But if we decide that the Viet Cong cannot be beaten in a satisfactory time frame without invading North Vietnam or using nuclear bombs there, Russian concern with the Chinese problem—which from the perspective of the United States must always seem a two-edged sword—could generate retaliation in Southeast Asia or elsewhere. Failure to act in the face of a threat to the existence of an established Communist state would constitute de facto resignation from the leadership of the international movement. The Soviet Union's assiduous efforts to array the various Communist parties against the Chinese evidence its belief that their support is highly relevant to the struggle. Moreover, it is worth recalling that the ideological foundations of the Russian state, which embraces so many disparate and not wholly assimilated nationalities, are transnational. A state apparatus resting on such foundations should not be expected to reject suddenly all values which transcend traditional national interests.

Just prior to the initiation of our air campaign against North Vietnam and the transfer of the main burden of land warfare to U.S. troops, there seems to have been an inclination in the intellectual community to conclude that the United States and the Soviet Union had tacitly agreed to keep civil conflicts limited both in terms of the level and geographic scope of the violence.[9] The main threats to the peace then envisioned nestled in places like Berlin, Cuba, and Quemoy and Matsu, where the threat to the existing political status was almost wholly external.

The escalation of the Vietnamese war has eviscerated assumptions about the willingness of at least the United States to accept serious inhibitions on her actual military capacity to intervene successfully in a civil war. We have successively rejected what seemed, before and during the 1964 election

---

8. *See* B. BRODIE, ESCALATION AND THE NUCLEAR OPTION (1966).
9. *See, e.g.,* R. Falk, *World Revolution and International Order,* in REVOLUTION 154, 174:
   [T]hose internal wars that are fought to expand or to contain the expansion of the revolutionary bloc are *tolerated* as a proper arena of conflict; norms to keep these conflicts both subnuclear and physically within the boundaries of a single state are increasingly recognized and are accepted as binding by the opposing actors.

campaign,[10] to be fixed limitations on the level of violence that would be deemed appropriate.[11] Now there is a distinct proclivity for identifying appropriate parameters as any parameters within which we will be able to destroy the insurgent armed forces.

Assuming, without predicting, that we ultimately extricate ourselves from Vietnam rather than shuffling coolly into an international cataclysm, the question which will then engage the pundits and statesmen will be how to avoid the next one. Some undoubtedly will argue that Vietnam is unique. The primary factor causing the steady expansion of conflict in Vietnam was the inability of the United States to extirpate the revolutionary movement quickly. This inability has in large measure been a function of terrain, a contiguous sanctuary and entrepôt, long-term Communist domination of the nationalist movement, the lack of political community in South Vietnam, a divisive war of independence, religious conflict, an influx of refugees in the postwar period, and United States indecision about the strength of its commitment.

I seriously doubt that the same mix is required for the production of another prolonged civil conflict in which United States materiel may seem insufficient to assure a counter-revolutionary triumph. In Thailand, the first stage of civil conflict is already at hand.[12] In Indonesia, the Communist Party may have been extinguished, but Sukarno apparently retains a powerful following outside Jakarta.[13] Is civil war unimaginable? The size of the territory, the terrain, and the varied divisions within the national community provide a sufficient basis for prolonged conflict. If the left wing could achieve de facto control over a sizeable area, declare itself independent or legitimate, secure recognition from certain states, and then initiate guerilla war elsewhere in the islands with Chinese aid, would the situation be wholly dissimilar to Vietnam, at least from the American point of view? The island of Borneo is certainly a

---

10. On Sept. 25, 1964, President Johnson said: "We don't want our American boys to do the fighting for Asian boys. We don't want to get involved in a nation with 700 million people and get tied down in a land war in Asia. . . ." Quoted in T. Wicker, *Into the Quicksand*, N.Y. Times, Nov. 27, 1966, § 4, at 13, col. 6.

11. *Cf.* R. Falk, *U.S. in Vietnam: Rationale and Law*, 13 DISSENT 275, 282 (1966):
In a sense, then, the war arising out of the 1954 arrangements at Geneva, if its outcome is measured by the original parameters of conflict, has long since been lost; in fact, several successive such "wars" have been "lost." The appearance of defeat has been somewhat avoided by changing the parameters of conflict through a series of very critical escalations of the U.S. military commitment, especially in terms of the numbers of American troops and the extension of violence to North Vietnam through bombing.

12. *See* N.Y. Times, Nov. 27, 1966, § 1, at 4, col. 1.

13. *See, e.g.,* A. Friendly, *Still No Answer to the Sukarno Question*, N.Y. Times, Oct. 30, 1966, § 4, at 6, col. 4:
General Suharto, Chairman of the Cabinet Presidium and Javanese par excellence, cannot help but be conscious of the durability of the President's [Sukarno's] popularity in the central and eastern portions of the island where 70 per cent of Indonesia's 107 million people live.
D. Warner, *Indonesia's Unfinished Revolution*, THE REPORTER, July 14, 1966, at 32: "He [Suharto] is well aware of the continuing support for Sukarno in Central and East Java and its potential danger."

potential center for protracted conflict between allegedly revolutionary and counter-revolutionary actors. And coming a good deal closer to home, who can be certain that the inevitable changing of the guard in the Iberian peninsula will not ignite intense civil strife? In sum, only Pollyanna could be confident that Vietnam cannot in essence be repeated if there are no significant changes in the means available to the international community for restricting the participation of third parties in civil wars.

What changes could be effected? Hope might lie in clarification and modification of the norms of participation. At a minimum, any useful norm must be evaluated by the following criteria:

> (1) Is there a reasonable prospect that it will be openly or tacitly accepted? This prospect normally will vary inversely with the norm's deviation from existing practice and any asymmetrical advantages it may bestow.
> (2) If accepted, does it reduce the probability of great power confrontation?
> (3) Is it sufficiently unambiguous so that serious violations are readily identifiable? If it is swollen with the potential for conflicting interpretations, violations are encouraged.
> (4) Will it facilitate geographic containment of the violence?

If more than one norm satisfied these criteria, they would then be tested by the more peripheral values of the international system, which include, I hope, minimization of damage to the area being contested.

The Classical View

The classical view—to which official Washington clings with rational rigidity—that outside states are free to help the incumbent early in a civil war and are obliged to refrain from helping the insurgents[14] does not satisfy the criteria. Aside from the dangerous ambiguity of just when the insurgency has achieved sufficient status to require equal treatment, the norm simply is not respected. It is wholly out of joint with actual practice. Even we, normally a major beneficiary, ignore it when it seems even modestly confining (unless someone far cleverer than I can drag Guatemala and the Bay of Pigs within its penumbra).[15]

---

14. *See* 2 L. OPPENHEIM, INTERNATIONAL LAW § 298, at 660 (7th ed. 1952).
15. *See* W. Friedmann, *United States Policy and the Crisis of International Law*, 59 AM. J. INT'L L. 857, 866 (1965):
> But above all it is a matter of grave and fundamental doubt whether the widespread but always controversial view that in civil war situations only the government but not the rebels are entitled to ask for foreign assistance retains any justification under contemporary conditions. Neither the United States nor any other country has been consistent in the application of this doctrine—as is shown, for example, by the conflicting policies with regard to Viet-Nam, Guatemala (1954) and Cuba—nor is the turbulent condition of mankind, when numerous states are in a state of social turmoil, compatible with a doctrine of 'legitimacy.' The latter becomes an instrument to prevent social change, which is a vital aspect of national self-determination. (Article 2(7), U.N. Charter).

Beyond all that, the "norm" makes a net contribution to the locus of forces impelling confrontation. Foreign aid to the rebels is treated as an act of aggression against the entire nation. In states whose governments identify with the fortunes of the incumbent, it becomes relatively easy to convince the public that the issue is not the relative merits and capacities of the internal antagonists, but the sanctity of international law. Moreover, as public attention focuses on the external aid rendered to the rebels, it becomes far easier to cultivate the idea that they are mere instruments of the foreign power. When the struggle is cast in these terms, acceptance of insurgent victory seems a pusillanimous withdrawal at High Noon. In other words, the traditional approach generates or facilitates generation of moral pressure to escalate.

The problem does not inhere in the notion of "legitimacy" but in its misapplication. One expedient reason for recognizing the legitimacy of incumbents in the good old days[16] was that they generally were strong enough to retaliate if some third party attempted to aid rebels. Moreover, despite their many inadequacies as rulers, the incumbents did in fact provide the order and organization which were preconditions to material progress. In addition, a rebellion, or even a coup, was an infrequent occurrence and was generally unsuccessful. Beyond expediency there stood the powerful sense of common concerns shared by the social and economic groups which dominated the principal powers. Today, not only the emotional or ideological but the expedient reasons for treating incumbents, in a majority of the world's independent states, as possessors of the traditional attributes of legitimacy have become historic relics.

International society is populated by a substantial number of feeble governments which simply are incapable of organizing their people. In the absence of foreign intervention, rebellions will occur frequently and will often succeed, and there is no capacity to resist the intrusion of Great (and even not so great) Powers, much less to retaliate in any serious fashion. Material progress is merely the stuff of which political rhetoric is woven. With respect to such regimes, the concept of legitimacy cannot command respect in the international community. Nor is it acceptable when applied to states which violate minimum human rights. The South African regime is legitimate by the traditional standards of international law, but if legitimacy means no aid to insurgents, then the rule is being, or, when expedient, will be, disregarded by an easy majority of the nations of the world. And since in international law, unlike domestic law, the inability of a rule to control conduct reduces it to the status of a non-rule, it seems fair to conclude that our oft-propounded view

---

16. In those days, of course, only a few states really counted. The norms then articulated by the theoreticians of international law were designed to reflect and preserve an international order dominated by the major political entities of Europe.

simply does not reflect the state of the law. Perhaps that is one reason why even we do not take it too seriously.[17]

THE NORMLESS PRESENT

What can replace it? The central truth of the matter is that today there are no real norms governing intervention by third parties in civil wars, and, as long as the United States insists on its right to intervene in any revolution with whatever scale of force is required to suppress it, no coherent norm for the regulation of intervention can be articulated. At least I cannot think of any norms which would have provided a legal umbrella for all of our recent interventions and would still even begin to meet the criteria for an efficacious norm listed above.

If the test for the legitimate introduction of counter-revolutionary combat forces were whether the revolutionaries have received substantial external assistance, our intervention in the Dominican Republic could not be justified. There, we were unable to establish anything more than marginal involvement by domestic Communists, and that can be established in almost any conceivable social and political revolution. Revolutions are always perilous enterprises. We have enhanced that peril by arming conservative governments in many parts of the world. No longer is it pitchfork against musket. Few reformers faced by the Wessin y Wessins of the Third World will afford the luxury of rejecting the aid of the far left, particularly in light of its normally high morale and, more important, its superior access to arms.

If the test were whether foreign combat units were fighting with the insurgents (as in Laos), our intervention in Vietnam would be of doubtful legality. On balance, the available evidence seems to support the proposition that infiltration by North Vietnamese army units began after our own forces evolved from the role of non-participating advisors.[18]

I prefer to hope that the current assessment of American interest will be

---

17. I obviously am not suggesting that a militarily weak state with a feeble apparatus for governing cannot be the subject of aggression. To deny the legitimacy of incumbents for purposes of measuring the obligations of other states *in case of civil war* is not to question the legitimacy of the nation.

18. *See* N.Y. Times, Dec. 14, 1966, at 3, col. 6 (quoting Leonard C. Meeker, legal adviser to the State Department):

Hanoi began to "infiltrate ethnic southerners in South Vietnam as early as 1957," totalling about 40,000 by late 1964.

"Beginning in late 1964, the infiltrating units consisted essentially of North Vietnamese soldiers organized in regular army units."

Cf. Hearings 52:

SECRETARY RUSK: From November of 1964 until January of 1965 they moved the 325th Division of the North Vietnamese Army down to South Vietnam. . . .

SENATOR GORE: Was that before or after we moved forces into South Vietnam?

SECRETARY RUSK: Well, the division moved after we had put, had reinforced our own forces there.

replaced by one which evaluates more realistically both the immediate and prospective dangers to peace inherent in proxy conflict between the United States and the Communist powers, and the dangers to our national interests posed by radical insurgency. A reassessment may be facilitated by the open search for norms to limit the reverberations of civil conflict.

NONINTERVENTION

Perhaps the most obvious norm would be a flat preclusion of participation. This norm might be thought to labor under only two major defects: it would be unenforceable and unacceptable. The sheer problem of definition would seriously jeopardize effective application. Does a norm of nonparticipation preclude the extension of military assistance to a "legitimate government" prior to the outbreak of civil war? If so, it would compel termination of our entire program of military assistance, hardly a consummation which the United States will devoutly wish. What is military assistance? Does it include the sale of military equipment on commercial terms? Does nonparticipation preclude economic aid?

Particularly in revolutionary civil war, economic aid, even where it does not simply screen military aid, plays a critical and asymmetric role. It can be delivered in far larger quantities to the government forces who normally hold the ports and airfields. It permits those who have no ideological appeal and cannot espouse the reforms which might in themselves command enthusiasm to buy loyalty directly or to obtain it indirectly by creating new social classes whose prosperity is linked to the influx of aid. It generates revenue for the payment of troops and administrators and the construction of military facilities and communications networks which will expedite the movement of troops and equipment and improve tactical planning. Norms which allocate uneven benefits rarely evoke the will to comply.

The training of personnel presents another gritty problem of interpretation. In significant measure we have supported our theory of aggression in Vietnam on the ground that the North Vietnamese have trained South Vietnamese cadres. If nothing else, this constitutes candid recognition of the importance of effective training programs. Does nonparticipation require the termination of training programs for military men alone? What about police? civilian communications experts? administrators? In a civil war where the insurgents are guerillas, one able administrator may be worth a dozen generals. An effective norm of nonparticipation could easily be found to preclude many of the training programs in which we currently engage.

When does the norm become operative? For the disciples of Mao, Guevara, and Giap, the war begins when the first band takes to the hills. The government will label this first phase "banditry," and its assessment may be consistent with the traditional distinctions. The international lawyer is accustomed to thinking of civil war as a large-scale revolt with a substantial territorial base. In the two centuries before our own, civil wars were normally fought between different regions or between colonies and the mother country. In class struggle, the war is everywhere, though it may be open in one place and underground in another. Moreover, strategy has changed. Rebels in the Third World are wedded to a strategy of movement and time. The possession of territory is subordinated to conservation of the armed force. By the time the revolutionary forces have secured a large territorial base, the government may already be on the frontier of strategic defeat, its morale rotted, the whole edifice merely a shove away from disintegration.

It would be frivolous to deny that in any practical sense the civil war began at a far earlier date. Yet it would be equally naive to conclude that civil war was under way the first time some rural militiaman had his throat slit. Thus, any attempt to use the actual date of commencement of a revolutionary civil war fought with guerilla tactics for the activation of a norm is futile.

Even if states could agree on a definition of nonparticipation, I cannot conceive of one which would be generally acceptable as the substance of a norm. Ideological passion has made trust a rare possession. The United States undoubtedly would feel that whatever its definition, nonparticipation would seriously alter the existing revolutionary equilibrium, because it would be far easier for the party aiding the insurgents to evade the norm. International inspection is bound to be more effective in the capital than in the bush. On the other hand, if economic aid were not precluded, the Russians might legitimately object for the reasons suggested earlier. But if it were precluded, both we and most underdeveloped states would find the proposed norm unacceptable; development planning will be not an art but a joke if the aid tap is likely to be shut off periodically and unpredictably. The whole idea is ludicrous.

A Prohibition on Tactical Support

A more realistic possibility is a flat prohibition of participation in tactical operations, either openly or through the medium of advisors or volunteers. In concrete terms this means that a country could not send its own forces on patrol in support of indigenous military units. Indeed, its forces could not even enter a zone in which combat with enemy units was foreseeable, either to fight, advise, or transport. In Vietnam, this rule would have pretty much restricted the United States presence to a few cities and the North Vietnamese presence to those areas in which government troops would not venture without military support from the United States. Outside the "war zone," a country would be precluded by this test from manning air defense installations—though it could supervise their initial disposition—or guarding installations, other than those occupied by its own men. On the other hand, it could staff training centers and provide advisors for the indigenous high command.

In Vietnam, we moved unequivocally beyond this point toward the end of 1961. During December our first helicopter units had arrived to carry Vietnamese troops into battle.[19] At that time or shortly thereafter, American personnel began to fly tactical missions in support of South Vietnamese forces, to man river patrol boats, and to join foot patrols.[20] But we still clung to the quaint notion that victory for the South Vietnamese could be achieved without the introduction of independently organized units of the American armed forces.

Under the proposed norm, a country would be legally free to extend any type or quantity of aid other than forms of assistance which could involve its personnel in actual combat. There would be no justification for a state allied with the incumbent government to attack a state aiding the insurgents within the allowed limits; such aid would not constitute an act of aggression against the country in which the civil war was being fought.

Is there reason to believe that such a norm might be accepted? It is certainly consistent in rationale, though not in detail, with Washington's Vietnam position as late as 1964: the war had to be won by the Vietnamese people; they had to bear the ultimate burden of combat.[21] When they (the "friendly" Vietnamese) demonstrated their incapacity to bear that burden successfully, however, we picked it up. It may be that our breach of our own guidelines was a consequence of the degree to which we had become involved symbolically in the fortunes of the incumbents, at least in part by committing our own elite troops on the battlefield, although in the guise of mere advisors. My critical assumption here is that until a major power commits its own forces, victory for the insurgents is not a psychologically unacceptable outcome, at least once the concept of the "legitimate incumbent" is deactivated.[22]

---

19. See N.Y. Times, Dec. 12, 1961, at 21, col. 1 (by Jacques Nevard):
Two United States Army helicopter companies arrived here today [Saigon, 12/11]. The helicopters, to be flown and serviced by United States troops, are the first direct military support by the United States for South Vietnam's war against Communist guerilla forces.
20. See N.Y. Times, Dec. 20, 1961, at 1, col. 1, 12, col. 3 (by Jack Raymond):
United States military men in South Vietnam were understood today to be operating in battle areas with South Vietnamese forces that are fighting Communist guerrillas.
Although the Americans, who are in uniform, are not engaged in actual combat operations, they are authorized to shoot back if fired upon.
American soldiers will be manning transport planes and some amphibious vessels. They will also be operating radio communications from strategic places.
21. In a CBS television interview on September 2, 1963, President Kennedy said:
In the final analysis it's their war. They're the ones who have to win it or lose it. We can help them, give them equipment, we can send our men out there as advisers, but they have to win it, the people of Vietnam, against the Communists.
N.Y. Times, Sept. 3, 1963, at 1, col. 8.
22. Secretary of Defense McNamara's reported opposition to the use of U.S. helicopter units in support of Thai counter-insurgency efforts (N.Y. Times, Nov. 3, 1966, at 1, col. 4) may indicate that this assumption is shared in some official circles.

The norm's acceptability in the West may also vary with the felt validity of my assumption that any government which enjoys significant support from substantial sections of the populace will defeat any insurgency if it has an unlimited draw on materiel and foreign training facilities for its officers and administrators. More than an assumption, it is an empirical conclusion based on the successful suppression or at least containment of radical leftist insurgencies in Greece, Colombia, Venezuela, Peru, the Philippines, and Burma. I think the record suggests that insurgency will succeed only where the rebels enjoy significant popular support and have organizational capacities distinctly, probably overwhelmingly, superior to the incumbents.[23]

However it may vary from our own policies, the norm does appear to codify Soviet and Chinese practice. Despite past martial polemics, neither the Chinese nor the Russians have dispatched troops to aid insurrectionary forces. Revolutionists around the world have fought and died alone. They have received varying quantities of materiel, foreign training, and advisors at central headquarters. But when it has come to the grisly business of combat, both champions of wars of national liberation have at most been willing to stand in the corner and pass an occasional sponge over the battered fighter's head. And by avoiding the risks attendant on military involvement, they have in all cases except, to this date, Vietnam accepted the liquidation of the revolutionary enterprise. The most recent Chinese pronouncement on wars of national liberation justifies a policy of limited intervention. In the September 3, 1965, issue of the *Peking Review*, Lin Piao, Mao's heir apparent, stated:

> The liberation of the masses is accomplished by the masses themselves—this is a basic principle of Marxism-Leninism. Revolution or people's war in any country is the business of the masses in that country and should be carried out primarily by their own efforts; there is no other way.
>
> . . .
>
> In order to make a revolution and to fight a people's war and be victorious, it is imperative to adhere to the policy of self-reliance, rely on the strength of the masses in one's own country and prepare to carry on the fight independently even when all material aid from outside is cut off. If one does not operate by one's own efforts, does not independently ponder and solve the problems of the revolution in one's own country and does not rely on the strength of the masses, but leans wholly on foreign aid—even though this be aid from socialist countries which persist in revolution—no victory can be won, or be consolidated even if it is won.[24]

A particularly dangerous consequence of our conversion of the struggle in South Vietnam into a war with North Vietnam (albeit one fought for quite

---

23. *Cf.* W. Friedmann, *supra* note 15: "The [traditional rule] becomes an instrument to prevent social change, which is a vital aspect of national self-determination. (Article 2 (7), U.N. Charter)."

24. *See* Lin Piao, *supra* note 4, at 19, 22.

limited objectives and with relatively restrained means, thus far) has been the introduction of Soviet advisers to assist in organizing local air defense. But the continued failure of the Soviet Union to participate more effectively by means, for example, of "volunteer" pilots and the continued emphasis on the advisory role of Soviet air defense personnel,[25] strengthens my conviction that despite their proclaimed enthusiasm for wars of national liberation, the Russians have little appetite for direct participation.

Will serious violations of the norm be readily identifiable? Definition should be greatly facilitated by the use of military terminology with a fairly well-established content.[26] As must be true of any norm operative in a severely adversary context, there inevitably will be some disputed points. But it is difficult to envision any persuasive interpretative split on fundamental matters. The possibility of combat is the crucial distinction. Any entry, whether by land, sea, or air, into war zones—*i.e.*, any area in which organized units of both rebel and government forces are located, or, a fortiori, entry of a third power's personnel into an area occupied solely by hostile indigenous troops—must be prohibited. Participation in the aiming and firing of air defense systems is combat. Offshore bombardment also must be precluded, for, even if one were to adopt the casuistic argument that the war zone does not extend to the high seas if forces operating there are, as a practical matter, immune to attack, bombardment is a tactical support function.

Experience in Vietnam appears to support the conclusion that foreign forces cannot move into war zones in substantial numbers without being identified, even where they are racially indistinguishable. Troops that do not wear distinctive uniforms must still carry some form of identification simply to ensure recognition by friendly units. Moreover, it seems improbable that codes, manuals, and all the other normal identifying accouterments of a military unit can either be left behind or committed to memory. In any event, the United States has certainly purported to possess an effective capability to identify foreign units. And United States forces were clearly unable to participate operationally for very long without irrefutable identification.

In addition to confining the violence geographically and imposing qualitative limits on intervention which would tend to prevent escalation to a point where rules are irrelevant, this norm would, I think, radically reduce the potential level of damage to the "host" country. Educational limitations will prevent either side from disposing of fire power on a scale comparable to the capability of major military powers. The grave cultural damage which is the inevitable concomitant of the presence of large numbers of foreign troops will also be avoided.

---

25. "[T]he newspaper [*Krasnaya Zvezda*, the Soviet Defense Ministry's newspaper] took pains to emphasize that Vietnamese crews had fired the missiles, with the Russians standing by as observers." N.Y. Times, Oct. 3, 1966, at 1, col. 1.

26. Alternatively, the norm could be broken up into a series of specific prohibitions.

Since peace is to most men more attractive than war, however limited, meliorative answers to the insistent belligerence of nations often have less appeal than prophylactic strategies. An effort merely to limit the scale of violence may also find an unreceptive audience among peace partisans because of the apprehension that norms which are accepted at the temporal rim of conflict have a way of being discarded as states approach its hub. I am hardly immune to that apprehension, but I do find it rather difficult to regard some of the more audacious alternatives with even a semblance of optimism about their acceptability.

Perhaps there will be occasions when, because the danger of direct confrontation between the nuclear powers will be on the very surface of a civil conflict or because of exigent events in other parts of the world, the United Nations will be permitted to intervene. And in certain areas, genuine regional organizations, embodying a real consensus on fundamental issues, may develop an adequate rationale and physical capability for the localization of civil strife.

But consistently effective multi-national intervention probably must await profound, indeed revolutionary, changes not simply in the climate of contemporary affairs, but in notions about national sovereignty and right cherished by the mass of men and the states they more or less rule. Today, many of these passionately held notions are more than a mere obstacle to containing the violent outbreaks which are an incident of life in a revolutionary system; they are actually a prime cause of that violence.[27] Faced with such intransigent facts, the realist is a man of somewhat meager hopes. To him, even modest proposals may seem naive.

---

27. *See* R. Falk, *World Revolution and International Order*, in REVOLUTION 154, 176-77.

Misperception of Aggression in Vietnam

RALPH K. WHITE

In the Vietnam war each side declares that it has to fight because of obvious, self-evident "aggression" by the other side. On each side there are images of a Hitler-like enemy, brutally, calculatingly bent on conquest. On each side there is a feeling that it would be weak and cowardly to let the enemy's aggression be rewarded by success; each side feels: "If we are men we cannot let this aggression go unpunished."

The thesis of this article is that both are wrong. There has been no aggression on either side—at least not in the sense of a cold-blooded, Hitler-like act of conquest. The analogies of Hitler's march into Prague, Stalin's takeover of Eastern Europe, and the North Korean attack on South Korea are false analogies. There is a better analogy in the outbreak of World War I, when, as historical scholarship has shown, both sides stumbled and staggered into the war in a spirit of self-defense (or defense of national pride against "intolerable humiliation") rather than in a spirit of deliberate conquest. (See Robert North's article in this issue.) In Vietnam each side, though by no means free from moral guilt, is far from being as diabolical as its enemies picture it, since both believe that whatever crimes they may commit are justified by the magnitude of the emergency. Each knows that

Ralph K. White is professor of psychology and a member of the Institute for Sino-Soviet Studies at George Washington University. He is the co-author of *Autocracy and Democracy: An Experimental Inquiry*. His study of "Images in the Context of International Conflict: Soviet Perceptions of the U.S. and the U.S.S.R." appeared in a recently published volume, *International Behavior*.

it has not "willed" this war. On each side ordinary human beings have become gradually entangled, hating the war and all the suffering associated with it, honestly believing that their manhood requires them to resist the "aggression" of the enemy. But the enemy's "aggression," in the sense in which it has been assumed to exist, has not existed.[1]

For reasons that will be discussed, it follows that the only honorable peace would be a compromise peace in which each side could feel it had held out against the aggressor's onslaught and had managed to preserve at least the bare essentials of what it was fighting to defend.

Can They Believe It When They Call Us "Aggressors"?

President Johnson has said, "The first reality is that North Vietnam has attacked the independent nation of South Vietnam. Its object is total conquest. . . . Let no one think for a moment that retreat from Vietnam would bring an end to the conflict. The battle would be renewed in one country and then another. The central lesson of our time is that the appetite of aggression is never satisfied."[2] Secretary McNamara has said, "The prime aggressor is North Vietnam."[3] Secretary Rusk has repeatedly declared that the whole purpose of our intervention would disappear the moment the North Vietnamese decided to "let their neighbors alone."

The great majority of the American people do not seriously doubt these statements; even among those who doubt the wisdom of our attempting to resist aggression in Southeast Asia there are many who do not doubt that Communist aggression has occurred. Those who do feel that it is our responsibility to resist the aggression that they regard as self-evident are likely to have ready answers to what they suppose to be the arguments against this belief. They may ask: "Can you deny that North Vietnam has sent troops and weapons to the South? Can you deny that the Viet Cong cadres are Communists, controlled by other Communists in Hanoi and perhaps in Peking? Can you deny that war by assassination in the villages is aggression, in principle, as much as is war by invasion of troops across a border?" And when they find that their opponents, while making certain qualifications (e.g., with regard to the completeness of the control of the Viet Cong by Hanoi), do not try to deny the essential truth of any of these

---

[1] A much more detailed and documented presentation of this thesis is contained in Ralph K. White, "Misperception and the Vietnam War," *Journal of Social Issues*, Vol. XXII, No. 3 (1966), pp. 1-167.

[2] Johns Hopkins speech, Apr. 7, 1965.

[3] Speech before the National Security Industrial Assn., Mar. 26, 1964.

things, they are likely to feel that their case is well established and that Communist aggression is indeed self-evident.

A visitor from Mars would be struck by the close parallel between all of this and the attitudes that are continually expressed on the other side. According to Ho Chi Minh, "It is crystal clear that the United States is the aggressor who is trampling under foot the Vietnamese soil."[4] According to Chou En-lai, "America is rapidly escalating the war in an attempt to subdue the Vietnamese people by armed force."[5] And according to Leonid Brezhnev, "Normalization of our relations [with the U.S.] is incompatible with the armed aggression of American imperialism against a fraternal Socialist country—Vietnam."[6] To the extent that they mean what they say, aggression by us seems as obvious to them as aggression by them seems to us.

That, then, is the essential question: to what extent do they mean what they say?

To most Americans, probably, the charge that *we* are aggressors seems like outrageous nonsense, so transparently false that honest men all over the world must put it down immediately as a propaganda trick by the Communists to cover up their own aggression. The thief is crying "Stop thief!" and must be doing it simply to distract attention from his own crime.

It is precisely here, though, that the perceptions of most Americans are, in my judgment, basically mistaken. The charge that we have been aggressors—inadvertent aggressors, without for a moment intending to be—is not outrageous nonsense. It is no more false than our charge that the Communists have been aggressors. Both charges are psychologically false, since neither side has committed conscious, deliberate, Hitler-like.aggression. But both charges are in a less essential sense true, since both sides, in the belief that they have been defending themselves, have engaged in certain actions which the other side, seeing them within a radically different frame of reference, could easily perceive as aggressive.

That this is true on the American side needs no demonstration. Certain actions of the Communists, notably the campaign of assassination in the villages and the sending of troops from the North to the South, have seemed to most Americans, interpreting them within an American frame of refer-

---

[4] Interview with Felix Greene, quoted in *The Washington Post*, Dec. 14, 1965, pp. A 1, A 16.

[5] Speech in Peking, reported in *The New York Times*, May 1, 1966, p. 4.

[6] Speech to the Central Committee of the CPSU, reported in *The Washington Post*, Sept. 30, 1965, A 16.

ence, to be flagrantly, self-evidently aggressive. What most Americans have almost wholly failed to realize is that we too have done things which, when perceived within the Communists' radically different frame of reference, have probably seemed to them to be just as flagrantly and self-evidently aggressive. This failure to see how our own actions are perceived by the Communists is the essence of our misperception.

Most of the rest of this article will be devoted to an exploration of the reasons for believing that the Communists do see our behavior as aggressive. The argument is twofold. (1) There are at least eight important kernels of truth in the Communist case against us—eight types of evidence that, when strongly focused upon by a Communist mind and interpreted within a Communist frame of reference, could seem to substantiate his charge of American aggression. (2) There is ample reason to believe that the lenses through which the Communists see reality have a high enough degree of refraction to do the rest of the job. They are quite capable of focusing strongly on these kernels of truth, interpreting them solely within a Communist frame of reference, failing to realize that we see them within a quite different frame of reference, ignoring or misinterpreting all the kernels of truth on our side, and therefore coming up with a black-and-white picture in which their role is wholly defensive and ours is aggressive. The chief reason to think they are capable of this much distortion lies in the fact that most American minds—presumably less dogmatic, more evidence-oriented—have been capable of a similar degree of distortion in the opposite direction. The very fact that so many Americans have denied, misinterpreted, soft-pedaled or simply ignored these eight important kernels of truth on the Communist side is sufficient evidence that the capacity to misperceive in this way is not inherently Communist. It is human. In other situations the Communists have, on the whole, shown much more of it than we have, but in the case of Vietnam the amount of distortion that apparently exists in Communist minds, i.e., the amount of it that they would need in order to believe most of what they say, is no greater than the amount in the minds of most Americans.

What is needed, then, is a careful examination of the "eight kernels of truth." We can hardly understand either the sincerity of Communist thinking or the distortions and blind spots in our own until we focus steadily on the facts that to them seem decisively important.

Three Reasons Why They Think South Vietnam "Belongs" to Them

The usage of the term "aggression" in the Communists' discourse suggests that in their minds, as in ours, it is applied when either or both of two conditions exist: (1) when they believe, rightly or wrongly, that country A is using force to take land that "belongs" to country B; and (2) when they believe, rightly or wrongly, that most of the people on that land want to be part of country B. The "eight kernels of truth" mentioned above include three types of evidence that, in my judgment, actually do tend to support their claim that South Vietnam "belongs" to them (reasons other than the belief that the people are on their side) and five types of evidence supporting their claim that most of the people are on their side.

Perhaps it should be repeated: this is not an argument that South Vietnam *does* "belong" to them, or that most of the people *are* on their side. It seems to me that the first of these propositions, when closely analyzed, is largely meaningless, and that the second, though very meaningful, cannot be clearly answered on an empirical basis and is probably somewhat less than half true, since most people in South Vietnam probably do not want to be ruled either by Hanoi or by Saigon. This is simply an argument that the facts are complex and ambiguous enough to disprove completely our prevailing American assumption that there has been deliberate, unequivocal Communist aggression, and to make it highly probable that the Communists *think* South Vietnam belongs to them and the people are on their side.[7]

What does "belonging" mean, psychologically? On what grounds does any group come to feel that a certain piece of land obviously "belongs" to it and not to someone else? Though at first glance the concept seems simple, on closer examination it turns out to be extraordinarily complex and elusive. Such an examination is needed, too, in view of the fact that an endless amount of bad blood and of violent conflict has been generated at the places in the world where two or more groups have had conflicting assumptions about what belongs to whom: the Thirteen Colonies, the Confederate States, Cuba, Bosnia-Herzegovina, Alsace-Lorraine, Austria, the Sudetenland, the Polish Corridor, Danzig, the Baltic states, Taiwan, Quemoy, Tibet, the Sino-Indian border, Indochina, Algeria, Kashmir, Cyprus, Israel. When the territorial self-image of one country overlaps with the territorial self-image of another, trouble seems to be almost inevitable, and such overlapping is hard to avoid because nations differ in their criteria of what constitutes ownership or "belonging." Sometimes, as in our American feeling about the Revolutionary War and the Southern feeling about the Civil War, the criterion is a belief about what most of the

---

[7] For a more balanced picture of the evidence on both sides, see White, *op. cit.*, especially pp. 19-44, 46-50, 89-90, and 106-16.

people in the area want. Sometimes, as in the British feeling about our Revolutionary War and the Northern feeling about the Civil War, it is a compound of habit, respect for tradition and legality, national pride, beliefs (which may be very deeply held) about what is best for all concerned, including minority groups such as the slaves in the American South or the Catholics in South Vietnam, and perhaps anxiety about what may happen elsewhere if violent attacks on the legally established order are allowed to succeed. There is always a tendency to accept whatever definition of "belonging" makes a given piece of land clearly belong to one's own nation or to an ally.

If we ask ourselves why most Americans assume that South Vietnam belongs to the Saigon Government and does not belong to the Viet Cong or to the Communist Government in the North, perhaps the best single answer would be that since 1954 we have regarded this as an established, accepted fact. Since 1954 we have had a mental image of Vietnam as having been divided, as Korea was, between a Communist North and a southern portion that was still part of the free world—perhaps precariously so, but for that reason all the more in need of being shored up and defended. Probably in the minds of most well-informed Americans there has been no belief that most of the people in South Vietnam want the kind of government they have had in Saigon. On that score there have been embarrassing doubts. But the doubts have usually been fairly well resolved in various ways, e.g., by the belief that most of the people in South Vietnam belong to a large, politically apathetic middle group that only wants peace and would gladly go along with whichever side seems likely to be the winner —from which many infer that there is no popular will which needs to be considered, and that we are therefore free to decide the matter on other grounds. Or the doubts may be resolved by the belief that in the long run a government sponsored by us would permit a genuine development of democracy and national independence, whereas no Communist government would do so; or by the belief that permitting a Communist use of force to succeed in South Vietnam would encourage the "wars of liberation" favored by Communist China and therefore endanger both peace and freedom throughout the world. But all of these points also encounter controversy, and when tired of such controversy many Americans, including Dean Rusk, fall back on the solid, simple, and (they feel) unanswerable proposition that there are Communist soldiers fighting on land that does not "belong" to them. "We will stay until they decide to let their neighbors alone." And the seeming obviousness of this "belonging," since it cannot be based on assumptions about what the people want, is probably based primarily on the fact that for at least twelve years there has been, on our maps and in our minds, a division between the Communist North and the non-Communist South. We see this as the established, accepted, natural order of things.

In doing so we ignore three facts that in Communist minds are much more important than the division of the country that occurred in 1954.

1. *The division of the country has its only legal basis in the Geneva Conference of 1954, and at that conference it was explicitly agreed that it would last only two years.* The Communist-led Viet Minh stopped fighting on the basis of what seemed to be a firm agreement that there would be an all-Vietnamese vote in 1956 (which they fully expected to win) that would unify the country, establishing both unity and full independence without further bloodshed. According to the respected French historian Philippe Devillers, "The demarcation line was to be purely provisional; the principle of Vietnamese unity was not questioned, and the idea of partition was officially rejected with indignation by both sides. When military forces were regrouped and administrative divisions laid down, national unity would be restored by free general elections."[8]

Informed Americans are now embarrassingly aware (though a great many reasonably well-informed Americans were not clearly aware of it until perhaps two or three years ago) that in 1956 Diem, apparently with American backing, refused to permit the elections that had been provided for by the Geneva Agreement. To be sure, neither he nor we had signed those agreements, and there were other persuasive reasons for not permitting the elections at that time or at any time since then. But that is not the present point at issue; the point is that, having in effect rejected the Geneva Agreement by not carrying out one of its key provisions, Diem and the United States deprived themselves of any right to invoke the Geneva Agreement as a legal or moral sanction for the division of the country. With Diem's decision not to press for a plebiscite under international supervision even in "his own" southern part of the country, he forfeited—at least in Communist eyes—not only all claim to the kind of legitimacy that genuine popular endorsement would have provided, but also all claim to invoke the Geneva Conference's endorsement of the 17th Parallel as a basis for his own rule in the South. In effect he proclaimed *de facto* control— "possession is nine-tenths of the law"—as his sole basis of legitimacy.

In the same year—and this is a fact that very few Americans know,

---

[8] Philippe Devillers, "The Struggle for Unification of Vietnam," *China Quarterly*, No. 9 (1962), pp. 2-23.

though it is of great importance to the villagers in South Vietnam who became members of the Viet Cong—Diem abolished the fine old semi-democratic Vietnamese system of electing village councils and mayors, which had survived even during the period of French rule. Both of these actions by Diem must have seemed to the Communists to be flagrantly anti-democratic, anti-Vietnamese, and a violation of the agreement on the basis of which they had laid down their arms. It was only *after* both had occurred, in 1957, that the Viet Cong began their campaign of assassination of government-appointed officials in the villages. From their standpoint, the decisive acts of armed aggression against them occurred in 1956, and anything they have done since then has only been defensive.

2. *In the years between 1950 and 1954, when the United States was supplying money and arms on a large scale to the French, the French were fighting against a clear majority of the Vietnamese people.*

The years before 1954 represent another major blind spot in the thinking of most Americans, though they are probably ever present in the thinking of the Vietnamese Communists. For them those years were as terrible and as heroic as the years of World War II were for the Communists in the Soviet Union.

Few Americans realize that in 1945 and 1946, when the postwar world was settling down to its present division between East and West, Vietnam was not so divided. Instead, it was enjoying the first flush of what seemed to be independence from the rule of France, under Ho Chi Minh's leadership. Since he was a Communist, this meant that the boundary between the two worlds was at that time the boundary of Vietnam itself. Vietnam as a whole had in a sense "gone Communist" when it accepted Ho's leadership. It was, then, the West that stepped over the boundary and used force on the far side of it. France began then, and continued until 1954—with massive American financial help after 1950—to try to reimpose her rule. Although there was talk of a new autonomous role for the three states of Indochina within the French Union, the anti-French majority of the Vietnamese could be forgiven for regarding this war as naked aggression on the part of France, aided greatly by the United States. The term "imperialist," which sounds so strange in American ears when applied to ourselves, does not sound so strange in the ears of Vietnamese who regarded French rule as imperialist and had much reason to associate alien intruding Frenchmen with alien intruding Americans. As for the word "aggressor," it is difficult to escape the conclusion that, by any definition of the term, we were committing aggression in Vietnam from 1950 to 1954. We were financing the use of force on land that did not "belong" to us—or to the

French—by any criterion that we would now accept, and we were doing it against what now clearly seems to have been a majority of the people.

On this last point we have the testimony of many people, including President Eisenhower. As he put it in a much-quoted passage, "I have never talked or corresponded with a person knowledgeable in Indochinese affairs who did not agree that had elections been held as of the time of the fighting, possibly 80 per cent of the populace would have voted for the Communist Ho Chi Minh as their leader rather than Chief of State Bao Dai."[9]

Since President Eisenhower's statement has often been misinterpreted it should be noted that he did not say that Ho Chi Minh would probably have won by 80 per cent in the elections that Diem refused to hold in 1956. He said "possibly;" he carefully said "had elections been held as of the time of the fighting," i.e., in 1954 or earlier, not in 1956, when Diem's prospect of victory would have been much brighter; and he specified as Ho's hypothetical opponent Bao Dai, who was generally regarded as a weak French stooge, rather than Diem, who at that time was regarded even by many of his enemies as an honest man and a staunch anti-French patriot. But on the point that is now at issue—whether the help we gave to the French was in effect a use of force against a majority of the Vietnamese people—President Eisenhower's statement would seem to be decisive.

Why did we do it? Our reasons were understandable if not valid. In 1950 the Communists had just won in China; they were starting the Korean war, and it looked as if desperate measures were necessary in order to keep all of East and Southeast Asia from succumbing to the Communist juggernaut. Perhaps President Truman was honest enough to say to himself that even aggression against the Vietnamese was justified by the magnitude of the emergency. If present-day Americans are able to be equally honest and to remember clearly the situation as it was then, it will help them to understand how present-day Vietnamese Communists could really regard us as aggressors.

3. *The Communist-led majority of the Vietnamese people had actually won their war for independence in 1954.*

Though they were supported to some extent by arms from China, the arms their enemies gained from the United States and from France were far more formidable. Consequently, one of the clearest indications that a large majority of the Vietnamese people did support Ho lies in the fact

[9] Dwight D. Eisenhower, *Mandate for Change* (Garden City, N.Y.: Doubleday and Co., Inc., 1963), p. 372.

that his ragged, relatively poorly armed troops did finally win. The battle of Dienbienphu was decisive, and it was generally agreed at the time that if the Viet Minh had wanted to fight a few months more they could have had the whole country.

This is an important part of the psychological background of the Geneva Agreements, and of everything that has happened since. In this respect the situation was very different from the situation in Korea in 1945, when the boundary at the 38th Parallel was first established, or in Korea in 1953, when a military stalemate finally led to a new and roughly similar truce line. In 1953 there was a military stalemate in Korea and the Communists had no basis at all for setting their hearts on unifying the country on their terms. In Vietnam they did. The Vietnamese Communists and the many non-Communists who fought with them had every reason to feel that the prize for which they had struggled and sacrificed through nine heartbreaking years of war was finally theirs: a unified, independent country. Then, by what must have seemed to them a form of chicanery, with the face of America appearing where the face of France had been, and with both Diem and John Foster Dulles blandly claiming that they were not bound by the decisions made at Geneva, a full half of the prize they felt they had fairly won was snatched from them.

Apart from any question of what the people want, then, the Vietnamese Communists have three additional reasons for feeling that South Vietnam "belongs" to them and not to the government established and maintained by us in Saigon: the artificial division of the country at the 17th Parallel was legally and morally invalid after 1956; their war for independence was supported by a large majority of the people; they won that war.

Five Reasons Why They Think the People of South Vietnam Are on Their Side

Since Communists have repeatedly said that any people has a right to fight a "war of liberation" against colonial overlords, no matter how much the rule of the overlords may be sanctioned by tradition and legality, it is clear that their decisive criterion of "aggression" (if they are consistent with their official statements) must be whether "the people" oppose it or not. The following five types of evidence, of which they are probably much more aware than the average American, are therefore relevant to the question of their sincerity on this point.

1. *There are many reasons to think that Vietnamese nationalism is now mobilized, and has been mobilized for some twenty years, much more in*

favor of Ho Chi Minh than in favor of the French-backed or American-backed government in Saigon.

In Vietnam, perhaps more than in any other developing country, the Communists have apparently succeeded in fusing Communism with nationalism, and especially with the cause of national unity. The long and finally victorious struggle against the French was conducted primarily under Communist leadership by peasants who regarded their leaders more as patriots than as Communists.[10] President Eisenhower's statement, quoted above, is very relevant here.[11]

It should be noted too that the more and more conspicuous role of America on the Saigon Government side since 1960 has been such as to mobilize the xenophobic nationalism of the Vietnamese in a new way. Since 1960 American aid to Saigon has become far greater and more obvious, while Chinese aid to the Communists has been on a much smaller scale. There are many big-nosed white faces now on the Government side of the war, while those on the Viet Cong side are authentically Vietnamese, even though now a considerable and very potent fraction of them have come down from the North. The Viet Cong guerrillas have been helped by their own countrymen, while the Government has incurred what is probably a much greater stigma by accepting massive help from white foreigners who cannot even speak Vietnamese.

2. *The peasants want land, and many of them have had land taken away from them by the Government.*

Although there is a village-centered peasant nationalism, it may well be that another motive—hunger—is even more basic in the typical peasant's make-up. He wants to safeguard the bowl of rice that represents his next meal, and the rice field that represents next year's meals for himself, his wife, and his children. From the standpoint of many peasants in the southern part of South Vietnam, especially the Mekong Delta, their rice and their rice fields have been under attack not only by the crop-destroying chemicals that have been dropped (in some areas) by Government planes, but also by the absentee landlords who have in many instances demanded between thirty and fifty per cent of the crop. This fact of absentee landlordism in the

---

[10] Bernard Fall, *The Two Vietnams* (New York: Frederick A. Praeger, 1964), pp. 104-29; Ellen Hammer, *The Struggle for Indochina* (Stanford: Stanford University Press, 1954); Jean Lacouture, *Vietnam Between Two Truces* (New York: Random House, 1966), pp. 5, 8, and 32.

[11] On the importance and nature of Vietnamese nationalism, see George A. Carver, Jr., "The Real Revolution in South Viet Nam," *Foreign Affairs*, Vol. XLIII, No. 3 (1965), especially pp. 399 and 403.

South is little known in the United States. It has been estimated that in South Vietnam proper (Cochin China, roughly the southern one-third of the country) only two per cent of the people owned forty-five per cent of the land before 1945.[12] Land reform since then has not greatly changed the situation. Some has occurred under Diem and his successors, but it was preceded by a drastic reclaiming of land that the Viet Minh, when it was in control of large areas in South Vietnam, had given to the peasants outright. Land reform by the present government has been a pale imitation of land reform under the Communist-led Viet Minh.

3. *Probably much more physical suffering has been imposed on the peasants by the Government and its American allies than by the Viet Cong.*

On this point Americans have had misperceptions of two quite different kinds. On the one hand there is the misperception of those Americans who, shocked by occasional television pictures of weeping mothers, roughly handled prisoners, and deliberately burned villages, have failed to realize that the atrocities of the Viet Cong, less accessible to Western photographers and less vividly depicted, are just as real. Public disembowelment of "enemies of the people" and of their wives and children is only one of the revolting procedures employed by them, and it has seldom found its way to our American newspaper pages or television screens. On the other hand, there is the misperception of those Americans who, focusing primarily on the widely discussed Viet Cong assassinations of teachers, health workers, and Government-appointed village officials, have often remained ignorant of the highly probable fact that, because of the nature of guerrilla and counter-guerrilla war, the sheer volume of suffering inflicted by the Government has been considerably greater than that inflicted by the Viet Cong.

There are two reasons for this. The more familiar one is that the present process of using American firepower and mobility to break the back of the Viet Cong has meant—despite genuine efforts to minimize it—a large amount of killing, maiming, and sometimes napalming of villagers who, whether "innocent" from our point of view or not, certainly regard themselves as innocent.[13] In a culture that values family loyalty as much as the Vietnamese culture does, this deeply affects not only those who have suffered from it themselves but also those who have seen a parent or other relative suffer or die.

The less familiar reason for it is that, in the conduct of counter-guerrilla

---

[12] Fall, *op. cit.*, pp. 308-11.
[13] Major-General Edward G. Lansdale, "Viet Nam: Do We Understand Revolution?" *Foreign Affairs*, Vol. XLIII, No. 1 (1964), p. 81.

operations, it is urgently necessary to obtain intelligence about the identity of the guerrilla fighters and where they are hiding. South Vietnamese soldiers have interpreted this as justifying a large-scale use of torture to obtain information not only from captured Viet Cong prisoners themselves but also from wives and relatives of men suspected of being in the Viet Cong. There is the water torture, the electric-current torture, the wire-cage torture—all widely used—and there are other kinds even less well-known in the United States (perhaps chiefly because of unofficial self-censorship by most of our information gatherers in Saigon) but well documented by observers such as Bernard Fall, Malcolm Browne, and Robin Moore.[14]

The ignorance and apathy of the great majority of the American public with regard to this ugliest aspect of the war represent in themselves a puzzling and very disturbing psychological phenomenon. Bernard Fall in 1965 spoke about "the universally callous attitude taken by almost everybody toward the crass and constant violations of the rules of war that have been taking place . . . . To me the moral problem which arises in Vietnam is that of torture and needless brutality to combatants and civilians alike."[15] But the fact of widely used torture has not been cited here as an accusation against the United States. As we have seen, some of the Viet Cong atrocities have been at least as bad. The direct participants in the torture have as a rule been South Vietnamese, not Americans, and during the past year (partly as a result of the article by Bernard Fall quoted above) the American military authorities have provided American troops with clear instructions not only as to the applicability of the 1949 Convention on the humane treatment of prisoners but also as to the long-run counterproductive character of the torturing of prisoners and their relatives. The fact is cited here because it provides such an emotionally compelling kernel of truth in the Communist case against the Saigon Government, as well as for the Communist thesis that the common people *must* hate that government. Simply by focusing on this and ignoring similar atrocities on the Communist side a Communist could arrive at that conclusion.

4. *There has been a great deal of inefficiency and corruption on the part of the local officials appointed by the Saigon Government.*

The tradition of exploitation and cheating of the peasants by Government-appointed officials is perhaps no worse than in a number of other

---

[14] Bernard Fall, "Vietnam Blitz: A Report on the Impersonal War," *The New Republic*, Oct. 9, 1965, pp. 18-21; Malcolm W. Browne, *The New Face of War* (New York: Bobbs-Merrill, 1965), pp. 114-18; Robin Moore, *The Green Berets* (New York: Avon Books, 1965), pp. 46-50.

[15] Fall, *ibid.*, pp. 19-20.

Asian countries, including pre-Communist China; but it is very bad,[16] and it does contrast with the Viet Cong's tradition of comparative honesty and concern with the welfare of the rank-and-file peasants.[17] Inefficiency is also clearly very common, in contrast with the quite extraordinary efficiency (in some ways) of the Viet Cong; and in many relatively inaccessible villages the choice is not between the Viet Cong type of village government and that of the Saigon officials, but between Viet Cong government and virtually no government at all. In these villages the Viet Cong cadres fill a political vacuum and provide an alternative to anarchy. To be sure, they themselves have helped to produce the anarchy by assassinating Government-appointed village leaders. But their tactics have not been the only cause of anarchy, and they themselves are probably more aware, indeed inordinately aware, of their own comparative honesty and efficiency, which "must" bring the peasants over to their side.

None of this, it may be noted, is incompatible with the fact, now well documented, that in the years since 1963 the Viet Cong's high-handed methods of taxation and recruitment among the peasants have become more and more burdensome. The comparative honesty and efficiency of Viet Cong functionaries are linked with an essentially authoritarian attitude and a willingness to subordinate peasant welfare to the progress of the war. But *in their minds* the peasant's resentment of such tactics is probably underestimated, while his appreciation of their more positive contributions is probably overestimated.

5. *The Viet Cong has a record of remarkable military success against enormous obstacles, and it seems unlikely that such success could have been achieved without widespread popular support.*

Americans sometimes forget or underestimate the great advantage that the anti-Communist forces have enjoyed from the standpoint of weapons, especially since America began in 1950 to give large-scale material help to the French. The total amount of such help has clearly been much greater than the material help the Viet Cong has received from the North. Moreover, few Americans realize that the rebellion did not begin in the part of South Vietnam near Laos and the Ho Chi Minh Trail, where an appreciable amount of help from the North might have been possible. It began primarily in the far South, in the Mekong Delta, where it was necessary to use mainly homemade or captured weapons. The rebels therefore had to

[16] M. Mok, "In They Go—To the Reality of This War," *Life*, Nov. 26, 1965, p. 71.
[17] Malcolm Browne, *op. cit.*, pp. 121-28; Viet Cong Soldiers' Diaries, quoted in *The Vietnam Reader*, ed. by M. G. Raskin and Bernard Fall (New York: Random House, 1965), p. 227.

make up in organization, dedication, and extent of popular support for the Government's great advantage in material equipment.[18] Still another fact frequently forgotten in America (or never learned) is that the rebellion began to a significant extent in 1957,[19] at least three years before its surprising success—with little outside help—led the Communist authorities in the North to give it a significant amount of material help.

It is true that one major compensating advantage possessed by the Viet Cong has been the tactical advantage of concealment and surprise that has led to the conventional estimate that counter-guerrilla forces must have a ten-to-one numerical superiority over guerrilla forces in order to defeat them. But what is sometimes forgotten is that the guerrillas' tactical advantage exists to this high degree only when they have the active support of most of the people (which they could hardly get by intimidation alone) in helping them to conceal themselves, in helping to supply them with the intelligence they need in order to have the full advantage of surprise, and in denying to the counter-guerrilla forces the same kind of intelligence.

Here too there are important counterarguments on the anti-Communist side. In particular the use of intimidation by the Viet Cong to clinch their hold on the peasants must account for much of the peasant cooperation that has occurred. But here again it is important to note that the Communists themselves are probably overinclined to discount or ignore those counterarguments. The military successes of the Viet Cong against far better armed opponents have been remarkable enough to enable Communists to say to themselves: "The people *must* be on our side."

* * * *

There are at least five reasons, then, to think that the Communists believe most of the people are on their side: nationalistic resentment of intrusion by white Americans, land hunger, resentment of torture and other physical suffering caused by the Government, the corruption of officials, and the military success of the Viet Cong against great material odds.

Together with the three additional reasons reviewed earlier for thinking they feel that South Vietnam is part of "their" country, these five seem quite adequate to make it probable that doctrinaire Communists, already predisposed against the United States, do believe it when they call us "aggressors." However mistaken this proposition may be (and I happen to

---

[18] Fall, *The Two Vietnams*, p. 317; Lacouture, *op. cit.*, pp. 21-23.
[19] Carver, *op. cit.*, p. 406.

think it is largely mistaken, on the basis of evidence that has hardly been touched upon here), the Communists probably *believe* it is true.[20]

A Sensible and Honorable Compromise

The preceding discussion is a diagnosis of the problem, not a prescription for its solution. In the light of this diagnosis, though, my own feeling is that the most sensible and honorable policy for the United States is to seek a compromise peace. It is the only kind of peace that would allow *both* sides to feel that they had preserved from the aggressor's grasp the bare essentials of what they were fighting to defend.

It could take various forms. One is a coalition government, with efforts by other countries to keep the coalition from being dominated by the organized, dedicated Communist minority within it. Such a coalition could be the outcome of negotiations, if genuine negotiations become possible, or it might conceivably be set up by our side unilaterally, with a real effort to give the Viet Cong and all other elements of the population power commensurate with their actual strength. Or it could take the form of a partition of the South along lines reflecting the balance of military power at the time the partition occurs. This too could be done with negotiations if possible but without negotiations if necessary—unilaterally, by a decision to concentrate our military strength on consolidating non-Communist control of large contiguous areas (not small "enclaves") while withdrawing from overexposed, hard-to-hold areas elsewhere. Free migration into and out of each area might follow, as it did in the partition that followed the 1954 agreement.

As to the relative merits of different types of compromise peace there are complex pro's and con's, and this is not the place to discuss them. What is argued here is that a search for *some* feasible form of compromise peace is the only sensible and honorable policy for the United States.

When each side believes the other to be the aggressor, both are sure to regard any compromise as unsatisfactory, since each will see a compromise as granting to the aggressor some part of his ill-gotten gains. Each wants to ensure that the aggressor is not rewarded by any expansion whatsoever. In this case, for instance, we Americans and our Vietnamese allies would hate to accept a compromise that we defined as granting to the Communists any expansion of power, either by gaining some land south of the

---

[20] Douglas Pike, *Viet Cong* (Cambridge, Mass.: M.I.T. Press, 1966), p. 378. Although Pike is very skeptical of the proposition that most of the people support the Viet Cong, he speaks of the party's "mystic belief in the power *and loyalty* of the people." Italics added.

17th Parallel or by gaining some power in a coalition government. The Communists would similarly regard with dismay a compromise peace that left the American "aggressors" still firmly ensconced on Vietnamese soil and still (as they would see it) ruling a large part of the country through their lackeys in Saigon. To them it would seem like a bitter and futile end to their twenty years of struggle to drive the alien white intruders into the sea.

As long as both sides rigidly adhere to this principle, a compromise is clearly impossible. However, *if* there is no clear break in the present military stalemate and the bloody, inhuman war continues with no end in sight, each side may lower its sights and begin to consider seriously whether some form of compromise would necessarily be cowardly and dishonorable. Probably both sides would even then be grimly determined never to surrender. "Surrender is unthinkable." But each side might become aware that it had a hierarchy of preferences. Three choices might emerge instead of only two: surrender (unthinkable), a compromise peace, and unending war, instead of surrender (unthinkable) and victory. Among these three choices a compromise peace might then seem the least intolerable.

What are the bare essentials of what each side is fighting to defend? Are they incompatible? Or would it be possible for both sides simultaneously to preserve what they care about most?

On our side, it seems to me, there are two things that a large majority of the American people regard as essential: to avoid a significant "domino" process in other parts of the world, and to preserve a tolerable life for our anti-Communist friends in Vietnam. The first of these is believed to be a matter of defending both freedom and peace: the freedom of other countries that are vulnerable to the Chinese strategy of takeover by "wars of liberation," and the peace that would be endangered elsewhere if a Communist victory in Vietnam led Communists everywhere to be more aggressive. The second is more a matter of honor and commitment. We feel that our words and actions have established a commitment to our anti-Communist allies, and that if we abandoned them to the untender mercies of the Viet Cong we would be doing a shameful thing. The validity of these two points will not be debated here; it is necessary only to recognize that most of the Americans who would be involved in the decision do care about both of them, and care deeply.

On the Communist side there are as yet no verbal indications of a hierarchy of preferences. On the surface there is only a fervent, monolithic insistence that the American aggressors must be wholly eliminated from the scene; and since we feel that any complete withdrawal by us would both accentuate the domino process and leave our anti-Communist friends helpless in the face of the organized, dedicated, vengeful Viet Cong, there is little chance of a compromise on this basis. It seems likely, though, that beneath the surface they do have a hierarchy of preferences. Perhaps, if convinced that the alternative is not victory but unending war, they would prefer peace with undisturbed control of some large fraction (say a half) of the population of South Vietnam. This would mean that they could stay alive, go back to the increasingly urgent business of cultivating their rice paddies, and preserve the way of life in which they have invested so much effort and sacrifice. The Communists in the North would be spared further bombing and the danger of a wider war, and although they would have failed in their great objective of unifying the country under their own control, they could salvage some pride in the thought that they had held their own against a much more powerful aggressor.

On each side, then, a compromise peace might be interpreted as salvaging the bare essentials of what that side was fighting to defend. It therefore seems psychologically feasible if we pursue it intelligently and persistently.

It also seems more honorable than any other alternative. By keeping the American flag flying in South Vietnam and stubbornly refusing to retreat from our present power position we would be balancing the power of Communist China on its periphery and fulfilling our obligation to the small non-Communist countries that are threatened by Communist takeover. We would also be fulfilling our obligation to preserve the life and livelihood of our non-Communist friends in Vietnam itself. But if we attempted by force of arms to conquer the parts of South Vietnam in which most of the people regard us as alien aggressors—and the evidence suggests that a very large proportion of the people in certain areas see us in that light—we would be in conflict with the principle of self-determination. It is not in the American tradition to impose abject surrender on brave men who believe, rightly or wrongly, that they are defending their homeland against aggression by us.

IV. DOCUMENTARY APPENDICES

OFFICIAL DOCUMENTS *

AGREEMENTS RELATING TO THE SITUATION IN VIET-NAM [1]

AGREEMENT BETWEEN THE COMMANDER-IN-CHIEF OF THE FRENCH UNION FORCES IN INDO-CHINA AND THE COMMANDER-IN-CHIEF OF THE PEOPLE'S ARMY OF VIET-NAM ON THE CESSATION OF HOSTILITIES IN VIET-NAM [2]

Signed at Geneva, July 20, 1954

CHAPTER I

Provisional Military Demarcation Line and Demilitarised Zone

ARTICLE 1

A PROVISIONAL military demarcation line shall be fixed, on either side of which the forces of the two parties shall be regrouped after their withdrawal, the forces of the People's Army of Viet Nam to the north of the line and the forces of the French Union to the south.

The provisional military demarcation line is fixed as shown on the map attached (see Map No. 1).[3]

It is also agreed that a demilitarised zone shall be established on either side of the demarcation line, to a width of not more than 5 kms. from it, to act as a buffer zone and avoid any incidents which might result in the resumption of hostilities.

ARTICLE 2

The period within which the movement of all forces of either party into its regrouping zone on either side of the provisional military demarcation line shall be completed shall not exceed three hundred (300) days from the date of the present Agreement's entry into force.

ARTICLE 3

When the provisional military demarcation line coincides with a waterway, the waters of such waterway shall be open to civil navigation by both parties wherever one bank is controlled by one party and the other bank by the other party. The Joint Commission shall establish rules of navigation for the stretch of waterway in question. The merchant shipping and other

---

* Obtained and prepared by R. R. Baxter of the Board of Editors.

1 These documents are reproduced at this time because of the interest currently being taken in the legality of the activities of the United States in Viet-Nam. See p. 565 above.

2 Great Britain, Misc. No. 20 (1954) (Cmd. 9239) at 27; 161 Brit. and For. State Papers 818 (1954).

3 Not reproduced.

civilian craft of each party shall have unrestricted access to the land under its military control.

ARTICLE 4

The provisional military demarcation line between the two final regrouping zones is extended into the territorial waters by a line perpendicular to the general line of the coast.

All coastal islands north of this boundary shall be evacuated by the armed forces of the French Union, and all islands south of it shall be evacuated by the forces of the People's Army of Viet Nam.

ARTICLE 5

To avoid any incidents which might result in the resumption of hostilities, all military forces, supplies and equipment shall be withdrawn from the demilitarised zone within twenty-five (25) days of the present Agreement's entry into force.

ARTICLE 6

No person, military or civilian, shall be permitted to cross the provisional military demarcation line unless specifically authorised to do so by the Joint Commission.

ARTICLE 7

No person, military or civilian, shall be permitted to enter the demilitarised zone except persons concerned with the conduct of civil administration and relief and persons specifically authorised to enter by the Joint Commission.

ARTICLE 8

Civil administration and relief in the demilitarised zone on either side of the provisional military demarcation line shall be the responsibility of the Commanders-in-Chief of the two parties in their respective zones. The number of persons, military or civilian, from each side who are permitted to enter the demilitarised zone for the conduct of civil administration and relief shall be determined by the respective Commanders, but in no case shall the total number authorised by either side exceed at any one time a figure to be determined by the Trung Gia Military Commission or by the Joint Commission. The number of civil police and the arms to be carried by them shall be determined by the Joint Commission. No one else shall carry arms unless specifically authorised to do so by the Joint Commission.

ARTICLE 9

Nothing contained in this chapter shall be construed as limiting the complete freedom of movement, into, out of or within the demilitarised zone, of the Joint Commission, its joint groups, the International Commission to be set up as indicated below, its inspection teams and any other persons, supplies or equipment specifically authorised to enter the demilitarised zone by the Joint Commission. Freedom of movement shall be permitted across the territory under the military control of either side over any road or waterway which has to be taken between points within the demilitarised zone when such points are not connected by roads or waterways lying completely within the demilitarised zone.

CHAPTER II

Principles and procedure governing implementation of the present Agreement

ARTICLE 10

The Commanders of the Forces on each side, on the one side the Commander-in-Chief of the French Union forces in Indo-China and on the other side the Commander-in-Chief of the People's Army of Viet Nam, shall order and enforce the complete cessation of all hostilities in Viet Nam by all armed forces under their control, including all units and personnel of the ground, naval and air forces.

ARTICLE 11

In accordance with the principle of a simultaneous cease-fire throughout Indo-China, the cessation of hostilities shall be simultaneous throughout all parts of Viet Nam, in all areas of hostilities and for all the forces of the two parties.

Taking into account the time effectively required to transmit the cease-fire order down to the lowest echelons of the combatant forces on both sides, the two parties are agreed that the cease-fire shall take effect completely and simultaneously for the different sectors of the country as follows:

Northern Viet Nam at 8:00 a.m. (local time) on 27th July, 1954.
Central Viet Nam at 8:00 a.m. (local time) on 1st August, 1954.
Southern Viet Nam at 8:00 a.m. (local time) on 11th August, 1954.

It is agreed that Peking mean time shall be taken as local time.

From such time as the cease-fire becomes effective in Northern Viet Nam, both parties undertake not to engage in any large-scale offensive action in any part of the Indo-Chinese theatre of operations and not to commit the air forces based on Northern Viet Nam outside that sector. The two parties also undertake to inform each other of their plans for movement from one regrouping zone to another within twenty-five (25) days of the present Agreement's entry into force.

ARTICLE 12

All the operations and movements entailed in the cessation of hostilities and regouping must proceed in a safe and orderly fashion:

(a) Within a certain number of days after the cease-fire Agreement shall have become effective, the number to be determined on the spot by the Trung

Gia Military Commission, each party shall be responsible for removing and neutralising mines (including river and sea mines), booby traps, explosives and any other dangerous substances placed by it. In the event of its being impossible to complete the work of removal and neutralisation in time, the party concerned shall mark the spot by placing visible signs there. All demolitions, mine fields, wire entanglements and other hazards to the free movement of the personnel of the Joint Commission and its joint groups, known to be present after the withdrawal of the military forces, shall be reported to the Joint Commission by the Commanders of the opposing forces;

(b) From the time of the cease-fire until regrouping is completed on either side of the demarcation line:

(1) The forces of either party shall be provisionally withdrawn from the provisional assembly areas assigned to the other party.

(2) When one party's forces withdraw by a route (road, rail, waterway, sea route) which passes through the territory of the other party (see Article 24), the latter party's forces must provisionally withdraw three kilometres on each side of such route, but in such a manner as to avoid interfering with the movements of the civil population.

ARTICLE 13

From the time of the cease-fire until the completion of the movements from one regrouping zone into the other, civil and military transport aircraft shall follow air corridors between the provisional assembly areas assigned to the French Union forces north of the demarcation line on the one hand and the Laotian frontier and the regrouping zone assigned to the French Union forces on the other hand.

The position of the air corridors, their width, the safety route for single-engined military aircraft transferred to the south and the search and rescue procedure for aircraft in distress shall be determined on the spot by the Trung Gia Military Commission.

ARTICLE 14

Political and administrative measures in the two regrouping zones, on either side of the provisional military demarcation line:

(a) Pending the general elections which will bring about the unification of Viet Nam, the conduct of civil administration in each regrouping zone shall be in the hands of the party whose forces are to be regrouped there in virtue of the present Agreement.

(b) Any territory controlled by one party which is transferred to the other party by the regrouping plan shall continue to be administered by the former party until such date as all the troops who are to be transferred have completely left that territory so as to free the zone assigned to the party in question. From then on, such territory shall be regarded as transferred to the other party, who shall assume responsibility for it.

Steps shall be taken to ensure that there is no break in the transfer of responsibilities. For this purpose, adequate notice shall be given by the withdrawing party to the other party, which shall make the necessary arrangements, in particular by sending administrative and police detachments to prepare for the assumption of administrative responsibility. The length of such notice shall be determined by the Trung Gia Military Commission. The transfer shall be effected in successive stages for the various territorial sectors.

The transfer of the civil administration of Hanoi and Haiphong to the authorities of the Democratic Republic of Viet Nam shall be completed within the respective time-limits laid down in Article 15 for military movements.

(c) Each party undertakes to refrain from any reprisals or discrimination against persons or organisations on account of their activities during the hostilities and to guarantee their democratic liberties.

(d) From the date of entry into force of the present Agreement until the movement of troops is completed, any civilians residing in a district controlled by one party who wish to go and live in the zone assigned to the other party shall be permitted and helped to do so by the authorities in that district.

ARTICLE 15

The disengagement of the combatants, and the withdrawals and transfers of military forces, equipment and supplies shall take place in accordance with the following principles:

(a) The withdrawals and transfers of the military forces, equipment and supplies of the two parties shall be completed within three hundred (300) days, as laid down in Article 2 of the present Agreement;

(b) Within either territory successive withdrawals shall be made by sectors, portions of sectors or provinces. Transfers from one regrouping zone to another shall be made in successive monthly instalments proportionate to the number of troops to be transferred;

(c) The two parties shall undertake to carry out all troop withdrawals and transfers in accordance with the aims of the present Agreement, shall permit no hostile act and shall take no step whatsoever which might hamper such withdrawals and transfers. They shall assist one another as far as this is possible;

(d) The two parties shall permit no destruction or sabotage of any public property and no injury to the life and property of the civil population. They shall permit no interference in local civil administration;

(e) The Joint Commission and the International Commission shall ensure that steps are taken to safeguard the forces in the course of withdrawal and transfer;

(f) The Trung Gia Military Commission, and later the Joint Commission, shall determine by common agreement the exact procedure for the disengagement of the combatants and for troop withdrawals and transfers, on the basis of the principles mentioned above and within the framework laid down below:

1. The disengagement of the combatants, including the concentration of the armed forces of all kinds and also each party's movements into the pro-

visional assembly areas assigned to it and the other party's provisional withdrawal from it, shall be completed within a period not exceeding fifteen (15) days after the date when the cease-fire becomes effective.

The general delineation of the provisional assembly areas is set out in the maps [4] annexed to the present Agreement.

In order to avoid any incidents, no troops shall be stationed less than 1,500 metres from the lines delimiting the provisional assembly areas.

During the period until the transfers are concluded, all the coastal islands west of the following lines shall be included in the Haiphong perimeter:

meridian of the southern point of Kebao Island,
northern coast of Ile Rousse (excluding the island), extended as far as the meridian of Campha-Mines,
meridian of Campha-Mines.

2. The withdrawals and transfers shall be effected in the following order and within the following periods (from the date of the entry into force of the present Agreement):

Forces of the French Union

Hanoi perimeter	80 days
Haiduong perimeter	100 days
Haiphong perimeter	300 days

Forces of the People's Army of Viet Nam

Ham Tan and Xuyenmoc provisional assembly area	80 days
Central Viet Nam provisional assembly area—first instalment	80 days
Plaine des Joncs provisional assembly area	100 days
Central Viet Nam provisional assembly area—second instalment	100 days
Pointe Camau provisional assembly area	200 days
Central Viet Nam provisional assembly area—last instalment	300 days

CHAPTER III

Ban on the introduction of fresh troops, military personnel, arms and munitions. Military bases

ARTICLE 16

With effect from the date of entry into force of the present Agreement, the introduction into Viet Nam of any troop reinforcements and additional military personnel is prohibited.

It is understood, however, that the rotation of units and groups of personnel, the arrival in Viet Nam of individual personnel on a temporary duty basis and the return to Viet Nam of the individual personnel after short

[4] Not reproduced.

periods of leave or temporary duty outside Viet Nam shall be permitted under the conditions laid down below:

(*a*) Rotation of units defined in paragraph (*c*) of this article) and groups of personnel shall not be permitted for French Union troops stationed north of the provisional military demarcation line laid down in Article 1 of the present Agreement during the withdrawal period provided for in Article 2.

However, under the heading of individual personnel not more than fifty (50) men, including officers, shall during any one month be permitted to enter that part of the country north of the provisional military demarcation line on a temporary duty basis or to return there after short periods of leave or temporary duty outside Viet Nam.

(*b*) "Rotation" is defined as the replacement of units or groups of personnel by other units of the same echelon or by personnel who are arriving in Viet Nam territory to do their overseas service there;

(*c*) The units rotated shall never be larger than a battalion—or the corresponding echelon for air and naval forces;

(*d*) Rotation shall be conducted on a man-for-man basis, provided, however, that in any one quarter neither party shall introduce more than fifteen thousand five hundred (15,500) members of its armed forces into Viet Nam under the rotation policy.

(*e*) Rotation units (defined in paragraph (*c*) of this article) and groups of personnel, and the individual personnel mentioned in this article, shall enter and leave Viet Nam only through the entry points enumerated in Article 20 below;

(*f*) Each party shall notify the Joint Commission and the International Commission at least two days in advance of any arrivals or departures of units, groups of personnel and individual personnel in or from Viet Nam. Reports on the arrivals or departures of units, groups of personnel and individual personnel in or from Viet Nam shall be submitted daily to the Joint Commission and the International Commission.

All the above-mentioned notifications and reports shall indicate the places and dates of arrival or departure and the number of persons arriving or departing;

(*g*) The International Commission, through its Inspection Teams, shall supervise and inspect the rotation of units and groups of personnel and the arrival and departure of individual personnel as authorised above, at the points of entry enumerated in Article 20 below.

ARTICLE 17

(*a*) With effect from the date of entry into force of the present Agreement, the introduction into Viet Nam of any reinforcements in the form of all types of arms, munitions and other war material, such as combat aircraft, naval craft, pieces of ordnance, jet engines and jet weapons and armoured vehicles, is prohibited.

(*b*) It is understood, however, that war material, arms and munitions which have been destroyed, damaged, worn out or used up after the cessation of hostilities may be replaced on the basis of piece-for-piece of the same type and with similar characteristics. Such replacements of war material, arms and ammunitions shall not be permitted for French Union troops stationed north of the provisional military demarcation line laid down in Article 1 of the present Agreement, during the withdrawal period provided for in Article 2.

Naval craft may perform transport operations between the regrouping zones.

(c) The war material, arms and munitions for replacement purposes provided for in paragraph (b) of this article, shall be introduced into Viet Nam only through the points of entry enumerated in Article 20 below. War material, arms and munitions to be replaced shall be shipped from Viet Nam only through the points of entry enumerated in Article 20 below.

(d) Apart from the replacements permitted within the limits laid down in paragraph (b) of this article, the introduction of war material, arms and munitions of all types in the form of unassembled parts for subsequent assembly is prohibited.

(e) Each party shall notify the Joint Commission and the International Commission at least two days in advance of any arrivals or departures which may take place of war material, arms and munitions of all types.

In order to justify the requests for the introduction into Viet Nam of arms, munitions and other war material (as defined in paragraph (a) of this article) for replacement purposes, a report concerning each incoming shipment shall be submitted to the Joint Commission and the International Commission. Such reports shall indicate the use made of the items so replaced.

(f) The International Commission, through its Inspection Teams, shall supervise and inspect the replacements permitted in the circumstances laid down in this article, at the points of entry enumerated in Article 20 below.

ARTICLE 18

With effect from the date of entry into force of the present Agreement, the establishment of new military bases is prohibited throughout Viet Nam territory.

ARTICLE 19

With effect from the date of entry into force of the present Agreement, no military base under the control of a foreign state may be established in the regrouping zone of either party; the two parties shall ensure that the zones assigned to them do not adhere to any military alliance and are not used for the resumption of hostilities or to further an aggressive policy.

ARTICLE 20

The points of entry into Viet Nam for rotation personnel and replacements of material are fixed as follows:

Zones to the north of the provisional military demarcation line: Laokay, Langson, Tien-Yen, Haiphong, Vinh, Dong-Hoi, Muong-Sen;

Zone to the south of the provisional military demarcation line: Tourane, Quinhon, Nhatrang, Bangoi, Saigon, Cap St. Jacques, Tanchau.

CHAPTER IV

Prisoners of War and Civilian Internees

ARTICLE 21

The liberation and repatriation of all prisoners of war and civilian internees detained by each of the two parties at the coming into force of the present Agreement shall be carried out under the following conditions:

(a) All prisoners of war and civilian internees of Viet Nam, French and other nationalities captured since the beginning of hostilities in Viet Nam during military operations or in any other circumstances of war and in any part of the territory of Viet Nam shall be liberated within a period of thirty (30) days after the date when the cease-fire becomes effective in each theatre.

(b) The term "civilian internees" is understood to mean all persons who, having in any way contributed to the political and armed struggle between the two parties, have been arrested for that reason and have been kept in detention by either party during the period of hostilities.

(c) All prisoners of war and civilian internees held by either party shall be surrendered to the appropriate authorities of the other party, who shall give them all possible assistance in proceeding to their country of origin, place of habitual residence or the zone of their choice.

CHAPTER V

Miscellaneous

ARTICLE 22

The Commanders of the Forces of the two parties shall ensure that persons under their respective commands who violate any of the provisions of the present Agreement are suitably punished.

ARTICLE 23

In cases in which the place of burial is known and the existence of graves has been established, the Commander of the Forces of either party shall, within a specific period after the entry into force of the Armistice Agreement, permit the graves service personnel of the other party to enter the part of Viet Nam territory under their military control for the purpose of finding and removing the bodies of deceased military personnel of that party, including the bodies of deceased prisoners of war. The Joint Commission shall determine the procedures and the time limit for the performance of this task. The Commanders of the Forces of the two parties shall communicate to each other all information in their possession as to the place of burial of military personnel of the other party.

ARTICLE 24

The present Agreement shall apply to all the armed forces of either party. The armed forces of each party shall respect the demilitarised zone and the territory under the military control of the other party, and shall commit no act and undertake no operation against the other party and shall not engage in blockade of any kind in Viet Nam.

For the purposes of the present article, the word "territory" includes territorial waters and air space.

ARTICLE 25

The Commanders of the Forces of the two parties shall afford full protection and all possible assistance and co-operation to the Joint Commission and its joint groups and to the International Commission and its Inspection Teams in the performance of the functions and tasks assigned to them by the present Agreement.

ARTICLE 26

The costs involved in the operations of the Joint Commission and joint groups and of the International Commission and its Inspection Teams shall be shared equally between the two parties.

ARTICLE 27

The signatories of the present Agreement and their successors in their functions shall be responsible for ensuring the observance and enforcement of the terms and provisions thereof. The Commanders of the Forces of the two parties shall, within their respective commands, take all steps and make all arrangements necessary to ensure full compliance with all the provisions of the present Agreement by all elements and military personnel under their command.

The procedures laid down in the present Agreement shall, whenever necessary, be studied by the Commanders of the two parties and, if necessary, defined more specifically by the Joint Commission.

CHAPTER VI

Joint Commission and International Commission for Supervision and Control in Viet Nam

ARTICLE 28

Responsibility for the execution of the Agreement on the cessation of hostilities shall rest with the parties.

An International Commission shall ensure the control and supervision of this execution.

ARTICLE 30

In order to facilitate, under the conditions shown below, the execution of provisions concerning joint actions by the two parties, a Joint Commission shall be set up in Viet Nam.

ARTICLE 31

The Joint Commission shall be composed of an equal number of representatives of the Commanders of the two parties.

ARTICLE 32

The Presidents of the delegations to the Joint Commission shall hold the rank of General.

The Joint Commission shall set up joint groups, the number of which shall be determined by mutual agreement between the parties. The joint groups shall be composed of an equal number of officers from both parties. Their location on the demarcation line between the regrouping zones shall be determined by the parties whilst taking into account the powers of the Joint Commission.

ARTICLE 33

The Joint Commission shall ensure the execution of the following provisions of the Agreement on the cessation of hostilities:

(a) A simultaneous and general cease-fire in Viet Nam for all regular and irregular armed forces of the two parties.

(b) A regroupment of the armed forces of the two parties.

(c) Observance of the demarcation lines between the regrouping zones and of the demilitarised sectors.

Within the limits of its competence it shall help the parties to execute the said provisions, shall ensure liaison between them for the purpose of preparing and carrying out plans for the application of these provisions, and shall endeavour to solve such disputed questions as may arise between the parties in the course of executing these provisions.

ARTICLE 34

An International Commission shall be set up for the control and supervision over the application of the provisions of the agreement on the cessation of hostilities in Viet Nam. It shall be composed of representatives of the following states: Canada, India and Poland.

It shall be presided over by the Representative of India.

ARTICLE 35

The International Commission shall set up fixed and mobile inspection teams, composed of an equal number of officers appointed by each of the above-mentioned states. The mixed teams shall be located at the following points: Laokay, Langson, Tien-Yen, Haiphong, Vinh, Dong-Hoi, Muong-Sen, Tourane, Quinhon, Nhatrang, Bangoi, Saigon, Cap St. Jacques, Tranchau. These points of location may, at a later date, be altered at the request of the Joint Commission, or of one of the parties, or of the International Commission itself, by agreement between the International Commission and the command of the party concerned. The zones of action of the mobile teams shall be the regions bordering the land and sea frontiers of Viet Nam, the demarcation lines between the regrouping zones and the demilitarised zones. Within the limits of these zones they shall have the right to move freely and shall receive from the local civil and military authorities all facilities they may require for the fulfilment of their tasks (provision of personnel, placing at their disposal documents needed for supervision, summoning witnesses necessary for holding enquiries, ensuring the security and freedom of movement of the inspection teams, &c . . .). They shall have at their disposal such modern means of transport, observation and communication as they may require. Beyond the zones of action as defined above, the mobile teams may, by agreement with the command of the party concerned, carry out other movements within the limits of the tasks given them by the present Agreement.

ARTICLE 36

The International Commission shall be responsible for supervising the proper execution by the parties of the provisions of the Agreement. For this purpose it shall fulfil the tasks of control, observation, inspection and investigation connected with the application of the provisions of the Agreement on the cessation of hostilities, and it shall in particular:

(*a*) Control the movement of the armed forces of the two parties, effected within the framework of the regroupment plan.

(*b*) Supervise the demarcation lines between the regrouping areas, and also the demilitarised zones.

(*c*) Control the operations of releasing prisoners of war and civilian internees.

(*d*) Supervise at ports and airfields as well as along all frontiers of Viet Nam the execution of the provisions of the agreement on the cessation of hostilities, regulating the introduction into the country of armed forces, military personnel and of all kinds of arms, munitions and war material.

ARTICLE 37

The International Commission shall, through the medium of the inspection teams mentioned above, and as soon as possible either on its own initiative, or at the request of the Joint Commission, or of one of the parties, undertake the necessary investigations both documentary and on the ground.

ARTICLE 38

The inspection téams shall submit to the International Commission the results of their supervision, their investigation and their observations; furthermore they shall draw up such special reports as they may consider necessary or as may be requested from them by the Commission. In the case of a disagreement within the teams, the conclusions of each member shall be submitted to the Commission.

ARTICLE 39

If any one inspection team is unable to settle an incident or considers that there is a violation or a threat of a serious violation, the International Commission shall be informed; the latter shall study the reports and the conclusions of the inspection teams and shall inform the parties of the measures which should be taken for the settlement of the incident, ending of the violation or removal of the threat of violation.

ARTICLE 40

When the Joint Commission is unable to reach an agreement on the interpretation to be given to some provision or on the appraisal of a fact, the International Commission shall be informed of the disputed question. Its recommendations shall be sent directly to the parties and shall be notified to the Joint Commission.

ARTICLE 41

The recommendations of the International Commission shall be adopted by majority vote, subject to the provisions contained in Article 42. If the votes are divided, the chairman's vote shall be decisive.

The International Commission may formulate recommendations concerning amendments and additions which should be made to the provisions of the Agreement on the cessation of hostilities in Viet Nam, in order to ensure a more effective execution of that Agreement. These recommendations shall be adopted unanimously.

ARTICLE 42

When dealing with questions concerning violations, or threats of violations, which might lead to a resumption of hostilities, namely:

(a) Refusal by the armed forces of one party to effect the movements provided for in the regroupment plan;

(b) Violation by the armed forces of one of the parties of the regrouping zones, territorial waters, or air space of the other party;

the decisions of the International Commission must be unanimous.

ARTICLE 43

If one of the parties refuses to put into effect a recommendation of the International Commission, the parties concerned or the Commission itself shall inform the members of the Geneva Conference.

If the International Commission does not reach unanimity in the cases provided for in Article 42, it shall submit a majority report and one or more minority reports to the members of the Conference.

The International Commission shall inform the members of the Conference in all cases where its activity is being hindered.

ARTICLE 44

The International Commission shall be set up at the time of the cessation of hostilities in Indo-China in order that it should be able to fulfil the tasks provided for in Article 36.

ARTICLE 45

The International Commission for Supervision and Control in Viet Nam shall act in close co-operation with the International Commissions for Supervision and Control in Cambodia and Laos.

The Secretaries-General of these three Commissions shall be responsible for co-ordinating their work and for relations between them.

ARTICLE 46

The International Commission for Supervision and Control in Viet Nam may, after consultation with the International Commissions for Supervision and Control in Cambodia and Laos and having regard to the development of the situation in Cambodia and Laos, progressively reduce its activities.　Such a decision must be adopted unanimously.

ARTICLE 47

All the provisions of the present Agreement, save the second sub-paragraph of Article 11, shall enter into force at 2400 hours (Geneva time) on 22nd July, 1954.

Done in Geneva at 2400 hours on the 20th of July, 1954, in French and in Vietnamese, both texts being equally authentic.

For the Commander-in-Chief of the French Union Forces in Indo-China:

DELTIEL,
Brigadier-General.

For the Commander-in-Chief of the People's Army of Viet Nam:

TA–QUANG–BUU,
Vice-Minister of National Defence
of the Democratic Republic of Viet Nam.[5]

5 The annexes to the agreement are not reproduced.

FINAL DECLARATION OF THE GENEVA CONFERENCE ON THE PROBLEM
OF RESTORING PEACE IN INDO-CHINA [6]

Geneva, July 21, 1954

1. The Conference takes note of the Agreements ending hostilities in Cambodia, Laos and Viet Nam and organising international control and the supervision of the execution of the provisions of these Agreements.

2. The Conference expresses satisfaction at the ending of hostilities in Cambodia, Laos and Viet Nam; the Conference expresses its conviction that the execution of the provisions set out in the present declaration and in the Agreements on the cessation of hostilities will permit Cambodia, Laos and Viet Nam henceforth to play their part, in full independence and sovereignty, in the peaceful community of nations.

3. The Conference takes note of the declarations made by the Governments of Cambodia and of Laos of their intention to adopt measures permitting all citizens to take their place in the national community, in particular by participating in the next general elections, which, in conformity with the constitution of each of these countries, shall take place in the course of the year 1955, by secret ballot and in conditions of respect for fundamental freedoms.

4. The Conference takes note of the clauses in the Agreement on the cessation of hostilities in Viet Nam prohibiting the introduction into Viet Nam of foreign troops and military personnel as well as of all kinds of arms and munitions. The Conference also takes note of the declarations made by the Governments of Cambodia and Laos of their resolution not to request foreign aid, whether in war material, in personnel or in instructors except for the purpose of the effective defence of their territory and, in the case of Laos, to the extent defined by the agreements on the cessation of hostilities in Laos.

5. The Conference takes note of the clauses in the Agreement on the cessation of hostilities in Viet Nam to the effect that no military base under the control of a foreign state may be established in the regrouping zones of the two parties, the latter having the obligation to see that the zones allotted to them shall not constitute part of any military alliance and shall not be utilised for the resumption of hostilities or in the service of an aggressive policy. The Conference also takes note of the declarations of the Governments of Cambodia and Laos to the effect that they will not join in any agreement with other states if this agreement includes the obligation to participate in a military alliance not in conformity with the principles of the Charter of the United Nations or, in the case of Laos, with the principles of the Agreement on the cessation of hostilities in Laos or, so long as their security is not threatened, the obligation to establish bases on Cambodian or Laotian territory for the military forces of foreign Powers.

[6] Great Britain, Misc. No. 20 (1954) (Cmd. 9239) at 9; 161 Brit. and For. State Papers 359 (1954).

6. The Conference recognises that the essential purpose of the Agreement relating to Viet Nam is to settle military questions with a view to ending hostilities and that the military demarcation line is provisional and should not in any way be interpreted as constituting a political or territorial boundary. The Conference expresses its conviction that the execution of the provisions set out in the present declaration and in the Agreement on the cessation of hostilities creates the necessary basis for the achievement in the near future of a political settlement in Viet Nam.

7. The Conference declares that, so far as Viet Nam is concerned, the settlement of political problems, effected on the basis of respect for the principles of independence, unity and territorial integrity, shall permit the Vietnamese people to enjoy the fundamental freedoms, guaranteed by democratic institutions established as a result of free general elections by secret ballot. In order to ensure that sufficient progress in the restoration of peace has been made, and that all the necessary conditions obtain for free expression of the national will, general elections shall be held in July 1956, under the supervision of an international commission composed of representatives of the member states of the International Supervisory Commission, referred to in the Agreement on the cessation of hostilities. Consultations will be held on this subject between the competent representative authorities of the two zones from 20th July, 1955, onwards.

8. The provisions of the Agreement on the cessation of hostilities intended to ensure the protection of individuals and of property must be most strictly applied and must, in particular, allow everyone in Viet Nam to decide freely in which zone he wishes to live.

9. The competent representative authorities of the Northern and Southern zones of Viet Nam, as well as the authorities of Laos and Cambodia, must not permit any individual or collective reprisals against persons who have collaborated in any way with one of the parties during the war, or against members of such persons' families.

10. The Conference takes note of the declaration of the Government of the French Republic to the effect that it is ready to withdraw its troops from the territory of Cambodia, Laos and Viet Nam, at the request of the governments concerned and within periods which shall be fixed by agreement between the parties except in the cases where, by agreement between the two parties, a certain number of French troops shall remain at specified points and for a specified time.

11. The Conference takes note of the declaration of the French Government to the effect that for the settlement of all the problems connected with the re-establishment and consolidation of peace in Cambodia, Laos and Viet Nam, the French Government will proceed from the principle of respect for the independence and sovereignty, unity and territorial integrity of Cambodia, Laos and Viet Nam.

12. In their relations with Cambodia, Laos and Viet Nam, each member of the Geneva Conference undertakes to respect the sovereignty, the independence, the unity and the territorial integrity of the above-mentioned states, and to refrain from any interference in their internal affairs.

13. The members of the Conference agree to consult one another on any question which may be referred to them by the International Supervisory Commission, in order to study such measures as may prove necessary to ensure that the Agreements on the cessation of hostilities in Cambodia, Laos and Viet Nam are respected.

UNITED STATES DECLARATION ON INDOCHINA [7]

Statement made by Under Secretary of State Walter B. Smith at the concluding Indochina plenary session at Geneva, July 21, 1954

As I stated on July 18, my Government is not prepared to join in a declaration by the Conference such as is submitted. However, the United States makes this unilateral declaration of its position in these matters:

Declaration

The Government of the United States being resolved to devote its effort to the strengthening of peace in accordance with the principles and purposes of the United Nations takes note of the agreements concluded at Geneva on July 20 and 21, 1954 between (a) the Franco-Laotian Command and the Command of the Peoples Army of Viet-Nam; (b) the Royal Khmer Army Command and the Command of the Peoples Army of Viet-Nam; (c) Franco-Vietnamese Command and the Command of the Peoples Army of Viet-Nam and of paragraphs 1 to 12 inclusive of the declaration presented to the Geneva Conference on July 21, 1954 declares with regard to the aforesaid agreements and paragraphs that (i) it will refrain from the threat or the use of force to disturb them, in accordance with Article 2 (4) of the Charter of the United Nations dealing with the obligation of members to refrain in their international relations from the threat or use of force; and (ii) it would view any renewal of the aggression in violation of the aforesaid agreements with grave concern and as seriously threatening international peace and security.

In connection with the statement in the declaration concerning free elections in Viet-Nam my Government wishes to make clear its position which it has expressed in a declaration made in Washington on June 29, 1954, as follows:

> In the case of nations now divided against their will, we shall continue to seek to achieve unity through free elections supervised by the United Nations to insure that they are conducted fairly.

With respect to the statement made by the representative of the State of Viet-Nam, the United States reiterates its traditional position that peoples are entitled to determine their own future and that it will not join in an arrangement which would hinder this. Nothing in its declaration just made is intended to or does indicate any departure from this traditional position.

[7] 31 Dept. of State Bulletin 162 (1954).

We share the hope that the agreements will permit Cambodia, Laos and Viet-Nam to play their part, in full independence and sovereignty, in the peaceful community of nations, and will enable the peoples of that area to determine their own future.

SOUTHEAST ASIA COLLECTIVE DEFENSE TREATY [8]

*Signed at Manila, September 8, 1954; entered into force as to the
United States, February 19, 1955*

The parties to this Treaty,

Recognizing the sovereign equality of all the parties,

Reiterating their faith in the purposes and principles set forth in the
Charter of the United Nations and their desire to live in peace with all
peoples and all governments,

Reaffirming that, in accordance with the Charter of the United Nations,
they uphold the principle of equal rights and self-determination of peoples,
and declaring that they will earnestly strive by every peaceful means to
promote self-government and to secure the independence of all countries
whose peoples desire it and are able to undertake its responsibilities,

Desiring to strengthen the fabric of peace and freedom and to uphold the
principles of democracy, individual liberty and the rule of law, and to
promote the economic well-being and development of all peoples in the
treaty area,

Intending to declare publicly and formally their sense of unity, so that
any potential aggressor will appreciate that the parties stand together in
the area, and

Desiring further to coordinate their efforts for collective defense for the
preservation of peace and security,

Therefore agree as follows:

ARTICLE I

The parties undertake, as set forth in the Charter of the United Nations,
to settle any international disputes in which they may be involved by
peaceful means in such a manner that international peace and security and
justice are not endangered, and to refrain in their international relations
from the threat or use of force in any manner inconsistent with the purposes of the United Nations.

ARTICLE II

In order more effectively to achieve the objectives of this Treaty, the
parties, separately and jointly, by means of continuous and effective self-

[8] 6 U.S. Treaties 81, T.I.A.S., No. 3170, 209 U.N. Treaty Series 28.   The parties to
the treaty are Australia, France, New Zealand, Pakistan, Philippines, Thailand, the
United Kingdom, and the United States.

help and mutual aid will maintain and develop their individual and collective capacity to resist armed attack and to prevent and counter subversive activities directed from without against their territorial integrity and political stability.

ARTICLE III

The parties undertake to strengthen their free institutions and to cooperate with one another in the further development of economic measures, including technical assistance, designed both to promote economic progress and social well-being and to further the individual and collective efforts of governments toward these ends.

ARTICLE IV

1. Each party recognizes that aggression by means of armed attack in the treaty area against any of the parties or against any state or territory which the parties by unanimous agreement may hereafter designate, would endanger its own peace and safety, and agrees that it will in that event act to meet the common danger in accordance with its constitutional processes. Measures taken under this paragraph shall be immediately reported to the Security Council of the United Nations.

2. If, in the opinion of any of the parties, the inviolability or the integrity of the territory or the sovereignty or political independence of any party in the treaty area or of any other state or territory to which the provisions of paragraph 1 of this article from time to time apply is threatened in any way other than by armed attack or is affected or threatened by any fact or situation which might endanger the peace of the area, the Parties shall consult immediately in order to agree on the measures which should be taken for the common defense.

3. It is understood that no action on the territory of any state designated by unanimous agreement under paragraph 1 of this article or on any territory so designated shall be taken except at the invitation or with the consent of the government concerned.

ARTICLE V

The parties hereby establish a Council, on which each of them shall be represented, to consider matters concerning the implementation of this Treaty. The Council shall provide for consultation with regard to military and any other planning as the situation obtaining in the treaty area may from time to time require. The Council shall be so organized as to be able to meet at any time.

ARTICLE VI

This Treaty does not affect and shall not be interpreted as affecting in any way the rights and obligations of any of the parties under the Charter of the United Nations or the responsibility of the United Nations for the maintenance of international peace and security. Each party declares that none of the international engagements now in force between it and any other of the parties or any third party is in conflict with the provisions of this Treaty, and undertakes not to enter into any international engagement in conflict with this Treaty.

ARTICLE VII

Any other state in a position to further the objectives of this Treaty and to contribute to the security of the area may, by unanimous agreement of the parties, be invited to accede to this Treaty. Any state so invited may become a party to the Treaty by depositing its instrument of accession with the Government of the Republic of the Philippines. The Government of the Republic of the Philippines shall inform each of the parties of the deposit of each such instrument of accession.

ARTICLE VIII

As used in this Treaty, the "treaty area" is the general area of Southeast Asia, including also the entire territories of the Asian parties, and the general area of the Southwest Pacific not including the Pacific area north of 21 degrees 30 minutes north latitude. The parties may, by unanimous agreement, amend this article to include within the treaty area the territory of any state acceding to this Treaty in accordance with Article VII or otherwise to change the treaty area.

ARTICLE IX

1. This Treaty shall be deposited in the archives of the Government of the Republic of the Philippines. Duly certified copies thereof shall be transmitted by that government to the other signatories.

2. The Treaty shall be ratified and its provisions carried out by the parties in accordance with their respective constitutional processes. The instruments of ratification shall be deposited as soon as possible with the Government of the Republic of the Philippines, which shall notify all of the other signatories of such deposit.

3. The Treaty shall enter into force between the states which have ratified it as soon as the instruments of ratification of a majority of the signatories shall have been deposited, and shall come into effect with respect to each other state on the date of the deposit of its instrument of ratification.

ARTICLE X

This Treaty shall remain in force indefinitely, but any party may cease to be a party one year after its notice of denunciation has been given to the Government of the Republic of the Philippines, which shall inform the governments of the other parties of the deposit of each notice of denunciation.

ARTICLE XI

The English text of this Treaty is binding on the parties, but when the parties have agreed to the French text thereof and have so notified the Government of the Republic of the Philippines, the French text shall be equally authentic and binding on the Parties.

UNDERSTANDING OF THE UNITED STATES OF AMERICA

The United States of America in executing the present Treaty does so with the understanding that its recognition of the effect of aggression and armed attack and its agreement with reference thereto in Article IV, paragraph 1 apply only to communist aggression but affirms that in the event of other aggression or armed attack it will consult under the provisions of Article IV, paragraph 2.

In witness whereof, the undersigned Plenipotentiaries have signed this Treaty.[9]

Done at Manila, this eighth day of September, 1954.

PROTOCOL TO THE SOUTHEAST ASIA COLLECTIVE DEFENSE TREATY [10]

*Signed at Manila, September 8, 1954; entered into force
as to the United States, February 19, 1955*

Designation of States and Territory as to which Provisions of
Article IV and Article III Are To Be Applicable

The parties to the Southeast Asia Collective Defense Treaty unanimously designate for the purposes of Article IV of the Treaty the states of Cambodia and Laos and the free territory under the jurisdiction of the state of Vietnam.

The parties further agree that the above mentioned states and territory shall be eligible in respect of the economic measures contemplated by Article III.

This Protocol shall enter into force simultaneously with the coming into force of the Treaty.

IN WITNESS WHEREOF, the undersigned Plenipotentiaries have signed this Protocol to the Southeast Asia Collective Defense Treaty.[11]

Done at Manila, this eighth day of September, 1954.

9 Signatures not reproduced.
10 6 U.S. Treaties 87, T.I.A.S., No. 3170, 209 U.N. Treaty Series 36.
11 Signatures not reproduced.

DECLARATION ON THE NEUTRALITY OF LAOS

The Governments of the Union of Burma, the Kingdom of Cambodia, Canada, the People's Republic of China, the Democratic Republic of Viet-Nam, the Republic of France, the Republic of India, the Polish People's Republic, the Republic of Viet-Nam, the Kingdom of Thailand, the Union of Soviet Socialist Republics, the United Kingdom of Great Britain and Northern Ireland and the United States of America, whose representatives took part in the International Conference on the Settlement of the Laotian Question, 1961–1962;

Welcoming the presentation of the statement of neutrality by the Royal Government of Laos of July 9, 1962, and taking note of this statement, which is, with the concurrence of the Royal Government of Laos, incorporated in the present Declaration as an integral part thereof, and the text of which is as follows:

THE ROYAL GOVERNMENT OF LAOS,

Being resolved to follow the path of peace and neutrality in conformity with the interests and aspirations of the Laotian people, as well as the principles of the Joint Communiqué of Zurich dated June 22, 1961, and of the Geneva Agreements of 1954,[1] in order to build a peaceful, neutral, independent, democratic, unified and prosperous Laos,
Solemnly declares that:

(1) It will resolutely apply the five principles of peaceful co-existence in foreign relations, and will develop friendly relations and establish diplomatic relations with all countries, the neighbouring countries first and foremost, on the basis of equality and of respect for the independence and sovereignty of Laos;

(2) It is the will of the Laotian people to protect and ensure respect for the sovereignty, independence, neutrality, unity, and territorial integrity of Laos;

(3) It will not resort to the use or threat of force in any way which might impair the peace of other countries, and will not interfere in the internal affairs of other countries;

(4) It will not enter into any military alliance or into any agreement, whether military or otherwise, which is inconsistent with the neutrality of the Kingdom of Laos; it will not allow the establishment of any foreign military base on Laotian territory, nor allow any country to use Laotian territory for military purposes or for the purposes of interference in the internal affairs of other countries, nor recognise the protection of any alliance or military coalition, including SEATO.[2]

(5) It will not allow any foreign interference in the internal affairs of the Kingdom of Laos in any form whatsoever;

(6) Subject to the provisions of Article 5 of the Protocol, it will require the withdrawal from Laos of all foreign troops and military personnel, and will not allow any foreign troops or military personnel to be introduced into Laos;

---

[1] For texts, see *American Foreign Policy, 1950–1955: Basic Documents*, vol. I, Department of State publication 6446, p. 775.
[2] Southeast Asia Treaty Organization.

(7) It will accept direct and unconditional aid from all countries that wish to help the Kingdom of Laos build up an independent and autonomous national economy on the basis of respect for the sovereignty of Laos;

(8) It will respect the treaties and agreements signed in conformity with the interests of the Laotian people and of the policy of peace and neutrality of the Kingdom, in particular the Geneva Agreements of 1962, and will abrogate all treaties and agreements which are contrary to those principles.

This statement of neutrality by the Royal Government of Laos shall be promulgated constitutionally and shall have the force of law.

The Kingdom of Laos appeals to all the States participating in the International Conference on the Settlement of the Laotian Question, and to all other States, to recognise the sovereignty, independence, neutrality, unity and territorial integrity of Laos, to conform to these principles in all respects, and to refrain from any action inconsistent therewith.

Confirming the principles of respect for the sovereignty, independence, unity and territorial integrity of the Kingdom of Laos and non-interference in its internal affairs which are embodied in the Geneva Agreements of 1954;

Emphasising the principle of respect for the neutrality of the Kingdom of Laos;

Agreeing that the above-mentioned principles constitute a basis for the peaceful settlement of the Laotian question;

Profoundly convinced that the independence and neutrality of the Kingdom of Laos will assist the peaceful democratic development of the Kingdom of Laos and the achievement of national accord and unity in that country, as well as the strengthening of peace and security in South-East Asia;

1. Solemnly declare, in accordance with the will of the Government and people of the Kingdom of Laos, as expressed in the statement of neutrality by the Royal Government of Laos of July 9, 1962, that they recognise and will respect and observe in every way the sovereignty, independence, neutrality, unity and territorial integrity of the Kingdom of Laos.

2. Undertake, in particular, that

(a) they will not commit or participate in any way in any act which might directly or indirectly impair the sovereignty, independence, neutrality, unity or territorial integrity of the Kingdom of Laos;

(b) they will not resort to the use or threat of force or any other measure which might impair the peace of the Kingdom of Laos;

(c) they will refrain from all direct or indirect interference in the internal affairs of the Kingdom of Laos;

(d) they will not attach conditions of a political nature to any assistance which they may offer or which the Kingdom of Laos may seek;

(e) they will not bring the Kingdom of Laos in any way into any military alliance or any other agreement, whether military or otherwise, which is inconsistent with her neutrality, nor invite or encourage her to enter into any such alliance or to conclude any such agreement;

(*f*) they will respect the wish of the Kingdom of Laos not to recognise the protection of any alliance or military coalition, including SEATO;

(*g*) they will not introduce into the Kingdom of Laos foreign troops or military personnel in any form whatsoever, nor will they in any way facilitate or connive at the introduction of any foreign troops or military personnel;

(*h*) they will not establish nor will they in any way facilitate or connive at the establishment in the Kingdom of Laos of any foreign military base, foreign strong point or other foreign military installation of any kind;

(*i*) they will not use the territory of the Kingdom of Laos for interference in the internal affairs of other countries;

(*j*) they will not use the territory of any country, including their own for interference in the internal affairs of the Kingdom of Laos.

3. Appeal to all other States to recognise, respect and observe in every way the sovereignty, independence and neutrality, and also the unity and territorial integrity, of the Kingdom of Laos and to refrain from any action inconsistent with these principles or with other provisions of the present Declaration.

4. Undertake, in the event of a violation or threat of violation of the sovereignty, independence, neutrality, unity or territorial integrity of the Kingdom of Laos, to consult jointly with the Royal Government of Laos and among themselves in order to consider measures which might prove to be necessary to ensure the observance of these principles and the other provisions of the present Declaration.

5. The present Declaration shall enter into force on signature and together with the statement of neutrality by the Royal Government of Laos of July 9, 1962, shall be regarded as constituting an international agreement. The present Declaration shall be deposited in the archives of the Governments of the United Kingdom and the Union of Soviet Socialist Republics, which shall furnish certified copies thereof to the other signatory States and to all the other States of the world.

In witness whereof, the undersigned Plenipotentiaries have signed the present Declaration.

Done in two copies in Geneva this twenty-third day of July one thousand nine hundred and sixty-two in the English, Chinese, French, Laotian and Russian languages, each text being equally authoritative.

PROTOCOL TO THE DECLARATION ON THE NEUTRALITY OF LAOS

The Governments of the Union of Burma, the Kingdom of Cambodia, Canada, the People's Republic of China, the Democratic Republic of Viet-Nam, the Republic of France, the Republic of India, the Kingdom of Laos, the Polish People's Republic, the Republic of Viet-Nam, the Kingdom of Thailand, the Union of Soviet Socialist Republics, the United Kingdom of Great Britain and Northern Ireland and the United States of America;

Having regard to the Declaration on the Neutrality of Laos of July 23, 1962;

Have agreed as follows:

ARTICLE 1

For the purposes of this Protocol

(a) the term "foreign military personnel" shall include members of foreign military missions, foreign military advisers, experts, instructors, consultants, technicians, observers and any other foreign military persons, including those serving in any armed forces in Laos, and foreign civilians connected with the supply, maintenance, storing and utilization of war materials;

(b) the term "the Commission" shall mean the International Commission for Supervision and Control in Laos set up by virtue of the Geneva Agreements of 1954 and composed of the representatives of Canada, India and Poland, with the representative of India as Chairman;

(c) the term "the Co-Chairmen" shall mean the Co-Chairmen of the International Conference for the Settlement of the Laotian Question, 1961–1962, and their successors in the offices of Her Britannic Majesty's Principal Secretary of State for Foreign Affairs and Minister for Foreign Affairs of the Union of Soviet Socialist Republics respectively;

(d) the term "the members of the Conference" shall mean the Governments of countries which took part in the International Conference for the Settlement of the Laotian Question, 1961–1962.

ARTICLE 2

All foreign regular and irregular troops, foreign para-military formations and foreign military personnel shall be withdrawn from Laos in the shortest time possible and in any case the withdrawal shall be completed not later than thirty days after the Commission has notified the Royal Government of Laos that in accordance with Articles 3 and 10 of this Protocol its inspection teams are present at all points of withdrawal from Laos. These points shall be determined by the Royal Government of Laos in accordance with Article 3 within thirty days after the entry into force of this Protocol. The inspection teams shall be present at these points and the Commission shall notify the Royal Government of Laos thereof within fifteen days after the points have been determined.

ARTICLE 3

The withdrawal of foreign regular and irregular troops, foreign paramilitary formations and foreign military personnel shall take place only along such routes and through such points as shall be determined by the Royal Government of Laos in consultation with the Commission. The Commission shall be notified in advance of the point and time of all such withdrawals.

ARTICLE 4

The introduction of foreign regular and irregular troops, foreign paramilitary formations and foreign military personnel into Laos is prohibited.

ARTICLE 5

Note is taken that the French and Laotian Governments will conclude as soon as possible an arrangement to transfer the French military installations in Laos to the Royal Government of Laos.

If the Laotian Government considers it necessary, the French Government may as an exception leave in Laos for a limited period of time a precisely limited number of French military instructors for the purpose of training the armed forces of Laos.

The French and Laotian Governments shall inform the members of the Conference, through the Co-Chairmen, of their agreement on the question of the transfer of the French military installations in Laos and of the employment of French military instructors by the Laotian Government.

ARTICLE 6

The introduction into Laos of armaments, munitions and war material generally, except such quantities of conventional armaments as the Royal Government of Laos may consider necessary for the national defence of Laos, is prohibited.

ARTICLE 7

All foreign military persons and civilians captured or interned during the course of hostilities in Laos shall be released within thirty days after the entry into force of this Protocol and handed over by the Royal Government of Laos to the representatives of the Governments of the countries of which they are nationals in order that they may proceed to the destination of their choice.

ARTICLE 8

The Co-Chairmen shall periodically receive reports from the Commission. In addition the Commission shall immediately report to the Co-Chairmen any violations or threats of violations of this Protocol, all significant steps which it takes in pursuance of this Protocol, and also any other important information which may assist the Co-Chairmen in carrying out their functions. The Commission may at any time seek help from the Co-Chairmen in the performance of its duties, and the Co-Chairmen may at any time make recommendations to the Commission exercising general guidance.

The Co-Chairmen shall circulate the reports and any other important information from the Commission to the members of the Conference.

The Co-Chairmen shall exercise supervision over the observance of this Protocol and the Declaration on the Neutrality of Laos.

The Co-Chairmen will keep the members of the Conference constantly informed and when appropriate will consult with them.

ARTICLE 9

The Commission shall, with the concurrence of the Royal Government of Laos, supervise and control the cease-fire in Laos.

The Commission shall exercise these functions in full co-operation with the Royal Government of Laos and within the framework of the Cease-Fire Agreement or cease-fire arrangements made by the three political forces in Laos, or the Royal Government of Laos. It is understood that responsibility for the execution of the cease-fire shall rest with the three parties concerned and with the Royal Government of Laos after its formation.

ARTICLE 10

The Commission shall supervise and control the withdrawal of foreign regular and irregular troops, foreign para-military formations and foreign military personnel. Inspection teams sent by the Commission for these purposes shall be present for the period of the withdrawal at all points of withdrawal from Laos determined by the Royal Government of Laos in consultation with the Commission in accordance with Article 3 of this Protocol.

ARTICLE 11

The Commission shall investigate cases where there are reasonable grounds for considering that a violation of the provisions of Article 4 of this Protocol has occurred.

It is understood that in the exercise of this function the Commission is acting with the concurrence of the Royal Government of Laos. It shall carry out its investigations in full co-operation with the Royal Government of Laos and shall immediately inform the Co-Chairmen of any violations or threats of violations of Article 4, and also of all significant steps which it takes in pursuance of this Article in accordance with Article 8.

ARTICLE 12

The Commission shall assist the Royal Government of Laos in cases where the Royal Government of Laos considers that a violation of Article 6 of this Protocol may have taken place. This assistance will be rendered at the request of the Royal Government of Laos and in full co-operation with it.

ARTICLE 13

The Commission shall exercise its functions under this Protocol in close co-operation with the Royal Government of Laos. It is understood that the Royal Government of Laos at all levels will render the Commission all possible assistance in the performance by the Commission of these functions and also will take all necessary measures to ensure the security of the Commission and its inspection teams during their activities in Laos.

ARTICLE 14

The Commission functions as a single organ of the International Conference for the Settlement of the Laotian Question, 1961–1962. The members of the Commission will work harmoniously and in co-operation with each other with the aim of solving all questions within the terms of reference of the Commission.

Decisions of the Commission on questions relating to violations of Articles 2, 3, 4 and 6 of this Protocol or of the cease-fire referred to in Article 9, conclusions on major questions sent to the Co-Chairmen and all recommendations by the Commission shall be adopted unanimously. On other questions, including procedural questions, and also questions relating to the initiation and carrying out of investigations (Article 15), decisions of the Commission shall be adopted by majority vote.

ARTICLE 15

In the exercise of its specific functions which are laid down in the relevant articles of this Protocol the Commission shall conduct investigations (directly or by sending inspection teams), when there are reasonable grounds for considering that a violation has occurred. These investigations shall be carried out at the request of the Royal Government of Laos or on the initiative of the Commission, which is acting with the concurrence of the Royal Government of Laos.

In the latter case decisions on initiating and carrying out such investigations shall be taken in the Commission by majority vote.

The Commission shall submit agreed reports on investigations in which differences which may emerge between members of the Commission on particular questions may be expressed.

The conclusions and recommendations of the Commission resulting from investigations shall be adopted unanimously.

ARTICLE 16

For the exercise of its functions the Commission shall, as necessary, set up inspection teams, on which the three member-States of the Commission shall be equally represented. Each member-State of the Commission shall ensure the presence of its own representatives both on the Commission and on the inspection teams, and shall promptly replace them in the event of their being unable to perform their duties.

It is understood that the dispatch of inspection teams to carry out various specific tasks takes place with the concurrence of the Royal Government of Laos. The points to which the Commission and its inspection teams go for the purposes of investigation and their length of stay at those points shall be determined in relation to the requirements of the particular investigation.

ARTICLE 17

The Commission shall have at its disposal the means of communication and transport required for the performance of its duties. These as a rule will be provided to the Commission by the Royal Government of Laos for payment on mutually acceptable terms, and those which the Royal Government of Laos cannot provide will be acquired by the Commission from other sources. It is understood that the means of communication and transport will be under the administrative control of the Commission.

ARTICLE 18

The costs of the operations of the Commission shall be borne by the members of the Conference in accordance with the provisions of this Article.

(a) The Governments of Canada, India and Poland shall pay the personal salaries and allowances of their nationals who are members of their delegations to the Commission and its subsidiary organs.

(b) The primary responsibility for the provision of accommodation for the Commission and its subsidiary organs shall rest with the Royal Government of Laos, which shall also provide such other local services as may be appropriate. The Commission shall charge to the Fund referred to in sub-paragraph (c) below any local expenses not borne by the Royal Government of Laos.

(c) All other capital or running expenses incurred by the Commission in the exercise of its functions shall be met from a Fund to which all the members of the Conference shall contribute in the following proportions:

The Governments of the People's Republic of China, France, the Union of Soviet Socialist Republics, the United Kingdom and the United States of America shall contribute 17·6 per cent each.

The Governments of Burma, Cambodia, the Democratic Republic of Viet Nam, Laos, the Republic of Viet Nam and Thailand shall contribute 1·5 per cent each.

The Governments of Canada, India and Poland as members of the Commission shall contribute 1 per cent each.

ARTICLE 19

The Co-Chairmen shall at any time, if the Royal Government of Laos so requests, and in any case not later than three years after the entry into force of this Protocol, present a report with appropriate recommendations on the question of the termination of the Commission to the members of the Conference for their consideration. Before making such a report the Co-Chairmen shall hold consultations with the Royal Government of Laos and the Commission.

ARTICLE 20

This Protocol shall enter into force on signature.

It shall be deposited in the archives of the Governments of the United Kingdom and the Union of Soviet Socialist Republics, which shall furnish certified copies thereof to the other signatory States and to all other States of the world.

In witness whereof, the undersigned Plenipotentiaries have signed this Protocol.

Done in two copies in Geneva this twenty-third day of July one thousand and nine hundred and sixty-two in the English, Chinese, French, Laotian and Russian languages, each text being equally authoritative.

Security Council Hears U.S. Charge of
North Vietnamese Attacks:

Statement by Adlai E. Stevenson, U.S. Representative
in the Security Council, August 5, 1964[1]

I HAVE asked for this urgent meeting to bring to the attention of the Security Council acts of deliberate aggression by the Hanoi regime against naval units of the United States.

Naval vessels of my Government, on routine operations in international waters in the Gulf of Tonkin, have been subjected to deliberate and repeated armed attacks. We therefore have found it necessary to take defensive measures.

The major facts about these incidents were announced last night by the President of the United States and communicated to other governments at the same time I was instructed to request this meeting. I shall recount these facts for you, Mr. President, in chronological order so that all the members may have all the information available to my Government.

At 8:08 a.m. Greenwich meridian time, August 2, 1964, the United States destroyer *Maddox* was on routine patrol in international waters in the Gulf of Tonkin, proceeding in a southeasterly direction away from the coast about 30 miles at sea from the mainland of North Viet-Nam. The *Maddox* was approached by three high-speed North Vietnamese torpedo boats in attack formation. When it was evident that these torpedo boats intended to take offensive action, the *Maddox*, in accordance with naval practice, fired three warning shots across the bows of the approaching vessels. At approximately the same time, the aircraft carrier *Ticonderoga*, which was also in international waters and had been alerted to the impending attack, sent out four aircraft to provide cover for the *Maddox*, the pilots being under orders not to fire unless they or the *Maddox* were fired upon first.

Two of the attacking craft fired torpedoes, which the *Maddox* evaded by changing course. All three attacking vessels directed machine gun fire at the *Maddox*. One of the attacking vessels approached for close attack and was struck by fire from the *Maddox*. After the attack was broken off, the *Maddox* continued on a southerly course in international waters.

Now, Mr. President, clearly this was a deliberate armed attack against

1 Department of State *Bulletin*, Aug. 24, 1964, pp. 272-274.

a naval unit of the United States Government on patrol in the high seas —almost 30 miles off the mainland. Nevertheless, my Government did its utmost to minimize the explosive potential of this flagrant attack in the hopes that this might be an isolated or uncalculated action. There was local defensive fire. The United States was not drawn into hasty response.

On August 3 the United States took steps to convey to the Hanoi regime a note calling attention to this aggression, stating that United States ships would continue to operate freely on the high seas in accordance with the rights guaranteed by international law, and warning the authorities in Hanoi of the "grave consequences which would inevitably result from any further unprovoked offensive military action against United States forces." This notification was in accordance with the provisions of the Geneva accords.

Our hopes that this was an isolated incident did not last long. At 2:35 p.m. Greenwich meridian time, August 4, when it was nighttime in the Gulf of Tonkin, the destroyers *Maddox* and *C. Turner Joy* were again subjected to an armed attack by an undetermined number of motor torpedo boats of the North Vietnamese navy. This time the American vessels were 65 miles from shore, twice as far out on the high seas as on the occasion of the previous attack. This time numerous torpedoes were fired. That attack lasted for over 2 hours.

There no longer could be any shadow of doubt that this was a planned, deliberate military aggression against vessels lawfully present in international waters. One could only conclude that this was the work of authorities dedicated to the use of force to achieve their objectives, regardless of the consequences.

My Government therefore determined to take positive but limited and relevant measures to secure its naval units against further aggression. Last night aerial strikes were thus carried out against North Vietnamese torpedo boats and their support facilities. This action was limited in scale, its only targets being the weapons and facilities against which we had been forced to defend ourselves. Our fervent hope is that the point has now been made that acts of armed aggression are not to be tolerated in the Gulf of Tonkin any more than they are to be tolerated anywhere else.

I want to emphasize that the action we have taken is a limited and measured response, fitted precisely to the attack that produced it, and that the deployments of additional U.S. forces to Southeast Asia are designed solely to deter further aggression. This is a single action designed to make unmistakably clear that the United States cannot be diverted by military attack from its obligations to help its friends establish and protect their independence. Our naval units are continuing their routine patrolling on the high seas with orders to protect themselves with all appropriate means against any further aggression. As President Johnson said last night, "We still seek no wider war."

Mr. President, let me repeat that the United States vessels were in international waters when they were attacked.

Let me repeat that freedom of the seas is guaranteed under long-accepted international law applying to all nations alike.

Let me repeat that these vessels took no belligerent actions of any kind until they were subject to armed attack.

And let me say once more that the action they took in self-defense is the right of all nations and is fully within the provisions of the Charter of the United Nations.

The acts of aggression by the North Vietnamese in the Gulf of Tonkin make no sense whatsoever standing alone. They defy rational explanation except as part of a larger pattern with a larger purpose. As isolated events, the kidnapping of village officials in the Republic of South Viet-Nam makes no sense either. Neither does the burning of a schoolhouse—or the sabotage of an irrigation project—or the murder of a medical worker—or the random bomb thrown into a crowd of innocent people sitting in a cafe.

All these wanton acts of violence and destruction fit into the larger pattern of what has been going on in Southeast Asia for the past decade and a half. So does the arming of terrorist gangs in South Viet-Nam by the regimes in Hanoi and Peiping. So does the infiltration of armed personnel to make war against the legitimate government of that nation. So does the fighting in Laos—and all the acts of subversion—and all the propaganda—and the sabotage of the international machinery established to keep the peace by the Geneva agreements—and the deliberate, systematic, and flagrant violations of those agreements by two regimes which signed them and which by all tenets of decency, law, and civilized practice are bound by their provisions.

The attempt to sink United States destroyers in international waters is much more spectacular than the attempt to murder the mayor of a village in his bed at night. But they are both part of the pattern, and the pattern is designed to subjugate the people of Southeast Asia to an empire ruled by means of force of arms, of rule by terror, of expansion by violence.

Mr. President, it is only in this larger view that we can discuss intelligently the matter that we have brought to this Council.

In his statement last night, President Johnson concluded by emphasizing that the mission of the United States is peace. Under the explicit instructions of President Johnson, I want to repeat that assurance in the Security Council this afternoon: Our mission is peace.

We hoped that the peace settlement in 1954 would lead to peace in Viet-Nam. We hoped that that settlement, and the supplementary Geneva accords of 1962, would lead to peace in Laos. Communist governments have tried aggression before—and have failed. Each time the lesson has had to be learned anew.

We are dealing here with a regime that has not yet learned the lesson that aggression does not pay, cannot be sustained, and will always be thrown back by people who believe, as we do, that people want freedom and independence, not subjection and the role of satellite in a modern empire.

In Southeast Asia we want nothing more, and nothing less, than the assured and guaranteed independence of the peoples of the area. We are in Southeast Asia to help our friends preserve their own opportunity to be free of imported terror, alien assassination, managed by the North Viet-Nam Communists based in Hanoi and backed by the Chinese Communists from Peiping.

Two months ago, when we were discussing in this Council the problems created on the Cambodia-South Viet-Nam frontier by the Communist Viet Cong, I defined our peace aims in Southeast Asia. I repeat them today:

There is a very easy way to restore order in Southeast Asia. There is a very simple, safe way to bring about the end of United States military aid to the Republic of Viet-Nam.

Let all foreign troops withdraw from Laos. Let all states in that area make and abide by the simple decision to leave their neighbors alone. Stop the secret subversion of other people's independence. Stop the clandestine and illegal transit of national frontiers. Stop the export of revolution and the doctrine of violence. Stop the violations of the political agreements reached at Geneva for the future of Southeast Asia.

The people of Laos want to be left alone.

The people of Viet-Nam want to be left alone.

The people of Cambodia want to be left alone.

When their neighbors decide to leave them alone—as they must—there will be no fighting in Southeast Asia and no need for American advisers to leave their homes to help these people resist aggression. Any time that decision can be put in enforcible terms, my Government will be only too happy to put down the burden that we have been sharing

578

STATEMENT OF ADLAI STEVENSON TO SECURITY COUNCIL

with those determined to preserve their independence. Until such assurances are forthcoming, we shall stand for the independence of free peoples in Southeast Asia as we have elsewhere.

That is what I said to this Council in May. That is what I repeat to this Council in August.

When the political settlements freely negotiated at the conference tables in Geneva are enforced, the independence of Southeast Asia will be guaranteed. When the peace agreements reached long ago are made effective, peace will return to Southeast Asia and military power can be withdrawn.

Southeast Asia Resolution[1]

Whereas naval units of the Communist regime in Vietnam, in violation of the principles of the Charter of the United Nations and of international law, have deliberately and repeatedly attacked United States naval vessels lawfully present in international waters, and have thereby created a serious threat to international peace; and

Whereas these attacks are part of a deliberate and systematic campaign of aggression that the Communist regime in North Vietnam has been waging against its neighbors and the nations joined with them in the collective defense of their freedom; and

Whereas the United States is assisting the peoples of southeast Asia to protect their freedom and has no territorial, military or political ambitions in that area, but desires only that these peoples should be left in peace to work out their own destinies in their own way: Now, therefore, be it

Resolved by the Senate and House of Representatives of the United States of America in Congress assembled, That the Congress approves and supports the determination of the President, as Commander in Chief, to take all necessary measures to repel any armed attack against the forces of the United States and to prevent further aggression.

SEC. 2. The United States regards as vital to its national interest and to world peace the maintenance of international peace and security in southeast Asia. Consonant with the Constitution of the United States and the Charter of the United Nations and in accordance with its obligations under the Southeast Asia Collective Defense Treaty, the United States is, therefore, prepared, as the President determines, to take all necessary steps, including the use of armed force, to assist any member or protocol state of the Southeast Asia Collective Defense Treaty requesting assistance in defense of its freedom.

SEC. 3. This resolution shall expire when the President shall determine that the peace and security of the area is reasonably assured by international conditions created by action of the United Nations or otherwise, except that it may be terminated earlier by concurrent resolution of the Congress.

[1] Text of Public Law 88-408 (H.J. Res. 1145), 78 Stat. 384, approved Aug. 10, 1964.

Comparison of Resolutions Relating to the Maintenance of Peace and Security in Various Areas*

Southeast Asia	Cuba	Formosa	Middle East
Whereas naval units of the Communist regime in Viet-Nam, in violation of the Charter of the United Nations and of international law, have deliberately and repeatedly attacked U.S. naval vessels lawfully present in international waters, and have thereby created a serious threat to international peace; Whereas these attacks are part of a deliberate and systematic campaign of aggression that the Communist regime in North Viet-Nam has been waging against its neighbors and the nations joined with them in the collective defense of their freedom; Whereas the United States is assisting the peoples of Southeast Asia to protect their freedom and has no territorial, military or political ambitions in that area but desires only that they should be left in peace to work out their own destinies in their own way: Now, therefore, be it	Whereas President James Monroe, announcing the Monroe Doctrine in 1823, declared that the United States would consider any attempt on the part of European powers "to extend their system to any portion of this hemisphere as dangerous to our peace and safety"; and Whereas in the Rio Treaty of 1947 the parties agreed that "an armed attack by any State against an American State shall be considered as an attack against all the American States, and, consequently, each one of the said contracting parties undertakes to assist in meeting the attack in the exercise of the inherent right of individual or collective self-defense recognized by article 51 of the Charter of the United Nations"; and Whereas the Foreign Ministers of the Organization of American States at Punta del Este in January 1962 declared "The present Government of Cuba has identified itself with the principles of Marxist-Leninist ideol-	Whereas the primary purpose of the United States in its relations with all other nations, is to develop and sustain a just and enduring peace for all; and Whereas certain territories in the West Pacific under the jurisdiction of the Republic of China are now under armed attack, and threats and declarations have been and are being made by the Chinese Communists that such armed attack is in aid of and in preparation for armed attack on Formosa and the Pescadores; Whereas such armed attack if continued would gravely endanger the peace and security of the West Pacific area and particularly of Formosa and the Pescadores; and Whereas the secure possession by friendly governments of the Western Pacific Island chain, of which Formosa is a part, is essential to the vital interests of the United States and all friendly nations in or bordering upon the Pacific Ocean; and Whereas the President of the United	

* Committee on Foreign Relations, United States Senate, 89th Congress, 2d Session, Background Information Relating to Southeast Asia and Vietnam (2d revised edition), March 1966 Washington, U.S. Government Printing Office 1966.

Southeast Asia	Cuba	Formosa	Middle East

Cuba

ogy, has established a political, economic, and social system based on that doctrine, and accepts military assistance from continental Communist powers, including even the threat of military intervention in America on the part of the Soviet Union"; and

Whereas the international Communist movement has increasingly extended into Cuba its political, economic, and military sphere of influence: Now, therefore, be it

Formosa

States on Jan. 6, 1955, submitted to the Senate for its advice and consent to ratification a Mutual Defense Treaty between the United States of America and the Republic of China, which recognizes that an armed attack in the West Pacific area directed against territories, therein described, in the region of Formosa and the Pescadores, would be dangerous to the peace and safety of the parties to the treaty: Therefore be it

Southeast Asia

Resolved by the Senate and House of Representatives of the United States of America in Congress assembled, That the Congress approves and supports the determination of the President, as Commander-in-Chief, to take all necessary measures to repel any armed attack against the forces of the United States and to prevent further aggression.

Cuba

Resolved by the Senate and House of Representatives of the United States of America in Congress assembled, That the United States is determined—

(a) to prevent by whatever means may be necessary, including the use of arms, the Marxist-Leninist regime in Cuba from extending, by force or the threat of force, its aggressive or subversive activities to any part of this hemisphere;

(b) to prevent in Cuba the creation or use of an externally supported military capability endangering the security of the United States; and

(c) to work with the Organization of American States and with freedom-loving Cubans to support the aspirations of the

Formosa

Resolved by the Senate and House of Representatives of the United States of America in Congress assembled, That the President of the United States be and he hereby is authorized to employ the Armed Forces of the United States as he deems necessary for the specific purpose of securing and protecting Formosa and the Pescadores against armed attack, this authority to include the securing and protection of such related positions and territories of that area now in friendly hands and the taking of such other measures as he judges to be required or appropriate in assuring the defense of Formosa and the Pescadores.

Middle East

Resolved by the Senate and House of Representatives of the United States of America in Congress assembled, That the President be and hereby is authorized to cooperate with and assist any nation or group of nations in the general area of the Middle East desiring such assistance in the development of economic strength dedicated to the maintenance of national independence.

Southeast Asia	Cuba	Formosa	Middle East

Cuban people for self-determination.

Southeast Asia

Sec. 2. The United States regards as vital to its national interest and to world peace the maintenance of international peace and security in Southeast Asia. Consonant with the Constitution and the Charter of the United Nations and in accordance with its obligations under the Southeast Asia Collective Defense Treaty, the United States is, therefore, prepared, as the President determines, to take all necessary steps, including the use of armed force, to assist any protocol or member state of the Southeast Asia Collective Defense Treaty requesting assistance in defense of its freedom.

Middle East

Sec. 2. The President is authorized to undertake in the general area of the Middle East, military assistance programs with any nation or group of nations of that area desiring such assistance. Furthermore, the United States regards as vital to the national interest and world peace the preservation of the independence and integrity of the nations of the Middle East. To this end, if the President determines the necessity thereof, the United States is prepared to use armed forces to assist any nation or group of such nations requesting assistance a g a i n s t a r m e d aggression from any country controlled by international communism: *Provided,* That such employment shall be consonant with the treaty obligations of the United States and with the Constitution of the United States.

Southeast Asia

This resolution shall expire when the President shall determine that the peace and security of the area is reasonably assured by international conditions created by action of the United Nations or otherwise, and shall so report to the Congress, except that it may be terminated earlier by a concurrent resolution of the two Houses.

Formosa

This resolution shall expire when the President shall determine that the peace and security of the area is reasonably assured by international conditions created by action of the United Nations or otherwise, and shall so report to the Congress.

Middle East

This joint resolution shall expire when the President shall determine that the peace and security of the nations in the general area of the Middle East are reasonably assured by international conditions created by action of the United Nations or otherwise except that it may be terminated earlier by a concurrent resolution of the two Houses of Congress.

THE LEGALITY OF UNITED STATES PARTICIPATION IN THE DEFENSE OF VIET-NAM

MARCH 4, 1966

1. THE UNITED STATES AND SOUTH VIET-NAM HAVE THE RIGHT UNDER INTERNATIONAL LAW TO PARTICIPATE IN THE COLLECTIVE DEFENSE OF SOUTH VIET-NAM AGAINST ARMED ATTACK

In response to requests from the Government of South Viet-Nam, the United States has been assisting that country in defending itself against armed attack from the Communist North. This attack has taken the forms of externally supported subversion, clandestine supply of arms, infiltration of armed personnel, and most recently the sending of regular units of the North Vietnamese army into the South.

International law has long recognized the right of individual and collective self-defense against armed attack. South Viet-Nam and the United States are engaging in such collective defense consistently with international law and with United States obligations under the United Nations Charter.

A. South Viet-Nam Is Being Subjected to Armed Attack by Communist North Viet-Nam

The Geneva accords of 1954 established a demarcation line between North Viet-Nam and South Viet-Nam.[1] They provided for withdrawals of military forces into the respective zones north and south of this line. The accords prohibited the use of either zone for the resumption of hostilities or to "further an aggressive policy."

During the 5 years following the Geneva conference of 1954, the Hanoi regime developed a covert political-military organization in South Viet-Nam based on Communist cadres it had ordered to stay in the South, contrary to the provisions of the Geneva accords. The activities of this covert organization were directed toward the kidnaping and assassination of civilian officials—acts of terrorism that were perpetrated in increasing numbers.

In the 3-year period from 1959 to 1961, the North Viet-Nam regime infiltrated an estimated 10,000 men into the South. It is estimated that 13,000 additional personnel were infiltrated in 1962, and, by the end of 1964, North Viet-Nam may well have moved over 40,000 armed and unarmed guerrillas into South Viet-Nam.

The International Control Commission reported in 1962 the findings of its Legal Committee:

> . . . there is evidence to show that arms, armed and unarmed personnel, munitions and other supplies have been sent from the Zone in the North to the Zone in the South with the objective of supporting, organizing and carrying out hostile activities, including armed attacks, directed against the Armed Forces and Administration of the Zone in the South.
> . . . there is evidence that the PAVN [People's Army of Viet Nam] has allowed the Zone in the North to be used for inciting, encouraging

[1] For texts, see American Foreign Policy, 1950–1955; Basic Documents, Vol. I, Department of State publication 6446, p. 750. [See also pp. 629–646 below.—Ed.]

and supporting hostile activities in the Zone in the South, aimed at the overthrow of the Administration in the South.

Beginning in 1964, the Communists apparently exhausted their reservoir of Southerners who had gone North. Since then the greater number of men infiltrated into the South have been native-born North Vietnamese. Most recently, Hanoi has begun to infiltrate elements of the North Vietnamese army in increasingly larger numbers. Today, there is evidence that nine regiments of regular North Vietnamese forces are fighting in organized units in the South.

In the guerrilla war in Viet-Nam, the external aggression from the North is the critical military element of the insurgency, although it is unacknowledged by North Viet-Nam. In these circumstances, an "armed attack" is not as easily fixed by date and hour as in the case of traditional warfare. However, the infiltration of thousands of armed men clearly constitutes an "armed attack" under any reasonable definition. There may be some question as to the exact date at which North Viet-Nam's aggression grew into an "armed attack," but there can be no doubt that it had occurred before February 1965.

B. International Law Recognizes the Right of Individual and Collective Self-Defense Against Armed Attack

International law has traditionally recognized the right of self-defense against armed attack. This proposition has been asserted by writers on international law through the several centuries in which the modern law of nations has developed. The proposition has been acted on numerous times by governments throughout modern history. Today the principle of self-defense against armed attack is universally recognized and accepted.[2]

The Charter of the United Nations, concluded at the end of World War II, imposed an important limitation on the use of force by United Nations members. Article 2, paragraph 4, provides:

> All Members shall refrain in their international relations from the threat or use of force against the territorial integrity or political independence of any state, or in any other manner inconsistent with the Purposes of the United Nations.

In addition, the charter embodied a system of international peacekeeping through the organs of the United Nations. Article 24 summarizes these structural arrangements in stating that the United Nations members:

> . . . confer on the Security Council primary responsibility for the maintenance of international peace and security, and agree that in carrying out its duties under this responsibility the Security Council acts on their behalf.

However, the charter expressly states in article 51 that the remaining provisions of the charter—including the limitation of article 2, paragraph

---

[2] See, e.g., Jessup, A Modern Law of Nations, 163 ff. (1948); Oppenheim, International Law, 297 ff. (8th ed., Lauterpacht, 1955). And see, generally, Bowett, Self-Defense in International Law (1958). [Footnote in original.]

4, and the creation of United Nations machinery to keep the peace—in no way diminish the inherent right of self-defense against armed attack. Article 51 provides:

> Nothing in the present Charter shall impair the inherent right of individual or collective self-defense if an armed attack occurs against a Member of the United Nations, until the Security Council has taken the measures necessary to maintain international peace and security. Measures taken by Members in the exercise of this right of self-defense shall be immediately reported to the Security Council and shall not in any way affect the authority and responsibility of the Security Council under the present Charter to take at any time such action as it deems necessary in order to maintain or restore international peace and security.

Thus, article 51 restates and preserves, for member states in the situations covered by the article, a long-recognized principle of international law. The article is a ''saving clause'' designed to make clear that no other provision in the charter shall be interpreted to impair the inherent right of self-defense referred to in article 51.

Three principal objections have been raised against the availability of the right of individual and collective self-defense in the case of Viet-Nam: (1) that this right applies only in the case of an armed attack on a United Nations member; (2) that it does not apply in the case of South Viet-Nam because the latter is not an independent sovereign state; and (3) that collective self-defense may be undertaken only by a regional organization operating under chapter VIII of the United Nations Charter. These objections will now be considered in turn.

C. The Right of Individual and Collective Self-Defense Applies in the Case of South Viet-Nam Whether or Not That Country Is a Member of the United Nations

1. South Viet-Nam enjoys the right of self-defense

The argument that the right of self-defense is available only to members of the United Nations mistakes the nature of the right of self-defense and the relationship of the United Nations Charter to international law in this respect. As already shown, the right of self-defense against armed attack is an inherent right under international law. The right is not conferred by the charter, and, indeed, article 51 expressly recognizes that the right is inherent.

The charter nowhere contains any provision designed to deprive nonmembers of the right of self-defense against armed attack.[3] Article 2,

---

[3] While nonmembers, such as South Viet-Nam, have not formally undertaken the obligations of the United Nations Charter as their own treaty obligations, it should be recognized that much of the substantive law of the charter has become part of the general law of nations through a very wide acceptance by nations the world over. This is particularly true of the charter provisions bearing on the use of force. Moreover, in the case of South Viet-Nam, the South Vietnamese Government has expressed its ability and willingness to abide by the charter, in applying for United Nations membership. Thus it seems entirely appropriate to appraise the actions of South Viet-Nam in relation to the legal standards set forth in the United Nations Charter. [Footnote in original.]

paragraph 6, does charge the United Nations with responsibility for insuring that nonmember states act in accordance with United Nations "Principles so far as may be necessary for the maintenance of international peace and security." Protection against aggression and self-defense against armed attack are important elements in the whole charter scheme for the maintenance of international peace and security. To deprive nonmembers of their inherent right of self-defense would not accord with the principles of the organization, but would instead be prejudicial to the maintenance of peace. Thus article 2, paragraph 6—and, indeed, the rest of the charter —should certainly not be construed to nullify or diminish the inherent defensive rights of nonmembers.

2. The United States has the right to assist in the defense of South Viet-Nam although the latter is not a United Nations member

The cooperation of two or more international entities in the defense of one or both against armed attack is generally referred to as collective self-defense. United States participation in the defense of South Viet-Nam at the latter's request is an example of collective self-defense.

The United States is entitled to exercise the right of individual or collective self-defense against armed attack, as that right exists in international law, subject only to treaty limitations and obligations undertaken by this country.

It has been urged that the United States has no right to participate in the collective defense of South Viet-Nam because article 51 of the United Nations Charter speaks only of the situation "if an armed attack occurs *against a Member of the United Nations.*" This argument is without substance.

In the first place, article 51 does not impose restrictions or cut down the otherwise available rights of United Nations members. By its own terms, the article preserves an inherent right. It is, therefore, necessary to look elsewhere in the charter for any obligation of members restricting their participation in collective defense of an entity that is not a United Nations member.

Article 2, paragraph 4, is the principal provision of the charter imposing limitations on the use of force by members. It states that they:

> . . . shall refrain in their international relations from the threat or use of force against the territorial integrity or political independence of any state, or in any other manner inconsistent with the Purposes of the United Nations.

Action taken in defense against armed attack cannot be characterized as falling within this proscription. The record of the San Francisco conference makes clear that article 2, paragraph 4, was not intended to restrict the right of self-defense against armed attack.[4]

One will search in vain for any other provision in the charter that would preclude United States participation in the collective defense of a non-

[4] See 6 UNCIO Documents 459. [Footnote in original.]

member. The fact that article 51 refers only to armed attack "against a Member of the United Nations" implies no intention to preclude members from participating in the defense of nonmembers. Any such result would have seriously detrimental consequences for international peace and security and would be inconsistent with the purposes of the United Nations as they are set forth in article 1 of the charter.[5] The right of members to participate in the defense of nonmembers is upheld by leading authorities on international law.[6]

D. The Right of Individual and Collective Self-Defense Applies Whether or Not South Viet-Nam Is Regarded as an Independent Sovereign State

1. South Viet-Nam enjoys the right of self-defense

It has been asserted that the conflict in Viet-Nam is "civil strife" in which foreign intervention is forbidden. Those who make this assertion have gone so far as to compare Ho Chi Minh's actions in Viet-Nam with the efforts of President Lincoln to preserve the Union during the American Civil War. Any such characterization is an entire fiction disregarding the actual situation in Viet-Nam. The Hanoi regime is anything but the legitimate government of a unified country in which the South is rebelling against lawful national authority.

The Geneva accords of 1954 provided for a division of Viet-Nam into two zones at the 17th parallel. Although this line of demarcation was intended to be temporary, it was established by international agreement, which specifically forbade aggression by one zone against the other.

The Republic of Viet-Nam in the South has been recognized as a separate international entity by approximately 60 governments the world over. It has been admitted as a member of a number of the specialized agencies of the United Nations. The United Nations General Assembly in 1957 voted to recommend South Viet-Nam for membership in the organization, and its admission was frustrated only by the veto of the Soviet Union in the Security Council.

In any event there is no warrant for the suggestion that one zone of a temporarily divided state—whether it be Germany, Korea, or Viet-Nam— can be legally overrun by armed forces from the other zone, crossing the

---

[5] In particular, the statement of the first purpose:

To maintain international peace and security, and to that end: to take effective collective measures for the prevention and removal of threats to the peace, and for the suppression of acts of aggression or other breaches of the peace, and to bring about by peaceful means, and in conformity with the principles of justice and international law, adjustment or settlement of international disputes or situations which might lead to a breach of the peace. . . . [Footnote in original.]

[6] Bowett, Self-Defense in International Law, 193–195 (1958); Goodhart, "The North Atlantic Treaty of 1949," 79 Recueil Des Cours, 183, 202–204 (1951, vol. II), quoted in 5 Whiteman's Digest of International Law, 1067–1068 (1965); Kelsen, The Law of the United Nations, 793 (1950); see Stone, Aggression and World Order, 44 (1958). [Footnote in original.]

internationally recognized line of demarcation between the two.   Any such doctrine would subvert the international agreement establishing the line of demarcation, and would pose grave dangers to international peace.

The action of the United Nations in the Korean conflict of 1950 clearly established the principle that there is no greater license for one zone of a temporarily divided state to attack the other zone than there is for one state to attack another state.   South Viet-Nam has the same right that South Korea had to defend itself and to organize collective defense against an armed attack from the North.   A resolution of the Security Council dated June 25, 1950, noted "with grave concern the armed attack upon the Republic of Korea by forces from North Korea," and determined "that this action constitutes a breach of the peace."

2.   The United States is entitled to participate in the collective defense of South Viet-Nam whether or not the latter is regarded as an independent sovereign state

As stated earlier, South Viet-Nam has been recognized as a separate international entity by approximately 60 governments.   It has been admitted to membership in a number of the United Nations specialized agencies and has been excluded from the United Nations Organization only by the Soviet veto.

There is nothing in the charter to suggest that United Nations members are precluded from participating in the defense of a recognized international entity against armed attack merely because the entity may lack some of the attributes of an independent sovereign state.   Any such result would have a destructive effect on the stability of international engagements such as the Geneva accords of 1954 and on internationally agreed lines of demarcation. Such a result, far from being in accord with the charter and the purposes of the United Nations, would undermine them and would create new dangers to international peace and security.

E. The United Nations Charter Does Not Limit the Right of Self-Defense to Regional Organizations

Some have argued that collective self-defense may be undertaken only by a regional arrangement or agency operating under chapter VIII of the United Nations Charter.   Such an assertion ignores the structure of the charter and the practice followed in the more than 20 years since the founding of the United Nations.

The basic proposition that rights of self-defense are not impaired by the charter—as expressly stated in article 51—is not conditioned by any charter provision limiting the application of this proposition to collective defense by a regional arrangement or agency.   The structure of the charter reinforces this conclusion.   Article 51 appears in chapter VII of the charter, entitled "Action With Respect to Threats to the Peace, Breaches of the Peace, and Acts of Aggression," whereas chapter VIII, entitled "Regional Arrangements," begins with article 52 and embraces the two following articles.

The records of the San Francisco conference show that article 51 was deliberately placed in chapter VII rather than chapter VIII, "where it would only have a bearing on the regional system."[7]

Under article 51, the right of self-defense is available against any armed attack, whether or not the country attacked is a member of a regional arrangement and regardless of the source of the attack. Chapter VIII, on the other hand, deals with relations among members of a regional arrangement or agency, and authorizes regional action as appropriate for dealing with "local disputes." This distinction has been recognized ever since the founding of the United Nations in 1945.

For example, the North Atlantic Treaty has operated as a collective security arrangement, designed to take common measures in preparation against the eventuality of an armed attack for which collective defense under article 51 would be required. Similarly, the Southeast Asia Treaty Organization was designed as a collective defense arrangement under article 51. Secretary of State Dulles emphasized this in his testimony before the Senate Foreign Relations Committee in 1954.

By contrast, article 1 of the Charter of Bogotá (1948), establishing the Organization of American States, expressly declares that the organization is a regional agency within the United Nations. Indeed, chapter VIII of the United Nations Charter was included primarily to take account of the functioning of the inter-American system.

In sum, there is no basis in the United Nations Charter for contending that the right of self-defense against armed attack is limited to collective defense by a regional organization.

F. The United States Has Fulfilled Its Obligations to the United Nations

A further argument has been made that the members of the United Nations have conferred on United Nations organs—and, in particular, on the Security Council—exclusive power to act against aggression. Again, the express language of article 51 contradicts that assertion. A victim of armed attack is not required to forgo individual or collective defense of its territory until such time as the United Nations organizes collective action and takes appropriate measures. To the contrary, article 51 clearly states that the right of self-defense may be exercised "*until* the Security Council has taken the measures necessary to maintain international peace and security."[8]

[7] 17 UNCIO Documents 288. [Footnote in original.]

[8] An argument has been made by some that the United States, by joining in the collective defense of South Viet-Nam, has violated the peaceful settlement obligation of article 33 in the charter. This argument overlooks the obvious proposition that a victim of armed aggression is not required to sustain the attack undefended while efforts are made to find a political solution with the aggressor. Article 51 of the charter illustrates this by making perfectly clear that the inherent right of self-defense is impaired by "Nothing in the present Charter," including the provisions of article 33. [Footnote in original.]

As indicated earlier, article 51 is not literally applicable to the Viet-Nam situation since South Viet-Nam is not a member.   However, reasoning by analogy from article 51 and adopting its provisions as an appropriate guide for the conduct of members in a case like Viet-Nam, one can only conclude that United States actions are fully in accord with this country's obligations as a member of the United Nations.

Article 51 requires that:

> Measures taken by Members in the exercise of this right of self-defense shall be immediately reported to the Security Council and shall not in any way affect the authority and responsibility of the Security Council under the present Charter to take at any time such action as it deems necessary in order to maintain or restore international peace and security.

The United States has reported to the Security Council on measures it has taken in countering the Communist aggression in Viet-Nam.   In August 1964 the United States asked the Council to consider the situation created by North Vietnamese attacks on United States destroyers in the Tonkin Gulf.[9]   The Council thereafter met to debate the question, but adopted no resolutions.   Twice in February 1965 the United States sent additional reports to the Security Council on the conflict in Viet-Nam and on the additional measures taken by the United States in the collective defense of South Viet-Nam.[10]   In January 1966 the United States formally submitted the Viet-Nam question to the Security Council for its consideration and introduced a draft resolution calling for discussions looking toward a peaceful settlement on the basis of the Geneva accords.[11]

At no time has the Council taken any action to restore peace and security in Southeast Asia.   The Council has not expressed criticism of United States actions.   Indeed, since the United States submission of January 1966, members of the Council have been notably reluctant to proceed with any consideration of the Viet-Nam question.

The conclusion is clear that the United States has in no way acted to interfere with United Nations consideration of the conflict in Viet-Nam. On the contrary, the United States has requested United Nations consideration, and the Council has not seen fit to act.

G. International Law Does Not Require a Declaration of War as a Condition Precedent To Taking Measures of Self-Defense Against Armed Attack

The existence or absence of a formal declaration of war is not a factor in determining whether an international use of force is lawful as a matter of international law.   The United Nations Charter's restrictions focus on the manner and purpose of its use and not on any formalities of announcement. It should also be noted that a formal declaration of war would not place any

---

[9] For a statement made by U. S. Representative Adlai E. Stevenson in the Security Council on Aug. 5, 1964, see BULLETIN of Aug. 24, 1964, p. 272.

[10] For texts, see *ibid.*, Feb. 22, 1965, p. 240, and Mar. 22, 1965, p. 419.

[11] For background and text of draft resolution, see *ibid.*, Feb. 14, 1966, p. 231.

obligations on either side in the conflict by which that side would not be bound in any event. The rules of international law concerning the conduct of hostilities in an international armed conflict apply regardless of any declaration of war.

H. Summary

The analysis set forth above shows that South Viet-Nam has the right in present circumstances to defend itself against armed attack from the North and to organize a collective self-defense with the participation of others. In response to requests from South Viet-Nam, the United States has been participating in that defense, both through military action within South Viet-Nam and actions taken directly against the aggressor in North Viet-Nam. This participation by the United States is in conformity with international law and is consistent with our obligations under the Charter of the United Nations.

II. THE UNITED STATES HAS UNDERTAKEN COMMITMENTS TO ASSIST SOUTH VIET-NAM IN DEFENDING ITSELF AGAINST COMMUNIST AGGRESSION FROM THE NORTH

The United States has made commitments and given assurances, in various forms and at different times, to assist in the defense of South Viet-Nam.

A. The United States Gave Undertakings at the End of the Geneva Conference in 1954

At the time of the signing of the Geneva accords in 1954, President Eisenhower warned "that any renewal of Communist aggression would be viewed by us as a matter of grave concern," at the same time giving assurance that the United States would "not use force to disturb the settlement." [12] And the formal declaration made by the United States Government at the conclusion of the Geneva conference stated that the United States "would view any renewal of the aggression in violation of the aforesaid agreements with grave concern and as seriously threatening international peace and security." [13]

B. The United States Undertook an International Obligation To Defend South Viet-Nam in the SEATO Treaty

Later in 1954 the United States negotiated with a number of other countries and signed the Southeast Asia Collective Defense Treaty.[14] The treaty contains in the first paragraph of article IV the following provision:

> Each Party recognizes that aggression by means of armed attack in the treaty area against any of the Parties or against any State or territory which the Parties by unanimous agreement may hereafter designate, would endanger its own peace and safety, and agrees that

[12] For a statement made by President Eisenhower on June 21, 1954, see *ibid.*, Aug. 2, 1954, p. 163.　　　[13] For text, see *ibid.*, p. 162.
[14] For text, see *ibid.*, Sept. 20, 1954, p. 393 [reprinted below, p. 646].

it will in that event act to meet the common danger in accordance with its constitutional processes. Measures taken under this paragraph shall be immediately reported to the Security Council of the United Nations.

Annexed to the treaty was a protocol stating that:

> The Parties to the Southeast Asia Collective Defense Treaty unanimously designate for the purposes of Article IV of the Treaty the States of Cambodia and Laos and the free territory under the jurisdiction of the State of Vietnam.

Thus, the obligations of article IV, paragraph 1, dealing with the eventuality of armed attack, have from the outset covered the territory of South Viet-Nam.   The facts as to the North Vietnamese armed attack against the South have been summarized earlier, in the discussion of the right of self-defense under international law and the Charter of the United Nations. The term ''armed attack'' has the same meaning in the SEATO treaty as in the United Nations Charter.

Article IV, paragraph 1, places an obligation on each party to the SEATO treaty to ''act to meet the common danger in accordance with its constitutional processes'' in the event of an armed attack.   The treaty does not require a collective determination that an armed attack has occurred in order that the obligation of article IV, paragraph 1, become operative.   Nor does the provision require collective decision on actions to be taken to meet the common danger.   As Secretary Dulles pointed out when transmitting the treaty to the President, the commitment in article IV, paragraph 1, ''leaves to the judgment of each country the type of action to be taken in the event an armed attack occurs.'' [15]

The treaty was intended to deter armed aggression in Southeast Asia. To that end it created not only a multilateral alliance but also a series of bilateral relationships.   The obligations are placed squarely on ''each Party'' in the event of armed attack in the treaty area—not upon ''the Parties,'' a wording that might have implied a necessity for collective decision.   The treaty was intended to give the assurance of United States assistance to any party or protocol state that might suffer a Communist armed attack, regardless of the views or actions of other parties.   The fact that the obligations are individual, and may even to some extent differ among the parties to the treaty, is demonstrated by the United States understanding, expressed at the time of signature, that its obligations under article IV, paragraph 1, apply only in the event of *Communist* aggression, whereas the other parties to the treaty were unwilling so to limit their obligations to each other.

Thus, the United States has a commitment under article IV, paragraph 1, in the event of armed attack, independent of the decision or action of other treaty parties.   A joint statement issued by Secretary Rusk and Foreign Minister Thanat Khoman of Thailand on March 6, 1962,[16] reflected this understanding:

---

[15] For text, see *ibid.*, Nov. 29, 1954, p. 820.
[16] For text, see *ibid.*, March 26, 1962, p. 498.

The Secretary of State assured the Foreign Minister that in the event of such aggression, the United States intends to give full effect to its obligations under the Treaty to act to meet the common danger in accordance with its constitutional processes. The Secretary of State reaffirmed that this obligation of the United States does not depend upon the prior agreement of all other parties to the Treaty, since this Treaty obligation is individual as well as collective.

Most of the SEATO countries have stated that they agreed with this interpretation. None has registered objection to it.

When the Senate Committee on Foreign Relations reported on the Southeast Asia Collective Defense Treaty, it noted that the treaty area was further defined so that the "Free Territory of Vietnam" was an area "which, if attacked, would fall under the protection of the instrument." In its conclusion the committee stated:

> The committee is not impervious to the risks which this treaty entails. It fully appreciates that acceptance of these additional obligations commits the United States to a course of action over a vast expanse of the Pacific. Yet these risks are consistent with our own highest interests.

The Senate gave its advice and consent to the treaty by a vote of 82 to 1.

C. The United States Has Given Additional Assurances to the Government of South Viet-Nam

The United States has also given a series of additional assurances to the Government of South Viet-Nam. As early as October 1954 President Eisenhower undertook to provide direct assistance to help make South Viet-Nam "capable of resisting attempted subversion or aggression through military means."[17] On May 11, 1957, President Eisenhower and President Ngo Dinh Diem of the Republic of Viet-Nam issued a joint statement[18] which called attention to "the large build-up of Vietnamese Communist military forces in North Viet-Nam" and stated:

> Noting that the Republic of Viet-Nam is covered by Article IV of the Southeast Asia Collective Defense Treaty, President Eisenhower and President Ngo Dinh Diem agreed that aggression or subversion threatening the political independence of the Republic of Viet-Nam would be considered as endangering peace and stability.

On August 2, 1961, President Kennedy declared that "the United States is determined that the Republic of Viet-Nam shall not be lost to the Communists for lack of any support which the United States Government can render."[19] On December 7 of that year President Diem appealed for additional support. In his reply of December 14, 1961, President Kennedy recalled the United States declaration made at the end of the Geneva con-

---

[17] For text of a message from President Eisenhower to President Ngo Dinh Diem, see *ibid.*, Nov. 15, 1954, p. 735.

[18] For text, see *ibid.*, May 27, 1957, p. 851.

[19] For text of a joint communique issued by President Kennedy and Vice President Chen Cheng of the Republic of China, see *ibid.*, Aug. 28, 1961, p. 372.

ference in 1954, and reaffirmed that the United States was "prepared to help the Republic of Viet-Nam to protect its people and to preserve its independence." [20] This assurance has been reaffirmed many times since.

III. ACTIONS BY THE UNITED STATES AND SOUTH VIET-NAM ARE JUSTIFIED UNDER THE GENEVA ACCORDS OF 1954

A. Description of the Accords

The Geneva accords of 1954 [21] established the date and hour for a cease-fire in Viet-Nam, drew a "provisional military demarcation line" with a demilitarized zone on both sides, and required an exchange of prisoners and the phased regroupment of Viet Minh forces from the south to the north and of French Union forces from the north to the south. The introduction into Viet-Nam of troop reinforcements and new military equipment (except for replacement and repair) was prohibited. The armed forces of each party were required to respect the demilitarized zone and the territory of the other zone. The adherence of either zone to any military alliance, and the use of either zone for the resumption of hostilities or to "further an aggressive policy," were prohibited. The International Control Commission was established, composed of India, Canada and Poland, with India as chairman. The task of the Commission was to supervise the proper execution of the provisions of the cease-fire agreement. General elections that would result in reunification were required to be held in July 1956 under the supervision of the ICC.

B. North Viet-Nam Violated the Accords From the Beginning

From the very beginning, the North Vietnamese violated the 1954 Geneva accords. Communist military forces and supplies were left in the South in violation of the accords. Other Communist guerrillas were moved north for further training and then were infiltrated into the South in violation of the accords.

C. The Introduction of United States Military Personnel and Equipment Was Justified

The accords prohibited the reinforcement of foreign military forces in Viet-Nam and the introduction of new military equipment, but they allowed

---

[20] For text of an exchange of messages between President Kennedy and President Diem, see *ibid.*, Jan. 1, 1962, p. 13.

[21] These accords were composed of a bilateral cease-fire agreement between the "Commander-in-Chief of the People's Army of Viet Nam" and the "Commander-in-Chief of the French Union forces in Indo-China," together with a Final Declaration of the Conference, to which France adhered. However, it is to be noted that the South Vietnamese Government was not a signatory of the cease-fire agreement and did not adhere to the Final Declaration. South Viet-Nam entered a series of reservations in a statement to the conference. This statement was noted by the conference, but by decision of the conference chairman it was not included or referred to in the Final Declaration. [Footnote in original.]

replacement of existing military personnel and equipment. Prior to late 1961 South Viet-Nam had received considerable military equipment and supplies from the United States, and the United States had gradually enlarged its Military Assistance Advisory Group to slightly less than 900 men. These actions were reported to the ICC and were justified as replacements for equipment in Viet-Nam in 1954 and for French training and advisory personnel who had been withdrawn after 1954.

As the Communist aggression intensified during 1961, with increased infiltration and a marked stepping up of Communist terrorism in the South, the United States found it necessary in late 1961 to increase substantially the numbers of our military personnel and the amounts and types of equipment introduced by this country into South Viet-Nam. These increases were justified by the international law principle that a material breach of an agreement by one party entitles the other at least to withhold compliance with an equivalent, corresponding, or related provision until the defaulting party is prepared to honor its obligations.[22]

In accordance with this principle, the systematic violation of the Geneva accords by North Viet-Nam justified South Viet-Nam in suspending compliance with the provision controlling entry of foreign military personnel and military equipment.

D. South Viet-Nam Was Justified in Refusing To Implement the Election Provisions of the Geneva Accords

The Geneva accords contemplated the reunification of the two parts of Viet-Nam. They contained a provision for general elections to be held in July 1956 in order to obtain a "free expression of the national will." The accords stated that "consultations will be held on this subject between the competent representative authorities of the two zones from 20 July 1955 onwards."

There may be some question whether South Viet-Nam was bound by these election provisions. As indicated earlier, South Viet-Nam did not sign the cease-fire agreement of 1954, nor did it adhere to the Final Declaration of the Geneva conference. The South Vietnamese Government at that

---

22 This principle of law and the circumstances in which it may be invoked are most fully discussed in the Fourth Report on the Law of Treaties by Sir Gerald Fitzmaurice, articles 18, 20 (U.N. doc. A/CN.4/120(1959)) II Yearbook of the International Law Commission 37 (U.N. doc. A/CN.4/SER.A/1959/Add.1) and in the later report by Sir Humphrey Waldock, article 20 (U.N. doc. A/CN.4/156 and Add. 1–3 (1963)) II Yearbook of the International Law Commission 36 (U.N. doc. A/CN.4/SER.A/1963/Add.1). Among the authorities cited by the fourth report for this proposition are: II Oppenheim, International Law 136, 137 (7th ed. Lauterpacht 1955); I Rousseau, Principes généraux du droit international public 365 (1944); II Hyde, International Law 1660 et seq. (2d ed. 1947); II Guggenheim, Traité de droit international public 84, 85 (1935); Spiropoulos, Traité théorique et pratique de droit international public 289 (1933); Verdross, Völkerrecht, 328 (1950); Hall, Treatise 21 (8th ed. Higgins 1924); 3 Accioly, Tratado de Direito Internacional Publico 82 (1956–57). See also draft articles 42 and 46 of the Law of Treaties by the International Law Commission, contained in the report on the work of its 15th session (General Assembly, Official Records, 18th Session, Supplement No. 9(A/5809)). [Footnote in original.]

time gave notice of its objection in particular to the election provisions of the accords.

However, even on the premise that these provisions were binding on South Viet-Nam, the South Vietnamese Government's failure to engage in consultations in 1955, with a view to holding elections in 1956, involved no breach of obligation. The conditions in North Viet-Nam during that period were such as to make impossible any free and meaningful expression of popular will.

Some of the facts about conditions in the North were admitted even by the Communist leadership in Hanoi. General Giap, currently Defense Minister of North Viet-Nam, in addressing the Tenth Congress of the North Vietnamese Communist Party in October 1956, publicly acknowledged that the Communist leaders were running a police state where executions, terror, and torture were commonplace. A nationwide election in these circumstances would have been a travesty. No one in the North would have dared to vote except as directed. With a substantial majority of the Vietnamese people living north of the 17th parallel, such an election would have meant turning the country over to the Communists without regard to the will of the people. The South Vietnamese Government realized these facts and quite properly took the position that consultations for elections in 1956 as contemplated by the accords would be a useless formality.[23]

IV. THE PRESIDENT HAS FULL AUTHORITY TO COMMIT UNITED STATES FORCES IN THE COLLECTIVE DEFENSE OF SOUTH VIET-NAM

There can be no question in present circumstances of the President's authority to commit United States forces to the defense of South Viet-Nam. The grant of authority to the President in article II of the Constitution extends to the actions of the United States currently undertaken in Viet-Nam. In fact, however, it is unnecessary to determine whether this grant standing alone is sufficient to authorize the actions taken in Viet-Nam. These actions rest not only on the exercise of Presidential powers under article II but on the SEATO treaty—a treaty advised and consented to by the Senate—and on actions of the Congress, particularly the joint resolution of August 10, 1964. When these sources of authority are taken together—article II of the Constitution, the SEATO treaty, and actions by the Congress—there can be no question of the legality under domestic law of United States actions in Viet-Nam.

A. The President's Power Under Article II of the Constitution Extends to the Actions Currently Undertaken in Viet-Nam

Under the Constitution, the President, in addition to being Chief Executive, is Commander in Chief of the Army and Navy. He holds the prime

---

23 In any event, if North Viet-Nam considered there had been a breach of obligation by the South, its remedies lay in discussion with Saigon, perhaps in an appeal to the co-chairmen of the Geneva conference, or in a reconvening of the conference to consider the situation. Under international law, North Viet-Nam had no right to use force outside its own zone in order to secure its political objectives. [Footnote in original.]

responsibility for the conduct of United States foreign relations. These duties carry very broad powers, including the power to deploy American forces abroad and commit them to military operations when the President deems such action necessary to maintain the security and defense of the United States.

At the Federal Constitutional Convention in 1787, it was originally proposed that Congress have the power "to make war." There were objections that legislative proceedings were too slow for this power to be vested in Congress; it was suggested that the Senate might be a better repository. Madison and Gerry then moved to substitute "to declare war" for "to make war," "leaving to the Executive the power to repel sudden attacks." It was objected that this might make it too easy for the Executive to involve the nation in war, but the motion carried with but one dissenting vote.

In 1787 the world was a far larger place, and the framers probably had in mind attacks upon the United States. In the 20th century, the world has grown much smaller. An attack on a country far from our shores can impinge directly on the nation's security. In the SEATO treaty, for example, it is formally declared that an armed attack against Viet-Nam would endanger the peace and safety of the United States.

Since the Constitution was adopted there have been at least 125 instances in which the President has ordered the armed forces to take action or maintain positions abroad without obtaining prior congressional authorization, starting with the "undeclared war" with France (1798–1800). For example, President Truman ordered 250,000 troops to Korea during the Korean war of the early 1950's. President Eisenhower dispatched 14,000 troops to Lebanon in 1958.

The Constitution leaves to the President the judgment to determine whether the circumstances of a particular armed attack are so urgent and the potential consequences so threatening to the security of the United States that he should act without formally consulting the Congress.

B. The Southeast Asia Collective Defense Treaty Authorizes the President's Actions

Under article VI of the United States Constitution, "all Treaties made, or which shall be made, under the Authority of the United States, shall be the supreme Law of the Land." Article IV, paragraph 1, of the SEATO treaty establishes as a matter of law that a Communist armed attack against South Viet-Nam endangers the peace and safety of the United States. In this same provision the United States has undertaken a commitment in the SEATO treaty to "act to meet the common danger in accordance with its constitutional processes" in the event of such an attack.

Under our Constitution it is the President who must decide when an armed attack has occurred. He has also the constitutional responsibility for determining what measures of defense are required when the peace and safety of the United States are endangered. If he considers that deployment of U. S. forces to South Viet-Nam is required, and that military measures against the source of Communist aggression in North Viet-Nam are necessary, he is constitutionally empowered to take those measures.

The SEATO treaty specifies that each party will act "in accordance with its constitutional processes."

It has recently been argued that the use of land forces in Asia is not authorized under the treaty because their use to deter armed attack was not contemplated at the time the treaty was considered by the Senate. Secretary Dulles testified at that time that we did not intend to establish (1) a land army in Southeast Asia capable of deterring Communist aggression, or (2) an integrated headquarters and military organization like that of NATO; instead, the United States would rely on "mobile striking power" against the sources of aggression.   However, the treaty obligation in article IV, paragraph 1, to meet the common danger in the event of armed aggression, is not limited to particular modes of military action. What constitutes an adequate deterrent or an appropriate response, in terms of military strategy, may change; but the essence of our commitment to act to meet the common danger, as necessary at the time of an armed aggression, remains.   In 1954 the forecast of military judgment might have been against the use of substantial United States ground forces in Viet-Nam. But that does not preclude the President from reaching a different military judgment in different circumstances, 12 years later.

C. The Joint Resolution of Congress of August 10, 1964, Authorizes United States Participation in the Collective Defense of South Viet-Nam

As stated earlier, the legality of United States participation in the defense of South Viet-Nam does not rest only on the constitutional power of the President under article II—or indeed on that power taken in conjunction with the SEATO treaty.   In addition, the Congress has acted in unmistakable fashion to approve and authorize United States actions in Viet-Nam.

Following the North Vietnamese attacks in the Gulf of Tonkin against United States destroyers, Congress adopted, by a Senate vote of 88–2 and a House vote of 416–0, a joint resolution containing a series of important declarations and provisions of law.[24]

Section 1 resolved that "the Congress approves and supports the determination of the President, as Commander in Chief, to take all necessary measures to repel any armed attack against the forces of the United States and to prevent further aggression." Thus, the Congress gave its sanction to specific actions by the President to repel attacks against United States naval vessels in the Gulf of Tonkin and elsewhere in the western Pacific. Congress further approved the taking of "all necessary measures . . . to prevent further aggression." This authorization extended to those measures the President might consider necessary to ward off further attacks and to prevent further aggression by North Viet-Nam in Southeast Asia.

The joint resolution then went on to provide in section 2:

> The United States regards as vital to its national interest and to world peace the maintenance of international peace and security in

[24] For text, see BULLETIN of Aug. 24, 1964, p. 268.

southeast Asia. Consonant with the Constitution of the United States and the Charter of the United Nations and in accordance with its obligations under the Southeast Asia Collective Defense Treaty, the United States is, therefore, prepared, as the President determines, to take all necessary steps, including the use of armed force, to assist any member or protocol state of the Southeast Asia Collective Defense Treaty requesting assistance in defense of its freedom.

Section 2 thus constitutes an authorization to the President, in his discretion, to act—using armed force if he determines that is required—to assist South Viet-Nam at its request in defense of its freedom. The identification of South Viet-Nam through the reference to "protocol state" in this section is unmistakable, and the grant of authority "as the President determines" is unequivocal.

It has been suggested that the legislative history of the joint resolution shows an intention to limit United States assistance to South Viet-Nam to aid, advice, and training. This suggestion is based on an amendment offered from the floor by Senator [Gaylord] Nelson which would have added the following to the text:

> The Congress also approves and supports the efforts of the President to bring the problem of peace in Southeast Asia to the Security Council of the United Nations, and the President's declaration that the United States, seeking no extension of the present military conflict, will respond to provocation in a manner that is "limited and fitting." Our continuing policy is to limit our role to the provision of aid, training assistance, and military advice, and it is the sense of Congress that, except when provoked to a greater response, we should continue to attempt to avoid a direct military involvement in the Southeast Asian conflict.[25]

Senator [J. W.] Fulbright, who had reported the joint resolution from the Foreign Relations Committee, spoke on the amendment as follows:

> It states fairly accurately what the President has said would be our policy, and what I stated my understanding was as to our policy; also what other Senators have stated. In other words, it states that our response should be appropriate and limited to the provocation, which the Senator states as "respond to provocation in a manner that is limited and fitting," and so forth. We do not wish any political or military bases there. We are not seeking to gain a colony. We seek to insure the capacity of these people to develop along the lines of their own desires, independent of domination by communism.
>
> The Senator has put into his amendment a statement of policy that is unobjectionable. However, I cannot accept the amendment under the circumstances. I do not believe it is contrary to the joint resolution, but it is an enlargement. I am informed that the House is now voting on this resolution. The House joint resolution is about to be presented to us. I cannot accept the amendment and go to conference with it, and thus take responsibility for delaying matters.
>
> I do not object to it as a statement of policy. I believe it is an accurate reflection of what I believe is the President's policy, judging from his own statements. That does not mean that as a practical matter I can accept the amendment. It would delay matters to do so.

25 110 Cong. Rec. 18459 (Aug. 7, 1964). [Footnote in original.]

would cause confusion and require a conference, and present us with all the other difficulties that are involved in this kind of legislative action. I regret that I cannot do it, even though I do not at all disagree with the amendment as a general statement of policy.[26]

Senator Nelson's amendment related the degree and kind of U. S. response in Viet-Nam to "provocation" on the other side; the response should be "limited and fitting." The greater the provocation, the stronger are the measures that may be characterized as "limited and fitting." Bombing of North Vietnamese naval bases was a "limited and fitting" response to the attacks on U. S. destroyers in August 1964, and the subsequent actions taken by the United States and South Viet-Nam have been an appropriate response to the increased war of aggression carried on by North Viet-Nam since that date. Moreover, Senator Nelson's proposed amendment did not purport to be a restriction on authority available to the President but merely a statement concerning what should be the continuing policy of the United States.

Congressional realization of the scope of authority being conferred by the joint resolution is shown by the legislative history of the measure as a whole. The following exchange between Senators Cooper and Fulbright is illuminating:

> MR. COOPER [John Sherman Cooper]. . . . The Senator will remember that the SEATO Treaty, in article IV, provides that in the event an armed attack is made upon a party to the Southeast Asia Collective Defense Treaty, or upon one of the protocol states such as South Vietnam, the parties to the treaty, one of whom is the United States, would then take such action as might be appropriate, after resorting to their constitutional processes. I assume that would mean, in the case of the United States, that Congress would be asked to grant the authority to act.
>
> Does the Senator consider that in enacting this resolution we are satisfying that requirement of article IV of the Southeast Asia Collective Defense Treaty? In other words, are we now giving the President advance authority to take whatever action he may deem necessary respecting South Vietnam and its defense, or with respect to the defense of any other country included in the treaty?
>
> MR. FULBRIGHT. I think that is correct.
>
> MR. COOPER. Then, looking ahead, if the President decided that it was necessary to use such force as could lead into war, we will give that authority by this resolution?
>
> MR. FULBRIGHT. That is the way I would interpret it. If a situation later developed in which we thought the approval should be withdrawn it could be withdrawn by concurrent resolution.[27]

26 *Ibid.*

27 110 Cong. Rec. 18409 (Aug. 6, 1964). Senator [Wayne] Morse, who opposed the joint resolution, expressed the following view on August 6, 1964, concerning the scope of the proposed resolution:

Another Senator thought, in the early part of the debate, that this course would not broaden the power of the President to engage in a land war if he decided that he wanted to apply the resolution in that way.

That Senator was taking great consolation in the then held belief that, if he voted for the resolution, it would give no authority to the President to send many troops into Asia.

The August 1964 joint resolution continues in force today. Section 2 of the resolution provides that it shall expire "when the President shall determine that the peace and security of the area is reasonably assured by international conditions created by action of the United Nations or otherwise, except that it may be terminated earlier by concurrent resolution of the Congress." The President has made no such determination, nor has Congress terminated the joint resolution.[28]

Instead, Congress in May 1965 approved an appropriation of $700 million to meet the expense of mounting military requirements in Viet-Nam. (Public Law 89–18, 79 Stat. 109.) The President's message asking for this appropriation stated that this was "not a routine appropriation. For each Member of Congress who supports this request is also voting to persist in our efforts to halt Communist aggression in South Vietnam."[29] The appropriation act constitutes a clear congressional endorsement and approval of the actions taken by the President.

On March 1, 1966, the Congress continued to express its support of the President's policy by approving a $4.8 billion supplemental military authorization by votes of 392–4 and 93–2. An amendment that would have limited the President's authority to commit forces to Viet-Nam was rejected in the Senate by a vote of 94–2.

D. No Declaration of War by the Congress Is Required To Authorize United States Participation in the Collective Defense of South Viet-Nam

No declaration of war is needed to authorize American actions in Viet-Nam. As shown in the preceding sections, the President has ample authority to order the participation of United States armed forces in the defense of South Viet-Nam.

Over a very long period in our history, practice and precedent have confirmed the constitutional authority to engage United States forces in hostilities without a declaration of war. This history extends from the undeclared war with France and the war against the Barbary pirates at the end of the 18th century to the Korean war of 1950–53.

I am sure he was quite disappointed to finally learn, because it took a little time to get the matter cleared, that the resolution places no restriction on the President in that respect. If he is still in doubt, let him read the language on page 2, lines 3 to 6, and page 2, lines 11 to 17. The first reads:

> The Congress approves and supports the determination of the President, as Commander in Chief, to take all necessary measures to repel any armed attack against the forces of the United States and to prevent further aggression.

It does not say he is limited in regard to the sending of ground forces. It does not limit that authority. That is why I have called it a predated declaration of war, in clear violation of article I, section 8, of the Constitution, which vests the power to declare war in the Congress, and not in the President.

What is proposed is to authorize the President of the United States, without a declaration of war, to commit acts of war. (110 Cong. Rec. 18426-7 (Aug. 6, 1964)). [Footnote in original.]

[28] On March 1, 1966, the Senate voted, 92–5, to table an amendment that would have repealed the joint resolution. [Footnote in original.]

[29] For text, see BULLETIN of May 24, 1965, p. 822.

James Madison, one of the leading framers of the Constitution, and Presidents John Adams and Jefferson all construed the Constitution, in their official actions during the early years of the Republic, as authorizing the United States to employ its armed forces abroad in hostilities in the absence of any congressional declaration of war. Their views and actions constitute highly persuasive evidence as to the meaning and effect of the Constitution. History has accepted the interpretation that was placed on the Constitution by the early Presidents and Congresses in regard to the lawfulness of hostilities without a declaration of war. The instances of such action in our history are numerous.

In the Korean conflict, where large-scale hostilities were conducted with an American troop participation of a quarter of a million men, no declaration of war was made by the Congress. The President acted on the basis of his constitutional responsibilities. While the Security Council, under a treaty of this country—the United Nations Charter—recommended assistance to the Republic of Korea against the Communist armed attack, the United States had no treaty commitment at that time obligating us to join in the defense of South Korea. In the case of South Viet-Nam we have the obligation of the SEATO treaty and clear expressions of congressional support. If the President could act in Korea without a declaration of war, *a fortiori* he is empowered to do so now in Viet-Nam.

It may be suggested that a declaration of war is the only available constitutional process by which congressional support can be made effective for the use of United States armed forces in combat abroad. But the Constitution does not insist on any rigid formalism. It gives Congress a choice of ways in which to exercise its powers. In the case of Viet-Nam the Congress has supported the determination of the President by the Senate's approval of the SEATO treaty, the adoption of the joint resolution of August 10, 1964, and the enactment of the necessary authorizations and appropriations.

V. CONCLUSION

South Viet-Nam is being subjected to armed attack by Communist North Viet-Nam, through the infiltration of armed personnel, military equipment, and regular combat units. International law recognizes the right of individual and collective self-defense against armed attack. South Viet-Nam, and the United States upon the request of South Viet-Nam, are engaged in such collective defense of the South. Their actions are in conformity with international law and with the Charter of the United Nations. The fact that South Viet-Nam has been precluded by Soviet veto from becoming a member of the United Nations and the fact that South Viet-Nam is a zone of a temporarily divided state in no way diminish the right of collective defense of South Viet-Nam.

The United States has commitments to assist South Viet-Nam in defending itself against Communist aggression from the North. The United States gave undertakings to this effect at the conclusion of the Geneva conference in 1954. Later that year the United States undertook an international obligation in the SEATO treaty to defend South Viet-Nam against Communist armed aggression. And during the past decade the United States has given additional assurances to the South Vietnamese Government.

The Geneva accords of 1954 provided for a cease-fire and regroupment of contending forces, a division of Viet-Nam into two zones, and a prohibition on the use of either zone for the resumption of hostilities or to "further an aggressive policy." From the beginning, North Viet-Nam violated the Geneva accords through a systematic effort to gain control of South Viet-Nam by force. In the light of these progressive North Vietnamese violations, the introduction into South Viet-Nam beginning in late 1961 of substantial United States military equipment and personnel, to assist in the defense of the South, was fully justified; substantial breach of an international agreement by one side permits the other side to suspend performance of corresponding obligations under the agreement. South Viet-Nam was justified in refusing to implement the provisions of the Geneva accords calling for reunification through free elections throughout Viet-Nam since the Communist regime in North Viet-Nam created conditions in the North that made free elections entirely impossible.

The President of the United States has full authority to commit United States forces in the collective defense of South Viet-Nam. This authority stems from the constitutional powers of the President. However, it is not necessary to rely on the Constitution alone as the source of the President's authority, since the SEATO treaty—advised and consented to by the Senate and forming part of the law of the land—sets forth a United States commitment to defend South Viet-Nam against armed attack, and since the Congress—in the joint resolution of August 10, 1964, and in authorization and appropriations acts for support of the U. S. military effort in Viet-Nam—has given its approval and support to the President's actions. United States actions in Viet-Nam, taken by the President and approved by the Congress, do not require any declaration of war, as shown by a long line of precedents for the use of United States armed forces abroad in the absence of any congressional declaration of war.

(54 Dept. of State Bulletin 474 (1966) ; Congressional Record, March 10, 1966, p. 5274.)

President Reviews U.S. Position on Bombing of North Viet-Nam

Following is the text of a letter from President Johnson to Senator Henry M. Jackson, which was released by the White House on March 2.[1]

March 1, 1967

DEAR SENATOR JACKSON: In further reference to our discussions at dinner on the evening of the 18th concerning the reasons for and effects of bombing, I wish to review for you the following.

We are bombing North Viet Nam because it is violating two solemn international agreements. In 1954 Hanoi agreed that North Viet Nam would not be "used for the resumption of hostilities or to further an aggressive policy."

In 1962 Hanoi agreed to withdraw all its military forces from Laos; to refrain from reintroducing such forces; and not to use the territory of Laos to interfere in the internal affairs of other countries.

Let me quote to you the recommendation made by General Maxwell Taylor to President Kennedy in his report of November 3, 1961, after Hanoi had violated the Geneva Declaration of 1954 but before the Geneva Declaration of 1962 was finally negotiated.

"While we feel that the program recommended represents those measures which should be taken in our present knowledge of the situation in Southeast Asia, I would not suggest that it is the final word. Future needs beyond this program will depend upon the kind of settlement we obtain in Laos and the manner in which Hanoi decides to adjust its conduct to that settlement. If the Hanoi decision is to continue the irregular war declared on South Viet-Nam in 1959 with continued infiltration and covert support of guerrilla bands in the territory of our ally, we will then have to decide whether to accept as legitimate the continued guidance, training and support of a guerrilla war across an international boundary, while the attacked react only inside their borders. . . .

"It is my judgment and that of my colleagues that the United States must decide how it will cope with Khrushchev's "wars of liberation" which are really para-wars of guerrilla aggression. This is a new and dangerous Communist technique which bypasses our traditional political and military responses. While the final answer lies beyond the

---

[1] *Weekly Compilation of Presidential Documents* dated Mar. 6; the letter was read to the Senate by Senator Jackson on Mar. 2.

scope of this report, it is clear to me that the time may come in our relations to Southeast Asia when we must declare our intention to attack the source of guerrilla aggression in North Viet-Nam and impose on the Hanoi Government a price for participating in the current war which is commensurate with the damage being inflicted on its neighbors to the south."

Not for one day after the Geneva Declaration of 1962 was signed did Hanoi meet its commitment or honor its earlier commitment of 1954. Aggression against South Viet Nam was continued throughout 1962, 1963, and 1964. Its forces were never withdrawn from Laos and Laos was violated in order to attack South Viet Nam.

When I became President and surveyed the problem faced by our nation, I reserved judgment on the decision which General Taylor forecast in 1961 we might have to make. But the fact was that the North Vietnamese continued illegally to infiltrate arms and men across international frontiers. And in 1964 they radically expanded this course of action. The trails became roads. Bands of infiltrators became regular military units.

Neither of the co-chairmen of the Geneva Conference—Great Britain and the Soviet Union—proved able to stop this violation; nor did the three members of the International Control Commission—India, Canada, and Poland.

With this failure of the international machinery designed to enforce the Geneva agreements we were thrown back, therefore, on our treaty responsibilities. Under the SEATO Treaty, presented to the Senate by President Eisenhower and ratified overwhelmingly, we had agreed that in the face of "armed attack in the treaty area" we would "act to meet the common danger."

By February 1965 it was unmistakably clear there was armed attack in the most literal sense: South Viet Nam was almost lost to that armed attack. And in that month, on the recommendation of the National Security Council, I decided that we had to "meet the common danger" by bringing our air power to bear against the source of the aggression.

We never believed aerial attack on North Viet Nam would, alone, end the war. We did, however, have three objectives.

The first was to back our fighting men and our fighting allies by demonstrating that the aggressor could not illegally bring hostile arms and men to bear against them from the security of a sanctuary.

Second, we sought to impose on North Viet Nam a cost for violating its international agreements.

Third, we sought to limit or raise the cost of bringing men and supplies to bear against the South.

All three of these important objectives have been achieved.

First, you should note that the military leaders now responsible for
the safety and morale of our men in the field, without exception, back
our bombing of the North. The same is true of the military and political leaders of those fighting side by side with us; that is to say, the
leaders of Australia, Korea, New Zealand, Philippines, Thailand, and
Viet Nam. They all know that it is right and necessary for us to refuse
to accept North Viet Nam as a sanctuary at a time when the government
in Hanoi is explicitly violating its international commitments and conducting aggression across international borders.

Second, we are, with remarkably limited cost in civilian lives, imposing a major cost on North Viet Nam for its violation of international
agreements.

Our attacks on military targets in North Viet Nam have diverted
about half a million men to cope with effects of our attacks. They are
repairing the lines of supply and are engaged in anti-aircraft and coastal
defense. This figure approximates the total number of men we now
have fighting in Southeast Asia. It is not much less than the number of
men South Viet Nam has had to mobilize to deal with the guerrilla
attack in the South.

At the cost of about 500 gallant American airmen killed, captured,
or missing, we are bringing to bear on North Viet Nam a burden
roughly equivalent to that which the Communists are imposing through
guerrilla warfare on the South—and we are doing it with far fewer
civilian casualties in the North.

Finally, the bombing of North Viet Nam has raised the cost of bringing an armed man or a ton of supplies illegally across the border from
the North to the South. Substantial casualties are inflicted on infiltrators and substantial tonnages of supplies are destroyed en route. Those
who now reach the South arrive after harassment which lowers their
effectiveness as reinforcements.

The bombing in the North is an action undertaken by your Government only after the most careful reflection. It is a response to a serious
and systematic and protracted violation of international agreements.
It is having significant consequences for those who chose to violate the
agreements. It is an integral part of our total policy which aims not
to destroy North Viet Nam but to force Hanoi to end its aggression
so that the people of South Viet Nam can determine their own future
without coercion.

Both the reasons for—and the results of—the bombing of North Viet Nam make it imperative that we continue to use this instrument of support for our men and our allies. It will end when the other side is willing to take equivalent action as part of a serious effort to end this war and bring peace to the people of Southeast Asia.

I take no satisfaction from the number of infiltrators killed on their way to South Viet Nam, from the number of trucks or of boats or of railroad cars destroyed or the tons of supplies destroyed. I take no satisfaction from the suffering of the people of North Viet Nam. I take no satisfaction from the fact that they have had to abandon their plans for economic and social development. I repeat what I said in Baltimore in April 1965[2]—I look forward to the day when the government and people of North Viet Nam can join, in peace, their fellows in Southeast Asia in developing and modernizing that region so full of energy and resources and promise. And on that day they will have—if they wish—the support of the United States in providing for their people an environment of progress. But right now I wish friend and neutral and adversary to know that we shall persist with our operations in the South—we shall persist with our operations in the North—until those who launched this aggression are prepared to move seriously to reinstall the agreements whose violation has brought the scourge of war to Southeast Asia.

Sincerely,

LYNDON B. JOHNSON

[2] BULLETIN of Apr. 26, 1965, p. 606.

The Duty Not to Intervene in Matters Within the Domestic Jurisdiction of Any State, in Accordance with the Charter

A. Written proposals and amendments

202. Five written proposals concerning the third principle considered by the Special Committee were submitted by *Czechoslovakia* (A/AC. 119/L.6), by *Yugoslavia* (A/AC.119/L.7), by the *United Kingdom of Great Britain and Northern Ireland* (A/AC.119/L.8), by *Mexico* (A/AC.119/L.24), and by *Ghana, India* and *Yugoslavia* (A/AC.119/L. 27). On the submission of the latter joint proposal, *Yugoslavia*, as one of the co-sponsors, withdrew its original proposal. *Guatemala* introduced an amendment (A/AC.119/L.25) to the *United Kingdom* proposal. An amendment to the *United Kingdom* proposal was also submitted by the *United States* (A/AC.119/L.26). These proposals and amendments were as follows:

203. *Proposal by Czechoslovakia* (A/AC.119/L.6)
   "The Principle of Non-Intervention
   "1. States shall refrain from any direct or indirect intervention under any pretext in the internal or external affairs of any other State. In particular, any interference or pressure by one State or group of States for the purpose of changing the social or political order in another State shall be prohibited.
   "2. States shall refrain from any acts, manifestations or attempts aimed at a violation of the territorial integrity or inviolability of any State.
   "3. States shall refrain from exerting pressure by any means, including the threat to sever diplomatic relations, in order to compel one State not to recognize another State."

204. *Proposal by Yugoslavia* (A/AC.119/L.7)
   "Non-Intervention
   "1. No State or group of States has the right to intervene, directly or indirectly, for any reason whatsoever, in the internal or external affairs of any other State.
   "2. Accordingly, States shall refrain from any form of interference or attempted threat against the independence or right to sovereign equality of any other State and in particular its right to select its political economic and social system and to pursue the development thereof.

"3. States shall therefore especially refrain from:

(a) using or encouraging the use of coercive measures of a political or economic character to force the sovereign will of another State either in the field of its internal or external relations, in order to obtain advantages of any kind;

(b) attempting to impose a political or social system on another State;

(c) interfering in civil strife in another State;

(d) organizing, assisting, fomenting, inviting, or tolerating subversive or terrorist activities against another State;

(e) interfering with or hindering in any form or manner the free disposition of the natural wealth and resources of another State."

205. *Proposal by the United Kingdom* (A/AC.119/L.8) *and amendments by Guatemala* (A/AC.119/L.25) and the *United States* (A/AC. 119/L.26):

Proposal by the United Kingdom

"*Statement of principles*

"1. Every State has the right to political independence and territorial integrity.

"2. Every State has the duty to respect the rights enjoyed by other States in accordance with international law, and to refrain from intervention in matters within the domestic jurisdiction of any other State."

"Commentary

"Non-intervention

" (1) The basic principle in paragraph 1 is reflected in the United Nations Charter, for example, in Article 2, paragraph 4.

" (2) The first part of paragraph 2 expresses the duty of States correlative to the right enjoyed by them under paragraph 1.

"The second part of paragraph 2, which expresses the classic doctrine of non-intervention to be found in numerous multilateral, regional and bilateral treaties, is a particular application of the first part. The wording does, however, leave certain questions unresolved, as, for example, what is meant by 'intervention' and what is meant by 'matters within the domestic jurisdiction.' In the context of inter-State relations, 'intervention' connotes in general forcible or dictatorial interference.

" (3) In considering the scope of 'intervention,' it should be recognized that in an interdependent world, it is inevitable and desirable that States will be concerned with and will seek to influence the actions and policies of other States, and that the objective of international law is not to prevent such activity but rather to ensure that it is compatible with the sovereign equality of States and self-determination of their peoples.

" (4) It would, therefore, be impossible to give an exhaustive definition of what constitutes 'intervention.' Much of the classic conception of intervention has been absorbed by the prohibition of the threat or use of force against the political independence or territorial integrity of States in accordance with Article 2, paragraph 4, of the Charter. There are, however, other forms of intervention, in particular the use of clandestine activities to encompass the overthrow of the Government of another State, or to secure an alteration in the political and economic structure of that State, which illustrate the dangers of attempting an exhaustive definition of what constitutes 'intervention.'

" (5) In the event that a State becomes a victim of unlawful intervention practised or supported by the Government of another State, it has the right to request aid and assistance from third States, which are correspondingly entitled to grant the aid and assistance requested. Such aid and assistance may, if the unlawful intervention has taken the form of subversive activities leading to civil strife in which the dissident elements are receiving external support and encouragement, include armed assistance for the purpose of restoring normal conditions."

206. The amendment submitted by *Guatemala* (A/AC.119/L.25) to the *United Kingdom* proposal was to the following effect:

" (1) Replace paragraph 2 by the following:
"2. Every State has the duty to respect the rights enjoyed by other States in accordance with international law. Correlatively, the fundamental rights of States are not subject to impairment in any form."

" (2) Add the following new paragraph 3:
"3. No State or group of States has the right to intervene, directly or indirectly for any reason whatever in matters within the domestic jurisdiction of States. In consequence, the principle of non-intervention bars not only the use of armed force but also any other form of interference of an economic or political nature designed to force the sovereign will of another State."

207. The *United States* submitted the following amendment (A/AC. 119/L.26) to the *United Kingdom* proposal:

" (1) In paragraph 2 under 'Statement of Principles,' insert, after 'intervention,' the words 'contrary to the Charter.' "

" (2) Add a new paragraph 3 under 'Statement of Principles':

"3. The United Nations is not authorized to intervene in matters which are essentially within the domestic jurisdiction of any State, and nothing in the Charter requires any Member to submit such matters to settlement under the Charter; but this principle is subject to the authority granted the Security Council under Chapter VII of the Charter concerning action with respect to threats to the peace, breaches of the peace, and acts of aggression."

" (3) In paragraph (2) under 'Commentary,' delete everything after 'The second part of paragraph 2' and substitute:

"makes clear that the obligation referred to springs from Article 2, paragraph 4, of the Charter, which constitutes a limitation of State action. The scope of the word 'intervention' is indicated by the wording of Article 2, paragraph 4. However, the concept of 'domestic jurisdiction' is not expressly included in Article 2, paragraph 4."

" (4) Substitute a new paragraph (3) under 'Commentary,' as follows:

"3. Paragraph 3 reflects the content of Article 2, paragraph 7, of the Charter. Article 2, paragraph 7, contains the only express reference in the Charter regarding non-intervention. However, it may be noted that neither in Article 2, paragraph 7, nor elsewhere in the Charter is there any express definition of either 'intervention' or 'domestic jurisdiction.' "

" (5) In paragraph (4) under 'Commentary,' delete 'therefore,' after 'it would' in the first line. Delete everything after 'exhaustive definition of what constitutes intervention' and substitute:

"or 'domestic jurisdiction.' In considering the scope of 'intervention,' it should be recognized that, in an interdependent world, it is inevitable and desirable that States will be concerned with and will seek to influence the actions and policies of other States, and that the objective of international law is not to prevent such activity but rather to ensure that it is compatible with the sovereign equality of States and self-determination of their peoples."

208. *Proposal by Mexico* (A/AC.119/L.24)

"*Principle C: The duty not to intervene in matters within the domestic jurisdiction of any State, in accordance with the Charter*

"1. Every State has the duty to refrain from intervening, alone or in concert with other States, directly or indirectly, for any reason whatever, in the internal or external affairs of any other State. The foregoing principle prohibits any form of interference or attempted threat against the personality of the State or against its political, economic and cultural elements.

"2. Consequently, every State has the duty to refrain from carrying out any of the acts specified hereunder, as also any other acts which may possibly be characterized as intervention:

" (1) The use or encouragement of the use of coercive measures of an economic or political nature in order to force the sovereign will of another State and obtain from the latter advantages of any kind;

" (2) Permitting, in the areas subject to its jurisdiction, or promoting or financing anywhere:

(a) The organization or training of land, sea or air armed forces of any type having as their purpose incursions into other States;

(b) Contributing, supplying or providing arms or war materials to be used for promoting or aiding a rebellion or seditious movement in any State, even if the latter's Government is not recognized; and

(c) The organization of subversive or terrorist activities against another State;

" (3) Making the recognition of Governments or the maintenance of diplomatic relations dependent on the receipt of special advantages;

" (4) Preventing or attempting to prevent a State from freely disposing of its natural riches or resources;

" (5) Imposing or attempting to impose on a State a specific form of organization or government;

" (6) Imposing or attempting to impose on a State the concession to foreigners of a privileged situation going beyond the rights, means of redress and safeguards granted under the municipal law to nationals."

209. *Proposal by Ghana, India and Yugoslavia* (A/AC.119/L.27)

"*Principle C: Non-intervention*

"1. No State or group of States has the right to intervene, directly or indirectly, for any reason whatsoever, in the internal or external affairs of any other State; nor to interfere in the right of any State to choose and develop its own political, economic and social order in the manner most suited to the genius of its people.

"2. Accordingly no State may use or encourage the use of coercive measures of an economic or political character to force the sovereign will of another State and obtain from it advantages of any kind. In particular States shall not:

> (a) organize, assist, foment, incite or tolerate subversive or terrorist activities against another State or interfere in civil strife in another State;
>
> (b) interfere with or hinder, in any form or manner, the promulgation or execution of laws in regard to matters essentially within the competence of any State;
>
> (c) use duress to obtain or maintain territorial agreements or special advantages of any kind; and
>
> (d) recognize territorial acquisitions or special advantages obtained by duress of any kind by another State."

210. *Mexico* also submitted to the Special Committee a working paper (A/AC.119/L.23) containing the inter-American texts relating to the principle of non-intervention and expressed the hope that elements might be found in those texts which could be used by the Special Committee for the more effective discharge of its task. The working paper referred to Articles 15-17 of the Charter of the Organization of American States, 1948, to Article 1 of the Convention relating to Duties and Rights of States in the Event of Civil Strife, 1928, and to the Draft instrument on violations of the principle of non-intervention, prepared by the Inter-American Juridical Committee, 1959.

Declaration on the Inadmissibility of Intervention in the Domestic Affairs of States and the Protection of Their Independence and Sovereignty[1]

Resolution Adopted by the United Nations General Assembly at its 1408th Plenary Meeting, December 21, 1965

The General Assembly,

Deeply concerned at the gravity of the international situation and the increasing threat to universal peace due to armed intervention and other direct or indirect forms of interference threatening the sovereign personality and the political independence of states,

Considering that the United Nations, in accordance with their aim to eliminate war, threats to the peace and acts of aggression, created an Organization, based on the sovereign equality of states, whose friendly relations would be based on respect for the principle of equal rights and self-determination of peoples and on the obligation of its Members to refrain from the threat or use of force against the territorial integrity or political independence of any state,

Recognizing that, in fulfilment of the principle of self-determination, the General Assembly, in the Declaration on the Granting of Independence to Colonial Countries and Peoples contained in Resolution 1514 (XV) of 14 December 1960, stated its conviction that all peoples have an inalienable right to complete freedom, the exercise of their sovereignty and the integrity of their national territory, and that, by virtue of that right, they freely determine their political status and freely pursue their economic, social and cultural development,

Recalling that in the Universal Declaration of Human Rights the General Assembly proclaimed that recognition of the inherent dignity and of the equal and inalienable rights of all members of the human family is the foundation of freedom, justice and peace in the world, without distinction of any kind,

Reaffirming the principle of non-intervention, proclaimed in the charters of the Organization of American States, the League of Arab States and the Organization of African Unity and affirmed at the conferences held at Montevideo, Buenos Aires, Chapultepec and Bogotá, as well as in the decisions of the Asian-African Conference at Bandung,

[1] Res. 2131 (XX), U.N. Doc. A/RES/2131 (XX)/Rev. 1 (1966); adopted on the report of the First Committee (U.N. Doc. A/6220) (1953); General Assembly, 20th Sess., Official Records, Supp. No. 14 (A/6014), p. 11. The Declaration was adopted by a roll-call vote of 109 in favor to none against, with one abstention (United Kingdom).

the First Conference of Heads of State or Government of Non-Aligned Countries at Belgrade, in the Programme for Peace and International Co-operation adopted at the end of the Second Conference of Heads of State or Government of Non-Aligned Countries at Cairo, and in the declaration on subversion adopted at Accra by the Heads of State and Government of the African States,

Recognizing that full observance of the principle of the non-intervention of states in the internal and external affairs of other states is essential to the fulfilment of the purposes and principles of the United Nations,

Considering that armed intervention is synonymous with aggression and, as such, is contrary to the basic principles on which peaceful international co-operation between states should be built,

Considering further that direct intervention, subversion and all forms of indirect intervention are contrary to these principles and, consequently, constitute a violation of the Charter of the United Nations,

Mindful that violation of the principle of non-intervention poses a threat to the independence, freedom and normal political, economic, social and cultural development of countries, particularly those which have freed themselves from colonialism, and can pose a serious threat to the maintenance of peace,

Fully aware of the imperative need to create appropriate conditions which would enable all states, and in particular the developing countries, to choose without duress or coercion their own political, economic and social institutions,

In the light of the foregoing considerations, solemnly declares:

1. No state has the right to intervene, directly or indirectly, for any reason whatever, in the internal or external affairs of any other state. Consequently, armed intervention and all other forms of interference or attempted threats against the personality of the state or against its political, economic and cultural elements, are condemned.

2. No state may use or encourage the use of economic, political or any other type of measures to coerce another state in order to obtain from it the subordination of the exercise of its sovereign rights or to secure from it advantages of any kind. Also, no state shall organize, assist, foment, finance, incite or tolerate subversive, terrorist or armed activities directed towards the violent overthrow of the régime of another state, or interfere in civil strife in another state.

3. The use of force to deprive peoples of their national identity

constitutes a violation of their inalienable rights and of the principle of non-intervention.

4. The strict observance of these obligations is an essential condition to ensure that nations live together in peace with one another, since the practice of any form of intervention not only violates the spirit and letter of the Charter of the United Nations but also leads to the creation of situations which threaten international peace and security.

5. Every state has an inalienable right to choose its political, economic, social and cultural systems, without interference in any form by another State.

6. All states shall respect the right of self-determination and independence of peoples and nations, to be freely exercised without any foreign pressure, and with absolute respect to human rights and fundamental freedoms. Consequently, all states shall contribute to the complete elimination of racial discrimination and colonialism in all its forms and manifestations.

7. For the purpose of the present Declaration, the term "state" covers both individual states and groups of states.

8. Nothing in this Declaration shall be construed as affecting in any manner the relevant provisions of the Charter of the United Nations relating to the maintenance of international peace and security, in particular those contained in Chapters VI, VII, and VIII.

Hanoi's Four Points

THE UNSWERVING policy of the DRV Government is to respect strictly the 1954 Geneva agreements on Vietnam and to implement correctly their basic provisions as embodied in the following points:

1—Recognition of the basic national rights of the Vietnamese people —peace, independence, sovereignty, unity, and territorial integrity. According to the Geneva agreements, the U.S. Government must withdraw from South Vietnam U.S. troops, military personnel, and weapons of all kinds, dismantle all U.S. military bases there, and cancel its military alliance with South Vietnam. It must end its policy of intervention and aggression in South Vietnam. According to the Geneva agreements, the U.S. Government must stop its acts of war against North Vietnam and completely cease all encroachments on the territory and sovereignty of the DRV.

2—Pending the peaceful reunification of Vietnam, while Vietnam is still temporarily divided into two zones the military provisions of the 1954 Geneva agreements on Vietnam must be strictly respected. The two zones must refrain from entering into any military alliance with foreign countries and there must be no foreign military bases, troops, or military personnel in their respective territory.

3—The internal affairs of South Vietnam must be settled by the South Vietnamese people themselves in accordance with the program of the NFLSV without any foreign interference.

4—The peaceful reunification of Vietnam is to be settled by the Vietnamese people in both zones, without any foreign interference.

This stand of the DRV Government unquestionably enjoys the approval and support of all peace and justice-loving governments and peoples in the world. The government of the DRV is of the view that the stand expounded here is the basis for the soundest political settlement of the Vietnam problem.

If this basis is recognized, favorable conditions will be created for the peaceful settlement of the Vietnam problem, and it will be possible to consider the reconvening of an international conference along the pattern of the 1954 Geneva conference on Vietnam.

The DRV Government declares that any approach contrary to the aforementioned stand is inappropriate; any approach tending to secure U.N. intervention in the Vietnam situation is also inappropriate. Such approaches are basically at variance with the 1954 Geneva agreements on Vietnam.

Washington's Fourteen Points
January 7, 1966

THE following statements are on the public record about elements which the United States believes can go into peace in Southeast Asia:

1. The Geneva Agreements of 1954 and 1962 are an adequate basis for peace in Southeast Asia;

2. We would welcome a conference on Southeast Asia or on any part thereof;

3. We would welcome "negotiations without preconditions" as the 17 nations put it;

4. We would welcome unconditional discussions as President Johnson put it;

5. A cessation of hostilities could be the first order of business at a conference or could be the subject of preliminary discussions;

6. Hanoi's four points could be discussed along with other points which others might wish to propose;

7. We want no U.S. bases in Southeast Asia;

8. We do not desire to retain U.S. troops in South Viet-Nam after peace is assured;

9. We support free elections in South Viet-Nam to give the South Vietnamese a government of their own choice;

10. The question of reunification of Viet-Nam should be determined by the Vietnamese through their own free decision;

11. The countries of Southeast Asia can be non-aligned or neutral if that be their option;

12. We would much prefer to use our resources for the economic reconstruction of Southeast Asia than in War. If there is peace, North Viet-Nam could participate in a regional effort to which we would be prepared to contribute at least one billion dollars;

13. The President has said "The Viet Cong would not have difficulty being represented and having their views represented if for a moment Hanoi decided she wanted to cease aggression. I don't think that would be an unsurmountable problem."

14. We have said publicly and privately that we could stop the bombing of North Viet-Nam as a step toward peace although there has not been the slightest hint or suggestion from the other side as to what they would do if the bombing stopped.

Civil War Panel

RICHARD J. BARNET, Director, Institute for Policy Studies; author of *Who Wants Disarmament?*

THOMAS EHRLICH, Associate Professor of Law, Stanford Law School.

RICHARD A. FALK, *Chairman*, Civil War Panel; Milbank Professor of International Law and Practices, Princeton University.

TOM J. FARER, Assistant Professor of Law, Columbia University.

LAWRENCE S. FINKELSTEIN, Dean of Graduate School, Brandeis University; former Deputy Assistant Secretary of Defense.

WOLFGANG FRIEDMANN, Professor of Law, Columbia University; author of *The Changing Structure of International Law.*

G. W. HAIGHT, Member of New York Bar.

ELIOT D. HAWKINS, Member of New York Bar.

BRUNSON MACCHESNEY, Professor of Law, Northwestern University; former President of the American Society of International Law.

MYRES S. MCDOUGAL, Sterling Professor of Law, Yale University; former President of the American Society of International Law; co-author of *Law and Minimum World Public Order.*

JOHN NORTON MOORE, Associate Professor of Law, University of Virginia.

STEPHEN SCHWEBEL, Executive Director of the American Society of International Law and Professor of International Law at the School of Advanced International Studies, The Johns Hopkins University; former Assistant Legal Adviser of the Department of State.

JOHN R. STEVENSON, Member of New York Bar and President of the American Society of International Law.

HOWARD J. TAUBENFELD, Professor of Law, Southern Methodist University; co-author of *Controls for Outer Space.*

Contemporary Contributors

NEILL H. ALFORD, JR., Professor of Law, University of Virginia.

WILLIAM BURKE, Professor of Law, Ohio State University; co-author of *The Public Order of the Oceans.*

RICHARD A. FALK, *Chairman*, Civil War Panel; Milbank Professor of International Law and Practices, Princeton University.

TOM J. FARER, Assistant Professor of Law, Columbia University; Member of Civil War Panel.

ROGER FISHER, Professor of Law, Harvard University.

WOLFGANG FRIEDMANN, Professor of Law, Columbia University; author of *The Changing Structure of International Law*; Member of Civil War Panel.

MANFRED HALPERN, Professor of Politics, Princeton University; author of *The Politics of Social Change in the Middle East and North Africa*.

LEONARD MEEKER, Legal Adviser to the Secretary of State of the United States Government.

JOHN NORTON MOORE, Associate Professor of Law, University of Virginia; Member of Civil War Panel.

DANIEL G. PARTAN, Professor of Law, Boston University.

QUENTIN L. QUADE, Professor of Political Science, Marquette University.

WALT W. ROSTOW, Special Assistant to the President of the United States.

DEAN RUSK, Secretary of State.

U THANT, Secretary General of the United Nations.

RALPH WHITE, Professor of Psychology and member of the Institute for Sino-Soviet Studies, George Washington University.

QUINCY WRIGHT, Professor of Law Emeritus, University of Chicago; author of *A Study of War*.

Permissions*

MANFRED HALPERN, "The Morality and Politics of Intervention." Reprinted by permission of the publisher from *International Aspects of Civil Strife*, edited by James N. Rosenau, Princeton, Princeton University Press, 1964, pp. 249-88.

WILLIAM BURKE, "The Legal Regulation of Minor International Coercion: A Framework of Inquiry." Reprinted by permission of the publisher from *Essays on Intervention*, edited by Roland J. Stanger, Mershon Center for Education in National Security, Ohio State University, 1964, pp. 87-125.

QUENTIN QUADE, *The U.S. and Wars of National Liberation*. Reprinted by permission of the author and publisher, New York, Council on Religion in International Affairs.

ROGER FISHER, "Intervention: Three Problems of Policy and Law." Reprinted by permission of the publisher from *Essays on Intervention*, edited by Roland J. Stanger, Mershon Center for Education in National Security, Ohio State University, 1964, pp. 464-71.

WOLFGANG FRIEDMANN, "Intervention, Civil War and the Role of International Law." Reprinted by permission of the author and publisher from *Proceedings American Society of International Law 1965*, Washington, D. C., American Society of International Law, pp. 67-75.

DANIEL G. PARTAN, "Legal Aspects of the Vietnam Conflict." Reprinted by permission of the author and publisher from *Boston University Law Review*, Boston, No. 46, 1966, pp. 281-316.

JOHN NORTON MOORE, "The Lawfulness of Military Assistance to the Republic of Viet-Nam." Reprinted by permission of the author and publisher from *American Journal of International Law*, Vol. 61, 1967, pp. 1-34.

QUINCY WRIGHT, "Legal Aspects of the Viet-Nam Situation." Reprinted by permission of the author and publisher from *American Journal of International Law*, Vol. 60, 1966, pp. 750-69.

WOLFGANG FRIEDMANN, "Law and Politics in the Vietnamese War: A Comment." Reprinted by permission of the author and publisher from *American Journal of International Law*, Vol. 61, 1967, pp. 776-84.

* Permissions are listed to correspond to the sequence of the materials included in this volume.

Index

Acheson, Dean, 159, 294
aggression, 40, 42n, 46, 69, 92, 103, 110, 117f, 131, 146, 158-59, 170, 223, 225n, 228, 363, 375, 446, 507, 509, 511, 515, 523-27, 532, 537f, 539-40; charges of, 222, 225; and collective self-defense, 221-29
Algeria, 4, 33
Algerian War, 9
Alliance for Progress, 64, 131, 509
American policy, see U.S. policy
Apple, R. W., 481n
Ardrey, Robert, 429n
armed attack, 3, 68, 164, 179f, 182, 194f, 243, 248, 326, 375, 418f, 419, 471; and defensive response, 417-30; by D.R.V. on R.V.N., 225n, 243-49, 471; conceptions of, 286f, 354-55, 363n; and NATO Treaty, 172, 172n; and North Vietnam assistance to N.L.F., 397, 472, 477-78; and SEATO Treaty, 170ff; and U.N. Charter, Article 51, 179, 224-25; and U.S. in Vietnam, 170, 179-81, 189
armed force, 137
armed interference, 142
Ashmore, Harry, 454n, 455n
Ataturk, Kimal, 64
Atlee, Clement, 168
Auriol, Vincent, 203, 203n

Bao Dai, 202, 202n, 203, 203n, 209n, 273, 273n, 275, 277, 277n, 278, 278n, 282n, 283, 464n, 531
Batista, F., 127
Bator, Victor, 259n, 412, 465, 465n
Bay of Pigs, 64, 298, 366, 378, 489. See also Cuba, Kennedy, J. F., Khrushchev, N.
belligerents, 157; and N.L.F., 220; recognition of, 156, 178, 178n, 220
Benda, Julien, 159
Berle, A. A., 315n
Bidault, Georges, 410
Bogota, Charter of, Article 15, 68; Article 16, 68
bombing, see U.S. in Vietnam
Boulding, Kenneth, 507
Bowett, Derek W., 84, 300
Brezhnev, Leonid, 525

Brodie, Bernard, 512
Brown, George, 258n
Browne, Malcolm, 535
Brownlie, I., 248, 250, 419, 430n, 473f
Burchett, Wilfred, 424n
Burke, William T., 82n
Buttinger, Joseph, 481n, 483, 484

Cambodia, SEATO Treaty, 169; violation of borders, 173, 173n
Carver, George A., 356
Castro, Fidel, 153, 156, 365, 378, 457n, 489
Central Intelligence Agency, see CIA
Chamoun, Camille, 45-47
Charter, see United Nations Charter
Chayes, Abram J., 350n
Che Guevera, 132, 133, 517
Chehab, Emir Fouad, 49
Chiang Kai-shek, 139, 144, 204, 279n
China, aggression, 110; and American imperialism, 106, 111; and Communist victory in South Vietnam, 110; revolution in, 332; and U.S. policy of containment, 112, 113; and Vietcong, 120; and wars of national liberation, 105, 106; and world domination, 115-16. See also Communism
Chou En-lai, 281n, 409n, 525
Chuach, Frank, 275n, 510n
Churchill, Winston, 153
CIA (Central Intelligence Agency), 47, 54, 56f, 479, 489-90
civil strife, defined and analyzed, 366-67, 458; and assistance, 402, 423-24, 435-36; and extra-territorial considerations, 490; and incumbent regime, 490; and intervention and counter-intervention patterns, 491; and self-determination, 437. See also civil war, conflict, internal war, intra-state conflict
civil war, 3, 4, 6, 6n, 20, 21, 197, 220, 264, 517; assistance to either or both sides, 156f, 267; assistance to incumbent, 265-67, 268, 313, 367, 514; assistance to insurgents, 265, 267, 313, 377, 429, 514; compliance with laws of war, 20-21; definition, 19-20; illegal intervention, 227-28; and in-